THOMAS HARDY'S PUBLIC VOICE

THOMAS HARDY'S PUBLIC VOICE

The Essays, Speeches, and Miscellaneous Prose

Edited by Michael Millgate

CLARENDON PRESS · OXFORD

OXFORD

UNIVERSITY PRESS

Great Clarendon Street, Oxford ox2 6DP

Oxford University Press is a department of the University of Oxford.
It furthers the University's objective of excellence in research, scholarship,
and education by publishing worldwide in

Oxford New York

Athens Auckland Bangkok Bogotá Buenos Aires Cape Town
Chennai Dar es Salaam Delhi Florence Hong Kong Istanbul Karachi
Kolkata Kuala Lumpur Madrid Melbourne Mexico City Mumbai Nairobi
Paris São Paulo Shanghai Singapore Taipei Tokyo Toronto Warsaw

and associated companies in Berlin Ibadan

Oxford is a registered trade mark of Oxford University Press
in the UK and certain other countries

Published in the United States
by Oxford University Press Inc., New York

British Library Cataloguing in Publication Data

Data available

Library of Congress Cataloging in Publication Data
Hardy, Thomas, 1840–1928.
Thomas Hardy's public voice : the essays, speeches, and miscellaneous prose / edited by
Michael Millgate.
p. cm.
Includes bibliographical references and index.
I. Millgate, Michael. II. Title.

PR4742.M54 2001 828'.808—dc21 2001021216

ISBN 0–19–818526–X

1 3 5 7 9 10 8 6 4 2

Typeset by Graphicraft Limited, Hong Kong
Printed in Great Britain
on acid-free paper by
Biddles Ltd,
Guildford and King's Lynn

ACKNOWLEDGEMENTS

This project was originally conceived early in 1971, at the moment when the editors of *The Collected Letters of Thomas Hardy*, then still at the planning stage, decided to restrict the contents of that edition to items of personal correspondence. The companion edition devoted to Hardy's public letters that I projected shortly afterwards has greatly expanded over the ensuing years, and the process of conceptual broadening and practical accumulation has, I fear, been too long and too sporadic for me to recall without risk of omission all those who have made direct or indirect contributions to it. I offer my thanks and sincerest apologies, therefore, to anyone whose name I fail to mention in the following paragraphs.

I am deeply grateful to the private owners and collectors who have graciously allowed me to consult and, on occasion, reproduce manuscript and other unique materials in their possession, notably Frederick B. Adams, David Holmes, Peter Lennon, Henry Lock, Christopher Pope, the late Richard L. Purdy, Gregory Stevens-Cox, and the late James Stevens-Cox. I have also visited many libraries in the search for printed and manuscript forms of the items included in this edition, and take this opportunity to record my warm thanks to the following institutions for permitting access to relevant materials in their collections and to the staffs of those institutions for much assistance and good advice: Bancroft Library, University of California, Berkeley (especially Peter Hanff); Beinecke Rare Book and Manuscript Library, Yale University (especially Vincent Giroud); Albert A. and Henry W. Berg Collection, New York Public Library, Astor, Lenox, and Tilden Foundations; British Library (especially Elizabeth James); British Library, Newspaper Library, Colindale; Brotherton Collection, University of Leeds (especially Christopher Sheppard); Colby College Library, Waterville, Maine (especially Patience-Anne W. Lenck and Nancy S. Reinhardt); Dorset County Library, Dorchester, Dorset; Dorset County Museum (especially Roger Peers, Richard de Peyer, Lilian

Swindall, and Judith Stinton); Eton College School Library (especially Michael Meredith and Helen Garton); English Folk Dance Society, Cecil Sharp House; Fisher Rare Book Library (especially Richard Landon, Kathryn Martyn, Elisabeth Anne Jocz, and Luba Frastacky) and Robarts Library, University of Toronto; Glasgow University Library; Harry Ransom Humanities Research Center, University of Texas (especially Cathy Henderson); Houghton Library, Harvard University; King's College Library, Cambridge; London Library; Magdalene College, Cambridge; Mount Saint Vincent University; National Library of Scotland, Edinburgh; Princeton University Library (especially Alexander Wainwright and Mark Farrell); Rationalist Press Association (especially the late Nicholas Walter); Royal Society for the Encouragement of Arts, Manufactures and Commerce (especially Susan Bennett); Victoria and Albert Museum, London; Wiltshire Record Office (especially Penelope Rundle).

Essential to the completion of the edition have been the permissions for the use of previously unpublished Hardy materials kindly granted by the copyright holder, the Miss E. A. Dugdale Will Trust, and the generous financial support received in the form of research grants from the Social Sciences and Humanities Research Council of Canada. For permission to include, as an Appendix, a modified version of an article that originally appeared in the pages of *The Thomas Hardy Journal*, I am grateful to the Thomas Hardy Society and especially Simon Curtis, the *Journal*'s editor.

In so far as the present edition began as an offshoot of *The Collected Letters of Thomas Hardy*, I have, of course, been deeply indebted to the wisdom and scholarship of two friends now sadly deceased, my then co-editor, Richard Little Purdy, and Catharine Carver, the copy-editor *extraordinaire* who saw most of the successive volumes of the edition through to publication. I also gladly acknowledge the help given by Freda Gough, who did the bulk of the typing for the *Collected Letters*, and by those—some now in senior academic positions—who as graduate students assisted in the production of the edition: Christine Bacque, Maureen Clarke, Edward J. Esche, Marjorie Garson, Gary Harrington, Kate Lawson, April London, Christine Pouget, and especially Martin Kreiswirth, Keith Lawson, Lawrence Miller, and Leslie Mann. Among those who have contributed more recently and more directly to various aspects of the present edition I am happy to acknowledge the excellent work done by Leslie Mann (again), Gail Richardson, Margaret Webster,

Adrian Bond, Ian Singer, Ian Dennis, Luke Tromly, and Mary Newberry.

For advice and assistance of all kinds I very much wish to thank Frederick and Marie-Louise Adams, Henry Auster, Frances Austin, Gordon and Celia Barclay, Claudius and Audrey Beatty, Jo Ann Boydston, Tony Bradbury, Eleanor Cook, Jane Cooper, Peter W. Coxon, Gillian Fenwick, Simon Gatrell, James Gibson, the late Desmond Hawkins, Robert H. Hirst, Linda Hughes, Heather Jackson, J. R. de J. Jackson, W. J. Keith, Charles Lock, Michael Meredith, W. W. Morgan, Norman Page, Michael Rabiger, Robert Robson, S. P. Rosenbaum, Mark Simons, the late Malcolm Tomkins, Keith Wilson, Donald Winslow, Judith Wittenberg, and Marjorie G. Wynne.

Among those who have made sustained and particular contributions to the edition it gives me pleasure to mention and thank: Elizabeth James, for practical help beyond the call of custodial duty; Ann and Anthony Thwaite, for unfailing encouragement and hospitality; Michiyuki Omomo, for meticulous research into Japanese materials; David Holmes, for generous practical help and richly informed advice; Pamela Dalziel, for wise editorial counsel and immensely helpful readings of the introductory matter and specimen entries; Peter Lennon, for so enthusiastically sharing his numerous Hardy discoveries in the pages of British and American magazines; Frances Whistler, for expert and sensitive editorial surveillance; and, as always, Bill and Vera Jesty, for the constancy of their friendship, hospitality, and ready assistance. Barbara Rosenbaum's published work on Hardy's literary remains has been an invaluable resource; I have gratefully profited from the annotations to Harold Orel's long-standing edition of *The Personal Writings of Thomas Hardy* more often than might be suggested by my specific invocations of his name; and I am, as always, profoundly indebted to my wife, Jane Millgate, for both her personal support and her professional expertise. Finally, my special thanks on this occasion go to Bernard Jones, who has so generously made available to me the scholarly results of his own long-pursued researches into Hardy's public writings and further enriched the present edition by closely reading and commenting upon the entire text in typescript.

M.M.

Toronto
December 2000

CONTENTS

Contents   xv

ABBREVIATIONS

Adams	Frederick B. Adams, personal collection
Beinecke	Beinecke Rare Book and Manuscript Library, Yale University
Biography	Michael Millgate, *Thomas Hardy: A Biography* (New York: Random House; Oxford: Oxford University Press, 1982)
BL	British Library
Career	Michael Millgate, *Thomas Hardy: His Career as a Novelist* (1971; Basingstoke: Macmillan Press, 1994)
CL	*Collected Letters of Thomas Hardy*, ed. Richard L. Purdy and Michael Millgate, 7 vols. (Oxford: Clarendon Press, 1978–88)
CPW	*The Complete Poetical Works of Thomas Hardy*, ed. Samuel Hynes, 5 vols. (Oxford: Clarendon Press, 1982–95)
DCM	Dorset County Museum, Dorchester, Dorset
Eton	Eton School Library, Eton College
Hardy on Stage	Keith Wilson, *Thomas Hardy on Stage* (Basingstoke: Macmillan Press, 1995)
Houghton	Houghton Library, Harvard University
Index	Barbara Rosenbaum, *Index of English Literary Manuscripts. Volume IV, 1800–1900. Part 2, Hardy–Lamb* (London and New York: Mansell Publishing, 1990)
Interviews and Recollections	*Thomas Hardy: Interviews and Recollections*, ed. James Gibson (Basingstoke: Macmillan Press, 1999)
Letters EFH	*Letters of Emma and Florence Hardy*, ed. Michael Millgate (Oxford: Clarendon Press, 1996)
Life and Art	Thomas Hardy, *Life and Art*, ed. Ernest Brennecke, Jr. (New York: Greenberg, 1925)
LW	Thomas Hardy, *The Life and Work of Thomas Hardy*, ed. Michael Millgate (London and Basingstoke: Macmillan Press, 1984)
LN	*The Literary Notebooks of Thomas Hardy*, ed. Lennart A. Björk, 2 vols. (London and Basingstoke: Macmillan Press, 1984)
Millgate	Collection of the editor
Orel	*Thomas Hardy's Personal Writings*, ed. Harold Orel (Lawrence: University of Kansas Press, 1966)
PN	*The Personal Notebooks of Thomas Hardy*, ed. Richard H. Taylor (London and Basingstoke: Macmillan Press, 1978)

Princeton	Princeton University Library
Purdy	Richard Little Purdy, *Thomas Hardy: A Bibliographical Study* (Oxford: Clarendon Press, 1954)
Shakespeare	*The Riverside Shakespeare*, ed. G. Blakemore Evans (Boston: Houghton Mifflin, 1974) (the source for all quotations and references)
Texas	Harry Ransom Humanities Research Center, University of Texas
Wessex edn	*The Works of Thomas Hardy in Prose and Verse*, 24 vols (London: Macmillan, 1912–31)

INTRODUCTION

Thomas Hardy has generally been viewed as an intensely private figure, shy of publicity and even of people, self-isolated in his Dorsetshire home, and much more cautious and conservative in his personal outlook than might have been expected of the author of *Tess of the d'Urbervilles* and *Jude the Obscure*. What the present edition reveals is that Hardy's public utterances were not only more numerous than previously assumed but took many different forms and addressed a wide variety of literary, social, and political issues. Hardy's prefaces to his own works are excluded, on the grounds that they properly belong with the books they introduce and are, indeed, widely available in those contexts. But his separately published essays, speeches, letters to newspapers, contributions to magazine 'symposia', and other acknowledged participations in public discourse are here fully described, edited, and annotated, together with the many unsigned items, ranging from obituaries and marriage-notices to promotional puffs and planted paragraphs in literary gossip columns, that have now been securely or tentatively identified. Also described, though not systematically reproduced, are Hardy's designs for tombstones and memorials, his acts of assistance to other writers, and numerous examples of his lending his (immensely famous) name to causes and organizations of which he approved, most often by becoming a co-signatory of letters and petitions initiated and written by others.

The search for such materials—initially stimulated by the decision of the editors of *The Collected Letters of Thomas Hardy* to exclude letters written specifically for publication—has led to the identification of numerous items not mentioned in Purdy's bibliography and to the discovery of other previously unknown utterances that might in any case have eluded bibliographical categorization. All such categories are here discarded in favour of an organization of all the items, whatever their content or technical character, into a single chronological sequence that enables Hardy's engagement in public issues to be viewed as a continuous process that nonetheless displayed shifts in approach, emphasis, and direction at different stages of his career. In particular, the so-called minor writings represented in Harold Orel's edition of *Thomas Hardy's Personal Writings* only by summaries or brief quotations are incorporated, fully edited, at their appropriate chronological locations. By listing, describing, and—in most instances—quoting such a wide range of texts, the edition seeks both to consolidate and to expand existing knowledge of Hardy's non-fictional writings, and in so doing to sharpen awareness of the ways in which he endeavoured to reconcile his professional imperatives, as an author making his living by his writings, with his possession of strong personal views on some of the most controversial social and moral issues of the time. Even in his final decades of fame and acknowledged literary pre-eminence he continued to manage both his career and his public life without assistance from accountants or publicists and with only very occasional recourse to the services of literary agents.

I

Although so much new material has become available for the edition, it has not been easy to apply rigid criteria to the determination of what should be included and what omitted. The basic operative definition —Hardy's identifiable prose contributions to public discourse—has proved by no means unproblematic in practice, and the inclusion or exclusion of several items has had to be determined on the basis of very thin contextual evidence or of 'special-case' considerations. Hardy's fame, for example, ensured that a good many letters originating as personal correspondence quickly found their way into print, and in such instances it is often impossible to establish whether Hardy actively desired, retrospectively approved, or passively accepted publication— or was simply never consulted in the matter. When a letter is addressed directly to a newspaper editor or, conversely, has 'Not for publication' written across the top of it, the situation is straightforward enough. But it is not at all clear that Hardy expected to see in print such letters as those in which he declined honorary membership of the Robert Louis Stevenson Club or acknowledged birthday greetings sent by the Vice-Chancellor of Cambridge University. Hardy certainly consented to the quotation in a newspaper advertisement of his extravagant private praise for Theodore Watts-Dunton's little fantasy called *Christmas at the Mermaid*, but it may be doubted whether that consent was altogether willingly given. Inevitably, however, such contemporaneous acts of publication acquired the *de facto* status of public gestures, and they have therefore been included in this edition—even when identical or variant texts are already available in the *Collected Letters*. Not so included, on the other hand, are the clearly private letters that Hardy allowed to be published, often many years later, in the posthumous biographies of such friends as Bishop Handley Moule.

Hardy's speeches—in one sense his quintessential public utterances—have presented problems of their own. Although Hardy is said as a young architect in London to have entertained his colleagues during slow afternoons with 'short addresses or talks on poets and poetry',[1] he certainly evaded almost all of the many invitations to speak that were thrust upon him in his later years. Lecturing, he declared in 1904, 'is beyond my powers and province',[2] and he consistently refused dinner engagements if there seemed the slightest risk of their involving a speech of any kind. A few brief and even impromptu efforts are certainly on record: according to a *Dorset Daily Echo* reporter, 'the tensest silence' followed Hardy's unexpectedly getting to his feet to say a few congratulatory words at the very end, or indeed *after* the very end, of a Dorchester Debating and Dramatic Society essay competition in March 1925.[3] But such accounts rarely specify—even in the third person, let alone the first—what Hardy actually said, a typical instance being the *Dorset County Chronicle*'s report of Hardy's response to the thanks accorded him, early in 1918, for entertaining the Hardy Players to tea following a performance of *The Mellstock Quire*: 'Mr. Hardy made a pleasant acknowledgment, and expressed his appreciation of the excellent manner in which the play had been performed.'[4] Sufficient unto that particular occasion, no doubt, was the report thereof, but it is certainly disappointing to know no more of Hardy's speech in honour of George Meredith at the July 1895 Omar Khayyàm Club dinner than that he 'wittily and sweetly described his first meeting with Mr. Meredith in "a dusty back room at Chapman and Hall's" '.[5]

[1] *LW*, p. 49.   [2] *CL* vii. 135.   [3] *Dorset Daily Echo*, 1 April 1925, p. 4.
[4] *Dorset County Chronicle*, 7 February 1918, p. 7.   [5] *Daily Chronicle*, 15 July 1895, p. 7.

Full texts fortunately survive—sometimes in more than one version —for Hardy's more formal speeches, although it seems somehow characteristic that the longest of these, 'Memories of Church Restoration', was actually delivered by someone else, while another, written to be read out at a meeting of the Society of Dorset Men in London, was never delivered at all, so much of the available time having been taken up by speakers who were personally present. Although that particular speech was eventually published, not everything written by Hardy for possible publication did in fact appear in his lifetime. Known items, such as his architectural prize essay of 1862, are identified, however, and, when the relevant texts remain available—as in the case of the surviving typescript of Hardy's unused preface to a posthumous volume of poems by Laurence Hope (i.e. Violet Nicolson)—they have been included in the edition at their approximate chronological location. Representation of the large number of Thomas Hardy entries published in the biographical dictionaries of the day has been complicated by the proliferation of minimally variant versions across the span of Hardy's long life and by the difficulty of determining what input, if any, Hardy himself might have had into the content and wording of any particular entry. The pragmatic editorial response has been to reproduce the Thomas Hardy entry from the first modern issue of *Who's Who*, published in 1897, on the grounds that it was based directly on information supplied by Hardy himself,[6] and also, for purposes of comparison, the entry incorporating the last of the many revisions he made during the course of his lifetime. Also reproduced is Hardy's initial appearance in the 1879 issue of *Men of the Time*, the principal predecessor of *Who's Who*, chiefly because of its early date and inclusion of details later accounts omit, but also because Hardy is known to have supplied the editors with personal information for a subsequent issue.

The edition also contains a number of hitherto unrevealed examples of Hardy's skill at what might now be called manipulation of the media. Through genial encounters at the Society of Authors, the Savile Club, and some of the many dining clubs of the day, Hardy established relationships of mutual convenience with such prominent journalists and editors as William Moy Thomas, Edmund Yates, Clement Shorter, and James Milne. When, therefore, he had an item of news to make public, a book to promote, a criticism to counter, a minor score to settle, his

---

[6] In the *Who's Who* files still retained by the publisher, Adam and Charles Black.

preferred course was not to speak out directly in his own person but rather to nudge one of his journalist friends into speaking out on his behalf, generally supplying a wording that could be used or adapted for the purpose—a paragraph ready for the planting. The journalists, for their part, were always eager for items of literary gossip and willing enough to reciprocate: Milne, of the *Daily Chronicle* and the *Book Monthly*, is identified in Hardy's address book as a 'literary paragraphist', Lindsay Bashford, of the *Daily Mail*, as an 'enquirer for lit[erary] news'.[7] When Yates and Moy Thomas were asked by Hardy in 1890 to challenge the negative comments that had been made about a charity performance by the American actress Ada Rehan, and especially about the verses Hardy had written for her to speak at the end of the performance, they responded in their respective columns with what are in this edition called 'inspired' paragraphs, directly reflective of both the substance and the actual wording of Hardy's request. Over the years Clement Shorter, as editor of the *Sphere*, included in his regular 'Literary Letter' column, without attribution and often without rephrasing, numerous items that Hardy had in fact supplied. And when Jemima Hardy died in 1904, her son found no difficulty in silently placing obituaries and portraits of her in several newspapers and magazines—loyally insisting that his sister Mary's painting was the best likeness. Hardy, clearly, was not above log-rolling and mild self-promotion, and there were plenty of people glad to be of service to so prominent a figure.

Hardy was much given to action by indirection. Pamela Dalziel has shown, in her edition of his *Excluded and Collaborative Stories*, how he became a concealed partner—a kind of Conradian 'secret sharer'—in some of the fictional writings of Florence Henniker and Florence Dugdale, and the present edition calls attention not only to his having assisted and indeed influenced Agnes Grove in her writings on contemporary social issues but also to the similar—if differently motivated— partnerships entered into with commentators on his own writings. In August 1906 Hardy told Henry Woodd Nevinson: 'As to the article on my books that you contemplate writing, the only condition I make is that I do not personally appear in it as saying this or that: though I shall, of course, not mind giving any explanation of what may be obscure in them—that you may print it without saying how you arrived at your

---

[7] Address book in Dorset County Museum.

elucidations.'[8] Topographers such as Bertram Windle and Hermann Lea were similarly provided with usable information—Lea on at least one occasion receiving and using some prefabricated text—and the literary critics Samuel Chew and Harold Child both published revised editions of their books about Hardy on the basis of corrections and suggestions that Hardy himself had supplied. A mutually satisfactory exchange was thus accomplished, Hardy achieving without fuss (if with some trouble) the correction of perceived errors while the writers involved were happy to be chided in private rather than in public and gratified to have the task of revision simultaneously authorized and eased.

These silent interventions of Hardy's are recorded, within the overall chronological sequence of the edition, in individual descriptive paragraphs that are unaccompanied by text and thus take the form of disembodied headnotes. Textless headnotes of this kind are also used to identify the public statements—mostly letters to newspapers and magazines—that Hardy signed in association with others. Because he neither initiated nor wrote the letters he co-signed,[9] they might be considered 'arm's-length' gestures; as documents, however, written precisely to attract attention and address current issues, they in fact exposed him as a prominent signatory very nearly as much as an individual letter would have done. Hardy's fame and reputation as a writer with a social conscience clearly put him under frequent pressure to participate in such public gestures, and those examples that have been discovered—there are undoubtedly others—are remarkable both for their number and for their range. It is perhaps not surprising that he should have associated himself with messages of congratulation to Ibsen on his seventieth birthday, to Tolstoy on his eightieth, and to Meredith at both seventy and eighty, and with appeals for the Keats–Shelley Memorial in Rome and the placement of a memorial to Byron in Poets' Corner. It is more striking to find him co-signing letters that protest against the threatened execution of Maxim Gorky in 1905, deplore the laying of ritual murder charges against Jews in Russia, advocate the establishment of a Jewish state in Palestine, and express concern over the future

---

[8] *CL* iii. 223.

[9] It is possible that in November 1890 James R. Osgood drafted at TH's suggestion the letter in defence of Harper & Brothers that was jointly signed by TH, William Black, and Walter Besant (*CL* i. 218–20).

of the British film industry. Despite his reputation for not having been swept away by patriotic fervour during the First World War, Hardy was one of the fifty-two authors who signed an orthodox declaration in support of British war aims in September 1914, and one of the thousand 'Representatives of the Brain-Power of the Nation' who in October 1916 put their names to the full-page launching in *The Times* of a campaign that deplored the damage being done by alcohol to the war effort and urged the government to 'suspend all drink licences throughout the Kingdom for the period of the war'.[10]

There remain some aspects of Hardy's activity in the public world that are not reflected in this edition, or only very selectively represented. No attempt is made to list his numerous unpublicized participations in attempts to obtain Civil List pensions or Royal Literary Fund grants for writers such as Charlotte Mew, Charles Montagu Doughty, W. E. Henley, Lascelles Abercrombie, and W. B. Yeats, and for the members of writers' families—William Barnes's daughter Laura, for example, and the widows of John Davidson and John Churton Collins—who found themselves in financial difficulties. Interviews, too, are omitted as a category. Important as they can be for their glimpses and echoes of the ideas and personalities of men and women long dead, they are perhaps best considered as a genre unto themselves and treated together as a group.[11] From an editorial standpoint there is in virtually every interview a basic irresolvable doubt as to the authenticity of what is represented as the direct speech of the interviewee,[12] and in the late-Victorian period the popularity of the journalistic interview undoubtedly led to widespread plagiarization of existing interviews and even to outright invention. Hardy wrote 'faked' or 'mostly faked' against several of the interviews inserted into his 'Personal' scrapbook,[13] and he complained to newspaper editors on more than one occasion about interviews that had been obtained under what he considered to be false pretences. This edition does, however, print the surviving draft of

[10] *The Times*, 27 October 1916, p. 6.

[11] A large number of Hardy interviews are represented in *Interviews and Recollections*, but the edition does not claim to be comprehensive and the interviews included are not always reproduced in their entirety.

[12] A recent article on the editing of Victorian interviews concludes that, at best, the filtering of everything through the interviewer makes it difficult to feel confidence in the validity of 'using such interviews as if they convey the actual words of their nominal subjects' (Patrick G. Scott and William B. Thesing, 'Conversations with Victorian Writers: Some Editorial Questions', *Documentary Editing*, 11 (June 1989), p. 38).   [13] Scrapbook in Dorset County Museum.

Hardy's prepared response to the journalist (James Milne) who came to interview him about the fate of Stonehenge in 1899.[14] It also identifies (without quotation) two other interviews to which he may perhaps have made written contributions, and a third, with William Archer, that was written down by Archer but made available to Hardy for correction and revision both before it went to the printer and when it was in proof.[15]

II

It is obvious from the number and variety of his public utterances that Hardy, at least in his later years, was rarely in want of a platform. Requests, invitations, and honorific gestures of every kind flooded in upon him simply by virtue of the immense respect in which, as a writer of acknowledged greatness, he was increasingly held from the early 1890s to his death in January 1928. On the other hand, many of those who sought Hardy's support clearly did so not just because he was a famous writer but because he had written specific works—notably *Tess of the d'Urbervilles*, *Jude the Obscure*, some of the early 'philosophical' poems, and later *The Dynasts*—in which they found assurance of a sensitive social and humanitarian conscience and a deeply pondered world-view, hence, they believed, a predisposition in favour of their own particular cause. Hardy's instinct and general policy seem always to have been to respond positively whenever there seemed no reason to do otherwise—as he said of joining a Shakespeare Memorial Committee in 1905, even when he 'saw no great good' in particular causes he generally 'saw no harm' in them either[16]—and it is clear from the major literary essays (including the various pieces on William Barnes), from 'The Dorsetshire Labourer', and from 'Memories of Church Restoration' that he gladly embraced opportunities to write on issues that directly concerned him. However, among the very many appeals that he received there were, of course, causes that he could not support, societies that he did not join, letters to newspapers that he declined to co-sign, and requests that he simply ignored—and any comprehensive examination of his participation in public life would need to take such instances of inaction or outright negativity fully into account.

---

[14] See Purdy, p. 306; the draft is in Dorset County Museum. The printed version of the interview is available in Orel, pp. 196–200.

[15] *CL* ii. 279, 280, 281; iii. 76; the interview itself is included in Archer's *Real Conversations* (London: William Heinemann, 1904), pp. 29–50.   [16] *CL* iii. 156.

On some issues, such as censorship, his position seems to have shifted somewhat over time. In the late nineteenth century, for example, he was an open supporter of Henry Vizetelly, imprisoned for publishing Zola's novels in England, and a strong protestor, in his 'Candour in English Fiction' essay, against the restrictive pressures exerted by the periodical press and the circulating libraries on the freedom of expression in the Victorian novel. Early in the twentieth century, however, he failed to back up John Lane over the threatened suppression of a translation of Hermann Sudermann's *Song of Songs*, and his letter supporting John Galsworthy's representations on stage censorship before a parliamentary committee in 1909 was rather ineffectually anecdotal—to the point that a commentator in the *Academy* could call it 'about the finest defence of the censorship that it would be possible to set up'.[17] And when he felt uncertain or insufficiently informed about an issue, he would sometimes delay his reply—deliberately or otherwise—until the moment for action had passed.[18] In 1912, for example, he was asked to join in a protest against the Lord Chamberlain's refusal to license Eden Phillpotts's play *The Secret Woman* unless specific changes were made,[19] but by the time he had quibbled over the wording of the document everybody else had signed it in its original form.

Such hesitations were not necessarily groundless, however. He clearly believed that neither *The Secret Woman* nor the particular translation of *The Song of Songs* provided sufficiently solid bases for serious challenges to the censorship laws.[20] He thought *The Secret Woman* undistinguished as a play, the changes demanded by the Lord Chamberlain easy to accommodate, and the letter of protest overstated, while his view of the Sudermann situation was subsequently endorsed by Lane's decision to bring out the book in an entirely new translation. What seems to have been operative in these instances was not so much a cautious avoidance of direct confrontation as a kind of quasi-puritanical truth-telling compulsion that Hardy sometimes compromised but never quite lost. Heinemann's decision not to use Hardy's preface to Laurence Hope's posthumous poems was surely influenced by its

---

[17] *Academy*, 14 August 1909, p. 413.

[18] In 1907, for instance, he failed to sign a statement on slavery in Angola, because (so he told its sponsor) he put it aside 'to read up, and then forgot' (*CL* iii. 363).   [19] *CL* iv. 200–1, 202–3.

[20] TH told George Moore, who had challenged his position in respect of Sudermann: 'If a protest over interference has to be made, it would be a wiser policy to do it in connection with some safer book' (*CL* iv. 133).

lukewarm praise of the poems themselves and its distinctly discordant insistence that it was always a mistake for women to use male pseudonyms—as, of course, Laurence Hope herself had done. Even his anonymously printed article on Florence Henniker must have left its adored subject distinctly disappointed by its observations on her novels and stories: of her latest novel Hardy observed that 'the growing strength in character-drawing makes the reader indifferent to the absence of a well-compacted plot'.[21]

A particular criticism of Hardy has been that he gave little public expression to his support for the women's suffrage cause. As late as 1916 he was still refusing to become publicly associated with the movement.[22] Relevant in this context, however, is his remarkable November 1906 letter to Millicent Fawcett, who had invited him to contribute to a pamphlet containing pro-suffrage statements by leading men of the day. His personal support of the cause, he explained, was real enough, but it was grounded in the belief that the consequence of its success would be

to break up the present pernicious conventions in respect of manners, customs, religion, illegitimacy, the stereotyped household (that it must be the unit of society), the father of a woman's child (that it is anybody's business but the woman's own, except in cases of disease or insanity), sport (that so-called educated men should be encouraged to harass & kill for pleasure feeble creatures by mean stratagems), slaughter-houses (that they should be dark dens of cruelty), & other matters which I got into hot water for touching on many years ago.[23]

Not surprisingly, Mrs Fawcett omitted Hardy's letter from her pamphlet, on the grounds that 'John Bull [was] not ripe for it at present'.[24] Three years later he told Agnes Grove of his fear 'that it would be really injuring the women's cause if I were to make known exactly what I think may be the result of their success—a result I don't object to, but which one half your supporters certainly would'.[25]

Hardy frequently insisted that his profession as a novelist required him to occupy in public a position of detachment, political neutrality, and non-involvement in organizations dedicated to social causes. In 1897 he made the point with unusual specificity and force when explaining to an American correspondent why he was unable to supply a magazine article on 'the marriage laws': 'The fact is that I am compelled

---

[21] 'The Hon. Mrs. Henniker', *Illustrated London News*, 18 April 1894, p. 195.
[22] *CL* v. 186.　　[23] *CL* iii. 238.
[24] M. Fawcett to TH, 4 December 1906 (DCM).　　[25] *CL* iv. 3.

by disposition, habit, & limitations to confine my writing to mere delineations of what I see, or fancy I see, in life, leaving to others the expression of views on such spectacles, & the consideration of how to right, remedy, or prevent the wrongs which some of them undoubtedly are.'[26] Hardy had in reality published a short article on the marriage laws in 1894, at the time of _Jude_, and he was to publish another, rather unfortunately timed, in 1912, the year of his first wife's death. Both are frank in their criticism of the existing legislation, but their arguments are pursued only up to a point well short of the profound radicalism revealed in the letter to Millicent Fawcett. While Hardy clearly preferred to remain silent on such troublesome questions, there evidently were occasions when he felt impelled to speak out: indeed, the symposium on divorce to which he contributed in 1912 was itself prompted by parliamentary proposals for revision of the current marriage laws, so that he would have thought of himself as contributing to the possibility of practical change.

Hardy was never a strident campaigner, however, and at times he spoke with a perceptible weariness induced by the sheer recalcitrance of the universe, as when he declared in the spring of 1914: 'Altogether the world is such a bungled institution from a humane point of view that a grief more or less hardly counts.'[27] As the years passed, his appetite and energy for public debate declined still further, its dangers and costs looming ever larger in his imagination. He had long known that 'when you begin a newspaper correspondence there is no telling when you will end',[28] and in 1920 he declined to support a call for peace in Ireland not just because he had despaired of the Irish situation but because he had grown weary of the stresses of controversy itself: 'If one begins that sort of thing he must be prepared to go on, or to get the worst of it, & at my age I am not able to go on, apart from the fact that I have kept outside politics all my life.'[29] Receiving a similar appeal from Walter de la Mare some seven months later, Hardy returned the document unsigned, 'believing such protests useless, &, in any event, my signature no help to them'.[30]

When, in 1923, he refused a request from Dorothy Allhusen, one of his oldest friends, for money to assist in repairing the church at Stoke Poges, an embarrassed Florence Hardy wrote back: 'I hope you will not be too vexed with T.H. for his obstinacy. He is an old man, & was never

---

[26] _CL_ ii. 154.   [27] _CL_ v. 30.   [28] _CL_ iii. 113.   [29] _CL_ vi. 53.   [30] _CL_ vi. 94.

very easy to persuade I think.'[31] Wearying, finally, even of his own most cherished issue, Hardy instructed May O'Rourke, the Max Gate secretary, to reply as follows to an early 1926 request that he send a supportive message to a protest meeting against the lifelong caging of animals and birds: 'Mr Hardy wishes me to say that he has already notified in public prints, &c, his opposition to the practice of keeping animals & birds in captivity. A message from him was therefore not necessary, & undesirable, since it is a mistake to be over-emphatic even in a good cause.'[32] That it was a mistake to be over-emphatic even in a good cause had always been Hardy's essential position—it has the ring of one of his mother's minatory pronouncements—and its implied tension, or perhaps compromise, between testifying and keeping silent was finally, and characteristically, endorsed by his ghost-writing much the most substantial of his non-fictional utterances for posthumous publication over the name of his wife.

III

The two volumes that Florence Hardy duly produced—*The Early Life of Thomas Hardy 1840–1891* and *The Later Years of Thomas Hardy 1892–1928*, originally published by Macmillan in 1928 and 1930 respectively—quoted extensively from many of the non-fiction pieces published by Hardy during his lifetime. Even so, there is ample evidence that Hardy had actively considered the possibility of publishing—within the context of a complete edition of his works—a volume specifically devoted to what he referred to as his 'Miscellanies' or his 'Miscellanea'. It is not clear whether he had in fact planned such a gathering prior to the 1925 New York publication, over his name, of *Life and Art: Essays, Notes, and Letters Collected for the First Time*, a compilation mostly of pieces not copyright in the United States that had been put together by the American critic Ernest Brennecke, Jr., the author of a recent biography that Hardy was already seeking to discredit. But when he wrote in April 1925 to discourage the British publishing house of T. Fisher Unwin from distributing *Life and Art* within the United Kingdom, he certainly claimed that he had 'for a long time . . . discussed with the Macmillans when my miscellanies (which would contain the major part of the said "Life & Art") shall be published in the uniform series of my works, for the sake of completeness'.

---

[31] *Letters EFH*, p. 202.   [32] *CL* vii. 12.

He went on to insist that the project, though postponed, 'must ultimately be done',[33] and there does indeed survive, among the Sydney Cockerell papers in the Victoria and Albert Museum, a Hardy manuscript with a cover-sheet that reads 'List of Miscellaneous Articles by Thomas Hardy—in case they should be required for reprinting in His Complete Works'. The two-page manuscript itself bears the heading:

Miscellanea: by *Thomas Hardy*

a list of all, or nearly all, that it would be desirable to publish, is here given, in case publication should be decided upon.
a copy of most of these articles is contained in the bundle with which this is enclosed.

The list itself is not in fact confined to non-fiction prose, in that it includes the early sketch 'How I Built Myself a House' and 'The Three Wayfarers', Hardy's own dramatization of his short story 'The Three Strangers'.[34] But all the other items are reproduced in the present edition, and several had already been reprinted—as, indeed, had 'How I Built Myself a House'—in *Life and Art*: for example, the three literary essays, the Barnes obituary, 'The Dorsetshire Labourer', the 1878 and 1883 letters on the use of dialect in novels, and what Hardy lists as 'Humours (or Memories?) of Church Restoration'. Hardy adds deprecatory comments on some of the pieces—'Why I Don't Write Plays' is 'apparently hardly worth preserving', the Tolbort obituary 'probably not worth reprinting'—and suggests the use of only one of his three critical articles on Barnes, 'as they are more or less similar'. It is clear, however, that the list was drawn up with some care, that it post-dates *Life and Art*—which is invoked on several occasions and even suggested as a source for the texts of one or two otherwise elusive items—and that it identifies the non-fiction writings that Hardy in his last years thought worthy of preservation. Few of his more outspoken and controversial writings are listed, but the possibility that they had been forgotten or regretted is countered by the reappearance of several such pieces in *Early Life* and *Later Years* (subsequently re-edited as *Life and Work*).

It does not appear that the list and accompanying 'bundle' of copies were sent to Macmillan while Hardy was still alive. Following Hardy's

---

[33] *CL* vi. 322. Florence Hardy, writing to Cockerell on 11 June 1925 (Beinecke), reported her husband as saying that Macmillan had not seemed interested in publishing such a volume.

[34] According to Florence Hardy, writing to Cockerell on 1 July 1929 (Beinecke), Hardy had said that the play was bound to be printed some day and might therefore go into 'the volume of miscellaneous articles'.

death in January 1928, however, Sydney Cockerell, as co-literary executor, insisted to Florence Hardy, the other literary executor, that a tougher line should be taken in dealings with the Macmillan house, and it was presumably at Cockerell's suggestion that, when Florence went to discuss the publication of *Winter Words* with Daniel Macmillan in London on 17 February 1928, she took with her what she called 'the collection of articles that my husband had tied together for a volume of miscellanies'.[35] Macmillan evidently took charge of the bundle, which he had politely expressed an interest in seeing,[36] and sent off to Charles Whibley, the firm's principal reader of literary works, the typed copy of Hardy's original list that Florence had also brought with her. When, however, Whibley returned the list to Macmillan (it is not clear that he saw the collection of texts), it was with the recommendation that only eight of the items should be retained, the remainder being too brief or trivial 'for publication in a permanent form'.[37]

Daniel Macmillan sent Cockerell a copy of Whibley's comments on the projected 'Miscellanea' volume, together with the list that Whibley had annotated, and indicated his firm's willingness to publish, 'on the usual terms', some such shortened version of 'Mr. Hardy's essays and addresses'.[38] Cockerell in his reply expressed his entire agreement with Whibley's report, asked for 'the usual terms' to be spelled out, and proposed that Macmillan in the meantime should keep the submitted copies of the articles Whibley had selected and return the others to himself.[39] Cockerell was evidently bypassing Florence and taking matters very much into his own hands; even so, little progress towards actual publication seems to have been made—perhaps because Cockerell was dissatisfied with the terms Macmillan offered, perhaps because Macmillan realized that the essays chosen would make up into only a very short book, or perhaps because everyone became preoccupied with the difficult gestation of the official biography. When the subject was reopened—apparently by Cockerell—early in 1929, Florence Hardy wrote Daniel Macmillan a distinctly negative letter on 23 January 1929

[35] Florence Hardy to D. Macmillan, 11 February 1928 (BL, Add. MS 54926, fo. 48).

[36] BL, Macmillan papers, Add. MS 55667.

[37] Attachment to D. Macmillan to Cockerell, 15 March 1928 (Beinecke). Whibley selected the three literary essays, the three critical pieces on Barnes (merged into and counting as one), 'Dorset in London', 'Memories of Church Restoration', 'Some Romano-British Relics Found at Max Gate', and 'The Dorsetshire Labourer'.

[38] D. Macmillan to Cockerell, 15 March 1928 (Beinecke).

[39] Cockerell to D. Macmillan, 16 March 1928 (Millgate).

to the effect that she had been advised 'by an eminent critic long ago' that Hardy's essays should not be published 'until after judgement had been formed upon his work as a whole—that is to say not until after three or four years'.[40] Macmillan, as he told Cockerell on 5 February 1929, was by this time 'very doubtful whether it would serve any good purpose to publish such a volume at all', and effectively closed the matter by adding: 'We certainly should not be keen to do so ourselves, though of course if you and Mrs. Hardy wished it done we should naturally be prepared to fall in with your wishes.'[41]

Macmillan had meanwhile returned the 'rejected' items to Cockerell, as requested, on 19 March 1928, and two and a half months later he put into the office safe the 'selected' residue of Hardy's original submission.[42] And there, apparently, it remained for many years. In July 1965, however, the Macmillan publishing house moved from the building in St Martin's Street it had occupied since 1897, abandoning much of the office furniture in the process. The weekend before the demolition men moved in, the vacated premises were visited by Nicholas Barker, who had joined Macmillan the previous May and had spent most of his time since then in travelling and familiarizing himself with all aspects of the firm's operations. Reaching the old roll-top desk at which he himself had sat during his very occasional visits to the building, he removed its miscellaneous contents—including a little bundle of magazines and loose pages, held together by a tightly buckled red and yellow cloth strap, that he found at the back of one of the drawers—and put them, unexamined, into a sack that he then took home and left in his garage. It was not until six years later that Barker finally opened the sack and discovered that the little bundle in fact contained the fascinating remnants of Hardy's 'Miscellanea' proposal, the collection of corrected proofs and typescripts, newspaper pages and magazine copies (e.g. of the issue of *Longman's Magazine* in which 'The Dorsetshire Labourer' had first appeared), typed copies of Hardy's list, and a few items of correspondence that Daniel Macmillan had in 1928 consigned to the office safe. Barker later made an anonymous donation of the materials to a sale being organized by the Friends of the National Library, and as Lot 89 they were purchased en bloc at Sotheby's on 9 June 1981 by Bertram Rota on behalf of David Holmes, dealer in manuscripts and devoted Hardyan, by whom

[40] Florence Hardy to D. Macmillan, 23 January 1929 (BL, Add. MS 54926, fos. 94–5).
[41] D. Macmillan to Cockerell, 5 February 1929 (Beinecke).
[42] Annotations to Macmillan office copy of Hardy's list (Millgate).

they have for the most part been distributed, by sale and gift, to a series of appropriate destinations.[43]

The lukewarm response on all sides to Hardy's 'Miscellanea' project immediately following his death evidently led not only to its remaining unpublished but to its becoming, in effect, forgotten. Purdy does not mention it, nor do any of the Hardy biographies; Harold Orel seems similarly to have been unaware of it; and indeed I know of no printed references to it other than the Sotheby catalogue entry, descriptions of individual items in catalogues issued by David Holmes and Maggs, and the brief accounts of the project and some of the 'bundle' items provided by Barbara Rosenbaum in her admirably comprehensive survey of Hardy's manuscripts.[44] I certainly knew nothing of it until it was brought to my attention by David Holmes some years after I had begun collecting items for inclusion in *Public Voice*. Since that time, however, my awareness of the 'Miscellanea' material, enhanced by the discovery of the original manuscript of Hardy's list, has translated into a satisfying sense of completing a volume that Hardy had wanted and confidently projected but been obliged to leave unrealized at his death.

The scale and breadth of the present edition, however, clearly exceed anything that Hardy himself could have imagined, or would perhaps have wished. He neither sought a major public role for himself, nor saw it as one that he could, as a novelist and poet, effectively perform, and he would certainly have considered unimportant many of the items here included. But what can now be thoroughly understood and firmly said is that he was throughout his career persistently and sensitively aware of both the immediate preoccupations and the deeper rhythms of his time, that he remained open and potentially responsive to requests that he lend his name or voice to specific organizations and issues, and that he was above all faithful to the causes such as cruelty to animals that he had made most particularly his own.

---

[43] It was from David Holmes that I first heard the outlines of this story, but for its more intimate details I am indebted to Nicholas Barker himself.

[44] *Index*, pp. 19, 149, 151, 168, 171, 172.

EDITORIAL PROCEDURES

This edition is devoted to the collection and, whenever appropriate, the reproduction of a wide range of public utterances and interventions for which Thomas Hardy was responsible during his lifetime. It excludes his prefaces and annotations to his own writings on the grounds that these 'belong' with the works to which they refer. It includes, on the other hand, all the separately published items of non-fiction prose for which Hardy is known to have been responsible: e.g. essays, speeches, obituaries, letters to newspapers, invited contributions to newspaper and magazine symposia, introductions and prefaces to other people's works, and even the occasional advertising 'puff'. It further extends to the identification—though not in general the reproduction—of public letters and other documents that he co-signed but did not himself write and of other, unsigned, items for which he can be shown to have been certainly or very probably responsible: e.g. corrections or additions to other people's writings. 'Inspired' (i.e. initiated but anonymous) contributions to the literary news and gossip columns of his day are reproduced when there is clear textual evidence for his participation, but simply listed when there is not. Also listed are some of the more interesting of the many societies and causes to which he publicly lent his name, one or two pieces of his writing no longer extant (hence not reproducible), and occasional instances in which he clearly intended to make a public gesture but was for some reason (e.g. delay on his part or a change in the situation being addressed) prevented from doing so.

Each of the texts in this edition possesses a distinct textual history and is introduced by a headnote in which that history—sometimes complex, sometimes involving a single witness—is concisely summarized, documented, and, when necessary, contextualized. Because of the edition's primary concern with Hardy's acts of direct public address, the utterances themselves are represented whenever feasible by the forms in which they were first made public—most often in the pages of a newspaper or magazine, and generally within a few days of their composition. The headnotes also record (selectively when numerous) other printings of the same item within Hardy's lifetime, and footnotes (generally reserved for explanatory and historical annotation) are deployed as necessary to register the more significant variants occurring in earlier or later authoritative forms (e.g. manuscripts and proofs or the posthumously published but essentially autobiographical *Life and Work*). In view, however, of the exposure of so many of the included items to such standard hazards of periodical publication as house-styling and editorial truncation, the pressures of deadlines and the errors of compositors, it has not seemed useful to supply comprehensive lists of discrepant readings.

Whenever it has seemed appropriate to reproduce an item in a form other than the one in which it was first printed—because, for example, it reappeared in an authorially revised version shortly after its initial publication, or was left partly or wholly unpublished during Hardy's lifetime—the procedures adopted are specified in the headnote. And in those instances when Hardy made a public communication that did not involve any textual performance on his part—as when he simply added his name to a letter composed by someone else—the headnote is allowed to stand alone, without an accompanying text, as a description and record of the event. Reference has been made to three or four interview situations in which Hardy is known or believed to have supplied material in written form, but interviews are, as a category, excluded. The inscriptions Hardy designed for tombstones and other public memorials are treated in more discursive fashion in an appendix.

Items are printed in a single chronological sequence throughout, in so far as that sequence can be precisely established. The placing of published items is determined by their date of first publication; that of unpublished items and those involving a silent—hence, in many cases, indeterminate—contribution on Hardy's part is in general dependent upon their likely date of composition or initiation. The wording and spelling of all quoted texts are precisely followed, but punctuation and layout have been lightly modified in order to reduce the incidence of essentially meaningless variations resulting from the styling and editing of the many books and periodicals concerned. Letters quoted from newspapers and magazines are regularized as to the placement of addresses, dates, salutations, and signatures; first paragraphs are taken flush to the left-hand margin, except in the case of letters that have retained recognizable elements of an epistolary format; book and periodical titles are given in italics, the titles of articles and poems in

Roman within quotation marks; and the capitalization standard in many newspapers and periodicals for headings to articles and signatures to letters is retained only to the extent of initial capitals. When the source is a Hardy manuscript (other than a published facsimile), ampersands have been expanded and working revisions within the manuscript left unrecorded.

Most of the items here reproduced were originally published without specific titles—e.g. as contributions to 'symposia', paragraphs within literary gossip columns, or letters grouped with others under such headings as 'Correspondence' or 'Letters to the Editor'. In the present edition the titles of individual items are of three kinds, identifiable by their distinctive typographical formats: those titles presumed to have originated with an editor or sub-editor appear within single quotation marks; those supplied by the present editor are surrounded by square brackets; those chosen by Hardy himself are free both of brackets and of quotation marks. The presence of question marks before and after a title signals that the attribution to Hardy is questionable in some respect that the headnote will explain.

1856

[1856.01]

[?The Alms-House Clock?]

Hardy in his last decades narrated somewhat differing versions (e.g. 1910.05; *LW*, p. 37) of how, as an architect's pupil, he tricked 'a Dorchester paper' into publishing 'an anonymous skit' on the disappearance of the clock that hung—and hangs still—from the former Napper's Mite alms-house in South Street, Dorchester, almost immediately opposite the office of John Hicks, the architect to whom he was apprenticed. No item precisely corresponding to Hardy's recollection of a paragraph 'in the form of plaintive letter from the ghost of the clock' has yet been discovered, but 'The Town Clocks', *Dorset County Chronicle*, 17 January 1856, p. 464 (see *Biography*, pp. 53–4), is tentatively reprinted below as seeming a somewhat stronger candidate than 'A Pump Complaining', *Southern Times*, 1 March 1856, p. 140 (reprinted *Dorset County Chronicle*, 6 March 1856, p. 614), suggested and printed by Purdy, pp. 291–2. Both possibilities, however, inconveniently pre-date the beginning of Hardy's apprenticeship to Hicks in July 1856. Rendered almost certainly irrelevant by its still earlier date is the recollection of Charles Lacey, an almost exact contemporary, of Hardy's having amused his Dorchester schoolfellows with 'a little poem' about an occasion when the hands of the South-street clock fell off (London *Evening Standard*, 12 January 1928, p. 1).

We wish to draw the attention of the proper authorities to the irregularity of the various public time-pieces in this our good town of Dorchester. For a long time past they have not marked the 'flight of time' accurately, and have appeared determined, by some wrongheaded principle of action to keep those who consult them in a constant state of doubt and perplexity. The Trinity Clock scorns the society of its neighbour St Peter's, and obstinately refuses to keep company with it; while the South-street Clock has an infinite contempt for both, and keeps on its own course; but whether it determines the hour of the day by the sun, or by railway time,[1] or by a system of its own, it is impossible to tell. Now, in the midst of such perversity, what can the public do? So many things are dependent on the time being marked accurately, that it is of the utmost importance that the guides we use should be of the best possible description, and not likely to lead us astray. We hope that this remonstrance will be listened to in the proper quarter, so that for the future there will be 'no more complaining in our streets'[2] of the eccentric behaviour of our Town Clocks.

[1856.02]

[?Accounts of Church-Restoration?]

In *Life and Work*, p. 37, Hardy claimed that, during the years (1856–62) when he was an apprentice and, later, an assistant to the Dorchester architect John Hicks, he 'prepared for the grateful reporter of the *Dorset Chronicle*' a number of 'accounts of church-restoration carried out by Hicks'. Purdy, p. 293, identifies several *Dorset County Chronicle* reports of the reopenings of Dorset churches worked on by Hicks during the period in question, and Hardy's use of the term 'prepared' would seem to suggest that some of them could incorporate passages of his own writing. But while such reports are often extensive and technically well informed, as C. J. P. Beatty showed when quoting—in *Thomas Hardy and the Restoration of Rampisham Church, Dorset* (Bridport, Dorset: privately printed, 1991), pp. 25–9—the *Dorset County Chronicle* account, 10 March 1859, p. 625, of the Rampisham parish church reopening, it is impossible to tell what just contribution, direct or otherwise, Hardy may in fact have made to any of them. See, however, 1870.01, 1891.04.

---

[1] The railway, running to a standardized timetable, had reached Dorchester in 1847; cf. 'London time' (1886.02).　　[2] Slightly adapted from Psalm 144: 14.

1857

[1857.01]

[Unpublished Juvenilia]

Surviving in the Dorset County Museum is a slim notebook of Hardy's headed 'A Chronological List of Thomas Hardy's Works in verse & prose—Giving date of writing, where known, and date of publication'. The list, which does not go beyond 1909, is in fact devoted almost exclusively to verse, but the very first entry, 'Written in 1857–1860', includes—in addition to ' "Domicilium"—a Poem in Blank Verse'—three prose items: 'A criticism of the "Essays of Elia" ', 'A criticism of Tennyson's Idylls', and 'A criticism of Tennyson's The Princess'. All are described as 'destroyed unprinted', and there is no way of determining their length, character, or degree of completion. Hardy seems also to have written prose as well as verse while he was in London between 1862 and 1867. His friend Horace Moule (1922.04) pushed him in the direction of journalism and praised in 1864 the 'chatty description of the Law Courts and their denizens' he had recently written (*Biography*, p. 86), and his writing at this period is perhaps typified—as it is almost uniquely represented—by his first publication, the fictional sketch 'How I Built Myself a House', published in *Chambers's Journal*, March 1865. See Hardy, *The Excluded and Collaborative Stories*, edited by Pamela Dalziel (Oxford: Clarendon Press, 1992), pp. [10]–23.

1863

[1863.01]

On the Application of Coloured Bricks and Terra Cotta to Modern Architecture

Hardy, working in London from 1862 to 1867 as an assistant architect in the office of Arthur Blomfield, won the Silver Medal of the Royal Institute of British Architects with this essay in 1863. He was distressed, however, by the judges' decision to withhold the cash portion of the prize—on the grounds that he had not dealt sufficiently with all aspects of the topic assigned—and is said to have taken the essay out of the Institute's library and never returned it (*Biography*, pp. 79–80). Despite its success in the competition, therefore, the essay was never published, and no copy is now known to be extant: Hardy did tell Edmund Gosse in July 1893 that he believed he had the manuscript 'in some drawer' (*CL* ii. 24), but in his 'Chronological List' (DCM) the item is described as 'lost', a frequent Hardyan euphemism for 'destroyed'. See *Journal of the Royal Institute of British Architects*, 24 April 1920, p. 296. Purdy, p. 293.

[1870.01]

[?Reopening of Turnworth Church?]

Hardy's claim (1856.02) to have assisted a *Dorset County Chronicle* reporter in writing informed accounts of the reopenings of 'restored' Dorset churches does not indicate whether he resumed such collaborations following his return to architectural work in Dorset in 1867. It certainly seems likely, however, that he was the source of the exceptionally detailed architectural information incorporated into the *Dorset County Chronicle*'s report, 28 April 1870, p. 8, of the reopening of Turnworth Church in north-east Dorset—a project designed by Hicks, taken over by the Weymouth architect, G. R. Crickmay, after Hicks's death, and completed for Crickmay under Hardy's close and apparently almost exclusive supervision (*Biography*, pp. 115–16). The technical portion of that report—amounting to roughly two-thirds of the whole—is reprinted below, not as representing Hardy's own writing (though it may in part be his) but as providing some insight into his architectural expertise and aesthetic at this relatively late point in his first career. See also 1891.04.

The operations which have been brought thus satisfactorily to a termination consist of an entire rebuilding of the church, with the exception of the tower. The old building was in the plan of a simple parallelogram, the walls being much thrust outward with the weight of the roof, which, together with their dilapidated condition, rendered them very insecure, and left no alternative but to take them completely down. The plan of enlargement may be approximately described as the erection of a nave, chancel, and porch, covering the whole site of the old structure; a north aisle and a chancel aisle being built on new ground taken in from the churchyard; a vestry is screened off at the east end. The tower, which is the only portion of the original edifice left standing, is somewhat less perfect in proportion and outline than are the majority of this class that we find attached to the village churches of the county; and this fact, added to some fear for its stability, suggested a doubt as to whether it would be advisable to let it remain; but the consideration that antiquity, however bald, has a claim upon our respect, and a charm which is vainly sought for in the most elaborate modern production, a careful bonding together of the weak portions was undertaken and successfully completed. An examination of the few fragments of work in the old church walls—and chiefly of a window on the north side—which were at all characteristic of a style, determined the architect in his choice of Early English features as the type that it would be desirable to follow in the new design, at the same time giving to the details, and notably to the carving,[1] some of the spirit and crispness which have been of late years imported into English work by the closer study of continental examples of the same date. This mode of treatment is most perceptible in the arcade dividing the nave from the aisle. The necessity of keeping the piers low and yet of good proportion is a difficulty which was experienced no less by the mediæval designers of village churches than by their modern imitators (as an inspection of such buildings will show), and this rendered the variety of style here adopted as desirable on grounds of utility as on those of appearance. The new church affords sitting accommodation for about 150 persons, including the school children, for whom seats have been fitted up under the tower. The roofs of the nave and aisles are open-timbered, and supported by framed trusses, which in their turn spring from carved stone corbels in the walls. The chancel roof assumes a polygonal shape, the angles being emphasised by moulded ribs dividing the whole surface into panels. These are backed by close diagonal boarding, foliated perforations enriching the lower portion immediately above the cornice. The lectern is of polished oak, a moulded base, which sustains coupled columns and richly-carved capitals with brackets above supporting the book-board, the prayer-desk being of a somewhat similar design. The pulpit, constructed also of oak, is polygonal in form. A credence stands on the north side of the chancel, within the sacrarium, the outline being a moulded equilateral arch springing from a slab enriched at the front with carved leaves. On the opposite side the window bench has been kept low and designed to form a sedile. The steps here are of polished Purbeck marble, and the whole of the chancel

---

[1] TH's name appears on an album of photographs (DCM) of the newly carved capitals in the nave, and he was almost certainly responsible for their design: see John Newman and Nikolaus Pevsner, *Dorset* (Harmondsworth: Penguin Books, 1972), p. 431.

floor is laid with Minton's encaustic tiles. We may add that the use of 'cathedral glass' in the windows gives them the semi-opacity desirable in those of ecclesiastical edifices, and softens the light of the interior. Mr G. R. Crickmay, of Weymouth, was the architect under whose super-intendence the building was begun and completed, the original plans having been prepared by the late Mr John Hicks, of Dorchester. The builder was Mr Augustine Green, of Blandford, who has executed the work in a most praiseworthy manner. The carving was by Messrs. Boulton and Son, of Cheltenham, and shows all the usual vigour and finish by which their work is distinguishable.

1874

[1874.01]

[Wedding Announcement]

Given the hostility of Hardy's family to his marriage, it was presumably Hardy himself who composed the following announcement and inserted it into the *Dorset County Chronicle*, 24 September 1874, p. 20. The class distinctions encoded in the difference between 'Mr T. Hardy' and 'J. A. Gifford, Esq.' are noted in *Biography*, p. 164.

HARDY–GIFFORD. Sept. 17, at St Peter's Church, Paddington, by the Rev. E. H. Gifford, D.D., hon. canon of Worcester, uncle of the bride, Thomas Hardy, of Celbridge-place, Westbourne Park, London, son of Mr T. Hardy, of Bockhampton, to Emma Lavinia, younger daughter of J. A. Gifford, Esq., of Kirland, Cornwall.

[1874.02]

[Response to Toast of Whitefriars Club]

The Whitefriars Club, a convivial association of writers and journalists, published privately in 1900 a retrospective volume, *The Whitefriars' Chronicles*, edited by T. Heath Joyce. One of the contributors, Charles E. Pearce, a prolific author of light fiction, recalled (p. 40) that Hardy had been the principal guest at a dinner held by the Club at its usual haunt, The Mitre Inn, Fleet Street, shortly after the first appearance of *Far from the Madding Crowd* in volume form—presumably, therefore, in the last weeks of 1874. According to Pearce, 'The rule of no toasts was departed from, and Hardy's health was drunk. He made no pretence to be an after-dinner speaker, and his response was brief and formal.' Hardy was sent a copy of *The Whitefriars' Chronicles* upon being elected to honorary membership of the club in 1901 and made reference to the 1874 dinner in his letter of acceptance (1901.03).

1875

[?Speech at Shotover Dinner?]

On 6 May 1875 (*CL* i. 37) Hardy accepted an invitation to attend a dinner being given in Oxford on 11 May 1875 by the editors of a satirical undergraduate magazine called *The Shotover Papers, Or, Echoes from Oxford*, published in thirteen numbers between 23 February 1874 and 9 February 1875. No commitment to speak is mentioned in Hardy's letter, nor does any reference to the occasion appear in *Life and Work*, but the dinner itself was briefly reported in the *Oxford Undergraduate's Journal*, 13 May 1875, p. 69, and a printed programme (Beinecke) lists Hardy as responding, along with the poet Austin Dobson (1840–1921), to the toast of 'Literature'.

[1877.01]

[Using the Dorset Dialect]

In 1877 the English Dialect Society issued a supplement, edited by the Revd Walter W. Skeat and J. H. Nodal and published by Trübner & Co., to its earlier *A Bibliographical List of the Works That Have Been Published, or Are Known to Exist in MS., Illustrative of the Various Dialects of English*, edited by Skeat alone and published by Trübner in 1873. The supplement, also called *A Bibliographical List*, includes *Far from the Madding Crowd* and *The Hand of Ethelberta* under the heading of 'Dorsetshire' (p. 174) and quotes on the same page the following slightly truncated text of the letter (DCM) that Hardy had written on 24 August 1876 in response to an enquiry (DCM) from Nodal, the Society's honorary secretary. For Hardy's subsequent comments on the use of dialect in his novels, see 1878.02 and 1881.01.

The dialect of the peasants in my novels is, as far as it goes, that of this county [Dorset][1]; but it is necessary to state that I have not, as a rule, reproduced in the dialogues such words as would, from their approximation to received English, seem to a London reader to be mere mispronunciations. But though I have scarcely preserved peculiarities of accent and trifling irregularities with such care as could have been wished for purposes of critical examination, the characteristic words which occur are in every case genuine, as heard from the lips of the natives. *A Pair of Blue Eyes* should be excepted from this explanation. The scene of that story is laid in Cornwall, with the dialect of which I am imperfectly acquainted.

---

[1] Not present in TH's MS but inserted within square brackets into the text as published.

1878

[1878.01]

'Thomas Hardy'

On 9 May 1878 Hardy forwarded to Edward Abbott (1841–1908), editor of the Boston *Literary World*, a 'few notes' for the biographical sketch of himself that Abbott had earlier proposed (*CL* i. 56). The manuscript (Bowdoin College) is in Emma Hardy's hand, but it bears a few alterations in her husband's hand and had presumably been drafted or dictated by him in the first instance. The unsigned sketch, headed 'World Biographies. Thomas Hardy', was extensively revised and in places rewritten prior to its publication, as below, in the *Literary World*, 1 August 1878, p. 46; its numerous departures from the readings of the manuscript—possibly the result of proof corrections made by Hardy himself—have been selectively footnoted. Purdy, p. 295.

Mr Thomas Hardy, the English novelist, was born in 1840, in a lonely old-fashioned house in Dorsetshire on the margin of a wood, in the rear of which stretched a heath for several miles. One is reminded of the spot by the opening scene in his latest story, *The Return of the Native*.[1] In his seventeenth year he was articled as pupil to an architect, who had an extensive practice in ecclesiastical architecture, it being about the time when the passion for church 'restoration' was in full vigor. Mr Hardy came in for a good share of this work, and under color of restoring and renovating for a good cause was instrumental in obliterating many valuable records in stone of the history of quiet rural parishes, much to his regret in later years. His attention, however, during this period was not wholly devoted to architecture, literature receiving his attention to a

---

[1] 'One ... *Native*.' Sentence absent from the MS and—since the novel was not published in volumes until November 1878—perhaps added in proof.

considerable extent, and his higher education being looked after by an able classical scholar and Fellow of Queen's College, Cambridge.[2] Mr Hardy first took up his permanent residence in London in 1862. His knowledge of Gothic art became greatly advanced by the opportunity this change afforded him of designing under the direction of Mr[3] A. W. Bloomfield, the well-known architect, son of a late bishop of London; but his interest soon turned more particularly in the direction of pictures, and he made use of every opportunity which the International Exhibition of that year and public and private galleries afforded to extend his knowledge of the various schools of art, ancient and modern. During this very year Mr Hardy wrote an essay on Architecture, which took the prize medal[4] of the Royal Institute of British Architects; and some time later he was awarded the prize offered by the late Sir William Tite, M.P., for architectural design. These successes encouraged in him the purpose of becoming an art critic, and to fit himself for that office he undertook special studies; but his early taste for romantic literature having meanwhile revived, he sent a first attempt[5] in fiction to a London magazine. It was at once accepted, and his career was determined; though his love of art has been by no means abandoned. Mr Hardy's first complete novel was[6] *Desperate Remedies* (1871), which in some quarters was applauded and in others loudly[7] condemned. *Under the Greenwood Tree* followed in 1872, a story which, though well received on all sides, was some time in making its way into notice. Both of the foregoing were published anonymously. In 1873 appeared *A Pair of Blue Eyes*, which attracted a good deal of attention; and in 1874 *Far from the Madding Crowd*, the latter first running its course in the pages of the *Cornhill Magazine*. *The Hand of Ethelberta* succeeded this in the same periodical a few months later, and *The Return of the Native*, Mr Hardy's sixth novel, is now reaching American readers through the pages of *Harper's Monthly*.[8]

[2] Horace Moule; the reading 'Queen's' (correctly 'Queens'') is in the MS.

[3] TH added 'now Sir' in pencil to the cutting of the article inserted into his 'Personal' scrapbook (DCM). For 'Bloomfield' MS reads (correctly) 'Blomfield'.

[4] MS reads 'prize and medal'; possible proof change by TH, who in 1863 won the RIBA prize medal but not the cash portion of the award (see 1863.01).

[5] For 'a first attempt' MS reads 'a short attempt'.

[6] For 'and his . . . was' MS reads 'and fiction thence forward became his hobby. But he did not altogether neglect art and visited several of the great collections of paintings in Continental Capitals from time to time. The first complete novel from his hands was'.

[7] For 'loudly' MS reads 'as loudly'.

[8] The serial, in *Harper's New Monthly Magazine*, ran from February 1878 to January 1879.

[1878.02]

'Dialect in Novels'

An unsigned review of *The Return of the Native* in the *Athenaeum* of 23 November 1878, pp. 654–5, criticized the dialogue of the rural characters as being 'pitched throughout in too high a key to suit the talkers'. Hardy's letter of reply, shorn of address and date, appeared as below in the next issue of the *Athenaeum*, 30 November 1878, p. 688; the original is not known to be extant. Reprinted in Lionel Johnson, *The Art of Thomas Hardy* (London: Elkin Mathews and John Lane, 1894), p. xvii, and *Life and Art*, p. 113. Purdy, p. 295.

A somewhat vexed question is reopened in your criticism of my story, *The Return of the Native*; namely, the representation in writing of the speech of the peasantry when that writing is intended to show mainly the character of the speakers, and only to give a general idea of their linguistic peculiarities.

An author may be said to fairly convey the spirit of intelligent peasant talk if he retains the idiom, compass, and characteristic expressions, although he may not encumber the page with obsolete pronunciations of the purely English words, and with mispronunciations of those derived from Latin and Greek. In the printing of standard speech hardly any phonetic principle at all is observed; and if a writer attempts to exhibit on paper the precise accents of a rustic speaker he disturbs the proper balance of a true representation by unduly insisting upon the grotesque element; thus directing attention to a point of inferior interest, and diverting it from the speaker's meaning, which is by far the chief concern where the aim is to depict the men and their natures rather than their dialect forms.

[1879.01]

[?Entry in *Men of the Time*?]

> Reproduced below is the first appearance of an entry for 'Thomas Hardy' in what was then the leading biographical reference work in Britain: *Men of the Time: A Dictionary of Contemporaries*, 10th edn. (London: George Routledge and Sons, 1879), pp. 488–9. A similar entry, appropriately expanded, appeared in each successive edition of the work until it expired, as *Men and Women of the Time*, with the Fifteenth Edition of 1899. The editorial preface to the Tenth Edition does not claim that the information used in individual entries has necessarily been obtained from or approved by their subjects, but the contents and emphases of the Hardy entry are similar to those of 1878.01 and strongly indicative of Hardy's own participation. He certainly mentions *Men of the Time* in a letter of 1881 (*CL* i. 96), and Barbara Rosenbaum (*Index*, HrT 1584.5) notes an unpublished letter (National Library of Scotland) in which he supplied information about himself to the Fourteenth Edition of 1895.

HARDY, THOMAS, novelist, was born June 2, 1840, at a village in Dorsetshire, and educated at different schools. He was destined for the architectural profession, and in his 17th year was articled as pupil to an architect practising in the county-town, during which period an able classical scholar gave attention to his higher education. After serving his time he went to London, and, allying himself with the modern school of Gothic artists, acquired additional experience in design under Mr Arthur Blomfield, M.A., F.R.I.B.A., son of the late Bishop Blomfield. His first literary performance was an essay on Coloured Brick and Terracotta Architecture, which received the prize and medal of the Institute of British Architects in 1863; he also was awarded in the same year Sir W. Tite's prize for architectural design. He now formed the idea of becoming an art-critic, and engaged in further studies for that purpose, but printed nothing. After hesitating for a few years between architecture and literature, he at length tried his hand on a work of fiction, which was published in 1871, and was equally praised and condemned. In 1872 he published the rural tale entitled *Under the Greenwood Tree*, and in 1873 *A Pair of Blue Eyes*, both of which were well received. These were followed, in 1874, by his best-known novel, *Far from the Madding Crowd*, and by *The Hand of Ethelberta*, in 1876.

[1879.02]

[Review of William Barnes's Poems]

One of Hardy's earliest admirers and supporters was Charles Kegan Paul (1828–1902), vicar of the Dorset village of Sturminster Marshall from 1862 to 1874, and subsequently co-founder of the publishing firm of Kegan Paul, Trench, & Co. When Paul became editor of the *New Quarterly Magazine* in 1879, he lost no time in publishing two of Hardy's short stories and persuading him to write a review of a book his own firm had just brought out, *Poems of Rural Life in the Dorset Dialect*, by the Revd William Barnes, philologist, schoolmaster, Dorset dialect poet, and rector of Winterborne Came. Hardy was perhaps embarrassed by the element of log-rolling involved—he certainly never wrote another book review—and by his own mixed feelings about Barnes's work and example, but he nevertheless adapted substantial portions of the review for his obituary of Barnes in 1886 (1886.02) and even for the second chapter of *Tess of the d'Urbervilles* in 1891. The text below is not that of the review as it appeared, anonymously, in the *New Quarterly Magazine*, new series 2 (October 1879), pp. 469–73, but that of the much longer original version represented by the set of lightly corrected galley proofs (formerly in the possession of David Holmes, later described in Bernard Quaritch's catalogue 1120, item 57) that Hardy preserved for potential publication among his 'Miscellanea'. Footnotes identify those sections of the review that actually appeared in the *New Quarterly* after it had received a severe, arguably justified, and almost certainly editorial pruning. What appear to be Hardy's deliberate departures from the wording of Barnes's poems have also been footnoted, but errors in Barnes's dialectal spellings and diacritical marks—left uncorrected by Hardy at least in this uniquely surviving set of proofs—have been silently emended to accord with the readings of the edition Hardy was reviewing; page references in the footnotes are to the same edition. Purdy, p. 295.

Poems of Rural Life in the Dorset Dialect. By William Barnes. (London: C. Kegan Paul & Co., 1879.)

Seldom does a new edition come before the public with better claims to a hearty welcome than this of Mr Barnes's Poems, which have now for the first time been all collected in one volume. When, twenty years ago,[1] the first instalment of these now well-known lyrics was put forth from the remote and peaceful home of their author, they were received with somewhat hazy notions as to their merits. The quaint archaic spelling of the original edition puzzled the stranger's eye to an extent with which his industry was unwilling to cope. But by the adoption of a modified style of spelling in the next edition, which has ever since been adhered to, this difficulty was to a great extent removed, and acquaintance[2] has been made far and wide with a writer whose exceptional knowledge of rustic life is as unquestionable as his power to cast his memories of that life in beautiful and pleasing form.

Though these poems are distinguished on the title-page by the name of the county generally from whose recesses their scenes and characters are derived, the more precise source of their inspiration is a limited district lying to the north and north-west of Dorsetshire, and having marked characteristics of its own. This fertile and sheltered tract of country, in which the fields are never brown, and the springs never dry, is bounded on the south by the bold chalk ridge that embraces the prominences of Hambledon Hill, Bulbarrow,[3] Nettlecombe Tout, Dogbury, and High Stoy. The tourist from the coast who, after plodding for ten or fifteen miles over chalk downs and cornlands, suddenly reaches the verge of one of these escarpments, is surprised and delighted to behold extended like a map beneath him a country differing absolutely from that which he has passed through. Behind him the hills are open, the sun blazes down upon fields so large as to give an unenclosed look to the landscape, the lanes are white, the hedges low, the atmosphere colourless. Here in the valley the world seems to be constructed upon a smaller and more delicate scale; the fields are mere paddocks,

---

[1] The initial collection of *Poems in the Dorset Dialect* was published in 1844, but Bernard Jones has suggested that TH may first have encountered Barnes's work in *Hwomely Rhymes* (1859).

[2] For 'When, twenty . . . and acquaintance' *New Quarterly* substitutes: 'Since the first instalment of these now well-known lyrics was put forth from the remote and peaceful home of their author, twenty years ago, acquaintance'.

[3] TH's alterations of 'Okeford Hill' to 'Bulbarrow', here and lower in the same paragraph, constitute his only substantive proof corrections.

so reduced that from this height their hedgerows appear like a network of dark green threads spread out upon the paler green of the grass. The atmosphere is cool, and is so tinged with azure that what artists call the middle distance partakes also of that hue, while the horizon northwards is of the deepest ultramarine. The arable land has nearly disappeared; with but few exceptions the landscape is a broad rich mass of grass and trees, swelling over minor hills and dales. The scene is one which rivals, and in many points surpasses, those much lauded views of Surrey and Buckinghamshire from Richmond Hill and the terrace at Windsor Castle. It is the Vale of Blackmore or Blackmoor; and the portion immediately beneath us—included in the triangle formed by Sherborne, Shaftesbury, and Bulbarrow—is the abiding place of the people whose daily duties, sayings, and innermost emotions have been laid bare in these poems; the spot is also the early home of the poet himself.

The district is of historic no less than of topographical interest. The Vale was known in former times as the Forest of White Hart, from a curious legend of King Henry the Third's reign,[4] in which the killing by a certain Thomas de la Lynd of a beautiful white hart which the king had run down and spared, was made the occasion of a heavy fine. In those days, and till comparatively recent times, the country was densely wooded. Even now traces of its earlier condition are to be found in the old oak copses and irregular belts of timber that yet survive upon its slopes, and the hollow-trunked trees that shade so many of its pastures.

It is true that among the sketches of men and women which abound in the volume, we sometimes find them housed in hamlets lying nominally beyond the vale; but to our minds these characters are in a great measure Blackmore people away from home, bearing with them still the well-marked traits which distinguish the Vale population from that of the neighbouring uplands.[5] Unlike the bucolic poets of old time, Mr Barnes does not merely use the beauties of nature as a background, reserving the whole front for the rustic characters, their manners, their emotions, and their simplicities. Moved by the pervading instinct of the nineteenth century, he gives us whole poems of still life, brief and unaffected, but realistic as a Dutch picture. In these the slow green river Stour, with its deep pools whence the trout leaps to the May-fly undisturbed by anglers,

---

[4] Henry III, born 1207, reigned from 1216 until his death in 1272.

[5] *New Quarterly* omits 'It is true . . . uplands.' The omitted sentence, however, together with some passages from the published text, was incorporated almost verbatim into the seventh paragraph of TH's *Athenaeum* obituary of Barnes (1886.02).

is found to be the dearest river of his memories, and the inspirer of some of his happiest effusions. Its multitudinous patches of water-lilies yellow and white, its pollard willows, its heavy headed bulrushes, are for ever haunting him; and such is the loving fidelity with which that stream is depicted, that one might almost construct a bird's-eye view of its upper course by joining together the vignettes that are given of this and that point in its length:[6]

> Where the woak do overspread,
> The grass begloom'd below his head,
> An' water, under bowèn zedge,
> A-springèn vrom the river's edge,
> Do ripple, as the win' do blow,
> An' sparkle, as the sky do glow;
> An' grey-leav'd withy-boughs do cool,
> Wi' darksome sheädes, the clear-feäced pool.[7]

Not only the river, but the woodland, the orchard, the lane, the old house, the porch, the hand-post, and so on, are each presented in turn— the latter objects in a style of humorous half-fetichism which accords remarkably well with the dialect and tone of thought common to the labourers in that nook. 'The wold waggon' is an instance:

> Upon his head an' taïl wer pinks,
> A-païnted all in tangled links;
> His two long zides were blue,—his bed
> Bent slightly upward at the head;
> His reäves rose upward in a bow
> Above the slow hind-wheels below.
> Vour hosses wer a-kept to pull
> The girt wold waggon when 'twer vull:
>
> .   .   .   .   .   .
>
> But he, an' all his hosses too,
> 'V a-ben a-done vor years agoo.[8]

Where figures are introduced the sketch is, of course, proportion- ately more animated. Every one who has crossed a newly sown field in autumn must feel the aptness of the lines,

---

[6] *New Quarterly* breaks off with a period at this point, resuming several paragraphs later at 'Mr Barnes frequently . . .'.

[7] Lines 1–8 of 'John Bleäke at Hwome at Night' (p. 245); line 1 correctly begins 'No; where . . .'.   [8] Lines 15–22, 47–8, of 'The Wold Waggon' (pp. 141–2).

An' there the screamèn bird-bwoy shook
Wi' little zun-burnt hand,
His clacker at the bright-wing'd rook,
About the zeeded land.[9]

Such passages as the following—which reads like a peasant's reply to Shelley's 'A widow bird sat mourning'[10]—are constantly reminding us how much of descriptive beauty depends merely upon bringing out some new feature of an old-familiar spectacle:

A zingèn drush do swaÿ
Up an' down upon a spraÿ,
An' cast his sheäde upon the window square.[11]

That peculiar colourless time of the early year when the days are beginning to lengthen, and sunlight increases without bringing warmth, was perhaps never more vividly brought to mind than by the poem called 'The Turn o' the Days':—

O the wings o' the rook wer a-glitterèn bright,
As he wheel'd on above, in the zun's evenèn light,
An' noo snow wer a-left, but in patches o' white,
    On the hill at the turn o' the days.
An' along on the slope wer the beäre-timber'd copse,
Wi' the dry wood a-sheäkèn, wi' red-twiggèd tops.
Vor the dry-flowèn wind, had a-blow'd off the drops
    O' the raïn, at the turn o' the days.

There the stream did run on, in the sheäde o' the hill,
So smooth in his flowèn, as if he stood still,
An' bright wi' the skylight, did slide to the mill,
    By the meäds, at the turn o' the days.
An' up by the copse, down along the hill brow,
Wer vurrows a-cut down, by men out at plough,
So straïght as the zunbeams, a-shot drough the bough
    O' the tree at the turn o' the days.

---

[9] Lines 14–17 of 'Wheat' (p. 312); the uncorrected proof-reading 'there' (for 'while') in line 14 presumably represents TH's deliberate rephrasing.

[10] Correctly 'A widow bird sate mourning', the song in Scene 5 of Shelley's unfinished *Charles the First*.

[11] Lines 36–8 of 'Knowlwood' (p. 239); TH was presumably responsible for the adjustments to lines 36–7, which correctly read 'While a zingèn drush do swaÿ, John, | Up an' down upon a spraÿ, John,'.

Then the boomèn wold clock in the tower did mark
His vive hours, avore the cool evenèn wer dark,
An' ivy did glitter a-clung round the bark
   O' the tree, at the turn o' the days.
An' womèn a-fraïd o' the road in the night,
Wer a-heästenèn on to reach hwome by the light,
A-castèn long sheädes on the road, a-dried white,
   Down the hill, at the turn o' the days.

The father an' mother did walk out to view
The moss-bedded snow-drop, a-sprung in the lew,
An' hear if the birds wer a-zingèn anew,
   In the boughs, at the turn o' the days.
An' young vo'k a-laughèn wi' smooth glossy feäce,
Did hie over vields, wi' a light-vooted peäce,
To friends where the tow'r did betoken a pleäce
   Among trees, at the turn o' the days.[12]

Mr Barnes frequently introduces compound epithets into his descriptive passages; and though many of these show a considerable divergence from the ordinary speech of the people, they are in themselves singularly precise, and often beautiful, definitions of the thing signified. Such expressions as 'the blue-hill'd worold',[13] 'the wide-horn'd cow',[14] true as they may be in the general, apply with double force to the highly-tinged horizon which bounds the Blackmore landscape, and the breed of cow which composes its dairies. And so of single adjectives. When 'the rustlèn copse'[15] is spoken of in connection with early winter, it should be known that the particular copse signified is an oak copse, and that the dead oak leaves of young underwood linger on their branches far into the winter weather, giving out to the wind the distinctive sound of which the writer has taken note.

We pass on to those more important lyrics which are entirely concerned with human interests and human character. The incidents are those of everyday life, cottagers' sorrows and cottagers' joys, but they are tinged throughout with that golden glow—'the light that never was'[16]—which

---

[12] Complete text of 'The Turn o' the Days' (pp. 322–3); stanza breaks, absent from the proofs, have here been inserted. *New Quarterly* text resumes at beginning of next paragraph with 'Mr Barnes . . .'.   [13] From line 6 of 'The New House A-gettèn Wold' (p. 370).

[14] From line 7 ('wide horn'd cows') of 'Milkèn Time' (p. 247).

[15] From line 2 of second stanza of 'I'm Out of Door' (p. 416).

[16] William Wordsworth, 'Elegiac Stanzas: Suggested by a Picture of Peele Castle, in a Storm, Painted by Sir George Beaumont', stanza 4, lines 3–4: 'The light that never was, on sea or land, | The consecration, and the Poet's dream'.

art can project upon the commonest things. They abound with touches of rare and delicate beauty; though that inequality of power which has been the misfortune of all writers and singers from Homer downwards becomes more visible among these than elsewhere. Indeed, there are some which have a questionable right to stand beside such a poem as the following, for instance, which is to our thinking of rare intensity as an expression of grief; the turn of thought in the sixth line of each stanza being particularly fine:

THE WIFE A-LOST

Since I noo mwore do zee your feäce,
　Up steäirs or down below,
I'll zit me in the lwonesome pleäce,
　Where flat-bough'd beech do grow:
Below the beeches' bough, my love,
　Where you did never come,
An' I don't look to meet ye now,
　As I do look at hwome.

Since you noo mwore be at my zide,
　In walks in zummer het,
I'll goo alwone where mist do ride,
　Drough trees a-drippèn wet:
Below the raïn-wet bough, my love,
　Where you did never come,
An' I don't grieve to miss ye now,
　As I do grieve at hwome.

Since now bezide my dinner-bwoard
　Your vaïce do never sound,
I'll eat the bit I can avword,
　A-vield upon the ground;
Below the darksome bough, my love,
　Where you did never dine,
An' I don't grieve to miss ye now,
　As I at hwome do pine.[17]

There is another on the same subject which is equally pathetic, called 'Woak Hill', but it is too long to quote here. In 'The Beäten Path' the fact that the village beauty died some time ago is brought forward by simply presenting the condition of things left behind her:

---

[17] Stanzas 1–3 (of 4) of 'The Wife A-Lost' (p. 295). The *New Quarterly* text breaks off at this point and resumes at 'Pictures of the lives . . .'.

The rwose wer doust that bound her brow;
The moth did eat her Zunday ceäpe;
Her frock wer out o' fashion now;
Her shoes wer dried up out o' sheäpe.[18]

There is no surer mark of poetical genius than the power shown in
these four lines of suggesting pathetic meanings without attempting any
conscious analysis of them. The manner has been called superficial and
easy in comparison with the analytical method; but excellence in this
style is in truth as difficult as it is precious, and is one of the rarest accom-
plishments of modern poets. The kindred observation of features, which
to the cursory beholder are so trifling as to be seen and not regarded,
but which, when brought into notice, are found to convey the essence
of a scene or emotion, shows itself on every page of these Dorset poems.
The memory is assisted in recalling a passing fox-hunt by the mention
of 'shaking ground'[19] as its accompaniment; or, to go to the other
extreme, an old countryman's staff is qualified by the epithet 'glossy-
knobbed'.[20] The simplicity here shown is not only the simplicity of the
natural man but that of the classical artist.[21]

Pictures of the lives of Hellenic or Sicilian fishermen and goatherds,
refined into sheer severity of outline by the atmosphere of two thousand
intervening years,[22] have been reproduced by modern poets as subjects
more worthy of treatment than similar ones of to-day; but they mostly
lack these life-giving touches and the human interest which is present in
the homely verse that flows without effort from Mr Barnes's pen. That
the life of a modern peasant is not too hopelessly ingrained in prose
for poetic treatment he has plainly shown. Farm life as, regulated by
the seasons, it varies from day to day through the year, is truthfully
reflected; and we are at every step indirectly reminded wherein lies that
poetry which, in spite of the occasional sting of poverty, is inseparable from
such a condition of life. It lies less in the peasant's residence among fields
and trees than in his absolute dependence on the moods of the air, earth,
and sky. Sun, rain, wind, snow, dawn, darkness, mist, are to him, now as
ever, personal assistants and obstructors, masters and acquaintances,

---

[18] Lines 5–8 of the fifth stanza of 'The Beäten Path' (p. 430).
[19] From line 4 ('sheäkèn ground') of the second stanza of 'Not Goo Hwome To-night' (p. 424).
[20] From line 3 ('glossy-knobbèd') of the second stanza of 'The Beäten Path' (p. 429).
[21] *New Quarterly* text resumes in next line with 'Pictures of . . .'.
[22] The allusion is to the idyls of Theocritus.

with whom he comes directly into contact, whose varying tempers must be well-considered before he can act with effect.

Unlike Burns,[23] Béranger,[24] and other poets of the people, Mr Barnes never assumes the high conventional style, and entirely leaves alone ambition, pride, despair, and other of the strong passions which move mankind, great and small. His rustics are, as a rule, happy people, and very seldom feel the painful sting of the rest of modern mankind, the disproportion between the desire for serenity and the power of obtaining it.[25] Whether the subtle sentiment of some of their utterances is not of a nature too refined to come from the minds of such men as they are shown to be in other places, may be doubted; but the blending of such thoughts with homely speech is artistically done, and may well pass unquestioned if it increases the scope of the poems in embodying the pathos of human life. This, after all, is the attribute upon which they must depend for their endurance, and as such is independent of the compass of a dialect.

There is not a town, and there is scarcely a village, in the county of Dorset where these poems have not been publicly read by their author and others to audiences of every grade, and the appreciative manner in which they are received by those hearers to whom the dialect is the only tongue, fully testifies to Mr Barnes's general truth of observation and handling. That this is the audience for whom he primarily writes is plain. On some occasions it is perhaps a matter to be regretted, since in those lyrics which have an inner meaning, it frequently leads him to conclude with a verse expressing in direct phrase a moral which would be more gratefully received by the ordinary reader if he were allowed to discover it for himself.[26]

Those who do not care for subtleties of dialect, and who regard pronunciation as of very little account beside meaning, may not see the necessity, in the more pathetic poems, for giving the precise sound of the rough sibilant by the use of *z*, especially as the Dorset *hr* is only approximately rendered by the common *r*, the particular objection to *z* being

---

[23] For Hardy's early reading of Robert Burns (1759–96), see *Thomas Hardy's 'Studies, Specimens &c.' Notebook*, ed. Pamela Dalziel and Michael Millgate (Oxford: Clarendon Press, 1994), p. 112, etc.

[24] Paul Jean de Béranger (1780–1857), French poet; a copy of his *Œuvres*, 2 vols. (Paris, 1876) was in the Max Gate library.

[25] The *New Quarterly* text breaks off here, resuming at 'But we have not exhausted . . .'.

[26] These questionable views of TH's are largely restated in the Preface to his 1908 selection of Barnes's poems: see 1908.09.

that the natural grotesqueness, which is the misfortune rather than the fault of that letter, is apt to injure the effect of tender diction upon readers who scan it for the first time. Such an objection, of course, is invalid within the boundaries of the county to whose inhabitants the sounds are as familiar in their hours of sadness as in times of laughter and jest.[27]

But we have not exhausted the various moods from grave to gay which find voice in this volume. An almost perfect expression of the Arcadian lover's ecstasy occurs in the lines called 'In the Spring'.

> My love is the maïd ov all maïdens,
>   Though all mid be comely,
> Her skin's lik' the jessamy blossom
> A-spread in the Spring.
>   .   .   .   .   .   .
>
> O grey-leafy pinks o' the geärden,
>   Now bear her sweet blossoms;
> Now deck wi' a rwose-bud, O briar,
>   Her head in the Spring.
>
> O light-rollèn wind blow me hither,
>   The väice ov her talkèn,
> Or bring vrom her veet the light doust,
>   She do tread in the Spring.
>
> O zun, meäke the gil'cups all glitter,
>   In goold all around her;
> An' meäke o' the deäisys' white flowers
>   A bed in the Spring.
>
> O whissle, gäy birds, up bezide her,
>   In drong-wäy, an' woodlands,
> O zing, swingèn lark, now the clouds,
>   Be a-vled in the Spring.[28]

'Blackmore Maïdens', conceived in the same spirit, is an example of the class of ballad typified by Sir Walter Scott's 'O Brignall Banks',[29] to which, indeed, it is no unfit companion—

---

[27] *New Quarterly* text resumes in next line with 'But we . . .'.

[28] *New Quarterly* breaks off here and resumes at 'Such songs as these—'. Omitted from the quotation are the first and seventh stanzas of 'In the Spring' (pp. 349–50); *New Quarterly* reads 'whistle' for 'whissle' and chooses, understandably, to omit the commas following 'hither', 'doust', 'glitter', and 'clouds'.

[29] The song, 'O, Brignall banks are wild and fair', in Canto Third, stanzas 16–18, of Scott's *Rokeby*.

If you vrom Wimborne took your road,
    To Stower or Paladore,
An' all the farmers' housen show'd
    Their daughters at the door;
You'd cry to bachelors at hwome—
    'Here, come: 'ithin an hour
You'll vind ten maïdens to your mind,
    In Blackmwore by the Stour.'

If you could zee their comely gaït,
    An' prettÿ feäces' smiles,
A-trippèn on so light o' waïght,
    An' steppèn off the stiles;
A-gwaïn to church, as bells do swing
    An' ring 'ithin the tow'r,
You'd own the pretty maïdens' pleäce
    Is Blackmwore by the Stour.

An' if you looked 'ithin their door,
    To zee em in their pleäce,
A-doèn house-work up avore
    Their smilèn mother's feäce;
You'd cry—'Why, if a man would wive
    An' thrive, 'ithout a dow'r,
Then let en look en out a wife
    In Blackmwore by the Stour.'

As I upon my road did pass
    A school-house back in Maÿ,
There out upon the beäten grass
    Wer maïdens at their plaÿ;
An' as the pretty souls did tweil
    An' smile, I cried, 'The flow'r
O' beauty, then, is still in bud
    In Blackmwore by the Stour.'[30]

Such songs as these—the *vers de société* of the Blackmore rustic world
—make us regret that Mr Barnes has not swept that gay chord a little
oftener.[31] His purely humorous compositions are more abundant, and of
these there is none so well appreciated on local platforms as the ballad of

---

[30] Stanzas 3, 2, 4, and 5 of 'Blackmwore Maïdens' (pp. 185–6); TH has omitted the first stanza
and reversed the order of the second and third stanzas. *New Quarterly* text resumes in next line with
'Such songs . . .'.

[31] *New Quarterly* breaks off at this point and resumes, beginning a new sentence and paragraph,
at 'Enough has been said . . .'.

'The Shy Man'. In this and other portrait-poems certain typical worthies of the neighbourhood appear and reappear till we know them as personal acquaintances, respect their peculiarities, and glance over their weaknesses. John Bleake, good Meäster Gwillett, Meäster Collins,[32] are among their number: and until a very few years ago they might have been met anywhere between Shaftesbury and Bubbdown Hill. But modern change has tended to obliterate all such quaint old copyholders and lifeholders —'liviers' as they were sometimes termed—who occupied a position between that of the large farmer and the mere peasant—

> Ov eight good hwomes, where, I can mind
> Vo'k liv'd upon their land, John,
> But dree be now a-left behind;
> The rest ha' vell in hand, John,
> An' all the happy souls they ved
> Be scatter'd vur an' wide.
> An' zome o'm be a-wantèn bread,
> Zome, better off, ha' died.[33]

Unfortunately, as must always be the case with descriptive poetry which embodies local speech, tone, and personal detail to such an extent as is done in these pages, much is lost to the outside reader, who only looks into them to revive his general recollections of country life. But[34] enough has been said to show how many are the passages of true poetic beauty that will reveal themselves here, even in a superficial reading by persons to whom the Dorset *r* and *z* are unknown utterances.

---

[32] Figures invoked in, respectively, 'Bleäke's House in Blackmwore', 'The Shy Man', and 'Good Meäster Collins'.

[33] The first 8 lines (of 11) of stanza 5 (p. 165) of 'The Hwomestead a-vell into Hand'.

[34] *New Quarterly* text resumes at next word, thus: 'Enough has . . .'.

1881

[1881.01]

'Papers of the Manchester Literary Club'

In an unsigned review of the annual volume of *Papers of the Manchester Literary Club*, published in the *Spectator*, 8 October 1881, pp. 1277–9, Hardy was criticized, along with the Scottish novelist George Macdonald, for his excessive use of dialect. Hardy's response invoked the offending passage about 'linguistic puzzles', commented on Dorset speech in terms clearly indebted to the philological ideas of William Barnes, and importantly supplemented the statements of his own literary method in 'Using the Dorset Dialect' (1877.01) and 'Dialect in Novels' (1878.02). No manuscript of the letter is known to survive; the text below is that of its publication in the correspondence section of the *Spectator*, 15 October 1881, p. 1308. Reprinted in *Life and Art*, pp. 114–15. Purdy, p. 295.

The Avenue, Wimborne, Dorset, October 11th.

Sir,

In your last week's article on the *Papers of the Manchester Literary Club*, there seems a slight error, which, though possibly accidental, calls for a word of correction from myself. In treating of dialect in novels, I am instanced by the writer as one of two popular novelists 'whose thorough knowledge of the dialectical peculiarities of certain districts has tempted them to write whole conversations which are, to the ordinary reader, nothing but a series of linguistic puzzles'.[1] So much has my practice been the reverse of this (as a glance at my novels will show), that I have been reproved for too freely translating dialect-English into readable English, by those of your contemporaries who attach more

---

[1] Accurately quoted from the *Spectator*, 8 October 1881, p. 1278.

importance to the publication of local niceties of speech than I do. The rule of scrupulously preserving the local idiom, together with the words which have no synonym among those in general use, while printing in the ordinary way most of those local expressions which are but a modified articulation of words in use elsewhere, is the rule I usually follow; and it is, I believe, generally recognised as the best, where every such rule must of necessity be a compromise, more or less unsatisfactory to lovers of form. It must, of course, be always a matter for regret that, in order to be understood, writers should be obliged thus slightingly to treat varieties of English which are intrinsically as genuine, grammatical, and worthy of the royal title[2] as is the all-prevailing competitor which bears it; whose only fault was that they happened not to be central, and therefore were worsted in the struggle for existence, when a uniform tongue became a necessity among the advanced classes of the population.

I am, Sir, &c.,
Thomas Hardy.

---

[2] The term 'Queen's English' (= standard English) had been put into circulation by Henry Alford's *A Plea for the Queen's English*, first published (as *The Queen's English*) in 1863.

1882

[1882.01]

[Pinero's *The Squire*]

When Arthur Wing Pinero's play *The Squire* was first presented at the St James's Theatre, London, on 29 December 1881, it was immediately recognized as displaying marked similarities to Hardy's novel, *Far from the Madding Crowd*, of five years earlier. 'The Theatres' column of the *Daily News*, 2 January 1882, p. 2, published the following letter of Hardy's together with letters from his collaborator, Joseph Comyns Carr, and from Pinero; Hardy wrote also to *The Times* (1882.02), as did Carr, and a lively controversy ensued as to Pinero's guilt or innocence as a plagiarist. Hardy's original letter, apparently sent as a telegram to W. Moy Thomas (1828–1910), dramatic critic of the *Daily News*, is not known to survive, but Thomas's reply of 1 January 1882 (DCM) expressed regret that by adding some words to the message prior to its publication he had made 'a slight hash of the construction' (see note). Purdy, pp. 295–6.

Wimborne, Dorset, Saturday. [31 December 1881]

Sir,

The critics, who have so unanimously traced the 'new and original' play at the St James's Theatre to my novel, *Far from the Madding Crowd*, are probably unaware of a fact more singular than that of mere adaptation; namely, that a play written by myself, based on that novel, and modified by Mr Comyns Carr to a form still nearer that of *The Squire*, was some months ago submitted to the management of the St James's Theatre, accepted by them, and some time afterwards rejected. Had my dramatisation of the novel never been in the hands of the St James's company; had they by their own choice read the novel and transformed it into such a play as is now produced, I should have said nothing;

but having had their attention drawn to the theme by my play; having practically adapted it; having been able to learn from it how sundry difficulties of the novel were to be got over for the stage, I venture to say that the whole transaction of producing *The Squire*, without my knowledge and after studying my play, and to do all this without a single allusion to my work in the playbill,[1] is quite unjustifiable, and would be a discredit to the management of any theatre. I shall feel obliged by your publishing this protest in your Monday article on 'The Theatres'.

Yours faithfully,
Thomas Hardy.

[1882.02]

' "The Squire" at the St. James's Theatre'

Hardy's second public letter about Pinero's *The Squire* appeared as follows—under the above editorial heading, and in company with other letters on the same topic—in *The Times*, 2 January 1882, p. 6. The manuscript of the letter is not known to survive, but it seems clearly to have been written later than the undated letter (1882.01) published in the *Daily News* on the same day. Purdy, p. 296.

Wimborne, Dorset, Jan. 1.

Sir,

My attention has been drawn to the play entitled *The Squire*, now just produced at the St James's Theatre, by a somewhat general declaration on the part of the daily Press that the play is an unacknowledged adaptation of my novel, *Far from the Madding Crowd*. I should have read this announcement with no strong feelings had my labours in connexion with the subject been limited to writing the novel; but the aspect of the matter is changed by the fact, of which the spectators were ignorant, that the managers of the St James's Theatre have had in their hands, not only the novel accessible to everybody, but a manuscript play of my own based on the novel. I had long been impressed with the notion that the central idea of the story—a woman ruling a farm and marrying a soldier

---

[1] It seems likely that the words 'and . . . playbill' were those added by Moy Thomas.

secretly, while unselfishly beloved through evil and through good report by her shepherd or bailiff—afforded a promising theme for the stage. I accordingly dramatized the story, read the play to Mr Comyns Carr, the art critic, who kindly improved it, and offered the play to the theatre above mentioned. I suggested to him that the rank of the personages should be raised, particularly that Sergeant Troy should appear as a lieutenant, and that in this case the names should be changed, and he told me that the suggestion was duly reported to the theatre. Moreover, a gipsy, who does not exist in the novel, was introduced into our play, and I see that a gipsy figures in *The Squire*. I then learnt that the play was verbally accepted and would soon appear; then, that it was rejected. Silence ensued till *The Squire* is proclaimed by many observers as in substance mine. My drama is now rendered useless, for it is obviously not worth while for a manager to risk producing a piece if the whole gist of it is already to be seen by the public at another theatre.[2]

I am, yours faithfully,
Thomas Hardy.

[1882.03]

[Advertisement for *Two on a Tower*]

Hardy was dissatisfied with the advertising of his novel *Two on a Tower* at the time of its publication in late October 1882, and on 27 November he wrote to the publishers, Sampson Low, Marston, Searle, & Rivington, to emphasize 'the novelty of the story' and ask that future announcements should 'appear in your list as written on the enclosed paper' (*CL* i. 109). Although the enclosure itself has not survived, its content is almost certainly represented by the following excerpt from Sampson Low's advertisement in the *Athenaeum*, 2 December 1882, p. 746. Purdy, p. 44.

---

[2] TH and Carr did nonetheless stage their version of *Far from the Madding Crowd* both in the provinces and in London during the early months of 1882, although it was less successful than *The Squire*. See Pamela Dalziel, 'Whose *Mistress*? Hardy's Theatrical Collaboration', *Studies in Bibliography*, 48 (1995), pp. 248–59; James F. Stottlar, 'Hardy vs. Pinero: Two Stage Versions of *Far from the Madding Crowd*', *Theatre Survey*, 18 (November 1977), pp. 23–43; and Suleiman M. Ahmad, *Far from the Madding Crowd* in the British Provincial Theatre,' *Thomas Hardy Journal*, 16 (February 2000), pp. 70–83.

TWO ON A TOWER. By Thomas Hardy. 3 vols. 31*s.* 6*d.*

Being the story of the unforeseen relations into which a lady and a youth many years her junior were drawn by studying the stars together; of her desperate situation through generosity to him; and of the reckless *coup d'audace* by which she effected her deliverance.

[1882.04]

'English Authors and American Publishers'

> This letter, published as below in the *Athenaeum*, 23 December 1882, pp. 848–9, was a late contribution to a controversy over the treatment of British authors by the New York publishing house of Harper and Brothers. Hardy's personal reference is to his novel *A Laodicean*, not published in volume form by Harper's but serialized in 13 instalments in the newly launched European Edition of *Harper's New Monthly Magazine* between December 1880 and December 1881. Purdy, p. 296.

Savile Club, Dec. 19, 1882.

It must be in the experience of so many English authors that the Messrs. Harper treat openly and fairly with them for their works, that iteration of the fact in print is hardly necessary. Moreover, that enterprising firm, having latterly taken up the only proper position for the Colossus among publishers that it is said to be, by planting one foot on this side of the Atlantic,[3] has thereby made itself more directly amenable to the customs of the English press than ever, and can have no possible wish to treat our writers cavalierly. For my own part, I may state—not to mention the *bona fides* of the Messrs. Harper in ordinary transactions— that some time ago I agreed to supply them with the advance sheets of a novel for so much money, the said novel to be no shorter than a specified length, while if longer there was to be no additional payment. When finished, the story, planned without reference to the agreement, turned out to be one-third longer than the guaranteed length; and I was greatly

---

[3] Harper and Brothers, long represented in London by the British publishing house of Sampson Low, had in 1880 sent over R. R. Bowker (see 1888.03) as its own London representative (*CL* i. 77).

surprised, and not less charmed, to receive from them the proportionate third above the price agreed on. It is said that other publishers delight in paying an author more than he expects to get, but I believe the excellent practice is not yet universal.

Thomas Hardy.

1883

[1883.01]

'Two on a Tower'

An unsigned review of *Two on a Tower* in the *St James's Gazette*, 16 January 1883, p. 14, combined warm praise of Hardy's work with disapproval of his having assigned his fictional Bishop of Melchester a role that might be interpreted as an insult to the Church of England. Hardy's distinctly disingenuous reply (of which no manuscript seems to have survived) was printed as below in the *St James's Gazette*, 19 January, p. 14. On that same date Frederick Greenwood (1830–1909), the paper's editor, wrote to Hardy to regret the review and insist that he personally was 'one of your most sincere and most convinced admirers' (DCM). Purdy, pp. 296–7.

Savile Club, Jan. 18.

Sir,

In your candid review of *Two on a Tower* you express an opinion that in some quarters the choice of a bishop as a victim (in a situation which, for unknown reasons, is supposed to have a ludicrous side) may be regarded as a studied insult to the Church.

Will you allow me to state that, however the choice may be regarded, no thought of such an insult was present to my mind in contriving the situation. Purely artistic conditions necessitated an episcopal position for the character alluded to, as will be apparent to those readers who are at all experienced in the story-telling trade. Indeed, that no *arrière-pensée* of the sort suggested had existence should be sufficiently clear to everybody from the circumstance that one of the most honourable characters in the book, and the hero's friend, is a clergyman, and that the heroine's most tender qualities are woven in with her religious feelings.

I am, Sir, your obedient servant,

Thomas Hardy.

[1883.02]

[Study and Stimulants]

> Hardy's contribution to Alfred Arthur Reade's compilation, *Study and Stimulants; Or, the Use of Intoxicants and Narcotics in Relation to Intellectual Life, as Illustrated by Personal Communications on the Subject, from Men of Letters and of Science* (Manchester: A. Heywood and Son, 1883), p. 66, was in fact constructed by Reade from two separate letters, the first, dated 27 February 1882 (David Holmes), commenting on the uses of tobacco, and the second, dated 5 December 1882 (Washington University, St Louis), returning a proof of those first comments and adding remarks on the uses of alcohol. In conflating the two letters, Reade omitted the addresses, salutations, and valedictions of both, the date of the first, and the opening sentence and brief postscript of the second. The slightly variant version of Hardy's second letter published in *Life and Work*, p. 163, clearly derives from a retained draft. The text below is that of *Study and Stimulants*. Purdy, p. 264.

Dec. 5, 1882.

I fear that the information I can give on the effect of tobacco will be less than little: for I have never smoked a pipeful in my life, nor a cigar. My impression is that its use would be very injurious in my case; and so far as I have observed, it is far from beneficial to any literary man. There are, unquestionably, writers who smoke with impunity, but this seems to be owing to the counterbalancing effect of some accident in their lives or constitutions, on which few others could calculate.[1] I have never found alcohol helpful to novel-writing[2] in any degree. My experience goes to prove that the effect of wine, taken as a preliminary to imaginative work, is[3] to blind the writer to the quality of what he produces rather than to raise its quality. When walking much out of doors, and particularly when on Continental rambles, I occasionally drink a glass or two of claret or mild ale. The German beers seem really beneficial at these times of exertion, which (as wine seems otherwise) may be owing to

---

[1] The passage from the 27 February letter ends at this point; omitted are the opening words of the 5 December letter: 'In answer to your inquiry I can say that'.

[2] So reads TH's 5 December letter; *LW*'s replacement of 'novel-writing' by 'literary production' presumably represents a deliberate revision rather than the reinstatement of a reading in the draft.

[3] *LW* reads 'work, as it is called, is'. The words 'as it is called', struck through in TH's original letter, evidently survived in his draft.

some alimentary qualities they possess, apart from their stimulating property. With these rare exceptions, I have taken no alcoholic liquor for the last two years.

T. Hardy.

[1883.03]

'Pictures in Elementary Schools'

Mary Elizabeth Christie (1847–1906), of the Art for Schools Association, published in the *Journal of Education*, new series 5 (June 1883), p. 201, a letter, headed as above, that described and advocated a scheme for 'supplying elementary schools with photographs and engravings of good pictures'. Hardy was listed among those expressing 'general approval' of the proposal, having consented to the use of his name in a letter to Christie of 11 April 1883 (*CL* i. 116–17), unpublished at the time but later included, apparently from a draft, in *Life and Work*, pp. 164–5. Christie's *Journal of Education* letter was reprinted in her posthumous *A Tardiness in Nature and Other Papers*, edited by Maud Withers (Manchester: at the University Press, 1907), pp. 23–8, Hardy being named on p. 28.

[1883.04]

The Dorsetshire Labourer

This important essay was written during the early months of 1883 in response to an invitation originally received the previous July (*CL* i. 107). The topic had become politically sensitive following the Liberal government's promise to extend the franchise to agricultural workers (*CL* i. 123–4), and Hardy indicated his personal sympathies by sending copies of the essay to Gladstone, the Prime Minister, and to John Morley, a leading member of the party's more radical wing. He nonetheless insisted in his covering letter to Morley that 'Though a Liberal, I have endeavoured to describe the state of things without political bias' (*CL* i. 118–19). Since Hardy's manuscript (DCM) carries a note by Charles J. Longman, the editor of *Longman's Magazine*, instructing the printer to send copies of the proofs to himself and to Andrew Lang as well as to the author, it seems unlikely that Hardy was

exclusively responsible for the numerous minor discrepancies between
that manuscript and the text that was published in *Longman's Magazine*,
2 (July 1883), pp. 252–69, and is reproduced below. Hardy never reprinted
the essay—perhaps because he drew extensively upon it when writing *Tess of
the d'Urbervilles*—but he authorized the printing of two short extracts to
accompany his contribution to H. Rider Haggard's *Rural England* (1902.10)
and included a copy of *Longman's Magazine* for July 1883 (Millgate) among
the materials selected for his projected 'Miscellanea' volume. A pamphlet
version of the essay—reset, dated 1884, retitled *The Dorset Farm Labourer
Past and Present*, and bearing the imprint of the Dorset Agricultural Workers'
Union, Dorchester—survives in a very few copies (e.g. Adams, BL, Beinecke,
Princeton) and seems, as Purdy observes, authentic in certain respects, distinctly questionable in others. Its occasional differences from the *Longman's*
text seem for the most part to be the result of compositorial error, and the
corrections on the copy stamped 'ROUGH PROOF' (Beinecke) are not in
Hardy's hand; even so, the few substantive changes could conceivably have
been authorial and are recorded in footnotes below. Reprinted in *Life and
Art*, pp. 20–47. Purdy, pp. 49–50.

It seldom happens that a nickname which affects to portray a class
is honestly indicative of the individuals composing that class. The few
features distinguishing them from other bodies of men have been seized
on and exaggerated, while the incomparably more numerous features
common to all humanity have been ignored. In the great world this wild
colouring of so-called typical portraits is clearly enough recognised.
Nationalities, the aristocracy, the plutocracy, the citizen class, and many
others, have their allegorical representatives, which are received with
due allowance for flights of imagination in the direction of burlesque.

But when the class lies somewhat out of the ken of ordinary society
the caricature begins to be taken as truth. Moreover, the original is held
to be an actual unit of the multitude signified. He ceases to be an abstract
figure and becomes a sample. Thus when we arrive at the farm-labouring
community we find it to be seriously personified by the pitiable picture
known as Hodge; not only so, but the community is assumed to be a
uniform collection of concrete Hodges.

This supposed real but highly conventional Hodge is a degraded
being of uncouth manner and aspect, stolid understanding, and snail-
like movement. His speech is such a chaotic corruption of regular
language that few persons of progressive aims consider it worth while to
enquire what views, if any, of life, of nature, or of society, are conveyed
in these utterances. Hodge hangs his head or looks sheepish when

spoken to, and thinks Lunnon a place paved with gold. Misery and fever lurk in his cottage, while, to paraphrase the words of a recent writer on the labouring classes, in his future there are only the workhouse and the grave.[4] He hardly dares to think at all. He has few thoughts of joy, and little hope of rest. His life slopes into a darkness not 'quieted by hope'.[5]

If one of the many thoughtful persons who hold this view were to go by rail to Dorset, where Hodge in his most unmitigated form is supposed to reside, and seek out a retired district, he might by and by certainly meet a man who, at first contact with an intelligence fresh from the contrasting world of London, would seem to exhibit some of the above-mentioned qualities. The latter items in the list, the mental miseries, the visitor might hardly look for in their fulness, since it would have become perceptible to him as an explorer, and to any but the chamber theorist, that no uneducated community, rich or poor, bond or free, possessing average health and personal liberty, could exist in an unchangeable slough of despond,[6] or that it would for many months if it could. Its members, like the accursed swine, would rush down a steep place and be choked in the waters.[7] He would have learnt that wherever a mode of supporting life is neither noxious nor absolutely inadequate, there springs up happiness, and will spring up happiness, of some sort or other. Indeed, it is among such communities as these that happiness will find her last refuge on earth, since it is among them that a perfect insight into the conditions of existence will be longest postponed.

That in their future there are only the workhouse and the grave is no more and no less true than that in the future of the average well-to-do householder there are only the invalid chair and the brick vault.

Waiving these points, however, the investigator would insist that the man he had encountered exhibited a suspicious blankness of gaze, a great uncouthness and inactivity; and he might truly approach the unintelligible if addressed by a stranger on any but the commonest subject. But suppose that, by some accident, the visitor were obliged to go home with this man, take pot-luck with him and his, as one of the family. For the nonce the very sitting down would seem an undignified performance, and at first, the ideas, the modes, and the surroundings generally, would be puzzling—even impenetrable; or if in a measure

---

[4] The reference is evidently to Richard Jefferies, *Hodge and his Masters* (London: Smith, Elder, 1880), ii. 307–12; cf. *Career*, pp. 207–9.

[5] Robert Browning, *Sordello*, Book the First, line 370.

[6] John Bunyan, *The Pilgrim's Progress*.   [7] Matt. 8: 32.

penetrable, would seem to have but little meaning. But living on there for a few days the sojourner would become conscious of a new aspect in the life around him. He would find that, without any objective change whatever, variety had taken the place of monotony; that the man who had brought him home—the typical Hodge, as he conjectured—was somehow not typical of anyone but himself. His host's brothers, uncles, and neighbours, as they became personally known, would appear as different from his host himself as one member of a club, or inhabitant of a city street, from another. As, to the eye of a diver, contrasting colours shine out by degrees from what has originally painted itself of an unrelieved earthy hue, so would shine out the characters, capacities, and interests of these people to him. He would, for one thing, find that the language, instead of being a vile corruption of cultivated speech, was a tongue with a grammatical inflection rarely disregarded by his entertainer, though his entertainer's children would occasionally make a sad hash of their talk. Having attended the National School they would mix the printed tongue as taught therein with the unwritten, dying, Wessex English that they had learnt of their parents, the result of this transitional state of theirs being a composite language without rule or harmony.[8]

Six months pass, and our gentleman leaves the cottage, bidding his friends good-bye with genuine regret. The great change in his perception is that Hodge, the dull, unvarying, joyless one, has ceased to exist for him. He has become disintegrated into a number of dissimilar fellow-creatures, men of many minds, infinite in difference; some happy, many serene, a few depressed; some clever, even to genius, some stupid, some wanton, some austere; some mutely Miltonic, some Cromwellian;[9] into men who have private views of each other, as he has of his friends; who applaud or condemn each other; amuse or sadden themselves by the contemplation of each other's foibles or vices; and each of whom walks in his own way the road to dusty death.[10] Dick the carter, Bob the shepherd, and Sam the ploughman, are, it is true, alike in the narrowness of their means and their general open-air life; but they cannot be rolled together again into such a Hodge as he dreamt of, by any possible enchantment. And should time and distance render an abstract being, representing the field labourer, possible again to the mind of the

---

[8] Here, as elsewhere in the essay, TH is deeply indebted to the ideas of William Barnes.

[9] Thomas Gray, *Elegy Written in a Country Churchyard*, stanza 15.

[10] Shakespeare, *Macbeth*, v. v. 3.

inquirer (a questionable possibility) he will find that the Hodge of current conception no longer sums up the capacities of the class so defined.

The pleasures enjoyed by the Dorset labourer may be far from pleasures of the highest kind desirable for him. They may be pleasures of the wrong shade. And the inevitable glooms of a straitened hard-working life occasionally enwrap him from such pleasures as he has; and in times of special storm and stress the 'Complaint of Piers the Ploughman'[11] is still echoed in his heart. But even Piers had his flights of merriment and humour; and ploughmen as a rule do not give sufficient thought to the morrow[12] to be miserable when not in physical pain. Drudgery in the slums and alleys of a city, too long pursued, and accompanied as it too often is by indifferent health, may induce a mood of despondency which is well-nigh permanent; but the same degree of drudgery in the fields results at worst in a mood of painless passivity. A pure atmosphere and a pastoral environment are a very appreciable portion of the sustenance which tends to produce the sound mind and body, and thus much sustenance is, at least, the labourer's birthright.

If it were possible to gauge the average sufferings of classes, the probability is that in Dorsetshire the figure would be lower with the regular farmer's labourers—'workfolk' as they call themselves—than with the adjoining class, the unattached labourers, approximating to the free labourers of the middle ages, who are to be found in the larger villages and small towns of the county—many of them, no doubt, descendants of the old copyholders who were ousted from their little plots when the system of leasing large farms grew general. They are, what the regular labourer is not, out of sight of patronage; and to be out of sight is to be out of mind when misfortune arises, and pride or sensitiveness leads them to conceal their privations.

The happiness of a class can rarely be estimated aright by philosophers who look down upon that class from the Olympian heights of society. Nothing, for instance, is more common than for some philanthropic lady to burst in upon a family, be struck by the apparent squalor of the scene, and to straightway mark down that household in her notebook as a frightful example of the misery of the labouring classes. There are two distinct probabilities of error in forming any such estimate. The first is that the apparent squalor is no squalor at all. I am credibly

---

[11] i.e. *Piers Plowman*, the 14th-century poem by William Langland.   [12] Matt. 6: 34.

informed that the conclusion is nearly always based on *colour*. A cottage in which the walls, the furniture, and the dress of the inmates reflect the brighter rays of the solar spectrum is read by these amiable visitors as a cleanly, happy home; while one whose prevailing hue happens to be dingy russet, or a quaint old leather tint, or any of the numerous varieties of mud colour, is thought necessarily the abode of filth and Giant Despair.[13] 'I always kip a white apron behind the door to slip on when the gentlefolk knock, for if so be they see a white apron they think ye be clane,' said an honest woman one day, whose bedroom floors could have been scraped with as much advantage as a pigeon-loft; but who, by a judicious use of high lights, shone as a pattern of neatness in her patrons' eyes.

There was another woman who had long nourished an unreasoning passion for burnt umber, and at last acquired a pot of the same from a friendly young carpenter. With this pigment she covered every surface in her residence to which paint is usually applied, and having more left, and feeling that to waste it would be a pity as times go, she went on to cover other surfaces till the whole was consumed. Her dress and that of the children were mostly of faded snuff-colour, her natural thrift inducing her to cut up and re-make a quantity of old stuffs that had been her mother's; and to add to the misery, the floor of her cottage was of Mayne brick[14]—a material which has the complexion of gravy mottled with cinders. Notwithstanding that the bed-linen and under-clothes of this unfortunate woman's family were like the driven snow,[15] and that the insides of her cooking utensils were concave mirrors, she was used with great effect as the frightful example of slovenliness for many years in that neighbourhood.

The second probability arises from the error of supposing that actual slovenliness is always accompanied by unhappiness. If it were so, a windfall of any kind would be utilised in most cases in improving the surroundings. But the money always goes in the acquisition of something new, and not in the removal of what there is already[16] too much of, dirt. And most frequently the grimiest families are not the poorest; nay,

[13] Bunyan, *The Pilgrim's Progress*.

[14] i.e. brick made—by the Hardy family, among others—in and near the Dorset village of Broadmayne. See Donald Young, 'Brickmaking in Dorset', *Proceedings of the Dorset Natural History and Antiquarian Society*, 93 (1971), pp. 213–41, where bricks from Broadmayne are described as 'drab brown' (p. 218).

[15] Shakespeare, *The Winter's Tale*, IV. iv. 218.   [16] For 'already' pamphlet reads 'always'.

paradoxical as it may seem, external neglect in a household implies something above the lowest level of poverty. Copyholders, cottage free-holders, and the like, are as a rule less trim and neat, more muddling in their ways, than the dependent labourer; and yet there is no more comfortable or serene being than the cottager who is sure of his roof. An instance of probable error through inability to see below the surface of things occurred the other day[17] in an article by a lady on the peasant proprietors of Auvergne.[18] She states that she discovered these persons living on an earth floor, mixed up with onions, dirty clothes, and the 'indescribable remnants of never stirred rubbish'; while one of the houses had no staircase, the owners of the premises reaching their bedrooms by climbing up a bank, and stepping in at the higher level.[19] This was an inconvenient way of getting upstairs; but we must guard against the inference that because these peasant proprietors are in a slovenly condition, and certain English peasants who are not propri-etors live in model cottages copied out of a book by the squire, the latter are so much happier than the former as the dignity of their architecture is greater. It were idle to deny that, other things being equal, the family which dwells in a cleanly and spacious cottage has the probability of a more cheerful existence than a family narrowly housed and draggle-tailed. It has guarantees for health which the other has not. But it must be remembered that melancholy among the rural poor arises primarily from a sense of the incertitude and precariousness of their position. Like Burns's field-mouse, they are overawed and timorous[20] lest those who can wrong them should be inclined to exercise their power. When we know that the Damocles' sword of the poor is the fear of being turned out of their houses by the farmer or squire, we may wonder how many scrupulously clean English labourers would not be glad with half-an-acre of the complaint that afflicts these unhappy freeholders of Auvergne.

It is not at all uncommon to find among the workfolk philosophers who recognise, as clearly as Lord Palmerston did, that dirt is only matter in the wrong place.[21] A worthy man holding these wide views had

---

[17] For 'occurred the other day' pamphlet reads 'occurs'.

[18] Frances Parthenope, Lady Verney, 'Peasant Properties in Auvergne. Jottings in Auvergne', *Contemporary Review*, 42 (December 1882), pp. 954–72.   [19] Verney, p. 957.

[20] Burns, 'To a Mouse, On turning her up in her Nest, with the Plough, November, 1785'.

[21] Henry John Temple, 3rd Viscount Palmerston (1784–1865), Prime Minister 1855–65; the occasion of his remark has not been identified.

put his clean shirt on a gooseberry bush one Sunday morning, to be aired in the sun, whence it blew off into the mud, and was much soiled. His wife would have got him another, but, 'No,' he said, 'the shirt shall wear his week. 'Tis fresh dirt, anyhow, and starch is no more.'

On the other hand, true poverty—that is, the actual want of necessaries—is constantly trying to be decent, and one of the clearest signs of deserving poverty is the effort it makes to appear otherwise by scrupulous neatness.

To see the Dorset labourer at his worst and saddest time, he should be viewed when attending a wet hiring-fair at Candlemas,[22] in search of a new master. His natural cheerfulness bravely struggles against the weather and the incertitude; but as the day passes on, and his clothes get wet through, and he is still unhired, there does appear a factitiousness in the smile which, with a self-repressing mannerliness hardly to be found among any other class, he yet has ready when he encounters and talks with friends who have been more fortunate. In youth and manhood, this disappointment occurs but seldom; but at threescore and over, it is frequently the lot of those who have no sons and daughters to fall back upon, or whose children are ingrates, or far away.

Here, at the corner of the street, in this aforesaid wet hiring-fair, stands an old shepherd. He is evidently a lonely man. The battle of life has always been a sharp one with him, for, to begin with, he is a man of small frame. He is now so bowed by hard work and years that, approaching from behind, you can scarcely see his head. He has planted the stem of his crook in the gutter, and rests upon the bow, which is polished to silver brightness by the long friction of his hands. He has quite forgotten where he is and what he has come for, his eyes being bent on the ground. 'There's work in en,' says one farmer to another, as they look dubiously across; 'there's work left in en still; but not so much as I want for my acreage'. 'You'd get en cheap,' says the other. The shepherd does not hear them, and there seem to be passing through his mind pleasant visions of the hiring successes of his prime—when his skill in ovine surgery laid open any farm to him for the asking, and his employer would say uneasily in the early days of February, 'You don't mean to leave us this year?'

[22] i.e. the commemoration of the Purification of the Virgin Mary. In Dorchester the hiring-fair —as evoked in chap. 23 of *The Mayor of Casterbridge*—was always held on Old Candlemas Day, 14 February, although introduction of the Gregorian calendar in 1752 had technically brought Candlemas Day forward to 2 February. See *Career*, pp. 99–100, 397–8.

But the hale and strong have not to wait thus, and having secured places in the morning, the day passes merrily enough with them.

The hiring-fair of recent years presents an appearance unlike that of former times. A glance up the high street of the town on a Candlemas-fair day twenty or thirty years ago revealed a crowd whose general colour was whitey-brown[23] flecked with white. Black was almost absent, the few farmers who wore that shade being hardly discernible. Now the crowd is as dark as a London crowd. This change is owing to the rage for cloth clothes which possesses the labourers of to-day. Formerly they came in smock-frocks and gaiters, the shepherds with their crooks, the carters with a zone of whipcord round their hats, thatchers with a straw tucked into the brim, and so on. Now, with the exception of the crook in the hands of an occasional old shepherd, there is no mark of speciality in the groups, who might be tailors or undertakers' men, for what they exhibit externally. Out of a group of eight, for example, who talk together in the middle of the road, only one wears corduroy trousers. Two wear cloth pilot-coats and black trousers, two patterned tweed suits with black canvas overalls, the remaining four suits being of faded broadcloth. To a great extent these are their Sunday suits; but the genuine white smock-frock of Russia duck and the whitey-brown one of drabbet,[24] are rarely seen now afield, except on the shoulders of old men. Where smocks are worn by the young and middle-aged, they are of blue material. The mechanic's 'slop'[25] has also been adopted; but a mangy old cloth coat is preferred; so that often a group of these honest fellows on the arable has the aspect of a body of tramps up to some mischief in the field, rather than its natural tillers at work there.[26]

That peculiarity of the English urban poor (which M. Taine ridicules, and unfavourably contrasts with the taste of the Continental working-people)—their preference for the cast-off clothes of a richer class to a special attire of their own[27]—has, in fact, reached the Dorset farm folk. Like the men, the women are, pictorially, less interesting than they used to be. Instead of the wing bonnet like the tilt of a waggon, cotton gown, bright-hued neckerchief, and strong flat boots and shoes, they (the

---

[23] Both here and later in the paragraph 'whitey-brown', the reading of TH's MS, has been preferred to the printed text's 'whity-brown'.

[24] 'Duck . . . drabbet': work clothes made of untwilled linen.

[25] A loose outer garment worn by urban workmen.

[26] For 'work there.' pamphlet reads 'their work.'.

[27] Hippolyte Taine, *Notes on England*, trans. W. F. Rae (London: Strahan, 1872), p. 39; see *LN* i. 108–9 (items 1026–7).

younger ones at least) wear shabby millinery bonnets and hats with beads and feathers, 'material' dresses, and boot-heels almost as foolishly shaped as those of ladies of highest education.

Having 'agreed for a place', as it is called, either at the fair, or (occasionally) by private intelligence, or (with growing frequency) by advertisement in the penny local papers, the terms are usually reduced to writing: though formerly a written agreement was unknown, and is now, as a rule, avoided by the farmer if the labourer does not insist upon one. It is signed by both, and a shilling is passed to bind the bargain. The business is then settled, and the man returns to his place of work, to do no more in the matter till Lady Day, Old Style—April 6.[28]

Of all the days in the year, people who love the rural poor of the south-west should pray for a fine day then. Dwellers near the highways of the county are reminded of the anniversary surely enough. They are conscious of a disturbance of their night's rest by noises beginning in the small hours of darkness, and intermittently continuing till daylight— noises as certain to recur on that particular night of the month as the voice of the cuckoo on the third or fourth week of the same. The day of fulfilment[29] has come, and the labourers are on the point of being fetched from the old farm by the carters of the new. For it is always by the waggon and horses of the farmer who requires his services that the hired man is conveyed to his destination; and that this may be accomplished within the day is the reason that the noises begin so soon after midnight. Suppose the distance to be an ordinary one of a dozen or fifteen miles. The carter at the prospective place rises 'when Charles's Wain is over the new chimney',[30] harnesses his team of three horses by lantern light, and proceeds to the present home of his coming comrade. It is the passing of these empty waggons in all directions that is heard breaking the stillness of the hours before dawn. The aim is usually to be at the door of the removing household by six o'clock, when the loading of goods at once begins; and at nine or ten the start to the new home is made. From this hour till one or two in the day, when the other family

[28] Lady Day, commemorating the Annunciation of the Virgin Mary, was one of the legally significant 'quarter days' by which contracts were customarily dated; according to the Gregorian calendar (New Style) it fell on 25 March, but for the Dorchester hiring agreements the old date (cf. Candlemas) was still retained.

[29] i.e. the effective date for hiring agreements entered into at the Candlemas fair; cf. Barnes's poem 'Leädy-Day, an' Riddèn House'.

[30] Shakespeare, *1 Henry IV*, ii. i. 2, where the time indicated is earlier than 4 a.m.; the constellation is more commonly known as the Plough.

arrives at the old house, the cottage is empty, and it is only in that short interval that the interior can be in anyway cleaned and lime-whitened for the new comers, however dirty it may have become, or whatever sickness may have prevailed among members of the departed family.

Should the migrant himself be a carter there is a slight modification in the arrangement, for carters do not fetch carters, as they fetch shepherds and general hands. In this case the man has to transfer himself. He relinquishes charge of the horses of the old farm in the afternoon of April 5, and starts on foot the same afternoon for the new place. There he makes the acquaintance of the horses which are to be under his care for the ensuing year, and passes the night sometimes on a bundle of clean straw in the stable, for he is as yet a stranger here, and too indifferent to the comforts of a bed on this particular evening to take much trouble to secure one. From this couch he uncurls himself about two o'clock, a.m. (for the distance we have assumed), and, harnessing his new charges, moves off with them to his old home, where, on his arrival, the packing is already advanced by the wife, and loading goes on as before mentioned.

The goods are built up on the waggon to a well-nigh unvarying pattern, which is probably as peculiar to the country labourer as the hexagon to the bee. The dresser, with its finger-marks and domestic evidences thick upon it, stands importantly in front, over the backs of the shaft horses, in its erect and natural position, like some Ark of the Covenant, which must not be handled slightingly or overturned.[31] The hive of bees is slung up to the axle of the waggon, and alongside it the cooking pot or crock, within which are stowed the roots of garden flowers. Barrels are largely used for crockery, and budding gooseberry bushes are suspended by the roots; while on the top of the furniture a circular nest is made of the bed and bedding for the matron and children, who sit there through the journey. If there is no infant in arms, the woman holds the head of the clock, which at any exceptional lurch of the waggon strikes one, in thin tones. The other object of solicitude is the looking-glass, usually held in the lap of the eldest girl. It is emphatically spoken of as *the* looking-glass, there being but one in the house, except possibly a small shaving-glass for the husband. But labouring men are not much dependent upon mirrors for a clean chin. I have seen many men shaving in the chimney corner, looking into the

---

[31] 2 Sam. 6: 6–7.

fire; or, in summer, in the garden, with their eyes fixed upon a gooseberry-bush, gazing as steadfastly as if there were a perfect reflection of their image—from which it would seem that the concentrated look of shavers in general was originally demanded rather by the mind than by the eye. On the other hand, I knew a man who used to walk about the room all the time he was engaged in the operation, and how he escaped cutting himself was a marvel. Certain luxurious dandies of the furrow, who could not do without a reflected image of themselves when using the razor, obtained it till quite recently by placing the crown of an old hat outside the window-pane, then confronting it inside the room and falling to—a contrivance which formed a very clear reflection of a face in high light.

The day of removal, if fine, wears an aspect of jollity, and the whole proceeding is a blithe one. A bundle of provisions for the journey is usually hung up at the side of the vehicle, together with a three-pint stone jar of extra strong ale; for it is as impossible to move house without beer as without horses. Roadside inns, too, are patronised, where, during the halt, a mug is seen ascending and descending through the air to and from the feminine portion of the household at the top of the waggon. The drinking at these times is, however, moderate, the beer supplied to travelling labourers being of a preternaturally small brew; as was illustrated by a dialogue which took place on such an occasion quite recently. The liquor was not quite to the taste of the male travellers, and they complained. But the landlady upheld its merits. ' 'Tis our own brewing, and there is nothing in it but malt and hops,' she said, with rectitude. 'Yes, there is,' said the traveller. 'There's water.' 'Oh! I forgot the water,' the landlady replied. 'I'm d——d if you did, mis'ess,' replied the man; 'for there's hardly anything else in the cup'.

Ten or a dozen of these families, with their goods, may be seen halting simultaneously at an out-of-the-way inn, and it is not possible to walk a mile on any of the high roads this day without meeting several. This annual migration from farm to farm is much in excess of what it was formerly. For example, on a particular farm where, a generation ago, not more than one cottage on an average changed occupants yearly, and where the majority remained all their lifetime, the whole number of tenants were changed at Lady Day just past, and this though nearly all of them had been new arrivals on the previous Lady Day. Dorset labourers now look upon an annual removal as the most natural thing in the world, and it becomes with the younger families a pleasant excitement. Change is also a certain sort of education. Many advantages accrue to the labourers from the varied experience it brings, apart from the discovery of the best market for their abilities. They have become shrewder and sharper men of the world, and have learnt how to hold their own with firmness and judgment. Whenever the habitually-removing man comes into contact with one of the old-fashioned stationary sort, who are still to be found, it is impossible not to perceive that the former is much more wide awake than his fellow-worker, astonishing him with stories of the wide world comprised in a twenty-mile radius from their homes.

They are also losing their peculiarities as a class; hence the humorous simplicity which formerly characterised the men and the unsophisticated modesty of the women are rapidly disappearing or lessening, under the constant attrition of lives mildly approximating to those of workers in a manufacturing town. It is the common remark of villagers immediately above the labouring class, who know the latter well as personal acquaintances, that 'there are no nice homely workfolk now as there used to be'. There may be, and is, some exaggeration in this, but it is only natural that, now different districts of them are shaken together once a year and redistributed, like a shuffled pack of cards, they have ceased to be so local in feeling or manner as formerly, and have entered on the condition of inter-social citizens, whose city stretches the whole county over. Their brains are less frequently than they once were 'as dry as the remainder biscuit after a voyage',[32] and they vent less often the result of their own observations than what they have heard to be the current ideas of smart chaps in towns. The women have, in many districts, acquired the rollicking air of factory hands. That seclusion and immutability, which was so bad for their pockets, was an unrivalled fosterer of their personal charm in the eyes of those whose experiences had been less limited. But the artistic merit of their old condition is scarcely a reason why they should have continued in it when other communities were marching on so vigorously towards uniformity and mental equality. It is only the old story that progress and picturesqueness do not harmonise. They are losing their individuality, but they are widening the range of their ideas, and gaining in freedom. It is too much to expect them to remain stagnant and old-fashioned for the pleasure of romantic spectators.

But, picturesqueness apart, a result of this increasing nomadic habit of the labourer is, naturally, a less intimate and kindly relation with

[32] Shakespeare, *As You Like It*, ii. vii. 38–40.

the land he tills than existed before enlightenment enabled him to rise above the condition of a serf who lived and died on a particular plot like a tree. During the centuries of serfdom, of copyholding tenants, and down to twenty or thirty years ago, before the power of unlimited migration had been clearly realised, the husbandman of either class had the interest of long personal association with his farm. The fields were those he had ploughed and sown from boyhood, and it was impossible for him, in such circumstances, to sink altogether the character of natural guardian in that of hireling. Not so very many years ago, the landowner, if he were good for anything, stood as a court of final appeal in cases of the harsh dismissal of a man by the farmer. 'I'll go to my lord' was a threat which overbearing farmers respected, for 'my lord' had often personally known the labourer long before he knew the labourer's master. But such arbitrament is rarely practicable now. The landlord does not know by sight, if even by name, half the men who preserve his acres from the curse of Eden.[33] They come and go yearly, like birds of passage, nobody thinks whence or whither. This dissociation is favoured by the customary system of letting the cottages with the land, so that, far from having a guarantee of a holding to keep him fixed, the labourer has not even the stability of a landlord's tenant; he is only tenant of a tenant, the latter possibly a new comer, who takes strictly commercial views of his man and cannot afford to waste a penny on sentimental considerations.

Thus, while their pecuniary condition in the prime of life is bettered, and their freedom enlarged, they have lost touch with their environment, and that sense of long local participancy which is one of the pleasures of age. The old *casus conscientiæ*[34] of those in power—whether the weak tillage of an enfeebled hand ought not to be put up with in fields which have had the benefit of that hand's strength—arises less frequently now that the strength has often been expended elsewhere. The sojourning existence of the town masses is more and more the existence of the rural masses, with its corresponding benefits and disadvantages. With uncertainty of residence often comes a laxer morality, and more cynical views of the duties of life. Domestic stability is a factor in conduct which nothing else can equal. On the other hand, new varieties of happiness evolve themselves like new varieties of plants, and new charms may have arisen among the classes who have been driven to adopt the remedy

[33] i.e. thorns and thistles: Gen. 3: 18.   [34] Roughly translateable as 'moral issue'.

of locomotion for the evils of oppression and poverty—charms which compensate in some measure for the lost sense of home.

A practical injury which this wandering entails on the children of the labourers should be mentioned here. In shifting from school to school, their education cannot possibly progress with that regularity which is essential to their getting the best knowledge in the short time available to them. It is the remark of village school-teachers of experience,[35] that the children of the vagrant workfolk form the mass of those who fail to reach the ordinary standard of knowledge expected of their age. The rural schoolmaster or mistress enters the schoolroom on the morning of the sixth of April, and finds that a whole flock of the brightest young people has suddenly flown away. In a village school which may be taken as a fair average specimen, containing seventy-five scholars, thirty-three vanished thus on the Lady Day of the present year. Some weeks elapse before the new comers drop in, and a longer time passes before they take root in the school, their dazed, unaccustomed mood rendering immediate progress impossible; while the original bright ones have by this time themselves degenerated into the dazed strangers of other districts.

That the labourers of the country are more independent since their awakening to the sense of an outer world cannot be disputed. It was once common enough on inferior farms to hear a farmer, as he sat on horseback amid a field of workers, address them with a contemptuousness which could not have been greatly exceeded in the days when the thralls of Cedric wore their collars of brass.[36] Usually no answer was returned to these tirades; they were received as an accident of the land on which the listeners had happened to be born, calling for no more resentment than the blows of the wind and rain. But now, no longer fearing to avail himself of his privilege of flitting, these acts of contumely have ceased to be regarded as inevitable by the peasant. And while men do not of their own accord leave a farm without a grievance, very little fault-finding is often deemed a sufficient one among the younger and stronger. Such ticklish relations are the natural result of generations of unfairness on one side, and on the other an increase of knowledge, which has been kindled into activity by the exertions of Mr Joseph Arch.[37]

---

[35] TH's sisters both taught in village schools at the beginning of their careers.

[36] Walter Scott, *Ivanhoe*, ch. 1.

[37] Joseph Arch (1826–1919), founder of the National Agricultural Labourers' Union and Member of Parliament.

Nobody who saw and heard Mr Arch in his early tours through Dorsetshire will ever forget him and the influence his presence exercised over the crowds he drew. He hailed from Shakespeare's county,[38] where the humours of the peasantry have a marked family relationship with those of Dorset men; and it was this touch of nature,[39] as much as his logic, which afforded him such ready access to the minds and hearts of the labourers here. It was impossible to hear and observe the speaker for more than a few minutes without perceiving that he was a humourist—moreover, a man by no means carried away by an idea beyond the bounds of common sense. Like his renowned fellow-dalesman Corin, he virtually confessed that he was never in court, and might, with that eminent shepherd, have truly described himself as a 'natural philosopher', who had discovered that 'he that wants money, means, and content, is without three good friends'.[40]

'Content' may for a moment seem a word not exactly explanatory of Mr Arch's views; but on the single occasion, several years ago, on which the present writer numbered himself among those who assembled to listen to that agitator,[41] there was a remarkable moderation in his tone, and an exhortation to contentment with a reasonable amelioration, which, to an impartial auditor, went a long way in the argument. His views showed him to be rather the social evolutionist—what M. Emile de Laveleye would call a 'Possibilist'[42]—than the anarchic irreconcileable. The picture he drew of a comfortable cottage life as it should be, was so cosy, so well within the grasp of his listeners' imagination, that an old labourer in the crowd held up a coin between his finger and thumb exclaiming, 'Here's zixpence towards that, please God!' 'Towards what?' said a bystander. 'Faith, I don't know that I can spak the name o't, but I know 'tis a good thing,' he replied.

The result of the agitation, so far, upon the income of the labourers, has been testified by independent witnesses with a unanimity which

---

[38] Warwickshire.

[39] Shakespeare, *Troilus and Cressida*, iii. iii. 175: 'One touch of nature makes the whole world kin'.

[40] Shakespeare, *As You Like It*, iii. ii. 32, 24–6, etc.; it is in fact Touchstone who calls the shepherd Corin 'a natural philosopher'.

[41] TH probably heard Arch speak at the Dorchester Candlemas Fair, 14 February 1873: see *Career*, pp. 98–100.

[42] Émile Louis Victor, Baron de Laveleye (1822–92), Belgian economist; the French *possibilistes*—somewhat like the British Fabians—were socialists committed to gradual rather than revolutionary change, hence prepared to collaborate with non-socialist parties in order to achieve immediate reforms. See *LN* i. 150–2, for TH's transcription of extended extracts from an article of Laveleye's in the *Fortnightly Review* of 1 April 1883.

leaves no reasonable doubt of its accuracy. It amounts to an average rise of three shillings a week in wages nearly all over the county. The absolute number of added shillings seems small; but the increase is considerable when we remember that it is three shillings on eight or nine —*i.e.*, between thirty and forty per cent. And the reflection is forced upon everyone who thinks of the matter, that if a farmer can afford to pay thirty per cent. more wages in times of agricultural depression than he paid in times of agricultural prosperity, and yet live, and keep a carriage, while the landlord still thrives on the reduced rent which has resulted, the labourer must have been greatly wronged in those prosperous times. That the maximum of wage has been reached for the present is, however, pretty clear; and indeed it should be added that on several farms the labourers have submitted to a slight reduction during the past year, under stress of representations which have appeared reasonable.

It is hardly necessary to observe that the quoted wages never represent the labourer's actual income. Beyond the weekly payment—now standing at eleven or twelve shillings—he invariably receives a lump sum of 2*l.* or 3*l.* for harvest work. A cottage and garden is almost as invariably provided, free of rent,[43] with, sometimes, an extra piece of ground for potatoes in some field near at hand. Fuel, too, is frequently furnished, in the form of wood faggots. At springtime, on good farms, the shepherd receives a shilling for every twin reared, while the carter gets what is called journey-money, that is, a small sum, mostly a shilling, for every journey taken beyond the bounds of the farm. Where all these supplementary trifles are enjoyed together, the weekly wage in no case exceeds eleven shillings at the present time.

The question of enough or not enough often depends less upon the difference of two or three shillings a week in the earnings of the head of a family than upon the nature of his household. With a family of half a dozen children, the eldest of them delicate girls, nothing that he can hope to receive for the labour of his one pair of hands can save him from many hardships during a few years. But with a family of strong boys, of ages from twelve to seventeen or eighteen, he enjoys a season of prosperity. The very manner of the farmer towards him is deferential; for home-living boys, who in many cases can do men's work at half the wages, and without requiring the perquisites of house, garden-land, and so on, are treasures to the employer of agricultural labour. These

---

[43] For 'free of rent' pamphlet, p. 17, reads 'rent free'.

precious lads are, according to the testimony of several respectable labourers, a more frequent cause of contention between employer and man than any other item in their reckonings. As the boys grow, the father asks for a like growth in their earnings; and disputes arise which frequently end in the proprietor of the valuables taking himself off to a farm where he and his will be better appreciated. The mother of the same goodly row of sons can afford to despise the farmer's request for female labour; she stays genteelly at home, and looks with some superciliousness upon wives who, having no useful children, are obliged to work in the fields like their husbands. A triumphant family of the former class, which recently came under notice, may be instanced. The father and eldest son were paid eleven shillings a week each, the younger son ten shillings, three nearly grown-up daughters four shillings a week each, the mother the same when she chose to go out, and all the women two shillings a week additional at harvest; the men, of course, receiving their additional harvest-money as previously stated, with house, garden, and allotment free of charge. And since '*sine prole*'[44] would not frequently be written of the Dorset labourer if his pedigree were recorded in the local history like that of the other county families, such cases as the above are not uncommon.

Women's labour, too, is highly in request, for a woman who, like a boy, fills the place of a man at half the wages, can be better depended on for steadiness. Thus where a boy is useful in driving a cart or a plough, a woman is invaluable in work which, though somewhat lighter, demands thought. In winter and spring a farm-woman's occupation is often 'turnip-hacking'—that is, picking out from the land the stumps of turnips which have been eaten off by the sheep—or feeding the threshing-machine, clearing away straw from the same, and standing on the rick to hand forward the sheaves. In mid-spring and early summer her services are required for weeding wheat and barley (cutting up thistles and other noxious plants with a spud), and clearing weeds from pasture-land in like manner. In later summer her time is entirely engrossed by haymaking—quite a science, though it appears the easiest thing in the world to toss hay about in the sun. The length to which a skilful raker will work and retain command over her rake without moving her feet is dependent largely upon practice, and quite astonishing to the uninitiated.

---

[44] 'Without offspring'.

Haymaking is no sooner over than the women are hurried off to the harvest-field. This is a lively time. The bonus in wages during these few weeks, the cleanliness of the occupation, the heat, the cider and ale, influence to facetiousness and vocal strains. Quite the reverse do these lively women feel in the occupation which may be said to stand, emotionally, at the opposite pole to gathering in corn: that is, threshing it. Not a woman in the county but hates the threshing-machine. The dust, the din, the sustained exertion demanded to keep up with the steam tyrant are distasteful to all women but the coarsest. I am not sure whether, at the present time, women are employed to feed the machine, but some years ago a woman had frequently to stand just above the whizzing wire drum, and feed from morning to night—a performance for which she was quite unfitted, and many were the manœuvres to escape that responsible position. A thin saucer-eyed woman of fifty-five, who had been feeding the machine all day, declared on one occasion that in crossing a field on her way home in the fog after dusk, she was so dizzy from the work as to be unable to find the opposite gate, and there she walked round and round the field, bewildered and terrified, till three o'clock in the morning, before she could get out. The farmer said that the ale had got into her head, but she maintained that it was the spinning of the machine. The point was never clearly settled between them; and the poor woman is now dead and buried.

To be just, however, to the farmers, they do not enforce the letter of the Candlemas agreement in relation to the woman, if she makes any reasonable excuse for breaking it; and indeed, many a nervous farmer is put to flight by a matron who has a tongue with a tang, and who chooses to assert, without giving any reason whatever, that, though she had made fifty agreements, 'be cust if she will come out unless she is minded'— possibly terrifying him with accusations of brutality at asking her, when he knows 'how she is just now'. A farmer of the present essayist's acquaintance, who has a tendency to blush in the presence of beauty, and is in other respects a bashful man for his years, says that when the ladies of his farm are all together in a field, and he is the single one of the male sex present, he would as soon put his head into a hornet's nest as utter a word of complaint, or even a request beyond the commonest.

The changes which are so increasingly discernible in village life by no means originate entirely with the agricultural unrest. A depopulation is going on which in some quarters is truly alarming. Villages used to contain, in addition to the agricultural inhabitants, an interesting and better-informed class, ranking distinctly above those—the blacksmith, the carpenter, the shoemaker, the small higgler, the shopkeeper (whose stock-in-trade consisted of a couple of loaves, a pound of candles, a bottle of brandy-balls and lumps of delight, three or four scrubbing-brushes, and a frying-pan), together with nondescript-workers other than farm-labourers, who had remained in the houses where they were born for no especial reason beyond an instinct of association with the spot. Many of these families had been life-holders,[45] who built at their own expense the cottages they occupied, and as the lives dropped, and the property fell in, they would have been glad to remain as weekly or monthly tenants of the owner. But the policy of all but some few philan-thropic landowners is to disapprove of these petty tenants who are not in the estate's employ, and to pull down each cottage as it falls in, leaving standing a sufficient number for the use of the farmer's men and no more. The occupants who formed the back-bone of the village life have to seek refuge in the boroughs. This process, which is designated by statisticians as 'the tendency of the rural population towards the large towns', is really the tendency of water to flow uphill when forced. The poignant regret of those who are thus obliged to forsake the old nest can only be realised by people who have witnessed it—concealed as it often is under a mask of indifference. It is anomalous that landowners, who are showing unprecedented activity in the erection of comfortable cottages for their farm labourers, should see no reason for benefiting in the same way these unattached natives of the village who are nobody's care. They might often expostulate in the words addressed to King Henry the Fourth by his fallen subject:—

> Our house, my sovereign liege, little deserves
> The scourge of greatness to be used on it;
> And that same greatness, too, which our own hands
> Have holp to make so portly.[46]

The system is much to be deplored, for every one of these banished people imbibes a sworn enmity to the existing order of things, and not a few of them, far from becoming merely honest Radicals, degenerate

---

[45] Lifehold was a form of tenancy that expired at the death of the longest-lived of (usually two or three) named individuals; the Hardy family's Higher Bockhampton cottage was so held at the time of TH's birth and such tenancies provide plot elements in *The Woodlanders* and other of his works.

[46] Shakespeare, *1 Henry IV*, I. iii. 10–13; the speaker is Thomas Percy, Earl of Worcester.

into Anarchists, waiters on chance, to whom danger to the State, the town—nay, the street they live in, is a welcomed opportunity.

A reason frequently advanced for dismissing these families from the villages where they have lived for centuries is that it is done in the interests of morality; and it is quite true that some of the 'liviers'[47] (as these half-independent villagers used to be called) were not always shining examples of churchgoing, temperance, and quiet walking. But a natural tendency to evil, which develops to unlawful action when excited by contact with others like-minded, would often have remained latent amid the simple isolated experiences of a village life. The cause of morality cannot be served by compelling a population hitherto evenly distributed over the country to concentrate in a few towns, with the inevitable results of overcrowding and want of regular employment. But the question of the Dorset cottager here merges in that of all the houseless and landless poor, and the vast topic of the Rights of Man, to consider which is beyond the scope of a merely descriptive article.[48]

[1883.05]

'The Late Mr. T. W. H. Tolbort, B.C.S.'

> Shortly after Hardy's return to Dorchester to live in the summer of 1883 he found himself attending the deathbed of Hooper Tolbort (1841–83), a well-remembered friend and rival of his youth (*Biography*, pp. 70–1, 241–2). Tolbort died on 4 August, and Hardy's signed obituary, full of interesting references to his own as well as to Tolbort's early life, appeared as below in the *Dorset County Chronicle*, 16 August 1883, p. 10. In the absence of a surviving manuscript, it is impossible to be certain whether the heading was Hardy's or, as assumed here, editorial. Purdy, p. 297, mentions an offprint seen at Max Gate in the 1930s.

Dorchester, August 14th, 1883.

There has just silently passed away in this town a remarkable man, whose presence here, except for the brief notice in your obituary column of last week, would probably have been unknown to the majority of the

---

[47] Living in houses or cottages held on lifehold leases: cf. 1927.07.
[48] For 'a merely descriptive article' pamphlet, p. 21, reads 'this essay'.

inhabitants, notwithstanding that he was a native of Dorchester, and but a few years ago familiar to every townsman. I refer to Mr Tolbort, of the Bengal Civil Service, Deputy Commissioner of Umballa. His career has been in many respects so noteworthy that I trust the few facts of his life which I here hastily put on paper as an inadequate tribute to his memory will be acceptable to your readers.

Thomas William Hooper Tolbort was born at Dorchester in 1841, and received his general education at the Rev. W. Barnes' school in South-street.[49] It was proposed that he should be brought up to the business of a chemist and druggist, and he was accordingly apprenticed with his uncle, Mr Froud, who then occupied the shop which is now kept by his successor, Mr Evans.[50] But the easy circumstances of young Tolbort's situation left him much spare time, which he devoted entirely to study. I distinctly remember—for I knew him well both at this period and afterwards—his marvellous passion for the acquisition of languages, and how he was to be discovered poring over grammars at all hours and seasons—often to the injury of his health. About this date he became intimate with a man whose insight and kindly counsel gave direction to the energies of more than one Dorchester youth—I mean the late Mr Horace Moule, of Queen's College, Cambridge.[51] By his advice Tolbort was led to present himself as a candidate at the Oxford Middle-class Examination,[52] where he took a first place among nine hundred candidates. Stimulated by this success he turned his thoughts to India and the Indian Civil Service, and with a view to enlarging his opportunities for study took up his residence in London in the autumn of 1861. In 1862 I frequently met him there, where he was still following his old course, and, when he did not come to me, I used to find him either at his rooms or at an Institute in Edward-street, scribbling translations into and from dead and living languages. One day Mr Moule, who had also come up to town, brought me the news of Tolbort's success in the Indian Examination, and produced a copy of the *Times*,[53] where our friend's

[49] William Barnes's school was next door to the building in which TH served his apprenticeship to the architect John Hicks; it is referred to again in 1886.02 and 1902.13.

[50] Albert John Evans, Dorchester chemist; his son (see 1909.09) dramatized several of Hardy's novels for performance.

[51] For the importance of Horace Mosley Moule (1832–73) in TH's own life and career, see *Biography*, pp. 66–70, etc., and TH's headnote to the 1922 reprinting of Moule's poem 'Ave Caesar' (1922.04). The college is correctly 'Queens''.

[52] External examinations conducted by the Oxford Delegates of Local Examinations from 1858 onwards; see John Roach, *Public Examinations in England 1850–1900* (Cambridge: at the University Press, 1971), pp. 77–99, etc.   [53] Issue of 7 August 1862, p. 10.

name stood at the head of the list, followed by 200 of lower rank. The next year he came out first in the second Indian examination, and in due course proceeded to Calcutta, where, two months after his arrival, he passed the examination in native languages and obtained his commission.

The greater part of his life in India was spent in the Punjaub, and the later place of his residence there was at Umballa. In 1875 he married Clare, daughter of the late Sir H. Cunliffe, Bart., of Acton Park, Denbighshire, and enjoyed a period of happy domestic life, diversified by extensive travel, devoting his leisure to various linguistic productions, among which were the transliteration into the Roman character of a Persian translation of Robinson Crusoe, and a similarly Romanised edition of the Arabian Nights in the Urdú language.[54] He was called to the bar at Lincoln's Inn in 1877. Four years after his marriage—viz., in 1879, Mrs Tolbort died of typhoid fever at Kasuli; and from this date other shadows began gradually to steal over him, though he did not, or would not for a long time, perceive their true significance. Symptoms of consumption, which he seemed to regard only as passing ailments, appeared in him at longer or shorter intervals, till in 1881 or 1882 it was deemed advisable that he should winter in Algiers. Having a two years' leave of absence he passed a part of last summer in Dorchester, when his haggard look was observed by his nearest relative with alarm and apprehension. To Dorchester he again returned about three weeks ago, shattered in health, but still full of plans for the future. A sudden accession of his dreadful cough broke down his fragile frame completely, and in five days after his arrival he was dead. Even on the last day that sanguine mood which so often prevails in those who are the victims of this malady permitted him to entertain only a slight suspicion that his death-warrant had come; and there is on this account intense pathos in the words which now lie before me—the last he ever wrote— directions jotted down in pencil (for he could not speak) in a hand remarkably firm and flowing for one in his dying condition. The words are 'I daresay I shall get over this all right, but in case anything should happen to me before my book is printed I would ask you to get it published for me. . . . The papers are all on the table in the next room— a big heap of them. . . .' The omitted sentences are merely details as to the terms to be made with his publisher, and the book referred to is the

---

[54] Copies of both *Rábinsan Krúso* and *Alif Laila* are in the British Library.

MS. of a work entitled 'The Portuguese in India', which will, I trust, shortly see the light.[55]

In addition to this work the hobby of Tolbort's late years was the scheme for using Roman type for printing the vernaculars of India and other Oriental tongues, so as to obviate the almost insurmountable difficulty and expense of printing them in native character—a difficulty to which, he contended, was largely due the present inferiority of the Muhammadan world to the Christian. 'Is it not remarkable', he asks in the preface to *Rabinsan Kruso*, 'that the decided[56] superiority of the Christian world should only have become manifest during the last four centuries—in other words, since the invention of the printing press?'

But his ardent projects for the quickening of Oriental progress by transliterating the crabbed characters into the easily reproducible Roman must be left to other hands. His work has been stopped—too soon. Yet there may be a slight satisfaction in the thought that, without antecedent intention, he lies buried, not far away in an Indian soil, but beside his mother at the most beautiful spot in the Dorchester Cemetery, within view of the hills and woods that his childhood knew well.

Although Tolbort was, in a certain sense, a supreme product of the great modern apparatus, competitive examination, he was by no means a mere thing of its manufacture. Long before his mind turned to Indian competition he had conceived the idea of becoming a sort of universalist in knowledge; and, in addition to competitive studies that resulted in a power to speak and write in nine tongues, he gave considerable attention to such subjects as photography,[57] shorthand, chemistry, and what not.[58] But his genius, as far as it showed itself, was receptive rather than productive, though there is reason to suppose that had his life been longer spared he would have given to the world in his maturer years much valuable original work.

---

[55] Tolbort in 1872 and 1874 had already published two papers on the Portuguese in India in the *Journal of the Asiatic Society of Bengal*. His projected book-length manuscript, however, was never published, perhaps because TH found it was less complete than Tolbort had allowed himself to believe. Caroline Tolbort, a cousin (probably the 'nearest relation' mentioned earlier), wrote to TH on 28 December 1886 (DCM) to enquire as to the fate of Tolbort's papers, but it is not known what TH said or did in response.   [56] In *Rábinsan Krúso* itself 'decided' is italicized.

[57] Tolbort's death certificate shows that he died at 9 South Street, Dorchester, the home of John Pouncy, a notable photographic pioneer.

[58] Cf. *LW*, p. 168: 'Tolbort lived and studied as if everything in the world were so very much worth while. But what a bright mind has gone out at one-and-forty!'

1884

[1884.01]

Some Romano-British Relics Found at Max Gate, Dorchester

Hardy originally read this paper—a frankly amateur account of discoveries made during the digging of the foundations of his new house—at a meeting of the Dorset Natural History and Antiquarian Field Club held in the new building of the Dorset County Museum on 13 May 1884. The paper was promptly reported, under the heading 'The "Find" in Fordington-field', in the *Dorset County Chronicle*, 15 May 1884, p. 5, but for some reason—possibly related to local unease with Hardy's newly asserted middle-class pretensions as symbolized by Max Gate itself—it was omitted from the appropriate volume of the *Proceedings of the Dorset Natural History and Antiquarian Field Club*. The text below is that of its eventual appearance, slightly revised (see foot-notes) and bearing what was presumably Hardy's own title, in the *Proceedings*, 11 (Dorchester: Printed at the 'Dorset County Chronicle' Office, 1890), pp. [78]–81. An offprint, paginated [1]–4, was simultaneously issued in pamphlet form (copy, DCM). Purdy, p. 61.

I have been asked to give an account of a few relics of antiquity lately uncovered in digging the foundations of a house at Max Gate,[1] in Fordington Field. But, as the subject of archæology is one to a great extent foreign to my experience, my sole right to speak upon it at all, in the presence of the professed antiquarians around, lies in the fact that I am one of the only two persons[2] who saw most of the remains *in situ*, just as they were laid bare, and before they were lifted up from their rest of,

---

[1] Max Gate was not finished until the middle of 1885 and for 'house . . . Field' *Chronicle* text reads 'house in Fordington Field'.

[2] Since Max Gate was built by the Hardy family's building firm, the other person involved in the discoveries was presumably TH's father or brother or a workman in their employ.

I suppose, fifteen hundred years. Such brief notes as I have made can be given in a few words. Leaving the town by the south-eastern or Wareham Road we come first, as I need hardly observe, to the site of the presumably great Romano-British cemetery upon Fordington Hill. Proceeding along this road to a further distance of half-a-mile, we reach the spot on which the relics lay. It is about fifty yards back from the road-side, and practically a level, bearing no immediate evidence[3] that the natural contour of the surface has ever been disturbed more deeply than by the plough.[4] But though no barrow or other eminence rises there it should, perhaps, be remarked that about three hundred yards due east from the spot stands the fine and commanding tumulus called Conquer Barrow (the name of which, by the way, seems to be a corruption of some earlier word). On this comparatively level ground we discovered, about three feet below the surface, three human skeletons in separate and distinct graves. Each grave was, as nearly as possible, an ellipse in plan, about 4ft. long and 2½ft. wide, cut vertically into the solid chalk. The remains bore marks of careful interment. In two of the graves, and, I believe, in the third, a body lay on its right side, the knees being drawn up to the chest, and the arms extended straight downwards, so that the hands rested against the ankles. Each body was fitted with, one may almost say, perfect accuracy into the oval hole, the crown of the head touching the maiden chalk at one end and the toes at the other, the tight-fitting situation being strongly suggestive of the chicken in the egg shell. The closest examination failed to detect any enclosure for the remains, and the natural inference was that, save their possible cerements, they were deposited bare in the earth. On the head of one of these, between the top of the forehead and the crown, rested a fibula or clasp of bronze and iron, the front having apparently been gilt. This is, I believe, a somewhat unusual position for this kind of fastening, which seemed to have sustained a fillet for the hair.[5]

In the second grave a similar one was found, but as it was taken away without my knowledge I am unable to give its exact position when unearthed. In the third grave nothing of the sort was discovered after a careful search.

In the first grave a bottle of white clay, nearly globular, with a handle, stood close to the breast of the skeleton, the interior being stained as

---

[3] For 'no . . . evidence' *Chronicle* reads 'no evidence'.
[4] Excavations conducted in the 1980s during the construction of the Dorchester Bypass revealed that the land on which Max Gate now stands was once the site of an extensive pre-Roman causeway camp.   [5] The words 'which . . . hair' added in 1890.

if by some dark liquid. The bottle, unfortunately, fell into fragments on attempting to remove it. In the same cavity, touching the shin bones of the occupant, were two urns of the material known as grey ware, and of a design commonly supposed to be characteristic of Roman work of the third or fourth century. It is somewhat remarkable that beside them was half, and only a half, a third urn, with a filmy substance like black cobweb adhering to the inner surface.

In the second cavity were four urns, standing nearly upright like the others, two being of ordinary size, and two quite small. They stood touching each other, and close to the breast of the skeleton; these, like the former, were empty, except of the chalk which had settled into them by lapse of time; moreover, the unstained white chalk being in immediate contact with the inner surface of the vessels was nearly a proof that nothing solid had originally intervened. In the third grave two other urns of like description were disclosed.

Two yards south from these graves a circular hole in the native chalk was uncovered, measuring about two feet in diameter and five feet deep. At the bottom was a small flagstone; above this was the horn, apparently of a bull, together with teeth and bones of the same animal. The horn was stumpy and curved, altogether much after the modern shorthorn type, and it has been conjectured that the remains were possibly those of the wild ox formerly inhabiting this island. Pieces of a black bituminous substance were mixed in with these, and also numerous flints, forming a packing to the whole. A few pieces of tile, and brick of the thin Roman kind, with some fragments of iridescent glass were also found about the spot.

There was naturally no systematic orientation in the interments—the head in one case being westward, in the other eastward, and in the third, I believe, south-west. It should be mentioned that the surface soil has been cleared away to a distance extending 50ft. south and west from where these remains were disinterred; but no further graves or cavities have been uncovered—the natural chalk lying level and compact—which seems to signify that the site was no portion of a regular Golgotha,[6] but an isolated resting-place reserved to a family, set, or staff; such outlying tombs having been common along the roadsides near towns in those far-off days—a humble Colonial imitation, possibly, of the system of sepulture along the Appian Way.[7]

---

[6] Burial ground, as in Matt. 27: 33: 'Golgotha, that is to say, a place of a skull.'

[7] The words 'a humble . . . Way' are absent from the *Chronicle* report of 1884; their presence here is doubtless related to TH's having visited Italy in 1887.

In spite of the numerous vestiges that have been discovered from time to time of the Roman city which formerly stood on the site of modern Dorchester, and which are still being unearthed daily by our local Schliemann,[8] one is struck with the fact that little has been done towards piecing together and reconstructing these evidences into an unmutilated whole—such as has been done, for instance, with the evidences of Pompeian life—a whole which should represent Dorchester in particular and not merely the general character of a Roman station in this country—composing a true picture by which the uninformed could mentally realise the ancient scene with some completeness.

It would be a worthy attempt to rehabilitate, on paper, the living Durnovaria[9] of fourteen or fifteen hundred years ago—as it actually appeared to the eyes of the then Dorchester men and women, under the rays of the same morning and evening sun which rises and sets over it now. Standing, for instance, on the elevated ground near where the South-Western Station is at present, or at the top of Slyer's Lane,[10] or at any other commanding point, we may ask what kind of object did Dorchester then form in the summer landscape as viewed from such a point; where stood the large buildings, where the small,[11] how did the roofs group themselves, what were the gardens like, if any, what social character had the streets, what were the customary noises, what sort of exterior was exhibited by these hybrid Romano-British people, apart from the soldiery? Were the passengers up and down the ways few in number, or did they ever form a busy throng such as we now see on a market day? These are merely the curious questions of an outsider to initiated students of the period. When we consider the vagueness of our mental answers to such inquiries as the above, we perceive that much is still left of this fascinating investigation which may well occupy the attention of the Club in future days.

---

[8] Heinrich Schliemann (1822–90), the German archaeologist who excavated the traditional site of Troy; the specific allusion is to the Dorchester antiquary Edward Cunnington (1825–1916), who conducted many amateur 'digs' in the Dorset area. The delay in the formal publication of TH's paper may have been related to his fairly transparent use of the locally influential Cunnington as the model for the dubious archaeologist in his story 'A Tryst at an Ancient Earthwork', initially published only in an American newspaper, the *Detroit Post*, on 15 March 1885, p. 13 (Purdy, p. 153; *Biography*, pp. 244–5).   [9] The Roman name for Dorchester.

[10] NE of Dorchester, where the road to Piddletrenthide crosses the ancient Ridgeway.

[11] The *Chronicle* reading 'where the small' has been preferred to the 'were they small' of *Proceedings*.

1886

[1886.01]

[?Thomas Hardy at Max Gate?]

An important and relatively early feature article on Hardy was 'Celebrities at Home. No. CCCCXL. Mr. Thomas Hardy at Max Gate, Dorchester', published in the *World* (London), 17 February 1886, pp. 6–7, and reprinted in the *Dorset County Chronicle*, 25 February 1886, pp. 3–4. Florence Hardy drew directly upon the article when revising *Life and Work* (pp. 508–9) following her husband's death, and Purdy, pointing to the presence of several offprints among Hardy's papers and to 'some internal evidence of style', has suggested that it might have been Hardy's own work. Since Hardy was clearly willing on occasion to supply journalists with prefabricated copy (cf. 1878.01, 1899.03), the writing may in part be his. Some passages, however, seem clearly to be the work of another hand, and while the article must certainly have been written with Hardy's active collaboration and approval, he was probably not in any substantial sense its author. The bulk of the article has recently been reproduced in *Interviews and Recollections*, pp. 20–3. Purdy, p. 264.

[1886.02]

The Rev. William Barnes, B.D.

Following Hardy's return to Dorchester and move to Max Gate, his friendship with William Barnes became a good deal closer, and when Barnes died on 7 October 1886 Hardy accepted an invitation (*CL* i. 153–4) to write the following signed obituary in the *Athenaeum*, 16 October 1886, pp. 501–2.

Working at some speed, he borrowed extensively from his own review of Barnes's *Poems of Rural Life in the Dorset Dialect* (1879.02)—an act of self-plagiarism that later obliged him (*CL* ii. 61, 62) to allow only the obituary, and not the review, to be reprinted in Lionel Johnson's *The Art of Thomas Hardy* (London: John Lane and Elkin Mathews, 1894), pp. xlix–lviii. Hardy mentioned the obituary in *Life and Work*, p. 190, noting that it was later drawn upon for the article on Barnes in the *Dictionary of National Biography* (1900.05), and included a tearsheet from the *Athenaeum* (Millgate) among the materials assembled for his projected 'Miscellanea' volume. Reprinted in *Life and Art*, pp. 48–55. Purdy, p. 297.

Until within the last year or two there were few figures more familiar to the eye in the county town of Dorset on a market day than an aged clergyman, quaintly attired in caped cloak, knee-breeches, and buckled shoes, with a leather satchel slung over his shoulders, and a stout staff in his hand. He seemed usually to prefer the middle of the street to the pavement, and to be thinking of matters which had nothing to do with the scene before him. He plodded along with a broad, firm tread, notwithstanding the slight stoop occasioned by his years. Every Saturday morning he might have been seen thus trudging up the narrow South Street, his shoes coated with mud or dust according to the state of the roads between his rural home and Dorchester, and a little grey dog at his heels, till he reached the four cross ways in the centre of the town. Halting here, opposite the public clock, he would pull his old-fashioned watch from its deep fob, and set it with great precision to London time.[1] This, the invariable first act of his market visit, having been completed to his satisfaction, he turned round and methodically proceeded about his other business.

This venerable and well-characterized man was William Barnes, the Dorsetshire poet and philologer, by whose death last week at the ripe age of eighty-six[2] the world has lost not only a lyric writer of a high order of genius, but probably the most interesting link between present and past forms of rural life that England possessed. The date of his birth at the very beginning of the century is less explanatory of his almost

---

[1] The rapid development of railways, telegraphs, etc., had made it necessary to standardize time on a national rather than a local basis: cf. 'railway time' (1856.01).

[2] Barnes, born in February 1801, was in fact 85 at the time of his death, but TH had evidently accepted (see next paragraph) the 1800 date supplied by Barnes's daughter Lucy Baxter (see 1902.13) in a letter (n.d., DCM) written hastily in the immediate aftermath of her father's death.

unique position in this respect than the remoteness, even from contemporary provincial civilization, of the pastoral recesses in which his
earlier years were passed—places with whose now obsolete customs
and beliefs his mind was naturally imbued. To give one instance of the
former tardiness of events in that part of the country: it was a day almost
within his remembrance when, amidst the great excitement and
applause of the natives, who swept the street with brooms in honour of
its arrival, a stage coach made its first entry into Sturminster Newton,
the little market town nearest to the hamlet of Bagbere, the home of his
parents.[3] And there used to come to a little bridge, close to his father's
door, till quite recently, a conjuror or 'white wizard', who cured afflicted
persons by means of the toad-bag—a small piece of linen having a limb
from a living toad sewn up inside, to be worn round the sufferer's neck
and next his skin, the twitching movements of which limb gave, so it was
said, 'a turn' to the blood of the wearer, and effected a radical change
in his constitution.[4]

Born so long ago as February 22nd, 1800 (1801 has been given, but I
believe incorrectly),[5] amid such surroundings, a thorough son of the
soil, and endowed with great retentiveness and powers of observation,
it is no wonder that Barnes became a complete repertory of forgotten
manners, words, and sentiments, a store which he afterwards turned
to such good use in his writings on ancient British and Anglo-Saxon
speech, customs, and folklore; above all, in the systematic study of his
native dialect, as a result of which he has shown the world that far from
being, as popularly supposed, a corruption of correct English, it is a distinct branch of Teutonic speech, regular in declension and conjugation,
and richer in many classes of words than any other tongue known to
him. As an instance of the latter he used to mention the pronouns with
particular pride, there being no fewer than four demonstratives to set
against the current English two. He would also instance any natural
object, such as a tree, and show that there were double the number of
names for its different parts in the Dorset dialect to those available in
the standard tongue.

It was a proud day for young William Barnes when, some time in the
year 1814 or 1815, a local solicitor, the late Mr Dashwood, entered the

---

[3] Based on a note (*LW*, p. 117) made by TH in 1877 while he was himself living in Sturminster
Newton. [4] Another of TH's Sturminster Newton notes: *LW*, p. 115.
[5] The 1801 birthdate is now universally accepted.

village school and inquired if there was a boy clever enough with his pen to come and copy deeds in his office in a clerkly hand. The only lad who at all approximated to such a high description was Barnes, and the scene of testing him with the long quill pen and paper, and his selection by the lawyer, must have been one to which Mulready[6] alone could have done justice. The youth thus found himself at a solicitor's desk, and, what was more, in a position to help himself in some degree to the grammars and glossaries his soul desired, and by whose diligent perusal at odd hours through many laborious years he became familiar with an astonishing number of languages and dialects. A more notable instance of self-help has seldom been recorded, considering the date in the century, the young man's circumstances, and the remote place of his residence, for it appears that he still lived on at the hamlet, walking to and from the town —or rather townlet—every day. In later years academic scholars were sometimes found to remark upon the unsystematic character of his linguistic attainments, but it cannot be gainsaid that he was almost always ready with definite and often exclusive information on whatever slightly known form of human speech might occur to the mind of his questioner, from Persian to Welsh, from the contemporary vernaculars of India to the tongues of the ancient British tribes. Over and above these subjects, his mind was occupied after his removal to Dorchester, to judge from his letters to old local newspapers, with investigations of Roman remains, theories on the origin of Stonehenge, and kindred archæological matters; while among his other hobbies about this time was engraving on wood and on silver, crests and initials upon old pieces of plate in the neighbourhood still remaining to testify to his skill in the art.

Though Barnes's first practical step in life had brought him to the office of a solicitor, his instincts were towards tuition; and when, some years later, he had become well settled in the county town he opened a school. As schoolmaster he was fairly successful from the first, and as time went by and he obtained, as a ten years' man, his university degree and took orders,[7] the school grew highly popular. It was during this period—from early in the forties onwards—that he wrote at intervals

---

[6] William Mulready (1786–1863), the genre painter.

[7] Under the prevailing regulations Barnes was able to gain a Bachelor of Divinity degree at Cambridge in 1850 after enrolling as a part-time student over a ten-year period, keeping three university terms, and passing a series of examinations.

the first, second, and third series of those sweet rustic poems by which his name will be best remembered.[8]

He used to tell an amusing story of his experience on relinquishing the school at Dorchester[9] to retire to the country rectory of Winterbourne Came, in which he has ended his days. About the very week of his translation, so to call it, the name of one of his pupils appeared in the *Times* and other papers at the head of the Indian examination list, a wide proportion of marks separating it from the name following.[10] The novelty of these lists lent a keen interest to them in those days,[11] and the next morning Mr Barnes was deluged with letters from all parts of the country requesting him at almost any price to take innumerable sons, and produce upon them the same successful effect. 'I told them it took two to do it,' he would say, adding, 'Thus a popularity which I had never known during the working years of my life came at almost the first moment when it was no longer of use to me.'

To many readers of these pages the charming idyls known as Barnes's 'Poems in the Dorset Dialect' are too familiar to need description or eulogy. Though locally distinguished on the title-page by the name of the county at large, the chief scenes of their inspiration lie more precisely in the limited district to the north and north-west of Dorsetshire, that is to say in the secluded Vale of Blackmore, whose margin formed the horizon of his boyhood, and was, as he himself sings in one of the poems, the end of the world to him then. This fertile and sheltered tract of country, where the fields are never brown and the springs never dry, is bounded on the south by the bold chalk ridge that embraces the prominences of Hambledon Hill, Bulbarrow, Nettlecombe Tout, Dogbury, and High-Stoy. The prospect northwards from each of these heights is one which rivals, and in many points surpasses, those much admired views of Surrey and Buckinghamshire from Richmond Hill and the terrace at Windsor Castle, while the portion of the landscape immediately beneath the spectator is the abiding-place of the people whose daily

---

[8] The earliest volume of Barnes's *Poems of Rural Life in the Dorset Dialect* was published in London by John Russell Smith in 1844; TH reviewed the single-volume collected edition of the three series when it was published by C. Kegan Paul & Co. in 1879 (1879.02).

[9] The school, in South Street, next door to the office of John Hicks, the architect to whom TH was apprenticed, is also invoked in 1883.05 and 1902.13.

[10] *The Times*, 7 August 1862, p. 10; the name was that of T. W. H. Tolbort, whose obituary TH later wrote (1883.05).

[11] Competitive examinations for entry into the Indian Civil Service had only recently been introduced.

doings, sayings, and emotions have been crystallized in the poet's verse. Occasionally, it is true, we find among the men and women presented in Mr Barnes's volumes some who are housed in hamlets lying nominally beyond the Vale, but to my mind these characters are in a great measure Blackmore people away from home, bearing with them still the well-marked traits which distinguish the Vale population from that of the neighbouring uplands. The same may be said of his backgrounds and scenery. Moreover, when, moved by the pervading instinct of the nineteenth century, he gives us whole poems of still life, unaffected and realistic as a Dutch picture, the slow green river Stour of the same valley, with its deep pools, whence the trout leaps to the may-fly undisturbed by anglers, is found to be the stream dearest to his memory and the inspirer of some of his happiest effusions.[12]

Unlike Burns, Béranger, and other poets of the people, Mr Barnes never assumed the high conventional style; and he entirely leaves alone ambition, pride, despair, defiance, and other of the grander passions which move mankind great and small. His rustics are, as a rule, happy people, and very seldom feel the sting of the rest of modern mankind—the disproportion between the desire for serenity and the power of obtaining it. One naturally thinks of Crabbe in this connexion;[13] but though they touch at points, Crabbe goes much further than Barnes in questioning the justice of circumstance. Their pathos, after all, is the attribute upon which the poems must depend for their endurance; and the incidents which embody it are those of everyday cottage life, tinged throughout with that 'light that never was',[14] which the emotional art of the lyrist can project upon the commonest things. It is impossible to prophesy, but surely much English literature will be forgotten when 'Woak Hill' is still read for its intense pathos, 'Blackmore Maidens' for its blitheness, and 'In the Spring' for its Arcadian ecstasy.[15]

Notwithstanding the wide appreciation of his verse both here and in America, so largely local were the poet's interests that it may be questioned if the enthusiasm which accompanied his own readings of his works in the town-halls of the shire was not more grateful to him than the admiration of a public he had never seen. The effect, indeed, of his recitations upon an audience well acquainted with the *nuances* of the

---

[12] For this paragraph cf. paragraphs 2 and 4 of 1879.02.

[13] George Crabbe (1754–1832), whose work TH much admired: see e.g. 1905.15 and *LW*, p. 351.   [14] Wordsworth, 'Elegiac Stanzas'; cf. 1879.02, n. 16.

[15] For this paragraph cf. paragraph 14 of 1879.02.

dialect—impossible to impart to outsiders by any kind of translation—can hardly be imagined by readers of his lines acquainted only with English in its customary form. The poet's own mild smile at the boisterous merriment provoked by his droll delivery of such pieces as 'The Shy Man', 'A Bit o' Sly Coorten', and 'Dick and I' returns upon the memory as one of the most characteristic aspects of a man who was nothing if not genial; albeit that, while the tyranny of his audience demanded these broadly humorous productions, his own preferences were for the finer and more pathetic poems, such as 'Wife a-lost', 'Woak Hill', and 'Jaäy a-past'.

To those who knew Mr Barnes in his prime it may have been a matter for conjecture why a man of his energies should not at some point or other of his career have branched off from the quiet byways of his early manhood into the turmoils of the outer world, particularly as his tastes at that time were somewhat general, and the direction of his labours was dictated in the main by his opportunities. The explanation seems to be that the poetic side of his nature, though not always dominant, was but faintly ruled by the practical at any time, that his place-attachment was strong almost to a fault, and that his cosmopolitan interests, though lively, were always subordinate to those local hobbies and solicitudes whence came alike his special powers and his limitations.

Few young people who have seen him only in latter years, since the pallor and stoop of old age overcame him, can realize the robust, upright form of his middle life, the ruddy cheek, and the bright quick eye. The last, indeed, dimmed but slightly, and even on his death-bed his zest for the subject of speech-form was strong as ever. In one of his latest conversations he became quite indignant at the word 'bicycle'. 'Why didn't they call it "wheel-saddle"?' he exclaimed.

Though not averse to social intercourse, his friendships extended over but a small area of society. But those who, like the present writer, knew him well and long, entertained for him a warm affection; while casual visitors from afar were speedily won to kindly regard by the simplicity of his character, his forbearance, and the charming spurts of youthful ardour which would burst out as rays even in his latest hours.

1887

[1887.01]

'Fine Passages in Verse and Prose'

> Hardy's response to an invitation to choose 'the one passage in all poetry which seems the finest, and also the one passage in prose which appears of its kind the best', was printed, along with others, in the *Fortnightly Review*, new series 42 (August 1887), p. 304, beneath the editorial heading 'Fine Passages in Verse and Prose; Selected by Living Men of Letters (No. 1)'. The *Fortnightly* also quoted, pp. 304–6, three of the five passages that Hardy— evading the strict terms of his assignment—had ventured to name; these have not been reprinted here but are identified in the footnotes. Purdy, p. 297.

I should have replied sooner, but the words, 'The one passage in all poetry which seems to me the finest' quite bewildered my mind by their immensity. I should say that there is no one passage finest; that the various kinds of best poetry are not reducible to a common standard. 'There is one glory of the sun, and another glory of the moon, and another of the stars.'[1] I know that you ask 'what *seems* the finest'; but that seeming varies with the time and mood, and according to the class of poetry that is for the nonce nearest to the tone of our situation.

I have very often felt (but not always) that one of the most beautiful of English lyrics is Shelley's 'Lament', 'O world, O life, O time';[2] and of descriptive poetry I do not know that anything has as yet been fairly able to oust our old friends in *Childe Harold*—*e.g.* C. III., stanzas 85 to 87.[3]

---

[1] 1 Cor. 15: 41, which reads 'and another glory of the stars'.
[2] Despite its brevity, this was not one of the passages quoted.
[3] Quoted in full by the *Fortnightly*; Purdy (p. 297) notes that the passage may have had personal associations for TH.

I know this is an old-fashioned taste; but it is a well-considered relapse on my part, for though in past years I have been very modern, in this matter I begin to feel that mere intellectual subtlety will not hold its own in time to come against the straightforward expression of good feeling.

With regard to prose the task is somewhat more practicable, and yet how hopeless! But I will go thus far: I think that the passages in Carlyle's *French Revolution* on the silent growth of the oak[4] have never been surpassed by anything I have read, except perhaps by his sentences on night in a city,[5] as specimens of contemplative prose (if they may be so called); and that in narrative prose the chapter of the Bible (2 Sam. xviii.)[6] containing the death of Absalom is the finest example of its kind that I know, showing beyond its power and pathos the highest artistic cunning.

[1887.02]

[Assistance to Barnes Biography]

Hardy knew and liked William Barnes's daughter Lucy Baxter, who wrote on art under the pseudonym of 'Leader Scott', and would later produce an affectionate obituary (1902.13) on the occasion of her death. Responding on 13 December 1886 (*CL* i. 157–8) to her letter from Florence of 7 December (DCM), he welcomed her intention to write a biography of her father and promised to send her anything he recalled from his own conversations with Barnes that might be 'of general interest'. Hardy is among those thanked in the Preface, p. ix, to the resulting volume, *The Life of William Barnes, Poet and Philologist* (London: Macmillan, 1887), published by Lucy Baxter over her own name, and two anecdotes (pp. 278, 309) are directly attributed to him.

---

[4] Two paragraphs quoted by the *Fortnightly* from Carlyle's *The French Revolution*, vol. 1, book second, ch. 1, 'Astræa Redux'.
[5] Part of paragraph quoted by the *Fortnightly* from Carlyle's *Sartor Resartus*, book 1, ch. 3.
[6] Not quoted by the *Fortnightly*.

1888

[1888.01]

[Speaking from the Bench]

Edward C. Sampson's invaluable article, 'Thomas Hardy—Justice of the Peace', *Colby Library Quarterly*, 13 (December 1977), pp. 263–74, shows that Hardy took the necessary oaths to qualify as a borough magistrate in 1884 and as a county magistrate in 1894 (the oaths themselves are quoted on pp. 264–5 and 267), and that he sat on the bench or as a grand-juror for the Assizes on numerous occasions between 1884 and 1919. As Sampson points out, the reports of such occasions in the local newspapers rarely quoted or even mentioned individual justices, but this by no means insignificant aspect of Hardy's involvement in public affairs can at least be represented by the two references to him in the *Dorset County Chronicle*, 1 March 1888, p. 4, as presiding at the Borough Petty Sessions in Dorchester on 27 February 1888. Before the court was a case in which the defendant, accused of refusing to pay a special tax, argued that the tax itself was illegal: in the first of the extracts reproduced below Hardy is quoted as asking whether it was a test case that had been brought before the court; in the second, following the line of asterisks, he is reported as pronouncing the court's verdict. See also *Collected Letters*, iii. 23, iv. 232, and v. 267.

Mr Hardy: Was it by general consent this case was selected?

*   *   *   *   *

After a brief consultation Mr Hardy, who presided, said it appeared the rate was legal, and therefore it should be enforced.

[1888.02]

'The Profitable Reading of Fiction'

Invited by Lorettus S. Metcalf (1837–1920), founder and first editor of the New York *Forum*, to write a 4,000-word essay on 'The Profitable Reading of Fiction' for a forty guinea fee, Hardy on 30 September 1887 (*CL* i. 168) accepted the proposal but asked for time in which to clear off existing commitments. As of 10 January 1888 he was still working on what he referred to as a piece of 'heavier writing' that he had 'unluckily promised an Editor' (*CL* i. 172), but its arrival in New York was acknowledged by Metcalf on 3 February (DCM), and it was published, as below (American spellings retained), in the *Forum*, 5 (March 1888), pp. [57]–70. Hardy never reprinted this first and most leisurely of his specifically literary essays, but he did list it among the contents of a possible volume of 'Miscellanea', adding that, since he could find no copy of the *Forum* printing, Ernest Brennecke's unauthorized *Life and Art* could serve as an alternative source. Reprinted in *Life and Art*, pp. 56–74. Purdy, p. 298.

When the editor of this review courteously offered me space in his pages to formulate a few general notions upon the subject of novel reading, considered with a view to mental profit, I could not help being struck with the timeliness of the theme; for in these days the demand for novels has risen so high, in proportion to that for other kinds of literature, as to attract the attention of all persons interested in education. But I was by no means persuaded that one whose own writings have largely consisted in books of this class was in a position to say anything on the matter, even if he might be supposed to have anything to say. The field, however, is so wide and varied that there is plenty of room for impersonal points of regard; and I may as well premise that the remarks which follow, where not exclusively suggested by a consideration of the works of dead authors, are mere generalizations from a cursory survey, and no detailed analysis, of those of to-day.

If we speak of deriving good from a story, we usually mean something more than the gain of pleasure during the hours of its perusal. Nevertheless, to get pleasure out of a book is a beneficial and profitable thing, if the pleasure be of a kind which, while doing no moral injury, affords relaxation and relief when the mind is overstrained or sick of itself. The prime remedy in such cases is change of scene, by which change of the material scene is not necessarily implied. A sudden shifting of the mental perspective into a fictitious world, combined with rest, is well known to be often as efficacious for renovation as a corporeal journey afar.

In such a case the shifting of scene should manifestly be as complete as if the reader had taken the hind seat on a witch's broomstick. The town man finds what he seeks in novels of the country, the countryman in novels of society, the indoor class generally in outdoor novels, the villager in novels of the mansion, the aristocrat in novels of the cottage.

The narrative must be of a somewhat absorbing kind, if not absolutely fascinating. To discover a book or books which shall possess, in addition to the special scenery, the special action required, may be a matter of some difficulty, though not always of such difficulty as to be insuperable; and it may be asserted that after every variety of spiritual fatigue there is to be found refreshment, if not restoration, in some antithetic realm of ideas which lies waiting in the pages of romance.

In reading for such hygienic purposes it is, of course, of the first consequence that the reader be not too critical. In other words, his author should be swallowed whole, like any other alterative pill. He should be believed in slavishly, implicitly. However profusely he may pour out his coincidences, his marvelous juxtapositions, his catastrophes, his conversions of bad people into good people at a stroke, and *vice versâ*, let him never be doubted for a moment. When he exhibits people going out of their way and spending their money on purpose to act consistently, or taking a great deal of trouble to move in a curious and roundabout manner when a plain, straight course lies open to them; when he shows that heroes are never faithless in love, and that the unheroic always are so, there should arise a conviction that this is precisely according to personal experience. Let the invalid reverse the attitude of a certain class of critics—now happily becoming less numerous—who only allow themselves to be interested in a novel by the defeat of every attempt to the contrary. The aim should be the exercise of a generous imaginativeness, which shall find in a tale not only all that was put there by the author, put he it never so awkwardly, but which shall find there what was never inserted by him, never foreseen, never contemplated. Sometimes these additions which are woven around a work of fiction by the intensive power of the reader's own imagination are the finest parts of the scenery.

It is not altogether necessary to this tonic purpose that the stories chosen should be 'of most disastrous chances, of moving accidents by flood and field'.[1] As stated above, the aim should be contrast. Directly the circumstances begin to resemble those of the reader, a personal connection, an interest other than an imaginative one, is set up, which results in an intellectual stir that is not in the present case to be desired. It sets his serious thoughts at work, and he does not want them stimulated just now; he wants to dream.

So much may be said initially upon alleviating the effects of overwork and carking care by a course of imaginative reading. But I will assume that benefit of this sort is not that which is primarily contemplated when we speak of getting good out of novels, but intellectual or moral profit to active and undulled spirits.

It is obvious that choice in this case, though more limited than in the former, is by no means limited to compositions which touch the highest level in the essential constituents of a novel—those without which it would be no novel at all—the plot and the characters. Not only may the book be read for these main features—the presentation, as they may collectively be called—but for the accidents and appendages of narrative; and such are of more kinds than one. Excursions into various philosophies, which vary or delay narrative proper, may have more attraction than the regular course of the enactment; the judicious inquirer may be on the look-out for didactic reflection, such as is found in large lumps in *Rasselas*;[2] he may be a picker-up of trifles[3] of useful knowledge, statistics, queer historic fact, such as sometimes occur in the pages of Hugo; he may search for specimens of the manners of good or bad society, such as are to be obtained from the fashionable writers; or he may even wish to brush up his knowledge of quotations from ancient and other authors by studying some chapters of *Pelham*[4] and the disquisitions of Parson Adams in *Joseph Andrews*.[5]

Many of the works which abound in appurtenances of this or a kindred sort are excellent as narrative, excellent as portraiture, even if in spite rather than in consequence of their presence. But they are the exception. Directly we descend from the highest levels we find that the majority are not effectual in their ostensible undertaking, that of giving

---

[1] Shakespeare, *Othello*, I. ii. 134–5.

[2] *The History of Rasselas, Prince of Abyssinia* (1759), moral fable by Samuel Johnson.

[3] Cf. Shakespeare, *A Winter's Tale*, IV. iii. 26: 'a snapper-up of unconsidered trifles'.

[4] *Pelham; or, The Adventures of a Gentleman*, a novel (1828) by Edward George Earle Lytton Bulwer-Lytton, 1st Baron Lytton.

[5] *The Adventures of Joseph Andrews and his Friend Mr Abraham Adams* (1742), the novel by Henry Fielding (see 1908.05).

us a picture of life in action; they exhibit a machinery which often works awkwardly, and at the instigation of unlikely beings. Yet, being packed with thoughts of some solidity, or more probably sprinkled with smart observations on men and society, they may be read with advantage even by the critical, who, for what they bring, can forgive the audible working of the wheels and wires and carpentry, heard behind the performance, as the wires and trackers of a badly constructed organ are heard under its tones.

Novels of the latter class—formerly more numerous than now—are the product of cleverness rather than of intuition; and in taking them up—bearing in mind that profit, and not amusement, is the student's aim—his manifest course is to escape from the personages and their deeds, gathering the author's wit or wisdom nearly as it would have presented itself if he had cast his thoughts in the shape of an essay.

But though we are bound to consider by-motives like these for reading fiction as praiseworthy enough where practicable, they are by their nature of an illegitimate character, more or less, and apart from the ruling interest of the genuine investigator of this department of literature. Such ingredients can be had elsewhere in more convenient parcels. Our true object is a lesson in life, mental enlargement from elements essential to the narratives themselves and from the reflections they engender.

Among the qualities which appertain to representations of life, construed, though not distorted, by the light of imagination—qualities which are seldom shared by views *about* life, however profound—is that of self-proof or obviousness. A representation is less susceptible of error than a disquisition; the teaching, depending as it does upon intuitive conviction, and not upon logical reasoning, is not likely to lend itself to sophistry. If endowed with ordinary intelligence, the reader can discern, in delineative art professing to be natural, any stroke greatly at variance with nature, which, in the form of moral essay, *pensée*, or epigram, may be so wrapped up as to escape him.

Good fiction may be defined here as that kind of imaginative writing which lies nearest to the epic, dramatic, or narrative masterpieces of the past. One fact is certain: in fiction there can be no intrinsically new thing at this stage of the world's history. New methods and plans may arise and come into fashion, as we see them do; but the general theme can neither be changed, nor (what is less obvious) can the relative importance of its various particulars be greatly interfered with. The higher passions must ever rank above the inferior—intellectual tendencies above animal, and moral above intellectual—whatever the treatment, realistic or ideal. Any system of inversion which should attach more importance to the delineation of man's appetites than to the delineation of his aspirations, affections, or humors, would condemn the old masters of imaginative creation from Æschylus to Shakespeare. Whether we hold the arts which depict mankind to be, in the words of Mr Matthew Arnold, a criticism of life,[6] or, in those of Mr Addington Symonds, a revelation of life,[7] the material remains the same, with its sublimities, its beauties, its uglinesses, as the case may be. The finer manifestations must precede in importance the meaner, without such a radical change in human nature as we can hardly conceive as pertaining to an even remote future of decline, and certainly do not recognize now.

In pursuance of his quest for a true exhibition of man, the reader will naturally consider whether he feels himself under the guidance of a mind who sees further into life than he himself has seen; or, at least, who can throw a stronger irradiation over subjects already within his ken than he has been able to do unaided. The new light needs not to be set off by a finish of phraseology or incisive sentences of subtle definition. The treatment may be baldly incidental, without inference or commentary. Many elaborate reflections, for example, have been composed by moralizing chroniclers on the effect of prosperity in blunting men's recollection of those to whom they have sworn friendship when they shared a hard lot in common. But the writer in Genesis who tells his legend of certain friends in such adverse circumstances, one of whom, a chief butler, afterward came to good fortune, and ends the account of this good fortune with the simple words, 'Now the chief butler did not remember Joseph, but forgat him',[8] brings out a dramatic sequence on ground prepared for assent, shows us the general principle in the particular case, and hence writes with a force beyond that of aphorism or argument. It is the force of an appeal to the emotional reason rather than to the logical reason; for by their emotions men are acted upon, and act upon others.

If it be true, as is frequently asserted, that young people nowadays go to novels for their sentiments, their religion, and their morals, the

[6] TH's source for this central Arnoldian tenet was probably Arnold's 'Wordsworth' essay in *Macmillan's Magazine*, 40 (July 1879), p. 199; see *LN* i. 119 (item 1105).

[7] John Addington Symonds, 'Matthew Arnold's Selections from Wordsworth', *Fortnightly Review*, NS 26 (November 1879), p. 690; see *LN* i. 125 (item 1148).

[8] Somewhat misquoted from Gen. 40: 23.

question as to the wisdom or folly of those young people hangs upon their methods of acquisition in each case. A deduction from what these works exemplify by action that bears evidence of being a counterpart of life, has a distinct educational value; but an imitation of what may be called the philosophy of the personages—the doctrines of the actors, as shown in their conversation—may lead to surprising results. They should be informed that a writer whose story is not a tract in disguise has as his main object that of characterizing the people of his little world. A philosophy which appears between the inverted commas of a dialogue may, with propriety, be as full of holes as a sieve if the person or persons who advance it gain any reality of humanity thereby.

These considerations only bring us back again to the vital question how to discriminate the best in fiction. Unfortunately the two hundred years or so of the modern novel's development have not left the world so full of fine examples as to make it particularly easy to light upon them when the first obvious list has been run through. The, at first sight, high-piled granary sifts down to a very small measure of genuine corn. The conclusion cannot be resisted, notwithstanding what has been stated to the contrary in so many places, that the scarcity of perfect novels in any language is because the art of writing them is as yet in its youth, if not in its infancy. Narrative art is neither mature in its artistic aspect, nor in its ethical or philosophical aspect; neither in form nor in substance. To me, at least, the difficulties of perfect presentation in both these kinds appear of such magnitude that the utmost which each generation can be expected to do is to add one or two strokes toward the selection and shaping of a possible ultimate perfection.

In this scarcity of excellence in novels as wholes the reader must content himself with excellence in parts; and his estimate of the degree to which any given modern instance approximates to greatness will, of course, depend not only upon the proportion that the finer characteristics bear to the mass, but upon the figure cut by those finer characteristics beside those of the admitted masterpieces as yet. In this process he will go with the professed critic so far as to inquire whether the story forms a regular structure of incident, accompanied by an equally regular development of character—a composition based on faithful imagination, less the transcript than the similitude of material fact. But the appreciative, perspicacious reader will do more than this. He will see what his author is aiming at, and by affording full scope to his own insight, catch the vision which the writer has in his eye, and is endeavoring to project upon the paper, even while it half eludes him.

He will almost invariably discover that, however numerous the writer's excellencies, he is what is called unequal; he has a specialty. This especial gift being discovered, he fixes his regard more particularly thereupon. It is frequently not that feature in an author's work which common repute has given him credit for; more often it is, while co-existent with his popular attribute, overshadowed by it lurking like a violet in the shade of the more obvious, possibly more vulgar, talent, but for which it might have received high attention. Behind the broad humor of one popular pen he discerns startling touches of weirdness; amid the colossal fancies of another he sees strokes of the most exquisite tenderness; and the unobtrusive quality may grow to have more charm for him than the palpable one.

It must always be borne in mind, despite the claims of realism, that the best fiction, like the highest artistic expression in other modes, is more true, so to put it, than history or nature can be.[9] In history occur from time to time monstrosities of human action and character explicable by no known law which appertains to sane beings; hitches in the machinery of existence, wherein we have not yet discovered a principle, which the artist is therefore bound to regard as accidents, hindrances to clearness of presentation, and, hence, weakeners of the effect. To take an example from sculpture: no real gladiator ever died in such perfect harmony with normal nature as is represented in the well-known Capitoline marble.[10] There was always a jar somewhere, a jot or tittle of something foreign in the real death-scene, which did not essentially appertain to the situation, and tended toward neutralizing its pathos; but this the sculptor omitted, and so consecrated his theme. In drama likewise. Observe the characters of any sterling play. No dozen persons who were capable of being animated by the profound reasons and truths thrown broadcast over *Hamlet* or *Othello*, of feeling the pulse of life so accurately, ever met together in one place in this world to shape an end. And, to come to fiction, nobody ever met an Uncle Toby who was Uncle Toby[11] all round; no historian's Queen Elizabeth was ever so perfectly a woman as the fictitious Elizabeth of *Kenilworth*.[12] What is called the idealization of characters is, in truth, the making of them too real to be possible.

It may seem something of a paradox to assert that the novels which most conduce to moral profit are likely to be among those written

---

[9] Cf. 1891.01, paragraph 4.
[10] The statue of 'The Dying Gladiator' in the Capitoline Museum in Rome.
[11] In Laurence Sterne's novel *The Life and Opinions of Tristram Shandy* (1759–67).
[12] Walter Scott's novel of 1821.

without a moral purpose. But the truth of the statement may be realized if we consider that the didactic novel is so generally devoid of *vraisemblance* as to teach nothing but the impossibility of tampering with natural truth to advance dogmatic opinions. Those, on the other hand, which impress the reader with the inevitableness of character and environment in working out destiny, whether that destiny be just or unjust, enviable or cruel, must have a sound effect, if not what is called a good effect, upon a healthy mind.

Of the effects of such sincere presentation on weak minds, when the courses of the characters are not exemplary, and the rewards and punishments ill adjusted to deserts, it is not our duty to consider too closely. A novel which does moral injury to a dozen imbeciles, and has bracing results upon a thousand intellects of normal vigor, can justify its existence; and probably a novel was never written by the purest-minded author for which there could not be found some moral invalid or other whom it was capable of harming.

To distinguish truths which are temporary from truths which are eternal, the accidental from the essential, accuracies as to custom and ceremony from accuracies as to the perennial procedure of humanity, is of vital importance in our attempts to read for something more than amusement. There are certain novels, both among the works of living and the works of deceased writers, which give convincing proof of much exceptional fidelity, and yet they do not rank as great productions; for what they are faithful in is life garniture and not life. You are fully persuaded that the personages are clothed precisely as you see them clothed in the street, in the drawing-room, at the assembly. Even the trifling accidents of their costume are rendered by the honest narrator. They use the phrases of the season, present or past, with absolute accuracy as to idiom, expletive, slang. They lift their tea-cups or fan themselves to date. But what of it, after our first sense of its photographic curiousness is past? In aiming at the trivial and the ephemeral they have almost surely missed better things. A living French critic goes even further concerning the novelists of social minutiæ. 'They are far removed', says he, 'from the great imaginations which create and transform. They renounce free invention; they narrow themselves to scrupulous exactness; they paint clothes and places with endless detail.'[13]

---

[13] Somewhat miquoted from Hippolyte Taine, *History of English Literature*, trans. H. van Laun (Edinburgh: Edmonston and Douglas, 1873), ii. 258.

But we must not, as inquiring readers, fail to understand that attention to accessories has its virtues when the nature of its regard does not involve blindness to higher things; still more when it conduces to the elucidation of higher things. The writer who describes his type of a jeweled leader of society by saying baldly how much her diamonds cost at So-and-So's, what the largest of them weighed and measured, how it was cut and set, the particular style in which she wore her hair, cannot convey much profit to any class of readers save two—those bent on making a purchase of the like ornaments or of adorning themselves in the same fashion; and, a century hence, those who are studying the costumes and expenditure of the period. But, supposing the subject to be the same, let the writer be one who takes less of a broker's view of his heroine and her adornments; he may be worth listening to, though his simplicity be quite childlike. It is immaterial that our example is in verse:

> 'Be you not proud of that rich hair
> Which wantons with the love-sick air;
> Whenas that ruby which you wear,
> Sunk from the tip of your soft ear,
> Will last to be a precious stone
> When all your world of beauty's gone.'—*Herrick*.[14]

And thus we are led to the conclusion that, in respect of our present object, our concern is less with the subject treated than with its treatment. There have been writers of fiction, as of poetry, who can gather grapes of thorns and figs of thistles.[15]

Closely connected with the humanizing education found in fictitious narrative which reaches to the level of an illuminant of life, is the æsthetic training insensibly given by familiarity with story which, presenting nothing exceptional in other respects, has the merit of being well and artistically constructed. To profit of this kind, from this especial source, very little attention has hitherto been paid, though volumes have been written upon the development of the æsthetic sense by the study of painting and sculpture, and thus adding to the means of enjoyment. Probably few of the general body denominated the reading public consider, in their hurried perusal of novel after novel, that, to a masterpiece in story there appertains a beauty of shape, no less than to a masterpiece in pictorial or plastic art, capable of giving to the trained mind an equal

---

[14] Robert Herrick, 'To Dianeme' ('Sweet, be not proud of those two eyes').
[15] Adapted from Matt. 7: 16.

pleasure. To recognize this quality clearly when present, the construction of the plot, or fable, as it used to be called, is to be more particularly observed than either in a reading for sentiments and opinions, or in a reading merely to discover the fates of the chief characters. For however real the persons, however profound, witty, or humorous the observations, as soon as the book comes to be regarded as an exemplification of the art of story-telling, the story naturally takes the first place, and the example is not noteworthy as such unless the telling be artistically carried on.

The distinguishing feature of a well-rounded tale has been defined in various ways, but the general reader need not be burdened with many definitions. Briefly, a story should be an organism. To use the words applied to the epic by Addison, whose artistic feeling in this kind was of the subtlest, 'nothing should go before it, be intermixed with it, or follow after it, that is not related to it'.[16] Tested by such considerations as these there are obviously many volumes of fiction remarkable, and even great, in their character-drawing, their feeling, their philosophy, which are quite second-rate in their structural quality as narratives. Instances will occur to every one's mind; but instead of dwelling upon these it is more interesting to name some which most nearly fulfill the conditions. Their fewness is remarkable, and bears out the opinion expressed earlier in this essay, that the art of novel-writing is as yet in its tentative stage only. Among them *Tom Jones*[17] is usually pointed out as a near approach to perfection in this as in some other characteristics; though, speaking for myself, I do not perceive its great superiority in artistic form over some other novels of lower reputation. The *Bride of Lammermoor*[18] is an almost perfect specimen of form, which is the more remarkable in that Scott, as a rule, depends more upon episode, dialogue, and description, for exciting interest, than upon the well-knit interdependence of parts. And the first thirty chapters of *Vanity Fair*[19] may be instanced as well-nigh complete in artistic presentation, along with their other magnificent qualities.

Herein lies Richardson's real if only claim to be placed on a level with Fielding: the artist spirit that he everywhere displays in the structural

---

[16] *Spectator*, no. 267 (5 January 1712), in *The Spectator*, ed. Donald F. Bond, 5 vols. (Oxford: Clarendon Press, 1965), ii. 541: 'An Action is entire when it is compleat in all its Parts; or as *Aristotle* describes it, when it consists of a Beginning, a Middle, and an End. Nothing should go before it, be intermix'd with it, or follow after it, that is not related to it.'

[17] *The History of Tom Jones* (1749), the novel by Henry Fielding.

[18] The novel by Walter Scott published in 1819 in the Third Series of *Tales of My Landlord*.

[19] The novel (1847–8) by William Makepeace Thackeray.

parts of his work and in the interaction of the personages, notably those of *Clarissa Harlowe*.[20] However cold, even artificial, we may, at times, deem the heroine and her companions in the pages of that excellent tale, however numerous the twitches of unreality in their movements across the scene beside those in the figures animated by Fielding, we feel, nevertheless, that we are under the guidance of a hand which has consummate skill in evolving a graceful, well-balanced set of conjunctures, forming altogether one of those circumstantial wholes which, when approached by events in real life, cause the observer to pause and reflect, and say, 'What a striking history!' We should look generously upon his deficiency in the robuster touches of nature, for it is the deficiency of an author whose artistic sense of form was developed at the expense of his accuracy of observation as regards substance. No person who has a due perception of the constructive art shown in Greek tragic drama can be blind to the constructive art of Richardson.

I have dwelt the more particularly upon this species of excellence, not because I consider it to rank in quality beside truth of feeling and action, but because it is one which so few non-professional readers enjoy and appreciate without some kind of preliminary direction. It is usually the latest to be discerned by the novel consumer, and it is often never discerned by him or her at all. Every intelligent reader with a little experience of life can perceive truth to nature in some degree; but a great reduction must be made for those who can trace in narrative the quality which makes the Apollo and the Aphrodite a charm in marble.[21] Thoughtful readers are continually met with who have no intuition that such an attribute can be claimed by fiction, except in so far as it is included in style.

The indefinite word style may be made to express almost any characteristic of story-telling other than subject and plot, and it is too commonly viewed as being some independent, extraneous virtue or varnish with which the substance of a narrative is artificially overlaid. Style, as far as the word is meant to express something more than literary finish, can only be treatment, and treatment depends upon the mental attitude of the novelist; thus entering into the very substance of a narrative, as into that of any other kind of literature. A writer who is not a mere

---

[20] *Clarissa; or, The History of a Young Lady* (1747–9), the novel by Samuel Richardson.

[21] TH presumably refers to the so-called Apollo Belvedere in the Vatican museum and the (lost) Aphrodite of Praxiteles, commonly regarded as ideal representations of the human body.

imitator looks upon the world with his personal eyes, and in his peculiar moods; thence grows up his style, in the full sense of the term.

> 'Cui lecta potenter erit res,
> Nec facundia deseret hunc, nec lucidus ordo.'[22]

Those who would profit from the study of style should formulate an opinion of what it consists in by the aid of their own educated understanding, their perception of natural fitness, true and high feeling, sincerity, unhampered by considerations of nice collocation and balance of sentences, still less by conventionally accepted examples. They will make the discovery that certain names have, by some accident or other, grown to be regarded as of high, if not of supreme merit in the catalogue of exemplars, which have no essential claims, in this respect, to be rated higher than hundreds of the rank and file of literature who are never mentioned by critic or considered by reader in that connection. An author who has once acquired a reputation for style may write English down to the depths of slovenliness if he choose, without losing his character as a master; and this probably because, as before observed, the quality of style is so vague and inapprehensible as a distinct ingredient that it may always be supposed to be something else than what the reader perceives to be indifferent.

Considerations as to the rank or station in life from which characters are drawn can have but little value in regulating the choice of novels for literary reasons, and the reader may leave thus much to the mood of the moment. I remember reading a lecture on novels by a young and ingenious, though not very profound, critic, some years ago, in which the theory was propounded that novels which depict life in the upper walks of society must, in the nature of things, be better reading than those which exhibit the life of any lower class, for the reason that the subjects of the former represent a higher stage of development than their less fortunate brethren.[23] At the first blush this was a plausible theory; but when practically tested it is found to be based on such a totally erroneous conception of what a novel is, and where it comes

---

[22] TH supplied his own footnote to the *Forum* text: 'Hor. "De Arte Poetica," 40.' (properly, lines 40–1). E. W. Blakeney translates: 'He who makes every effort to select his theme aright will be at no loss for choice words or lucid arrangement' (*Horace on the Art of Poetry* (London: Scholartis Press, 1928), p. 42).

[23] This view was not uncommon in the Victorian period and TH may simply have invented the unidentified critic.

from, as not to be worth a moment's consideration. It proceeds from the assumption that a novel is the thing, and not a view of the thing. It forgets that the characters, however they may differ, express mainly the author, his largeness of heart or otherwise, his culture, his insight, and very little of any other living person, except in such an inferior kind of procedure as might occasionally be applied to dialogue, and would take the narrative out of the category of fiction; *i.e.*, verbatim reporting without selective judgment.

But there is another reason, disconnected entirely from methods of construction, why the physical condition of the characters rules nothing of itself one way or the other. All persons who have thoughtfully compared class with class—and the wider their experience the more pronounced their opinion—are convinced that education has as yet but little broken or modified the waves of human impulse on which deeds and words depend. So that in the portraiture of scenes in any way emotional or dramatic—the highest province of fiction—the peer and the peasant stand on much the same level; the woman who makes the satin train and the woman who wears it. In the lapse of countless ages, no doubt, improved systems of moral education will considerably and appreciably elevate even the involuntary instincts of human nature; but at present culture has only affected the surface of those lives with which it has come in contact, binding down the passions of those predisposed to turmoil as by a silken thread only, which the first ebullition suffices to break. With regard to what may be termed the minor key of action and speech—the unemotional, every-day doings of men—social refinement operates upon character in a way which is oftener than not prejudicial to vigorous portraiture, by making the exteriors of men their screen rather than their index, as with untutored mankind. Contrasts are disguised by the crust of conventionality, picturesqueness obliterated, and a subjective system of description necessitated for the differentiation of character. In the one case the author's word has to be taken as to the nerves and muscles of his figures; in the other they can be seen as in an *écorché*.[24]

The foregoing are a few imperfect indications how, to the best of my judgment, to discriminate fiction which will be the most desirable reading for the average man or woman of leisure, who does not wish the occupation to be wholly barren of results except in so far as it may

---

[24] An anatomical model (lit. 'flayed').

administer to the pleasure of the hour. But, as with the horse and the stream in the proverb, no outside power can compel or even help a reader to gain good from such reading unless he has some natural eye for the finer qualities in the best productions of this class. It is unfortunately quite possible to read the most elevating works of imagination in our own or any language, and, by fixing the regard on the wrong sides of the subject, to gather not a grain of wisdom from them, nay, sometimes positive harm. What author has not had his experience of such readers?— the mentally and morally warped ones of both sexes, who will, where practicable, so twist plain and obvious meanings as to see in an honest picture of human nature an attack on religion, morals, or institutions. Truly has it been observed that 'the eye sees that which it brings with it the means of seeing'.[25]

[1888.03]

[?Assistance to R. R. Bowker?]

Richard Rogers Bowker (1848–1933), the American publisher and bibliographer, came to London in the summer of 1880 as the representative of *Harper's New Monthly Magazine*, and was soon on friendly terms with Hardy, who had undertaken to contribute *A Laodicean* for serial publication in the first volume of a new European edition of the magazine (*CL* i. 77–94, *passim*). Bowker subsequently wrote for the May and June 1888 issues of *Harper's* a two-part survey, 'London as a Literary Centre', that included first-hand accounts of many writers of the day, Hardy among them. The description of Hardy's working habits in the June instalment (vol. 77, pp. 8–9) is detailed and obviously well informed, and James Gibson, quoting extensively from it in *Interviews and Recollections*, pp. 13–14, very reasonably infers that it must have been based on notes supplied by Hardy himself. That Hardy was Bowker's source there can be no doubt, but several other authors are portrayed with similar intimacy and the likelihood that Bowker obtained his information from conversations with Hardy and his wife is strongly suggested by the account of a visit to them at Tooting recorded in E. McClung Fleming, *R. R. Bowker: Militant Liberal* (Norman: University of Oklahoma Press, 1952), pp. 146–7, and partly quoted in *Biography*, p. 209.

---

[25] A modification of a passage, itself within quotation marks, in the opening paragraph of Part First, Book 1, ch. 2 ('Realised Ideals') of Thomas Carlyle's *The French Revolution*.

[1888.04]

[The Waterloo Ball]

Hardy's fascination with the Napoleonic period was of long standing, and in 1876, travelling in Germany and Belgium with his wife, he had visited the battlefield of Waterloo and tried, in Brussels, to solve the much-debated question of where precisely the Duchess of Richmond had held her famous ball on the eve of the battle, 17 June 1815. That search is recalled and the mystery concisely reviewed in the footnote at the beginning of *The Dynasts*, Part Third, Act VI, Scene ii. As Purdy suggests, the following letter to the editor, published under the heading 'The Waterloo Ball' in *The Times*, 17 December 1888, p. 4, may well correspond, by some trick of memory, to the untraced letter on the same subject that Hardy later recalled having written 'to some London paper' while still in Brussels in 1876 (*LW*, p. 114). Purdy, p. 298.

Savile Club.

Sir,

The intermittent correspondence in your columns, initiated by Sir William Fraser,[26] about the so-called Waterloo Ball, brings us, if I have read it aright, to the following position concerning that romantic event:—That the contradiction between the declared recollections of Lady de Ros and those of her sister the Lady Louise Tighe[27] as to its site, is the real and the apparently hopeless obstacle to forming a conclusion upon the matter.

May not these statements be reconciled by assuming that the Duchess of Richmond, during her stay in Brussels, gave more than one ball, or that at least, in addition to the great last ball, a small dance or two took place, and that one of these, magnified by a child's imagination, may have been the occasion within the recollection of the younger sister?

I have the honour to be, Sir, your obedient servant,

Thomas Hardy.

[26] Sir William Fraser, Bt (1826–98), later the author of *Words on Wellington: The Duke—Waterloo—The Ball* (London: John C. Nimmo, 1889); his letter headed 'The Waterloo Ball' had appeared in *The Times*, 25 August 1888, p. 12.

[27] Georgiana, widow of William, Lord de Ros, and Louisa, widow of the Rt Hon. William Frederick Fownes Tighe, were respectively the third and fifth daughters of Charles Lennox, 4th Duke of Richmond and Lennox, and his wife Charlotte, daughter of the 4th Duke of Gordon. Their memories of living in Brussels with their parents, the givers of the ball, in 1815, had been invoked during the *Times* correspondence—notably by their niece, Lady Constance Russell, in the issue of 14 December 1888, p. 10.

1889

[1889.01]

[Notes to Philip Henry Gosse's Dorset Reminiscences]

At the request of his friend Edmund Gosse (1849–1928), Hardy on 26 October 1888 (*CL* i. 181) supplied three notes about Dorset customs to an autobiographical essay, 'A Country Day-School Seventy Years Ago', found by Gosse among the papers of his recently deceased father, the zoologist Philip Henry Gosse (1810–88), who had lived as a boy in the Dorset seaport of Poole. When the essay was published in *Longman's Magazine*, 13 (March 1889), pp. 512–24, the wording of Hardy's notes—reproduced below from pp. 516, 517, and 523—had been significantly revised, presumably by Hardy himself, from that of his letter to Gosse. When, however, the second and third notes were included in *Life and Work*, pp. 231–2, their original readings were largely restored, Hardy having evidently relied upon a retained draft of the 1889 letter. See Douglas Wertheimer, 'Some Hardy Notes on Dorset Words and Customs', *Notes and Queries*, 219 (January 1974), p. 26.

[*On a game called 'ducks off', popular among children in Poole:*]
Still played, Mr Thomas Hardy tells me, as 'cobbs off', in the interior of the county.—E.G.

[*On 'Shicsack Day' as a name for Oak-apple Day, 29 May:*]
Mr Hardy says: 'It is still called "Sic-sac day" by the peasantry; I have no notion what the words mean.'

[*On Dorset dialect and 'the Teutonic form "Ich"':*]
Mr Thomas Hardy writes to me: 'This and kindred words, e.g. "Ich woll", "er woll", "er war" (I will, he will, he was), &c., are still used by old people in north-west Dorset and Somerset. (Vide Grammer Oliver's conversation in *The Woodlanders*, which is an attempted reproduction.) I

heard "Ich" only last Sunday,[1] but it is dying rapidly. I know nobody now under seventy who speaks so, and those above it use the form only in their impulsive moments.' It does not appear to occur in Mr Barnes's Vale of Blackmore dialect-poems.[2]—E.G.

[1889.02]

[In Support of Henry Vizetelly]

On 29 May 1889 the publisher Henry Vizetelly (1820–94) was sentenced to three months' imprisonment for bringing out translations of novels by Émile Zola and other French writers. A petition to the Home Secretary for Vizetelly's release was organized by Vizetelly's son, Ernest, and Hardy was among the many signatories whose names were listed on a single printed sheet loosely inserted into copies of Robert Buchanan's pamphlet, *On Descending into Hell: A Letter Addressed to the Right Hon. Henry Matthews, Q.C., Home Secretary, Concerning the Proposed Suppression of Literature* (London: George Redway, 1889). Hardy's name also appears in the (incomplete) list of the petition's supporters published in Ernest Vizetelly's *Émile Zola, Novelist and Reformer: An Account of his Life and Work* (London: John Lane The Bodley Head, 1904), p. 298. Henry Vizetelly was not released but served his full term in deteriorating health, and in 1891, three years before Vizetelly's death, Hardy co-signed a successful application to the Royal Literary Fund on his behalf. See Donald Mason, 'The Doll of English Fiction: Hardy, Zola and the Politics of Convention' (Ph.D. thesis, McMaster University, Ontario, 1994).

[1889.03]

'How Authors Write'

The American journal the *Phonographic World*, founded in 1885, was primarily devoted to the study and practice of phonography or shorthand, especially the phonetic shorthand system invented by Sir Isaac Pitman (1813–97). Its interests, however, soon extended to the typewriter, then

[1] Presumably from one or both of his parents, whom he habitually visited at Higher Bockhampton on Sundays.

[2] Bernard Jones confirms Barnes's avoidance of the 'Ich' form but adds that Barnes's reasons for doing so are not entirely clear.

coming increasingly into commercial use, and early in 1889 (so the March 1889 number reported, p. 134) 'letters were addressed to many of the most distinguished writers in the country, asking whether in actual composition, it was their custom to use the pen, or to record their "thoughts" through the medium of the typewriter, or stenographer'. Hardy's letter, one of a handful of British responses, appeared as below in the *Phonographic World*, 4 (July 1889), p. 252. Purdy, p. 298.

Savile Club, London, W., April 6, 1889.

In reply to your inquiry as to my method of transferring thoughts to paper, I beg to state that I write them in longhand. I have occasionally dictated: but not to a shorthand writer.[3] As you request any further particulars, I may add that several years ago I studied shorthand with a view to taking notes; but on examining several systems I found that the scientific systems were not sufficiently practicable, and the practicable systems not sufficiently scientific. The two systems which most attracted me were Taylor's and Pitman's. I found that Taylor's *un*improved—*i.e.*, as published by Taylor himself in the last century[4]—was a good old system; but as improved by more recent stenographers it was completely ruined.[5] It seemed to me, however, after examining some dozen popular forms, that the system which successfully grapples with the vowel difficulty has yet to be invented. I have never used a typewriter.

Thomas Hardy.

[1889.04]

[Memorial to Wilkie Collins]

In a letter published in *The Times*, 3 October 1889, p. 8, Harry Quilter, art critic and editor of the *Universal Review*, solicited subscriptions to a projected

---

[3] TH dictated much of the serial text of *A Laodicean* to his wife during his 1880–1 illness (*LW*, p. 150).

[4] Samuel Taylor's *An Essay Intended to Establish a Standard for an Universal System of Stenography* was published in 1786; Sir Isaac Pitman's system, developed from Taylor's, was first published in his *Stenographic Sound-Hand* (1837).

[5] TH's copy, however, of *Taylor's System of Stenography, or Short-hand Writing: Revised and Improved*, ed. John Henry Cooke (London: Simpkin, Marshall, 1856), is annotated 'T.H. | The best system' (DCM).

memorial to Wilkie Collins (died 23 September 1889) and gave a provisional listing of the members of a supportive 'provisional committee'. Two days later (5 October, p. 8) *The Times* reported, at Quilter's request, that 'the names of George Meredith and Thomas Hardy have been added to the provisional committee'. For Hardy's subsequent involvement, see *CL* i. 210.

[1889.05]

'A British "Théâtre Libre" '

Hardy held strong opinions on the banality of contemporary drama, the elaborateness of Victorian staging, and the numbing effects of theatrical censorship, and was therefore warily supportive of the campaign of Jack T. Grein and C. W. Jarvis, co-editors of *The Weekly Comedy* (and co-authors of a never-performed adaptation of *The Woodlanders*), for the establishment of a British 'Théâtre Libre' along the lines of the existing Parisian exemplar. The *Weekly Comedy* editorial of 30 November 1889, p. 7, advocated a theatre 'free from the shackles of the censor, free from the fetters of convention, unhampered by financial considerations', and Hardy's undated letter, published on the same page, was one of several from dramatists and other literary figures who had been invited to respond to such a programme. Purdy, p. 298.

Savile Club.

Dear Sirs,

As I have no practical acquaintance with the management of theatres, I fear that my opinion on how an English 'free stage' is to be attempted will have very little value. Different people would, I suppose, attach different meanings to a 'free stage'. My impression of its objects and functions is simply that it should be a stage on which the plan of seeking to awaken interest by the traditionary formalisms that shape the ordinary modern play is superseded by aiming at a new interest, depending on startling convictions of fidelity to life. At the contemporary theatre we see life as it cannot be, though sometimes, perhaps, as it might advantageously be; we should then see life as it unfortunately turns out to be—as nearly, that is, as art, which is at bottom artifice, can and should convey such a spectacle.

Nowadays, persons who were devoted to the drama in their youth find as they approach middle age that they cannot by any possibility feel deeply interested in the regulation stage-presentation of life, their impressions usually being: First act—it may be so; second act—it surely is not so; third—it cannot be so; fourth—ridiculous to make it so; fifth—it will do for the children.

Moreover, the imagination should be appealed to rather than the bare eyesight. Could not something be done to weed away the intolerable masses of scenery and costume? A good many hundred people would travel a good many miles to see a play performed in the following manner:—The ordinary pit boarded over to make a stage, so that the theatre would approach in arrangement the form of an old Roman amphitheatre; the scenery being simply a painted canvas hung in place of the present curtain, the actors performing in front of it, and disappearing behind it when they go off the stage; a horizontal canvas for sky or ceiling; a few moveable articles of furniture, or trees in boxes, as the case may be indoors or out; the present stage being the green room.[6] The costumes to be suggestive of the time and situation, and not exclusively suggestive of what they cost. Spectators would then, sitting to a great extent round the actors, see the *play* as it was seen in old times, but as they do not see it now for its accessories.

Yours faithfully,
Thomas Hardy.

---

[6] For TH's rough sketch of such a theatre, as included in a letter to Grein of 24 July 1890, see *CL* i. 213.

1890

[1890.01]

'Candour in English Fiction'

Hardy was the third and final contributor, following the novelists Eliza Lynn Linton (1822–98) and Walter Besant (1836–1901), to a symposium on 'Candour in English Fiction' published in the *New Review*, 2 (January 1890), pp. [15]–21. His comments clearly sprang from past conflicts with editors and publishers over his treatment of the relations between the sexes and especially from his current difficulties in getting *Tess of the d'Urbervilles* into print. The *New Review* paid £12 for the essay (receipt, Leeds), but Hardy probably received nothing for the reprinting of the symposium (as from the *New Review*) in the *Eclectic Magazine* of New York, new series 51 (March 1890), pp. 315–18. No manuscript of the essay is known to survive, but the copy (Beinecke) of the January 1890 *New Review* that Hardy included among the contents of his projected 'Miscellanea' bears several pencil corrections in his hand; these are not incorporated into the following text, which is that of the essay as published, but the more significant have been recorded in the footnotes. Reprinted in *Life and Art*, pp. 75–84. Purdy, p. 299.

Even imagination is the slave of stolid circumstance; and the unending flow of inventiveness which finds expression in the literature of Fiction is no exception to the general law. It is conditioned by its surroundings like a river-stream. The varying character and strength of literary creation at different times may, indeed, at first sight seem to be the symptoms of some inherent, arbitrary, and mysterious variation; but if it were possible to compute, as in mechanics, the units of power or faculty, revealed and unrevealed, that exist in the world at stated intervals, an approximately even supply would probably be disclosed. At least there is no valid reason for a contrary supposition. Yet of the inequality in its realisations there can be no question; and the discrepancy would seem to lie in contingencies which, at one period, doom high expression to dumbness and encourage the lower forms, and at another call forth the best in expression and silence triviality.

That something of this is true has indeed been pretty generally admitted in relation to art-products of various other kinds. But when observers and critics remark, as they often do remark, that the great bulk of English fiction of the present day is characterised by its lack of sincerity, they usually omit to trace this serious defect to external, or even eccentric[1] causes. They connect it with an assumption that the attributes of insight, conceptive power, imaginative emotion, are distinctly weaker nowadays than at particular epochs of earlier date. This may or may not be the case to some degree; but, on considering the conditions under which our popular fiction is produced, imaginative deterioration can hardly be deemed the sole or even chief explanation why such an undue proportion of this sort of literature is in England a literature of quackery.[2]

By a sincere school of Fiction we may understand a Fiction that expresses truly the views of life prevalent in its time, by means of a selected[3] chain of action best suited for their exhibition. What are the prevalent views of life just now is a question upon which it is not necessary to enter further than to suggest that the most natural method of presenting them, the method most in accordance with the views themselves, seems to be by a procedure mainly impassive[4] in its tone and tragic in its developments.

Things move in cycles; dormant principles renew themselves, and exhausted principles are thrust by. There is a revival of the artistic instincts towards great dramatic motives—setting forth that 'collision between the individual and the general'[5]—formerly worked out with such force by the Periclean and Elizabethan dramatists, to name no other. More than this, the periodicity which marks the course of taste in civilised countries does not take the form of a true cycle of repetition, but what Comte, in speaking of general progress, happily characterises

---

[1] For 'even eccentric' the 'Miscellanea' copy reads 'at least excentric'.
[2] In the 'Miscellanea' copy Hardy wrote 'modify' against the last two lines of this paragraph.
[3] For 'a selected' the 'Miscellanea' copy reads 'an artistically selected'.
[4] For 'impassive' the 'Miscellanea' copy reads 'impersonal'.
[5] Unidentified, and perhaps not an actual quotation.

as 'a looped orbit':[6] not a movement of revolution but—to use the current word—evolution.[7] Hence, in perceiving that taste is arriving anew at the point of high tragedy, writers are conscious that its revived presentation demands enrichment by further truths—in other words, original treatment: treatment which seeks to show Nature's unconsciousness not of essential laws, but of those laws framed merely as social expedients by humanity, without a basis in the heart of things; treatment which expresses the triumph of the crowd over the hero, of the commonplace majority over the exceptional few.

But originality makes scores of failures for one final success, precisely because its essence is to acknowledge no immediate precursor or guide. It is probably to these inevitable conditions of further acquisition that may be attributed some developments of naturalism in French novelists of the present day, and certain crude results from meritorious attempts in the same direction by intellectual adventurers here and there among our own authors.

Anyhow, conscientious fiction alone it is which can excite a reflective and abiding interest in the minds of thoughtful readers of mature age, who are weary of puerile inventions and famishing for accuracy;[8] who consider that, in representations of the world, the passions ought to be proportioned as in the world itself.[9] This is the interest which was excited in the minds of the Athenians by their immortal tragedies, and in the minds of Londoners at the first performance of the finer plays of three hundred years ago. They reflected life, revealed life, criticised life. Life being a physiological fact, its honest portrayal must be largely concerned with, for one thing, the relations of the sexes, and the substitution for such catastrophes as favour the false colouring best expressed

---

[6] See *LN* i. 76, 323 (item 749 and n.), where TH summarizes (and illustrates) the relevant passage from the English translation of Auguste Comte's *Social Dynamics*, vol. iii of his four-volume *System of Positive Polity* (London: Longmans, Green, 1876), p. 60. The term 'looped orbit' is also invoked in the Apology prefixed to *Late Lyrics and Earlier* (1922): see *CPW* ii. 325.

[7] A marginal note in the 'Miscellanea' copy, '—an onward & an apparently backward', has not been arrowed in by TH. His apparent intention was to revise 'not . . . revolution' to read 'an onward and an apparently backward movement not of revolution'.

[8] For 'for accuracy' the 'Miscellanea' copy reads 'for poetized accuracy'.

[9] It is apparently with reference to this passage that TH has written at the foot of p. 16 of the 'Miscellanea' copy: ' "As soon as I observe that anyone, when judging of poetical representations, considers anything more important than the inner Necessity & Truth, I have done with him." Sch. to Goethe.' The quotation is from *Correspondence between Schiller and Goethe, from 1794 to 1805*, trans. L. Dora Schmitz, 2 vols. (London: George Bell and Sons, 1877–9), i. 58, of which TH had a copy in his library (Frank Hollings catalogue 212, item 166).

by the regulation finish that 'they married and were happy ever after', of catastrophes based upon sexual relationship as it is. To this expansion English society opposes a well-nigh insuperable bar.

The popular vehicles for the introduction of a novel to the public have grown to be, from one cause and another, the magazine and the circulating library; and the object of the magazine and circulating library is not upward advance but lateral advance; to suit themselves to what is called household reading, which means, or is made to mean, the reading either of the majority in a household or of the household collectively. The number of adults, even in a large household, being normally two, and these being the members which, as a rule, have least time on their hands to bestow on current literature, the taste of the majority can hardly be, and seldom is, tempered by the ripe judgment which desires fidelity. However, the immature members of a household often keep an open mind, and they might, and no doubt would, take sincere fiction with the rest but for another condition, almost generally co-existent: which is that adults who would desire true views for[10] their own reading insist, for a plausible but questionable reason, upon false views for the reading of their young people.

As a consequence, the magazine in particular and the circulating library in general do not foster the growth of the novel which reflects and reveals life. They directly tend to exterminate it by monopolising all literary space. Cause and effect were never more clearly conjoined, though commentators upon the result, both French and English, seem seldom if ever to trace their connection. A sincere and comprehensive sequence of the ruling passions, however moral in its ultimate bearings, must not be put on paper as the foundation of imaginative works, which have to claim notice through the above-named channels, though it is extensively welcomed in the form of newspaper reports. That the magazine and library have arrogated to themselves the dispensation of fiction is not the fault of the authors, but of circumstances over which they, as representatives of Grub Street, have no control.

What this practically amounts to is that the patrons of literature— no longer Peers with a taste—acting under the censorship of prudery, rigorously exclude from the pages they regulate subjects that have been made, by general approval of the best judges, the bases of the finest

---

[10] Comma following 'for' in *New Review* text has here been deleted; later in the sentence the period following 'reason' has here been corrected to a comma.

imaginative compositions since literature rose to the dignity of an art. The crash of broken commandments is as necessary an accompaniment to the catastrophe of a tragedy as the noise of drum and cymbals to a triumphal march. But the crash of broken commandments shall not be heard; or, if at all, but gently, like the roaring of Bottom—gently as any sucking dove, or as 'twere any nightingale, lest we should fright the ladies out of their wits.[11] More precisely, an arbitrary proclamation has gone forth that certain picked commandments of the ten shall be preserved intact—to wit, the first, third, and seventh; that the ninth shall be infringed but gingerly; the sixth only as much as necessary;[12] and the remainder alone[13] as much as you please, in a genteel manner.

It is in the self-consciousness engendered by interference with spontaneity, and in aims at a compromise to square with circumstances, that the real secret lies of the charlatanry pervading so much of English fiction. It may be urged that abundance of great and profound novels might be written which should require no compromising, contain not an episode deemed questionable by prudes. This I venture to doubt. In a ramification of the profounder passions the treatment of which makes the great style, something 'unsuitable' is sure to arise; and then comes the struggle with the literary conscience. The opening scenes of the would-be great story may, in a rash moment, have been printed in some popular magazine before the remainder is written; as it advances month by month the situations develop, and the writer asks himself, what will his characters do next? What would probably happen to them, given such beginnings? On his life and conscience, though he had not foreseen the thing, only one event could possibly happen, and that therefore he should narrate, as he calls himself a faithful artist. But, though pointing a fine moral, it is just one of those issues which are not to be mentioned in respectable magazines and select libraries. The dilemma then confronts him, he must either whip and scourge those characters into doing something contrary to their natures, to produce the spurious effect of their being in harmony with social forms and ordinances, or, by leaving them alone to act as they will, he must bring down the thunders of respectability upon his head, not to say ruin his editor, his publisher, and himself.

[11] Adapted from Shakespeare, *A Midsummer Night's Dream*, I. ii. 79–84.

[12] Exod. 20: 1–17: As numbered (and somewhat rephrased) in the Book of Common Prayer these commandments are as follows: (1) Thou shalt have none other gods but me; (3) Thou shalt not take the Name of the Lord thy God in vain; (7) Thou shalt not commit adultery; (9) Thou shalt not bear false witness against thy neighbour; (6) Thou shalt do no murder.

[13] For 'and the remainder alone' the *Miscellanea* copy substitutes 'the remainder you may'.

What he often does, indeed can scarcely help doing in such a strait, is, belie his literary conscience, do despite to his best imaginative instincts by arranging a *dénouement* which he knows to be indescribably unreal and meretricious, but dear to the Grundyist[14] and subscriber. If the true artist ever weeps it probably is then, when he first discovers the fearful price that he has to pay for the privilege of writing in the English language—no less a price than the complete extinction, in the mind of every mature and penetrating reader, of sympathetic belief in his personages.

To say that few of the old dramatic masterpieces, if newly published as a novel (the form which, experts tell us, they would have taken in modern conditions), would be tolerated in English magazines and libraries is a ludicrous understatement. Fancy a brazen young Shakespeare of our time—*Othello, Hamlet,* or *Anthony and Cleopatra* never having yet appeared—sending up one of those creations in narrative form to the editor of a London magazine, with the author's compliments, and his hope that the story will be found acceptable to the editor's pages; suppose him, further, to have the temerity to ask for the candid remarks of the accomplished editor upon his manuscript. One can imagine the answer that young William would get for his mad supposition of such fitness from any one of the gentlemen who so correctly conduct that branch of the periodical Press.[15]

Were the objections of the scrupulous limited to a prurient treatment of the relations of the sexes, or to any view of vice calculated to undermine the essential principles of social order, all honest lovers of literature would be in accord with them. All really true literature directly or indirectly sounds as its refrain the words in the *Agamemnon*: 'Chant Ælinon, Ælinon! but may the good prevail.'[16] But the writer may print

---

[14] Rigidly moralistic person, like Mrs Grundy in Thomas Morton's *Speed the Plough* (1800).

[15] *New Review*, p. 19, carries TH's own footnote—namely: 'It is, indeed, curious to consider what great works of the past the notions of the present day would aim to exclude from circulation, if not from publication, if they were issued as new fiction. In addition to those mentioned, think of the *King Œdipus* of Sophocles, the *Agamemnon* of Æschylus, Goethe's *Faust* and *Wilhelm Meister*, the *Prometheus* of Æschylus, Milton's *Paradise Lost*. The "unpleasant subjects" of the two first-named compositions, the "unsuitableness" of the next two, would be deemed equalled only by the profanity of the two last; for Milton, as it is hardly necessary to remind the reader, handles as his puppets the Christian divinities and fiends quite as freely as the pagan divinities were handled by the Greek and Latin imaginative authors.'

[16] The repeated chant ('Chant Sorrow, Sorrow! . . .') of the chorus in the *Agamemnon* of Æschylus; TH owned a copy of the Bohn Classics edition of the tragedies of Æschylus (now in the Frederick B. Adams collection); see W. R. Rutland, *Thomas Hardy: A Study of his Writings and their Background* (Oxford: Blackwell, 1938), p. 36.

the *not* of his broken commandment in capitals of flame; it makes no difference. A question which should be wholly a question of treatment is confusedly regarded as a question of subject.

Why the ancient classic and old English tragedy can be regarded thus deeply, both by young people in their teens and by old people in their moralities, and the modern novel cannot be so regarded; why the honest and uncompromising delineation which makes the old stories and dramas lessons in life must make of the modern novel, following humbly on the same lines, a lesson in iniquity, is to some thinkers a mystery inadequately accounted for by the difference between old and new.

Whether minors should read unvarnished fiction based on the deeper passions, should listen to the eternal verities in the form of narrative, is somewhat a different question from whether the novel ought to be exclusively addressed to those minors. The first consideration is one which must be passed over here; but it will be conceded by most friends of literature that all fiction should not be shackled by conventions concerning budding womanhood, which may be altogether false. It behoves us then to inquire how best to circumvent the present lording of nonage over maturity, and permit the explicit novel to be more generally written.

That the existing magazine and book-lending system will admit of any great modification is scarcely likely.[17] As far as the magazine is concerned it has long been obvious that as a vehicle for fiction dealing with human feeling on a comprehensive scale it is tottering to its fall; and it will probably in the course of time take up openly the position that it already covertly occupies, that of a purveyor of tales for the youth of both sexes, as it assumes that tales for those rather numerous members of society ought to be written.

There remain three courses by which the adult may find deliverance. The first would be a system of publication under which books could be bought and not borrowed, when they would naturally resolve themselves into classes instead of being, as now, made to wear a common livery in style and subject, enforced by their supposed necessities in addressing indiscriminately a general audience.

---

[17] TH's specific predictions were not realized, but the system in fact underwent major changes from 1895 onwards, with the replacement of the three-decker novel by the much cheaper one-volume novel and an associated decline in the importance both of magazine serialization and of the circulating library.

But it is scarcely likely to be convenient to either authors or publishers that the periodical form of publication for the candid story should be entirely forbidden, and in retaining the old system thus far, yet ensuring that the emancipated serial novel should meet the eyes of those for whom it is intended, the plan of publication as a *feuilleton* in newspapers read mainly by adults might be more generally followed, as in France. In default of this, or co-existent with it, there might be adopted what, upon the whole, would perhaps find more favour than any with those who have artistic interests at heart, and that is, magazines for adults; exclusively for adults, if necessary. As an offshoot there might be at least one magazine for the middle-aged and old.

There is no foretelling; but this (since the magazine form of publication is so firmly rooted) is at least a promising remedy, if English prudery be really, as we hope, only a parental anxiety. There should be no mistaking the matter, no half measures. *La dignité de la pensée*, in the words of Pascal,[18] might then grow to be recognised in the treatment of fiction as in other things, and untrammelled adult opinion on conduct and theology might be axiomatically assumed and dramatically appealed to. Nothing in such literature should for a moment exhibit lax views of that purity of life upon which the well-being of society depends; but the position of man and woman in nature, and the position of belief in the minds of man and woman—things which everybody is thinking but nobody is saying—might be taken up and treated frankly.

[1890.02]

'The Art of Authorship'

On 26 September 1887 the Revd George Bainton (1848–1925), a Congregational minister in Coventry, wrote (DCM) to ask Hardy for information about his working methods and early training that Bainton himself might invoke when lecturing to 'our young men' on 'the art of composition, and the means essential to secure a forcible and interesting style of expression'. Hardy replied on 11 October 1887 (*CL* i. 168–9), but evidently did not expect that his letter would eventually appear as below, stripped of its opening paragraph and of all its epistolary elements, in the 'Truthfulness to One's Self'

[18] Not perhaps a direct quotation: see Blaise Pascal, *Pensées sur la religion et sur quelques autres sujets*, ed. Louis Lafuma, 3 vols. (Paris: Éditions du Luxembourg, 1952), i. 142, 380, 411.

section of Bainton's compilation *The Art of Authorship* (London: James Clarke, 1890), pp. 320–1. The volume, published in May 1890, also contained responses from many other authors who had been similarly approached, and George Meredith was among the several who complained to the Society of Authors about Bainton's failure to seek permission prior to publication. Hardy himself, however, in an article on the controversy in the Society's journal *The Author*, 16 June 1890, pp. 44–7, was listed among a small group of writers not objecting to Bainton's tactics. Purdy, p. 299.

Any studied rules I could[19] not possibly give, for I know of none that are of practical utility. A writer's style is according to his temperament, and my impression is that if he has anything to say which is of value, and words to say it with, the style will come of itself.

[1890.03]

[Inspired Paragraph on Mrs Jeune's Holiday Fund]

Hardy was a devoted friend of the London hostess and social reformer Mary Jeune, later Lady St Helier (1845–1931), and in 1890—when he was still known only as a novelist—he took the public risk of writing some 'Lines' for delivery by the American actress Ada Rehan at the end of a special performance given at the Lyceum Theatre on 23 July in aid of Mrs Jeune's Holiday Fund for City Children. Irritated by disparaging newspaper reports of the event, and of his own verses, Hardy suggested to W. Moy Thomas, dramatic critic of the *Daily News* (see 1882.01), that his next column might contain, 'in your own phrase, & not in the form of a letter from me', a more positive account of the occasion (*CL* i. 214). But while the 'form' of Hardy's letter to Thomas is not reflected in the paragraph reproduced below from 'The Theatres' section of the *Daily News*, 28 July 1890, p. 2, the influence of its wording is very apparent.

In reference to the thin attendance[20] at the performance at the Lyceum on Wednesday afternoon for the benefit of Mrs Jeune's Holiday Fund,

[19] For 'Any . . . could' TH's original letter read 'Any detailed rules as to the formation of style I could'.

[20] The *Daily News*, 24 July, p. 5, had reported that the Lyceum stalls and pit were at least two-thirds empty.

we are assured that the amount realised was quite as much as was expected, being about one hundred pounds. The scanty attendance is partly accounted for by the fact that some who had supported the cause by paying for seats stayed away on account of the sultriness of the weather.

[1890.04]

[Inspired Paragraph on 'Lines' for Ada Rehan]

> On the same day as he wrote to Moy Thomas (1890.03) Hardy also wrote to Edmund Yates (1831–94), founder and editor of the *World*, to propose a form of words in which Yates, if he so wished, could take issue with the disparaging remarks on Hardy's 'Lines' for Ada Rehan that had appeared in the *Globe* newspaper the day following the performance. Comparison with Hardy's original letter to Yates (*CL* i. 214–15) shows that its wording was largely adopted for the following paragraph in the *World*, 30 July 1890, p. 25.

Surely, my good *confrère* of the 'oldest evening journal',[21] you were somewhat hard in your strictures on the verses written by Mr Thomas Hardy and spoken last week by Miss Rehan,[22] considering they were written for a charitable purpose, and, as I have reason to know, in great haste, while the accomplished lady who recited them was waiting for the MS.?

[1890.05]

[Co-Signed Defence of Harper & Brothers]

> In this letter, published in the *Athenaeum*, 22 November 1890, p. 701, the novelists Walter Besant (1836–1901), William Black (1841–98), and

---

[21] The *Globe* had been founded in 1803, earlier than any other London evening paper still in existence in 1890; it survived until the end of 1922, when it was incorporated into the *Evening Standard*.

[22] The *Globe*, 24 July 1890, p. 6, called the verses 'poor stuff, poetically—Johnsonian in heaviness of thought and sesquipedalian in verbal expression'.

Thomas Hardy came jointly to the defence of the American publishing house of Harper & Brothers in a controversy, ongoing since the *Athenaeum* of 4 October 1890, p. 452, over its dealings with the suddenly famous Rudyard Kipling. The letter itself, dated 17 November, was apparently drafted by the publisher James Ripley Osgood, who acted as the Harper's London agent (*CL* i. 218–19), Hardy's only contribution to its composition being a recommendation (*CL* i. 219, 220) that portions of the original draft should be omitted. Kipling's robust response, in the form of his poem 'The Rhyme of the Three Captains', appeared in the *Athenaeum*, 6 December, pp. 776–7. Reprinted in *Life and Art*, pp. 126–7.

1891

[1891.01]

'The Science of Fiction'

This most sharply focused of Hardy's literary essays appeared in the *New Review*, 4 (April 1891), pp. 315–19, as the third and final segment of a symposium on 'The Science of Fiction' in which the other participants were Walter Besant and the French novelist Paul Bourget (1852–1935). The *Eclectic Magazine* of New York reprinted the symposium (from the *New Review*) in its issue of June 1891—Hardy's contribution appearing on pp. 854–6—but no pre-publication form of the essay is known to survive and there are no textual markings in the copy of the *New Review* (Millgate) that Hardy submitted for inclusion in his projected 'Miscellanea' volume. In June 1928 Desmond MacCarthy made the obituary gesture of reprinting the essay, still dated 1891, in the first number of *Life and Letters*, pp. 12–16. The text below is that of the *New Review*. Reprinted in *Life and Art*, pp. 85–90. Purdy, p. 300.

Since Art is science with an addition, since some science underlies all Art, there is seemingly no paradox in the use of such a phrase as 'the Science of Fiction'. One concludes it to mean that comprehensive and accurate knowledge of realities which must be sought for, or intuitively possessed, to some extent, before anything deserving the name of an artistic performance in narrative can be produced.

The particulars of this science are the generals of almost all others. The materials of Fiction being human nature and circumstances, the science thereof may be dignified by calling it the codified law of things as they really are. No single pen can treat exhaustively of this. The Science of Fiction is contained in that large work, the cyclopædia of life.

In no proper sense can the term 'science' be applied to other than this fundamental matter. It can have no part or share in the construction of a

story, however recent speculations may have favoured such an application. We may assume with certainty that directly the constructive stage
is entered upon, Art—high or low—begins to exist.

The most devoted apostle of realism, the sheerest naturalist, cannot
escape, any more than the withered old gossip over her fire, the exercise
of Art in his labour or pleasure of telling a tale. Not until he becomes
an automatic reproducer of all impressions whatsoever can he be called
purely scientific, or even a manufacturer on scientific principles. If in
the exercise of his reason he select or omit, with an eye to being more
truthful than truth (the just aim of Art),[1] he transforms himself into a
technicist at a move.

As this theory of the need for the exercise of the Dædalian[2] faculty
for selection and cunning manipulation has been disputed, it may be
worth while to examine the contrary proposition. That it should ever
have been maintained by such a romancer as M. Zola, in his work on the
Roman Expérimental,[3] seems to reveal an obtuseness to the disproof
conveyed in his own novels which, in a French writer, is singular indeed.
To be sure that author—whose powers in story-telling, rightfully and
wrongfully exercised, may be partly owing to the fact that he is not a
critic—does in a measure concede something in the qualified counsel
that the novel should keep as close to reality *as it can*; a remark which
may be interpreted with infinite latitude, and would no doubt have been
cheerfully accepted by Dumas *père*[4] or Mrs Radcliffe.[5] It implies dis-
criminative choice; and if we grant that we grant all. But to maintain in
theory what he abandons in practice, to subscribe to rules and to work
by instinct, is a proceeding not confined to the author of *Germinal* and
La Faute de l'Abbé Mouret.[6]

The reasons that make against such conformation of story-writing to
scientific processes have been set forth so many times in examining the
theories of the realist, that it is not necessary to recapitulate them here.

---

[1] Cf. paragraph 9 below, and note; also 1888.02, paragraph 19.

[2] 'Of or after the style of Dædalus; skilful, ingenious, formed with art' (*OED*).

[3] Émile Zola (1840–1902), *Le Roman expérimental* (Paris: G. Charpentier, 1880), although TH's
knowledge of Zola's theories was perhaps chiefly based on his reading of articles in French journals:
see e.g. *LN* i. 384 (item 1321).

[4] Alexandre Dumas (1802–70), French dramatist and historical novelist, author of *Le Comte de
Monte Cristo*, etc.

[5] Mrs Ann Radcliffe (1764–1823), romantic novelist, author of *The Mysteries of Udolpho*, etc.

[6] For TH's close reading of these two novels in English translation, see *LN* ii. 473–5 (Appendix
items 180–201); he had copies of seven other Zola novels in his library, three of them in French.

Admitting the desirability, the impossibility of reproducing in its entirety the phantasmagoria of experience with infinite and atomic truth, without shadow, relevancy, or subordination, is not the least of them. The fallacy appears to owe its origin to the just perception that with our widened knowledge of the universe and its forces, and man's position therein, narrative, to be artistically convincing, must adjust itself to the new alignment, as would also artistic works in form and colour, if further spectacles in their sphere could be presented. Nothing but the illusion of truth can permanently please, and when the old illusions begin to be penetrated, a more natural magic has to be supplied.

Creativeness in its full and ancient sense—the making a thing or situation out of nothing that ever was before—is apparently ceasing to satisfy a world which no longer believes in the abnormal—ceasing at least to satisfy the van-couriers of taste; and creative fancy has accordingly to give more and more place to realism, that is, to an artificiality distilled from the fruits of closest observation.

This is the meaning deducible from the work of the realists, however stringently they themselves may define realism in terms. Realism is an unfortunate, an ambiguous word, which has been taken up by literary society like a view-halloo, and has been assumed in some places to mean copyism, and in others pruriency, and has led to two classes of delineators being included in one condemnation.

Just as bad a word is one used to express a consequence of this development, namely 'brutality', a term which, first applied by French critics, has since spread over the English school like the other.[7] It aptly hits off the immediate impression of the thing meant; but it has the disadvantage of defining impartiality as a passion, and a plan as a caprice. It certainly is very far from truly expressing the aims and methods of conscientious and well-intentioned authors who, notwithstanding their excesses, errors, and rickety theories, attempt to narrate the *vérité vraie*.[8]

---

[7] A specific French source for this term has not been found, and TH seems to have been exaggerating its prevalence (as distinct from *la bête humaine*) in British critical discourse. For an attack, however, on the 'brutal' aspects of French naturalism, see *Documents of Modern Literary Realism*, ed. George J. Becker (Princeton: Princeton University Press, 1963), p. 354.

[8] Colloquially, 'true truth'; TH, evidently with Zola's example in mind, seems to mean the artist's essential understanding of an external object prior to any interpretative or imaginative processing. Two years later the term was defined by Arthur Symons as 'the very essence of truth—the truth of appearances to the senses, of the visible world to the eyes that see it; and the truth of spiritual things to the spiritual vision' ('The Decadent Movement in Literature', *Harper's New Monthly Magazine*, 87 (November 1893), p. 859).

To return for a moment to the theories of the scientific realists. Every friend to the novel should and must be in sympathy with their error, even while distinctly perceiving it. Though not true, it is well found. To advance realism as complete copyism, to call the idle trade of story-telling a science, is the hyperbolic flight of an admirable enthusiasm, the exaggerated cry of an honest reaction from the false, in which the truth has been impetuously approached and overleapt in fault of lighted on.

Possibly, if we only wait, the third something, akin to perfection, will exhibit itself on its due pedestal. How that third something may be induced to hasten its presence, who shall say? Hardly the English critic.

But this appertains to the Art of novel-writing, and is outside the immediate subject. To return to the 'science'. . . . Yet what is the use? Its very comprehensiveness renders the attempt to dwell upon it a futility. Being an observative responsiveness to everything within the cycle of the suns that has to do with actual life, it is easier to say what it is not than to categorise its *summa genera*.[9] It is not, for example, the paying of a great regard to adventitious externals to the neglect of vital qualities, not a precision about the outside of the platter and an obtuseness to the contents. An accomplished lady once confessed to the writer that she could never be in a room two minutes without knowing every article of furniture it contained and every detail in the attire of the inmates, and, when she left, remembering every remark. Here was a person, one might feel for the moment, who could prime herself to an unlimited extent and at the briefest notice in the scientific data of fiction; one who, assuming her to have some slight artistic power, was a born novelist. To explain why such a keen eye to the superficial does not imply a sensitiveness to the intrinsic is a psychological matter beyond the scope of these notes; but that a blindness to material particulars often accompanies a quick perception of the more ethereal character-istics of humanity, experience continually shows.

A sight for the finer qualities of existence, an ear for the 'still sad music of humanity',[10] are not to be acquired by the outer senses alone, close as their powers in photography may be. What cannot be discerned by eye and ear, what may be apprehended only by the mental tactility that

---

[9] i.e. its defining characteristic.
[10] William Wordsworth, 'Lines Composed a Few Miles above Tintern Abbey', line 91.

comes from a sympathetic appreciativeness of life in all its manifestations, this is the gift which renders its possessor a more accurate delin-
eator of human nature than many another with twice his powers and
means of external observation, but without that sympathy. To see in half
and quarter views the whole picture, to catch from a few bars the whole
tune, is the intuitive power that supplies the would-be story-writer with
the scientific bases for his pursuit. He may not count the dishes at a feast,
or accurately estimate the value of the jewels in a lady's diadem; but
through the smoke of those dishes, and the rays from these jewels, he
sees written on the wall:—

> 'We are such stuff
> As dreams are made of, and our little life
> Is rounded with a sleep.'[11]

Thus, as aforesaid, an attempt to set forth the Science of Fiction in
calculable pages is futility; it is to write a whole library of human philosophy, with instructions how to feel.

Once in a crowd a listener heard a needy and illiterate woman saying
of another poor and haggard woman who had lost her little son years
before: 'You can see the ghost of that child in her face even now.'

That speaker was one who, though she could probably neither read
nor write, had the true means towards the 'Science' of Fiction innate
within her; a power of observation informed by a living heart. Had she
been trained in the technicalities, she might have fashioned her view of
mortality with good effect; a reflection which leads to a conjecture that,
perhaps, true novelists, like poets, are born, not made.

[1891.02]

'The Merry Wives of Wessex'

Irritated by a hostile review of *A Group of Noble Dames* under the heading
'The Merry Wives of Wessex' in the *Pall Mall Gazette* of 8 July 1891, p. 3,
Hardy wrote to the editor the same day to protest against what he saw as the
anonymous reviewer's overstated objections to the horrific aspects of
'Barbara of the House of Grebe'. The text below is that of the letter as it

---

[11] Shakespeare, *The Tempest*, IV. i. 156–8; the reading 'made of' is that of the *New Review*.

appeared, under the same supplied heading, in the *Pall Mall Gazette* of 10 July 1891, p. 2. Purdy, p. 300.

Mandeville-place, W. July 8.[12]

Sir,

On reading your notice of *A Group of Noble Dames*, I confess to a feeling of surprise that the critic of a paper which I had imagined to possess a certain virility should be shocked at the mere tale of a mutilated piece of marble, seeing what we have had of late years in mutilations and bloody bones, both fictitious and real. I have almost concluded that the *Pall Mall* reviewer must be a highly sensitive and beautiful young lady, who herself nourishes an unhappy attachment to a gentleman in some such circumstances as those of the story. If so, I admit that I have treated her ready imagination rudely; if not so, there must be something unusual in the telling of the story. This can hardly be the case, since to guard against the infliction of 'a hideous and hateful fantasy', as you call it, the action is thrown back into a second plane or middle distance, being described by a character to characters, and not point-blank by author to reader.[13] But supposing 'Barbara of the House of Grebe' to be indeed a grisly narrative. A good horror has its place in art. Shall we, for instance, condemn 'Alonzo the Brave'?[14] For my part I would not give up a single worm of his skull. With respect to the dames generally, I can assure you that these tales were fairly tested before they were offered to the genteel public. They have been read aloud by me, or told in drawing-rooms to ladies whose names, if I were to give them, would be a sufficient guarantee of their trustworthiness in ethical judgments; and the listeners were unanimous in recognizing no harm. To a modest query of my own concerning possible criticism they replied brusquely, 'Critics don't know.' I hope that opinion may be true for once of the *Pall Mall* critic in his estimate of 'Barbara'—the particular dame's history censured.

Yours, &c.,

Thomas Hardy.

[12] TH and his wife rented a flat at 12 Mandeville Place, Manchester Square, for the London 'season' (late spring and early summer) of 1891.

[13] The *Pall Mall* reviewer, in a reply signed 'Your sensitive and beautiful reviewer' and printed immediately below TH's letter, commented with some effectiveness on the 'aesthetic nicety' of this argument: 'If Mr. Hardy suggests a hateful picture to the imagination, it is none the less hateful because the machinery he uses happens to be more or less old-fashioned and inartistic.'

[14] The ballad 'Alonzo the Brave and the Fair Imogine' by Matthew Gregory Lewis (1775–1818), first published in Lewis's *The Monk* (1796).

[1891.03]

'The State Recognition of Authors'

> W. Robertson Nicoll (1851–1923), editor of the *Bookman*, wrote on 5 November 1891 (DCM) to invite Hardy's participation in an ongoing controversy (see the *Spectator*, 19 September 1891, pp. 380–1, and the *Author*, 1 October 1891, pp. 140–2) over the appropriateness of conferring titles and honours upon eminent literary figures. Hardy's reply, one of several, was published, undated as below, in the *Bookman*, 1 (December 1891), p. 98; a surviving rough draft (DCM) evidently served as copy for the letter's inclusion in *Life and Work*, p. 252 (cf. p. 352). Reprinted in *Life and Art*, p. 130. Purdy, p. 264.

Sir,

I daresay it would be very interesting that literature should be honoured by the State. But I don't see how it could be satisfactorily done.[15] The highest flights of the pen are often, indeed mostly,[16] the excursions and revelations of souls unreconciled to life; while the natural tendency of a government would be to encourage acquiescence in life as it is. However, I have not thought much about the matter.

Thomas Hardy.

[1891.04]

[Assistance to Revd W. Miles Barnes]

> The Revd William Miles Barnes (1840–1916), the son of the poet, was the rector of Winterborne Monkton, a village just south-west of Dorchester. He was on friendly terms with Hardy in the 1880s and 1890s, and in his article, 'A Brief Historical and Descriptive Sketch of the Churches in the Rural Deanery of Dorchester (Dorchester Portion)', published in the *Proceedings of the Dorset Natural History and Antiquarian Field Club*, 12 (1891), pp. 36–70, he stated that his descriptions of the twenty-three churches were based on 'personal inspection of the buildings, notes of their features being taken at the time, in which survey I received much kind assistance from Mr. T. Hardy'. It is not clear, however, that Hardy was at all involved in the writing of the article.

---

[15] Struck through in TH's draft is the original conclusion of this sentence: 'unless we had a political, social, theological and moral revolution every season'.

[16] For 'are often, indeed mostly' draft and *LW* read 'are mostly'.

1892

[1892.01]

[New Year's Greeting to American Women]

Having in its December 1891 issue featured Christmas messages from 'a number of England's famous women', the *Ladies' Home Journal* of Philadelphia included in its January 1892 issue a series of New Year greetings to the women of America from 'some of the great men of England'. Hardy's brief message, headed 'An English Author's Tribute', appeared as below in the *Ladies' Home Journal*, 9 (January 1892), p. 10, and was reprinted, with one trivial and evidently non-authorial variation, in the *Publishers' Circular*, 2 January 1892, p. 7 (cutting in Hardy's 'Personal' scrapbook, DCM).

American women seem to me[1] to be more earnest of purpose than those of European countries. I have been told that this opinion arises from my having met only the best American womankind. Be that as it may, such is my impression, and I am glad to record it upon this occasion of sending a New Year line to the women of your country.

[1892.02]

[?Partially Inspired Review of *Tess of the d'Urbervilles*?]

On 31 December 1891 Hardy sent to Edmund Yates, editor of the *World*, comments drawn 'from numerous unexpected letters' (*CL* i. 250) that might

---

[1] *Publishers' Circular* text omits 'to me'.

be used in defending the recently published *Tess of the d'Urbervilles* against accusations of its being hostile to women. Although the material supplied by Hardy was not used directly by the *World*, it almost certainly influenced the strong defence of Tess's 'purity' included in the anonymous review of the novel published in the *World*, 13 January 1892, p. 23.

[1892.03]

[Responses to Questionnaire on US Copyright]

Hardy had long been active in the cause of literary copyright. He was named in *The Times*, 11 May 1875, p. 10, as a member of a deputation that had called upon the Prime Minister, Disraeli, on behalf of the Association to Protect the Rights of Authors (*LW*, p. 109), and in *The Times*, 3 March 1887, p. 6, he was similarly identified as having participated in a conference on 'The Maintenance of Literary Property' organized by the Society of Authors (cf. *CL* i. 162). In 1891 he benefited greatly from the provisions of the United States Copyright Act, passed just in time for him to secure the American copyright of *Tess of the d'Urbervilles*, but commented on its continuing draw-backs in a letter to the New York *Critic* published in July of the following year (1892.14). Little seems discoverable, however, about either the occasion or the ultimate destination of the meagre answers Hardy jotted down (David Holmes) in response to a series of handwritten questions relating to the 1891 Act. Since 'The United Press' is printed at the top left-hand corner of each of the two sheets, the questions presumably originated with a journalist work-ing in London for the American news agency of that name, but no resulting article has been found. No date appears on either sheet, but Walter Besant's answers to the same questionnaire (sold with Hardy's at Sotheby's on 16 July 1974, lot 408) are dated 19 January 1892. In the text below the questions are given first, in italics, and Hardy's responses follow.

1. (a) *Do you regard the U.S. Copyright Act of 1891 as beneficial to British authorship, or the reverse?*
   (b) *Kindly explain in what manner the influence—whichever it may be— will, in your opinion, be felt.*

Ansr (a) Speaking conjecturally Yes.
(b) Have received as yet no information on which I can base an opinion.

T. H.

2. *Do you think that the position of the British author, as regards America, is appreciably improved by the act?*

vide 1 (a)

T. H.

3. *Should you wish to take advantage of the act for copyrighting any future work of your own?*

Ansr. Certainly

T. H.

[1892.04]

[?Inspired Letter about *Tess of the d'Urbervilles*?]

As published in the *Spectator*, 30 January 1892, p. 167, the undated letter below was signed with the initials 'C. L. H.' On the cutting inserted into Hardy's 'Personal' scrapbook (DCM), however, the 'C.' has been altered in ink to an 'E.', and it seems almost certain that the sender was Hardy's wife, Emma Lavinia Hardy, and that she was writing at her husband's request—and probably on the basis of his draft. Whether the incorrect initial was an error on the part of the *Spectator* or a deliberate disguise on the part of the author(s), it is impossible to tell.

Sir,

In the interest of dictionary-makers, may I be allowed to state that the apparently coarse word used by the heroine of *Tess of the D'Urbervilles* (Vol. I., p. 127, line 16), from which you draw an inference in your review of that novel,[2] has ceased in Somerset, Dorset, &c., to carry with it the coarse idea of its root-meaning, being spoken by the most modest to imply simply a company of slatternly, bickering, and generally unpleasant women?[3]

I am, Sir, &c.,

C. L. H.

---

[2] The *Spectator* reviewer, R. H. Hutton (23 January 1892, pp. 121–2), did not quote the offending phrase but observed that Tess's use of a 'coarse expression' in reference to Car Darch and her companions 'betrays perfectly well her knowledge of the dangers before her'.

[3] The word was 'whorage' (Wessex edn., p. 83); cf. the definition in William Barnes, *A Grammar and Glossary of the Dorset Dialect* (Berlin: A. Asher, 1863), p. 63: 'Horridge, Whorage. A house or nest of bad characters.'

[1892.05]

[Inspired Paragraph on *Tess of the d'Urbervilles*]

Writing to Norman MacColl, editor of the *Athenaeum*, on 9 February 1892 (*CL* i. 258), in the midst of the controversy surrounding the publication of *Tess of the d'Urbervilles*, Hardy took the opportunity to pass on some information about the origins of the novel that he hoped MacColl would make public. The following paragraph, essentially a third-person reworking of the first-person anecdote in Hardy's letter, duly appeared in the 'Literary Gossip' column of the *Athenaeum*, 13 February 1892, p. 215.

It will interest the admirers of *Tess of the D'Urbervilles* to know that the opening incident, which some critics denounced as unnatural,[4] took place under Mr Hardy's cycs. Hc was standing at the corner of a street in a small town in Dorsetshire when a tipsy man staggered past, saying, 'I've got a great family vault over at——.' Mr Hardy's curiosity was roused, and he found that the man's statement was true. He represented one of our oldest Norman families. The admirable novel which is now delighting the public grew up from this incident, supplemented by other facts.

[1892.06]

[?Columbus Album?]

On 11 April 1892 (DCM) Mary Augusta Ward, the novelist (1851–1920; better known as Mrs Humphry Ward), asked Hardy to contribute his signature and a quotation, inscribed on parchment, to a volume of autographs that would be preserved by the city of Milan in commemoration of the four hundredth anniversary of Columbus's arrival in America in 1892. Hardy agreed (*CL* i. 263), provided he was given guidance as to exactly what was required, but further information about his contribution, if any, has proved elusive.

---

[4] As TH's letter to MacColl makes clear, he had chiefly in mind the anonymous notice in the *Saturday Review*, 16 January 1892, p. 73, which charged, apropos of the opening chapter, that there was 'not one single touch of nature either in John Durbeyfield or in any other character in the book'.

[1892.07]

[List of Autobiographical Dates]

Among the several items relating to Hardy in the May 1892 issue of the *Book Buyer*, published in New York by Charles Scribner's Sons, is a list of dates, 'up to the time when he at last achieved a popular success as an author', that is directly attributed to Hardy and evidently corresponds, if perhaps not word for word, to the 'notes' that Hardy sent to Scribner's on 17 March 1892 (*CL* i. 260). Reproduced in the same issue were the photograph of himself that Hardy had sent with the 'notes' and a facsimile of the complimentary close and signature ('Yours very truly, Thomas Hardy') from his accompanying card. The text below is that of the *Book Buyer*, 9 (May 1892), pp. 152–3.

1856.—Articled to an ecclesiastical architect.

1858–9.—Wrote poems and critical essays on Tennyson, Coleridge, Lamb, etc.; none published.

1863.—Essay on Architecture received the Prize Medal of the Royal Institute of Architects.

1865.—First printed sketch appeared, being a short tale in *Chambers's Journal*, entitled 'How I Built Myself a House'.

1865–7.—Abandoned prose; read and wrote verse exclusively for nearly two years; none published; entered as student of modern languages at King's College, London.

1867–8.—Read divinity with a view to enter Church of England; abandoned for reasons of dogma.

1867–70.—Alternated between London and country as residence and between literature and architecture. During this interval a MS. by Mr Hardy was read by Mr John Morley (now the Right Hon. John Morley, M. P.), and also by Mr George Meredith, who each independently advised him to go on writing.

1870–71.—Wrote *Desperate Remedies* and *Under the Greenwood Tree*; published the former; a pecuniary loss on the publication; abandoned literature for architecture.

1872.—Unearthed MS. of *Under the Greenwood Tree*, and sold it to publisher for a small sum. Book well received.

1872.—Definite offer from a publisher for a serial story; abandoned architecture and wrote *A Pair of Blue Eyes*.

1874.—*Far from the Madding Crowd* appeared in *Cornhill Magazine*.[5]

[1892.08]

'A Professorial University for London'

Hardy was sympathetic to the campaign, led by Professor Karl Pearson (1857–1936), mathematician and biologist, for the University of London to be established as a centralized 'professorial' institution, on the German or Scottish model, rather than as a federation of semi-independent colleges. He agreed in April 1892 (*CL* i. 263) that his name should be added to 'the list of signatures' supportive of the formation of the Association for Promoting a Professorial University for London and reconfirmed that support on 12 June (*CL* i. 272), just prior to publication in *The Times*, 18 June 1892, p. 18, of a report headed 'A Professorial University for London' in which he was named as one of the Association's earliest members.

[1892.09]

[?'Mr. Thomas Hardy at Max Gate, Dorchester'?]

The status of this interview, published in *Cassell's Saturday Journal*, 25 June 1892, pp. 944–6, as part of a series entitled 'Representative Men at Home', was called somewhat into question by Richard Purdy's discovery—among papers seen at Max Gate prior to Florence Hardy's death—of a letter in which the *Journal*'s editor referred to it as 'your article on yourself'. As Purdy observed (p. 300), the interview appears to have been conducted in the standard fashion by an assigned interviewer, but Hardy's views do seem to have been more directly and reliably reported than on most such occasions, and he may well have written down some or even all of his answers (cf. 1899.03) for the interviewer's use. Extended extracts appear in *Interviews and Recollections*, pp. 36–8. Purdy, p. 300.

---

[5] The list ends at this point; a succeeding paragraph summarizing TH's subsequent career may also have derived from his notes but seems not to be in his words: e.g. *The Mayor of Casterbridge* is described as 'a biographical study of Michael Henchard'.

[1892.10]

[Death Notice for Thomas Hardy, Senior]

This formal announcement of the death of Hardy's father appeared in the 'Deaths' column of the *Dorset County Chronicle*, 28 July 1892, p. 16. The reference to 'the house of his birth' seems clear confirmation of Hardy's authorship. Purdy, p. 300.

HARDY.—July 20, at Bockhampton, in the house of his birth, Thomas Hardy, son of the late Thomas and Mary Hardy, of the same place, in his 81st year.

[1892.11]

[Memorial Leaflet for Thomas Hardy, Senior]

For his father's funeral in Stinsford church on 31 July 1892 Hardy prepared and had printed a single-sheet memorial leaflet, headed 'Stinsford Church, | July 31, 1892', that contained verses 3, 4, 5, and 6 of the Tate and Brady version of Psalm 90, described as 'The grave-side hymn of this parish down to about 1840', and a brief celebration in Latin (as below) of Thomas Hardy senior's twenty years of service as one of the church musicians. The leaflet also identified the tune ('St Stephen') to which the hymn was to be sung, and it appears from the draft (G. Stevens-Cox) sent to the printer that Hardy originally intended to include the tune's opening bars. Two days before the funeral Hardy sent the vicar of Stinsford one hundred copies of the leaflet (*CL* i. 279–80), and a few of these still survive (e.g. DCM, Berg).

In Memoriam Thomæ Hardy olim in hac ecclesia viginti annos musici. Ob: Jul: Die XX. A.D. MDCCCXCII, æt: suæ LXXXI.[6]

---

[6] 'In memory of Thomas Hardy formerly a musician in this church for twenty years. Died July 20 A. D. 1892, in his 81st year.'

[1892.12]

[Shelley Memorial Fund]

Hardy did not join—perhaps was not invited to join—with Tennyson, William Morris, and others in signing the letter in *The Times*, 15 July 1892, p. 6, which announced the creation of a Shelley Centenary Committee and Shelley Memorial Fund. On 27 July 1892, however, he told J. Stanley Little, an honorary secretary of both bodies, that he was enclosing a contribution towards the memorial and took 'much satisfaction in appending my name to the circular' (*CL* i. 278–9). No copy of the fund-raising circular has been located, but at the public meeting held at Horsham, Sussex (near Shelley's birthplace), on 4 August 1892 the chairman spoke of Hardy, absent because of his father's recent death, as one of those who had 'associated themselves heartily' with the centenary scheme (*The Times*, 5 August 1892, p. 11).

[1892.13]

'Why I Don't Write Plays'

Hardy was the first of nineteen contributors to a symposium entitled 'Why I Don't Write Plays' that ran daily in the *Pall Mall Gazette* between 31 August and 13 September 1892 in response to a suggestion by William Archer that more British novelists should also be writing for the stage. Hardy's comments were printed, as below, in the *Pall Mall Gazette*, 31 August 1892, p. [1], identically reprinted in the (weekly) *Pall Mall Budget*, 1 September 1892, p. 1313; and excerpted in *Harper's Bazar*, 24 September 1892, p. 771. Accompanying the *Pall Mall Budget* printing (cutting in Hardy's 'Personal' scrapbook, DCM) is a facsimile of what appears to be Hardy's draft, in which the answers to the questions are not numbered; the same facsimile was used as the frontispiece to *Life and Art* in 1925, but the whereabouts of the original remain unknown. Reprinted in *Life and Art*, pp. 116–17. Purdy, p. 301.

[*Preceding Hardy's comments were the questions to which contributors to the symposium had been asked to respond:*

(1) *Whether you regard the present divorce of fiction from the drama as beneficial or inimical to the best interests of literature and of the stage;*

(2) *Whether you, yourself, have at any time had, or now have, any desire to exercise your gifts in the production of plays as well as of novels; and, if not,*

(3) *Why you consider the novel the better or more convenient means for bringing your ideas before the public whom you address.*]

1. Inimical to the best interests of the stage: no injury to literature.

2. Have occasionally had a desire to produce a play, and have, in fact, written the skeletons of several. Have no such desire in any special sense just now.

3. Because, in general, the novel affords scope for getting nearer to the heart and meaning of things than does the play: in particular, the play as nowadays conditioned, when parts have to be moulded to actors, not actors to parts; when managers will not risk a truly original play; when scenes have to be arranged in a constrained and arbitrary fashion to suit the exigencies of scene-building, although spectators are absolutely indifferent to order and succession, provided they can have set before them a developing thread of interest. The reason of this arbitrary arrangement would seem to be that the presentation of human passions is subordinated to the presentation of mountains, cities, clothes, furniture, plate, jewels, and other real and sham-real appurtenances, to the neglect of the principle that the material stage should be a conventional or figurative arena, in which accessories are kept down to the plane of mere suggestions of place and time, so as not to interfere with the required high-relief of the action and emotions.

[1892.14]

[The American Editions of *Tess of the d'Urbervilles*]

A reviewer in the 9 July 1892 issue of the *Critic* (of New York), p. 13, pointed out that neither the first American edition of *Tess of the d'Urbervilles*, published in January 1892, nor the 'New and Revised' edition of May 1892 had included the authorial 'Explanatory Note' prefaced to the English first edition. Hardy's delayed reponse, published as below in the *Critic*, 10 September 1892, p. 134, under the editorial heading 'A Letter from Mr Thomas Hardy', was perhaps the occasion of the New York newspaper placard, 'Copyright with England: Hardy riled', that Hardy recalled when asked to make a statement about American copyright several years later (*CL* iii. 154). Reprinted in *Life and Art*, p. 129. Purdy, p. 301.

Max Gate, Dorchester, Aug. 26th, 1892.

A complaint has reached me from your pages to the effect that even in the revised and enlarged American edition of *Tess of the D'Urbervilles* I have thought fit to suppress the explanatory preface which appears in all the English editions.

I find it to be quite true that the preface is omitted; but you will perhaps allow me to assure your readers that such omission was not intentional on my part, but arose from circumstances of publication over which I had no control at the time.

I am now taking measures to attach to the American edition both the original preface and a new preface which is in preparation for the fifth English edition.

I may add in this connection that the necessity for (at least) simultaneous publication in America of English books, to secure copyright, renders it almost impossible that the latest addenda of an author should be incorporated in the foreign imprint. Could even a fortnight's grace be allowed, final touches, given just before going to press on this side, would not be excluded from American copies as they now are in so many cases.

Yours faithfully,

Thomas Hardy.

[1892.15]

'Fame's Tribute to Children'

Hardy's invited contribution to *Fame's Tribute to Children: Being a Collection of Autograph Sentiments Contributed by Famous Men and Women for this Volume. Done in Fac-simile and Published for the Benefit of the Children's Home, of the World's Columbian Exposition* (Chicago: A. C. McClurg and Company, 1892) took the form of a brief passage adapted, as follows (punctuation slightly adjusted), from Chapter 3 of *Tess of the d'Urbervilles*. A facsimile of his inscription of the passage occupies p. 37 of the original edition and p. 28 (where it faces Henry James's inscription of an extract from 'The Pupil') of the more cheaply produced second edition of 1893.

Little Children.

... 'Helpless creatures, who have never been asked if they wished for life on any terms, much less if they wished for it on ... hard conditions.' (From 'Tess of the D'Urbervilles.')[7]

Thomas Hardy.

Oct. 8. 1892

---

[7] Cf. *Tess* (Wessex edn.), p. 24: 'six helpless creatures who had never been asked if they wished for life on any terms, much less if they wished for it on such hard conditions as were involved in being of the shiftless house of Durbeyfield.'

1893

[1893.01]

[Inspired Paragraphs in the *Bookman*]

In a letter of 19 December 1892 (DCM) W. Robertson Nicoll (see 1891.03), editor of the London *Bookman*, solicited—specifically for publication—Hardy's reaction to current rumours of his ill-health (cf. *CL* i. 289). Hardy's reponse seems not to have survived, but its essence and much of its actual phrasing are evidently reflected, as below, in the 'News Notes' section of the *Bookman*, 3 (January 1893), p. [1]. The next paragraph of 'News Notes' is also reproduced—following the line of asterisks—as containing observations on the creation and development of the fictional Wessex that are also likely to have originated in material supplied by Hardy himself.

A paragraph has been going the round of the American papers in which it is stated that Mr Hardy has been 'sick unto death', and that great efforts have been made to keep the fact secret. There is no truth in the story. Mr Hardy is quite well, and the only illness he has had this year was a slight chill, caught in the early autumn by driving across the downs in the rain, which confined him to his room for a week.

*   *   *   *   *

Apropos of a recent novel, and in view of the growing familiarity of the word 'Wessex'—which in a late review is alluded to as a country possessing a peculiar 'charm' for the scene of a story—it may be well to remember that Wessex as a modern region, with its contemporary life and scenery, has no existence outside Mr Thomas Hardy's novels. The first use of the word in fiction occurred in the pages of *Far from the Madding Crowd*, which ran through the *Cornhill Magazine* in 1874, and from the vague conception that most people had of the boundaries of the kingdom referred to—at that time at least—it was well suited to the writer's purpose, which has been systematically followed out in all his succeeding stories, where we find the included counties particularised as 'North Wessex,' 'South Wessex,' 'Mid-Wessex,' and by other subdivisions.

[1893.02]

'Dorchester Street-Naming'

Hardy's interest in the history of Dorchester, the 'original' of his fictional Casterbridge, was strongly reflected in the following letter, published without a date and beneath a presumably editorial heading in the *Dorset County Chronicle*, 23 February 1893, p. 11. No action to revive the old names of streets and public places seems to have ensued on this occasion—despite the interest shown by the influential local figure Robert Pearce Edgcumbe (*CL* ii. 4)—but Hardy returned to the issue in 1902 when a new Dorchester guidebook was under discussion (*CL* iii. 17, 18–20, 28; see also 1905.16).

Max Gate.

I see in your current impression a suggestion by the Mayor of Dorchester that the street names of the town be re-painted and others added where wanting.[1] When this is done certain original and historic names now fast sinking into oblivion should be restored to particular localities, such a course being in the interests of the borough, which in summer-time derives a growing support from artistic, antiquarian, and descriptive visitors from far and near. Among these names would be the following:—The Bath Road (Grove Buildings); Gallow's-hill; Jail-lane; Lower-street (by the Baptist Chapel); Bowling-alley-walk; Bowling-green-street (Charles street); Bull-stake; Bull-stake-passage; The Bow; East Walls; West Walls; Holloway; and Standfast. Old inhabitants will remember more. Should genteel tastes object to unqualified restoration of these designations they might be painted as second titles.

T. H.

---

[1] As reported in the *Dorset County Chronicle*, 16 February 1893, p. 5.

[1893.03]

[Authorized Remarks on Family Background]

Hardy had read *The New Spirit* by Havelock Ellis (1859–1939) in the spring of 1890 (*LN* ii. 14–17) and was well aware of the appreciative assessment of his novels published by Ellis in the *Westminster Review* of April 1883. When, therefore, Ellis wrote on 9 July 1890 (DCM) to ask for background details relevant to an article about 'the ancestry of our chief recent poets and imaginative writers', Hardy immediately offered to supply the information either orally or in writing (*CL* vii. 113–14). The following passage from Ellis's 'The Ancestry of Genius', *Atlantic Monthly*, 71 (March 1893), pp. 386–7, clearly depends upon such information; what is unclear is the extent to which it incorporates Hardy's own wording.

Mr Thomas Hardy belongs to a Dorset family, which has not, apparently, encouraged foreign alliances, although the Hardys at a remote period are believed to have been a French family who emigrated from Jersey.[2] Of Mr Hardy's four grandparents, all belonged to Dorset except one, who came from Berkshire.[3] His paternal great-grandmother, Mr Hardy believes, was Irish.[4] On the paternal side, also, a black-haired ancestor left very distinct traces, while on the mother's side the race was fairer, and closer to the ordinary Wessex-Saxon type.

[1893.04]

'A Question of Priority'

The dramatic critic William Archer (1856–1928) revealed in the *Westminster Gazette*, 6 May 1893, pp. 1–2, that the play called *Alan's Wife*, first performed at the Independent Theatre, 28 April 1893, with Elizabeth Robins in the title role, had been adapted at his suggestion from a story ('Befriad' by Elin Ameen) that he had read in a Swedish paper. In the play the heroine personally baptizes her sickly baby before murdering it, and Archer commented that the original story 'was published long before Mr. Hardy's "Tess" and

---

[2] Cf. *LW*, p. 9.   [3] TH's father's mother, born Mary Head of Fawley, Berkshire.
[4] Although TH made similar statements on a number of occasions, it is not clear upon what, if any, evidence they were based, nor to which of his father's grandmothers they were meant to apply.

contains the baptism scene in full'. Hardy, always sensitive to suggestions of plagiarism, asked Archer for details of the story's publication. Reassured by the reply (*CL* ii. 8, 9), he sent the following letter to the *Westminster Gazette*, where it was published, under the editorial heading 'A Question of Priority', on 10 May 1893, p. 2. The letter was reprinted, its date expanded to 'May 9, 1893', as Appendix II of *Alan's Wife. Being Number Two of the Independent Theatre Series of Plays*, edited by J. T. Grein, with an introduction by William Archer (London: Henry and Co., 1893), p. [55]. Purdy, p. 304.

May 9.

Sir,

In Mr Archer's letter to you *apropos* of a play called 'Alan's Wife', he states that the story on which that play is founded, and which describes a baptism scene as in *Tess of the D'Urbervilles*, was published in a Swedish magazine before the English novel.

I learn from Mr Archer that the actual date of the Swedish magazine was January, 1891. This bears out his printed assertion, my baptism scene having appeared in the *Fortnightly Review* about May or June of the same year.[5]

The coincidence being somewhat an odd one, will you allow me to say that the chapters of *Tess* containing this incident were in the hands of Messrs. Tillotson and Sons, the syndicate-publishers of Bolton, so early as September, 1889, and were partly put into type by their printers at that date; though (for reasons that had nothing to do with the subject of the story) I asked the firm to allow me to withdraw the MS., which they consented to do. Later on in the same year it was read by some London editors.[6]

Messrs. Tillotson would, I have no doubt, testify to these facts if required, as would also the London editors; thus carrying us back to a date a year and a quarter before the publication of the Swedish tale—whatever that priority may be worth in a resemblance presumably accidental.

Yours faithfully,

Thomas Hardy.

[5] 'The Midnight Baptism: A Study in Christianity', *Fortnightly Review*, NS 49 (May 1891), pp. [659]–701. The episode was omitted from the serialization of *Tess* but reincorporated into the three-volume first edition of the novel published in November 1891; see Purdy, p. 69.

[6] The pre-publication adventures of *Tess* are most fully described in the introduction to the Clarendon Press edition, edited by Juliet Grindle and Simon Gatrell (Oxford: Clarendon Press, 1983).

[1893.05]

'A Plea for a Revived Pilgrimage'

In 1893 the indefatigable crusading journalist William Thomas Stead (1849–1912) used his editorship of the *Review of Reviews* to promote an ambitious scheme for revivifying the nation's sense of its history and values through organized pilgrimages to sites such as Hastings, Canterbury, Westminster Abbey, and Winchester that were associated with great events and figures of the past. Stead's programme included a 'Lecture on Thomas Hardy's Country (with limelight views)', to be given in Bournemouth by the novelist Walter Raymond, and Hardy was one of the many people to whom Stead wrote, sending details of the scheme and soliciting letters of support. Hardy wrote a positive but self-deprecating reply on 31 May (*CL* ii. 10) and Stead included the greater part of it, along with other endorsements, in his long article, 'The Wasted Wealth of King Demos. III.—His Past—A Plea for a Revived Pilgrimage', published in the June 1893 issue of the *Review of Reviews*, pp. [662]–74. Hardy's letter appeared, as below, on p. 673.

The idea of the Pilgrimage—at any rate to the haunts of men now dead, if not to spots brought into notice by the living—is an interesting one, and in these days, when all classes seem to be waiting for a lead in respect of emotions, dreams, views and religion might be carried out, I should think, rationally and systematically. The only real difficulty would lie probably in the mixing together of persons of different classes previously strangers. The various County Field Clubs are the only institutions known to me which faintly resemble what you would propose.

[1893.06]

'Contrainte et Liberté'

Hardy was one of several writers from different countries invited to respond to a question posed in the July 1893 issue of the Parisian journal *L'Ermitage: Revue mensuelle artistique et littéraire*: 'Quelle est la meilleur condition du bien social, une organisation spontanée et libre ou bien une organisation disciplinée et méthodique.' Although able to read French, Hardy always hesitated to write it, and the two paragraphs published in French under the heading 'Contrainte et Liberté' in *L'Ermitage*, 4 (November 1893), p. 260, were almost certainly translated by the editorial staff. The text below is that of the same two paragraphs as contained in Hardy's original letter of 14 August 1893, now in the Pierpont Morgan Library. Not reproduced here, because omitted from *L'Ermitage*, are the letter's specifically epistolary elements (address, date, signature, etc.), Hardy's identification of himself as the author of *Tess* and *Far from the Madding Crowd*, and his request for 'a copy of the paper in which the answers appear'. A draft of the letter survives (DCM) and was almost certainly Hardy's source for the reprinting of the item in *Life and Work*, p. 274—textually unrevised but accompanied by the wry retrospective comment: 'It is doubtful if this Utopian scheme possessed Hardy's fancy for any long time.' Purdy, p. 269.

In answer to your question dated July 1st, I beg leave to say that I consider a social system based on individual spontaneity to promise better for happiness than a curbed and uniform one under which all temperaments are bound to shape themselves to[7] a single pattern of living.

To this end I would have society divided into *groups of temperaments*, with a different code of observances for each group.

[1893.07]

[Testimonial for A. P. Watt]

Although Hardy's 10 January 1892 letter to the literary agent A. P. Watt (*CL* i. [251]) is clearly appreciative of Watt's efficient placement of his story 'On the Western Circuit', it is less clear that he envisioned Watt's publishing a fragment of that letter, for promotional purposes, in *Collection of Letters Addressed to A. P. Watt by Various Writers* (London: Literary Agency, 1893), p. 23. Hardy's letter reappeared in *Letters Addressed to A. P. Watt* (London: A. P. Watt & Son, 1894); that volume was itself several times reprinted and expanded by the inclusion of letters from new clients; and by 1924 Hardy's letter, itself unchanged, was appearing, as below, on p. 87 of what had become *Letters Addressed to A. P. Watt and his Sons 1883–1924*.

---

[7] For 'and uniform . . . themselves to' both draft and letter originally read 'and regulated one, under which all temperaments are bound to conform to'.

Maxgate, Dorchester. January 10th, 1892.

Dear Mr Watt,

. . . I enclose herewith the receipt, and have to thank you for saving me a considerable deal of trouble in arranging for the simultaneous publication of the story here and abroad. *By your management the pecuniary result is bettered, without mulcting any one.*[8]

Yours very truly,

Thomas Hardy.

A. P. Watt, Esq.

---

[8] This sentence is not underlined in TH's original.

[1894.01]

'Methods of Authors'

On 26 July 1884 Hardy responded (*CL* i. 128) to questions about his working habits contained in a circular sent out by Dr Hugo Erichsen, City Physician of Detroit, Michigan, from 1880 to 1890 and a frequent contributor to Detroit newspapers. Reproduced below are Hardy's answers as eventually published, together with those of several other writers, in Erichsen's *Methods of Authors* (Boston: The Writer Publishing Company, 1894), p. 107; the wording of Hardy's original letter was adapted in minor ways but not significantly misrepresented.

Thomas Hardy prefers the night for working, but finds the use of daytime advisable, as a rule. He follows no plan as to outline, and uses no stimulant excepting tea. His habit is to remove boots or slippers as a preliminary to work. He has no definite hours for writing, and only occasionally works against his will.

[1894.02]

'The Tree of Knowledge'

Hardy was one of thirteen contributors to a symposium in the June 1894 issue of the *New Review* that was headed 'The Tree of Knowledge' and focused primarily on what young women should know prior to marriage. The symposium appeared without a preamble, and apparently without any anticipatory announcement, but the principal issues the contributors had been asked to address emerge fairly clearly from Hardy's response. His deliberate expansion of those issues by calling into question the validity of marriage itself doubtless reflected his current preoccupation with the composition of *Jude the Obscure*—and perhaps with his own marital situation. The text below is that of the *New Review*, 10 (June 1894), p. 681. Reprinted in *Life and Art*, pp. 118–19. Purdy, p. 304.

To your first inquiry I would answer that a girl should certainly not be allowed to enter into matrimony without a full knowledge of her probable future in that holy estate, and of the possibilities which may lie in the past of the elect man.

I have not much faith in an innocent girl's 'discovery of the great mysteries of life' by means of 'the ordinary intercourse of society'.[1] Incomplete presentations, vicious presentations, meretricious and seductive presentations, are not unlikely in pursuing such investigations through such a channel. What would seem to be the most natural course is the answer to your second question: that a plain handbook on natural processes, specially prepared, should be placed in the daughter's hands, and, later on, similar information on morbid contingencies. Innocent youths should, I think, also receive the same instruction; for (if I may say a word out of my part) it has never struck me that the spider is invariably male and the fly invariably female.

As your problems are given on the old lines so I take them, without entering into the general question whether marriage, as we at present understand it, is such a desirable goal for all women as it is assumed to be; or whether civilisation can escape the humiliating indictment that, while it has been able to cover itself with glory in the arts, in literatures, in religions, and in the sciences, it has never succeeded in creating that homely thing, a satisfactory scheme for the conjunction of the sexes.

[1894.03]

The Hon. Mrs. Henniker

Hardy's intense friendship with the novelist Florence Henniker (1855–1923) began in May 1893 (*Biography*, pp. 335–41), and in the autumn of that year

---

[1] Quotations evidently from the questions posed by the *New Review*.

they collaborated in the composition and publication of a short story called 'The Spectre of the Real'—a process at once professional and deeply emotional authoritatively recounted by Pamela Dalziel in her edition of Hardy's *Excluded and Collaborative Stories* (Oxford: Clarendon Press, 1992), pp. [260]–88. A year later, by arrangement with the accommodating Clement Shorter (*CL* ii. 55, 59, 71), editor of the *Illustrated London News*, Hardy wrote and published the following sketch as an anonymous accompaniment to Mrs Henniker's photograph. The text below is that of the *Illustrated London News*, 18 August 1894, p. 195; Hardy's lightly corrected manuscript (Adams) is identically phrased and headed, if somewhat differently punctuated, and was probably used as setting copy. Purdy, p. 304.

Florence Ellen Hungerford Henniker, *née* Milnes, whose portrait is annexed, is the younger daughter of the first Lord Houghton[2] and sister of the present Lord Lieutenant of Ireland[3] and of the Hon. Lady Fitzgerald.[4] The literary bias which has almost resulted in placing Mrs Henniker on the list of professional authors may possibly be hereditary in her, for it manifested itself at an early age—a quaint devotional fervour, not uncommon in imaginative children, taking the form of an enthusiasm for the writing of hymns. Possibly also her having been surrounded through childhood and youth by literary personages of all classes and countries, whom her father was accustomed to entertain at Fryston Hall[5] and in London, made her early familiar with the idea of putting her thoughts upon paper. But it was not till within the last three or four years that she decided to publish as fiction the experiences of life gained in England and abroad by one who has certainly had good opportunities of observing it. Her first and wholly experimental novel, bearing the amateurish title of *Bid Me Good-bye*, was followed by a tale of stronger characterisation called *Sir George*, which has lately been republished in one volume. Last year Mrs Henniker issued a longer novel entitled *Foiled*, wherein the growing strength shown in character-drawing makes the reader indifferent to the absence of a well-compacted plot. A volume of short stories called *Outlines*,[6] published

---

[2] Better known as Richard Monckton Milnes (1809–85), politician, author, and biographer of Keats; he was created Baron Houghton in 1863.

[3] Robert Offley Ashburton Crewe-Milnes (1858–1945), 2nd Lord Houghton, later Marquess of Crewe.

[4] Amicia, wife of Sir Gerald Fitzgerald, Accountant-General of the Royal Navy.

[5] In Yorkshire, east of Leeds. See *LW*, p. 149, and James Pope-Hennessy, *Monckton Milnes: The Flight of Youth 1851–1885* (London: Constable, 1951), pp. 108–13.

[6] This volume was dedicated to TH.

this year, evidences a literary form and style sufficient to carry their author through more ambitious performances. Mrs Henniker has also written tales for the *Cornhill*, *Blackwood*, *English Illustrated*, and other magazines, and has published some scattered translations of French and Italian verse. Her note of individuality, her own personal and peculiar way of looking at life, without which neither aristocrat nor democrat, fair woman nor foul, has any right to take a stand before the public as author, may be called that of emotional imaginativeness,[7] lightened by a quick sense of the odd, and by touches of observation lying midway between wit and humour.

---

[7] TH's impression upon first meeting her was of a 'charming, *intuitive* woman' (*LW*, p. 270).

1895

[1895.01]

'The Duchy of Cornwall and Mr. Thomas Hardy'

Rosamund Tomson, the poet (1863–1911), with whom Hardy had been at least flirtatiously involved a few years earlier, published in the New York *Independent*, 22 November 1894, pp. [1]–2, an admiring article about him that was nevertheless a source of some embarrassment. Tomson asserted, presumably on the basis of a half-remembered personal conversation, that approval for the Duchy of Cornwall's sale of the land for Max Gate in 1883 had at first been denied by the responsible official and subsequently granted only through the personal intervention of the Prince of Wales. The story was picked up by the *Dorset County Chronicle*, 27 December 1894, p. 9; George Herriot, the Duchy official involved (see *CL* vii. 103), wrote on 9 January 1895 (DCM) to ask Hardy for an explanation; and on 10 January (*CL* ii. 66–7) Hardy responded with a comprehensive denial of Tomson's version of events. The following brief statement was also published, beneath the editorial heading 'The Duchy of Cornwall and Mr. Thomas Hardy', in the *Dorset County Chronicle*, 17 January 1895, p. 4. Purdy p. 305.

Mr Thomas Hardy's attention having been drawn to a paragraph from an American paper to which we gave currency a week or two ago, respecting the negotiations for a site for his house at Max Gate, he requests us to state that, so far from the Duchy agent having at first been applied to in vain, or having acted in any way adversely to his application, as stated in the paragraph, Mr Herriott[1] showed every courtesy from the beginning, forwarded the application in the readiest manner, and took great personal interest in the choice of the site.

---

[1] So misspelled in the *Dorset County Chronicle*.

[1895.02]

'Canadian Copyright'

Hardy's long-standing interest in copyright issues (cf. 1892.03) was confirmed by the appearance of his name, on the third page of a report headed 'Literary Property. I.—Canadian Copyright', *The Author*, 5 (1 April 1895), pp. 283–6, as one of the more than 1,500 signatories to a petition to the Colonial Secretary protesting the impact of recent Canadian copyright legislation on British authors and publishers. See 'Canadian Copyright', *The Times*, 30 May 1895, p. 12.

[1895.03]

[Speech at Omar Khayyàm Club Dinner]

On 13 July 1895 the Omar Khayyàm Club, chaired by Edward Clodd (1840–1930), held a special dinner at the Burford Bridge Hotel, Boxhill, Surrey, in honour of George Meredith, who lived nearby. At the end of the dinner, according to the *Daily Chronicle*, 15 July, p. 7, the first speeches were made by Clodd and Meredith, then Hardy, George Gissing, and three other speakers got successively to their feet 'under pressure of the knowledge that in a very few minutes the train was due at Boxhill Station by which many of the diners were to return to town'. But if Hardy's speech was necessarily brief, it was still more briefly summarized—as below—in the *Daily Chronicle* report. See 1909.06.

Replying for the guests, Mr Thomas Hardy wittily and sweetly described his first meeting with Mr Meredith in 'a dusty back room at Chapman and Hall's', when the author of *The Ordeal of Richard Feverel* was reader to the firm, and the author of *The Return of the Native* was just beginning his career. Mr Meredith spoke of Mr Hardy's work as 'promising', and thereby much encouraged his subsequent fellow-king of English literature.

[1895.04]

' "Hearts Insurgent" '

The serialization of Hardy's last novel, *Jude the Obscure*, ran in *Harper's New Monthly Magazine* from December 1894 to November 1895, first as *The Simpletons* and then, beginning with the second instalment, as *Hearts Insurgent*. The serial text had been extensively bowdlerized by Hardy himself in response to the editor's concern that his magazine 'contain nothing which could not be read aloud in any family circle' (Purdy, pp. 87, 90), and when an alert reader complained (*Daily Chronicle*, 24 September 1895, p. 3) about one of the resulting absurdities in the plot Hardy felt obliged to write back immediately in defence both of the serial and, more especially, of the first edition that would shortly be published. Hardy's letter appeared, as below, in the *Daily Chronicle*, 25 September 1895, p. 3, under the editorial heading ' "Hearts Insurgent" '. Purdy, p. 305.

Sept. 24.

Sir,

In answer to the inquiry in your impression of to-day concerning the story now appearing in *Harper's*, allow me to say that little or nothing has been omitted or modified without my knowledge, though I failed to see the necessity for some of the alterations, if for any. However, as abridged in the magazine I venture to think the novel a not uninteresting one for the general family circle, to which the magazine is primarily addressed—to use the editor's own words to me—while the novel as originally written, addressed mainly to middle-aged readers, and of less interest than as now printed to those young ladies for whose innocence we are all so solicitous, will be published in a volume a month hence, under a new title.[2]

Yours, &c.,

Thomas Hardy.

---

[2] *Jude the Obscure* was published in London by Osgood, McIlvaine & Co. (London agents of Harper & Brothers) on 1 November 1895, though dated 1896.

1896

[1896.01]

'Hymns that have Helped'

W. T. Stead, editor of the *Review of Reviews*, wrote to Hardy 12 December 1895 (DCM) to solicit a contribution to his forthcoming 'Penny Hymnal under the title of "Hymns that Have Helped Me"'. But Hardy's response— not known to survive except in the form of his pencilled draft (DCM)—was evidently too qualified for Stead's purposes. It did not appear among the group of replies published in the January 1896 *Review of Reviews*, and only the titles of Hardy's chosen hymns were included in Stead's *Hymns that have Helped. Being a Collection of those Hymns, Whether Jewish, Christian, or Pagan, which have been Found Most Useful to the Children of Men* (London: 'Review of Reviews' Office, [1896]), p. 117. Hardy felt that his position had been mis-represented—as he told Florence Henniker (*CL* ii. 139), he did like the hymns he had mentioned 'but had never found any help from them in the sense intended'—and when including his letter, as below, in *Life and Work*, pp. 290–1, he not only drew, with trivial adjustments, upon the text of his draft but made a significant addition to the second sentence. Purdy, p. 269.

I am unable to answer your inquiry as to 'Hymns that have helped me'.

But the undermentioned have always been familiar and favourite hymns of mine as poetry:—[1]

1. 'Thou turnest man, O Lord, to dust.' Ps. XC. v. 3, 4, 5, 6 (Tate and Brady.)[2]

---

[1] For 'mine as poetry' draft reads 'mine'.

[2] For 'Tate and Brady' draft reads 'Common Prayer': the metrical versions of the Psalms by Nicholas Brady (1659–1726) and Nahum Tate (1652–1715) were long included in the Book of Common Prayer. See Peter W. Coxon, 'Hardy's Favourite Hymns', *Thomas Hardy Journal*, 13 (May 1997), pp. 42–55. For Psalm 90, see also 1892.11.

2. 'Awake, my soul, and with the sun.' (Morning Hymn, Ken.)[3]
3. 'Lead, kindly Light.' (Newman.)[4]

[1896.02]

[Sources of *The Trumpet-Major*]

Publication of the revised 'Wessex Novels' edition of *The Trumpet-Major* in December 1895 prompted the revival of some old accusations of plagiarism that Hardy's Preface to the new edition had sought finally to refute. The New York *Critic*, for example, in its issue of 9 May 1896, p. 336, renewed its charge, dating from 28 January 1882, that the drilling scene in Chapter 23 of the novel was heavily indebted to Augustus Baldwin Longstreet's *Georgia Scenes*, first published in 1835. Hardy's response—published as below, under the editorial heading 'A Card from Mr Hardy', in the *Critic* of 4 July 1896, p. 8—essentially repeated what he had said in a letter of March 1882 to the American editor Thomas Bailey Aldrich (*CL* i. 103–4): that he knew nothing of Longstreet's work and had drawn for the drilling scene upon a section of C. H. Gifford's *History of the Wars Occasioned by the French Revolution*, published in 1817, believing it to be authentically descriptive of a mustering of recruits in the English countryside. In fact both Gifford and Longstreet had used, and acknowledged, the same piece of satirical fiction by a still earlier American writer. Hardy owned a copy of Gifford's work (DCM) but had perhaps resorted to an old notebook entry without realizing its closeness to its source. Purdy, p. 305.

London, June 9, 1896.

Sir:

My publishers have just sent me a cutting from *The Critic* of May 9, which contains a paragraph on a resemblance between the drilling scene in *The Trumpet Major*, and a scene in an American book published in 1840.

I know nothing of the latter work, but I have already stated in the preface to *The Trumpet Major* my authorities for many of the incidents it

---

[3] Thomas Ken (1637–1711), Bishop of Bath and Wells, the 'gentle-voiced prelate' of *Jude the Obscure* (Wessex edn.), p. 96; for the hymn, see *LW*, p. 16, and Coxon, pp. 47–50.

[4] John Henry Newman (1801–90), cardinal, whose writings TH always admired (see *LN* i. 241–3); for the hymn, see *Far from the Madding Crowd* (Wessex edn.), pp. 448–9, and Coxon, pp. 51–2.

contains,[5] mentioning that some of the details of this particular militia drill (apparently those referred to) were suggested by a similar description in Gifford's History of the War with Napoleon, published in London in 1817—a description which I understood to refer to the English peasantry. This book, and the Army Regulations for 1800–1815, which I consulted at the War Office, and contemporary newspapers, were the only printed matter I used to substantiate the many traditional accounts of rustic drilling that I obtained from old men and women who remembered those quaint performances, and who were living when I prepared this book.

Apologizing for occupying your space with such a trivial matter as a few sentences in a novel written twenty years ago, I am,

Yours faithfully,

Thomas Hardy.

[1896.03]

[Assistance to Agnes Grove]

Hardy first met—and was attracted to—the beautiful Agnes Grove (1863–1926), wife of Walter John Grove (later Sir Walter Grove, Bt), in September 1895 at Rushmore, the estate owned by her father, General Augustus Lane Fox Pitt-Rivers (1827–1900), the famous anthropologist and archaeologist. Early in the course of their ensuing friendship, Hardy took both pleasure and trouble in assisting Agnes Grove in her ambition to write and publish on contemporary social issues. A first attempt was rejected by the editor to whom Hardy had sent it (*CL* ii. 96, 101), but she was soon successful in placing a two-part essay in another journal chosen and approached by Hardy on her behalf: 'Our Children: What Children Should Be Told. i. On Religion. ii. On Physiology', *Free Review*, 6 (1 July 1896), pp. 393–9. That the essay was somewhat radical for its day, its views often close to Hardy's own, must in part have been the result of Hardy's having proposed the topic, read and commented on the essay itself in draft and in proof, and dealt directly with the editor of the *Free Review* (*CL* ii. 101, 114–18, 120, 123). He also helped his 'good little pupil' (*CL* ii. 117) to refine and publish a number of

---

[5] *The Trumpet-Major* (London: Osgood, McIlvaine, 1896), pp. v–vi: the comments in the May 1896 *Critic* had in fact been prompted by TH's preface. For the so-called '*Trumpet-Major* Notebook' (DCM), used by TH when gathering material for the novel, see *PN*, pp. [117]–86.

later pieces, and in the autumn of 1907 he read a set of proofs (Beinecke) for her book *The Social Fetich*, a primarily humorous commentary on contemporary speech and manners, of which he was himself the dedicatee. See *Biography*, pp. 454–5, and Desmond Hawkins, *Concerning Agnes: Thomas Hardy's 'Good Little Pupil'* (Gloucester: Alan Sutton, 1982), pp. 97–9, 122–5, etc.

[1896.04]

[Assistance to Bertram Windle's Guidebooks]

In September 1896 Hardy was asked by Bertram Windle (1858–1929), FRS, writer on anthropology, science, and medicine, to provide information about the 'Wessex' locations of his fiction for inclusion in a new edition of Murray's *Handbook for Residents and Travellers in Wilts and Dorset*. Hardy responded with a wealth of topographical detail, largely written out in Emma Hardy's hand (see *CL* ii. 131–4, and *Index*, HrT 1525), and Windle not only put this material to immediate use in the *Handbook* (London: John Murray, 1899; copy presented to Hardy with Murray's compliments in BL) but drew upon it more fully when collaborating with the artist Edmund H. New in *The Wessex of Thomas Hardy* (London: John Lane The Bodley Head, 1902), dedicating the volume to Hardy and thanking him in the preface for the 'generous assistance' that made it possible 'to speak with such certainty as to the identification of certain of the spots' (p. xi). The copy Windle and New signed and presented to Hardy was listed in Stonehill catalogue 141, item 113.

[1896.05]

[R. L. Stevenson Memorial Fund]

Writing on 3 December 1896 to the secretary-treasurer of the Stevenson Memorial Fund (*CL* vii. 129), Hardy supported the proposal that a memorial to Robert Louis Stevenson (1850–94) be erected in Edinburgh. When the general appeal for contributions was sent out some five months later, Hardy's name appeared in *The Times*, 27 May 1897, p. 10, among those on 'the first subscription list, which is issued with the appeal'.

1897

[1897.01]

[*Who's Who* Entry, 1897]

When *Who's Who* first appeared in its modern format as *Who's Who 1897: First Year of New Issue*, edited by Douglas Sladen (London: Adam & Charles Black, 1897), it included, on p. 361, the following entry for 'Thomas Hardy', based closely on the form (still preserved in the publishers' archives) that Hardy himself had completed, signed, and returned. The entry as printed, however, includes information not supplied on the form, and it seems likely that Hardy saw a proof and made additions to it. Footnotes below refer to Hardy's holograph responses on the original form and to small but significant changes made for the entry published in *Who's Who 1898*, p. 423. Hardy revised his entry on several subsequent occasions: corrections in his (currently unlocated) copies of *Who's Who* for 1907 and 1926 are mentioned in William P. Wreden Catalogue 11, items 135 and 136. But, rather than record the successive stages of what was primarily a process of biblio-graphical accretion, the present edition simply reproduces—for purposes of comparison—his final *Who's Who* entry of 1927 (1927.12).

HARDY, Thomas, J. P. for Dorset; novelist; *b.* Dorsetshire, 2 June 1840; articled to an ecclesiastical architect, 1857; studied Gothic archi-tecture in London, under Sir A. Blomfield, A. R. A., 1862–67; prizeman of Royal Institute of British Architects, 1863; the Architectural Association, 1863; relinquished architecture for literature, 1870–72;[1] *m.* Emma, *d.* of J. Gifford, niece of Archdeacon Gifford.[2] *Publications*: Desperate Remedies, 1871; Under the Greenwood Tree, 1872; A Pair of Blue Eyes, 1872–73; Far from the Madding Crowd, 1874; Hand of

---

[1] Changed to '1868–72' in 1898.

[2] Date of marriage, 1874, added in 1898; curiously, questions about marital status and children were not included in the form sent to TH, though such information was a standard element in the entries as published.

Ethelberta, 1876; Return of the Native, 1878; The Trumpet Major, 1879; A Laodicean, 1880–81; Two on a Tower, 1882; The Mayor of Casterbridge, 1884–85; The Woodlanders, 1886–87; Tess of the D'Urbervilles, 1891; Jude the Obscure, 1895; A Group of Noble Dames, Life's Little Ironies, Wessex Tales (various dates).[3] *Recreations*: forestry,[4] cycling, architecture. *Clubs*: Athenaeum, Savile, Authors'.[5]

[1897.02]

The Well-Beloved

Hardy's novel *The Well-Beloved* had a hostile reception in some quarters upon its first appearance in volume form in March 1897, and on 26 March (DCM) Lewis Hind (1862–1927), editor of the *Academy*, invited Hardy to reply in its pages to a peculiarly offensive review of *The Well-Beloved* published in the *World* of that date. Hardy declined the offer, insisting that 'Personal abuse best answers itself' (*CL* ii. 155), but two days later he sent for publication the letter that appeared, as below, in the *Academy*, 3 April 1897, p. 381, under the heading that he had himself supplied. As the facsimile reproduction in the *Library Chronicle of the University of Texas*, 7 (Summer 1962), p. [6], clearly shows, Hardy's original letter (Texas) served as printer's copy and was lightly edited in the process. The published letter was reprinted in *Life and Art*, pp. 133–4, and extracts from it appear in *Life and Work*, pp. 303–4. Purdy, p. 270.

Dorchester: March 29.[6]

After reading your review of *The Well-Beloved*[7] (more appreciative in feeling and generous towards its faults than such a slight story deserves), I think it would not be amiss to account for the ultra-romantic notion of the tale, which seems to come slightly as a surprise to readers. Not only was it published serially five years ago, but it was sketched many years before that date, when I was comparatively a young man, and interested in the Platonic Idea, which, considering its charm and its poetry, one could well wish to be interested in always.

---

[3] In 1898 the three short story collections were assigned their individual publication dates.

[4] Changed to 'arboriculture' in 1898.

[5] 'Authors'', is a scrawled addition to TH's 1897 form, apparently in a hand other than his own, and in 1898 the name of the club was omitted.

[6] TH used unheaded stationery, and although 'March 29' was simply moved from the end of his letter, 'Dorchester' was an editorial addition; editorially omitted, on the other hand, were his opening 'Sir' and closing 'Yours sincerely'.   [7] *Academy*, 27 March 1897, pp. 345–6.

Later on, in answer to a request from Mr Tillotson, of Bolton, for 'something light' for his syndicate,[8] the tale was taken in hand and adapted, the idea of perfection in woman[9] being made to grow upon the hero, an innocent and moral man throughout, as described, till it became a trouble to him rather than a delight.

In lately correcting and revising the chapters I saw that the visionary character of the conception, and, so to speak, the youthfulness of the plot, was what I should certainly not have been able to enter into at this time of my life, if it had not been shaped already. There is, of course, underlying the fantasy followed by the visionary artist the truth that all men are pursuing a shadow, the Unattainable, and I venture to hope that this may redeem the tragi-comedy[10] from the charge of frivolity, or of being built upon a baseless conceit, that may otherwise have been brought against it.

I may, perhaps, be allowed to state in addition, that 'Avice' is an old name common in the county, and that 'Caro' (like all the other surnames) is an imitation of a local name[11] which will occur to everybody who knows the place—this particular modification having been adopted because of its resemblance to the Italian for 'dear'.[12]

Thomas Hardy.

[1897.03]

[Inspired Comment on New York Staging of *Tess of the d'Urbervilles*]

As Keith Wilson makes clear in his *Thomas Hardy on Stage*, pp. 40–2, Hardy's reservations about Lorimer Stoddard's dramatization of *Tess of the d'Urbervilles* did not prevent him from taking satisfaction in the success of the New York production with Minnie Maddern Fiske in the title role and

---

[8]　Though initially written for the Tillotson & Son syndicate of Bolton (Purdy, pp. 94–5), the serial was actually published, as *The Pursuit of the Well-Beloved*, in the *Illustrated London News*.

[9]　For 'perfection in woman' TH's MS originally read 'beauty'.

[10]　For 'redeem the tragi-comedy' TH's MS originally read 'redeem the tale's first form of a tragi-comedy'.

[11]　Probably the name Lano, which occurs with some frequency in Portland records and on Portland tombstones.

[12]　To the cutting of this letter in his 'Personal' scrapbook (DCM) TH has added in holograph at this point: '[—i.e. "Well-Beloved".]'

contemplating its possible transplantation to London. A 'copyright' performance was held at the St James's Theatre on 1 March 1897 (*CL* ii. 149–50), and on 26 March 1897 he offered the theatre critic W. Moy Thomas 'a line or two which you may, or may not, like to insert in yr dramatic column' (Sotheby catalogue, 6 June 1929, lot 727). Thomas responded by printing the following brief item in 'The Theatres' section of the *Graphic* for 3 April 1897, p. 407. Clement Shorter (1857–1926), editor of several magazines, had earlier responded to a similar request from Hardy (*CL* ii. 151) by publishing in the *Sketch* of 17 March the cast list of the New York production and a photograph of Mrs Fiske herself.

New plays—and important new plays are coming to us from America. . . . The other piece is the American version of *Tess of the D'Urbervilles*, which will probably be brought over by the Fiske Company. Mr Thomas Hardy, who is greatly pleased by the production, informs me, as an instance of the thoroughness of the representation in New York, that the scenery has been painted, though without his knowledge, from drawings made on the actual scene of that pathetic story.

[1897.04]

'The Disappearance of an Englishman at Zermatt'

Hardy, holidaying with his wife in Switzerland, arrived at Zermatt on 28 June 1897 and promptly became interested in the recent mysterious disappearance from a nearby mountain path of James Robert Cooper, the father of Edith Cooper, one of the two authors known jointly as 'Michael Field'. The episode is recorded in *Life and Work*, p. 313, but Hardy never reprinted the following letter, published under an editorial heading in *The Times*, 8 July 1897, p. 10. Purdy, pp. 305–6.

Hôtel de la Paix, Geneva, July 3.

Sir,

I can add my own to Miss Cooper's surprise[13] that no public notice was taken of the disappearance of Mr Cooper on Thursday, June 24.

---

[13] A letter from Edith Cooper in *The Times* of 2 July, p. 10, expressed 'surprise . . . that the newspapers have not yet received any intimation of such an occurrence as this in such a place as Zermatt'.

I arrived at Zermatt on the Monday following, and on Tuesday and Wednesday found people speaking of the possible catastrophe with bated breath. 'Zermatt is a place of strange tragedies,' they said.

But I had no idea till now that no account of the disappearance had been sent to the Press.

Probably the matter will be cleared up before this reaches you, but I may say that I walked up to the Riffel Alp by the way Mr Cooper must have taken, and down again, examining narrowly such slight precipices as occur on each side of the very rough bridle path which forms the route, and I came to the conclusion that no human body could fall over at any point and lie invisible. My impression is that Mr Cooper must have diverged from the path for some reason or other. I ought to mention that a sinister rumour as to the cause of his not returning was told to me by some English ladies, though I do not think it probable in the circumstances.[14]

Yours truly,

Thomas Hardy.

[1897.05]

'The Best Scenery I Know'

Hardy, invited to contribute to an ongoing *Saturday Review* symposium on 'The Best Scenery I Know', characteristically evaded any direct expression of a personal choice, supplying instead a list of generally popular West of England views. The reprinting of this letter in *Life and Work*, p. 314, was evidently based upon Hardy's draft (DCM), and one obviously correct reading from that draft is incorporated below into the text of the letter's original publication in the *Saturday Review*, 7 August 1897, p. 140. Purdy, p. 270.

---

[14] The possibility of Cooper's having been murdered was in fact actively canvassed in investigations by Swiss and British authorities and in the correspondence columns of *The Times*—notably in a long letter from Edward Whymper, the famous climber, published on 24 July, p. 4. Edith Cooper, in *The Times* of 26 July, p. 4, accepted as reasonable the general conclusion that her elderly father must have fallen from a bridge or precipice along his presumed route, but some doubts remained even after the discovery of his body in late October: see 'Death in the Mountains', in *Works and Days: From the Journal of Michael Field*, ed. T. and D. C. Sturge Moore (London: John Murray, 1933), pp. 223–30.

9 July, 1897.

Sir,

I am unable to reply to your inquiry on 'The Best Scenery I know'.

A week or two ago I was looking at the inexorable faces of the Jungfrau and the Matterhorn; a few days later at the Lake of Geneva with all its soft associations. But which is 'best' of things that do not compare at all, and hence cannot be reduced to a common denominator?[15] At any given moment we like best what best meets the mood of that moment.

Not to be entirely negative, however, I may say that, in my own neighbourhood, the following scenes rarely or never fail to delight beholders:—

1. View from Castle Hill, Shaftesbury.
2. View from Pilsdon Pen.
3. New Forest vistas near Brockenhurst.
4. The river Dart.
5. The coast from Trebarwith Strand to Beeny Cliff, Cornwall.[16]

Yours truly,

Thomas Hardy.

[1897.06]

[Autograph Quotation in *Notables of Britain*]

One hundred and fifty men and women were chosen by W. T. Stead, editor of the *Review of Reviews*, for inclusion in *Notables of Britain: An Album of Portraits and Autographs of the Most Eminent Subjects of Her Majesty in the 60th Year of Her Reign* (London: 'Review of Reviews' Office, 1897). According to the book's Preface, p. 3, those selected were asked to write out in their own hands 'the saying, verse, watchword, maxim, or other quotation that had been most helpful to them in their career'. Hardy's holograph submission, transcribed below, appears in facsimile on page 168, facing his photograph. Donald J. Winslow, reporting this item in the *Thomas Hardy Journal*, 8 (May 1992), pp. 68–70, also drew attention to the short 'biography' of Hardy, presumably written by Stead, on p. 202 of the book: 'Born, 1840; one who

---

[15] So draft and *LW*; *Saturday Review* reads 'denomination'.
[16] The setting, thinly disguised, of *A Pair of Blue Eyes*.

was novelist laureate of Dorsetshire, who now aspires to pre-eminence in portraying the part which the passion of sex plays in men and women.'

'This is the chief thing: Be not perturbed, for all things are according to the nature of the universal.'

(Long's) M. Aurelius Antoninus.[17]

The foregoing is one passage, among others, that I have had much in mind.[18]

Thomas Hardy.

[1897.07]

[The Wessex Society of Manchester]

Hardy accepted the presidency of the Wessex Society of Manchester and District on 10 November 1897 (*CL* ii. 181), sent messages to the Society on 7 January 1902 (*CL* iii. 1) and 20 October 1904 (*CL* iii. 142), and late in 1907 supplied it with a verse motto (*LW*, p. 363). All of these items are cast in the form of personal letters, and no publication has been discovered for any of them. Because, however, they sometimes venture upon general pronouncements and seem clearly to have been addressed to an audience at least as large as the Society's membership, the October 1904 message will be reproduced in its chronological sequence (1904.17) by way of representing this aspect of Hardy's public presence.

[1897.08]

[The Discount on Books]

A symposium on 'The Booksellers, Some Novelists, and a Discount', published in the *St James's Budget Literary Supplement*, 19 November 1897,

---

[17] TH's copy of Marcus Aurelius Antoninus, *Thoughts of the Emperor*, trans. George Long (London: Bell and Daldy, 1862), was presented to him, inscribed with this quotation, by his friend Horace Moule on New Year's Day 1865 (Beinecke).

[18] Florence Hardy told Richard Purdy (notebooks, Beinecke) that TH kept his copy of *Thoughts of the Emperor* always by his bedside; see *LW*, p. 183, and *Tess* (Wessex edn.), p. 331.

pp. 18–20, sought to examine the current practice by which booksellers allowed customers a discount of threepence in the shilling (i.e. 25 per cent) on books purchased—so that a book published, say, at six shillings would in fact be sold at four shillings and sixpence. Publishers and booksellers were said to be broadly in favour of a reduction in the discount to twopence in the shilling, and the symposium was designed to elicit—pending a decision by the Society of Authors—the personal opinions of 'some of our most prominent novelists'. Hardy's brief and somewhat evasive response was printed, as below, on page 19.

Concerning the allowance or not of discount by retail booksellers I can only repeat what I have said on the question elsewhere[19]—that it seems to me to be entirely one for the booksellers and publishers themselves, turning on details of trading, and varying with conditions of locality, such as distance from centres, and so on, which authors can know very little about as a rule.

[1897.09]

[Assistance to Dorset Guidebook]

The writer Ascott Robert Hope Moncrieff (1846–1927), editor of the fourteenth edition of *Black's Guide to Dorset* (London: Adam and Charles Black, 1897), acknowledged in his preface (p. vi) the 'valuable advice and assistance' he had received from Hardy and one or two others. Hardy knew Moncrieff as a fellow-member of the Savile Club, and in a letter of 14 February 1897 (*CL* ii. 146) he agreed to Moncrieff's printing information he had supplied so long as it was not put in his own words or as a communication from himself. There are numerous references to Hardy's novels throughout the guide, and he must certainly have contributed to the systematic collation of fictitious and 'real' places on pp. 7–8.

---

[19] This reference has not been identified.

1898

[1898.01]

'Mr. George Meredith'

Hardy was one of thirty co-signatories of a letter of congratulation to George Meredith (1828–1909) on his seventieth birthday that was published, under the heading 'Mr. George Meredith', in *The Times*, 12 February 1898, p. 10— and probably elsewhere. Hardy's letters to Edmund Gosse early in January 1898 (*CL* ii. [184]–7) show that the message, though instigated by Gosse, was actually drafted by Leslie Stephen.

[1898.02]

'To Dr. Henrik Ibsen'

Edmund Gosse was a translator and ardent supporter of the plays of the Norwegian dramatist Henrik Ibsen, and in 1898 he collaborated with the theatrical critic William Archer in organizing a scheme by which subscribers contributed one guinea each to the purchase of a set of English silver that was presented to Ibsen on 20 March, his seventieth birthday. Hardy participated in the scheme (*CL* ii. 187) and is named in the list of forty subscribers included, together with the text of the letter of presentation, in *To Dr. Henrik Ibsen*, the four-page leaflet privately printed at the Chiswick Press, 20 March 1898 (copy in Brotherton Collection, University of Leeds).

1899

[1899.01]

'A Plea for the Horses'

W. T. Stead wrote on 4 January 1899 (DCM) to seek Hardy's support for a Crusade for Peace being launched by his new campaigning journal, *War Against War*. Hardy's response, with its emphasis on the fate of horses in wartime, was somewhat tangential to the main thrust of Stead's campaign, and when it appeared (as below) in *War Against War*, 20 January 1899, p. 21, it was separated from letters addressed more directly to the Crusade and given the editorial heading 'A Plea for the Horses'. Included in Hardy's 'Personal' scrapbook (DCM) is a cutting of an abbreviated reprinting of the letter, headed 'Armies without Cavalry', in the *Daily Chronicle*, 25 January 1899, p. 8. Slightly variant readings are found both in Hardy's draft (DCM) and in the two sentences from the second paragraph subsequently included in *Life and Work*, pp. 325–6. Purdy, p. 270.

January 10, 1899.

Dear Mr Stead,

I think that a practical beginning may soon be made in the cause of Peace, though the moving force thereto may be, for a time, less perhaps a conviction of the iniquity of War than of its absurdity.

As a preliminary, all civilised nations could at least show their humanity by covenanting that no horses shall be employed in battle, except for transport. Soldiers at worst know what they are doing, but these animals are denied even the poor possibilities of glory and reward as a compensation for their sufferings. The feasibleness of their disuse would largely depend on the truth of what has been asserted—that the cost of cavalry expended on infantry would produce more effective results.

Yours truly,
Thomas Hardy.

[1899.02]

'British Authors on French Literature'

Early in 1899 Hardy was one of several British writers who responded to an invitation from the Paris daily *Le Gaulois* to contribute to its weekly literary supplement, *Le Gaulois du dimanche*, an answer to the question: 'Which French authors now dead best represented in their works the distinctive genius of France?' The resulting symposium, headed 'Les Écrivains français jugés par les écrivains anglais', was published in French in *Le Gaulois du dimanche*, 11–12 February 1899, p. [1], and simultaneously in English, under the heading 'British Authors on French Literature', in the London *Morning Post*, 11 February 1899, p. 5–6—Hardy's curiously overcrowded contribution on p. 5 reappearing that same evening in the *St James's Gazette*, p. 15. Although the *Morning Post* article speaks of having received 'proofs of the answers' from *Le Gaulois*, its English version of Hardy's letter, given below, seems clearly to be the original, not a translation back from the French; it lacks, however, the salutation, valediction, address, and date ('janvier 1899') that were present—or perhaps supplied—in the French version. Purdy, p. 306.

Your question—Which are the French authors now dead whose works are, in my opinion, most characteristic of the genius of France?—is a difficult one to answer in a brief letter owing to the many-sidedness of that genius, the variety of lights given out by the innumerable facets into which French genius has shaped itself. My reading in your literature, moreover, has not been extensive. But I should say that the fewest names it would be possible to include in the list of these immortals[1] are those of Rabelais, Descartes, Corneille, Pascal, Molière, Montesquieu, Voltaire, Diderot, J. J. Rousseau, Béranger, Victor Hugo, Auguste Comte, George Sand, and H. de Balzac. I should also like to add Gautier and Dumas, father and son. Not one of those typical writers[2] could have been born of another Nation, and not one of them can be regarded as the echo of a predecessor.

And why not also add Villon, Racine, La Fontaine, Madame de Sévigné, Bossuet, Le Sage, Chateaubriand, De Musset, and Baudelaire? Each is characteristic. But one might go too far, and I send my selection for what it may be worth.

---

[1] The phrase 'of these immortals' has no counterpart in the *Gaulois* text.
[2] For 'typical writers' the *Gaulois* text reads 'écrivains originaux'.

[1899.03]

[On Stonehenge]

The death of Sir Edmund Antrobus, 3rd baronet, of Amesbury Abbey, on 1 April 1899 called into doubt the future of the ancient monument of Stonehenge, situated on land which Sir Edmund had owned. Rumours of its possible sale brought calls for its purchase by the nation, and the *Daily Chronicle*, 24 August 1899, p. 3, published an unsigned 'interview' with Hardy under the title 'Shall Stonehenge Go?', following it up on 25 August, p. 3, with a reprinting of the Stonehenge episode from Chapter 58 of *Tess*. After Hardy's death the *Daily Chronicle* item, considerably reworked, was included in *A Window in Fleet Street* (London: John Murray, 1931), pp. 253–64, by the journalist James Milne, with whom Hardy had been on friendly terms. It is clear, however, from an untitled five-page draft manuscript in Hardy's hand (Texas) that the *Daily Chronicle* piece was based almost word for word (invented interruptions apart) upon a series of reflections on the character, history, and present condition of Stonehenge that Hardy had written out prior to Milne's arrival. That draft, though never directly published, is reproduced below as representing what Hardy actually wrote; the version printed in the *Daily Chronicle* is available in Orel, pp. 196–200. Purdy, p. 306.

I am not entitled to the expression of any authoritative opinion on the question before the public at this moment on what is to be done about Stonehenge; as I have no more knowledge of the monument than is common to or obtainable by anybody who chooses to visit it.[3] That it should be made the sure property of the nation by government purchase now that an opportunity has arisen for doing so is, I think, beyond dispute.[4] What should next be done, or if anything else should be done, is a more difficult question.

What strikes a visitor accustomed to observe the effects of years and weather on ruins so exposed as these is that the dilapidation in progress is not so insignificant as may be cursorily imagined. Wet weather and frost are, as all know, the destructive factors in the case, and to the best of my recollection it is on the South-west face of the ruin that decay goes

---

[3] TH similarly cited lack of knowledge of recent developments as his reason for declining an invitation to write about Stonehenge in 1927: see *CL* vii. 73.

[4] Stonehenge was finally given to the nation in 1918 by C. H. E. Chubb of Salisbury, who had bought it following the death of Sir Edmund Antrobus, 4th baronet, in 1915.

on most rapidly. On this south west side Time nibbles year after year, and it is only owing to the shelter afforded by the south west walls to the rest of the structure that any of the columns are erect—all these being the ones to the north east. Indeed, to those persons who have had the misfortune to be on Salisbury Plain in a piercing downpour, and have noticed, or rather have felt, how the drops pass into them like arrows, it is a matter of wonder that the erection has stood so long. Apart from the effect of the water on the stones themselves, they are gradually under-mined by the trickling down of the rain they intercept, forming pools on the ground; so that the foundation sinks on the wettest side till the stone topples over. There are only three architraves now remaining supported on their proper pillars, and as these incline[5] the architraves will slip off.

The only possible way of protecting the ruin from these driving rains which will ultimately abrade and overthrow them would be by a belt of plantations. Against such planting there is to be urged that most people consider the gaunt nakedness of its situation to be a great part of the solemnity and fascination of Stonehenge. It is by no means certain, however, that the country immediately round it was originally bare and open on all sides, and if it were enclosed by a wood approaching no nearer than, say, ten chains to the bank of earth surrounding the stone-circle, the force of these disastrous winds and rains would be broken by the trees, and the duration of the ruin lengthened far beyond its pos-sible duration now. As cultivation and agricultural buildings have latterly advanced over the plain till they are quite near the spot, and interfere with its loneliness, the objection to such planting would be less, in that the trees would shut out these incongruities.

The size of the whole structure is considerably dwarfed to the eye by the openness of the place, and as with all such erections, a strong light detracts from its impressiveness. In the brilliant noonday sunlight in which most visitors repair thither, and surrounded by bicycles and sandwich papers, the scene is not to my mind attractive, but garish and depressing. In dull threatening weather however, and in the dusk of evening, its charm is indescribable. On a day of heavy cloud the sky seems almost to form a natural roof touching the pillars, and colours are revealed on the surfaces of the stones whose presence would not be suspected on a fine day. And if a gale of wind is blowing the strange

---

[5] The unnecessary MS alteration of 'incline' to 'decline' is in a non-authorial hand.

musical hum emitted by the place adds an effect which can never be forgotten.[6] To say that on moonlight nights it is also at its finest is a commonplace.

The problem of the purpose and date of Stonehenge could possibly be narrowed down from its present vagueness, if not settled, by a few days excavation near the spot. This, if done at all, should be carried out under the strictest supervision. Personally I confess to a liking for the state of dim conjecture in which we stand with regard to its history. All one can say is that the building was probably erected after the barrow-period of interment in these islands, from the fact that one or two barrows seem to have been interfered with in its construction.

[1899.04]

[Misrepresented Message on Dreyfus Affair]

Invited by the Paris journal *La Vogue* to comment on the latest developments in the Dreyfus affair, Hardy delayed his response and then, on 12 July 1899, told the editor (*CL* ii. 223) that 'at this late date, when discussion of the case has been so prolonged and exhaustive, I consider that any remarks of mine thereupon would be superfluous'. The journal's symposium, 'L'Affaire Dreyfus à l'étranger', published in its August 1899 issue (new series 3, pp. 106–20), did not include Hardy's letter, but reported on its final page: 'Quant au grand romancier anglais M. Thomas Hardy, il estime qu'on a déjà trop écrit sur ce sujet.' See also *CL* ii. 329.

[1899.05]

'Favourite Books of 1899'

Published in the *Academy*, 9 December 1899, p. 695, under the heading 'Favourite Books of 1899. Some Readers', were several replies to a request, 'sent out to a number of well-known men and women, both literary and practical', for the titles of the two books 'read with most interest and pleasure'

---

[6] Cf. *Tess* (Wessex edn.), p. 501.

during the past year. Hardy's response—first noted by Werner Bies in *Thomas Hardy Society Review*, 1 (1980), p. 193—appeared, as below, at the head of the list.

MR THOMAS HARDY.

Letters of Robert and Mrs Browning.[7]
Yeats's *Wind Among the Reeds.*[8]

[1899.06]

[Revision of Article in *Folk-Lore*]

Hardy is quoted or mentioned on three occasions in 'Dorset Folklore Collected in 1897', compiled by H. Colley March and published in the Folk-Lore Society journal *Folk-Lore*, 10 (December 1899), pp. 478–89. On an item about 'toad-doctors' (cf. *LW*, p. 115) he comments, ' "A toad-bag" is even now a common expression' (p. 480). To a report of a maypole having formerly been set up at Piddletrenthide he adds, 'And at many other villages in my childhood' (p. 481). The introduction to a group of local stories supplied by the wife of Major-General Charles Edward Astell of Piddlehinton states that 'Mr. Thomas Hardy has made some alterations in the spelling, so that the dialect may be the better represented' (p. 482). It was of this last item that Hardy had written to his folklorist friend Edward Clodd on 31 October 1898: 'I return the folklore proof through you in case I may have taken too many liberties with it, which you can *dele* at pleasure' (*CL* ii. 204).

[1899.07]

'A Christmas Ghost Story'

By the end of 1899 the war against the Boers in South Africa was well under way—and British public opinion patriotically inflamed. It was in this

---

[7] *The Letters of Robert Browning and Elizabeth Barrett Barrett, 1845–1846*, 2 vols. (London: Smith, Elder, 1899). The Brownings' son was much criticized for allowing publication of the letters, but TH later claimed to have encouraged him to do so: see Elliott Felkin, 'Days with Thomas Hardy', *Encounter*, 18 (April 1962), p. 30; also *CL* ii. 277.

[8] William Butler Yeats, *The Wind among the Reeds* (London: Elkin Mathews, 1899).

atmosphere that Hardy's poem 'A Christmas Ghost-Story', published in its
original eight-line form (*CPW* i. 121) in the *Westminster Gazette*, 23 December
1899, p. 5, was criticized in a *Daily Chronicle* leading article, 25 December,
p. 4, on the grounds that the soldier's ghost who wondered what had become
of the Christian message of peace was an unheroic figment of Hardy's imagination and 'not one of the Dublin fusiliers who cried amidst the storm of
bullets at Tugela, "Let us make a name for ourselves!"' Hardy's elegant
letter of reply, headed 'A Christmas Ghost Story' and dated 25 December,
appeared as below in the *Daily Chronicle*, 28 December, p. 8, and was rather
gracelessly acknowledged in an editorial on page 4. That he had devoted
much of Christmas Day to its composition is clear from his densely worked
surviving draft (DCM) and from the several corrections made even to the
letter as sent (Princeton). The letter was reprinted, together with the poem,
in the 29 December 1899 issue of W. T. Stead's *War Against War in South
Africa*, p. 166. Purdy, pp. 306–7.

Dec. 25.

Sir,

In your interesting leading article of this morning, on Christmas Day,
you appear to demur to the character of the soldier's phantom in my few
lines entitled 'A Christmas Ghost Story' (printed in the *Westminster
Gazette* for Dec. 23), as scarcely exhibiting the primary quality of, say,
a Dublin Fusilier, which is assumed to be physical courage; the said
phantom being plaintive, embittered, and sad at the prevalence of war
during a nominal Æra of peace. But surely there is artistic propriety—
and, if I may say so, moral and religious propriety—in making him, or it,
feel thus, especially in a poem intended for Christmas Day. One's
modern fancy of a disembodied spirit—unless intentionally humorous
—is that of an entity which has passed into a tenuous, impartial, sexless,
fitful, form of existence, to which bodily courage is a contradiction in
terms. Having no physical frame to defend or sacrifice, how can he show
either courage or fear? His views are no longer local; nations are all one
to him; his country is not bounded by seas, but is co-extensive with the
globe itself, if it does not even include all the inhabited planets of the sky.
He has put off the substance, and has put on, in part at any rate, the
essence of the Universal.

If we go back to the ancient fancy on this subject, and look into the
works of great imaginative writers, they seem to construct their soldier-
shades much on the same principle—often with a stronger infusion of
emotion, and less of sturdiness. The Homeric ghost of Patroclus was

plaintively anxious about his funeral rites,[9] and Virgil's military ghosts—though some of them certainly were cheerful, and eager for war news—were as a body tremulous and pensive.[10] The prophet Samuel, a man of great will and energy when on earth, was 'disquieted'[11] and obviously apprehensive when he was raised by the Witch of Endor[12] at the request of Saul. Moreover, the authors of these Latin, Greek, and Hebrew fantasies were ignorant of the teaching of Christmas Day, that which alone moved the humble Natal shade to speak at all.

In Christian times Dante makes the chief Farinata exhibit a fine scornfulness,[13] but even his Cæsar, Hector, Æneas, Saladin, and heroes of that stamp,[14] have, if I am not mistaken, an aspect neither sad nor joyful, and only reach the level of serenity. Hamlet's father, impliedly martial in life, was not particularly brave as a spectre.[15] In short, and speaking generally, these creatures of the imagination are uncertain, fleeting, and quivering, like winds, mists, gossamer-webs, and fallen autumn leaves; they are sad, pensive, and frequently feel more or less sorrow for the acts of their corporeal years.

Thus I venture to think that the phantom of a slain soldier, neither British nor Boer, but a composite, typical phantom, may consistently be made to regret on or about Christmas Eve (when even the beasts of the field kneel, according to a tradition of my childhood)[16] the battles of his life and war in general, although he may have shouted in the admirable ardor and pride of his fleshtime, as he is said to have done: 'Let us make a name for ourselves!'

Your obedient servant,

Thomas Hardy.

---

[9] Homer, *Iliad*, xxiii. 69–92.   [10] Virgil, *Aeneid*, vi. 477–93.   [11] 1 Sam. 28: 15.

[12] 1 Sam. 28: 7. Spelled 'En-dor' in Princeton MS, as in the Authorized Version.

[13] In Canto 10, lines 31–6, of the *Inferno* Farinata stands erect in hell, as if holding it in great disdain ('a gran dispitto').

[14] *Inferno*, Canto 4, lines 122–3, 129.

[15] *Hamlet*, I. i. 148–9: 'it started like a guilty thing | Upon a fearful summons'.

[16] Cf. TH's poem 'The Oxen' (*CPW* ii. 206) and *Tess* (Wessex edn.), p. 143.

1900

[1900.01]

[*The Sphere*]

Hardy had published fiction in both the *Illustrated London News* and the *English Illustrated Magazine* and was on terms of guarded friendliness with Clement Shorter, their energetic editor. Not surprisingly, therefore, he contributed a poem, 'At the War Office', to the first (27 January 1900) number of Shorter's new illustrated magazine, the *Sphere*, and sent the message of congratulation that was printed, along with many others, in the *Sphere*, 3 February 1900, p. 70, under the heading 'The Verdict of the Press and Public'. The initialled but undated holograph note (David Holmes) that Hardy actually sent to Shorter reads slightly differently from the published text reproduced below, his own original heading, 'The Sphere', having been editorially absorbed into the body of his message.

The title, THE SPHERE, is a very happy one. There is no suggestion of crudeness in the contents as might have been expected in a first number, and it seems to have struck into the pace on its sudden start as if it had been going for years.

[1900.02]

'*Tess* at the Coronet Theatre'

Although the Lorimer Stoddard stage adaptation of *Tess of the d'Urbervilles* had received a United Kingdom 'copyright' performance in March 1897 (see 1897.03), continuing uncertainty as to the likelihood of an actual London production was a major factor in Hardy's refusal, in November 1899 (*CL* ii. 239), to countenance an alternative dramatization by Hugh Arthur Kennedy. When, therefore, a staging of Kennedy's adaptation opened, still unauthorized, at the Coronet Theatre, Notting Hill Gate, on 19 February 1900, and was tepidly reviewed in *The Times*, 20 February, p. 9, Hardy promptly dissociated himself from the production in a letter published, as below, in *The Times* 21 February 1900, p. 4, under the editorial heading '*Tess* at the Coronet Theatre'. Kennedy replied (*The Times*, 8 March, p. 11) that he had understood that Hardy's permission would be forthcoming, and the play itself, transferred to the Comedy Theatre, ran until 28 April. See Marguerite Roberts, '*Tess*' *in the Theatre* (Toronto: University of Toronto Press, 1950), pp. l–lix. Purdy, p. 307.

Dorchester. Feb. 20.

Sir,

As I find I am naturally supposed to have something to do with the production of *Tess of the D'Urbervilles* at the Coronet Theatre last night, I shall be glad if you will allow me to state that I have not authorized such a dramatization, and that I am ignorant of the form it has taken, except in so far as I gather from the newspapers.

Yours faithfully,

Thomas Hardy.

[1900.03]

[?Obituary for Laurence W. Pike?]

Hardy was on friendly terms with Laurence Warburton Pike, JP, of Wareham, an active advocate of temperance and vegetarianism, an opponent of blood sports, and a vigorous campaigner for the compassionate treatment of horses wounded in battle—a cause which Hardy himself had very much at heart (cf. 1899.01 and *CL* ii. 232, 248). Pike died, aged 50, on 30 August 1900, and although Hardy did not write the *Dorset County Chronicle* obituary (6 September, p. 7), it is clear from his letters to Clement Shorter before and after Pike's death (*CL* ii. 265, 266) that he certainly supplied the photograph of Pike published in the 'Men and Women' section of the *Sphere*, 15 September 1900, p. 337, and was very probably the author of the brief unsigned obituary that appeared, as below, on the same page.

The death is announced of Mr Laurence W. Pike, J.P. for Dorset, who will be chiefly remembered as the writer of several letters to the *Times*[1] and other papers last year on the humane treatment of horses wounded in battle. Up to the time of his last illness he had continued his efforts to give shape to some practical scheme bearing on the object he had in view. Mr Pike had the courage of his convictions on many other matters, notably that of sporting, which, with rare self-denial, he had abandoned in the belief that such a form of recreation was unjustifiable.[2]

[1900.04]

The American National Red Cross Society

Frank D. Higbee, somewhat loosely associated with the American Red Cross, was visiting England in the autumn of 1900 in pursuit of an elaborate and in practice unworkable fundraising scheme which aimed to 'secure greetings to the United States on the dawn of the new century from as many of the rulers of civilized nations as possible, and dispose of [copies of] these greetings for cash to meetings which would be arranged for the night of Dec. 31 in every city of importance in the United States' (*New York Times*, 21 December 1900, p. 1). In a letter of 3 October 1900 (*CL* ii. 267) Hardy declined Higbee's request for a meeting but enclosed, on a separate sheet headed as above, a holograph testimonial to the Red Cross itself (Colby). That message seems never to have been used by the Red Cross, either at the time or at a later date; it was, however, quoted as an item of bibliographical interest under the heading 'Thomas Hardy Writes to the American Red Cross' in the *Biblio* (Pompano Lakes, NJ) for November–December 1925, p. 857, and included by Hardy himself in *Life and Work*, p. 330, on the basis of a retained draft (DCM). The text below is that of Hardy's original MS. Purdy, p. 270.

A society for the relief of suffering is entitled to every man's gratitude; and though, in the past century, material growth has been out of all proportion to moral growth, the existence of such a society as this

---

[1] Pike's first and most substantial letter on the subject appeared in *The Times*, 10 November 1899, p. 15.
[2] Cf. penultimate paragraph of TH's letter to Florence Henniker, 24 November 1899 (*CL* ii. 238).

leaves[3] one not altogether without hope that during the next hundred years the relations between our inward and our outward progress may become less of a reproach to civilization.

[1900.05]

[Assistance to William Barnes Entry in *DNB*]

The critic Thomas Seccombe (1866–1923), invited to write the article on William Barnes for the *Dictionary of National Biography*, sought Hardy's assistance in two letters of May 1900 (DCM), and it is clear from Hardy's letters to Seccombe on 21 October 1900 and to Florence Henniker the following day (*CL* ii. 269, 270) that he did indeed read and 'correct' the article at some stage of its production. The article as published includes an extended quotation from Hardy's obituary of Barnes (1886.02).

---

[3] For 'existence . . . leaves' draft and *LW* read 'existence of your Society leaves'.

1901

[1901.01]

[Revision of *Chambers's Encyclopædia* Entry]

Hardy wrote to W. and R. Chambers of Edinburgh, publishers of *Chambers's Encyclopædia*, on 16 July 1899 (National Library of Scotland) to ask if he might be given an opportunity to correct some errors in the references to himself in the 1895 edition—the identification of his birthplace as 'Upper Boghampton' having doubtless been a particular source of irritation. His representations were evidently effective, in that the 'Thomas Hardy' entry in the *Encyclopædia*'s 1901 edition (v. 556) is more than twice as long as that of 1895, spells 'Bockhampton' correctly, and includes a highly favourable critique of his work. What is not known is the extent to which Hardy himself participated in the revision process.

[1901.02]

[Revisions to William Archer Interview]

It is clear that William Archer's interview of Hardy in February 1901 was an arranged encounter between friends and that Hardy was given the opportunity to read and alter the text (*CL* ii. 279, 281) prior to its first publication as 'Real Conversations. Conversation II. With Mr. Thomas Hardy' in *Pall Mall Magazine*, 22 (April 1901), pp. 527–37, and again before it was collected, lightly revised, in Archer's *Real Conversations* (London: William Heinemann, 1904), pp. 29–50. He seems to have made only minor alterations on the first occasion and, on the second, to have added 'a very few words . . . where I thought they were required for clearness' (*CL* iii. 76). Extracts from the *Real Conversations* version of the interview are included in *Interviews and Recollections*, pp. 65–71.

[1901.03]

[Honorary Membership of the Whitefriars Club]

When Hardy accepted honorary membership of the Whitefriars Club (see 1874.02) he must have anticipated some degree of publicity, at least within the Club itself, and his acceptance letter of 17 March 1901 indeed appeared, as below, in the 'Club Notes' section of the *Whitefriars Journal*, 1 (March 1901), p. 11. The reasons for the invitation, and especially for its timing, were made sufficiently clear by the announcement, within the same 'Club Notes', of a forthcoming 'pilgrimage' to Wessex: see 1901.05.

Max Gate, Dorchester, March 17th, 1901.

Dear Mr Spurgeon,[1]

I have much pleasure in accepting honorary membership of the Whitefriars Club, though I feel it to be a distinction I have not deserved.

I remember the occasion on which I dined with the Club in 1874 according to the book of 'Chronicles' you kindly sent.[2] I am not quite sure whose guest I was, either Black's or Gibbon's,[3] the latter I think, as they were the only two members I knew.

Yours truly,

Thomas Hardy.

[1901.04]

'The Curse of Militarism'

The London journal *The Young Man* published in May 1901, pp. 145–9, an essay on 'The Curse of Militarism' by William Clarke (1852–1901), writer on contemporary political, social, and cultural issues. Hardy—along with Edward Clodd, Walter Crane, the Dean of Durham, and several others— was invited to respond, his brief comments appearing, as below, in the

---

[1] (Sir) Arthur Spurgeon (1861–1938), journalist and publisher, secretary of the Whitefriars Club at this date.   [2] i.e. *The Whitefriars' Chronicles*: see 1874.02.

[3] William Black (see 1890.05), Scottish novelist, with whom Hardy became friendly early in his own career (see e.g. *CL* i. 45); for Charles Gibbon (1843–90), another Scottish novelist, see *CL* iv. 77–8.

second instalment of the resulting symposium, also headed 'The Curse of Militarism', in *The Young Man*, 15 (June 1901), p. 191. Clarke's essay was later reprinted in *William Clarke: A Collection of his Writings*, edited by Herbert Burrows and John A. Hobson (London: Swan Sonnenschein, 1908). Purdy, p. 307.

I have read 'The Curse of Militarism', but have no remark of any value to make. Aggressiveness being one of the laws of nature, by condemning war we condemn the scheme of the universe; while by exalting war we exalt sentiments which all worthy religions agree in calling evil, and whose triumphs the world would do well to escape by self-annihilation.

[1901.05]

[Speech to the Whitefriars Club]

On 29 June 1901 members of the Whitefriars Club (see 1901.03) and their wives ventured out of London on a Wessex 'pilgrimage' that began at the Wool railway station, passed through Bere Regis, Puddletown, and Dorchester, and ended at Max Gate, where the pilgrims were entertained to afternoon tea and strawberries and cream. The party, about a hundred strong, was led by Clement Shorter, but most of the arrangements had been made by Clive Holland (i.e. Charles James Hankinson, 1866–1959), journalist and photographer. Speeches of thanks were made before the visitors left to take the train back to London, and a third-person report of Hardy's reply was included in the account of the day (unsigned but written by Clive Holland) that was published, as below, in the *Dorchester Telegram*, 2 July 1901, p. 4. That account was reprinted in the *Whitefriars Journal*, 1 (December 1901), pp. 7–15, with Hardy's speech on p. 14.

In brief acknowledgment, Mr Hardy said that he and Mrs Hardy were delighted to see so many guests. He likened the 'pilgrimage' to that of which Chaucer wrote, only that here to-day there was no 'poor man'.[4] [Laughter.] It was a surprise to him the club had arranged to see so much. Should they ever visit Dorset again, he would suggest that they start their drive at Bulbarrow, toward the north of the county, and

---

[4] Cf. the Prologue to the *Canterbury Tales*: 'A good man was ther of religioun | And was a poore Person of a town'.

proceed along the edge of the valley to Wynyard's Gap. This way would show them that Dorset had views which would compare even with the famous view from Richmond Hill, of which so much had lately been written. He did not know why Dorset had been so little thought of. Perhaps it was the result of a report which certain commissioners who were sent hither during the agitation against the Factory Acts gave. So depressing was their report of the industrial and social conditions of the county that it had seemed, unjustly, to cut Dorset quite off ever since.

[1901.06]

[The View from Richmond Hill]

Included in *Life and Work*, p. 332, is the text of a brief letter about the view from Richmond Hill that Hardy wrote to a correspondent named Frederic Chapman in June 1901. Although no contemporary appearance of the letter has been discovered, it certainly addressed an issue of public interest—see, for example, the reference to Richmond Hill in 1901.05 and letter headed 'The View from Richmond Hill' in *The Times*, 2 July 1901, p. 12—and may either have been published or at least intended for publication at the time. The text in *Collected Letters*, ii. 290 (from the MS at Mount Saint Vincent University), is identical with that in *Life and Work* except that in the latter the 'Lass' of Richmond Hill is referred to as 'her' rather than collectively with Richmond Hill itself as 'them'.

[1901.07]

[Abolition of the Royal Buckhounds]

Hardy was mentioned in the February 1900 issue of *Humanity: The Journal of the Humanitarian League*, p. 12, as one of more than 200 signatories to a recent memorial to the Prime Minister protesting against 'the so-called sport of hunting park deer' and urging disbandment of the pack of Royal Buckhounds, dogs specially bred to hunt male deer. The next year the new king, Edward VII, decided that the pack should indeed be abolished, and on 1 July 1901 the Humanitarian League held a meeting in London to celebrate that decision (*The Times*, 2 July 1901, p. 5). Hardy—responding to a request from Henry S. Salt (1851–1939), the author and humanitarian—sent a message that was read out at the meeting and printed as below in *Humanity*, 4 (August 1901), pp. 155–6. Hardy's holograph MS (Princeton) and draft (DCM) differ from the printed text only in retaining Salt's name at the foot of the letter as addressee. Purdy, p. 307.

Max Gate, Dorchester, June 27, 1901.

Dear Sir,

I am unable to send anything that could be read with advantage at the meeting, my views on sport in general being what are called extreme, that is, I hold it to be, in any case, immoral and unmanly to cultivate a pleasure in compassing the death of our weaker and simpler fellow-creatures by cunning, instead of learning to regard their destruction, if a necessity, as an odious task, akin to that, say, of the common hangman. In this view the hunting of tame stags is but a detail.

Yours truly,

Thomas Hardy.

[1901.08]

[Assistance to Clive Holland]

'A Pilgrimage to Wessex', an article by Clive Holland (see 1901.05) published in the New York *Critic*, 39 (August 1901), pp. 136–44, was reprinted verbatim from the booklet of the same title issued by the Whitefriars Club prior to its 29 June 1901 visit to Dorset and Max Gate, and the *Critic*'s headnote echoed the *Whitefriars Journal*, 1 (May 1901), pp. 10–11, in making extravagant claims for the authority of the article's references to *Tess of the d'Urbervilles*: 'The letterpress, so far as topography is concerned, has been revised by Mr. Hardy and bears his imprimatur. This article is, therefore, the first authorized statement ever published concerning the topographical features of the most famous of the Wessex novels.' Hardy's interventions, however, are likely to have been few and slight: he did for a time assist Holland in locating and photographing 'Wessex' locations—Holland's *Thomas Hardy, O.M.: The Man, his Works, and the Land of Wessex* (London: Herbert Jenkins, 1933) reproduces in facsimile a list in Hardy's hand of places in *Jude the Obscure*—but grew increasingly distrustful of his inquisitiveness (e.g. *CL* vi. 206–7).

[1901.09]

[The Beauty of Wessex]

Following the Whitefriars Club visit to Dorset on 29 June 1901 (see 1901.05), the *New York Times Saturday Review*, 6 July 1901, p. 485, printed a brief report—evidently originating with Clive Holland—to the effect that the interest of the scenery traversed by the 'pilgrims' did not arise 'from its own intrinsic beauty, but from the novelist's interpretation of it'. An irritated Hardy sent Clement Shorter a corrective paragraph, worried whether it should be published with or without attribution, or even published at all (*CL* ii. 297), and eventually allowed it to appear, as his own work, in Shorter's regular 'A Literary Letter', *Sphere*, 7 September 1901, p. 288. The same paragraph was published (as from the *Sphere*) in the *Academy* of the same date, p. [183], and both appearances were at least technically anticipated by its printing (again with acknowledgement to the *Sphere*) in the London *Literary World*, 6 September 1901, p. 161. The text below is that of the *Sphere*, emended in two instances (see footnotes) on the basis of the corrected proof that Hardy preserved in his 'Personal' scrapbook (DCM). Reprinted (as from the *Academy*) in *Life and Art*, p. 135. Purdy, p. 307.

This statement is rather unfair to Wessex, and, indeed, quite inaccurate, as will be evident when it is explained that the party of visitors did not go near the 'intrinsically romantic'[5] spots so imperfectly[6] described in the novels but, like almost all tourists, adhered for the most part to the London highway and the branch highway passing through the heath district,[7] which is rather impressive and lonely than 'romantic' or 'beautiful'. Had they, for instance, visited Shaston or Shaftesbury, Bullbarrow, Nettlecombe Tout, Dogbury[8] Hill, High Stoy, Cross in Hand, Bubb Down Hill, Toller Down, Wynyard's Gap, and a dozen other such places for inland scenery, and the coast cliffs between Swanage and Lyme Regis for marine, such a remark could not have been

---

[5] TH had evidently seen, not the *New York Times* report itself, but the elaborated paraphrase contained in an incorrectly identified cutting in his 'Personal' scrapbook (DCM). Shorter's brief introduction to TH's paragraph quotes from the same source the statement that the Whitefriars pilgrims 'found that the Wessex country was not intrinsically romantic and beautiful, but could only move through the illusions produced by the novelist'.

[6] For 'spots so imperfectly' *Sphere* reads 'spots imperfectly'.

[7] Proof shows that for 'the heath district' TH first wrote 'Egdon Heath'.

[8] For 'Dogbury' *Sphere* reads 'Dogberry', TH's proof correction having apparently been ignored.

made. But then, most of these spots lie miles out of the regular way, and few of them can be reached except on foot. The pilgrims were not absent from London much more than twelve hours altogether, returning there the same evening; and it is utterly impossible to see the recesses of this county in such a manner, not to mention those adjoining.

[1901.10]

[On Fordington St George]

Max Gate lay in the parish of Fordington St George, Hardy admired the architecture of the church and valued its association with the family of the Revd Henry Moule (1801–80), the vicar from 1829 until his death, and Emma Hardy regularly worshipped there. As a member of the church's Restoration Committee, Hardy supported in October 1901 an appeal for funds drafted by the current vicar, the Revd Sidney Boulter, but pencilled into the draft a paragraph assuring potential donors that 'no mischief to the architecture' was intended (*CL* ii. 301). No copy of the appeal as issued has yet been traced, but the inclusion of such a paragraph is mentioned in a pseudonymous letter to the *Dorset County Chronicle* quoted by C. J. P. Beatty in *Thomas Hardy: Conservation Architect. His Work for the Society for the Protection of Ancient Buildings* (Dorchester: Dorset Natural History and Archaeological Society, 1995) p. 31, and in a report on the church submitted to the Society for the Protection of Ancient Buildings in February 1903 by Hardy's friend the Revd Thomas Perkins, rector of Turnworth. Hardy collaborated with Perkins in writing that report—after first resigning from the Restoration Committee in protest against the extensive alterations that were in fact being planned (*CL* iii. 50)—and in November 1906 he wrote directly to the Society in response to an enquiry about the Fordington situation as it then stood (*CL* iii. 235–6). For a full account of Hardy's involvement in this episode, see Beatty, *Conservation Architect*, pp. 27–37.

[1901.11]

[?Inspired Statement in *Literature*?]

The weekly journal *Literature*, published by *The Times*, was the forerunner of *The Times Literary Supplement*, and Hardy evidently used the 'Notes of the Day' section of its issue of 9 November 1901, p. 432, as the platform for an indirect assertion—a week before the publication of his second volume of poems—of his continuing interest in the writing of novels and short stories.

Mr Thomas Hardy denies the statement of a contemporary[9] that he has given up writing novels.

[1901.12]

[On *Christmas at the Mermaid*]

Hardy's 2 December 1901 letter (*CL* ii. 304) to Theodore Watts-Dunton (1832–1914), Swinburne's friend and guardian, included extravagant praise of Watts-Dunton's poem, *Christmas at the Mermaid*, just reissued as a Christmas gift book. The letter had been private, but when Watts-Dunton asked (3 December 1901, DCM) if a sentence from it might be used in an advertisement for his book, Hardy evidently felt obliged to consent (*CL* ii. 304). The following paragraph—adapted from two sentences originally separated—duly appeared, prefaced by 'Mr. Thomas Hardy says', at the head of 'Some Press and Other Opinions' in John Lane's advertisement for *Christmas at the Mermaid* in the *Athenaeum*, 14 December 1901, p. 800. The first two paragraphs of the letter were subsequently quoted in their entirety both by James Douglas, *Theodore Watts-Dunton: Poet, Novelist, Critic* (London: Hodder and Stoughton, 1904), pp. 440–1, and by Thomas Hare and Arthur Compton-Rickett, *The Life and Letters of Theodore Watts-Dunton*, 2 vols. (London: T. C. & E. C. Jack, 1916), pp. 286–7.

I was carried back right into Armada times by David Gwynn's vivid story. The absence of Shakespeare from the 'Mermaid' strikes me as being one of the finest touches of the poem; and we feel him, in some curious way, more than if he had been there.

---

[9] i.e. a contemporary newspaper or magazine; the reference is presumably to an item in the 'News Notes' section of the *Bookman*, November 1901, p. 39, that read in part: 'Our readers will learn with dismay that Mr. Hardy has ceased to take interest in fiction, and does not mean to write any more novels.'

[1902.01]

The Abbey Gate-House, Cerne Abbas, Dorset

A brief unsigned article, headed 'The Abbey Gate-House, Cerne Abbas, Dorset', was published in the professional journal, the *Builder*, 8 February 1902, p. 132, as the accompaniment to a set of architectural drawings bearing the name of Emma Hardy's nephew Gordon Gifford, whom Hardy himself had instructed in the basics of architecture. The article is unsigned, but Hardy's authorship is effectively confirmed by the conclusion of his 13 January 1902 letter to the editor of the *Builder* (*CL* vii. 133): 'I need hardly add that the drawing and description are gratuitously offered, the spot being one in which I have long taken an interest, as you may know.' The article is reproduced below in its entirety, although it seems unlikely that Hardy was responsible for the final sentence.

The now melancholy and perishing townlet of Cerne Abbas (in Domesday Book 'Cernel',[1] or 'Cerneli'), about eight miles north from Dorchester, traces its ruin, like so many similar places, to the suppression of the Abbey in its midst; which was unhappily followed by the destruction of most of the conventual buildings. The drawing here given represents the chief fragment which remains standing.

The only relics of the Abbey Church itself are some broken mouldings lying in a farmhouse garden, portion of an altar-piece built up in a cottage wall, and some trefoiled work of almost Greek delicacy, now fixed over the churchyard doorway. From these fragments it appears that the church must have been much earlier in date than the gateway, and withal a beautiful example of the purest geometrical Decorated style. Not one stone of it now remains upon another, and those visitors

---

[1] Abbot's Cernel was TH's 'Wessex' name for Cerne Abbas.

to the lonely spot who care to attempt a mediæval problem may sit and conjecture from the position of the Abbey House, and the few other walls still erect, whereabouts could have been situate the church and cloisters—not an easy question to decide. The site is a cunningly chosen one in an attractive vale, and the buildings, when at their best, must have been among the fairest sights of Merrie England—fronted by fish-ponds, backed by vineyards (according to tradition), and by the lofty, green 'Giant's Hill'.

Some archæologists have doubted if the gateway could have been wide enough for the chief entrance to the Abbey; and have supposed it the entrance to the Abbots' house.[2] Its picturesque surroundings make it a favourites subject for sketchers, but so far as we are aware no drawing of it to scale is accessible. The present one is by Mr G. Gifford, of the office of Sir A. W. Blomfield & Sons,[3] from measurements taken by him on the spot. The drawing was sent to us by Mr Thomas Hardy, the eminent novelist, who lives in the neighbourhood and takes a great interest in its antiquities, and we have much pleasure in publishing it at his request.

[1902.02]

Victor Hugo

Asked by Dr Mario Borsa (14 February 1902, DCM) for a statement in celebration of the centenary of Victor Hugo's birth, Hardy responded with a brief message that was published—translated into Italian and accompanied by a facsimile of his signature—along with other such tributes in the Trieste newspaper *Il piccolo della sera*, 26 February 1902, under the heading 'Nel centenario di Vittor Hugo' (cutting in Hardy's 'Personal' scrapbook, DCM). The text below, however, is that of Hardy's draft (DCM): headed 'Victor Hugo', it corresponds closely to the Italian translation and was very slightly revised for inclusion in *Life and Work*, p. 334. Purdy, p. 270.

---

[2] This interpretation, partly restated in a letter printed in the next issue of the *Builder* (15 February 1902, p. 161), is now generally accepted: see *An Inventory of the Historical Monuments in the County of Dorset. Volume I: West Dorset* (London: Her Majesty's Stationery Office, 1952; rev. edn., 1973), pp. 77, 79, and plate 105.

[3] The London architectural firm for which TH himself had worked in the 1860s and to which he had recently recommended Gordon Gifford (*CL* ii. 245).

His memory must endure; for his[4] works are the Cathedrals of literary architecture, his imagination adding greatness to the colossal, and charm to the small.

[1902.03]

'The Wessex of Thomas Hardy'

> Hardy and his wife had gone to some trouble (*CL* ii. 131–3) to assist Bertram Windle (see 1896.04) in the preparation of his topographical survey *The Wessex of Thomas Hardy*, illustrated by Edmund H. New and published by John Lane in 1902. To Hardy's annoyance, the anonymous review of the book in the *Guardian* of 9 April 1902, p. 513, included an attack on himself as an over-praised 'writer of picturesque tales' who had demonstrated 'obvious ignorance of archæology' and fostered an erroneous identification of the historical Wessex with Dorsetshire. His letter of protest, published as below under the heading 'The Wessex of Thomas Hardy' in the *Guardian*, 16 April 1902, p. 551, was followed on the same page by an unrepentant rejoinder from the original reviewer. Purdy, pp. 307–8.

April 11, 1902.

Sir,

Some unusually distinct misstatements are made by your critic of *The Wessex of Thomas Hardy*, by Professor Windle, in your impression of the 9th inst.

He says:—

'Mr Hardy, by the application of this name [Wessex] to Dorsetshire has done an historical wrong which it will be very difficult to undo. . . . If Wessex . . . is to be identified with a special shire, every historian knows that the honour is due far more to Hampshire than to Dorsetshire.'

So far from my ever having identified Wessex with Dorsetshire, I have invariably shown that I do not so identify it, but make it to include six counties; I have described Winchester under the old name of Wintonceaster as its capital; have mentioned the Thames as its northern boundary; and, above all, have exhibited its area in a map whose outline

---

[4] For 'endure; for his' *LW* reads 'endure. His'.

coincides with that given to the old kingdom by historians of early England.

He says:—

'A passage is actually quoted [from a book of mine] as to the finding of a buried Roman soldier in a garden at Dorchester, which is absolute nonsense in every line so far as an interment of the Romano-British period is concerned.'

If it were nonsense it would not, perhaps, much matter in a work of imagination.[5] But it so happens that several such skeletons were unearthed by myself many years ago,[6] lying precisely as described, one having three urns and a bottle standing in contact with its breast and a fibula resting on its forehead. The urns, which I still possess, are of the well-known Romano-British pattern, of which many examples may be seen in museums; and the fibula also matches those usually found in such collections and labelled as of the same period.

Your reviewer's remarks upon the place-names, too, are full of misrepresentations, though I cannot here enter into the necessary detail for explaining why. Altogether I fail to see any justification for these inaccurate statements, which are made, moreover, concerning the writings of a person who is not the author of the book reviewed.[7]

Thomas Hardy.

[1902.04]

'M. Maeterlinck's Apology for Nature'

When *The Buried Temple* (London: George Allen, 1902)—a translation by Alfred Sutro of *Le Temple enseveli*, a volume of essays by the Belgian dramatist Maurice Maeterlinck (1862–1949)—was anonymously reviewed in the *Academy and Literature*, 3 May 1902, pp. 451–2, Hardy took strong exception to the following quotation from Maeterlinck: 'Nature does not appear to be just from our point of view; but we have absolutely no means of judging whether she be not just from her own. The fact that she pays no heed to the

---

[5] The reading 'fiction' for 'imagination' is found in what appears to be a contemporary typescript copy of this letter in TH's 'Personal' scrapbook (DCM). See *Index*, HrT 1600, where place of publication is incorrectly given as *Manchester Guardian*.

[6] Cf. 'Some Romano-British Relics' (1884.01).

[7] Scrapbook typescript adds 'I am, Sir, | Your obedient servant,'.

morality of our own actions does not warrant the inference that she has no morality, or that ours is the only one there can be' (p. 452). Hardy copied that passage and others from the review into one of his literary notebooks (*LN* ii. 125–6) and wrote the letter that appeared, as below, in the *Academy and Literature*, 17 May 1902, pp. 514–15, under the heading—presumably though not certainly editorial—'M. Maeterlinck's Apology for Nature'. A corrected proof of the letter was preserved in Hardy's 'Personal' scrapbook (DCM), even though the alterations seem not to be in his hand, and he probably drew upon it for the reprinting in *Life and Work*, pp. 338–9, where the title of Maeterlinck's book is incorrectly given as *Apology for Nature*. Reprinted in *Life and Art*, pp. 131–2. Purdy, p. 271.

Max Gate, Dorchester.

Sir,

In your review of M. Maeterlinck's book you quote with seeming approval his vindication of Nature's ways, which is (as I understand it) to the effect that, though she does not appear to be just from our point of view, she may practice a scheme of morality unknown to us, in which she is just. Now, admit but the bare possibility of such a hidden morality, and she would go out of court without the slightest stain on her character, so certain should we feel that indifference to morality was beneath her greatness.

Far be it from my wish to disturb any comforting fantasy, if it be[8] barely tenable. But alas, no profound reflection can be needed to detect the sophistry in M. Maeterlinck's argument, and to see that the original difficulty recognized by thinkers like Schopenhauer, Hartmann, Haeckel,[9] &c., and by most of the persons called pessimists, remains unsurmounted.

Pain has been, and pain is: no new sort of morals in Nature can remove pain from the past and make it pleasure for those who are its infallible estimators, the bearers thereof. And no injustice, however slight, can be atoned for by her future generosity, however ample, so long as we consider Nature to be, or to stand for, unlimited power. The exoneration of an omnipotent Mother by her retrospective justice becomes an absurdity when we ask, what made the foregone injustice necessary to Her Omnipotence?

---

[8] For 'if it be' *LW* (but not the proof) reads 'if it can be'.

[9] The German philosophers Artur Schopenhauer (1788–1860) and Eduard von Hartmann (1842–1906) and the German naturalist Ernst Haeckel (1834–1919) are all quoted and otherwise invoked in TH's *Literary Notebooks*.

So you cannot, I fear, save her good name except by assuming one of two things: that she is blind, and not a judge of her actions, or that she is an automaton, and unable to control them; in either of which assumptions, though you have the chivalrous satisfaction of screening one of her sex, you only throw responsibility a stage further back.

But the story is not new. It is true, nevertheless, that, as M. Maeterlinck contends, to dwell too long amid such reflections does no good, and that to model our conduct on Nature's apparent conduct, as Nietzsche would have taught, can only bring disaster to humanity.[10]

Yours truly,

Thomas Hardy.

[1902.05]

Edmund Kean in Dorchester [1]

During the early years of the new century Hardy's interest in local history was intensified by the writing of *The Dynasts*, the proliferation of books and articles about the topography of Wessex, and his involvement in plans for a new Dorchester guidebook (*CL* iii. 19–20). Signing himself 'History', he contributed in the spring of 1902 to a complicated controversy in the correspondence columns of the *Dorset County Chronicle* about early nineteenth-century Dorchester theatres and their associations with the famous actor Edmund Kean (1789?–1833; see *LW*, p. 339). A long letter by the historian A. M. Broadley in the issue of 15 May 1902, p. 11, was challenged in the issue of 22 May, p. 11, by a letter signed 'Dorset' that claimed to turn 'the hose of real facts upon the speculative sentimentality which is being excited over the connection of Edmund Kean with Dorchester'. Hardy's riposte to 'Dorset' was published, as below, in the *Dorset County Chronicle*, 29 May 1902, p. 11; a surviving draft (DCM) is annotated 'Sent May 26. 1902' and shows that the heading, 'Edmund Kean in Dorchester', was Hardy's own. The letter reappeared, slightly revised, in *Life and Work*, pp. 339–40. Purdy, p. 271.

Your correspondent 'Dorset', who proposes to 'turn the hose' upon the natural interest of Dorchester people in Edmund Kean, should, I think, first turn the hose upon his own uncharitableness. His contention

[10] An indication that TH's hostility to Nietzsche pre-dated the outbreak of war with Germany in 1914. See 1914.02 and especially 1914.05 and 1914.08.

amounts to this, that because one of the greatest, if not the very greatest, of English tragedians was not without blemish in his morals, no admiration is to be felt for his histrionic achievements, or regard for the details of his life. So, then, Lord Nelson should have no place in our sentiment, nor Burns, nor Byron—not even Shakespeare himself, nor, unhappily, many another great man whose flesh has been weak. With amusing maladroitness your correspondent calls himself by the name of the county which has lately commemorated King Charles the Second, of all people in the world[11]—a worthy who seduced scores of men's wives to Edmund Kean's one. Kean was, in truth, a sorely tried man, and it is no wonder that he succumbed.[12] The illegitimate child of a struggling actress, the vicissitudes and hardships of his youth and young manhood left him without moral ballast when the fire of his genius brought him success and adulation. The usual results followed, and owing to the publicity of his life it has been his misfortune ever since to have, like Cassius in *Julius Caesar*,

'All his faults observed,
Set in a note-book, learn'd and conn'd by rote'[13]

by people who show the Christian charity[14] of your correspondent!

History.[15]

[1902.06]

Edmund Kean in Dorchester [2]

Hardy's second letter on this topic appeared, with the same authorial heading, in the *Dorset County Chronicle*, 12 June 1902, p. 10, following another letter from 'Dorset' in the preceding issue, 5 June, p. 14. The surviving draft (DCM)—undated (though subsequently annotated 'June. 1902') and lacking a complimentary close—evidently served as copy for the reprinting in *Life and Work*, p. 340, of the letter's third, fourth, and fifth sentences. Purdy, p. 271.

[11] The square brackets placed in the draft around 'of all people in the world' presumably relate to, and date from, TH's omission of those words from *LW*.

[12] For 'he succumbed' *LW* (but not draft) reads 'he may have succumbed'.

[13] Shakespeare, *Julius Caesar*, iv. iii. 97–8.

[14] For 'Christian charity' *LW* (but not draft) reads 'Christian feeling'.

[15] Signature preceded in draft by 'Your obedient servant'.

Your correspondent 'Dorset' will find in the various volumes on the 'Life of Edmund Kean',[16] or in ordinary Cyclopædias (such as Chambers's), the reasons for concluding that he was the illegitimate son of an actress. 'Dorset's' apparent supposition that the open mistresses of Charles II., whose names are known to him, were the only ladies with whom that Monarch was intimate, needs no reply. One word as to the building in[17] which Kean performed in 1813. There can be little doubt that it was in the old theatre yet existing, stage[18] and all, at the back of Messrs. Godwin's china shop,[19] and for these, among other reasons. The theatre in North-square, built by Curme,[20] was not opened till February, 1828; while there are still dwellers in Dorchester who have known persons speak of seeing plays in the older theatre about 1821 or 1822, Kean's visit being thus only[21] a few years earlier. The building near the site of the present Masonic Hall, which has been mentioned as in use for a short time, was probably a temporary location in the interval between the occupation of the old and the new theatres.

History.

[1902.07]

'Maeterlinck and the Censor'

Hardy, prompted by Arthur Symons (*CL* iii. 25), joined Meredith, Swinburne, and several others in co-signing a letter protesting against the Lord Chamberlain's 'irrevocable' decision not to license a London production of *Monna Vanna*, a new play by the Belgian dramatist Maurice Maeterlinck that centred upon the willingness of a married woman to surrender her honour for her country's sake. The letter, headed as above, was published

[16] Draft does not have quotation marks round 'Life of Edmund Kean', TH evidently not having had a specific biography in mind.   [17] For 'building in' *LW* reads 'building [in Dorchester] in'.

[18] For 'existing, stage' *LW* reads 'existing [though not as such], stage'.

[19] Thomas Godwin's china shop, located in Dorchester at the south-east corner of the junction of Trinity Street with High West Street, retained until well into the twentieth century substantial evidence of its having once been a theatre (1924.05). See *An Inventory of the Historical Monuments in the County of Dorset. Volume Two: South-East, Part I* (London: Royal Commission on Historical Monuments [England], 1970), p. 123.

[20] Charles Curme, a local builder, was the son of Thomas Curme, who had built the first theatre in Dorchester late in the 18th century.

[21] For 'visit . . . only' draft reads 'visit being only', *LW* 'visit having been only'.

in *The Times*, 20 June 1902, p. 7; the copy Hardy actually signed is in the Beinecke Library, together with the responses of the other signatories. See Karl Beckson, *Arthur Symons: A Life* (Oxford: Clarendon Press, 1987), pp. 220 and 366, n. 30.

[1902.08]

Edmund Kean in Dorchester [3]

This third and last of Hardy's pseudonymous letters about Edmund Kean and the Dorchester theatres was published, as below, under the same heading as its predecessors, in the *Dorset County Chronicle*, 10 July 1902, p. 11. No draft of the letter seems to have survived, nor was it included in *Life and Work*—perhaps because Hardy became over time less confident as to the validity of his information and arguments. Purdy, p. 308.

Your other correspondents appear to have settled, at least to their absolute satisfaction,[22] that Edmund Kean's celebrated performance at Dorchester, before the agent from Drury Lane, took place at the theatre still standing in North-square. Now, anybody who chooses to consult at the British Museum or elsewhere a file of the *Dorset Chronicle* for 1828, will see in the impression for February 28th an account of the opening, on the Monday of that week, of the 'New Theatre built by Mr Curme[23] in North-square', the opening performance being by a Mr Lee, with the play of John Bull, &c.[24] The conclusion, therefore, is that Kean in 1813 acted in a theatre built fifteen years after he visited the town. This

[22] Hardy seems to have had chiefly in mind a letter from A. M. Broadley in the issue of 3 July 1902, p. 13.
[23] Corrected from the *Chronicle*'s 'Curma', evidently a compositorial error; for Curme, see 1902.06.
[24] TH's reference is to a report headed 'The Theatre' in the *Dorset County Chronicle*, 28 February 1828, p. [4], which he had read and recorded in his 'Facts' notebook (DCM) several years earlier. Unfortunately, he here misquotes his own note—in which the words 'in North Square, Dorchester' are followed by a question mark and placed within square brackets—and thus misrepresents the item itself, which certainly reported a new theatre as opening under Mr [Henry] Lee's management with a performance of *John Bull* [by George Colman the Younger] but nowhere identified its location. TH had perhaps been misled by an advertisement in the *Dorset County Chronicle*, 21 February 1828, p. [1], stating that tickets for the Loyalty Theatre, to be opened by Mr Lee on 25 February, were available from 'the Libraries' and from Mr Lee at Mrs Frampton's, North Square.

seems a more wonderful performance of Kean's than the play itself. All things may be possible in the eyes of some newspaper correspondents; but one would wish to know how Kean achieved his feat. Like Miss Rosa Dartle[25] I only ask for information.

History.

[1902.09]

'La Littérature anglaise et la guerre du Sud-Africain'

> Early in 1902 the *Revue Bleue* of Paris invited Hardy to contribute to a forthcoming article on the effect of the South African (or Boer) War on English literature by answering three questions: '1) if the war has had any effect; 2) if so, what kind of effect; 3) if not, why not?' (letter of the Vicomte de Rorthays, 24 January 1902, DCM). The article, 'La Littérature anglaise et la guerre du Sud-Africain', signed Gilbert Giluncy, appeared in the *Revue Bleue*, 4th series, 18 (16 August 1902), pp. 213–18, Hardy's letter (p. 213), in common with other responses from British figures, being translated into French and incorporated—as 'l'opinion du grand romancier, si essentiellement anglais'—within the structure of the article overall. The translation, however, omitted substantial segments of Hardy's original letter as represented by his unsigned holograph draft (DCM; the letter as sent is not known to survive), and that draft is therefore reproduced below in addition to the French text as published. Hardy's slightly modified quotation of his second answer in *Life and Work*, p. 334, is recorded in a footnote. Purdy, p. 270.

'Je crois, écrit-il, 1° que la guerre a très appréciablement influencé la littérature durant les deux dernières années; 2° que l'effet produit a été la vaste multiplication des livres sur la guerre elle-même, sur les guerres précédentes, d'œuvres d'*action* par opposition aux œuvres de *réflexion*,[26] et d'une grande quantité de poésies guerrières et patriotiques.

'Ces publications rejettent naturellement dans l'ombre celles qui s'inspirent d'un esprit plus calme et plus philosophique. Un trait caractéristique, d'importance secondaire, mais très curieux, parmi une certaine catégorie d'écrivains, est le déguisement, sous une terminologie

---

[25] In Dickens's *David Copperfield*.   [26] All italicizations as in the *Revue Bleue*.

chrétienne, de principes qui, sans être nécessairement inadmissibles au point de vue de la politique internationale, sont et demeurent anti-chrétiens parce que *inexorables* et *impérieux*.'

*   *   *   *   *

Feb 1. 1902

Dear Sir:

I fear that my casual opinion of the effect of the South African war on English literature will not be of much service to you. But, such as it is, I give it.

(1) I think that the war has very appreciably affected the literature of the past 2¼ years.

(2) The kind of effect produced has been the vast multiplication of books on the war itself, books on former wars, books of action as opposed to reflection, and large quantities of warlike and patriotic poetry.[27] These works naturally throw into the shade works that breathe a more quiet and philosophic[28] spirit—a curious minor feature in the case among a certain class of writers being the disguise under Christian terminology of principles not necessarily wrong from the point of view of international politics, but obviously Anti-Christian, because inexorable and masterful.

I am, Dear Sir,
Yours truly

[1902.10]

[Contribution to Haggard's *Rural England*]

H. Rider Haggard (1856–1925), famous as a novelist, was also deeply interested in agriculture, and in a letter of 6 March 1902 (DCM) he asked Hardy for some observations on 'the past, present and future' of the Dorset agricultural labourer and tenant farmer for inclusion in the 'Dorsetshire' chapter of his *Rural England: Being an Account of Agricultural and Social Researches Carried*

[27] *LW*, p. 334, quotes TH's second answer only, introducing it by a brief summary of the question and then replacing 'The kind . . . poetry' by 'A vast multiplication of books on the war itself, and the issue of large quantities of warlike and patriotic poetry'.

[28] Misspelled 'phlosophic' in draft.

Out in the Years 1901 & 1902, 2 vols. (London: Longmans, Green, 1902). Hardy evidently suggested that his response should be in the form of a letter (Haggard to Hardy, 11 March 1902, DCM), and his heavily worked draft (DCM), dated March 1902, shows that it was carefully considered. The discrepancies between that draft and the letter as published in *Rural England* presumably resulted from changes made by Hardy himself in the (unlocated) fair copy sent to Haggard or during subsequent proof correction. When including the letter in *Life and Work*, pp. 335–7, however, Hardy did so on the basis of the retained draft, making a number of fresh alterations in the process: the three versions—draft, *Rural England*, *Life and Work*—thus differ considerably, though without affecting Hardy's argument. The text below is that of *Rural England*, i. 282–5; footnotes draw attention to the more significant variations from *Life and Work* and from the original draft. *Rural England*, i. 285–6, also reprints extracts from Hardy's 'Dorsetshire Labourer' essay (1883.04), but these seem to have been selected by Haggard himself. Purdy, p. 270.

As to my opinion[29] on the past of the agricultural labourer in this county, I think, indeed know, that down to 1850 or 1855 his condition was in general one of great hardship. I say in general, for there have always been fancy farms, resembling St Clair's estate in *Uncle Tom's Cabin*, whereon they lived as smiling exceptions to those of their class all around them. I recall one such, the estate owner being his own farmer, and ultimately ruining himself by his hobby. To go to the other extreme; as a child I knew by sight a sheep-keeping boy who, to my horror, shortly afterwards died of want, the contents of his stomach at the autopsy being raw turnip only. His father's wages were 6*s.* a week, with about £2 at harvest, a cottage rent free, and an allowance of thorn faggots from the hedges as fuel. Between these examples came the great bulk of farms, whereon wages ranged from 7*s.* to 9*s.* a week, and perquisites were better in proportion.

Secondly, as to the present: things are of course widely different now. I am told that at the annual hiring-fair just past, the old positions were absolutely reversed, the farmers walking about and importuning the labourers to come and be hired instead of, as formerly, the labourers anxiously entreating the stolid farmers to take them on at any pittance. Their present life is almost without exception one of comfort, if the most ordinary thrift be observed. I could take you to the cottage of a

[29] Draft and *LW* are both dated March 1902 and begin 'My dear Haggard: As to your first question, my opinion'.

shepherd, not many miles from here, that has brass rods and carpeting to the staircase, and from the open door of which you hear a piano strumming within. Of course, bicycles stand by the doorway, while at night a large paraffin lamp throws out a perfect blaze of light upon the passer-by. The son of another labourer I know takes dancing lessons at a quadrille class in the neighbouring town.[30]

But changes at which we must all rejoice have brought other changes which are not so attractive. The labourers have become more and more migratory, the younger families in especial, who enjoy nothing so much as fresh scenery and new acquaintance. The consequences are curious and unexpected. For one thing, village tradition—a vast amount[31] of un-written folk-lore, local chronicle, local topography and nomenclature —is absolutely sinking, has nearly sunk, into eternal oblivion. I cannot recall a single instance of a labourer who still lives on the farm on which he was born, and I can only recall a few who have been five years on their present farm. Thus, you see, there being no continuity of envi-ronment in their lives, there is no continuity of information, the names, stories, and relics of one place being speedily forgotten under the incoming facts of the next. For example, if you ask one of the workfolk (they used always to be called 'workfolk' hereabout; 'labourers' is an imported word)[32] the names of surrounding hills, streams, the character and circumstances of people buried in particular graves, at what spots parish personages lie interred, questions on local fairies, ghosts, herbs, &c., they can give no answer; yet I can recall the time when the places of burial, even of the poor and tombless, were all remembered; the history of the squire's family[33] for 150 years back was known; such and such ballads appertained to such and such localities; ghost tales were attached to particular sites; and secret[34] nooks wherein wild herbs grew for the cure of divers maladies were pointed out readily.

On the subject of migration to the towns I think I have printed my opinions from time to time,[35] so that I will only say a word or two about it here. In this consideration the case of the farm labourers merges itself in the case of rural cottagers generally, including that of jobbing labourers,

---

[30] *LW* (only) adds 'Well, why not!'   [31] For 'amount' draft and *LW* read 'mass'.
[32] Struck through in the draft is the original conclusion of this sentence: 'word) about Napoleon's attempted invasion or even Monmouth's rebellion, the child will give for answer what-ever he or she may have learnt about Monmouth or Napoleon at school; but I can remember a time when to a question on the subject you got a traditional answer—that the rebellion ended at such a corner'.   [33] For 'the squire's family' *LW* (only) reads 'the parish and squire's family'.
[34] *LW* (only) omits 'secret', which is almost invisible in the draft.   [35] See e.g. 1883.04.

artisans, and nondescripts of all sorts who go to make up the body of
English villagery. That these people have removed to the towns of sheer
choice during the last forty years it would be absurd to say, except as to
that percentage of young, adventurous, and ambitious spirits among
them which is found in all societies. The prime cause of the removal is,
unquestionably, insecurity of tenure. If they do not escape this in the
towns, it is not fraught with such trying consequences to them as in a
village, where they may have to travel ten or twenty miles to find
another house and other work. Moreover, if in a town lodging an
honest man's daughter should have an illegitimate child, or his wife
take to drinking, he is not compelled to[36] pack up his furniture and get
his living elsewhere, as is, or was lately, too often the case in the country.
(I am neither attacking nor defending this order of things; I merely
relate it. The landlord sometimes had reason on his side, sometimes
not.)

Why such migrations to cities did not largely take place till within the
last forty years or so is, I think, in respect of farm labourers, that they had
neither the means nor the knowledge in old times that they have now.
And they had not the inclination, owing to the stability of villagers of the
other class, such as mechanics and small traders, who are the backbone
of village life. The tenure of these latter was before that date a fairly[37]
secure one, even if they were not in the possession of small freeholds.
The custom of granting leaseholds for three lives and other life-holding
privileges obtained largely in our villages, and though tenures by lifehold may not be ideally good or fair, they did at least subserve the purpose of keeping the native population at home. Villages in which there
is not now a single cottager other than a weekly tenant, were formerly
occupied almost entirely on the lifehold principle, the term extending
over seventy or a hundred years; and the young man who knows that he
is secure of his father's and grandfather's dwelling for his own lifetime,
thinks twice and three times before he embarks on the uncertainties of a
wandering career. Now, though, as I have said, these cottagers were not
often farm labourers, their permanence reacted on the farm labourers,
and made their lives with such associates richer in incident, better worth
living, and more reluctantly abandoned.[38]

---

[36] For 'compelled to' *LW* (only) reads 'compelled by any squire to'.

[37] For 'was . . . fairly' draft and *LW* read 'was, down to about fifty years ago, a fairly'.

[38] For 'such . . . abandoned' draft reads 'such associates better worth living', *LW* 'such comfortable associates better worth living'.

Thirdly, as to the future, and[39] the ultimate results from such a state of things, it hardly becomes me to attempt to prophesy here. That remedies exist for them, and are easily applicable, you will readily gather from what I have stated above.

[1902.11]

[Assistance to Hardy Entry in the *Encyclopædia Britannica*]

Hardy's letter to Arthur Symons of 28 September 1900 (*CL* ii. 267) speaks of his having gone to some trouble to provide the 'authoritative statement' of his ancestry and early life for which Symons (1865–1945) had asked (26 September, DCM) and on which he subsequently drew in writing the entry for 'Hardy, Thomas' in the *Encyclopædia Britannica*, 10th edn. (London: Adam and Charles Black, 1902), xxix. 224–5. The precise extent, however, of Symons's indebtedness to Hardy's information and phrasing is impossible to determine.

[1902.12]

[On the First Number of *T.P.'s Weekly*]

On 14 November 1902 Thomas Power O'Connor (1848–1929), already well known both as a journalist and as a Member of Parliament, published the first number of *T.P.'s Weekly*, priced at one penny. Though filled for the most part with lightweight gossip about books and writers, it also featured early in its career an abbreviated serialization of Joseph Conrad's *Nostromo*. Hardy, approached by O'Connor (13 November, DCM), with a request for a 'friendly send-off' to his new journal, duly joined George Meredith and many other literary and journalistic contemporaries in offering congratulations. His message, perhaps sent as a telegram, appeared as follows, under the heading 'Breaking the Record', in *T.P.'s Weekly*, 21 November 1902, p. 58.

[39] For 'future, and' *LW* (only) reads 'future, the evils of instability, and'.

It seems to me to have a thoughtfulness of tone and a real literary quality which must recommend it to all wise households.

[1902.13]

Recollections of 'Leader Scott'

Lucy Barnes, William Barnes's third daughter, married Samuel Thomas Baxter in 1868 and lived for the rest of her life in Florence, producing biographies, topographical pieces, and well-regarded studies of Italian art and architecture under the pseudonym of 'Leader Scott'. As Lucy Baxter she published in 1887 *The Life of William Barnes, Poet and Philologist* (see 1887.02). Hardy had known her as a young woman, and as a helpful guide during his visit to Florence with his wife in 1887 (*LW*, pp. 195, 199), and when news of her death arrived in November 1902 he willingly wrote the 'few recollections' of her (*CL* iii. 38) published in the *Dorset County Chronicle*, 27 November 1902, p. 5. The piece was published simultaneously in *The Times*, 27 November, p. 11, from copy supplied by the *Chronicle*, and Hardy told Edmund Gosse the next day: 'My few lines on "Leader Scott" were written *currente calamo* for our local people. If I had known that the Times would copy them I could have given them a little better shape' (*CL* iii. 39; see also *CL* iii. 40). Several extracts were published in *T.P.'s Weekly*, 5 December, p. 104, and Hardy himself sent copies of the proof to the *Academy and Literature*, where it was partly quoted, partly summarized, on 29 November, p. 568, and to the *Athenaeum*, which proved to have already commissioned another obituary of Mrs Baxter. The text below is that of the *Dorset County Chronicle*; a footnote records the addition which Hardy later wrote alongside the cutting of that printing inserted in his 'Personal' scrapbook (DCM). Purdy, p. 308.

Max Gate, Dorchester, Nov. 24th.

The information that I can give concerning the life and personality of this accomplished woman will, I fear, be of the most meagre description; for since her girlhood I have caught only passing glimpses of her at wide and wider intervals, just as one may discern through trees a bird in its flight, now here, now there, now a long way off, ere lost beyond the horizon.

Miss Lucy Barnes, of Dorchester, afterwards Mrs S. T. Baxter, of Florence, known to readers as 'Leader Scott', I can first remember as an attractive girl of nineteen or twenty, living at the house of her father, William Barnes, the poet and philologist. At that time of her life she was of sweet disposition, but provokingly shy, with plenty of brown hair, a tripping walk, a face pretty rather than handsome, and extremely piquant to a casual observer, having a nose tip-tilted to that slight Tennysonian degree[40] which is indispensable to a contour of such character. When she grew nervous she showed a momentary hesitation of speech, not reaching to a stammer, like that of an embarrassed child, which to myself and to many others was not the least of her attractive qualities. Her appearance, gracefulness, and marked gentleness, made her a typical 'Lucy', from whom the numerous Lucys in the novels of that date seemed to be drawn.

After she was twenty-two or three I lost sight of her for twenty years, but while in London I heard of her marriage and departure for Florence, and also knew of the books she published from time to time, which need not be enumerated here. I next met her at her father's rectory at Came, Dorset, in 1884 or 1885, she being then on one of her few visits to England—the last, I believe, that she ever paid to her native country. She was still girlish in manner, though by that date she had children in their teens.

During our stay in Florence in 1887 my wife and I saw her almost every day; and we made pilgrimages together to many spots of interest, she being, of course, as a long resident in Italy, an invaluable guide. Among these was the grave of Mrs Browning, who, to Mrs Baxter's regret, had died shortly before the latter's arrival in Florence. It was in Mrs Baxter's company also that I stood in the Piazza dell'Annunziata and gazed at the statue of the Grand-Duke Ferdinand I., opposite the Palazzo Riccardi-Menelli, we having been led there by the famous lines:

> 'There's a Palace in Florence the world knows well,
>   And a statue watches it from the Square',

which open the story told in 'The Statue and the Bust'.[41] In making this inspection an incident occurred which may be worth recalling. Having seen the statue we looked for the bust, but were[42] informed by an

---

[40] For 'that slight Tennysonian degree' *The Times* reads 'that faint degree'.

[41] By Robert Browning, one of TH's favourite poems.

[42] For 'bust, but were' TH's scrapbook insertion reads 'bust, (forgetting that the poem spoke of its "empty shrine") and were'; cf. *LW*, p. 200.

obliging waiter standing at a door hard by that it had unfortunately been taken down from a particular spot in the palace-façade which he pointed out. He added luminous details, and I gave him a lira for his information. On the first Sunday after my return to London I met Browning, and he was interested to hear of the incident. 'But that waiter!' he added with a hearty laugh. 'Why—I invented the bust!' It is, of course, just possible, though not likely, that Browning's memory was in error, and that the friendly waiter did not lie. Curiously enough, Mrs Baxter inclined to the opinion that there had been a bust, and that the waiter spoke the truth.

The view from her drawing-room in the Via Valfonda was a wide and beautiful one, and I hoped to revisit her there. But 'to-morrow, and to-morrow'![43]—I never saw her again. However, we corresponded with her at not unfrequent intervals. She appeared to retain all that old energy for literary work that she had inherited from her father, and her long acquaintance with Italy and Italian art and literature enabled her to produce those carefully-pondered books bearing thereon, of which the titles are well known.

She was deeply interested in the Florentines and I can remember her saying that the nobility of the Italian character was not fully realised in England; adding—how naturally!—'particularly that of the men'.

She died on November 10th last, at Villa Bianca, Via Settignanese, Florence, and was buried on the Wednesday following at the Cemetery of the Allori.

[1902.14]

'Favourite Books of 1902'

Supplied by the *Academy and Literature* with a printed, stamped, and pre-addressed postcard (Princeton) on which to complete a statement beginning 'The two new Books which have pleased and interested me most in 1902 are', Hardy altered the wording to read 'A new Book which has interested me in 1902 is', inserted ' "The Princess of Hanover" by Margaret L. Woods', and added his signature. The magazine severely pruned this response and

---

[43] Shakespeare, *Macbeth*, v. v. 19.

printed it, as below, together with numerous other selections, under the heading 'Favourite Books of 1902' in the *Academy and Literature*, 6 December 1902, p. 633.

MR THOMAS HARDY.

Margaret L. Woods's 'The Princess of Hanover.'[44]

---

[44] Margaret L. Woods (1856–1945), second daughter of George Granville Bradley, Dean of Westminster, was a novelist and poet whose work was sometimes compared to TH's. *The Princess of Hanover* (London: Duckworth, 1902) was a verse closet-drama, a form shortly to be adopted for *The Dynasts*, and Hardy was perhaps taking the opportunity to reassert the value of that form—as well as his respect for Woods's work—in opposition to a hostile review of *The Princess of Hanover* that he thought important enough to insert into one of his literary notebooks (*LN* ii. 130–3).

1903

[1903.01]

'The Decay of the Novel'

Hardy was one of several writers, American and British, invited by the editors of the New York *Critic* to comment on an article, 'The Decay of the Novel', by Benjamin Swift, published in its issue of January 1903, pp. 59–61. His distinctly perfunctory appropriation and endorsement of a single observation from Swift's penultimate paragraph appeared, as below, under the heading 'The Decay of the Novel', in the *Critic*, 42 (February 1903), p. 151.

The author writes with force and insight when he says that the immoral book is the book which hides truth and creates a fool's paradise and a mirage that misleads.[1]

[1903.02]

[On Capital Punishment]

Howard Maynard Shipley (1872–1934), writer on science, was at this date a graduate student at Stanford University, and on 11 March 1903 (DCM) he wrote from California to solicit Hardy's views on capital punishment for inclusion in a report he was preparing for his university's Department of Economics. Shipley placed two short articles on capital punishment with *Harper's Weekly*, 8 September and 29 December 1906, but no publication or invocation of Hardy's response has yet been discovered. Hardy's draft—

---

[1] Cf. Swift, p. 61: 'the immoral book *par excellence* is the book which hides truth and creates a fool's paradise and a mirage of life.'

undated but approximately assignable to early April 1903 (*CL* iii. 58)—served as the basis for his inclusion of the message in *Life and Work*, p. 341, and that text, very slightly revised from the draft, is reproduced below. Whether or not he fully understood Shipley's status and purpose, there seems no doubt that Hardy believed himself to be making a public statement based on his experience as an 'acting'—i.e. actively practising—magistrate who sometimes participated in the grand jury preliminaries to murder trials at the Dorset Assizes. For E.C. Sampson's article on Hardy as magistrate, see 1888.01.

As an acting magistrate I think that Capital Punishment operates as a deterrent from deliberate crimes against life to an extent that no other form of punishment can rival. But the question of the moral right of a community to inflict that punishment is one I cannot enter into in this necessarily brief communication.

[1903.03]

'Serial Rights in Stories'

Hardy's short story 'Benighted Travellers', originally sold to the Tillotson & Son fiction syndicate of Bolton in 1881 and published in the *Bolton Weekly Journal*, 17 December 1881, was in 1891 renamed 'The Honourable Laura' and included in *A Group of Noble Dames*. Tillotson, however, retained the serial rights to the story as 'Benighted Travellers' and Clement Shorter, though forewarned by Hardy (*CL* iii. 48), subsequently leased it under that title for publication in the 2 and 9 May 1903 issues of the *Sphere*. Hardy objected to Tillotson's taking 'an unfair advantage of the words "serial rights" that most authors use without realizing that they may be acted on 20 years after' (*CL* iii. 60; cf. *CL* iii. 66–7), and published the following letter of explanation and complaint in the *Athenaeum*, 16 May 1903, p. 626, under the heading 'Serial Rights in Stories'. Purdy, p. 308.

As I receive inquiries concerning my 'new story' in the *Sphere* for May 2nd and 9th, will you allow me space to say that, so far from being new, it is a resuscitated old story which appeared in a country journal[2] nearly twenty years ago, and that I am in no way responsible for its publication as if new?

---

[2] The *Bolton Weekly Journal*; Hardy here uses 'country' as synonymous with 'provincial'.

I make this an opportunity of reminding inexperienced writers of fiction that, in disposing of 'serial rights' in their productions, they should take care to limit the time during which such rights may be exercised.

Thomas Hardy.

[1903.04]

[Inspired Paragraph on *The Dynasts*] [1]

When Clement Shorter reported in his 'Literary Letter' column in the *Sphere*, 14 November 1903, p. 150, that Hardy had 'just completed a play in blank verse, a work he has had in hand at odd moments for the last six years', he was drawing upon, and partly quoting from, the letter Hardy had written to him on 2 November (*CL* iii. 82)—possibly with a view to instigating just such an announcement. Hardy was quite specific, however, in a further letter to Shorter—unlocated, but quoted in Davis and Orioli's catalogue 30 (Summer 1929), item 86—of 8 November 1903: 'By the way, you might say in print, (if you really think it worth while), that "the Drama is entirely literary and only nominally a play and arranged so that it will read as easily as a novel or narrative poem".' The following paragraph duly appeared at the conclusion of Shorter's 'Literary Letter' in the *Sphere*, 21 November 1903, p. 176.

Mr Thomas Hardy's new play is not written for the stage as has been suggested. It is a purely literary drama, and so arranged that it will read as a novel or a narrative poem, thus making a real addition to Mr Hardy's romantic works.

1904

[1904.01]

[Inspired Paragraphs on *The Dynasts*] [2]

Just ahead of the publication date for Part First of *The Dynasts*, 13 January 1904, Hardy was approached by James Milne (see 1899.03), now editor of the *Book Monthly* and literary editor of the *Daily Chronicle*, with a request for some usable information about this new departure. On 12 January Hardy sent in reply, as 'scraps' that might 'serve your purpose', what he called 'the impressions of almost the only person who has read the proofs' (*CL* iii. [97]). Because those 'scraps' have disappeared, it is impossible to tell how fully or precisely their contents were absorbed into the paragraphs published, as below, in the *Book Monthly*, February 1904, pp. 293–4, and (following the line of asterisks) March 1904, p. 370. It is, however, clear that Milne's 'friend', like Hardy's 'person', could have been none other than Hardy himself.

A friend who had the opportunity of reading Mr Thomas Hardy's *Dynasts* in proof, notes two points as being interesting in his literary art. The drama differs from Mr Hardy's previous works in prose and verse, in that the love interest is reduced to a vanishing point. This circumstance may appeal differently to the Young Person and to the Old Person. Again, the drama contains a scene[1] in which Pitt is attacked by Fox and Sheridan for the ineffectiveness of his military organisation. Pitt's answer is not unlike that of the present Ministry on their conduct of affairs in the South African war.

Some of the critics, in writing of *The Dynasts*, have spoken as if its number of acts and scenes were beyond all reason. It is worth pointing out, that if the scenes be examined, many of them are found to be only in dumb show. Should the proportion in the First Part be continued to

[1] Part First, Act I, Scene 3.

the end of the drama, there will be about a hundred speaking scenes in the nineteen acts.[2] To appeal to Shakespeare, his *Henry VI.* contains fifteen acts and nearly eighty scenes, several of them twice as long as any in *The Dynasts*, so far. Moreover, it is an acting play, while *The Dynasts* is entirely panoramic in intention. To speak in figures is often to get a needless impression of strangeness.

*   *   *   *   *

It has been a common assumption, in relation to Mr Hardy's drama, *The Dynasts*, that he has taken to the writing of verse quite recently, as a second thought, after years of prose. This must be for want of knowledge that the opposite is actually the fact. After spending many years of his early manhood in excursions into verse, the only kind of literature that attracted him, Mr Hardy, almost against his will, turned to novel writing for necessary and practical reasons. His production of poems and a blank-verse drama during the last few years is, therefore, merely a reversion to his first instincts.

[1904.02]

The Dynasts: A Rejoinder

Arthur Bingham Walkley, dramatic critic of *The Times* from 1900 to 1926, published an unsigned review of Part First of *The Dynasts* in *The Times Literary Supplement* of 15 January 1904, pp. 11–12. In a further unsigned article, headed '*The Dynasts*: A Suggestion', in the issue of 29 January, p. 30, he criticized Hardy's appropriation of dramatic conventions to undramatic and unperformable purposes and suggested that *The Dynasts* might be performed as a puppet play. Hardy's response appeared, as below, in *The Times Literary Supplement*, 5 February 1904, pp. 36–7, under a heading, '*The Dynasts*: A Rejoinder', that was probably of his own choosing. Samuel Hynes usefully prints both sides of the Hardy–Walkley exchange in *Complete Poetical Works*, v. 385–96. Purdy, p. 309.

---

[2] An act-by-act outline of Parts Second and Third of *The Dynasts* was included as a kind of appendix to the first edition of Part First.

Max Gate, Dorset, Feb. 2.

Sir,

The objections raised by your dramatic critic[3] to the stage-form adopted in *The Dynasts* for presenting a rapid mental vision of the Napoleonic wars—objections which I had in some degree anticipated in the preface to the book[4]—seem to demand a reply, inasmuch as they involve a question of literary art that is of far wider importance than as it affects a single volume. I regret that in the space of a letter I shall only be able to touch upon it briefly.

Your critic is as absolute as the gravedigger in *Hamlet*.[5] I understand his contention to be that to give a panoramic poem (which *The Dynasts* may perhaps be called) the form of a stage-drama—even a convention-alized form—or to give such a form to anything whatever that is intended for the study only, is false in principle. Whether the aim of *The Dynasts* was to dumbfound the worthy burgher (as your critic surmises in the French tongue)[6] or not, his theory certainly does dumbfound, or, as he would say, *épate*, the present writer. According to it one must conclude that such productions as Shelley's *Prometheus Unbound*, Byron's *Cain*, and many other unactable play-like poems are a waste of means, and, in his own words, 'may be read just as, *faute de mieux*, shoe-leather may be used as an article of diet'.[7]

His view would seem to be based on an assumption that in no cir-cumstances must an art borrow the methods of a neighbour art. Yet if there is one thing needful to the vitality of any art it is the freedom of the worker therein from the restraint of such scientific reasoning as would lay down this law, freedom from the *rationale* of every development that he adopts. The artistic spirit is at bottom a spirit of caprice, and in some of its finest productions in the past it could have given no clear reason why they were run in this or that particular mould, and not in some more obvious one. And if it could be proved that in *The Dynasts* nothing is gained, but much lost, by its form, that attempt would still have been legitimate.

[3] TH of course knew Walkley's name and had once met and 'rather liked' him (*CL* iii. 107).

[4] *The Dynasts . . . Part First* (London: Macmillan, 1904), pp. ix–x.

[5] Shakespeare, *Hamlet*, v. i. 136: 'How absolute the knave is!'

[6] Walkley had suggested that TH's 'whim' might be 'to *épater le bourgeois*'.

[7] TH's quotation from Walkley is accurate; *Prometheus Unbound* was published in 1820, *Cain* in 1821.

Nevertheless, if your reviewer's statement that the stage-form is inherently an unnatural one for reading, a waste of available means, were strictly accurate, I would concede to him the expediency, though not the obligation, of avoiding it in a book. But why, one asks, is it bad for reading? Because, I understand him to answer, it was invented for the stage. He might as well assert that bitter ale is bad drinking for England because it was invented for India. His critical hand is, indeed, subdued to what it works in[8] when he pens such a theory. It surely ought to have occurred to him that this play-shape is essentially, if not quite literally, at one with the instinctive, primitive, narrative shape. In legends and old ballads, in the telling of 'an owre true tale'[9] by country-folks on winter nights over a dying fire, the place and time are briefly indicated at the beginning in almost all cases; and then the body of the story follows as what he said and what she said, the action being often suggested by the speeches alone. This likeness between the order of natural recital and the order of theatrical utility may be accidental; but there it is; and to write Scene so-and-so, Time so-and-so, instead of Once upon a time, At such a place, is a trifling variation that makes no difference to the mental images raised. Of half-a-dozen people I have spoken to about reading plays, four say that they can imagine the enact-ment in a read play·better than in a read novel or epic poem. It is a matter of idiosyncrasy.

The methods of a book and the methods of a play, which he says are so different, are fundamentally similar. It must be remembered that the printed story is not a representation, but, like the printed play, a means of producing a representation, which is done in the one case by sheer imaginativeness, in the other by imaginativeness pieced out with material helps. Why, then, should not a somewhat idealized semblance of the latter means be used in the former case?

For a rather digressive reason your reviewer drags in the art of architecture.[10] In mercy to his own argument he should have left architecture alone. Like those of a play for reading, its features are continually determined by no mechanical, material, or methodic

---

[8] Shakespeare, Sonnet 111, lines 6–7: 'my nature is subdued | To what it works in, like the dyer's hand.'

[9] Quoted from the conclusion of ch. 34 of Scott's *The Bride of Lammermoor*.

[10] Walkley, arguing that the conventions and devices of fiction and drama should not be mixed within a single work, had invoked the proposition that in architecture 'structure is conditioned by material'.

necessities (which are confused together by your critic). As for mechanical necessities, that purest relic of Greek architecture, the Parthenon, is a conventionalized representation of the necessities of a timber house, many of which are not necessities in stone, such as the imitations of wood rafter-ends, beam-ends, and ceiling-joists. As for necessities of purpose, medieval architects constructed church-parapets with the embrasures of those of a fortress, and on the Continent planned the eastern ends of their Cathedrals in resemblance of a Roman Hall of Justice. In respect of necessities of method, that art, throughout its history, has capriciously subdued to its service, in sheer waywardness, the necessities of other arts, so that one can find in it a very magazine[11] of examples of my own procedure in *The Dynasts*. Capitals, cornices, bosses, and scores of other details, instead of confining their shapes to those strictly demanded by their office, borrow from the art of sculpture without scruple and without reason. Sculptured human figures are boldly taken, and, by the name of caryatids, are used as columns. In sculpture itself we find the painter's 'necessity' borrowed—a superficies[12]—and used for bas-reliefs, even though shapes are misrepresented by so doing. And if we turn to poetry we find that rhythm and rhyme are a non-necessitous presentation of language under conditions that in strictness appertain only to music.

But analogies between the arts are apt to be misleading, and having said thus much in defence of the form chosen, even supposing another to have been available, I have no room left for more than a bare assertion that there was available no such other form that would readily allow of the necessary compression of space and time. I believe that any one who should sit down and consider at leisure how to present so wide a subject within reasonable compass would decide that this was, broadly speaking, the only way.

Before concluding I should like to correct a misapprehension of your critic's, and of others, that I have 'hankerings after actual performance' of *The Dynasts*. My hankerings, if any, do not lie that way. But I fancy his do. His laborious search in cyclopædias for some means of performing it[13] plainly betray that he is dying to see the show; which is flattering. But if

---

[11] Ammunition store.   [12] Surface on which to work.

[13] Walkley, disdainfully suggesting that *The Dynasts* might be performed as a puppet show or shadow play, had cited from the *Encyclopædia Britannica* the example of a puppet theatre that had presented the battle of Trafalgar and other events of the Napoleonic Wars at country fairs in the 1830s.

he will look again at the last paragraph of the preface he will perceive that my remarks on performance refer to old English dramas only.[14]

Your obedient servant,

Thomas Hardy.

[1904.03]

The Dynasts: A Postscript

Hardy's letter in *The Times Literary Supplement* of 5 February 1904 (1904.02) provoked another unsigned piece by Walkley, '*The Dynasts* and the Puppets', in the issue of 12 February, p. 46. Walkley reinforced his earlier suggestion for performance of *The Dynasts* by puppets and returned to the question of why anyone writing a narrative to be read would deliberately 'forgo all the privileges of narrative art' and accept instead 'the restrictions proper to a spectacle'. Hardy's second riposte—published as below in *The Times Literary Supplement*, 19 February 1904, p. 53, with the presumably authorial heading '*The Dynasts*: A Postscript'—shifted the ground of the discussion by asserting that negative responses to *The Dynasts*, including Walkley's original review of 15 January, had been chiefly motivated by unexpressed theological objections (see *CL* iii. 98, 98–9, 107, 113). Walkley's two articles on *The Dynasts* were later merged into the single essay, '*The Dynasts* and the Puppets', included in his *Drama and Life* (London: Methuen, 1907), pp. 106–14. Purdy, p. 309.

Max Gate, Dorset, Feb. 16.

Sir,

Your critic has humorously conducted his discourse away from his original charge against *The Dynasts* into the quaint and unexpected channel of real performance by means of fantoccini, Chinese shadows,[15] and other startling apparatus. This is highly creditable to his ingenious

---

[14] In fact, as Walkley correctly observed in *The Times Literary Supplement*, 12 February 1902, p. 46, the example of mumming speech invoked in the Preface to Part First of *The Dynasts* is clearly intended to suggest a method of performing other apparently unstageable dramas—including, by implication, *The Dynasts* itself.

[15] Terms not in fact used by Walkley; '*fantoccini*' are (Italian) puppets, and 'Chinese shadows' ('les Ombres Chinoises') were performed, like Indonesian shadow plays, by passing flat figures between a light source and a translucent screen.

mind; yet we must remember that the whole fabric of his vision[16] arose only out of his altruistic desire to provide me with a means of escape from what he holds to be an untenable position. But I still absolutely deny it to be such, though I may seem ungrateful. I think I have shown that an attempt to write a spectacular poem (if he will allow me to use the expression for want of a better), more or less resembling a stage-play, though not one, has full artistic justification and is not 'false in principle', as he stated. He naturally continues to think the other way; and there I fear the matter must remain.

But the truth seems to be—if I may say a final word here on a point outside the immediate discussion—that the real offence of *The Dynasts* lies, not in its form as such, but in the philosophy which gave rise to the form. This is revealed by symptoms in various quarters, even (if I am not mistaken) by your critic's own faint tendency to harden his heart against the 'Immanent Will'. Worthy British Philistia, unlike that ancient Athens it professes to admire, not only does not ask for a new thing,[17] but even shies at that which merely appears at first sight to be a new thing. As with a certain King, the reverse of worthy, in the case of another play, some people ask, 'Have you read the argument? Is there no offence in't?'[18] There can hardly be, assuredly, on a fair examination. The philosophy of *The Dynasts*, under various titles and phases, is almost as old as civilization. Its fundamental principle, under the name of Predestination, was preached by St Paul. 'Being predestinated'—says the author of the Epistle to the Ephesians, 'Being predestinated according to the purpose of Him who worketh all things after the counsel of His own Will';[19] and much more to the same effect, the only difference being that externality is assumed by the Apostle rather than immanence. It has run through the history of the Christian Church ever since. St Augustine held it vaguely, Calvin held it fiercely, and, if our English Church and its Nonconformist contemporaries have now almost abandoned it to our men of science (among whom determinism is a commonplace), it was formerly taught by Evangelical divines of the finest character and conduct. I should own in fairness that I think this has been shrewdly recognized in some quarters whose orthodoxy is unimpeachable, where the philosophy of *The Dynasts* has been handled as sanely and as calmly as I could wish.

---

[16] Shakespeare, *The Tempest*, iv. i. 151. [17] Acts 17: 21.
[18] Shakespeare, *Hamlet*, iii. ii. 232–3. [19] Eph. 1: 11.

Nevertheless, as was said in the Preface, I have used the philosophy as a plausible theory only. Though, for that matter, I am convinced that, whether we uphold this or any other conjecture on the cause of things, men's lives and actions will be little affected thereby, these being less dependent on abstract reasonings than on the involuntary intersocial emotions, which would more probably be strengthened than weakened by a sense that humanity and other animal life (roughly, though not accurately, definable as puppetry) forms the conscious extremity of a pervading urgence, or will.

Your obedient servant,

Thomas Hardy.

[1904.04]

[Message to the Rationalist Press Association] [1]

Hardy had declined to become an Honorary Associate of the Rationalist Press Association in 1899 (*CL* ii. 223), and in 1920 he would resist inclusion in *A Biographical Dictionary of Modern Rationalists* (*CL* vii. 162). He was nevertheless on intimate terms with Edward Clodd, a leading Rationalist, and understood to be generally supportive of the cause: an article on his novels in the Association's journal, the *Literary Guide and Rationalist Review*, new series no. 90 (1 December 1903), pp. 185–6, pointed with approval to their 'frank Paganism' and 'scathing denunciation of God'. Invited to attend the annual dinner of the Association on 29 February 1904, Hardy couched his refusal in sympathetic terms—doubtless anticipating that his letter would be read out at the dinner and subsequently published. The text below is that of the letter as it appeared, together with several other such messages, in the *Literary Guide and Rationalist Review*, new series no. 94 (1 April 1904), p. 58.

I regret to say that I shall not be in London on Monday, and am unable to accept your kind invitation to the Annual Dinner. I do not, however, often go to dinners when I am there.

I think the cheap publications of the Association are a powerful means of spreading scientific knowledge among those who would not otherwise get at it. One must, of course, always hope that, in destroying superstition, emotional fancy—which may be called make-believe superstition—will not be destroyed along with it, adding, as it does, so largely to the interest of life.

I cannot close this letter without alluding to the lamented loss of your associate, Sir Leslie Stephen, whom I knew for thirty years.[20]

[1904.05]

[The Cruelty of Blood Sports]

Although the 'Swiftian' letter of 2 March 1904 to the Revd S. Whittell Key (1874–1948), Anglican clergyman and occasional author, is not known to have been published in Hardy's lifetime, his heavy corrections to the draft (Beinecke) indicate that it was written with considerable care, and the actual letter (Princeton) is marked as if for possible publication. Hardy himself included the item—so revised as to incorporate a reference to Darwin—in *Life and Work*, p. 345, and shortly after his death the sale of the letter at auction allowed a portion of its text to be picked up by the *Daily Mail*, 14 March 1929, p. 12, and thus reprinted in *Cruel Sports: The Official Journal of the League for the Prohibition of Cruel Sports*, 3 (April 1929), p. 59. The text below is reproduced from *Collected Letters*, iii. 110.

March 2. 1904

Dear Sir:

I am not sufficiently acquainted with the many varieties of sport to pronounce which is, quantitatively, the most cruel.

I can only say generally that the prevalence of those sports that consist in the pleasure of watching a fellow-creature, weaker and less favoured than ourselves, in its struggles to[21] escape the death-agony we mean to inflict by a treacherous contrivance, seems to me one[22] of the many convincing proofs that we have not yet emerged from barbarism.

In the present state of affairs there would appear to be no reason why the children,[23] say, of overcrowded families should not be used for sporting purposes. There would[24] be no difference in principle: moreover

---

[20] Stephen, an honorary associate of the Rationalist Press Association, died 22 February 1904; see 1906.14.   [21] For 'struggles to' *LW* reads 'struggles by nature's poor resources only to'.

[22] For 'by . . . one' *LW* reads 'by the treacherous contrivances of science, seems one'.

[23] For 'no . . . children' *LW* reads 'no logical reason why the smaller children'.

[24] For 'There would' *LW* reads 'Darwin has revealed that there would'.

these children would often escape lives intrinsically less happy than those of wild birds and animals.[25]

Yours truly

Thomas Hardy.

Revd S. Whittell Key, M. A.

[1904.06]

'La France est-elle en décadence?'

Louis Dumur (1860–1933), editor of the Parisian journal *L'Européen*, wrote on 19 November 1903 (DCM) to ask Hardy to contribute to an international symposium on the question of whether or not France was in a state of national decline. Hardy's reply, one of several published in French beneath the heading 'La France, est-elle en décadence?' in *L'Européen*, 26 March 1904, p. 4, is reproduced below. An English version of that reply (omitting the illustration) appeared in the *Daily Chronicle*'s report of the symposium, headed 'Is France Decadent?' and published 31 March 1904, p. 3, but since it had been translated back from the French it only approximately represented what Hardy had actually written. The second text below, following the line of asterisks, is therefore that of Hardy's surviving draft, dated 4 December 1903 (DCM), which was itself slightly altered for inclusion in *Life and Work*, p. 342; omitted, however, are those elements (date, salutation, valediction, name and position of addressee) that were not reproduced in any of the published texts. What particularly emerges from the juxtaposition is the way in which *L'Européen*, translating Hardy's 'serrated' as 'dentelée', turns the acute angles of his diagram into more consistently 'progressive' right angles. In *Life and Work* a fledged arrow points to the starting point of the diagram, which is serrated, as in Hardy's draft, but much more irregular. Purdy, p. 271.

Dorchester (Angleterre).

En réponse à votre demande, je dirai qu'à mon avis la France n'est pas en décadence. Son histoire me semble prendre la forme d'une ligne dentelée, come ceci:

---

[25] For 'and animals' *LW* reads 'and other animals'.

et un véritable jugement de ses tendences générales ne peut pas être fondé sur une observation momentanée; il doit s'étendre sur des périodes entières de variation.

Ce qui maintiendra la France en tant que nation, c'est sa faculté unique d'assimiler les idées nouvelles et de s'émanciper promptement de celles qui se trouvent être infructueuses.

*   *   *   *   *

Max Gate, Dorchester

In reply to your inquiry[26] I would say that I am not of opinion that France is in a decadent state. Her history seems to take the form of a serrated line, thus:

and a true judgment of her general tendency cannot be based on a momentary observation, but must extend over whole periods of variation.

What will sustain France as a nation is her[27] unique accessibility to new ideas, and her ready power of emancipation from those which reveal themselves to be effete.

[1904.07]

[Death Notice for Jemima Hardy]

There seems no reason to doubt Hardy's authorship of the formal death notice of his mother, Jemima Hardy (*née* Hand), published as below in the 'Deaths' column of the *Dorset County Chronicle*, 7 April 1904, p. 16.

HARDY.—April 3, at Upper Bockhampton, Jemima, widow of the late Thomas Hardy, in her 91st year.

---

[26] *LW* omits 'In . . . inquiry'.   [27] For 'is her' *LW* reads 'is, I think, her'.

[Obituary for Jemima Hardy]

> Hardy must certainly have written the unsigned obituary of his mother that appeared, as below, in *The Times*, 6 April 1904, p. 4. An abbreviated version of the same obituary, incorporated within a paragraph not otherwise written by Hardy, was printed in the *Dorset County Chronicle*, 7 April 1904, p. 4. Purdy, p. 309.

The death occurred on Easter Sunday, at her house near Dorchester, of Mrs HARDY, mother of Mr Thomas Hardy, the author, in her 91st year. She came[28] on the maternal side of an old yeoman stock, who were small landowners in Melbury Osmund, Dorset, for several centuries, till they became implicated in the Monmouth rising. Their house was entered after Sedgmoor by some of the soldiery, the two daughters escaping by a back staircase into the orchard. In the 'Presentment of Rebels to Chief Justice Jeffreys, 1685', the name of one of the family occurs, the charge being 'Absent from Home att the Tyme of the Rebellion', but he is not mentioned among those executed.[29] Mrs Hardy was a woman of strong character and marked originality, with the keenest love for literature; and much of her son's work in prose and verse was based upon her memories and opinions.

[1904.09]

[Supplement to Obituary for Jemima Hardy]

> 'The Office Window' section of the *Daily Chronicle* of 9 April 1904, p. 4, stated that it had received from Hardy, and was printing at his request, a note 'in correction of many erroneous statements concerning his aged mother'. The note was quoted in the London *Globe* that same evening (cutting in

---

[28] For 'The death . . . came' the *Chronicle* reads 'Mrs Hardy came'.

[29] Similar details of TH's mother's family background appear in *LW*, pp. 10–11, 362. See also TH's story 'The Duke's Reappearance', published in 1896, collected into *A Changed Man* in 1913 (Purdy, pp. 153, 155).

Hardy's 'Personal' scrapbook, DCM) and reprinted in full by the *Dorset County Chronicle*, 14 April 1904, p. 6, following its account of Jemima Hardy's funeral, and by the *Gentlewoman*, 16 April 1904, p. 544, where it was accompanied by a photograph. The text below is that of the *Daily Chronicle*. Purdy, p. 309.

The late Mrs Hardy, Mr Thomas Hardy's mother, was[30] a woman of character in many ways. The first book that she gave her son, after those merely for the nursery, was Dryden's Virgil,[31] for which she had a great liking. By the time that he was twelve she had him regularly instructed in Latin, and at fifteen in French by a governess. The house in which she died was built by the Hardys more than a century ago, but it passed out of their hands some years back.[32] Yet, though she was the owner of several comfortable freehold houses not far off, she preferred to remain in the original inconvenient one, which she was enabled to do, as long as she chose, by the courtesy of the present possessor.

[1904.10]

[Inspired Paragraph about Jemima Hardy] [1]

Asked by Clement Shorter to supply a portrait of Jemima Hardy for reproduction in one of the magazines he edited, Hardy on 8 April 1904 (*CL* iii. 118–19) sent for use in the *Sphere*—not, he insisted, in the *Tatler*—a photograph of a portrait painted by his sister Mary, commenting adversely in a postscript on the 'erroneous paragraphs' about his mother that had appeared in the press. Shorter took the hint, and when the portrait appeared in the 'Literary Letter' section of the *Sphere*, 23 April 1904, p. 92, the accompanying remarks drew heavily, as follows, on the obituary notices Hardy had already published and incorporated the substance and much of the wording of Hardy's 8 April postscript.

All who are indebted to Mr Thomas Hardy for some of the most genuine literature of our age will sympathise with him in the loss of his

---

[30] For 'The late . . . was' *Dorset County Chronicle* reads 'The late Mrs Hardy was'.
[31] i.e. John Dryden's translation of Virgil's works, first published in 1697; TH's copy, itself undated, is in DCM (cf. *LW*, p. 21).   [32] The Higher Bockhampton cottage, TH's birthplace.

mother, who died quite recently in her ninety-first year. Mrs Hardy came of an old yeoman stock which was implicated in the Monmouth rising. She was a woman of marked originality of character with a keen love of literature. From her Mr Hardy inherited some of his genius. Many erroneous paragraphs have gained currency during the last few days concerning her and her illustrious son. Mr Hardy was never at the Dorchester National School as was said, and his mother's tiny cottage is an eight-roomed homestead with an acre and a half of land attached to it. Further, Mrs Hardy has been ailing for a long time, so that her death was not unexpected. But all these points are comparatively trifling. The essential fact is that Mrs Hardy, senior, was a remarkable woman, venerated by all who knew her.

[1904.11]

[?Inspired Paragraph on Hardy Cottage?]

> In his zeal to correct misrepresentations of the conditions in which his mother had lived, Hardy evidently wrote also to Thomas Power O'Connor, editor of *T.P.'s Weekly* (cf. 1902.12). The letter itself has not been traced, but the following paragraph, published as below in *T.P.'s Weekly*, 29 April 1904, p. 565, shows clear signs of Hardy's instigation and indeed of his participation (e.g. 'hereabout'). A cutting of the item is in Hardy's 'Personal' scrapbook (DCM).

Some absurd paragraphs have been circulated as professing to describe the house of Mr Thomas Hardy's recently-deceased mother, in Dorset. I happen to know that the interior is cosy in the extreme, being that of an ordinary old country homestead of seven or eight rooms, with a range in the kitchen and grates elsewhere, the walls being twice as thick as those of a modern 'villa'. The stabling has been lately pulled down. Freestone floors and thatched roofs are common hereabout for antiquated country houses and parsonages, though not for the newer cottages, because of the expense, brick and slate being much cheaper.

[1904.12]

[?Inspired Paragraph about Jemima Hardy?] [2]

The photograph of Mary Hardy's portrait of Jemima Hardy that appeared in the *Graphic*, 16 April 1904, p. 519, was sent by Hardy to the editor, Thomas Heath Joyce, on 10 April 1904 (*CL* iii. 119), and there is every possibility that he also supplied much of the following paragraph, printed on the same page under the heading 'Our Portraits'.

By the death last week of Mrs Hardy, the aged mother of Mr Thomas Hardy, a noteworthy tie with the past is broken, by reason of the observant character of the woman who watched life for so long a time. Mrs Hardy's cognisance of events was clear and precise, extending from the death of the Princess Charlotte in 1817 to the recent discussions on the Education Bill. Inheriting from her mother a great taste for literature, Mrs Hardy permanently injured her sight by excessive reading, the books she liked being quite as largely those of a solid kind as of the lighter fiction. She was buried in the same grave with her deceased husband, in the churchyard described under the name of 'Mellstock' in Mr Hardy's novels and verses. Our portrait is from a painting by Mrs Hardy's daughter, Miss Mary Hardy.

[1904.13]

[?Inspired Paragraph about Jemima Hardy?] [3]

Hardy similarly supplied James Milne of the *Book Monthly* with a photograph of his sister's pencil sketch of their mother (*CL* iii. 125), and while direct evidence is again lacking, it seems safe to infer—from his previous exchanges with Milne and from the character of the passage itself—that he was very largely the author of the following account of Jemima Hardy's reading that appeared with the portrait sketch in the *Book Monthly*, 1 (May 1904), pp. 524–6.

It is possible to add something, to what has already been said, about Mr Thomas Hardy's mother, who died last month. Her strong literary bias brought her into kinship with letters, independently of the writings of her son. She was catholic in her taste for books, enjoying the philosophy of Johnson's *Rasselas*[33] in turn with the frivolities of Combe's *Doctor Syntax*.[34] She preferred *Marmion* to any of Scott's prose works,[35] of the latter liking *Kenilworth* the best. Byron, of course, she admired, influenced possibly by his vogue in her youth. It was *Vanity Fair* which she seemed to rate above all other novels by deceased writers.

Mrs Hardy appreciated Fielding, though she considered him 'low', too frequently: yet admitting that if there had been no Fielding there would probably have been no Thackeray. She held the *Mill on the Floss* to be the best of George Eliot's novels, caring less for *Adam Bede* by reason of the doctrinal part, which she regarded—perhaps unjustly—as an adroit manœuvre of the author to gain the ear of the orthodox. A friend of hers had reviewed it under the belief that it was written by an Evangelical parson.[36] Hutchins's *History of Dorset* perennially interested Mrs Hardy, and naturally, her people being mentioned thercin.[37] Shc lies in the churchyard described under the name of 'Mellstock' in the Wessex novels.

[1904.14]

'Tolstoy on War'

The Times, 27 June 1904, pp. 4–5, published the full text, in translation, of 'Bethink Yourselves' by Count Leo Tolstoy (1828–1910), a dissertation or—as Hardy called it—a philosophic sermon on war, written in the context of the ongoing Russo-Japanese conflict. A leading article in the same issue (p. 11) praised Tolstoy's earnestness and sincerity but strongly criticized what it saw as the crudeness of his logic and the inflammatory nature of his rhetoric. Hardy's prompt and strongly worded reaction was printed, as below, under the presumably editorial heading 'Tolstoy on War', in *The Times*, 28 June, p. 9, and he placed in his 'Personal' scrapbook (DCM)

---

[33] Cf. *LW*, p. 21.

[34] *The Tour of Doctor Syntax, in Search of the Picturesque*, the first of three 'Doctor Syntax' verse satires written by William Combe and illustrated by Rowlandson, first appeared in book form in 1812.   [35] A preference shared by TH himself: see *LW*, pp. 51, 250–1.

[36] Horace Moule, in the course of a positive review of *Adam Bede*, George Eliot's second book of fiction, in the *Saturday Review*, 26 February 1859, wrote of the author: 'He is evidently a country clergyman . . .' (p. 250).

[37] Christopher Swetman, a seventeenth-century ancestor of Jemima Hardy (*née* Hand), is mentioned in the Melbury Osmund section of John Hutchins, *The History and Antiquities of the County of Dorset*, 3rd edn., 4 vols. (Westminster: John Bowyer Nichols and Sons, 1861–70), iv. 439.

a cutting of the letter's reappearance—minus address, date, salutation, vale-
diction, and signature—on the front page of the *Star* that same afternoon.
The letter was subsequently included, minus address and date, in *Life and
Work*, p. 346. Purdy, p. 271.

The Athenæum, Pall-mall, S. W., June 27.

Sir,

I should like to be allowed space to express in the fewest words a
view of Count Tolstoy's philosophic sermon on war, of which you print
a translation in your impression of to-day and a comment in your
leading article.

The sermon may show many of the extravagances of detail to which
the world has grown accustomed in Count Tolstoy's later writings. It
may exhibit, here and there, incoherence as a moral system. Many
people may object to the second half of the dissertation—its special
application to Russia in the present war (on which I can say nothing).
Others may be unable to see advantage in the writer's use of theological
terms for describing and illustrating the moral evolutions of past ages.
But surely all these objectors should be hushed by his great argument,
and every defect in his particular reasonings hidden by the blaze of glory
that shines from his masterly general indictment of war as a modern
principle, with all its senseless and illogical crimes.

Your obedient servant,

Thomas Hardy.

[1904.15]

[On Modern Idealism]

Hardy replied on 20 June 1901 to a request from the Italian journalist
Arnaldo Cervesato (20 April 1901, DCM) for an expression of his views on
the revival of idealism in the modern world. It was not until three years later,
however, that an Italian translation of his letter—described as 'di colore, a dir
vero, un po' troppo enigmatico'—was published, along with many others,
in Cervesato's *Primavera d'idee* (Bari: Gius. Laterza & Figli, 1904), p. 231.
Hardy's original letter appeared in facsimile (p. 104) as an illustration to
Ulisse Ortensi's 'Letterati Contemporanei: Thomas Hardy' in the Italian
journal *Emporium*, 20 (July 1904), pp. 100–8, and was more recently in the
possession of David Holmes; also surviving is Hardy's identically worded

draft (DCM), presumably the source for the slightly abbreviated reprinting of the letter in *Life and Work*, p. 333. The first text below is that of *Primavera d'idee*, the second that of Hardy's original letter, shorn of those elements (address, date, salutation, valediction, signature) that Cervesato chose not to reproduce.

La mia riposta alla sua inchiesta sarà breve. Io non credo che vi sia per essere alcun risveglio sicuro degli antichi ideali transcendentali, ma credo che si possa sviluppare gradatamente un idealismo della fantasia, ossia un idealismo nel quale la fantasia non sia più truccata e mascherata come fede, ma sia accettata francamente ed onestamente come una consolazione immaginosa, non potendosi trovare una qualche consolazione sostanziale nella vita.

*   *   *   *   *

My reply to your inquiry must be brief.[38] I do not think that there will be any permanent revival of the old transcendental ideals, but that there may gradually be developed an Idealism of Fancy; that is, an idealism in which Fancy is no longer tricked out and made to masquerade as Belief, but is frankly and honestly accepted as an imaginative solace in the lack of any substantial solace to be found in life.

[1904.16]

[First Meeting of the Dorset Men in London]

The *Dorset County Chronicle*, 14 July 1904, p. 5, carried a long report of the meeting held in London on 7 July 1904 to consider the formation of 'an association of Dorset men in London'. Quoted along with other communications read out at the gathering was the following letter of apology and good wishes that Hardy had addressed to William Watkins (1863–1925), convenor of the meeting and subsequently honorary secretary of the new Society of Dorset Men in London. The report was reprinted in the *Society of Dorset Men in London* (Year-Book 1904–5), Hardy's letter appearing, as below, on pp. 17–18.

---

[38] *LW* omits this opening sentence.

The Athenæum, Pall Mall, S. W. July 5th, 1904.

My dear Sir,

I have only just received your circular and letter, owing to my having been in Town since the Spring. Though I shall not personally be able to attend the meeting of Dorset men on the 7th, I wish it every success in its object, and hope that such an Association may tend to free Dorset from the reproach one sometimes hears levelled against it—that of being one of the most narrow-minded of English counties.

Faithfully yours,
Thomas Hardy.

[1904.17]

[Message to the Wessex Society of Manchester]

Having agreed in 1897 to become the first president of the Wessex Society of Manchester (see 1897.07), Hardy was evidently expected to send greetings from time to time to the Society's members. The following letter was apparently published only to the extent of being read out at one of the Society's meetings, but—as promised at 1897.07—it is reproduced here (from *CL* iii. 142) as exemplifying a minor but not unimportant aspect of Hardy's public activity.

Max Gate, Dorchester. Oct. 20: 1904

Dear Sir:

It is a pleasure to hear of the continued prosperity of the Wessex Society of Manchester. Such Societies are a growing feature of our age, and they probably tend as much as anything to develop that spirit of kinship among men which, we may hope, will one day overrule national jealousies and obliterate the antagonisms of race.[39]

Yours truly
Thomas Hardy.

The President, Wessex Society, Manchester.

---

[39] In January 1902 TH had somewhat misquoted Southey in reminding the Society's members that 'Whatever strengthens local attachments strengthens both individual and national character' (*CL* iii. [1]).

Laurence Hope

'Laurence Hope' was the pseudonym of the poet Adela Florence (called Violet) Nicolson who had recently committed suicide in the Indian city of Madras following the death at the age of sixty-one of her husband, Lieutenant-General Malcolm Hassels Nicolson of the Bengal Army, twenty-two years her senior. Hardy had met Violet Nicolson for the first, and probably the only time, at the home of Blanche Alethea Crackanthorpe, and been much struck by her beauty and personality. She presented him with copies of her two published volumes of verse, *The Garden of Kama* and *Stars of the Desert*, and they corresponded after her return to India. Hardy seems to have thought her still younger than she actually was (*CL* iii. 142, 143), and his distress at the news of her death prompted the writing of the unsigned obituary published, as below, under the heading ' "Laurence Hope" ' in the *Athenaeum*, 29 October 1904, p. 591. Currently unlocated is the heavily corrected three-page draft of the obituary, once in the collection of Carroll A. Wilson and listed as no. 192 in *A Descriptive Catalogue of the Grolier Club Centenary Exhibition 1940 of the Works of Thomas Hardy, O. M. 1840–1928* (Waterville, Me.: Colby College Library, 1940). Purdy, p. 309.

We learn with much regret that the accomplished poet who was known to the world by the above pseudonym, but whose real name was Violet Nicolson, died by her own hand at Madras, on the 4th inst., as a result of the intense grief and depression which had settled upon her since the loss of her husband, Lieut.-General Malcolm[40] Nicolson, C. B., in August last.

There were those who saw in the volumes of verse that 'Laurence Hope' had already put forth great promise for any future productions of her pen. *The Garden of Kama*, which appeared in 1901, was described as a series of love lyrics from India,[41] and their tropical luxuriance and Sapphic fervour[42] attracted the attention of so many readers that a second and third edition of the book were demanded. The reviewers accepted these compositions by 'Mr Hope' for what they professed

[40] Spelled 'Malcom' in the *Athenaeum*.

[41] *The Garden of Kama, and Other Love Lyrics from India*, arranged in verse by Laurence Hope (London: William Heinemann, 1902 [1901]).

[42] The Grolier Catalogue notes of TH's revisions to the draft: 'The perfect phrase for her poetry, "Sapphic fervour", was not captured until a fourth attempt.'

to be, translations or imitations; but, remembering the *Sonnets from the Portuguese*,[43] we may at least go so far as to doubt if it will ever be precisely known how much in them was imitation and how much original work. The same remark may be made of the volume published last year, *Stars of the Desert*,[44] which shows a greater mastery of rhythm than she had before attained to, and a firmer intellectual grasp, with no loss of intensity. It is noticeable that on nearly the last page of her last book she writes:—

> If Fate should say, 'Thy course is run,'
>   It would not make me sad;
> All that I wished to do is done,
>   All that I would have, had.[45]

The author was still in the early noon of her life, vigour, and beauty, and the tragic circumstances of her death seem but the impassioned closing notes of her impassioned effusions.

---

[43] Although the title of Elizabeth Barrett Browning's sonnet sequence (1850) suggested that the poems were simply translations, they were in fact intensely personal.

[44] *Stars of the Desert*, by Laurence Hope (London: William Heinemann, 1903).

[45] TH quotes the first four lines of a six-line stanza from the sequence of poems about sexual love called 'The Court of Pomegranates'; the stanza concludes: 'My Lord has left his life with me, | And mine divinely glad!' (*Stars of the Desert*, pp. 150–1).

1905

[1905.01]

'Will Maxim Gorky be Hanged?'

A report headed 'Will Maxim Gorky Be Hanged?' in the *Morning Leader*, 31 January 1905, p. 4, placed the names of Swinburne, Meredith, and Hardy at the top of an otherwise alphabetical list of signatories to a protest—initiated by the *Morning Leader* itself—against the threatened execution in St Petersburg of the Russian novelist Maxim Gorky (pseudonym of Aleksei Maksimovich Peshkov, 1868–1936), who had been involved in the early stages of the abortive 1905 revolution. A cutting of the protest as reprinted in the *Morning Leader*, 1 February, p. 4, is in Hardy's 'Personal' scrapbook (DCM).

[1905.02]

[Disclaimer of Smithard Interview] [1]

Although Hardy had learned from long experience to be distrustful of interviewers, both confessed and unconfessed, he seems to have been deceived as to the intentions of a W. Smithard (otherwise unidentified) whose 'Thomas Hardy. A Talk with the Wessex Novelist at Casterbridge' was published in the *Daily Chronicle*, 8 February 1905, p. 4. Hardy's prompt disclaimer appeared, as below, under the heading 'Mr. Thomas Hardy', in the *Daily Chronicle*, 9 February 1905, p. 3, but the interview nevertheless reappeared, in part, in the *Dorset County Chronicle*, 16 February 1905, pp. 4–5. Extracts were again printed in the New York *Critic*, April 1905, pp. 305–6, but so also was the text of Hardy's letter of repudiation. Purdy, p. 310.

Dorchester, Feb. 8.

Sir,

In respect of the interview with myself that you print this morning, I should like to state that it was obtained through a misapprehension on my part, and does not accurately reflect my opinions.

I had no idea, when receiving the apparently artless visitor, who now signs the production, that he was an interviewer who would report my conversation.[1]

Thomas Hardy.

[1905.03]

[Disclaimer of Smithard Interview] [2]

When the *Dorset County Chronicle* reprinted the interview by W. Smithard from the London *Daily Chronicle* (see 1905.02), Hardy evidently felt obliged to issue a second disclaimer for local consumption. The surviving MS (G. Stevens-Cox) is headed 'To the Editor of the Dorset Chronicle' and signed as from 'Your obedient servant' but otherwise differs only in minor details from the letter printed, as below, under the heading 'The Interview with Mr. Hardy', in the *Dorset County Chronicle*, 23 February 1905, p. 13.

Max Gate, February 19th.

In reference to the interview with myself which you quote from a London paper in your last week's impression, it may be desirable to repeat to your readers, what has already been stated elsewhere, that the article was unauthorised, and is incorrect as to my views, being in some places 'faked',[2] so that I am not responsible for what it contains.

Thomas Hardy.

---

[1] The *Daily Chronicle* stated in an appended note that the article had been accepted 'in the belief that Mr Hardy had consented to its publication'.

[2] TH had evidently registered its substantial indebtedness to the interview published in the *Manchester Guardian*, 15 October 1904, p. 6.

[1905.04]

[Motto for Society of Dorset Men in London]

At the Inaugural Dinner of the Society of Dorset Men in London, 27 February 1905, as reported in the *Dorset County Chronicle*, 2 March 1905, p. 5 (subsequently reprinted in the Society's Year-Book for 1904–5, p. 41), the following message from Hardy was read out—to 'Laughter and loud applause'—by his friend Sir Frederick Treves, Bt, the eminent Dorchester-born surgeon who was serving as the Society's first president. The Society promptly adopted 'Who's afraid?' as its motto, later modifying it, with Hardy's approval, to the dialect form 'Who's A-Feär'd?' (Year-Book for 1925, p. 8). The text below is that of the *Dorset County Chronicle*.

It is a sign of the times that modest little Dorset should at last have the courage to stand up to great London and say, 'Who's afraid?'

[1905.05]

[Vice-Presidency of Dorset Men in London]

The letter of 25 February 1905 (*CL* iii. 158) that Hardy wrote to William Watkins, secretary to the Society of Dorset Men in London, when accepting the Society's vice-presidency is included here as having been read out by Watkins at the Society's inaugural meeting on 27 February 1905 and printed, as below, when the occasion was reported in the *Dorset County Chronicle*, 2 March 1905, p. 6. The same report appeared in *Society of Dorset Men in London* (Year-Book 1904–5), p. 54.

Max Gate, Dorchester, February 25th.

My dear Sir,

I am in receipt of your letter of yesterday, in which your committee honour me by a request that I should be associated with the Society of Dorset Men in London as a vice-president. I have much pleasure in assenting to their wish if my probable inability to be present at dinners or meetings does not incapacitate me for such a distinction.

I am, dear Sir, yours truly,

Thomas Hardy.

[1905.06]

[Aberdeen Honorary Degree]

Hardy included in *Life and Work*, p. 347, the following extract from what was evidently his preserved draft of a formal letter of thanks to the University of Aberdeen—presumably addressed to its then Principal, John Marshall Lang—on the occasion, in early March 1905, of his being offered an honorary doctor of laws degree (see *CL* iii. 159–60 and note). Although no publication of the letter has been discovered, Hardy presumably regarded it to some extent as a public document, and the extract seems in any case worth reprinting here as a reminder of his appearance at the degree ceremony itself, 7 April 1905, when he was cheered by the largely undergraduate audience but not required to respond with a speech of any kind. See Martin Ray, 'Thomas Hardy in Aberdeen', *Aberdeen University Review*, 56 (Spring 1995), pp. 58–69.

I am impressed by its coming from Aberdeen, for though a stranger to that part of Scotland to a culpable extent I have always observed with admiration the exceptional characteristics of the Northern University, which in its fostering encouragement of mental effort seems to cast an eye over these islands that is unprejudiced, unbiassed and unsleeping.

[1905.07]

[Birthday Dinner for Frederick Greenwood]

Hardy was named both in *The Times*, 14 March 1905, p. 11, and in Clement Shorter's 'Literary Letter' page in the *Sphere*, 18 March 1905, p. 282, as a member of the committee organizing a dinner to honour the 75th birthday of the prominent journalist Frederick Greenwood (see 1883.01), editor of the *Cornhill* 1862–8 and co-founder and for many years editor of the *Pall Mall Gazette*. In *Honouring Frederick Greenwood* (BL), the pamphlet about the dinner that Shorter had privately printed after the event, Hardy was again listed as a committee member and credited with having written 'one of the most sympathetic letters to the Committee'. He absented himself from the actual dinner, however, in order to be present at the honorary degree ceremony in Aberdeen (see 1905.06), and had told Shorter beforehand that he did not think it necessary 'to write a letter for printing, as [Greenwood] was an influential editor long before I was heard of, & it might seem patronizing' (*CL* iii. 165). See also 1905.09.

[1905.08]

'Far from the Madding Crowd: A Correction'

This letter, published as below in the *Spectator* of 29 April 1905, p. 638, was prompted by Hardy's sense that his early dealings with William Tinsley, the publisher of his first three novels, had been damagingly misrepresented by the *Spectator* review (22 April 1905, p. 596) of Edmund Downey's volume of book-selling reminiscences, *Twenty Years Ago* (London: Hurst and Blackett, 1905). Downey, however, responded in the *Spectator*, 6 May 1905, p. 672, that the actual quotation from Tinsley in *Twenty Years Ago*, pp. 20–1, did not in fact accuse Hardy of seeking to negotiate a better price for what became *Far from the Madding Crowd*. Hardy's MS (Beinecke) shows that the letter's date (25 April) was editorially omitted and the valediction standardized. Purdy, p. 310.

The Athenæum, Pall Mall, S. W.

Sir,

I see quoted in innumerable newspapers and reviews, including your own of April 22nd,[3] a statement in a recent book by Mr E. Downey, called *Twenty Years Ago*, to the effect that the novel, *Far from the Madding Crowd*, was offered to the late Mr W. Tinsley, and withdrawn because he would not 'give a rise' on another publisher's price for it. As an unpleasant question of an author's practice with publishers is suggested, I think it worth while to say, if you will allow me room, that the statement is untrue. The story was produced in response to a request from the late Sir Leslie Stephen, the editor, for a novel for the *Cornhill*, and the opening chapters were sent up to him from the country, and accepted—those to follow being taken on trust—without any negotiation elsewhere, or outside knowledge of the matter till after the contract had been entered into with the publishers of the *Cornhill*.

I am, Sir, &c.,

Thomas Hardy.

---

[3] MS shows 'of April 22nd' to have been inserted in another, presumably editorial, hand.

[Draft Paragraph Supplied to the *Sphere*]

Frederick Greenwood (see 1905.07) was displeased by Hardy's letter in the *Spectator*, 29 April 1905 (1905.08), and wrote privately to him that same day (typed transcript, Leeds) to reassert and justify his claim—made, for example, in the *Illustrated London News*, 1 October 1892, p. 431—to have first brought *Under the Greenwood Tree* to the attention of the *Cornhill* and so opened the way to the serialization of *Far from the Madding Crowd*. Clement Shorter had drawn his own irritated letter from Greenwood (typed transcript, Leeds) by saying in his *Sphere* 'Literary Letter', 22 April, p. 90—perhaps at Hardy's suggestion—that Greenwood's *Cornhill* story, 'Mr. Hardy assures me, is a pretty invention'. On 1 May 1905, therefore, the date of his personal reply to Greenwood (*CL* vii. 138–9), Hardy also drafted and sent to Shorter the following conciliatory statement—reproduced here from a typed transcript apparently made for Shorter at a later date (Leeds; see *Index*, HrT 1416.5)—and urged him to 'put a paragraph in your Literary Letter embodying what I have jotted down' (*CL* vii. 139). Shorter in fact devoted three paragraphs of his 'Literary Letter', *Sphere*, 13 May 1905, p. 162, to the topic, adapting rather than directly reproducing Hardy's draft and supplementing it from other sources, including the letter he had himself received from Greenwood.

Mr T.H's contradiction of a statement in Mr Downey's book of reminiscences that having been offered a price for *Far from the Madding Crowd*[4] for the *Cornhill Magazine*, he told it to the late Mr Tinsley to get him to bid higher, an unlikely statement on the face of it—has led to quite irrelevant comments. The *Daily News*[5] and other papers have found it difficult to reconcile Mr H's assertion that the late Sir Leslie Stephen, and nobody else, asked him for *F.M.C.* for the *Cornhill*, with the generally accredited statement that it was Mr F. Greenwood who obtained that story for the Magazine. But surely there is no contradiction here. The facts are, I believe, that Mr Greenwood, though he had discontinued editing the *Cornhill*, still retained a connection with it, and having read *Under the Greenwood Tree* suggested to Mr Stephen (who had succeeded him in the editorship) and to Mr George Smith the publisher, that a story by the author of that book would suit the *Cornhill*. They read it, and agreeing with Mr Greenwood, Mr Leslie Stephen (as he then was) wrote to Mr Hardy as he has declared.

---

[4] Corrected from the typescript's 'Maddening Crowd'.
[5] '*Far from the Madding Crowd*', *Daily News*, 29 April 1905, p. 6.

[1905.10]

[Contributions to Hermann Lea's *Handbook*]

Although Hardy was on friendly terms with Hermann Lea (1869–1952), photographer and aspiring author, he declined to authorize Lea's *A Handbook to the Wessex Country of Thomas Hardy's Novels and Poems* (London: Kegan Paul, Trench, Trübner; Bournemouth: Holland Rowbottom, [1905]). His numerous letters to Lea in *Collected Letters* nevertheless display a lively attentiveness to both the general and the specific statements being made in the little book. Lea seems gladly to have accepted Hardy's guidance (see e.g. *CL* iii. 137–8, with its list of Wessex place names), and his opening paragraphs (pp. [1]–2) incorporate word for word the definitions of the geographical scope of Wessex and the relationship between Wessex settings and actual places that Hardy supplied in his letter of 1 June 1905 (*CL* iii. 171–2). See 1913.04 for Hardy's contribution to Lea's more substantial *Thomas Hardy's Wessex* (1913).

[1905.11]

[Introduction to Tyndale Exhibition Catalogue]

Walter Tyndale (1855–1943), an artist specializing in watercolour, collaborated with the journalist Clive Holland (see 1901.05) in the production of *Wessex* (London: Adam & Charles Black, 1906), a topographical and historical survey of south-western England, written by Holland and generously illustrated by Tyndale's watercolours. During the summer of 1905, Tyndale exhibited the original paintings at the Leicester Galleries in London, prefacing the printed catalogue with an 'introductory letter' from Hardy, clearly written for that specific purpose. That letter, however, was not included in Tyndale's *Hardy Country Water-Colours* (London: A. & C. Black, [1920?]). The text below is that of the *Catalogue of an Exhibition of Water-Colours of Wessex (Thomas Hardy's Country) by Walter Tyndale* (London: Leicester Galleries, June–July 1905), pp. 5–6. Purdy, p. 310.

Hyde Park Mansions, W. June 5th, 1905.

Dear Mr Tyndale,

It was a pleasant surprise to me to find that you had been lingering unseen in the nooks and corners of Wessex, with no other object than to produce these many charming water-colour sketches of some of the typical scenery there.

Their number is beyond what I should have fancied you could paint even in the greater part of the whole year which I believe you have given to the work. Many a scorching sun and dripping cloud you must have suffered from to get so much material at such differing seasons in our uncertain climate.

You will remember, perhaps, the way in which I became aware of your presence in that part of the country, and of your intentions respecting it. Last November, was it not, when I broke from the meadow into the church-path, and observed your figure motionless under a tree, with the red and yellow leaves falling round you? You were endeavouring, so intently to get their true colours on to your paper that you did not per- ceive me till I drew close, wondering who the stranger was. It was one of those trifling incidents that leave a permanent picture in the mind—a picture which you yourself were not able to see, although you saw so many.

You ask me what I think of these impressions of Wessex. I am unfor- tunately unable to give any valuable critical opinion in the usual tech- nical sense; but to their fidelity, both in form and in colour, I can testify. And you seem to have conveyed in your renderings that under- picture, as one may say that mood or temperament, which pertains to each particular spot portrayed, and to no other on earth.

I am, yours truly,
Thomas Hardy.

[1905.12]

[Unpublished Preface to Posthumous Poems of Laurence Hope]

Following the death of 'Laurence Hope' (see 1904.18) in October 1904, her friend Blanche Crackanthorpe arranged with William Heinemann for the publication of a posthumous collection, *Indian Love*, and asked Hardy to supply a preface. That preface, however, was omitted from the volume as published (London, 1905)—probably because of its lukewarm tone, tactless conclusion, and heavy dependence on Hardy's already published obituary (1904.18)—and on 16 July 1905 (*CL* vii. 140) Hardy wrote angrily to Heinemann to demand an explanation, withdraw all permissions, and seek the return of his manuscript. What Heinemann evidently sent was the three-page typescript now in the Dorset County Museum, although a note on its (additional) cover-page, 'The only copy supplied by Mrs. Crackanthorpe', tends to suggest that it had itself been made—presumably by Mrs Crackanthorpe and for purposes of submission—from an original holograph MS. The few markings on the typescript in Hardy's hand are clearly retrospective: on the cover-page he wrote '(never published)'; to the title, 'Preface', he added '[to the posthumous poems of Laurence Hope, written by request]'; and at the foot of the final page he spelled out his name, '[Thos Hardy]', below his typed initials. As the sole textual witness now known to exist, the typescript becomes the necessary source of the text below.

The pages which follow contain the last productions in verse of the accomplished woman who chose to be known to the reading world by the pseudonym of 'Laurence Hope'. Many are now aware that her real name was Violet Nicolson, and that she was the young wife of a Lieutenant-General who died at Madras in August of last year. Her own death, in grief and depression at her loss, took place less than two months after that of her husband.

Now that for her, in poetry as in all else, the rest is silence,[6] one may feel a passing regret that by not using on her title page the name she actually bore—far from an unattractive one—or a distinctly feminine pseudonym if some disguise were her fancy, she should have refrained in her authorship from an avowal of sex which would have thrown light at the beginning on the sentiment of her canticles. In the long run women almost invariably lose more than they gain by masquerading on the literary stage in male attire.

It was the experience of the present writer to meet Violet Nicolson only once, and then in a room full of people; but in the half hour's intercourse she communicated to her interlocutor a distincter sense of an individuality than is usually conveyed by persons after many meetings, even when they possess it. The impression of her personality was that of one whose nature was not sufficiently renunciative to be likely to

---

[6] Shakespeare, *Hamlet*, v. ii. 358.

encounter the ordinary shocks of life without exceptional perturbation, distress, and rebellion. She was obviously not of those, if any there be, who can execute to their satisfaction the moral feat which delighted the Psalmist—to look upon the travail of their souls and be satisfied;[7] much the reverse, indeed.

There were readers who saw in the volumes that 'Laurence Hope' put forth, great promise for any future productions of her pen. *The Garden of Kama* which appeared in 1901, was described as a series of Love-lyrics from India, and their tropical luxuriance and sapphic fervour attracted the attention of so many readers that a second and third impression of the book were issued. The reviewers accepted these compositions by 'Mr Hope' for what they professed to be—translations or imitations; but remembering the *Sonnets from the Portuguese* we may at least go so far as to doubt if it will ever be precisely known how much in them was imitation and how much original work. The same remark may apply to the next volume that she published, some time in 1903, entitled *Stars of the Desert*, which shows a greater mastery of rhythm than she had before attained to, and a greater intellectual steadiness, without loss of ardency.[8]

In many pieces of the present collection the assumption, or reality, of imitation, is apparently still kept up. Now that the unexpected has happened, and a comparatively young figure makes her last recital in public as a disembodied phantom, beside whose sad intangibility the fires of the flesh are a grim incongruousness, we may wish that the choice of note or model in some of these emotional artistries could have been otherwise, even while recognizing their purely dramatic or per-sonative character. But all such would have fallen naturally into their evolutionary place and value had they been succeeded by less wayward performances of larger scope and schooled feeling, such as would in the probable order of things have come from her hand if she had survived to philosophic years. They are not without a pathetically humourous side when we are informed of the exemplary English domesticity of the writer's own life, and of the contributory if not primary cause of her death.

It is noticeable that on nearly the last page of the last book printed by herself she declares

---

[7] In fact, a reference to Isa. 53: 11.

[8] Entire paragraph taken almost verbatim from Hardy's obituary of 'Laurence Hope', although 'ardency' itself is an interesting substitution for the obituary's 'intensity'.

> If Fate should say, 'Thy course is run',
>   It would not make me sad;
> All that I wished to do is done,
>   All that I would have, had.

The author was still in the warm noon of her life, vigour, and beauty when she wrote thus; and the tragic circumstances of her end so shortly after seem but the impassioned closing notes of her impassioned effusions.[9]

[1905.13]

[Dorchester Sewage Works]

Hardy, distressed for some time by the odours emanating from new sewage disposal works in the vicinity of Max Gate, was much pleased by the success of R. R. Talbot, the owner of nearby Syward Lodge, in obtaining a High Court injunction restraining the Dorchester council from continuing with the construction work (*Dorset County Chronicle*, 3 August 1905, p. 9; see also 31 October 1901, pp. 12–13). The 'public' status of the following letter (included in *CL* iii. 179) is perhaps debateable: although Hardy obviously meant it to be read by the mayor and councillors, he may not have welcomed or even foreseen its publication, as below, in the *Dorset County Chronicle*, 10 August 1905, p. 12.

Max Gate, Dorchester, August 7th.

Dear Sir,

I see from one of the local papers that an appeal is contemplated from the judgment in the case of Talbot *v*. The Dorchester Corporation. I suggest that a meeting of the inhabitants be called before a step involving such a serious risk of their money be undertaken.[10]

Yours truly,

T. Hardy.

The Mayor of Dorchester.

[9] Final paragraph, including quotation, again taken almost verbatim from obituary, with 'warm noon' substituted for 'early noon'.

[10] The councillors rejected TH's advice and 'resented it as intrusive' (see *CL* iii. 179–80), although—as Sampson (see headnote to 1888.01) points out—such a meeting was eventually held.

[1905.14]

[Speech to the Institute of Journalists]

Some two hundred members of the Institute of Journalists, divided into two groups, paid a one-day visit to south Dorset, including Hardy's house at Max Gate, on 1 September 1905. The first group to arrive at Max Gate did little more than walk around the garden, but the second, and larger, group was entertained to tea in a marquee erected for the purpose, and Hardy and his wife both responded briefly to a proposed and twice-seconded vote of thanks. Hardy's speech—clearly reflective of his experience with the Whitefriars Club (see 1901.05, 1901.09)—was reported as follows in the *Dorset County Chronicle*, 7 September 1905, p. 5. *The Times*, 2 September, p. 5, also reported his remarks, but in the third person.

I have such very strong reasons for not making a speech that I will confine myself to a very few words, and simply say I am very glad to see you here. I wish you had a longer time, and that you could see more of the scenery of the county than you will be able to see to-day—the beautiful scenery that lies further in the middle of the county. If ever you should come this way again and will go along some of the prominences, such as Bulbarrow and High Stoy, and other places pretty well known, you will see we have some scenery worth showing.[11]

[1905.15]

'The Commemoration of Crabbe'

Hardy went to Aldeburgh, Suffolk, in late September 1907 to attend the (belated) celebrations of the 150th anniversary of the birth, in Aldeburgh, of the poet George Crabbe (1754–1832). He insisted in advance to his host, Edward Clodd, that he could take no active part in the event itself (*CL* vii. 141), and he certainly made no formal presentation of any kind; in the press, however, he was variously quoted as having declared, e.g., that Crabbe was 'the father of poetic realism' (*Guardian*, 25 June 1914, p. 808) and that he

---

[11] Bernard Jones has noted the echo of stanza 1, line 6, of Barnes's 'Praise o' Do'set': 'We've an ox or two wo'th showèn'.

'had sucked his earliest inspiration from Crabbe' (*Outlook*, 9 March 1907, p. 308)—which latter statement Hardy altered in his 'Personal' scrapbook (DCM) to read 'had learnt his earliest realism from Crabbe'. What Hardy may have said in conversation is unknown, but the only documentable source for these remarks yet discovered is the following sentence from a speech by Clement Shorter as quoted, under the heading 'The Commemoration of Crabbe', in *The Times*, 18 September 1905, p. 9.

To those who loved the novels of Mr Thomas Hardy, who was present, Mr Shorter stated that he had Mr Hardy's authority for saying that Crabbe had the most potent influence upon his work.[12]

[1905.16]

Foreword [to *Dorchester (Dorset) and its Surroundings*]

Hardy had submitted suggestions for a projected new Dorchester guidebook in April 1902 (*CL* iii. 19–20; *Index*, HrT 1568.5), and his readiness to supply a brief 'Foreword' to F. R. and Sidney Heath, *Dorchester (Dorset) and its Surroundings* (Dorchester: F. G. Longman; London: The Homeland Association, 1905), p. [7], was doubtless influenced by the book's designation as Dorchester's 'Official Guide' (see Sidney Heath, 'Thomas Hardy. By a Teacher who Knew Him', *Teacher's World*, 18 January 1928, p. 826) and its inclusion of 'Notes Respecting the Country Walks round Dorchester' by his recently deceased friend Henry J. Moule. Hardy's holograph MS (Texas; *Index*, HrT 1544) is headed 'Foreword' and corresponds precisely to the published text as reproduced below. The proof copy of the entire book (Texas; *Index*, HrT 1818) shows that Hardy also made several corrections and additions to the main body of the text, all of them incorporated prior to publication. Hardy acknowledged receipt of the published book on 21 November 1905 (*CL* iii. 188). Purdy, p. 310.

I have been asked by the compiler of this guide-book to examine the topographical and historical portions of his text; and having done so,

---

[12] *LW*, p. 351, speaks of TH's attending all the Aldeburgh events and 'honouring Crabbe as an apostle of realism who practised it in English literature three-quarters of a century before the French realistic school had been heard of'. See also *CL* v. 294.

I can say without hesitation that, so far as I am able to judge, he has embodied therein a quantity of closely-packed material, rich in anti-quarian and contemporaneous fact to a degree not common in so small a volume. This is particularly the case in the paragraphs which deal with the period of the Roman occupation and the mediæval and later centuries.

On the pages which refer to certain works of fiction and poems of recent date I naturally express no opinion.[13]

The book has the recommendation of containing a map of the town and its suburbs—a feature lacking, so far as I am aware, in all previous guides of the kind.[14] Natives of the ancient borough may smile at the idea of any sane person losing his way in a town of ten thousand inhabit-ants; yet I have been credibly informed that such is frequently the case, even amongst teetotallers; and I have myself met with one gentleman —a most ingenious and intelligent person—who suffered from the same misadventure, and complained bitterly of there being no readily accessible map for his guidance. The need is now supplied.

[13] In the proof copy TH nonetheless paid particular attention to statements about his own life, works, and 'Wessex' locations: e.g. he added of Colliton House 'This is Lucetta's house as to character, though not as to situation' (p. 75), and changed the identification of Little Hintock from Melbury Osmund to 'under High-Stoy' (p. 114).

[14] The provision of a map had been TH's first recommendation when a new Dorchester guide was being considered in 1902 (*CL* iii. 19).

1906

[1906.01]

'Anglo-German Relations'

At a time of political tension between Britain and Germany, *The Times*, 12 January 1906, p. 15, printed two letters under the above heading, the first an assertion of friendly feelings towards Great Britain signed by a group of German scientists, scholars, artists, and composers, the second a response in the same positive vein signed by a similarly wide-ranging group of leading British figures, Hardy among them. The artist William Rothenstein was active in obtaining the British signatures (*CL* iii. 193), but it appears from the archive of related material in the Berg collection of the New York Public Library that the letter was drafted by George Bernard Shaw, not himself a signatory. Hardy jotted down the main points of the draft on the back of Rothenstein's initial request of 19 December 1905 (DCM); the copy of the mimeographed draft that he actually signed is in the Berg.

[1906.02]

[?Inspired Paragraphs on Part Two of *The Dynasts*?]

Hardy's journalist friend James Milne was editor of the *Book Monthly* and book editor of the *Daily Chronicle*, and in the light of Hardy's known use of Milne as an unacknowledged mouthpiece (see e.g. 1899.03, 1904.01) it seems likely that he was in some sense the originator of the advance announcements of Part Two of *The Dynasts* published in Milne's 'Books of the Day' column, *Daily Chronicle*, 12 January 1906, p. 3, and (following the line of asterisks) in the *Book Monthly*, February 1906, p. 346.

Another volume of Mr Thomas Hardy's poetic drama of the Napoleonic period will be out at the end of January—Macmillan. It begins just before the battle of Jena, and carries the drama onward to the fighting at Torres Vedras. Mr Hardy has still another volume of this work to write before it is completed. Until then, at all events, no new novel by him—if, indeed, he writes any more fiction—need be expected.

*   *   *   *   *

An interesting book of the month will be the second part, 4s. 6d. net, of Mr Thomas Hardy's drama of the Napoleonic wars, *The Dynasts*. This volume opens with a scene in Fox's lodgings in Arlington Street, that statesman being described as 'a stout, swarthy man with shaggy eyebrows'. Then the drama passes to Paris, to Berlin, to Jena, and to the Spanish Peninsula, finally closing in London. Besides Napoleon, all the historical figures of that time are introduced in this work, which will be completed in a third volume.

[1906.03]

H.J.M.: Some Memories and Letters

Hardy was friendly with several of the seven sons of the Revd Henry Moule (1801–80), ingenious inventor and redoubtable evangelical Vicar of the Dorchester suburb of Fordington. His earliest and most intimate relationship was with the brilliant but unstable Horace Moule (see 1922.04), who committed suicide in 1873, but in later years he developed a close friendship with the eldest of the brothers, Henry Joseph Moule (1825–1904), who had a career in estate management outside Dorset, became Curator of the Dorset County Museum in the early 1880s, and is still actively remembered for his distinctive and evocative watercolour sketches of the local countryside. Hardy's affectionate reminiscence of his friend appeared, as below (omitting quotation marks around inset passages), in the new edition of Moule's *Dorchester Antiquities* (Dorchester: Henry Ling), pp. [7]–13, published in January 1906; though referred to within the volume as a 'preface', it is not so headed, presumably because the author's own preface had been retained from the edition of 1901. Also retained from that earlier edition were Hardy's drawing, p. 76, of an integral group of three linked fibulae found at Max Gate and his quoted comment, pp. 75–6: 'It seems to be of three metals —iron (at the hinge), bronze in the body and rings, and the pins gold.' Purdy, pp. 310–11,

My first distinct recollection of Henry Moule carries me back, through a long avenue of years, towards the middle of the last century. His figure emerges from the obscurity of forgotten and half-forgotten things somewhere between 1856 and 1860, when I recall him as he stood beside me while I was attempting a sketch from nature in water colours. He must have been about thirty, and had already become an adept in out-door painting. As I was but a youth, and by no means practised in that art, he criticized my performance freely.

How it happened that we were together thus I am quite unable to remember; also whether I had known him long. Possibly I had known him slightly for some time, for at this date there was a perennial discussion in progress between my father and his, the Vicar of Fordington, about a field which my father owned but had no use for, which the Vicar had a mind to take for experiments in his well-known hobby of spade husbandry. Every year the question was renewed, the field looked at, heads shaken, and the matter again shelved.

Anyhow, when I took up water-colouring, our common interest led him frequently to call at my home, to ascertain what further exercises I had been giving myself in that accomplishment. He was such an enthusiast in painting that, though he always insisted on calling himself a mere amateur, there is no doubt he would have achieved high results therein if he had chosen to make of it a profession instead of a pastime. To such a man my youthful and intermittent fancy for the same pursuit must have seemed unsatisfactory enough.

At this time he used to impress me as being rather taciturn than otherwise, which may seem strange to those who knew him only as the fluent conversationalist of later years. Another difference from more recent conceptions of him lay in the fact that his interests seemed to be not especially centred in Dorset and Dorset matters—further than that the county afforded good sketching ground. This may probably be explained by his experiences immediately preceding those years. Since leaving Cambridge he had travelled over a good deal of Europe, had lived away from Dorset even when in England, and had had his attention fixed on men and affairs quite dissociated from this county. Nobody could have supposed at that time that a day would come when his interests would extend but rarely beyond it.

Change took us both far from Dorset anon; him to Scotland and elsewhere as land-agent, and me to London in the study of architecture. For a long while I heard nothing of him, except indirectly through members of his family or of mine. But a continuous residence in London of several years having begun to tell upon my health I determined to go into the country for a time.[1] He heard of my plan, and wrote to me suggesting estate management as a change of occupation, which would give me plenty of air. The scheme did not suit me, but it had the advantage of renewing our intercourse for a brief season.

The curtain again dropped between us, and how our acquaintance was revived is a mere matter of conjecture. The vicissitudes of life carried me hither and thither between London, Dorset, Somerset, Surrey, Paris, Germany,[2] and elsewhere; but never a line can I discover from him during this long interval. That I saw him occasionally in the seventies is however possible. Not till 1881 does my record reach firm ground. I have before me a letter received from him in the July of that year, when I was temporarily at Wimborne[3] and he was at Weymouth, which shows that the silence between us had been broken:

Your kind invitation to visit you in your new abode has been by no means forgotten by me, and I write to make a proposal in connection with it.

If all goes well I shall be present at my brother Handley's[4] wedding at Cambridge on Aug. 16, and it has occurred to me that as I shall in any case be passing by Wimborne, it would be a capital chance for me to have the pleasure of reviving my acquaintance with you. Do tell me, then, if you shall be at home on the 17th or 18th, and if so, whether it will be convenient to you to receive me for a night. I wish I could bring Mrs Moule[5] with me, but unfortunately she will be obliged to remain at home.

I clearly recall the visit, and how I met him at the station on his arrival. I feared that after so many years I might not recognize him; but there was no difficulty in doing that, though he had changed of course, and so, no doubt, had I. We had a day or two of delightful intercourse, sitting up till the small hours, and one of the subjects of our conversation is alluded to in a letter from him a week or two after:

... I have been thinking much of what you say as to my pencil being brought into play in conjunction with your pen. I do heartily wish that it might come to pass somehow or other. ... If, as you think, landscape with smallish figures will do,

---

[1] TH worked in London as an assistant architect from 1862 to 1867.

[2] TH stayed only a few weeks in Somerset (specifically Yeovil) and made only holiday visits to France and Germany.   [3] TH and his wife lived in Wimborne from June 1881 to June 1883.

[4] Handley Carr Glyn Moule (1841–1920), Principal of Ridley Hall, Cambridge, 1880–99, Bishop of Durham (1901–20); he married Harriot Mary Elliott.

[5] Elizabeth Moule, *née* Young (1833–1915).

I trust that I should be able to do you justice. . . . Then again, I take much to Mrs Hardy's idea of a book on Dorset written by you with landscape and architectural illustrations by me. There I should be at home, I may say . . . I shall be glad to hear from you again on these matters.

Further correspondence ensued on the subject, but nothing came of it, there being doubts 'if Dorset pure and simple would pay'. It must be remembered that the date was nearly a quarter of a century back, when the county was not so popular as it is now. In concluding another letter thereon (October 1881) he adds:

I am so sorry that you had such poor weather for Scotland in general and Roslin in particular.[6] That charming wooded glen depends much on weather for its beauty. The weather in Scotland seems to have changed very locally this season. I was told on Saturday of two parties of tourists who spent August in Scotland— in different parts, it would seem; for one party had 27 wet days and four fine ones, and the other 27 fine and four wet!

After a visit to London and elsewhere, he wrote, the following March (1882):

It seems to me a very long time since last I heard from you. . . . There is one clause in your letter which ought to have been answered.

This, it appears, related to illustrations for magazines, for which he had a fancy just then, and he describes some of his experiments in wood engraving, pen-and-ink drawing, &c., concluding:

I saw the Electric Exhibition at the Crystal Palace,[7] and thought of what you had said of electric engineering being a good field. . . . I have always (ever since) thought of it for my elder boy, who is mighty at mechanism and that sort of thing. . . . To be sure it is early days as yet. He is only 15.[8]

It would be such a pleasure to see you both if you penetrate so far at any time. We could house you in a 'prophet's chamber'.[9]

---

[6] Hardy and his wife visited Scotland in August and September 1881 (*LW*, pp. 154–5).

[7] The International Electrical Exhibition at the Crystal Palace, in south London, opened in stages during January and February 1882.

[8] Moule's elder son, Henry Reginald Moule (1866–1932), in fact entered the Church, but seems to have been dismissed from his Northamptonshire benifice in 1906 following a mysterious 'disappearance'; his Memoir of his father was included in the new edition of *Dorchester Antiquities* together with an announcement—subsequently proved erroneous—that he had recently 'lost his life by drowning'.

[9] Joseph Wright's *English Dialect Dictionary* (1898–1905) defines 'prophet's chamber' as a room occupied by a minister.

New Year's Eve, 1883, stirred the muse in him, on the subject of bar-rows and flint arrow-heads, whereon I had touched in *The Return of the Native*, and he sent me a production in verse. The lines are strong and lyrical, as, *e.g.*, the following. They are supposed to be said or sung by the spirit of a departed Kelt who wanders on the heath in modern times:

> We sleep here lonely on the hill, and as we lie
> Seasons and years and ages slowly pass us by;
> And still they stand, our far-seen barrows on the heath,
> But men speak not the names of us who lie beneath.
> Ah! but our names were shouted loud on that brave day
> When here the astonished legion saw us turn at bay,
> And, shudd'ring, heard the spell poured forth in magic song
> That makes the foeman weak, but Keltic tribesmen strong!
> And when through helm and shield, and through close-jointed mail,
> Pierc'd our death-bearing flint-points, thick as storm of hail,
> Down went Centurion, Prætor, Eagle-bearer bold,
> But not the Eagle—passed in death to comrade's hold!
> But not the Eagle—over sullen slow retreat,
> Still shining, held on high to guide unwilling feet.
>
> .   .   .   .   .
>
> In purple robe his god-like state doth Cæsar keep—
> In purple pall 'tis meet his liegemen sleep.

The removal to Dorchester of both my friend and myself put an end to the necessity of correspondence. From such brief notes as passed between us thence onward I make a few extracts. One (Sept. 1894) is on how to get a good view of the Froom Valley for painting, with Wool Bridge house[10] in the middle distance; it shows that his zest for land-scape art was unabated:

It struck me as a hard problem, and I think so still. However, from an up-train on Wednesday, and a down one to-day, I looked my best to see if I could spy out a fitting spot. The result is that I have a hope—slight, however—that something might be done from a place North of a group of cottages, public house, &c., that you pass about a mile W. of Wool Station.

Later, writing about a view of the same meadows from Norris Mill, he flies off to another subject—one relating to my novel of *Jude*, then being published serially:

[10] Imagined by TH as the house to which Angel Clare took Tess on their wedding night.

It was a good lecture last evening on Christminster (?),[11] and it was a good stroke of policy to have it delivered. It will, I hope, induce some of our artizan friends to attend the lectures in January on the Colonies—lectures emanating from the beautiful city with which they may now claim some acquaintance.[12] It is a fine thing, this permeation of the land by the Universities. Here, yesterday, was Oxford Wells discoursing of Oxford grey colleges and Oxford extension work. Here, yesterday, was Cambridge C. Moule [the writer's brother][13] holding a Cambridge local examination.

Four or five more years of occasional meetings and brief notes lead up to a letter of October, 1902, which reached me when I was staying at Bath.[14] It is about a matter of folk-lore, on which he was keen, and he plunges into it without preface:

Have you heard, I wonder, of the hare 'incident', as the French would call it?

Yesterday a hare could think of nothing better to do than to run all up South Street, across Bull Stake, and up Pease Lane [the Dorchester Council, with doubtful wisdom, has obliterated these historic names].[15] At the top of the lane, opposite Miss A——'s stables,[16] someone killed it. People who saw it, or heard of it, said that this vagary was a sure sign that there would be a fire here within a week. So certain of this was a fireman that he said he was half inclined not to go to bed last night, as it was more than possible that he should be roused before morning by the fire-bell.

Well, it was not so prompt in fulfilment—this prophecy—as he feared. But it is a fact that this morning there was a fire, and, of all places, at Miss A——'s stable. Soon put out it was, I believe; but some of our friends in the bottom of their hearts have, very likely, a thought that the ghost of the hare had to do with it.

---

[11] In the Dorchester Town Hall, 20 December 1894, Moule proposed the vote of thanks to Joseph Wells, fellow and tutor of Wadham College, Oxford, following his lecture on 'Oxford University and its Part in the Life of England'. TH had introduced 'Christminster' for the first time in the December 1894 instalment of *The Simpletons* (i.e. *Jude the Obscure*) and Moule's question mark presumably reflected uncertainty as to whether Oxford was indeed the intended 'original'.

[12] A series of six fortnightly lectures on 'The Rise and Progress of the British Colonies' was delivered in Dorchester by J. A. R. Marriott, secretary of the Oxford University Extension delegacy, between February and April 1895.

[13] TH's interpolation and square brackets; Charles Walter Moule (1834–1921), a friend of TH's and one of H. J. Moule's younger brothers, became tutor and then president of Corpus Christi College, Cambridge.

[14] For TH's visit to Bath with his wife in October 1902, see *Biography*, 419–20.

[15] TH's interpolation and square brackets; for his advocacy of a revival of such street names, see 1893.02.

[16] The omitted name was that of Margaret Jane Ashley (died 1913, aged 75), who lived at Stratton Manor, High West Street, Dorchester, now known as Agriculture House. The stables were evidently at the back of the house, on what is now called Colliton Street.

Certe, post hoc; vix propter hoc.[17] But I can imagine you taking this very strange occurrence up, as you did South's elm-tree totem in *The Woodlanders*.

It will be perceived that he still writes as zestfully as ever. But a few months more brought about a sad change. I quote from a note sent in the spring of 1903, concerning a proposition Mrs Hardy had made that he should occupy our house while we were away in London:

It had been a weight on my mind, the yearly giving over of our dwelling to the indefatigable charwoman. I couldn't go a long journey—I couldn't go out of hail of the doctor—and lo! you two kind friends just exactly solve the puzzle—*dei ex machinâ*[18] indeed. . . . To an old decrepit fogey like me there will be a delight in having Conquer Barrow and the hedge-side track to Came Wood close at hand.

The plan was carried out, and he derived great benefit from the change, which reflected itself in his letters to me in London. He was daily finding prospects for sketches, old associations, naturally, enhancing their artistic charm; the year, moreover, being in the very act of putting forth the beauties of leafy June.

Twenty-acres, with its far views on three sides, I can hardly keep out of. This morning I found a spot in the middle cart-road from which I mean to make three sketches without moving, except to turn west, north, and east. Yesterday I did a little bit (first outdoor sketch since January).

It is a real satisfaction to me that you, coming from a nightingale be-sung home,[19] should also have the glorious song here at this house. Margie[20] heard a nightingale the night before last.

On the 16th of June he says:

My bulletin is not a confirmation of my former one, but something far exceeding it in favourable character. . . . I can hardly believe in the betterment which has taken place. I am quite a different being. *Deo gratias.*[21] My enjoyment of your country surroundings here has increased day by day, and also my delight in sketching bits thereof. The ever-changing 'distances' seen from various points, S., W., and N. from quite close, and E. from the other side of Mount Pleasant, are a never-failing joy to my heart.

I had visions of his comparative rejuvenation by occasional residence there. But little do we divine how the future means to handle us. Exactly

---

[17] 'Certainly, after this; [but] hardly on account of this.'
[18] Literally, 'gods from the machine'; i.e. miraculous intervenors.
[19] i.e. TH's Higher Bockhampton birthplace.
[20] Moule's daughter Margaret; she married the Revd Edward Charles Leslie in 1906.
[21] 'Thanks be to God.'

nine months from the date of this letter I was attending his funeral.[22] At the beginning, I think, of the March following, he was taken seriously ill. I was just starting to call at his house one day after, when news was brought by a member of his family that he was much better; and I decided to postpone my visit till the next day. Within a few hours it was too late. And thus abruptly was brought to an end a friendship of between forty and fifty years.

[1906.04]

[Assistance to Clive Holland]

Hardy seems always to have regarded Clive Holland with a certain degree of suspicion, and on 3 February 1906 he declined to write an introductory note for *Wessex*, a guidebook written by Holland, illustrated by Walter Tyndale, and published by Adam and Charles Black later that same year. At the same time—perhaps because he admired Tyndale's work (see 1905.11), or simply because he preferred statements about himself and his work to be accurate rather than otherwise—he did read the proofs he had been sent, make 'corrections of errors in absolute fact', and offer 'some suggestions' for Holland to adopt or reject as he chose (*CL* iii. 194–5).

[1906.05]

[On the Jewish Territorial Organization]

Israel Zangwill (1864–1926), author and journalist, best known for his novel *Children of the Ghetto* (1892), was a passionate Zionist and one of the founders of the Jewish Territorial Organization (ITO), which sought the establishment of a self-governing Jewish state, composed initially of refugees from persecution in Russia, that would be located—Palestine itself being then under Turkish rule—somewhere within the British Empire or under British protection. Late in 1905 Zangwill sent out to numerous British writers a letter descriptive of the ITO's aims and activities; his article, 'Letters and the

---

[22] For TH's moving description of Moule's funeral in a letter to another of his brothers, the Revd Arthur Moule, see *CL* iii. 114–16.

ITO', *Fortnightly Review*, new series 79 (April 1906), pp. [633]–47, quoted a
selection of the replies received, Hardy's sympathetic response appearing,
as below, on pp. 638–9. Hardy's draft (DCM), dated 10 November 1905,
clearly provided the textual basis for the letter's reappearance in *Life and
Work*, pp. 352–3, and Emma Hardy's personal letter to Zangwill in *Letters
of Emma and Florence Hardy*, p. 33, is also of interest. Purdy, p. 271.

Dear Mr Zangwill,

It would be altogether presumptuous in me—so entirely outside
Jewish life—to express any positive opinion on the scheme embodied in
the pamphlet you send to me. I can only say a word or two of the nature
of a fancy. To found an autonomous Jewish State or Colony, under
British suzerainty or not, wears the look of a good practical idea, and it
is possibly all the better for having no retrospective sentiment about it.
But I cannot help saying that this retrospective sentiment among Jews is
precisely the one I can best enter into (so that if I were a Jew I should be
a rabid Zionist, no doubt), and I feel that the idea of ultimately getting
to Palestine is the particular idea to make the imaginative among your
people enthusiastic—'like unto them that dream'—as one of you said
in a lyric which is among the finest in any language, to judge from its
moving power in a translation.[23] You, I suppose, read it in the original;
I wish I could. (This is a digression).

The only plan that seems to me to reconcile the traditional feeling
with the practical is that of regarding the proposed Jewish State on
virgin soil as a stepping-stone to Palestine. A Jewish colony, united and
strong and grown wealthy in, say, East Africa, could make a bid for
Palestine (as a sort of annexe)—say 100 years hence—with far greater
effect than the race as scattered all over the globe can ever do; and who
knows if by that time altruism may not have made such progress that the
then ruler or rulers of Palestine, whoever they may be, may even hand it
over to the expectant race, and gladly assist such part of them as may
wish to establish themselves there.[24]

This expectation, nursed throughout the formation and development
of the new territory, would at any rate be serviceable as an ultimate ideal
to stimulate action.

With such an idea lying behind the immediate one, perhaps the
Zionists would re-unite and co-operate with the new Territorialists.

---

[23] Ps. 126: 1: 'When the Lord turned again the captivity of Zion, we were like them that dream.'
[24] For 'assist . . . establish' draft and *LW* read 'assist them, or part of them, to establish'.

I have written, as I said, only a fancy.[25] But as I think you know, nobody outside Jewry can take much deeper[26] interest than I do in a people of such extraordinary history and character—who brought forth, moreover, a young reformer who, though only in the humblest walk of life, became the most famous personage the world has ever known.

Believe me,

Yours sincerely,

Thomas Hardy.

[1906.06]

'A Glimpse of John Stuart Mill'

John Stuart Mill (1806–73), the philosopher, retired from his position with the East India Company in 1858. Elected to the House of Commons in 1865 as a Member of Parliament for Westminster, he supported the policies of William Ewart Gladstone (especially at the time of the Second Reform Bill of 1867) but lost his seat in the general election of 1868. Hardy's vivid description of Mill's appearance as he spoke from the hustings in Covent Garden during the 1865 campaign serves also to evoke Hardy himself as the enthusiastic 'young man living in London' who went on, just two years later, to write *The Poor Man and the Lady*, a novel rejected by publishers because of what he himself later called its 'socialistic' tendencies. The letter first appeared, as below, beneath its presumably editorial heading, in *The Times*, 21 May 1906, p. 6; it was reprinted, without alteration, in *Life and Work*, pp. 355–6. Purdy, p. 271.

Hyde Park-mansions, May 20.

Sir,

This being the 100th anniversary of J. Stuart Mill's birth, and as writers like Carlyle, Leslie Stephen, and others have held that anything, however imperfect, which affords an idea of a human personage in his actual form and flesh, is of value in respect of him, the few following

---

[25] Zangwill comments in the article (p. 639): 'Mr. Hardy's fancy is the baldest fact. He has expressed in a nutshell my own views on every point of a complex question.'

[26] For 'take much deeper' draft and *LW* read 'take a deeper'.

words on how one of the profoundest thinkers of the last century appeared 40 years ago to the man in the street may be worth recording as a footnote to Mr Morley's admirable estimate of Mill's life and philosophy in your impression of Friday.[27]

It was a day in 1865, about 3 in the afternoon, during Mill's candidature for Westminster. The hustings had been erected in Coventgarden, near the front of St Paul's Church; and when I—a young man living in London—drew near to the spot, Mill was speaking. The appearance of the author of the treatise *On Liberty*[28] (which we students of that date knew almost by heart) was so different from the look of persons who usually address crowds in the open air that it held the attention of people for whom such a gathering in itself had little interest. Yet it was, primarily, that of a man out of place. The religious sincerity of his speech was jarred on by his environment—a group on the hustings who, with few exceptions, did not care to understand him fully, and a crowd below who could not. He stood bareheaded, and his vast pale brow, so thin-skinned as to show the blue veins, sloped back like a stretching upland, and conveyed to the observer a curious sense of perilous exposure. The picture of him as personified earnestness surrounded for the most part by careless curiosity derived an added piquancy—if it can be called such—from the fact that the cameo clearness of his face chanced to be in relief against the blue shadow of a church which, on its transcendental side, his doctrines antagonized. But it would not be right to say that the throng was absolutely unimpressed by his words; it felt that they were weighty, though it did not quite know why.

> Your obedient servant,
>
> Thomas Hardy.

[1906.07]

Memories of Church Restoration

Hardy's abandonment of architecture in the early 1870s was followed by a revulsion against the destructive consequences of the kind of church

---

[27] John Morley, 'John Stuart Mill', *The Times Literary Supplement*, 18 May 1906, pp. [173]–4.

[28] *On Liberty* (London: Parker, 1859); Hardy's heavily marked copy (London: Longmans, Green, 1867), apparently a late printing of the third edition of 1864, is in DCM.

'restoration' in which he had himself engaged, and in 1881 he joined the Society for the Protection of Ancient Buildings, founded by William Morris in 1877, and declared himself 'entirely in sympathy with its movements' (*CL* i. 95). As C. J. P. Beatty has shown in *Thomas Hardy: Conservation Architect* (see 1901.10), Hardy's architectural experience enabled him to assist the SPAB from time to time, and his long confessional paper, 'Memories of Church Restoration' (which Beatty prints and annotates), was read at the Society's annual general meeting on 20 June 1906—not by Hardy himself, who hated public speaking, but by his Savile Club acquaintance, Colonel Eustace Balfour, soldier and architect. The paper was widely reported and quoted (e.g. *The Times*, 21 June, p. 9; *Academy*, 30 June, pp. 612–13), and printed in full in *The Society for the Protection of Ancient Buildings . . . Twenty-Ninth Annual Report* (London, 1906), pp. 59–80. Because the *Report* went only to SPAB members, Hardy asked for its distribution to be delayed while he sought a wider audience for 'Memories'. Reginald Smith, editor of the *Cornhill*, promptly accepted the paper for 'concurrent' publication with the *Report* (4 July, DCM) but excluded the marginal glosses the *Report* had reproduced from Hardy's fair-copy holograph manuscript (Texas); the unglossed text duly appeared, somewhat revised, in *Cornhill Magazine*, 94 (August 1906), pp. 184–96, and was reprinted, as from the *Cornhill*, in the *Living Age* (Boston), 1 September 1906, pp. [515]–23, and subsequently in *Life and Art*, pp. 91–109.

Reconstruction of the early textual history of the paper is facilitated by the availability at Texas of not only Hardy's lightly revised manuscript but also his extensively corrected set of the *Report* galley proofs. Also surviving (Beinecke) is the set of tearsheets from the printed *Report* on which Hardy recorded his initial revisions for the *Cornhill*—although the unadopted alteration of the title, to 'Humours of Church Restoration', was almost certainly of later date. The changes between the *Report* and the *Cornhill* not so recorded were presumably made on a proof of the *Cornhill* printing itself. The absence from that printing of the marginal glosses—present in all the earlier witnesses and retained by Hardy when preserving the Beinecke tearsheets for inclusion in his projected 'Miscellanea' volume—significantly compromises its status as the embodiment of Hardy's matured intentions. In the following text, however, those 'final' readings of the *Cornhill* are appropriately, if unhistorically, united with the glosses of the *Report* in their original marginal locations. Purdy, p. 311.

Churches better untouched.

A melancholy reflection may have occurred to many people whose interests lie in the study of Gothic architecture. The passion for 'restoration' first became vigorously operative, say, three-quarters of a century ago; and if all the mediæval buildings in England had been left as they stood at that date, to incur whatever dilapidations might have befallen them at the hands of time, weather, and general neglect, this country would be richer in specimens to-day than it finds itself to be after the expenditure of millions in a nominal preservation during that period.

Active destruction under saving names has been effected upon so gigantic a scale that the concurrent protection of old structures, or portions of structures, by their being kept wind- and water-proof amid such operations counts as nothing in the balance. Its enormous magnitude is realised by few who have not gone personally from parish to parish through a considerable district, and compared existing churches there with records, traditions, and memories of what they formerly were. *Destruction has been on a gigantic scale.*

But the unhappy fact is nowadays generally admitted, and it would hardly be worth adverting to on this occasion if what is additionally assumed were also true, or approximately true: that we are wiser with experience, that architects, incumbents, church-wardens, and all concerned, are zealous to act conservatively by such few of these buildings as still remain untinkered, that they desire at last to repair as far as is possible the errors of their predecessors, and to do anything but repeat them. *Little wiser now.*

Such an assumption is not borne out by events. As it was in the days of Scott the First and Scott the Second—Sir Walter and Sir Gilbert[29]—so it is at this day on a smaller scale. True it may be that our more intelligent architects now know the better way, and that damage is largely limited to minor buildings and to obscure places. But continue it does, despite the efforts of this society; nor does it seem ever likely to stop till all tampering with chronicles in stone be forbidden by law, and all operations bearing on their repair be permitted only under the eyes of properly qualified inspectors.

At first sight it seems an easy matter to preserve an old building without hurting its character. Let nobody form an opinion on that point who has never had an old building to preserve.

In respect of an ancient church, the difficulty we encounter on the threshold, and one which besets us at every turn, is the fact that the building is beheld in two contradictory lights, and required for two *Incompatible purposes make the difficulty.*

---

[29] TH refers to Sir Walter Scott (1771–1832), the novelist and poet, and Sir George Gilbert Scott (1811–78), architect, perhaps the most energetic of the Victorian 'restorers', with whose work on Salisbury Cathedral TH was particularly familiar.

incompatible purposes. To the incumbent the church is a workshop; to[30] the antiquary it is a relic. To the parish it is a utility; to the outsider a luxury. How unite these incompatibles? A utilitarian machine has naturally to be kept going, so that it may continue to discharge its original functions; an antiquarian specimen has to be preserved without making good even its worst deficiencies. The quaintly carved seat that a touch will damage has to be sat in, the frameless doors with the queer old locks and hinges have to keep out draughts, the bells whose shaking endangers the graceful steeple have to be rung.

If the ruinous church could be enclosed in a crystal palace, covering it to the weathercock from rain and wind, and a new church be built alongside for services (assuming the parish to retain sufficient earnest-mindedness to desire them), the method would be an ideal one. But even a parish composed of opulent members of this society would be staggered by such an undertaking. No: all that can be done is of the nature of compromise. It is not within the scope of this paper to inquire how such compromises between users and musers may best be carried out, and how supervision, by those who really know, can best be ensured when wear and tear and the attacks of weather make interference unhappily unavoidable. Those who are better acquainted than I am with the possibilities of such cases can write thereon, and have, indeed, already done so for many years past. All that I am able to do is to look back in a contrite spirit at my own brief experience as a church-restorer, and, by recalling instances of the drastic treatment we then dealt out with light hearts to the unlucky fanes that fell into our hands, possibly help to prevent its repetition on the few yet left untouched.

The worst cases in past times.　　The policy of Thorough[31] in these proceedings was always, of course, that in which the old church was boldly pulled down from no genuine necessity, but from a wanton wish to erect a more modish[32] one. Instances of such I pass over in sad silence.[33] Akin thereto was the case in which a church exhibiting two or three styles was made uniform by removing the features of all but one style, and imitating that throughout in new work. Such devastations need hardly be dwelt on now. Except in

---

[30] For 'workshop; to' MS and *Report* read 'workshop or laboratory; to'.

[31] Although *Cornhill* reads 'thorough' the capital present in MS, *Report*, and tearsheets has here been restored. 'Thorough' was the term used by Thomas Wentworth, 1st Earl of Strafford (1593–1641), for the repressive measures with which he sought to restore the authority of Charles I in Ireland in the 1630s.　　　　[32] For 'modish' MS, *Report*, and tearsheets read 'stylish'.

[33] For 'Instances . . . silence.' MS, *Report*, and tearsheets read 'This I pass over in melancholy silence.'

the most barbarous recesses of our counties they are past. Their name alone is their condemnation.

The shifting of old windows, and other details irregularly spaced, and spacing them at exact distances, was an analogous process. The deportation of the original chancel-arch to an obscure nook, and the insertion of a wider new one to throw open the view of the choir, was also a practice much favoured, and is by no means now extinct. In passing through a village less than five years ago the present writer paused a few minutes to look at the church, and on reaching the door heard quarrelling within. The voices were discovered to be those of two men—brothers, I regret to state—who after an absence of many years had just returned to their native place to attend their father's funeral. The dispute was as to where the family pew had stood in their younger days. One swore that it was in the north aisle, adducing as proof his positive recollection of studying Sunday after Sunday the zigzag moulding of the arch before his eyes, which now visibly led from that aisle into the north transept. The other was equally positive that the pew had been in the nave. As the altercation grew sharper an explanation of the puzzle occurred to me, and I suggested that the old Norman arch we were looking at might have been the original chancel-arch, banished into the aisle to make room for the straddling new object in its place. Then one of the pair of natives remembered that a report of such a restoration had reached his ears afar, and the family peace was preserved, though not till the other had said 'Then I'm drowned if I'll ever come into the paltry church again, after having such a trick played upon me.'

Many puzzling questions are to be explained by these shiftings, and particularly in the case of monuments, whose transposition sometimes led to quaint results. The chancel of a church not a hundred and fifty miles from London has, I am told,[34] in one corner a vault containing a fashionable actor and his wife, in another corner a vault inclosing the remains of a former venerable vicar who abjured women and died a bachelor. The mural tablets, each over its own vault, were taken down at the refurbishing of the building, and refixed reversely, the stone of the theatrical couple over the solitary divine, and that of the latter over the pair from the stage. Should disinterment ever take place, which is not unlikely nowadays, the excavators will be surprised to find a lady beside

Shifting of old features.

Puzzling questions for Posterity.

---

[34] 'I am told' added in Beinecke tearsheets and *Cornhill*, presumably in order to 'distance' what remains a clear reference to Stinsford church, burial place of the 'handsome Irish comedian' (*LW*, p. 13) William O'Brien and his wife, born Lady Susan Fox-Strangways.

the supposed reverend bachelor, and the supposed actor without his wife. As the latter was a comedian he would probably enjoy the situation if he could know it, though the vicar's feelings might be somewhat different.[35]

Such facetious carelessness is not peculiar to our own country. It may be remembered that when Mrs Shelley wished to exhume her little boy William, who had been buried in the English cemetery at Rome, with the view of placing his body beside his father's ashes, no coffin was found beneath the boy's headstone, and she could not carry out her affectionate wish.[36]

Memorials banished for artistic reasons

This game of Monumental Puss-in-the-Corner, even when the outcome of no blundering, and where reasons can be pleaded on artistic or other grounds, is, indeed, an unpleasant subject of contemplation by those who maintain the inviolability of records. Instances of such in London churches will occur to everybody. One would like to know if any note has been kept of the original position of Milton's monument in Cripplegate Church, which has been moved more than once, I believe, and if the position of his rifled grave is now known. When I first saw the monument it stood near the east end of the south aisle.[37]

Sherborne Abbey affords an example on a large scale of the banishment of memorials of the dead, to the doubtful advantage of the living. To many of us the human[38] interest in an edifice ranks before its architectural interest, however great the latter may be; and to find that the innumerable monuments erected in that long-suffering building are all huddled away into the vestry is, at least from my point of view, a heavy mental payment for the clear nave and aisles. If the inscriptions could be read the harm would perhaps be less, but to read them is impossible without ladders, so that these plaintive records are lost to human notice. Many of the recorded ones, perhaps, deserve to be forgotten; but who shall judge?

And destroyed.

And unhappily it was oftenest of all the headstones of the poorer inhabitants—purchased and erected in many cases out of scanty means—that suffered most in these ravages. It is scarcely necessary to

---

[35] TH had played with this idea in his poem 'The Levelled Churchyard', first published in *Poems of the Past and the Present* (1901).

[36] TH's source was probably the footnote in Edward Dowden's *The Life of Percy Bysshe Shelley*, 2 vols. (London: Kegan Paul, Trench, 1886), ii. 268; his copy is now in the Frederick B. Adams collection.

[37] Milton was buried, and his monument erected, in the London church of St Giles's, Cripplegate, but the grave was vandalized in the eighteenth century. On the location of grave and monument, see Beatty, *Conservation Architect* (see 1901.10), pp. 79–80.

[38] For 'To many of us the human' all earlier texts read 'The human'.

particularise among the innumerable instances in which headstones have been removed from their positions, the churchyard levelled, and the stones used for paving the churchyard walks, with the result that the inscriptions have been trodden out in a few years.[39]

Next in harm to the re-designing of old buildings and parts of them came the devastations caused by letting restorations by contract, with a clause in the specification requesting the builder to give a price for 'old materials'—the most important of these being the lead of the roofs, which was to be replaced by tiles or slate, and the oak of the pews, pulpit, altar-rails, &c., to be replaced by deal. This terrible custom is, I should suppose, discontinued in these days. Under it the builder was directly incited to destroy as much as possible of the old fabric as had intrinsic value, that he might increase the spoil which was to come to him for a fixed deduction from his contract. Brasses have marvellously disappeared at such times, heavy brass chandeliers, marble tablets, oak carving of all sorts, leadwork above all. 'Old Materials.'

But apart from irregularities it was always a principle that anything later than Henry VIII. was Anathema, and to be cast out. At Wimborne Minster fine Jacobean canopies were removed from Tudor stalls for the offence only of being Jacobean. At an hotel in Cornwall, a tea-garden was, and possibly is still, ornamented with seats constructed of the carved oak from a neighbouring church—no doubt the restorer's honest perquisite. Church relics turned up in unexpected places. I remember once going into the stonemason's shed of a builder's yard, where, on looking round, I started to see the Creed, the Lord's Prayer, and the Ten Commandments, in gilt letters, staring emphatically from the sides of the shed. 'Oh, yes,' said the builder, a highly respectable man, 'I took 'em as old materials under my contract when I gutted St Michael and All Angels', and I put 'em here to keep out the weather: they might keep my blackguard hands serious[40] at the same time; but they don't.' A fair lady with a past was once heard[41] to say that she could not go to morning service at a particular church because the parson read one[42] of Destruction of good features For the crime of their date.

[39] TH's 'The Levelled Churchyard' (see n. 35 above) is again relevant.

[40] For 'serious' MS (only) reads 'from cussing' within the context of a passage extensively revised in Texas proofs; another version of this anecdote in *LW*, p. 129, identifies the builder as John Wellspring, of Dorchester.

[41] For 'A fair lady with a past was once heard' MS and *Report* read 'A lady once was heard'; TH's alteration on tearsheets reads as *Cornhill* but with 'matron' in place of 'lady'.

[42] For 'one' MS reads 'some', *Report* 'certain'. The Commandment was presumably the seventh, against adultery: see 1890.01, paragraph 9.

the Commandments with such accusatory emphasis: whether these that had become degraded to the condition of old materials were taken down owing to kindred objections one cannot know.

A use for old family vaults.

But many such old materials were, naturally, useless when once unfixed. Another churchwright whom I knew in early days was greatly incommoded by the quantity of rubbish that had accumulated during a restoration he had in hand, there being no place in the churchyard to which it could be wheeled. In the middle of the church was the huge vault of an ancient family supposed to be extinct, which had been broken into at one corner by the pickaxe of the restorers, and this vault was found to be a convenient receptacle for the troublesome refuse from the Ages. When a large number of barrow-loads had been tipped through the hole the labourer lifted his eyes to behold a tall figure standing between him and the light. 'What are you doing, my man?' said the figure blandly. 'A getting rid of the rubbage, sir,' replied the labourer. 'But why do you put it there?' 'Because all the folks have died out, so it don't matter what we do with their old bone cellar.' 'Don't you be too sure about the folks having died out. I am one of that family, and as I am very much alive, and that vault is my freehold, I'll just ask you to take all the rubbish out again.' It was said that the speaker had by chance returned from America, where he had made a fortune, in the nick of time to witness this performance, and that the vault was duly cleared and sealed up as he ordered.

The generous donor the instigator of mischief.

The 'munificent contributor' to the expense of restoration was often the most fearful instigator of mischief. I may instance the case of a Transition-Norman pier with a group of shafts, the capitals of which showed signs of crushing under the weight of the arches. By taking great care it was found possible to retain the abacus and projecting parts supporting it, sculptured with the vigorous curled leaves of the period, only the diminishing parts, or the bell of each capital, being renewed. The day after the re-opening of the church the lady who had defrayed much of the expense complained to the contractor of his mean treatment of her in leaving half the old capitals when he should have behaved handsomely, and renewed the whole. To oblige her the carver chipped over the surface of the old carving, not only in that pier, but in *all* the piers, and made it look as good as new.

No Clerk of Works fatal.

Poor forlorn parishes,[43] which could not afford to pay a clerk of works to superintend the alterations, suffered badly in these ecclesiastical

---

[43] For 'Poor . . . parishes' MS and *Report* read 'Poor parishes'.

convulsions. During the years they were raging at their height I jour-
neyed to a distant place to supervise a case, in the enforced absence of
an older eye. The careful repair of an interesting Early English window
had been specified; but it was gone. The contractor, who had met me on
the spot, replied genially to my gaze of concern: 'Well now, I said to   Builders' mis-
myself when I looked at the old thing, "I won't stand upon a pound or   apprehensions.
two: I'll give 'em a new winder now I am about it, and make a good
job of it, howsomever."' A caricature in new stone of the old window
had taken its place.

    In the same church was an old oak rood-screen of debased Per-
pendicular workmanship, but valuable, the original colouring and gild-
ing, though much faded, still remaining on the cusps and mouldings.
The repairs deemed necessary had been duly specified, but I beheld in
its place a new screen of deal, varnished to a mirror-like brilliancy.
'Well,' replied the builder, more genially than ever, 'I said to myself,
"Please God, now I am about it, I'll do the thing well, cost what it will!"'
'Where's the old screen?' I said, appalled. 'Used up to boil the work-
men's kittles; though 'a were not much at that!'[44]

    The reason for consternation lay in the fact that the bishop—a strict
Protestant—had[45] promulgated a decree concerning rood-screens—
viz., that though those in existence might be repaired, no new one would
be suffered in his diocese for doctrinal reasons.[46] This the builder knew
nothing of. What was to be done at the re-opening, when the bishop was
to be present, and would notice the forbidden thing? I had to decide
there and then, and resolved to trust to chance and see what happened.
On the day of the opening we anxiously watched the bishop's approach,
and I fancied I detected a lurid glare in his eye as it fell upon the illicit
rood-screen. But he walked quite innocently under it without noticing
that it was not the original. If he noticed it during the service he was
politic enough to say nothing.[47]

    I might dwell upon the mistakes of architects as well as of builders if   Mistakes of
there were time. That architects the most experienced could be cheated   Architects.

[44] Another version of this anecdote in *LW*, p. 82, identifies it (and presumably the anecdote in
the preceding paragraph) as referring to St Juliot Church in Cornwall, the scene of Hardy's first
meeting with Emma Lavinia Gifford.

[45] For 'bishop . . . had' *Report* reads 'bishop—strictly Protestant—had'; paragraph heavily
revised in Texas proofs.

[46] For 'diocese for doctrinal reasons.' all earlier texts read 'diocese.'

[47] This anecdote is linked to St Juliot church, but Beatty points out (*Conservation Architect*, p. 80)
that neither 'the bishop' nor TH himself was in fact present at the reopening ceremony.

to regard an accident of churchwardenry as high artistic purpose, was revealed to a body of architectural students, of which the present writer was one, when they were taken over Westminster Abbey in a peripatetic lecture by Sir Gilbert Scott.[48] He, at the top of the ladder, was bringing to our notice a feature which had, he said, perplexed him for a long time: why the surface of diapered stone before him should suddenly be discontinued at the spot he pointed out, when there was every reason for carrying it on. Possibly the artist had decided that to break the surface was a mistake; possibly he had died; possibly anything; but there the mystery was. 'Perhaps it is only plastered over!' broke forth in the reedy voice of the youngest pupil in our group. 'Well, that's what I never thought of,' replied Sir Gilbert, and taking from his pocket a clasp knife which he carried for such purposes, he prodded the plain surface with it. 'Yes, it *is* plastered over, and all my theories are wasted,' he continued, descending the ladder not without humility.

Abuses in rehanging of Bells.
    My knowledge at first hand of the conditions of church-repair at the present moment is very limited. But one or two prevalent abuses have come by accident under my notice. The first concerns the rehanging of church bells. A barbarous practice is, I believe, very general, that of cutting off the cannon of each bell—namely, the loop on the crown by which it has been strapped to the stock—and restrapping it by means of holes cut through the crown itself. The mutilation is sanctioned on the ground that, by so fixing it, the centre of the bell's gravity is brought nearer to the axis on which it swings, with advantage and ease to the ringing. I do not question the truth of this; yet the resources of mechanics are not so exhausted but that the same result may be obtained by leaving the bell unmutilated and increasing the camber of the stock, which, for that matter, might be so great as nearly to reach a right angle. I was recently passing through a churchyard where I saw standing on the grass a peal of bells just taken down from the adjacent tower and subjected to this treatment. A sight more piteous than that presented by these fine bells, standing disfigured in a row in the sunshine, like cropped criminals in the pillory, as it were ashamed of their degradation, I have never witnessed among inanimate things.

---

[48] Although TH was incorrect in stating (*LW*, p. 433) that he received his RIBA prize medal from Sir Gilbert Scott, he could certainly have participated, as a member of the Architectural Association, in one of the tours of Westminster Abbey Scott conducted for the Association during the 1860s (Beatty, *Conservation Architect*, p. 80).

Speaking of bells, I should like to ask cursorily why the old sets Destruction
of chimes have been removed from nearly all our country churches. The of chimes.
midnight wayfarer, in passing along the sleeping village or town, was
cheered by the outburst of a stumbling tune, which possessed the added
charm of being probably heeded by no ear but his own. Or, when lying
awake in sickness, the denizen would catch the same notes, persuading
him that all was right with the world. But one may go half across
England and hear no chimes at midnight now.[49]

I may here mention a singular incident in respect of a new peal of Singular
bells at a church whose rebuilding I was privy to, which occurred on incident of
bell-hanging.
the opening day many years ago. It being a popular and fashionable
occasion, the church was packed with its congregation long before the
bells rang out for service. When the ringers seized the ropes, a noise
more deafening than thunder resounded from the tower in the ears of
the sitters.[50] Terrified at the idea that the tower was falling they rushed
out at the door, ringers included, into the arms of the astonished bishop
and clergy, advancing, so it was said,[51] in procession up the churchyard
path, some of the ladies being in a fainting state. When calmness
was restored by the sight of the tower standing unmoved as usual, it was
discovered that the six bells had been placed 'in stay'—that is, in an
inverted position ready for the ringing, but in the hurry of preparation
the clappers had been laid inside though not fastened on, and at the first
swing of the bells they had fallen out upon the belfry floor.

After this digression I return to one other abuse of ecclesiastical Christmas
fabrics, that arising from the fixing of Christmas decorations. The bat- decorations.
talion of young ladies to whom the decking with holly and ivy is usually
entrusted, seem to be possessed with a fixed idea that nails may be driven
not only into old oak and into the joints of the masonry, but into the
freestone itself if you only hit hard enough. Many observers must have
noticed the mischief wrought by these nails. I lately found a fifteenth-
century arch to have suffered more damage during the last twenty years
from this cause than during the previous five hundred of its existence.
The pock-marked surface of many old oak pulpits is entirely the effect
of the numberless tin-tacks driven into them for the same purpose.

---

[49] Cf. Shakespeare, *2 Henry IV*, III. ii. 214.

[50] Earlier texts all read 'the startled sitters', and the *Cornhill*'s omission of 'startled' may have
been a compositorial error.

[51] The awkward insertion of 'so it was said' into the Beinecke tearsheets and the *Cornhill* was
perhaps another instance of Hardy's distancing himself from an identifiable event.

An ideal view
of restoration.

Such abuses as these, however, are gross, open, palpable,[52] and easy to be checked. Far more subtle and elusive ones await our concluding consideration, which I will rapidly enter on now. Persons who have mused upon the safeguarding of our old architecture must have indulged in a reflection which, at first sight, seems altogether to give away the argument for its material preservation. The reflection is that, abstractly,[53] there is everything to be said in favour of church renovation—if that really means the honest reproduction of old shapes in substituted materials. And this too, not merely when the old materials are perishing, but when they are only approaching decay.

It is easy to show that the essence and soul of an architectural monument does not lie in the particular blocks of stone or timber that compose it, but in the mere forms to which those materials have been shaped. We discern in a moment that it is in the boundary of a solid—its insubstantial superficies or mould—and not in the solid itself, that its right lies to exist as art. The whole quality of Gothic or other architecture —let it be a cathedral, a spire, a window, or what not—attaches to this, and not to the substantial erection which it appears exclusively to consist in. Those limestones or sandstones have passed into its form; yet it is an idea independent of them—an æsthetic phantom without solidity, which might just as suitably have chosen millions of other stones from the quarry whereon to display its beauties. Such perfect results of art as the aspect of Salisbury Cathedral from the north-east corner of the Close, the interior of Henry VII.'s Chapel at Westminster, the East Window of Merton Chapel, Oxford, would be no less perfect if at this moment, by the wand of some magician, other similar materials could be conjured into their shapes, and the old substance be made to vanish for ever.

This is, indeed, the actual process of organic nature herself, which is one continuous substitution. She is always discarding the matter, while retaining the form.

Restoration
practically
objectionable

Why this reasoning does not hold good for a dead art, why the existence and efforts of this Society are so amply justifiable, lies in two other attributes of bygone Gothic artistry—a material and a spiritual one. The first is uniqueness; such a duplicate as we have been considering can never be executed. No man can make two pieces of matter exactly alike.

---

[52] Cf. Shakespeare, *1 Henry IV*, II. iv. 225–6.
[53] Earlier texts all retain the evidently incorrect 'abstractedly'.

But not to shelter the argument behind microscopic niceties, or to imagine what approximations might be effected by processes so costly as to be prohibitive, it is found in practice that even such an easily copied shape as, say, a traceried window does not get truly reproduced. The old form inherits, or has acquired, an indefinable quality—possibly some deviation from exact geometry (curves were often struck by hand in mediæval work)—which never reappears in the copy, especially in the vast majority of cases where no nice approximation is attempted.

and well-nigh impossible.

The second, or spiritual, attribute which stultifies the would-be reproducer is perhaps more important still, and is not artistic at all. It lies in human association. The influence that a building like Lincoln or Winchester[54] exercises on a person of average impressionableness and culture is a compound influence, and though it would be a fanciful attempt to define how many fractions of that compound are æsthetic, and how many associative, there can be no doubt that the latter influence is more valuable than the former. Some may be of a different opinion, but I think the damage done to this sentiment of association by replacement, by the rupture of continuity, is mainly what makes the enormous loss this country has sustained from its seventy years of church restoration so tragic and deplorable. The protection of an ancient edifice against renewal in fresh materials is, in fact, even more of a social—I may say a humane—duty than an æsthetic one. It is the preservation of memories, history, fellowships, fraternities. Life, after all, is more than art, and that which appealed to us in the (maybe) clumsy outlines of some structure which had been looked at and entered by a dozen generations of ancestors outweighs the more subtle recognition, if any, of architectural qualities. The renewed stones at Hereford, Peterborough, Salisbury, St Albans, Wells,[55] and so many other places, are not the stones that witnessed the scenes in English Chronicle[56] associated with those piles. They are not the stones over whose face the organ notes of centuries 'lingered and wandered on as loth to die',[57] and the fact that they are not, too often results in spreading abroad the feeling I instanced in the anecdote of the two brothers.

Moreover fatal to human interest.

Moreover, by a curious irony, the parts of a church that have suffered the most complete obliteration are those of the closest personal relation—the woodwork, especially that of the oak pews of various

---

[54] i.e. Lincoln and Winchester cathedrals.   [55] 'Hereford . . . Wells': all cathedrals.

[56] i.e. in English history; TH seems not to have had any specific 'chronicle' in mind.

[57] Quoted from Wordsworth's sonnet, 'Inside of King's College Chapel, Cambridge'.

Georgian dates, with their skilful panellings, of which not a joint had started, and mouldings become so hard as to turn the edge of a knife. The deal benches with which these cunningly mitred and morticed framings have been largely replaced have already, in many cases, fallen into decay.

But the building is actually perishing.

But not all pewing was of oak, not all stonework and roof timbers were sound, when the renovators of the late century laid hands on them; and this leads back again to the standing practical question of bewildering difficulty which faces the protectors of Ancient Buildings—what is to be done in instances of rapid decay to prevent the entire disappearance of such as yet exists? Shall we allow it to remain untouched for the brief years of its durability, to have the luxury of the original a little while, or sacrifice the rotting original to instal, at least, a reminder of its design? The first impulse of those who are not architects is to keep, ever so little longer, what they can of the very substance itself at all costs to the future. But let us reflect a little. Those designers of the Middle Ages who were concerned with that original cared nothing for the individual stone or stick—would not even have cared for it had it acquired the history that it now possesses; their minds were centred on the aforesaid form, with, possibly, its colour and endurance, all which qualities it is now rapidly losing. Why then should we prize what they neglected, and neglect what they prized?

Conflict of the Æsthetic sense with the Antiquarian.

This is rather a large question for the end of a lecture. Out of it arises a conflict between the purely æsthetic sense and the memorial or associative. The artist instinct and the caretaking instinct part company over the disappearing creation. The true architect, who is first of all an artist and not an antiquary, is naturally most influenced by the æsthetic sense, his desire being, like Nature's, to retain, recover, or recreate the idea which has become damaged, without much concern about the associations of the material that idea may have been displayed in. Few occupations are more pleasant than that of endeavouring to re-capture an old design from the elusive hand of annihilation.

Thus if the architect have also an antiquarian bias he is pulled in two directions—in one by his wish to hand on or modify the abstract form, in the other by his reverence for the antiquity of its embodiment.

Architects have been much blamed for their doings in respect of old churches, and no doubt they have much to answer for. Yet one cannot logically blame an architect for being an architect—a chief craftsman, constructor, creator of forms—not their preserver.

If I were practising in that profession I would not, I think, undertake a church restoration in any circumstances. I should reply, if asked to do so, that a retired tinker or rivetter of old china, or some 'Old Mortality'[58] from the almshouse, would superintend the business better. In short, the opposing tendencies excited in an architect by the distracting situation can find no satisfactory reconciliation.[59]

Fortunately cases of imminent disappearance are not the most numerous of those on which the Society has to pronounce an opinion. The bulk of the work of preservation lies in organising resistance to the enthusiasm for newness in those parishes, priests, and churchwardens who regard a church as a sort of villa to be made convenient and fashionable for the occupiers of the moment; who say, 'Give me a wide chancel arch—they are "in" at present'; who pull down the west gallery to show the new west window, and pull out old irregular pews to fix mathematically spaced benches for a congregation that never comes. *But these are not the majority of cases.*

Those who are sufficiently in touch with these proceedings may be able to formulate some practical and comprehensive rules for the salvation of such few—very few—old churches, diminishing in number every day, as chance to be left intact owing to the heathen apathy of their parson and parishioners in the last century. The happy accident of indifferentism in those worthies has preserved their churches to be a rarity and a delight to pilgrims of the present day. The policy of 'masterly inaction'[60]—often the greatest of all policies—was never practised to higher gain than by these, who simply left their historic buildings alone. To do nothing, where to act on little knowledge is a dangerous thing,[61] is to do most and best. *Past indifference a present blessing.*

---

[58] A reference to the graveyard-haunting figure whose nickname provides the title of Walter Scott's novel *Old Mortality*.

[59] MS and *Report* read 'reconciliation. All that he can do is of the nature of compromise.'; the sentence is struck through in the Beinecke tearsheets.

[60] The phrase 'wise and masterly inactivity' appears in the opening section of Sir James Mackintosh's *Vindiciae Gallicae; A Defence of the French Revolution* (1791).

[61] Cf. Pope, *Essay on Criticism*, i. 215.

[1906.08]

[Message to Dorchester Visit of Society of Dorset Men]

The following letter to William Watkins (see 1904.16), founder and honorary secretary of the Society of Dorset Men in London, was read out at a civic luncheon given in Dorchester on 15 June 1906 to celebrate both the presentation of the ornate clock that still stands in the Borough Gardens and the organized visit being made to the county town that same day by members of the Society. The letter was quoted in full in the *Dorset County Chronicle*, 21 June 1906, p. 6, and in the *Society of Dorset Men in London* (Year-Book 1906–7), p. 45, and is included in *Collected Letters*, iii. 212. The text below is that of the *Dorset County Chronicle*.

1, Hyde Park-mansions, W., June 11th, 1906.

My dear Sir,

I much regret that circumstances should detain me here in London at the very time of the visit of the Society of Dorset Men to their native county and mine, especially as I gather from the itinerary that you will be driving near my house on your excursion round Dorchester. It would, indeed, have been most pleasant if I could have been at hand to welcome you to the neighbourhood. I shall, however, in a certain sense have done so already, in a rather lengthy speech of some 20 volumes, which I hope you will take as delivered on the occasion. I trust that the weather may be fine, and I could have wished that time had allowed you to penetrate into the further recesses of the county. This perhaps your enterprise may accomplish later on.

Yours very truly,

Thomas Hardy.

W. Watkins, Esq., Hon. Sec., Society of Dorset Men in London.

[1906.09]

'Keats–Shelley Memorial'

On 20 June 1906 (*CL* vii. 142) Hardy returned to the Keats–Shelley Memorial Association his signed copy of a letter soliciting contributions to a fund for the purchase and endowment of the house in the Piazza di Spagna, Rome, in which John Keats had died, and expressed his willingness that his name should 'appear in the press as one of the signatories'. It so appeared, along with the names of thirty others, when the letter was published, headed as above, in *The Times*, 3 July 1906, p. 11. Hardy had long been an active supporter of the Shelley Memorial Fund (*CL* i. 278–9, v. 28) and had already made his own donation to the new fund (*CL* iii. 200). Fourteen years later (draft to John I. Fraser, 25 March 1920, DCM) he agreed to his being named as a member of the committee seeking to acquire Wentworth Place, in Hampstead, as a Keats memorial, and was so identified in the *Morning Post*, 9 April 1920, p. 4. He also contributed his poem 'At a House in Hampstead' to *The John Keats Memorial Volume* published by the committee in 1921, and later sent a fair copy of the poem to be hung in what had been Keats's sitting-room (Purdy, pp. 216–17).

[1906.10]

[Inspired Statement on Wessex Locations]

Writing on 4 July 1906 to his journalist friend James Milne, Hardy declined to review Sir Frederick Treves's recently published *Highways and Byways in Dorset* for the *Daily Chronicle* but suggested that Milne might like to use in his regular 'Books of the Day' column—'of course to be put into your own words' (*CL* iii. 216)—the enclosed paragraph on the current proliferation of books on Wessex. Although the paragraph is on a separate sheet and in what may be the hand of Hardy's cousin Mary Antell, its authorship is confirmed by the presence of a correction in what is unmistakeably Hardy's own hand. Milne published the paragraph, as below, in 'Books of the Day', *Daily Chronicle*, 6 July 1906, p. 3, attributing it to 'a correspondent' and reorganizing Hardy's sentence structures without significantly altering his wording.

It is truly a 'little irony' that so many guide books to Wessex and the Wessex novels should be circulating just now; since in his earlier Wessex books mystifications were freely adopted by Mr Hardy. Any reader who examines the old editions can see that for himself, and no doubt it was the novelist's intention to throw readers off the scent if they thought of searching for real localities. These disguises having become useless were mostly removed later on, and a correct topography given, but that they were sufficient for the time may be gathered from the fact that in criticising *The Mayor of Casterbridge* the *Saturday Review* writer announced himself unable to judge of the situation of the real place, if there was a real place.[62]

[1906.11]

'A Commission on Spelling Reform'

When President Theodore Roosevelt in the summer of 1906 endorsed the policies of the American Spelling Reform Committee, headed by Brander Matthews, an editorial in the *Daily Chronicle*, 25 August 1906, p. 4, expressed the wish that he had first 'summoned an International Anglo-American Congress, in order to see if a common code of spelling could not have been agreed upon'. Hardy, asked by reply-paid telegram (DCM) if he would support the appointment of such a commission, sent back (draft, DCM) the telegraphic message reproduced below from the 'Office Window' column of the *Daily Chronicle*, 29 August 1906, p. 4. Purdy, p. 311.

Yes, commission to be of every nationality except our own. Am struck with the advantage of having this reform of English spelling taken in hand by an eminent American of Dutch extraction.[63] Where is the Oxford dictionary now?[64]

[1906.12]

'Memorial to the Duma'

Hardy was one of a large number of leading British figures—including more than 200 Members of Parliament—who signed a memorial to the new Russian parliament or *Duma*, established as a gesture towards democratization following the 1905 revolution. His name appears in the report, headed 'Memorial to the Duma', in *The Times*, 6 September 1906, p. 7, though it was not among the 'first signatories' listed when the text of the memorial was originally published in *The Times*, 24 July 1906, p. 5. Plans for delivery of the

[62] The unsigned review in the *Saturday Review*, 29 May 1886, p. 757, found the action of the novel improbable and set in a 'remote region—which we are unable to localize'.

[63] Theodore Roosevelt was of Dutch descent on his father's side.

[64] i.e. the *Oxford English Dictionary* (originally called the *New English Dictionary*), completed in 1928; only the volumes for the letters A–G had been published at this date.

memorial by a British deputation were eventually abandoned in the face of the outspoken hostility of Russian conservatives to what they represented as foreign interference in their country's internal affairs (see e.g. *The Times*, 19 October 1906, p. 3).

[1906.13]

[A Tower for Holy Trinity Church]

Canon Rowland Hill, rector of Holy Trinity Church, Dorchester, was presumably responsible for supplying the material for the following paragraph in the 'Ecclesiastical Intelligence' section of *The Times*, 6 September 1906, p. 5, although Hardy evidently supported Hill's initiative and may have deliberately written something that Hill could publish. Nearly three years later, the one complete sentence quoted by *The Times* was again quoted, slightly rephrased, in the *Morning Leader*, 3 May 1909, p. 7, as part of a brief article attached to a reproduction of Hardy's rough sketch and plan of the Holy Trinity project. That project seems never to have been seriously taken up, however, and the church remains towerless.

Mr Thomas Hardy has started a movement for adding a tower to the south-west side of Holy Trinity Church, Dorchester. In a letter to the rector (Canon Rowland Hill) Mr Hardy, who encloses a sketch of the proposed tower 'made in an idle moment',[65] says he hopes it may stimulate some wealthy lover of architecture to carry out the idea. He adds, 'The church is sadly deficient in external dignity at present, and no stranger passing by it can realize that such a large church stands there.'

[1906.14]

[Recollections of Leslie Stephen]

Leslie Stephen (1832–1904), philosopher, man of letters, and first editor of the *Dictionary of National Biography*, played an important role in Hardy's early career. As editor of the *Cornhill Magazine*, he oversaw the serialization of

---

[65] In a letter of 19 September 1906 (*CL* iii. 226) TH insisted that his sketch of the tower was 'not a considered design, but merely a rough outline on half a sheet of note-paper'.

Far from the Madding Crowd that first made Hardy famous, and their ensuing friendship contributed significantly to Hardy's lifelong habits of sceptical and indeed agnostic thought. Invited (2 May 1905, DCM) by the historian Frederic William Maitland (1850–1906) to contribute to the latter's *The Life and Letters of Leslie Stephen* (London: Duckworth, 1906), Hardy responded with the lengthy and affectionate reminiscence, interspersed with quotations from Stephen's letters, that is reproduced below from the published text. Hardy's original manuscript seems to have been destroyed, together with all but one of his letters to Maitland, but it is clear from Maitland's side of the correspondence (DCM) that Hardy responded promptly to requests and proof-read his contribution as printed. He also sent—and Maitland included (p. 278)—his sonnet about Stephen, 'The Schreckhorn', later praised by Virginia Woolf, Stephen's daughter, for its evocation of her father's appearance and personality (*Biography*, p. 172). Maitland printed the reminiscences in three segments, the first on pp. 263–4, the second on pp. 270–6, and the third on pp. 276–7, and these divisions are here indicated by lines of asterisks. In detaching Hardy's text from Maitland's contexts, however, it has seemed appropriate to reverse the order of the first and second segments—dealing respectively with events of 1875 and of 1872–4—and so restore what must surely have been the chronological sequence of Hardy's original narrative. Whether that narrative included an account of the *Cornhill* serialization of *The Hand of Ethelberta* is by no means clear. Such an account could well have been the source of the paragraph of brief quotations from Stephen's letters to Hardy about *The Hand of Ethelberta* introduced by Maitland as a transition between segments two and three (p. 276); it seems, on the other hand, significant that Maitland breaks off with the words 'But Mr Hardy must resume his tale.' The paragraph in any case contains none of Hardy's own words and is here omitted, along with three additional Stephen letters that Hardy seems to have supplied at Maitland's request (pp. 290–1, 393–4, 450–1). Hardy drew upon these reminiscences, supplemented by further extracts from Stephen's letters, for *Life and Work*, pp. 101–2, 108–9. Purdy, p. 264.

It was at the beginning of December 1872, on a wet and windy morning, when in a remote part of the country, that a letter stained with raindrops arrived for me in a handwriting so fine that it might have been traced by a pin's point.

Dear Sir,—I hear from Mr Moule[66] that I may address you as the author of *Under the Greenwood Tree*.

---

[66] Horace Moule.

I have lately read that story with very great pleasure indeed. I think the description of country life admirable, and, indeed, it is long since I have received more pleasure from a new writer.

It also occurred to me, and it is for this reason that I take the liberty of addressing you, that such writing would probably please the readers of the *Cornhill Magazine* as much as it has pleased me. *Under the Greenwood Tree* is, of course, not a magazine story. There is too little incident for such purpose; for, though I do not want a murder in every number, it is necessary to catch the attention of readers by some distinct and well-arranged plot.

If you are, as I hope, writing anything more, I should be very glad to have the offer of it for our pages. . . .

Yours truly,

Leslie Stephen.[67]

A reply that I could send him, when free—though that would not be for some time—a pastoral tale which I thought of calling *Far from the Madding Crowd*, in which the chief characters would be a woman-farmer, a shepherd, and a sergeant in the Dragoon Guards, brought another letter immediately. He said that the idea of the story attracted him, that he liked my proposed title for it, and that he hoped I would call and talk it over when next I came to town. An understanding having been come to by a further note or two that he should have the story if all went well (not a word of it being written as yet), no more passed between us then; and I had nothing from him till the April of next year (1873) when he inquired again:

Since I wrote to you last, circumstances have occurred which make it desirable for me to ask whether the novel of which you then spoke to me is in a sufficiently advanced state to allow of my seeing it with a view to its appearance in the *Cornhill*, and if so, at what time you would be able to let me publish the first number. It would not be necessary to have the whole story before beginning. . . . You spoke of coming to town in the spring. If you should be here I should be very glad to see you.

If I went up, however, I did not call, and must have replied that the MS. was very little advanced (the preceding story, *A Pair of Blue Eyes*, being barely finished), for later he says:

Since I wrote, arrangements have been nearly concluded which will, I think, obviate any necessity for hurrying you. . . . I should like to see a specimen of your

---

[67] This letter (DCM) is fully transcribed in Purdy, pp. 336–7. The omissions, both signalled and silent, from TH's letters were presumably determined by Maitland rather than by TH himself.

story before I go abroad, which will be in the middle either of June or July—most likely the latter.

In writing that I would endeavour to show him something of it before he left, I mentioned that I had just read an article of his in the current *Fortnightly Review*, and he alluded to it in his next: 'I am gratified by your approbation of my *Fortnightly* article. I have some more to say upon that matter in a forthcoming volume, which will, I fear or hope, shock the orthodox.'[68] As soon, therefore, as I could, I forwarded a few chapters of the story, with some succeeding ones in outline, which, briefly, he was pleased to characterise in terms that, coming from such a quarter, were more eulogistic than I was aware of. He hoped I should hurry on 'the elopement of the heroine' (which I had foreshadowed), and added a personal sentence: 'I am going abroad on Thursday or Friday next for a couple of months, being a good deal overworked and worried.' He was back again in South Kensington by September, and I sent on a few more chapters, written out at length, so that altogether he had about enough matter to make a first number, with something over. He replied there-on: 'I think that, so far as it has gone, it will suit us admirably. As a rule, it is desirable that I should see the whole MS. of a novel before definitely accepting it. Under the circumstances, however, and as I should wish to begin the publication of your novel before long, it may be desirable to decide at once.'

When I had come to terms with the publishers by an exchange of letters, he wanted to know whether, if he began to issue the story in the coming January number (which was sooner than previously proposed) I could keep in front of the printers month by month. I said I thought I could do so, and he sent the first number on to them, asking me to let him have the second soon, and again inviting me to come and see him, as I was about to run up to town, suggesting lunch-time.

I called, however, at some other hour; and on that day, owing to my remissness in not going sooner as he had wished, we met for the first time at 8 Southwell Gardens. He welcomed me with one hand, holding back the barking 'Troy' with the other. The dog's name I, of course, had never heard till then, and I said, 'That is the name of my wicked soldier-hero.' He answered caustically: 'I don't think my Troy will feel hurt at

---

[68] 'Are We Christians?', *Fortnightly Review*, 19 (March 1873), pp. 281–303; reprinted in Stephen's *Essays on Freethinking and Plainspeaking* (London: Longmans, Green, 1873). Footnoted by Maitland.

the coincidence, if yours doesn't.' I rejoined, 'There is also another coincidence. Another Leslie Stephen lives near here, I find.' 'Yes,' he said, 'he's the spurious one.'

Perceiving, what I had not gathered from his letters, that I had a character to deal with, I made some cheerful reply, and tried him further. We were looking out of the window, and I asked him what made him live in such a new street (he had lately removed thither), with pavements hardly laid, and the road-stones not rolled in. He said he had played as a child with his nurse in the fields hard by, and he fancied living on the spot, which was dear to him, though the building operations interfered with the sentiment much. I felt then that I liked him, which at first I had doubted. The feeling never changed.

I agreed to lunch on the next day, and arrived in a yellow fog which ate into the very bones. Mrs Stephen and Miss Thackeray[69] were present in shawls. We sat over the fire after lunch, and the closeness of the printers in the rear of my pen led Stephen to remark that *Vanity Fair* was written at the rate of five pages a day, *The Newcomes* at the rate of ten, and *Esmond* (I think) at the rate of three. We also talked of Carlyle, whom Stephen had visited on the previous day; and he illustrated by enactment the remarkable way in which the philosopher lit his pipe. Somehow we launched upon the subject of David and Saul. One of the ladies said that her best idea of Saul's character had been gained from Browning's poem of that name. I spoke to the effect that the Bible account would take a deal of beating, and that I wondered why the clergy did not argue the necessity of plenary inspiration from the marvellous artistic cunning with which so many Bible personages, like those of Saul and David, were developed, though in a comparatively unliterary age. Stephen, who had been silent, then said, 'Yes. But they never do the obvious thing'; presently adding in a dry grim tone, 'If you wish to get an idea of Saul and David you should study them as presented by Voltaire in his drama.'[70] Those who know that work will appreciate Stephen's mood.

He was pleased with the reception, in January, of *Far from the Madding Crowd*, and wrote to congratulate me. 'Besides the gentle *Spectator*,' he says, 'who thinks you must be George Eliot, because you know

---

[69] Stephen's first wife, Harriet (1840–75), was the daughter of William Makepeace Thackeray, the novelist and first editor of the *Cornhill*; her sister, Anne Isabella Thackeray, later Lady Ritchie (1837–1919), was herself a novelist and woman of letters.

[70] The five-act tragedy *Saul et David*, of which Voltaire himself once disclaimed authorship.

the names of the stars,[71] several good judges have . . . Moreover, the *Spectator* has really a good deal of critical feeling. I always like to be praised by it—and, indeed, by other people!'[72] A week later he alludes to the same review: 'I have been waiting for castigation at their hands for certain essays of mine,[73] but they have not yet condescended to mention me. I suppose the rod is in pickle.'

'I have ventured to leave out a line or two in the last batch of proofs', he wrote soon afterwards, 'from an excessive prudery of which I am ashamed; but one is forced to be absurdly particular. May I suggest that Troy's seduction of the young woman will require to be treated in a gingerly fashion when, as I suppose must be the case, he comes to be exposed to his wife? I mean that the thing must be stated, but that the words must be careful. Excuse this wretched shred of concession to popular stupidity; but I am a slave. I hope to see you soon.'[74] I wondered what had so suddenly caused in one, who had seemed anything but a prude, the 'excessive prudery' alluded to. But I did not learn till I saw him in April. Then he told me that an unexpected Grundian cloud, though no bigger than a man's hand[75] as yet, had appeared on our serene horizon. Three respectable ladies and subscribers, representing he knew not how many more, had written to upbraid him for an improper passage in a page of the story which had already been published.

I was struck mute, till I said, 'Well, if you value the opinion of such people, why didn't you think of them beforehand, and strike out the passage?' 'I ought to have, since it is their opinion, whether I value it or no,' he said with a half groan. 'But it didn't occur to me that there was anything to object to!' I reminded him that though three objectors who disliked the passage, or pretended to, might write their disapproval, three hundred who possibly approved of it would not take the trouble to write, and hence he might have a false impression of the public as a body. 'Yes; I agree. Still I suppose I ought to have foreseen these gentry, and have omitted it,' he murmured.

It may be added here, to finish with this detail (though it anticipates dates), that when the novel came out in volume-form the *Times* quoted

---

[71] The reference, identified by Maitland in a footnote, is to the *Spectator* review (3 January 1874, p. 22) of the first instalment of *Far from the Madding Crowd*.

[72] The original MS, dated 8 January 1874 (DCM), is fully transcribed in Purdy, p. 337.

[73] *Essays on Freethinking and Plainspeaking*. Footnoted by Maitland. See n. 68 above.

[74] The original MS, dated 12 March 1874 (DCM), is fully transcribed in Purdy, pp. 338–9.

[75] Cf. I Kings 18: 44: 'Behold, there ariseth a little cloud out of the sea, like a man's hand.'

in a commendatory review the very passage that had offended. As soon as I met him, I said, 'You see what the *Times* says about that paragraph; and you cannot say that the *Times* is not respectable.' He was smoking, and replied tardily: 'No; I can't say that the *Times* is not respectable.' I then urged that if he had omitted the sentences, as he had wished he had done, I should never have taken the trouble to restore them in the reprint, and the *Times* could not have quoted them with approbation. I suppose my manner was slightly triumphant; at any rate, he said, 'I spoke as editor, not as man. You have no more consciousness of these things than a child.'

To return to the April of that year. Speaking to him of a remarkably generous review of the previous book of mine, I asked him if in such a case one ought not to write and thank the reviewer. He smoked on half a minute. 'No, I don't see why you should thank him,' he said. 'I have criticised books in heaps for years and years, but nobody ever thanked me for a review.' After a pause, gloomily: 'Though perhaps the only feeling ever caused an author by a review of mine has been one of utter disgust!'

Far from the Madding Crowd having run its course, he asked me in December, if I could let him have another story. 'I am sorry that the *Madding Crowd* has come to an end,' he wrote, 'but all stories must end.'

*   *   *   *   *

One day [March 23, 1875],[76] I received from Stephen a mysterious note asking me to call in the evening, as late as I liked. I went, and found him alone, wandering up and down his library in slippers; his tall thin figure wrapt in a heath-coloured dressing-gown. After a few remarks on our magazine arrangements, he said he wanted me to witness his signature to what, for a moment, I thought was his will; but it turned out to be a deed renunciatory of holy orders, under the Act of 1870. He said grimly that he was really a reverend gentleman still, little as he might look it, and that he thought it as well to cut himself adrift of a calling for which, to say the least, he had always been utterly unfit. The deed was executed with due formality. Our conversation then turned upon theologies decayed and defunct, the origin of things, the constitution of matter, the unreality of time and kindred subjects. He told me that he had 'wasted'

---

[76] Square brackets in Maitland.

much time on systems of religion and metaphysics, and that the new theory of vortex rings[77] had a 'staggering fascination' for him.

* 　 * 　 * 　 * 　 *

As a relief from the *Ethelberta*, comedy, or satire, on the fusion of classes—which, by the way, was published thirty years too soon, and, following a pastoral tale, nonplussed the public—I had planned some tragic poems, being anxious to get back to verse if I could. But, he seemed disinclined, as editor, to take up the idea, and in 1877, on my starting another novel, *The Return of the Native*, we had some correspondence about its suitability for the *Cornhill*. But, though he liked the opening, he feared that the relations between Eustacia, Wildeve, and Thomasin might develop into something 'dangerous' for a family magazine, and he refused to have anything to do with it unless he could see the whole. This I never sent him; and the matter fell through. It was the last contribution that I ever offered him, so far as I can remember.

Our correspondence as editor and edited was thus broken off, but when I had published *The Trumpet Major*, he expressed, with some perversity I thought, his regret that I had not given him the opportunity of bringing it out. He said he liked stories in which 'Old George the Third was round the corner',[78] as in that one, but not those in which he was on the stage. 'Though', he added, in a saturnine tone, 'the heroine married the wrong man.' I replied that they mostly did. 'Not in magazines,' he answered.

After this I saw him but very occasionally, until at length a ten years' chasm of silence came between us in our pilgrimage—a silence which I shall always regret. Towards the latter part of the time, in 1897, I was in the Bernese Oberland, when the opening scenery revealed the formidable peak of the Great Schreckhorn,[79] which, as I knew, he had been the first to 'conquer' (to use his own word) as an Alpine climber in 1861, where he had been 'frequently flattened out against the rock like a beast of ill-repute nailed to a barn'.[80] Then and there I suddenly had a vivid sense of him, as if his personality informed the mountain—gaunt

[77] Vortex rings are mentioned in various scientific contexts in the middle years of the nineteenth-century, but the reference here is presumably to the hydrodynamic theory, originating with the German scientist Hermann Ludwig Ferdinand Helmholtz (1821–94), that liquid vortex rings constituted the fundamental molecular structure of the universe.

[78] Cf. Stephen's letter of 17 February 1879 (DCM), quoted in part in *LW*, p. 131.

[79] See *LW*, p. 311.

[80] Adapted from the essay, 'The Schreckhorn', in Stephen's *The Playground of Europe* (1871; London: Longmans, Green, 1904), p. 79.

and difficult, like himself. His frequent conversations on his experiences in the Alps recurred to me, experiences always related with modesty in respect of his own achievements, and with high commendation of the achievements of others, which were really no greater than his own. As I lay awake that night, the more I thought of the mountain, the more permeated with him it seemed: I could not help remarking to my wife that I felt as if the Schreckhorn were Stephen in person; and I was moved to begin a sonnet to express the fancy, which I resolved to post to him when I got home. However, thinking that he might not care for it, I did not do so.[81]

[1906.15]

[Assistance to H. W. Nevinson]

The journalist Henry Woodd Nevinson (1856–1941) had met Hardy at Clodd's house in Aldeburgh in 1903 and published an admiring article about him, supplemented by an extensive bibliography, in the *English Illustrated Magazine* that same year. When, in August 1906, he sought permission to visit Max Gate, Hardy responded warmly, specifying only that he not be quoted in any resulting article or cited as the source of any critical 'elucidations' such an article might offer (*CL* iii. 223). Nevinson's brief but valuable *Thomas Hardy* (London: George Allen & Unwin, 1941) makes it clear that Hardy talked freely during the two days they spent together, but while Nevinson drew upon his Dorchester visit in the article that immediately followed—'Thomas Hardy: The Son of Earth', *The Reader*, 10 November 1906, p. 69, subsequently collected in *Essays in Freedom* (London: Duckworth, 1909)—he was scrupulous in his observance of Hardy's injunction.

[1906.16]

[?Entry in Dorset Directory?]

It is not known whether Hardy contributed, either directly or indirectly, to the 'Thomas Hardy' entry in *Wilts and Dorset at the Opening of the Twentieth*

---

[81] Stephen almost certainly never saw the sonnet, which was first published in Maitland, p. 278, and first collected by TH in *Satires of Circumstance* (1914).

Century: Contemporary Biographies, ed. William Thomas Pike (Brighton: W. T. Pike, 1906), p. 244—reissued as *A Dictionary of Edwardian Biography: Dorset* (Edinburgh: Peter Bell, 1983). Although the entry consists for the most part of standard biographical information, the inclusion of one or two less familiar details (e.g. 'is a moderately good cyclist, and was formerly a fair swimmer') suggests the possibility of some personal involvement on Hardy's part.

[1906.17]

'Henry Mills Alden'

Henry Mills Alden (1836–1919), the American editor and author, was from 1869 until his death the managing editor of *Harper's Monthly Magazine*, in which Hardy published more of his works—novels, stories, and poems— than in any other journal on either side of the Atlantic. Although he seems never to have met Alden in person, Hardy was inevitably asked to join with other British and American authors in contributing congratulatory letters to the 70th birthday tribute to Alden published, as below, in *Harper's Weekly*, 15 December 1906, p. 1814. Hardy's original letter has not been located. Purdy, p. 311.

Max Gate, Dorchester, November 11, 1906.

Dear Mr Alden,

Please allow a small and distant voice among the many to con- gratulate you on a hale arrival at your seventieth year. That you have not been pricked to death during a long literary part of the term by the sharp thorns which lurk in all editorial cushions testifies to your staying powers physically and intellectually; that you have thriven upon them testifies to what my words will not reach.

How long ago it is since we first corresponded I cannot remember,[82] but it marks, I know, a large section of our lives. With my wishes for your continued happiness, I remain, always truly yours,

Thomas Hardy.

---

[82] Little of TH's correspondence with Harper and Brothers appears to have survived, but his connection with *Harper's Monthly* dated back to the American serialization of *The Return of the Native*, February 1878 to January 1879.

[1907.01]

[?Obituary Paragraphs on the Revd Thomas Perkins?]

> The Revd Thomas Perkins (1842–1907), rector of the Dorset village of Turnworth, was an amateur photographer and author of architectural guide-books whom Hardy—who had overseen the rebuilding of Turnworth church in 1869–70 (see 1870.01)—especially admired for 'his humane and disinterested views, and staunch support of the principle of justice for animals, in whose cause he made noble sacrifices, and spent time and money that he could ill afford' (*LW*, p. 359). Perkins's devotion to animals was also emphasized in the unattributed paragraphs published in two London papers shortly after his death on 23 March 1907, and Hardy may well have been their author. The first item, introduced by 'a correspondent writes', appeared as below in *The Times*, 29 March 1907, p. 7, the day following the formal obituary of 28 March. The second (following the line of asterisks) accompanied the photograph of Perkins reproduced in the *Sphere*, 13 April 1907, p. 27: Hardy had sent its editor, Clement Shorter, a 'picture' of Perkins on 3 April (*CL* iii. 250–1) and seems the likeliest source of the words Shorter quoted.

Mr Perkins was a man of interesting personality and wide interests, whose unceasing efforts in the cause of animals would alone be sufficient to single him out as one of the most unflaggingly humane characters of our time. He took numerous photographs illustrating animal life, and his rectory was quite a menagerie of forlorn animals that he had rescued from suffering and death from time to time.

*   *   *   *   *

The Rev. Thomas Perkins, M. A., rector of Turnworth, Dorset, who died on March 21 aged sixty-five, was 'a member of several learned societies, the author of many works on ecclesiastical architecture, the devoted friend of animals, the unwearying advocate of their rights and denouncer of their oppressors'.

[1907.02]

'Snake Feeding at the Zoo'

Cruelty to animals was an issue on which Hardy always felt, and wrote, strongly. In this instance he had been sent—presumably by Henry S. Salt (1851–1939), honorary secretary of the Humanitarian League 1891–1920— an advance offprint of 'The Zoological Society and its Snakes. A Question Not Answered', a protest against the feeding of live goats to pythons at the London Zoo that was about to appear as a Supplement to the League's journal, *The Humanitarian*, for June 1907. The following letter, written from the Hardys' temporary London address, appeared as below in the same issue: *The Humanitarian*, 3 (June 1907), p. 139. It omits the name of the addressee, 'The Committee of the Humanitarian League', but otherwise differs from the original MS (Princeton) only in details of punctuation and layout.

1, Hyde Park Mansions, W., May 13th, 1907.

Gentlemen,

I approve of the views expressed in the pamphlet on 'Snake-Feeding at the Zoo', which you have sent; though I consider snake-feeding to be but an infinitesimal part of the general blameworthiness of man in dealing with the weaker animals; *e.g.*, in killing them for food or as vermin with unnecessary barbarity, in making them work too laboriously; killing them for sport, keeping them in cages and hutches as so-called pets, making them perform at public exhibitions, etc., all which practices I should like to see prohibited except the two first, which can only be mitigated. These, unfortunately, the defects of the terrestrial scheme prevent our stopping—at any rate at present.

Yours very truly,

Thomas Hardy.

[1907.03]

[Message to the Rationalist Press Association] [2]

Hardy was invited, as an acknowledged sympathizer (see 1904.04), to attend the sixth annual dinner of the Rationalist Press Association in the spring of 1907. The Association's indefatigable founder and vice-chairman, Charles Albert Watts (1858–1946), evidently used such occasions to draw in potential members and supporters, and Hardy's letter was one of several read out at the dinner and subsequently printed, as below, in the report of the occasion published in the *Literary Guide and Rationalist Review*, new series no. 132 (1 June 1907), pp. 89–90.

Max Gate, Dorchester. April 11th, 1907.

Dear Sir,

I am sorry to be unable to be present at the dinner to which I have received the honour of an invitation, and for which I have to thank the Board.

You ask me to express an opinion on the educational work of the Association. I may say that I think it is doing great good in saving the time that young people waste in learning as facts masses of emotional fancy which they have to unlearn later on.

That the Rationalist Press does not attempt (so far as I have seen) to supply any other channels for the checked emotion is I suppose, no fault of an Association that limits itself to questions of reason. As, however, man cannot live by Rationalism alone, one can dream of a supplementary or complemental Association, which should supply the second half of human needs—objects for such emotion—which could be tended and nourished frankly as fancy, and not under its old name of faith.

Yours very truly,
Thomas Hardy.

[1907.04]

'Opinions on Japan'

In the summer of 1907 Hardy responded to a request from K. Minoura, proprietor of the Tokyo newspaper *Hochi Shimbun* and vice-president of the House of Representatives of the Imperial Diet, for a contribution to a series of letters representing 'the feelings and opinion in Christendom towards Japan and her people' (8 June 1907, DCM). Hardy's letter appeared in Japanese, under the heading 'Opinions on Japan, from prominent figures of the world', on the second page of the *Hochi Shimbun*, 24 September 1907; other contributors, on different dates, included William Jennings Bryan, the US Secretary of State, and Alfred Austin, the British Poet Laureate. Hardy's original letter has not been located, but his pencil draft (DCM) has served as the source of the text below, as it earlier provided the basis for the printing of the letter in *Life and Work*, p. 362.

Max Gate Dorchester Aug. 13. 1907

Dear Sir:

I am unable to express a well-defined opinion on Japan and her people. I can only express a hope, which is that your nation may not become absorbed in material ambitions masked by threadbare conventions, like the European nations and America, but that it may develop to an enlightened spirituality that shall become a shining example.

Yours very truly

T. H.

[1907.05]

[On Adelphi Terrace]

In the course of a personal letter to Clement Shorter of 24 January 1906 (*CL* iii. 194), Hardy reminiscenced about Adelphi Terrace, on the Thames Embankment, as it was in the 1860s, when he worked there in Arthur Blomfield's architectural office. In April 1907 Austin Brereton quoted three sentences from that letter in his book, *The Literary History of the Adelphi and its Neighbourhood* (London: Anthony Treherne, 1907), p. 216, citing the letter's (unidentified) recipient as authorization for the quotation. Whether

Hardy's permission for the quotation was also obtained is not known, but he did subsequently readapt the passage from Brereton for inclusion, as below, in his own *Life and Work*, p. 42. Purdy, p. 263.

I sat there drawing, inside the easternmost window of the front room on the first floor above the ground floor, occasionally varying the experience by idling on the balcony. I saw from there the Embankment and Charing-Cross Bridge built, and of course used to think of Garrick and Johnson. The rooms contained at that date fine Adam mantelpieces[1] in white marble, on which we used to sketch caricatures in pencil.

[1907.06]

'The Censorship of Plays'

The refusal of performance licences to such plays as Edward Garnett's *The Breaking Point* and Harley Granville Barker's *Waste* provoked the theatrical community to renewed criticism of the Office of Censorship and its practices: see Dennis Kennedy, *Granville Barker and the Dream of Theatre* (Cambridge: Cambridge University Press, 1985), pp. 91–8. Asked by J. M. Barrie (7 October 1907, DCM) to associate himself with a public letter of protest, Hardy jokingly objected that he could scarcely claim to be 'a dramatic author' (*CL* iii. 277); he nevertheless signed and promptly returned the copy Barrie had sent (Beinecke), and was duly named among many other signatories when the letter appeared, under the heading 'The Censorship of Plays', in *The Times*, 29 October 1907, p. 15.

[1907.07]

Forewords [The Society of Dorset Men in London]

At its annual meeting on 15 November 1907 the Society of Dorset Men elected Hardy—'much against my wish', as he told Florence Henniker

---

[1] Both Brereton and TH's original letter refer only to a single room and mantelpiece; the architects Robert, James, and William Adam built the Adelphi 1769–71.

(*CL* iii. 288)—as its second President, in succession to Sir Frederick Treves. Hardy was not at the meeting but did later supply some lightly reminiscential 'Forewords' (the term seems to have been his own) that were published, as below, in the *Society of Dorset Men in London* (Year-Book 1907–8), pp. [3]–4. The entire text, apart from the opening sentence, was reprinted (as from the Year-Book) in the *Daily Mail*, 10 March 1908, p. 5, under the heading 'Young Man from the Country'. Purdy, p. 311–12.

The Society of Dorset Men in London has entered upon the fourth year of its existence, and can no longer be regarded as a tender bantling whose every breath needs to be watched and counted, hopefully or the reverse. The idea of such a Society has become familiar to its members; and as the seasons pass, and a younger generation of exiles from the parent county duly succeeds to associateship, it will gradually cease to cross their minds that there ever was a time when 'neither vell nor mark' (to use a phrase from home)[2] of such an institution was apparent in the roaring loom of London life.

If it were worth doing, I could describe to those who are now in the full vigour of their activities in this City, and in the full flush of comradeship with brethren of the Society and others, what London seemed like to a Dorset young man who plunged into it alone more than forty-five years ago, in the somewhat reckless method of becoming a Londoner that was perhaps more common then than now. I might also describe what permanent residence in town meant to such a young man—living on from year to year, strolling up and down Holborn Hill before the Viaduct was constructed, wandering in the labyrinth of Seven Dials before the new Avenues were cut,[3] and hastening off to Drury Lane or the Princess's Theatre to see Phelps or Charles Kean[4] in a Shakespearean tragedy. So far as I can recollect, the last thing that such a young man ever thought of was association with persons coming from his own part of England, or even discovering their existence. Though obviously (it is astonishing how obvious a thing becomes when it has been carried out) nothing tends so largely to remove that isolation

---

[2] Dorset dialect: literally 'neither skin nor vestige', i.e. 'no trace'.

[3] Seven Dials, now (AD 2000) a tight traffic circle in Monmouth Street, was a notoriously crime-ridden area (Dickens's 'Tom All Alone's') prior to its 'clearance' in the latter half of the nineteenth century. Shaftesbury Avenue, to its north, was cut through in 1877–86, Garrick Street, to its south, in 1860, and Charing Cross Road, to its west, in 1887.

[4] For TH's recollections of the actors Samuel Phelps (1804–78) and Charles John Kean (1811?–68), second son of Edmund Kean, see respectively *LW*, pp. 54, 44.

which is so apt to depress, and harm—sometimes permanently—the lives of country beginners in London, as a Society like ours, at bottom it is but one symptom among many of the general growth of human altruism noticeable everywhere. I can, unhappily, recall cases in which such a Society would probably have saved from rack and ruin many a promising youth so circumstanced.

My impression is that though the members themselves are grateful to those energetic spirits who set the Society going—I can express the belief freely, since I myself had no part in doing it—those who are pre-eminently grateful do not live in London at all, or but a small minority of them. I refer to the mothers of the younger constituents of this body. The sleepless nights and anxious days that have been spent, not only by Dorset mothers, but by those of every other county, at the time of their youthful sons' first plunge into the City alone, would make a pathetic record if they could be revealed. Such anxieties—which would be intenser still if all the risks were realised—can never be entirely dispelled. But I think that our County Society, young as it is, is doing as much to allay them as can be accomplished by any similar means, and will do more as it unfolds itself in future years.

1908

[1908.01]

[Inspired Paragraph on *The Dynasts* Part Third]

Responding, on 15 January 1908, to a request from James Milne, the friendly editor of the *Book Monthly*, Hardy sent 'two or three details' of the forthcoming Part Third of *The Dynasts*, but added that he hoped their publication could not be regarded as 'the puff preliminary—a thing I should deprecate as you know' (*CL* vii. 144). The two paragraphs of Hardy's pencilled manuscript (Eton) subsequently appeared, slightly reworked, as an unattributed single paragraph in the 'Personal and Particular' section of the *Book Monthly*, 5 (February 1908), p. 321. The following reproduction includes Milne's introductory sentence, with its significant 'informed'.

An informed word on the third and final volume of Mr Thomas Hardy's poem, *The Dynasts*. The volume covers the time from the crossing of the Niemen by the Grand Army under Napoleon, on its fatal march to Moscow, to the midnight after Waterloo—a space of three years almost to a day in historic reality, though made to seem less in the drama, as would be expected. As the action includes the campaigns of Moscow, Leipzig, Vittoria and Waterloo, and thus deals with more events of magnitude than occur in the earlier parts, this one is somewhat longer. The Duchess of Richmond's romantic ball at Brussels[1] forms, of course, one of the fifty-three scenes of which the part consists, and no less than nine scenes are occupied with the battle of Waterloo itself. Altogether, on a hasty counting, from a hundred and thirty to a hundred and forty speaking characters appear, and a much larger number of 'walking' personages.

[1] See 1888.04.

[1908.02]

'Mr. Meredith's Birthday'

George Meredith in his last years was widely regarded as the greatest living English writer, and on 12 February 1908, p. 17, *The Times* published under the heading 'Mr. Meredith's Birthday' the text of an address, 'mounted on vellum', that was being presented to him on the occasion of his eightieth birthday by 'some of his friends and admirers'. The names of most of the signatories were listed alphabetically, but inscribed on the vellum itself, according to *The Times*, were the names of Hardy, Swinburne, John Morley, and Frederick Greenwood, Meredith's 'old friends and literary colleagues'. A less detailed report appeared in the *Daily News*, 12 February, p. 7, and doubtless in other papers as well. *Life and Work*, pp. 370–1, quotes Meredith's letter thanking Hardy for his participation in the address.

[1908.03]

'George Meredith'

H. W. Smith, of the *Daily News*, asked Hardy, 8 January 1908 (DCM), to contribute his views on George Meredith's achievements and 'place in the world of letters' for publication on the occasion of Meredith's eightieth birthday. Hardy had already signed the formal address being presented to Meredith (1908.02), and his brief but polite reply to Smith (*CL* iii. 295) seems clearly to have been intended as a simple refusal. An abbreviated version of that reply was nevertheless published, as below, in the *Daily News*, 12 February 1908, p. 4, as one of a series of messages under the heading 'George Meredith. Special Messages to "The Daily News"'. Purdy, p. 312.

I have known Mr Meredith for so long a time—forty years within a few months[2]—and his personality is such a living one to me, that I cannot reach a sufficiently detached point of view to write a critical estimate of his great place in the world of letters.

---

[2] They first met in March 1869 when Meredith was the reader, for Chapman & Hall, of the manuscript of TH's never-published first novel, *The Poor Man and the Lady* (see 1909.06; *LW*, pp. 62–4).

[1908.04]

[Addition to Promotional Leaflet for *The Dynasts*]

Early in 1908, following the appearance of Part Third of *The Dynasts*, Hardy's publishers sent him a proof of an eight-page advertising leaflet covering the entire work. Returning the proof to Frederick Macmillan on 26 April 1908, Hardy described the 'prospectus' as 'ingeniously drawn up' and the quotations from press notices 'judiciously chosen', but suggested that the readability of *The Dynasts* might be emphasized by adding an invented notice attributed to the 'Uncritical Public': 'It carries you on like an exciting novel' (*CL* vii. 145). He must therefore be presumed to have inspired, if not actually written, the following statement, printed in bold-faced type at the foot of the final page of the leaflet as issued (copy at Eton).

Many readers who have begun the drama with some hesitation have afterwards assured the author that they found it as exciting as a novel.

[1908.05]

Dorset in London

As President of the Society of Dorset Men in London for 1907–8 Hardy would normally have been expected to take the chair and give a speech at the Society's annual dinner on 11 May 1908. When first invited to become a Vice-President, however, he had warned of his 'probable inability to be present at dinners or meetings' (see 1905.05), and on this occasion he simply sent a copy of his speech to be read by the Society's secretary, William Watkins. But because the available time was taken up by speeches from people actually present, Hardy's presidential address—much to his annoyance (*LW*, p. 367)—was neither read nor quoted in the report of the dinner in the *Dorset County Chronicle*, 14 May 1908, pp. 5–6. It did appear separately, as below, under the authorial title 'Dorset in London', in *Society of Dorset Men in London* (Year-Book 1908–9), pp. [3]–7, preceded by a facsimile of five sentences from the manuscript. Curiously, the sentences in the facsimile—varying in one detail from the text as printed—were precisely those quoted in *The Times*, 15 December 1908, p. 4. The manuscript in its entirety was evidently sent back to Watkins in October 1908 to enable him to produce the facsimile (Watkins to Hardy, 9 and 12 October, DCM), but Watkins seems not to have returned it the second time (*LW*, p. 367) and its fate is unknown. When Watkins originally received the manuscript prior to the dinner he undertook (9 May, DCM) to have 'a typed copy' made and sent to Hardy within a few days' time, but the surviving ten-page typescript that Hardy corrected and preserved among his 'Miscellanea' materials (Beinecke) was apparently a copy made from the 1908–9 Year-Book. Purdy, pp. 312–13.

The Society of Dorset Men that has been formed in this City is now in the fifth year of its existence, and though a very little Society at first, it has grown to an astonishing degree during its moderate span of life. Much as it is indebted to its organisers and conductors for the attainment of its present position, there may be something in the character of the people composing it that has helped it on. A distinguished Scotchman,[3] devoted to psychological study, who knows Dorset very well, has been heard to remark that what I may call the cohesive feeling among Dorset county men away from home largely resembles that among his own folk north of the Tweed; and if he is right, this would go far to account for the Society's development by leaps and bounds.

No more curious change has come over London social life of late years than the rise of that almost total disregard of provincialism among its constituents and casual sharers which nowadays pervades the City. Incomers are allowed to preserve personal peculiarities that they formerly were compelled to stifle if they wished to be accepted. This is particularly the case in respect of local accents. A hundred or even fifty years ago the object of every sojourner in the Metropolis from the West—as from East, South and North—was to obliterate his local colour, and merge himself in the type Londoner as quickly as possible. But now Town society has become a huge menagerie, and at what are called the best houses visitors hear with no surprise twangs and burrs and idioms from every point of the compass. It is a state of disregard primarily owing, no doubt, to larger conceptions of life, coupled with the influx of Americans every season; though it is now extended to the provincial English, Scotch and Irish. In former times an unfamiliar accent was immediately noted as quaint and odd, even a feature of ridicule in novels, memoirs, and conversations of the date. So that while

---

[3] Probably TH's friend Sir George Brisbane Douglas, Bt (1856–1935); see *LW*, pp. 235, 250, etc.

it was the aim of every provincial, from the squire to the rustic, to get rid of his local articulation at the earliest moment, he now seems rather to pride himself on retaining it, being, in fact, virtually encouraged to do so.

Even dialect-words are respected. Within my own recollection it was, for instance, thought comical to hear in London a West of England man speak of the autumn as 'the fall'. But now that the American multi-millionaire also speaks of the autumn as the fall, the expression is voted poetical—which indeed it is.

Who knows that country accents and words may not some day be affected by smart society men in Town, like the newest pattern in waistcoats, and members of fashionable clubs go down to the shires with week-end tickets, to get a little private practice? Unless, on the other hand, all local differences become obliterated before that date by the amalgamating effect of perpetual intercourse arising out of endless facilities for travel.

After such a surmise as this, it may not be amiss if we indulge in a brief meditative survey of the many points of contact between our County and the City, and consider what the phrase 'Dorset in London' may be felt to mean. We may discover it to contain much more than is apparent at first sight.

For clearness, let us imagine ourselves in the situation of a young man just arrived in London from Dorsetshire, with a half-formed intention of making the capital the scene of his life's endeavours, and a prob-ability of finding there his home and his interests, possibly his grave. We will assume that he is in no hurry to make up his mind, is under no great stress of any sort, and can afford time to look about him.

He pauses, maybe, on Waterloo Bridge, and, Dorset people being impressionable, he experiences as he gazes at the picture before him a vivid sense of his own insignificance in it, his isolation and loneliness. He feels himself among strangers and strange things. Being, however, though impressionable, also a very thorough sort of person, he means to explore the town, and leaning against the parapet of the bridge he looks at his new map to find out his bearings. He perceives that, despite the first strangeness, there are three 'Dorset' Streets, a 'Dorset' Square, and one or two 'Dorset' Roads in the wilderness of brick and stone encamp-ments about him. Also a 'Weymouth' Street, a 'Blandford' Square and Street, a 'Bryanston' Square, Place and Street, a 'Melcombe' Place, a 'Portland' Place and Street, a 'Sherborne' Lane, a 'Cranbourne' Street, a 'Melbury' Road, a 'Bridport' Place, and even a 'Bindon' Road. Dorset, either directly, or indirectly through family titles, has certainly set its mark on London nomenclature.

The most conspicuous object before his eyes is St Paul's Cathedral, rising against the sky from Ludgate Hill. St Paul's is built of Portland stone. St Paul's seems, on reflection, to be almost as much Dorset as he is. To be sure, it has been standing here in London for more than two hundred years, but it stood, or rather lay, in Dorset probably two hundred thousand years before it got here. How thoroughly metropolitan it is; its façade thrills to the street noises all day long, and has done so for three or four human lifetimes. But through what a stretch of time did it thrill all day and all night in Portland to the tides of the West Bay, particularly when they slammed against the island during south-west gales, and sent reverberations into the very bottom quarry there. As if to prevent his ever forgetting this geological fact, some of the stones that were quarried for the Cathedral still remain, as is well known, in the lonely cove of the isle, squared and ready, though for some unaccountable reason they were never taken away, like their fellows, to adorn the largest city in the world.

Reflecting on this, he looks towards the Strand end of the bridge, where the lengthy front of Somerset House displays itself, one of the most satisfactory specimens of that order of architecture to be found in London, one which would, indeed, be almost perfect if it could be raised to a somewhat higher level. The substance of this dignified building also hails from Portland, and was buried for ages in the heart of the isle.

Once on this trail our imaginary Dorset young man moves along to follow it up. But, as we have not his leisure, we will not accompany him through all his wanderings to look at more specimens of Dorset stonework—the Whitehall Banqueting House, the Horse Guards, nearly all the churches of Wren, the General Post Office, and many other buildings. London, in brief, teems with edifices of importance executed in stone from Dorsetshire.

Should he still be in the mood, he may look for Dorset at a lower level—in the paving-blocks of the streets; though these, it is true, have largely given way to wood and asphalte[4] of late. Enormous quantities of these blocks came from another corner of the county—Swanage and the Isle of Purbeck.

---

[4] A frequent nineteenth-century spelling.

(I may observe parenthetically in respect of the 'Isle' of Portland and the 'Isle' of Purbeck, that our Dorset ancestors must have been as imaginative as Mr Wemmick in the matter of islands,[5] a brook that you can jump over, or a dribble through an isthmus of pebbles, having been enough, in their view, to entitle a merely peninsular spot to that geographical distinction.)

Not to dwell longer on the extent to which material London is a product of Dorsetshire, let us pass on to what may, perhaps, be still more significant instances of the fact that Dorset has made herself at home in no mean degree in the London of the past.

To begin where we began in our examination of the substantive part of the City—St Paul's. What probably attracts us most of all among the monuments within the building is that erected to Wellington, a design which has been declared, by better judges than I can pretend to be, to show absolute genius in all its features, to be one of the few instances, in a city where so much of the monumental work is bad, that touch real success in this difficult branch of art. And to whose mind does this fine work—the admiration of connoisseurs from all parts of the world—owe its existence? To the mind of a Dorset man, a man of Blandford, Alfred Stevens—one whose exceptional powers as a creator of beautiful forms were unhappily brought to an early end by the living death of paralysis, to England's great artistic loss.[6]

Our meditative friend may now turn aside to the bookstalls of the neighbourhood, and casually take down from a row of volumes a small one in old-fashioned binding. It contains poems which, as he glances through them, he finds to combine airy vivaciousness and humour in a manner altogether charming. There are whimsical epigrams and songs, graceful and witty sketches in rhyme, poetical qualities that, in the words of Austin Dobson, 'lift their possessor above every other writer of familiar verse'.[7] The author of all this grace and lightness is Matthew

---

[5] Wemmick, in Dickens's *Great Expectations*, ch. 25, has turned his suburban cottage into an island fortress, accessible only by a plank across 'a chasm about four feet wide and two deep'.

[6] Alfred Stevens (1818–75), artist, the son of a Blandford house-painter; see *LW*, pp. 390–1. The Wellington monument, unfinished at his death, is his best-known work.

[7] Dobson (see 1875.01) edited a selection of Matthew Prior's verse and published an essay on him in *Eighteenth-Century Vignettes*, but neither includes the words here quoted; Dobson's *D.N.B.* entry on Prior does, however, assert that 'in occasional pieces and familiar verse [he] has no rival in English'.

Prior, mostly called Matt, a man who was born at Wimborne. Should curiosity lead our enquirer on, he will discover the tomb of this elegant Dorset genius in Westminster Abbey.[8]

The same investigator may on some succeeding day find himself in Bloomsbury, standing in front of the Foundling Hospital. This institution, which he had always imagined to be eminently metropolitan, he learns to have been established by the indefatigable exertions of a native of Lyme Regis, Thomas Coram, whose name has been given to an adjoining street—one of the few instances in London of a street being called after a person who deserves commemoration.[9] Coram made such great personal sacrifices to further his darling project that he ruined himself by his efforts, and was reduced in his old age to dependence upon charitable subscriptions. His portrait by his friend Hogarth may be seen in the Hospital still, and it should make every Dorset native proud that such a philanthropic being first drew breath on our county's shore.

It would take us all night to dwell upon the history of every Dorset man who has added distinction to London in past times. It is only possible to give a name or two more. That of John Morton, Cardinal and Archbishop of Canterbury, occurs to me. He was Dorset born, hailing from Bere Regis, and was at one time a monk at Cerne Abbas. Bacon describes him as a wise and eloquent man, but in nature harsh and haughty; accepted by the King, envied of the nobility, and hated by the people.[10]

Ashley Cooper, the first Earl of Shaftesbury, is another notable of Dorset origin, having been born at Wimborne St Giles.[11] Conspicuous rather than good, the most prominent figure in the notorious Cabal Ministry, he is the chief character in 'Absalom and Achitophel', the immortal satire of Dryden, whose lines about him testify to his extraordinary ability, even while they mercilessly dissect him:—

---

[8] Matthew Prior (1664–1721), poet and diplomat.

[9] Thomas Coram (1668?–1751), merchant and philanthropist; the Foundling Hospital has since been pulled down, but Coram Street still runs between Woburn Place and Coram's Fields, where the Hospital formerly stood.

[10] John Morton (1420?–1500), Archbishop of Canterbury and cardinal; the description is taken almost verbatim from Francis Bacon, *History of the Reign of King Henry the Seventh*, in *Works*, ed. James Spedding *et al.* (New York: Hurd and Houghton, 1869), xi. 310.

[11] Anthony Ashley Cooper, first earl of Shaftesbury (1621–83), a central political figure during the Commonwealth and Restoration periods.

A fiery soul which working out its way,
Fretted the pigmy body to decay.
                 .   .   .   .

Great wits are, sure, to madness near allied,
And thin partitions do their bounds divide;
Else why should he, with wealth and honour blest
Refuse his age the needful hours of rest?
Punish a body which he could not please;
Bankrupt of life, yet prodigal of ease?[12]

Nor must I forget to mention, as a Dorset man who in his time was a
force in London and elsewhere, the Cromwellian Colonel Nathaniel
Whetham, whose life and times have lately been made the subject of
an interesting volume by two of his descendants.[13] He was born at
Burstock, near Broadwindsor, in 1604, and early became an important
man of affairs in the City. When the Civil Wars broke out he served
in the Parliamentary Army as a Colonel of Dragoons, and afterwards
became a Member of Parliament, but on the death of Cromwell he
retired to private life in the part of England from which he had sprung.

There are many others from the same little shire who have stepped
or ridden up to this City by the old road which comes through High
Street, Kensington, and on to Hyde Park Corner. One might almost
include Henry Fielding, who was a London magistrate as well as a writer
of novels and plays. Though not born in the county, he was closely
associated with North-East Dorset, having settled for some time at East
Stower.[14] That he knew Dorset like a native is apparent to any Dorset
man who makes himself familiar with this keen observer's humorous
scenes and dialogues. I may also include, since he has a monument in
Westminster Abbey, Sir Richard Bingham, of Bingham's Melcombe,
whom Strype calls 'a brave soldier', and Fuller describes as being *fortis
et felix* in all his undertakings'. He fought in the battles of Candia and
Lepanto, and was engaged in all sorts of adventures by land and sea.[15]

---

[12] John Dryden, 'Absalom and Achitophel', lines 156–7, 163–8.

[13] Nathaniel Whetham (1604–68), colonel on the Parliamentary side during the Civil War;
TH's reference is to Catherine During Whetham and William Cecil Dampier Whetham,
A History of the Life of Colonel Nathaniel Whetham (London: Longmans, Green, 1907).

[14] Fielding (1707–54), often claimed by TH as a Dorset writer (e.g. *CL* ii. 195, 196), was in fact
born in Somerset; he did, however, spend most of his early life in the Dorset village of East Stour
(as it is now spelled) and later subscribed himself as 'Henry Fielding of East Stour'.

[15] Sir Richard Bingham (1528–99), soldier and (repressive) governor of Connaught; TH's
references are apparently to bk. I, ch. 30, of John Strype, *Annals of the Reformation and Establishment
of Religion*, 2 vols. (Oxford: Clarendon Press, 1824), ii. 455—though the phrase there is 'great

Coming away from his monument the visitor may glance across to Lambeth, and, in addition to that of Cardinal-Archbishop Morton aforesaid, recall the name of Archbishop William Wake, who was born at Blandford in 1657.[16]

Having started on this line of inquiry in the assumed character of a newly-arrived young man, members of the Society can pursue it further in their own. It is an inquiry that may stouten[17] their hearts and set them girding their loins[18] anew. It will enable them to realise that certain men of Dorset have done no small things here in the past. Many of them were excellent things, others less excellent—much less; but all of them things which required energy, determination, and self-reliance. I think—at any rate I hope—that the investigation will tend to lessen that feeling of gloomy isolation to which young men of Dorset stock are peculiarly liable in an atmosphere not altogether exhilarating after their own air—say in days of fog, when the south-west county is known to be flooded with sunshine, or in those days of piercing rawness from the eastern marshes, that seems to eat into the bones, a rawness seldom or never felt in their own shire. They may gradually learn to take these inclemencies philosophically, and to decide, as those noted predecessors of theirs, good and bad, probably decided, that their true locality and anchorage is where what they can do best can best be done.

[1908.06]

[The Tolstoy Jubilee]

On 8 March 1908 Hardy told Charles Hagberg Wright, librarian of the London Library, that he wished to be 'at least nominally associated with the recognition of Tolstoy's 80th birthday' (*CL* iii. 303–4), and in *The Times*, 23 May 1908, p. 7, he is named as a member of the committee charged with preparing 'an address of congratulation' for signature by Tolstoy's English

soldier'—and Thomas Fuller, *The History of the Worthies of England*, ed. John Nichols, 2 vols. (London: F. C. and J. Rivington, 1811), i. 313. The battle of Candia (the Venetian name for Crete) was a siege lasting from 1645 to 1669, long after Lepanto (1572) and after Bingham's death; Fuller says only that Bingham fought 'in Candia'.

[16] William Wake (1657–1737), Archbishop of Canterbury 1716–37; Lambeth Palace was, and is, the Archbishop of Canterbury's London seat.   [17] i.e. 'to make stout' (*OED*).

[18] A frequent biblical phrase: e.g. 1 Kings 18: 46.

admirers and initiating the publication of 'a cheap edition of his writings in English'. The text of the address was included in a letter from Hagberg Wright published in *The Times*, 15 June 1908, p. 5, and in the issue of 10 September, p. 9, Edmund Gosse, the other principal organizer, reported that the list of more than 700 signatories was headed by the names of George Meredith, Thomas Hardy, Henry James, and J. M. Barrie. Wright went to Russia to make the presentation and reported his experiences in *The Times*, 17 September 1908, p. 6.

[1908.07]

Maumbury Ring

Maumbury Ring—or, more usually, Rings—the Roman amphitheatre in Dorchester, was partially excavated in the early autumn of 1908, with follow-up investigations over the next few years, and shown to have been of Neolithic origin. Hardy, who had used the amphitheatre as the setting for the reunion of Henchard and his wife in *The Mayor of Casterbridge*, was an interested observer of the digging being done in 1908 (*CL* iii. 335) and found himself mentioned in some of the reports of the work that appeared in *The Times* (e.g. 24 September 1908, p. 6; 29 September, p. 8). On 30 September (DCM) Charles Moberly Bell, of *The Times*, wrote and invited him to contribute some reflections of his own. The resulting article appeared under the presumably authorial title 'Maumbury Ring' in *The Times*, 9 October 1908, p. 11, and is reproduced below. Hardy's manuscript is not known to survive, but he preserved a tearsheet of the *Times* page (Millgate) among his 'Miscellanea'. Purdy, p. 312.

The present month sees the last shovelful filled in, the last sod replaced, of the excavations in the well-known amphitheatre at Dorchester, which have been undertaken at the instance of the Dorset Field and Antiquarian Club and others, for the purpose of ascertaining the history and date of the ruins. The experts have scraped their spades and gone home to meditate on the results of their exploration, pending the resumption of the work next spring. Mr St George Gray, of Taunton,[19] has superintended the labour, assisted by Mr Charles Prideaux, an

[19] Harold St George Gray (1872–1963), archaeologist, secretary of the Somersetshire Archaeological and Natural History Society and curator of its museum.

enthusiastic antiquary of the town,[20] who, with disinterested devotion
to discovery, has preferred to spend his annual holiday from his professional duties at the bottom of chalk trenches groping for *fibulæ* or arrow-
heads in a drizzling rain, to idling it away on any other spot in Europe.

As usual, revelations have been made of an unexpected kind. There
was a moment when the blood of us onlookers ran cold, and we shivered
a shiver that was not occasioned by our wet feet and dripping clothes.
For centuries the town, the county, and England generally, novelists,
poets, historians, guide-book writers, and what not, had been freely
indulging their imaginations in picturing scenes that, they assumed,
must have been enacted within those oval slopes; the feats, the contests,
animal exhibitions, even gladiatorial combats, before throngs of people

> Who loved the games men played with death,
> Where death must win[21]

—briefly, the Colosseum programme on a smaller scale. But up were
thrown from one corner prehistoric implements, chipped flints, horns,
and other remains, and a voice announced that the earthworks were of
the palæolithic or neolithic age, and not Roman at all!

This, however, was but a temporary and, it is believed, unnecessary
alarm. At other points in the structure, as has been already stated in *The
Times*,[22] the level floor of an arena, trodden smooth, and coated with
traces of gravel, was discovered with Roman relics and coins on its surface; and at the entrance and in front of the podium, a row of post-holes,
apparently for barriers, as square as when they were dug, together with
other significant marks, which made it fairly probable that, whatever the
place had been before Julius Cæsar's landing, it had been used as an
amphitheatre at some time during the Roman occupation. The obvious
explanation, to those who are not specialists, seems to be that here, as
elsewhere, the colonists, to save labour, shaped and adapted to their own
use some earthworks already on the spot. This was antecedently likely
from the fact that the amphitheatre stands on an elevated site—or, in
the enigmatic words of Hutchins, is 'artfully set on the top of a plain',[23]
—and that every similar spot in the neighbourhood has a tumulus

---

[20] Charles Sydney Prideaux, a dentist by profession, was curator of the Dorset County Museum
for a short period prior to his death in 1934 at the age of 61.

[21] Adapted ('Who' for 'She') from lines 65–6 of Swinburne's 'Faustine'.

[22] *The Times*, 24 September 1908, p. 6.

[23] John Hutchins, *The History and Antiquities of the County of Dorset*, 3rd edn., 4 vols
(Westminster: John Bowyer Nichols & Sons, 1861–70), ii. 796.

or tumuli upon it; or had till some were carted away within living memory.

But this is a matter on which the professional investigators will have their conclusive say when funds are forthcoming to enable them to dig further. For some reason they have hitherto left undisturbed the ground about the southern end of the arena, underneath which the *cavea* or vault for animals is traditionally said to be situated, though it is doubtful if any such vault, supposing it ever to have existed, would have been suffered to remain there, stones being valuable in a chalk district. And if it had been built of chalk blocks the frost and rains of centuries would have pulverized them by this time.

While the antiquaries are musing on the puzzling problems that arise from the confusion of dates in the remains, the mere observer who possesses a smattering of local history, and remembers local traditions that have been recounted by people now dead and gone, may walk round the familiar arena, and consider. And he is not, like the archaists, compelled to restrict his thoughts to the early centuries of our era. The sun has gone down behind the avenue on the Roman Via and modern road that adjoins, and the October moon is rising on the south-east behind the parapet, the two terminations of which by the north entrance jut against the sky like knuckles. The place is now in its normal state of repose and silence, save for the occasional bray of a motorist passing along outside in sublime ignorance of amphitheatrical lore, or the clang of shunting at the nearest railway station.[24] The breeze is not strong enough to stir even the grass-bents with which the slopes are covered, and over which the loiterer's footsteps are quite noiseless.

Like all such taciturn presences, Maumbury is less taciturn by night than by day, which simply means that the episodes and incidents associated therewith come back more readily to the mind in nocturnal hours. First, it recalls to us that, if probably Roman, it is a good deal more. Its history under the rule of the Romans would not extend to a longer period than 200 or 300 years, while it has had a history of 1,600 years since they abandoned this island, through which ages it may have been regarded as a handy place for early English council-gatherings, may have been the scene of many an exciting episode in the life of the Western kingdom. But for century after century it keeps itself closely curtained, except at some moments to be mentioned.

[24] Dorchester has two railway stations, Dorchester South being somewhat nearer to the amphitheatre than Dorchester West.

The civil wars of Charles I. unscreen it a little, and we vaguely learn that it was used by the artillery when the struggle was in this district, and that certain irregularities in its summit were caused then.[25] The next incident that flashes a light over its contours is Sir Christopher Wren's visit a quarter of a century later. Nobody knows what the inhabitants thought to be the origin of its elliptic banks—differing from others in the vicinity by having no trench around them—until the day came when, according to legend, Wren passed up the adjoining highway on his journey to Portland to select stone for St Paul's Cathedral, and was struck with the sight of the mounds.[26] Possibly he asked some rustic at plough there for information. That all tradition of their use as an amphitheatre had been lost is to be inferred from the popular name,[27] and one can quite understand how readily, as he entered and stood on the summit, a man whose studies had lain so largely in the direction of Roman architecture should have ascribed a Roman origin to the erection. That the offhand guess of a passing architect should have turned out to be true—and it does not at present seem possible to prove the whole construction to be prehistoric—is a remarkable tribute to his insight.

The curtain drops for another 40 years, and then Maumbury was the scene of as sinister an event as any associated with it, because it was a definite event. It is one which darkens its concave to this day. This was the death suffered there on March 21, 1705–6, of a girl who had not yet reached her nineteenth year. Here, at any rate, we touch real flesh and blood, and no longer uncertain visions of possible Romans at their games or barbarians at their sacrifices. The story is a ghastly one, but nevertheless very distinctly a chapter of Maumbury's experiences. This girl was the wife of a grocer in the town, a handsome young woman 'of good natural parts', and educated 'to a proficiency suitable enough to one of her sex, to which likewise was added dancing'.[28] She was tried and condemned for poisoning her husband, a Mr Thomas Channing, to whom she had been married against her wish by the compulsion of her parents. The present writer has examined more than once a report of

---

[25] The earthwork was fortified by the Parliamentarian forces holding Dorchester during the Civil War and its south-west bulge apparently originated as a gun platform of this period.

[26] Hutchins, *Dorset* ii. 795, mentions Wren's visit, but TH's source was probably, as he says, local 'legend'.   [27] TH presumably means 'Maumbury Ring' itself.

[28] TH's quotations are taken, somewhat freely, from his principal source, *Serious Admonitions to Youth, In a Short Account of the Life, Trial, Condemnation and Execution of Mrs. Mary Channing . . . with Practical Reflections* (London: Ben. Bragg, 1706), pp. 5, 4, 7.

her trial, and can find no distinct evidence that the thoughtless, pleasure-loving creature committed the crime, while it contains much to suggest that she did not. Nor is any motive discoverable for such an act. She was allowed to have her former lover or lovers about her by her indulgent and weak-minded husband, who permitted her to go her own ways, give parties, and supplied her with plenty of money. However, at the assizes at the end of July, she was found guilty, after a trial in which the testimony chiefly went to show her careless character before and after marriage. During the three sultry days of its continuance, she, who was soon to become a mother, stood at the bar—then, as may be known, an actual bar of iron—'by reason of which (runs the account) and her much talking, being quite spent, she moved the Court for the liberty of a glass of water'.[29] She conducted her own defence with the greatest ability, and was complimented thereupon by Judge Price, who tried her, but did not extend his compliment to a merciful summing-up. Maybe that he, like Pontius Pilate, was influenced by the desire of the townsfolk to wreak vengeance on somebody, right or wrong. When sentence was about to be passed, she pleaded her condition; and execution was postponed. Whilst awaiting the birth of her child in the old damp gaol by the river at the bottom of the town, near the White Hart inn, which stands there still, she was placed in the common room for women prisoners and no bed provided for her, no special payment having been made to her gaoler, Mr Knapton, for a separate cell. Someone obtained for her the old tilt of a wagon to screen her from surrounding eyes, and under this she was delivered of a son, in December. After her lying-in, she was attacked with an intermittent fever of a violent and lasting kind, which preyed upon her until she was nearly wasted away. In this state, at the next assizes, on the 8th of March following, the unhappy woman, who now said that she longed for death, but still persisted in her innocence, was again brought to the bar, and her execution fixed for the 21st.

On that day two men were hanged before her turn came, and then, 'the under-sheriff having taken some refreshment',[30] he proceeded to his biggest and last job with this girl not yet 19, now reduced to a skeleton by the long fever, and already more dead than alive. She was conveyed from the gaol in a cart 'by her father's and husband's houses',[31] so that the course of the procession must have been up High-East-street

---

[29] *Serious Admonitions*, p. 44, adds 'or small Beer, and was permitted to have what she pleased'.
[30] *Serious Admonitions*, p. 51.   [31] *Serious Admonitions*, p. 51.

as far as the Bow, thence down South-street and up the straight old Roman road to the Ring beside it. 'When fixed to the stake she justified her innocence to the very last, and left the world with a courage seldom found in her sex. She being first strangled, the fire was kindled about five in the afternoon, and in the sight of many thousands she was consumed to ashes.'[32] There is nothing to show that she was dead before the burning began, and from the use of the word 'strangled' and not 'hanged', it would seem that she was merely rendered insensible before the fire was lit. An ancestor of the present writer, who witnessed the scene, has handed down the information that 'her heart leapt out' during the burning, and other curious details that cannot be printed here. Was man ever 'slaughtered by his fellow man'[33] during the Roman or barbarian use of this place of games or of sacrifice in circumstances of greater atrocity?

A melodramatic, though less gruesome, exhibition within the arena was that which occurred at the time of the 'No Popery' riots, and was witnessed by this writer when a small child. Highly realistic effigies of the Pope and Cardinal Wiseman were borne in procession from Fordington Hill round the town, followed by a long train of mock priests, monks, and nuns, and preceded by a young man discharging Roman candles, till the same wicked old place was reached, in the centre of which there stood a huge rick of furze, with a gallows above. The figures were slung up, and the fire blazed till they were blown to pieces by fireworks contained within them.[34]

Like its more famous prototype, the Colosseum, this spot of sombre records has also been the scene of Christian worship, but only on one occasion, so far as the writer of these columns is aware, that being the Thanksgiving service for Peace a few years ago.[35] The surplices of the clergy and choristers, as seen against the green grass, the shining brass musical instruments, the enormous chorus of singing voices, formed

---

[32] Adapted from *Serious Admonitions*, p. 51.

[33] Quotation unidentified; possibly a vague memory of 'man—arrayed for mutual slaughter' in Wordsworth's 'Ode. The Morning of a Day Appointed for a General Thanksgiving'.

[34] TH's memories of the Dorchester disturbances are also evoked in *LW*, p. 26. The 'No Popery' riots of November and December 1850 were prompted by the decision of Pope Pius IX to establish for the Roman Catholic Church in England a diocesan episcopacy headed by Cardinal Nicholas Patrick Stephen Wiseman (1802–65) as Archbishop of Westminster.

[35] Peace between Britain and the Boer Republics was signed 31 May 1902; however, TH seems to have been remembering the service held in the amphitheatre on the day of King Edward VII's coronation, 9 August 1902, and devoted chiefly to giving thanks for the king's restoration to health.

not the least impressive of the congregated masses that Maumbury Ring has drawn into its midst during its existence of a probable eighteen hundred years in its present shape, and of some possible thousands of years in an earlier form.[36]

[1908.08]

Louis Napoleon, and the Poet Barnes

The original (Texas) of Hardy's 4 September 1908 letter (*CL* iii. 330) to the publisher John Lane is still accompanied by the manuscript, headed 'Louis Napoleon, & the Poet Barnes', of the extended anecdote published that November in F. H. Cheetham's *Louis Napoleon and the Genesis of the Second Empire* (London: John Lane The Bodley Head, 1909 [1908]) in the form of a last-minute Postscript printed on the two sides of an unpaginated leaf inserted between pages 378 and 379. Hardy's conversation with William Barnes took place in 1885, and while his notes, as included in *Life and Work*, pp. 181–2, are textually quite distinct from what he wrote in 1908, they were doubtless used to assist his memory on the later occasion. The text below is that of the Postscript, though omitting Cheetham's introductory sentence and with three misspellings corrected on the basis of Hardy's manuscript. Purdy, p. 312.

When the Rev. William Barnes, the Dorset poet, was a schoolmaster in Dorchester,[37] he had as usher a certain Mr Hann, a fair and rather choleric young man from the Vale of Blackmoor.[38] It was during the years that Louis Napoleon, afterwards the Emperor Napoleon III, was residing in London; and at this time he paid a visit to the Damers,[39] who

[36] Orel, p. 231, prints as TH's an additional paragraph about the excavations that in *The Times* is separated by a line from TH's article, printed in smaller type, and clearly the work of the representative of *The Times* who sent in the earlier reports.

[37] Barnes's Dorchester school lasted from 1835 to 1862, when he became Rector of Winterborne Came.

[38] Isaac Hann, aged 43 in 1861, ran a school of his own in Dorchester after Barnes's school closed; elsewhere (*LW*, p. 182) TH speaks of him as having probably been related to his own mother's family, the Hands, and as being, like them, 'peppery'.

[39] The reference here is to the family of Colonel George Lionel Dawson-Damer (1788–1856), who was born Dawson, third son of the Earl of Portarlington, and added the extinct Dorset family name of Damer in 1829. The Damers were active and generous patrons of William Barnes over an extended period.

then lived at Came House near the town. On Sundays after service it was the custom of the burghers of Dorchester to promenade in 'The Walks', as the boulevards are called that then, as now, encircle the older part of the town; and on one fine Sunday afternoon Barnes and his usher Hann promenaded with the rest. In the stream of people moving in the opposite direction was a party of gay strollers from Came House, which included among others Louis Napoleon. The latter, in a sort of freak, just as he was passing the aforesaid Mr Hann, put out his walking-cane between Hann's legs so unexpectedly that the latter staggered and nearly fell, which caused laughter among the other promenaders. Barnes (who told the story to me) said that the next thing of which he was conscious was of having Hann's coat tossed into his arms by his furious usher, and of seeing Hann in his shirt-sleeves spring in a pugilistic attitude in front of Louis Napoleon, and call upon him to defend himself before he was laid flat on the gravel. The gaiety around turned to consternation; Louis Napoleon, who realized by this time that he had mistaken his man, apologized profusely, and declared that the intrusion of the cane between Hann's legs had been a pure accident (though Mr Barnes said that he had seen, without doubt, that it was wilfully done). Hann by degrees cooled down under the politeness of the gentleman (whom he did not know), resumed his coat, and there the matter ended, to the great relief of the nervous ladies who were crowded near with their Prayer-books and Bibles, and the disappointment of the boys and the less genteel of the townsmen.

[1908.09]

Preface [to *Select Poems of William Barnes*]

On 14 January 1907 (DCM) Walter Raleigh (1861–1922), professor of English Literature at Oxford, wrote to Hardy on behalf of the Clarendon Press to solicit his participation in the preparation of a selected edition of the poems of William Barnes. Hardy in his reply (*CL* iii. 245) expressed enthusiasm for the project, but insisted that his current preoccupation with completion of *The Dynasts* prevented his doing more than offer advice on the choice of poems. When Raleigh renewed his request on 26 January 1908 (DCM), however, Hardy undertook the entire task of selection; six months later he agreed to write a short preface (*CL* iii. 292–3, 322); in the event, he also provided glossarial notes, although these are not reproduced in the present edition. Many of the ideas in Hardy's preface can be traced directly back to his earlier writings on Barnes (1879.02, 1886.02), and he set out in 1908 to be an interventionist editor, seeking and receiving permission from the Press to omit as he saw fit the 'unfortunate stanza or two of a prosy didactic nature that drag the poem as a whole down to a lower level' (*CL* iii. 292)—a textual policy whose questionable consequences are well demonstrated by W. J. Keith in 'Thomas Hardy's Edition of William Barnes', *Victorian Poetry*, 15 (Summer 1977), pp. 121–31. No manuscript or proof materials for Hardy's preface seem to have survived. The text that follows is that of the first edition of *Select Poems of William Barnes* (London: Henry Frowde, 1908), pp. [iii]–xii, emended to incorporate the single correction entered by Hardy in his study copy of the first printing (DCM; *Index* HrT 1560) and incorporated into the second 'edition' or rather printing of 1921 (dated 1922). The study copy also contains a number of other alterations and additions, but all are to the notes and none was in fact acted upon either in the second printing or in a third 'edition' (again printed from the original plates) published in 1933. The white spaces used in 1907 to indicate the divisions within the Preface have been retained. Purdy, pp. 135–7.

This volume of verse includes, to the best of my judgement, the greater part of that which is of the highest value in the poetry of William Barnes. I have been moved to undertake the selection by a thought that has overridden some immediate objections to such an attempt,—that I chance to be (I believe) one of the few living persons having a practical acquaintance with letters who knew familiarly the Dorset dialect when it was spoken as Barnes writes it, or, perhaps, who know it as it is spoken now. Since his death, education in the west of England as elsewhere has gone on with its silent and inevitable effacements, reducing the speech of this country to uniformity, and obliterating every year many a fine old local word. The process is always the same: the word is ridiculed by the newly taught; it gets into disgrace; it is heard in holes and corners only; it dies; and, worst of all, it leaves no synonym. In the villages that one recognizes to be the scenes of these pastorals the poet's nouns, adjectives, and idioms daily cease to be understood by the younger generation, the luxury of four demonstrative pronouns, of which he was so proud, vanishes by their compression into the two of common English, and the suffix to verbs which marks continuity of action is almost everywhere shorn away.

To cull from a dead writer's whole achievement in verse portions that shall exhibit him is a task of no small difficulty, and of some temerity.

There is involved, first of all, the question of right. A selector may say: These are the pieces that please me best; but he may not be entitled to hold that they are the best in themselves and for everybody. This opens the problem of equating the personality—of adjusting the idiosyncrasy of the chooser to mean pitch. If it can be done in some degree—one may doubt it—there has[40] to be borne in mind the continually changing taste of the times. But, assuming average critical capacity in the compiler, that he represents his own time, and that he finds it no great toil to come to a conclusion on which in his view are the highest levels and the lowest of a poet's execution, the complete field of the work examined almost always contains a large intermediate tract where the accomplishment is of nearly uniform merit throughout, selection from which must be by a process of sampling rather than of gleaning; many a poem, too, of indifferent achievement in its wholeness may contain some line, couplet, or stanza of great excellence; and contrariwise, a bad or irrelevant verse may mar the good remainder; in each case the choice is puzzled, and the balance struck by a single mind can hardly escape being questioned here and there.

A word may be said on the arrangement of the poems as 'lyrical and elegiac'; 'descriptive and meditative'; 'humorous'; a classification which has been adopted with this author in the present volume for the first time. It is an old story that such divisions may be open to grave objection, in respect, at least, of the verse of the majority of poets, who write in the accepted language. For one thing, many fine poems that have lyric moments are not entirely lyrical; many largely narrative poems are not entirely narrative; many personal reflections or meditations in verse hover across the frontiers of lyricism. To this general opinion I would add that the same lines may be lyrical to one temperament and meditative to another; nay, lyrical and not lyrical to the same reader at different times, according to his mood and circumstance. Gray's *Elegy* may be instanced as a poem that has almost made itself notorious by claiming to be a lyric in particular humours, situations, and weathers, and waiving the claim in others.

One might, to be sure, as a smart impromptu, narrow down the definition of lyric to the safe boundary of poetry that has all its nouns in the vocative case, and so settle the question by the simple touchstone of the grammar-book, adducing the *Benedicite* as a shining example.[41] But

---

[40] So the second printing; for 'there has to' the first printing reads 'there are to'.
[41] 'Benedicite, omnia opera', a canticle in the Morning Prayer service in the Book of Common Prayer; each stanza begins with a vocative 'O'.

this qualification would be disconcerting in its stringency, and cause a fluttering of the leaves of many an accepted anthology.

A story which was told the writer by Mr Barnes himself may be apposite here. When a pupil of his[42] was announced in the *Times* as having come out at the top in the Indian Service examination-list of those days, the schoolmaster was overwhelmed with letters from anxious parents requesting him at any price to make their sons come out at the top also. He replied that he willingly would, but that it took two to do it. It depends, in truth, upon the other person, the reader, whether certain numbers shall be raised to lyric pitch or not; and if he does not bring to the page of these potentially lyric productions a lyrical quality of mind, they must be classed, for him, as non-lyrical.

However, to pass the niceties of this question by. In the exceptional instance of a poet like Barnes who writes in a dialect only,[43] a new condition arises to influence considerations of assortment. Lovers of poetry who are but imperfectly acquainted with his vocabulary and idiom may yet be desirous of learning something of his message; and the most elementary guidance is of help to such students, for they are liable to mistake their author on the very threshold. For some reason or none, many persons suppose that when anything is penned in the tongue of the country-side, the primary intent is burlesque or ridicule, and this especially if the speech be one in which the sibilant has the rough sound, and is expressed by Z. Indeed, scores of thriving story-tellers and dramatists seem to believe that by transmuting the flattest conversation into a dialect that never existed, and making the talkers say 'be' where they would really say 'is', a Falstaffian richness is at once imparted to its qualities.

But to a person to whom a dialect is native its sounds are as consonant with moods of sorrow as with moods of mirth: there is no grotesqueness in it as such. Nor was there to Barnes. To provide an alien reader with a rough clue to the taste of the kernel that may be expected under the shell of the spelling has seemed to be worth while, and to justify a division into heads that may in some cases appear arbitrary.

In respect of the other helps—the glosses and paraphrases given on each page—it may be assumed that they are but a sorry substitute for the full significance the original words bear to those who read them without

[42] T. W. H. Tolbort; see 1883.05.

[43] TH here ignores, e.g., Barnes's *Poems of Rural Life in Common English* (London: Macmillan, 1868), although he owned a copy (DCM) inscribed to him by Barnes himself.

translation, and know their delicate ability to express the doings, joys and jests, troubles, sorrows, needs and sicknesses of life in the rural world as elsewhere. The Dorset dialect being—or having been—a tongue,[44] and not a corruption, it is the old question over again, that of the translation of poetry; which, to the full, is admittedly impossible. And further; gesture and facial expression figure so largely in the speech of husbandmen as to be speech itself; hence in the mind's eye of those who know it in its original setting each word of theirs is accompanied by the qualifying face-play which no construing can express.

It may appear strange to some, as it did to friends in his lifetime, that a man of insight who had the spirit of poesy in him should have persisted year after year in writing in a fast-perishing language, and on themes which in some not remote time would be familiar to nobody, leaving him pathetically like

A ghostly cricket, creaking where a house was burned;[45]

—a language with the added disadvantage by comparison with other dead tongues that no master or books would be readily available for the acquisition of its finer meanings. He himself simply said that he could not help it, no doubt feeling his idylls to be an extemporization, or impulse, without prevision or power of appraisement on his own part.

Yet it seems to the present writer that Barnes, despite this, really belonged to the literary school of such poets as Tennyson, Gray, and Collins, rather than to that of the old unpremeditating singers in dialect. Primarily spontaneous, he was academic closely after; and we find him warbling his native wood-notes[46] with a watchful eye on the predetermined score, a far remove from the popular impression of him as the naif and rude bard who sings only because he must,[47] and who submits the uncouth lines of his page to us without knowing how they come there. Goethe never knew better of his; nor Milton; nor, in their rhymes, Poe; nor, in their whimsical alliterations here and there, Langland and the versifiers of the fourteenth and fifteenth centuries.

In his aim at closeness of phrase to his vision he strained at times the capacities of dialect, and went wilfully outside the dramatization of peasant talk. Such a lover of the art of expression was this penman of

---

[44] As Barnes himself, writing as a philologist, always insisted.
[45] Quoted from stanza 12 of Browning's 'A Toccata of Galuppi's', one of TH's favourite poems.
[46] Cf. Milton, 'L'Allegro', line 134.   [47] Cf. Tennyson, *In Memoriam*, section 21, line 23.

a dialect that had no literature, that on some occasions he would allow art to overpower spontaneity and to cripple inspiration; though, be it remembered, he never tampered with the dialect itself. His ingenious internal rhymes, his subtle juxtaposition of kindred lippings and vowel-sounds, show a fastidiousness in word-selection that is surprising in verse which professes to represent the habitual modes of language among the western peasantry. We do not find in the dialect balladists of the seventeenth century, or in Burns (with whom he has sometimes been measured), such careful finish, such verbal dexterities, such searchings for the most cunning syllables, such satisfaction with the best phrase. Had he not begun with dialect, and seen himself recognized as an adept in it before he had quite found himself as a poet, who knows that he might not have brought upon his muse the disaster that has befallen so many earnest versifiers of recent time, have become a slave to the passion for form, and have wasted all his substance in whittling at its shape.

From such, however, he was saved by the conditions of his scene, characters, and vocabulary. It may have been, indeed, that he saw this tendency in himself, and retained the dialect as a corrective to the tendency. Whether or no, by a felicitous instinct he does at times break into sudden irregularities in the midst of his subtle rhythms and measures, as if feeling rebelled against further drill. Then his self-consciousness ends, and his naturalness is saved.

But criticism is so easy, and art so hard: criticism so flimsy, and the life-seer's voice so lasting. When we consider what such appreciativeness as Arnold's could allow his prejudice to say about the highest-soaring among all our lyricists;[48] what strange criticism Shelley himself could indulge in now and then; that the history of criticism is mainly the history of error, which has not even, as many errors have, quaintness enough to make it interesting, we may well doubt the utility of such writing on the sand. What is the use of saying, as has been said of Barnes, that compound epithets like 'the blue-hill'd worold', 'the wide-horn'd cow', 'the grey-topp'd heights of Paladore',[49] are a high-handed enlargement of the ordinary ideas of the field-folk into whose mouths they are put? These things are justified by the art of every age when they

[48] In his 'Byron' essay, *Macmillan's Magazine*, 43 (March 1881), p. 377, Matthew Arnold described Shelley as a 'beautiful and ineffectual angel, beating in the void his luminous wings in vain'.

[49] Quotations from, respectively, 'The New House A-Gettèn Wold', 'Milkèn Time', and 'Shaftesbury Feäir'.

can claim to be, as here, singularly precise and beautiful definitions of what is signified; which in these instances, too, apply with double force to the deeply tinged horizon, to the breed of kine, to the aspect of Shaftesbury Hill, characteristic of the Vale[50] within which most of his revelations are enshrined.

Dialect, it may be added, offered another advantage to him as the writer, whatever difficulties it may have for strangers who try to follow it. Even if he often used the dramatic form of peasant speakers as a pretext for the expression of his own mind and experiences—which cannot be doubted—yet he did not always do this, and the assumed character of husbandman or hamleteer enabled him to elude in his verse those dreams and speculations that cannot leave alone the mystery of things, —possibly an unworthy mystery and disappointing if solved, though one that has a harrowing fascination for many poets,—and helped him to fall back on dramatic truth, by making his personages express the notions of life prevalent in their sphere.

As by the screen of dialect, so by the intense localization aforesaid, much is lost to the outsider who by looking into Barnes's pages only revives general recollections of country life. Yet many passages may shine into that reader's mind through the veil which partly hides them; and it is hoped and believed that, even in a superficial reading, something more of this poet's charm will be gathered from the present selection by persons to whom the Wessex R and Z are uncouth misfortunes, and the dying words those of an unlamented language that need leave behind it no grammar of its secrets[51] and no key to its tomb.

September, 1908.

---

[50] The Vale of Blackmore, in north Dorset, where Barnes was born.
[51] TH seems to have overlooked Barnes's own studies of the Dorset dialect, among them *A Grammar and Glossary of the Dorset Dialect* (Berlin: A. Asher & Co., 1863).

1909

[1909.01]

[Messina Earthquake Message]

Early in 1909 Hardy was one of more than two hundred writers, artists, musicians, actors, and politicians from several countries who contributed to an album of messages of sympathy being put together as part of a campaign to raise funds for victims of the devastating earthquake that had killed more than 77,000 people in Messina and Reggio Calabria in December 1908. The album, bearing the printed title *Original Autograph Letters, Poems, Manuscript Music, etc.* and including (as no. 181) the autograph of Hardy's message below, was described in some detail in Maggs Bros. catalogues 501 of 1928 (item 479) and 560 of 1931 (item 605); it is now in the Houghton Library at Harvard.

> —'Incedimus per ignes
> Suppositos cineri doloso.'
> (Hor. Od. II. 1.)[1]
>
> Thomas Hardy.

[1909.02]

[Testimonial for Harry Pouncy]

Hardy was well pleased with the publicity given to his stories and poems by the lectures, slide shows, and dramatic performances (see *CL* iii. 279–81) of Harry Pouncy (1870–1925), a Dorchester journalist and lecturer, and in

---

[1] i.e. Horace, book II, ode 1. TH's version of the quotation substitutes 'incedimus' for Horace's 'incedis' and may be translated as: 'We walk on fires hidden beneath deceptive ashes.'

early January 1909 he fulfilled a promise (*CL* iii. 362–3) to write on Pouncy's behalf to Gerald Christy, proprietor of The Lecture Agency (*CL* iv. [1]). He presumably also gave permission for that letter to appear, undated as below, on the front of the Agency's promotional brochure for Pouncy's lectures. Inside the brochure a slightly rephrased extract from the same letter was supplemented by a few additional words ascribed to Hardy himself, 'I think that everybody enjoyed the entertainment', and a separate testimonial from his sister Mary, 'A charming lecture, abounding in tasteful touches'.

Max Gate, Dorchester.

Dear Sir,

I write to introduce to your notice Mr Harry Pouncy as a Lecturer and Entertainer.

He has given much pleasure to large audiences in this County (in which I have been included more than once), and it seems to many of us that he might extend his field of operations with advantage to the public and to himself.

Yours faithfully,

Thomas Hardy.

[1909.03]

[The Poe Centenary]

Charles William Kent (1860–1917), professor of English literature and belles lettres at the University of Virginia, wrote on 12 December 1908 (DCM) to invite Hardy's participation in the university's commemoration, 16–19 January 1909, of the centenary of the birth of Edgar Allan Poe. A shortened version of Hardy's reply was subsequently published in *The Book of the Poe Centenary*, edited by Charles W. Kent and John S. Patton (Charlottesville: University of Virginia, 1909), pp. 196–7, although for reasons that remain unclear it first appeared, in a slightly differing but identically abbreviated text, in *The Times*, 15 January 1909, p. 11, and was reprinted from there in the *Dorset County Chronicle*, 21 January, p. 4, and by Hardy himself in *Life and Work*, p. 370. The text below is that of Hardy's manuscript (University of Virginia), reproduced in its entirety; *The Book of the Poe Centenary* printed, verbatim, its second and third paragraphs only; the variant readings initiated by *The Times* are recorded in footnotes. Purdy, p. 271.

Max Gate, Dorchester. January 4. 1909.

Dear Sir:

I have to express my thanks to your Committee for the honour of their invitation to the Centenary celebration of the birth of Edgar Allan Poe, which distance makes it impossible for me to accept.

The University of Virginia does well to commemorate the birthday of this poet. Now that the lapse[2] of time has reduced the insignificant and petty details of his life to their true proportion beside the measure of his poetry, and softened the horror of the correct classes at his lack of respectability, that fantastic and romantic genius shows himself in all his rarity. His qualities, which would have been extraordinary anywhere, are altogether extraordinary[3] for the America of his date.

Why one who was in many ways disadvantageously circumstanced for the development of the art of poetry should have been the first to realize to the full the possibilities of the English language in rhyme and alliteration is not easily explicable. It is a matter of curious conjecture whether his achievements in verse would have been the same if the five years of childhood spent in England had been extended to adult life. That 'unmerciful disaster'[4] hindered those achievements from being carried further must be an endless regret to lovers of poetry.[5]

I beg to remain, dear Sir,

Yours very truly

Thomas Hardy.

To Dr Charles W. Kent, Chairman of the Poe Committee.

[1909.04]

[Unattributed Comment on Drama and the Novel]

In an article headed 'Novelist and Dramatist' in the *Morning Leader*, 23 January 1909, p. 4, William Archer, the theatrical critic, took up a question

---

[2] For 'that the lapse' *Times*, *Chronicle*, and *LW* read 'that lapse'.

[3] For 'are altogether extraordinary' *Times*, *Chronicle*, and *LW* read 'are much more extraordinary'.

[4] Quoted from Poe's 'The Raven', stanza 11; usually given as 'unmerciful Disaster'.

[5] For 'of poetry' *Times*, *Chronicle*, and *LW* read 'of good poetry'.

Hardy had put to him in a letter of 9 January (*CL* iv. 2), quoting most of the letter in doing so and identifying its author as '[a] novelist whose name, were I at liberty to mention it, would command the most unqualified respect'. Although Hardy did not write his letter specifically for publication, it was certainly his intention to prompt an article from Archer, and he knew in any case that anything he said to Archer, Shorter, Milne, and other friendly journalists and editors was likely to appear in print in some form.

Why do you never write[6] an article on the unfair and disproportionate difference of standard applied to works of the theatre and to those of us poor scribblers—I mean imaginative writers—who depend upon the Press for making our ideas known? A situation, for instance, which is a stale thing in a novel or dramatic poem,[7] is hailed as one of dazzling originality when, after some years, it has been imitated from that novel or poem, and appears behind the footlights. Surely a readjustment of terms is wanted here, so that the two arts might be reduced to common measure.

[1909.05]

Notes on Stinsford Church

Hardy's April 1909 report on the condition of Stinsford Church, headed as above, was written for the Stinsford Church Restoration Committee and typed in a small number of copies, probably no more than three. The known copies are currently owned by the Dorset County Museum, Frederick B. Adams, and C. J. P. Beatty (*CL* iv. 18–20). Although this item is listed among Hardy's prose works in *Index*, HrT 1528, it resembles his numerous letters to the Society for the Protection of Ancient Buildings—available both in *Collected Letters* and Beatty's *Conservation Architect* (see 1901.10)—in being intended for very limited private circulation only, and has therefore not been reproduced here.

---

[6] For 'Why . . . write' TH's letter reads 'why you never write': Archer, beginning the quotation in mid-sentence, slightly alters its structure and wording.

[7] Since TH had only recently completed publication of *The Dynasts*, this reference to dramatic poems constituted a significant clue to the quotation's authorship.

[1909.06]

[On the Death of Meredith]

> At the time of George Meredith's death, 18 May 1909, Hardy was in London and seeing a good deal of Florence Dugdale, currently a reporter for the *Standard* and *Evening Standard* newspapers. It therefore seems reasonable to assume—despite Hardy's reference to 'the Standard man' in a letter to the inquisitive Shorter (*CL* iv. 23)—that the following paragraphs from the column headed 'Mr. Meredith's Death' in the *Standard*, 19 May 1909, p. 9, were contributed by Florence Dugdale with the active assistance of Hardy himself.

Mr Thomas Hardy, whom Meredith's death has left the sole surviving representative of English literature at its greatest, was on his way to the Academy yesterday morning when he learned of the death of his valued friend.

'I have known Meredith for about forty years,' said Mr Hardy. 'I liked him greatly. He was, when I first met him, reader to Messrs Chapman and Hall, the publishers, who had their office then in Piccadilly, where the Royal Institute of Painters in Water Colours now stands.[8] I had submitted the manuscript of my first novel, which has never been published. It was a revolutionary thing, called *The Poor Man and the Lady*. Mr Chapman suggested that I should have a chat with their reader. Meredith was very kind and most enthusiastic. He gave me no end of good advice, most of which' (this with a quiet smile), 'I am bound to say he did not follow himself. He advised me not to "nail my colours to the mast" at so early a stage in my career. Only a fragment of that manuscript remains now.

'I remember that office so well. Such a dusty, untidy place![9]

'He, Meredith, sent me a message, only a short while ago, asking me to go down and see him. I meant to do so, but I put it off. That is how it always is.

'Both Meredith's and Swinburne's deaths have been a great shock to me. I knew Meredith long before I knew Swinburne.[10] It is very sad for

---

[8] And stands still (AD 2000), almost opposite the Royal Academy of Arts to which TH was headed.

[9] For other accounts of TH's 1868 encounter with Meredith, see 1927.09 and *LW*, pp. 62–4.

[10] Swinburne died 10 April 1909; on 25 May 1909 TH told Edward Clodd, 'Meredith I miss more as a man; Swinburne as a writer' (*CL* iv. 25).

two such men to pass away in so short an interval, hardly more than a month.'

[1909.07]

'The Dramatic Censorship'

The letter below was written at the request of John Galsworthy (1867–1933), the novelist and dramatist, and included—along with letters from Henry James, H. G. Wells, Israel Zangwill, Arnold Bennett, Joseph Conrad, and Maurice Hewlett—in the evidence given by Galsworthy on 12 August 1909 before the Joint Select Committee of the House of Lords and the House of Commons on the Stage Plays (Censorship). The text below is that of its first publication, as part of a report on the hearings headed 'The Dramatic Censorship', in *The Times*, 13 August 1909, p. 4. The letter was reprinted in the official *Report* of the Committee, published 2 November 1909, in *Censorship and Licensing* (London: *The Stage*, 1910), and in John Palmer's *The Censor and the Theatres* (London: T. Fisher Unwin, 1912). In the *Academy*, 14 August 1909, p. 413, it was quoted but scornfully characterized as 'about the finest defence of the censorship that it would be possible to set up'. See also *Collected Letters*, iv. 53. Reprinted (as from the *Academy*) in *Life and Art*, p. 128. Purdy, p. 313.

Max Gate, Dorchester, 26–7–09.

Dear Mr Galsworthy,

All I can say is that something or other—which probably is consciousness of the Censor—appears to deter men of letters, who have other channels for communicating with the public, from writing for the stage.

As an ounce of experience is worth a ton of theory, I may add that the ballad which I published in the *English Review* for last December, entitled 'A Sunday Morning Tragedy', I wished to produce as a tragic play before I printed the ballad form of it; and I went so far as to shape the scenes, actions, &c. But it then occurred to me that the subject—one in which the fear of transgressing convention overrules natural feeling to the extent of bringing dire disaster—an eminently proper and moral subject —would prevent my ever getting it on the boards, so I abandoned it.

Sincerely yours,

Thomas Hardy.

[1909.08]

[An Age of Freedom]

Fred Harsley, a lecturer in English at the University of Berlin, wrote to Hardy 9 August 1909 (DCM) on behalf of his psychologist colleague Dr Max Dessoir, who wanted to compile a small manuscript volume that would reflect the 'Weltanschauung' of 'twenty or thirty representative men in England and Germany' and so constitute 'an epitome' of contemporary 'culture and thought'. The fate of Dessoir's manuscript volume, intended for 'a certain festive occasion', is unknown, but Hardy's participation—perhaps prompted in part by Harsley's mentioning Kipling as among those who had already responded—is sufficiently confirmed by the survival of his ink draft, dated August 1909 (DCM), and the inclusion, as follows, of an accurate transcription of that draft—though not of its epistolary features—in *Life and Work*, p. 374.

We call our age an age of Freedom.[11] Yet Freedom, under her incubus of armaments, territorial ambitions smugly disguised as patriotism, superstitions, conventions of every sort, is of such stunted proportions in this her so-called time, that the human race is likely to be extinct before Freedom arrives at maturity.[12]

[1909.09]

[Speech on Dramatization of *Far from the Madding Crowd*]

Although Hardy greatly valued his privacy and was deeply reluctant to speak on formal occasions, he was by no means an entirely reclusive figure on his own Dorset ground. He was an active member of the Dorset County Museum, sat on the bench as a Justice of the Peace from time to time, served as a Governor of the Dorchester Grammar School, and took a lively interest

---

[11] Here and throughout his draft TH substituted 'Freedom' for the deleted 'Liberty'.

[12] Also present in the draft are TH's signature and address ('Dorchester: England'), the date ('August: 1909'), and the annotation 'Sent by request', followed by Dessoir's name and Berlin address.

in the dramatizations of his novels performed by the members of the Dorchester Debating and Dramatic Society. The local and national newspaper reports of these public appearance became more frequent as his fame grew, but such reports—e.g. the following item, headed '"Far from the Madding Crowd"', from *The Times*, 20 November 1909, p. 10—rarely recorded any of the actual words of the brief off-the-cuff speeches he sometimes found it necessary to deliver.

Mr Thomas Hardy attended two performances of the dramatized version of his novel at Dorchester yesterday.[13] After the *matinée* Mr Hardy went behind the scenes and had tea with the players, whom he warmly complimented. At the close of the second performance, when the members of the cast were assembled on the stage, he expressed his great pleasure at the manner in which they had acquitted themselves, and particularly the ripe and racy way in which the rustic characters had reproduced the humour of the Wessex folk. A cordial vote of thanks to Mr Hardy for allowing his novel to be dramatized and to Mr A. H. Evans, the dramatist,[14] was proposed by Dr Kerr, president of the Dorchester Debating Society, from the members of which the cast was chosen. Mr Hardy, in response, said that all the praise was due to Mr Evans.

[1909.10]

[Vivisection]

On 13 November 1922 Sue M. Farrell (1856–1940), wife of the publisher Clinton Pinckney Farrell, wrote to Hardy (DCM) in her capacity as founder and president of the Vivisection Investigation League of New York and asked if the statement he had contributed to an anti-vivisection booklet published by the League '[s]ome years ago' might reappear in a forthcoming second edition. Hardy annotated the letter 'Permission granted with pleasure.' It is unclear when *Vivisection: From the Viewpoint of Some Great Minds* (New York: Vivisection Investigation League, n.d.) was first published, but Hardy's statement on p. [16] is dated May 1909 and most of the other invited

---

[13] For details of this production of *Far from the Madding Crowd*, see *Hardy on Stage*, pp. 67–70.
[14] Alfred Herbert Evans (1862–1946), Dorchester chemist, also dramatized other of TH's novels and stories. He was the son of Alfred John Evans (see 1883.05) and the father of Maurice Evans, the Shakespearian actor.

contributions seem also to have been written in 1909. The *Vivisection* text is reproduced below, with its American spelling retained; the slight differences (recorded in footnotes) from the version included in *Life and Work*, pp. 373–4, appear in this instance to have been the result of conscious revision rather than of dependence on a now-vanished draft. Purdy, pp. 271–2.

The discovery of the law of evolution, which revealed that all organic creatures are of one family, shifted the centre of altruism from humanity to the whole conscious world collectively. Therefore the practice of vivisection, which might have been defended while the belief ruled that men and animals are essentially different, has been left by that discovery without any logical argument in its favor. And if the practice, to the extent merely of inflicting slight discomfort now and then, be defended on grounds of good[15] policy for animals as well as men, it is nevertheless in strictness a wrong, and stands precisely in the same category as would its[16] practice on men themselves.

[1909.11]

'Mr. Hardy's Poems'

Hardy, always sensitive to accusations of pessimism, took offence at the review of his new verse collection, *Time's Laughingstocks*, in the London *Daily News*, 13 December 1909, p. 4, and wrote immediately to the newspaper's editor, echoing in so doing some of the points he had sought to make the previous day in a private letter to his friend Edmund Gosse (*CL* iv. 65). The text below is that of the letter as it appeared, headed 'Mr. Hardy's Poems', in the *Daily News*, 15 December 1909, p. 6. Purdy, p. 313.

Dec. 13.

Sir,

I notice that, in reviewing *Time's Laughingstocks, and Other Verses*, after omitting the second part of the title, you say: 'Throughout . . . the outlook is that of disillusion and despair'—repeating the assertion more than once in slightly different words. If this were true it might be no bad

---

[15] For 'defended . . . good' *LW* reads 'defended [as I sometimes hold it may] on grounds of it being good'.   [16] For 'would its' *LW* reads 'would stand its'.

antidote to the grinning optimism nowadays affected in some quarters; but I beg leave to observe that of the ninety odd poems the volume contains, more than half do not answer to the description at all—as can be seen by a mere glance through it—while of the remainder many cannot be so characterised without exaggeration. I shall, therefore, feel obliged if you will correct the misstatement.

Yours, etc.,

Thomas Hardy.

1910

[1910.01]

[Inspired Paragraphs on Family Background]

Hardy was irritated to find in the popular magazine *T.P.'s Weekly*, 7 January 1910, p.18, what he considered an intrusive article about himself, 'Some Story-Book People. V. Thomas Hardy', written by Constance Smedley, author and feminist, whom he had found 'most bright and interesting' when she called at Max Gate in August 1907 (*CL* iii. 270). A letter of personal rather than public protest to the journal's editor (*CL* iv. 71) seems to have been effective in forestalling publication of the promised continuation of Smedley's article, and in another letter Clement Shorter was encouraged to question in the *Sphere* the morality of using biographical information obtained under false pretences (*CL* iv. 70). Hardy—who later wrote 'Lies' on the copy of Smedley's article inserted in his 'Personal' scrapbook (DCM)—overstated his refutations of Smedley's statements in his follow-up letter to Shorter of 17 January (*CL* iv. 71–2), and Shorter exaggerated them still further in adapting and expanding upon that letter in the following paragraphs from his 'Literary Letter', *Sphere*, 29 January 1910, p. 112.

Those who know Mr Hardy very well and something of his origin will smile at a description of him presented in a popular newspaper only the other day. 'The many-headed beast'[1] was there told that Mr Hardy came of 'a peasant stock', and that his mother lived in 'a tiny cottage' until her death.

There are many other quite unwarrantable references to Mr Hardy's home life in the article about as accurate as those I have quoted. But what are the facts? Mr Hardy's father was actually a well-known builder,

---

[1] i.e. the public: cf. Shakespeare, *Coriolanus*, II. iii. 16; Pope, *Imitations of Horace: Epistles*, I. i. 121; Tennyson, 'To——, After Reading a Life and Letters', line 20, etc.

whose contracts[2] with architects led to Mr Hardy himself being made one. This was why he entered the office in Adelphi Terrace of one of the best known of London architects, Sir Arthur Blomfield.

So far from coming of peasant stock, although that, of course, would be discredit to no man, Mr Hardy's family hailed from Jersey in the fifteenth century, and at one time owned thousands of acres in the county of Dorset. Mr Hardy's father was himself the owner of a considerable amount of land and some twenty houses at his death, all of which is now the property of the great novelist's elder brother.[3] Mr Hardy's mother came of a stock of yeomen landholders who were ruined in the Monmouth Rebellion.[4] As for 'the humble cottage' I am pleased to give a picture of it here. It is, as will be seen, a substantial farmhouse. In my native Norfolk they call such places 'halls'.[5]

[1910.02]

'Mr. Hardy's Swinburne Poem'

When Hardy's poem 'A Singer Asleep' was first published in the *English Review*, April 1910, pp. 1–3, its headnote read simply 'A. C. S.', and doubts arose as to whether the crucial reference to Algernon Charles Swinburne was sufficiently clear. On 3 April 1910, therefore, Hardy wrote to Lindsay Bashford, literary editor of the *Daily Mail*, to ask if he would publish 'the explanatory paragraph enclosed', Swinburne's memory being 'so important in poetry' (*CL* iv. 81). Since, however, that paragraph seems not to have survived, it is impossible to determine how far Bashford adopted its wording when placing the following item, headed 'Mr. Hardy's Swinburne Poem', in the *Daily Mail*, 5 April 1910, p. [5]. Purdy, p. 313.

[2] Shorter's 'contracts' is evidently a misreading of TH's 'contact' (see n. 4 below).

[3] TH's only brother, Henry (1851–1928), was in fact his junior by eleven years.

[4] Compare TH's 17 January letter: 'My father was, of course, a well-known builder of this county, whose contact with architects led to my being made one, & who came of an impoverished branch of the Dorset Hardys hailing from Jersey in the 15th century. They owned thousands of acres in the county at one time, but he was the only one who owned any at his death, & he not more than 30 acres & about 20 houses—all now owned by my brother. My mother's people were yeoman landholders ruined in the Monmouth Rebellion' (*CL* iv. 72).

[5] The size of the modest Higher Bockhampton cottage in which Hardy was born and his mother lived and died was somewhat exaggerated by the angle of the photograph in the *Sphere*; it was never in fact a farmhouse, and to call it a 'hall' was an absurdity of which Shorter was no doubt conscious.

Mr Thomas Hardy has a poem entitled 'The Singer Asleep', in com-memoration of Swinburne in the current number of the *English Review*. The first stanza is as follows:

> In this fair niche above the unslumbering sea
> That sentrys up and down all night, all day,
> From cove to promontory, from ness to bay,
> The Fates have fitly bidden that he should be
> Pillowed eternally.

The 'fair niche' is Bonchurch graveyard in the Isle of Wight, which is cut into the hill just above the sea and is now in all its budding beauty. Two or three weeks ago the poet's gravemound was replaced by a tomb-stone similar to those over his relatives.[6]

[1910.03]

[The Moral Rights of Animals]

This much reprinted letter was written on the occasion of the Humanitar-ian League's twentieth anniversary, addressed to the League's founder and honorary secretary, Henry S. Salt, and first published, as below, in the League's journal, the *Humanitarian*, 5 (May 1910), p. 35. The *Humanitarian* text corresponded word for word—omission of minor formal elements apart—to Hardy's original (Princeton) and was itself reprinted in *The Times*, 3 May 1910, p. 10, and in such other locations as the *Glasgow Herald*, 4 May 1910, p. 8—where it provoked negative comment (see 1910.04)—and the *Animals' Guardian*, 12 (June 1910), p. 114. The discrepant readings of *Life and Work*, pp. 376–7, evidently derive from Hardy's dependence on his retained draft (DCM). Purdy, p. 272.

The Athenæum, Pall Mall, S. W. April 10, 1910.

Sir,

I am glad to think that the Humanitarian League has attained the handsome age of twenty years—the Animals' Defence Department particularly.

---

[6] On 23 March 1910 TH visited Bonchurch with Florence Dugdale, who later recorded (*Letters EFH*, p. 152) his anger at finding that Swinburne's tombstone—like the tombs of his relatives—was topped by a cross.

Few people seem to perceive fully as yet that the most far-reaching consequence of the establishment of the common origin of all species is ethical; that it logically involved a readjustment of altruistic morals, by enlarging, as a necessity of rightness,[7] the application of what has been called 'The Golden Rule' from the area of mere mankind to that of the whole animal kingdom. Possibly Darwin himself did not quite perceive it.[8]

While man was deemed to be a creation apart from all other creations, a secondary or tertiary morality was considered good enough to practise towards[9] the 'inferior' races; but no person who reasons nowadays can escape the trying conclusion that this is not maintainable. And though we may not[10] at present see how the principle of equal justice all round is to be carried out in its entirety, I recognise that the League is grappling with the question.

Your obedient servant,

Thomas Hardy.[11]

[1910.04]

[Nature's Indifference to Justice]

When a leading article in the *Glasgow Herald*, 4 May 1910, p. 8, criticized Hardy's letter in the May issue of the *Humanitarian* (1910.03) for its 'over-neat idealism . . . characteristic of an intellectual and sensitive recluse', Sidney Trist, the editor of the *Animals' Guardian*, sent Hardy a copy, evidently in the hope of receiving a publishable reply. Hardy responded with a partly personal letter (*CL* iv. 90), but Trist deleted that portion of the document before printing it, as below, in the *Animals' Guardian* (June 1910), p. 114, immediately following Hardy's letter of 10 April (1910.03).

---

[7] *LW* (only) italicizes 'necessity of rightness'.

[8] For 'not quite perceive it' *LW* and draft read 'not wholly perceive it, though he alluded to it'.

[9] For 'enough to practise towards' *LW* and draft read 'enough towards'.

[10] For 'though we may not' *LW* and draft read 'though I myself do not'.

[11] TH's original letter adds 'The Secretary:| Humanitarian League'.

The Athenæum, 18th May, 1910.

Dear Mr Trist,

The remarks of *The Glasgow Herald* on my letter to *The Humanitarian* do not, I think, require any answer from me. They are merely an enlargement of my own conclusion—the difficulty of carrying out to its logical extreme the principle of equal justice to all the animal kingdom. Whatever humanity may try to do, there remains the stumbling block that nature herself is absolutely indifferent to justice, and how to instruct nature is rather a large problem.

. . . . .

The newspaper cutting I enclose is horribly suggestive.[12]

Very truly yours,

Thomas Hardy.

[1910.05]

['Edited' Article on His 70th Birthday]

Hardy specifically acknowledged to Edward Clodd, 17 June 1910 (*CL* iv. 98–9), that the unsigned article, 'Thomas Hardy. Great Writer's 70th Birthday', published in the London *Standard*, 2 June 1910, p. 8, had been written by Florence Dugdale, then working as a reporter for the *Standard*. Four years later, in the *Standard*, 11 February 1914, p. 10, a report of the Hardy–Dugdale marriage confirmed this attribution but added that the article had been 'edited by Mr. Hardy'—as seems likely enough in the light of its incorporation of private biographical information and of Florence Dugdale's acknowledgment (*Letters EFH*, p. 60) of Hardy's participation in the drafting of her article on Edward Clodd's seventieth birthday, published in the *Evening Standard*, 30 June 1910, p. 5. For Hardy's other secret collaborations with Dugdale, see Thomas Hardy, *The Excluded and Collaborative Stories*, edited by Pamela Dalziel (Oxford: Clarendon Press, 1992). Editorial subheadings have been omitted from the *Standard* text reproduced below.

---

[12] As reported by the *Animals' Guardian* the paragraph, headed 'Monkeys for Vivisection', was dated 'New York, May 13th.' and read as follows: 'According to this morning's papers, the officials of the medical research department of the Rockefeller Institute have just purchased no fewer than 200 monkeys for purposes of vivisection. The purchase is stated to be due to the strong public feeling that exists against the utilisation of dogs for vivisection.—Central News.'

To-day Mr Thomas Hardy, who is considered by many to be our greatest living poet and novelist, completes his seventieth year. To those who know him the fact seems almost incredible. His health and vigour remain unimpaired, and he retains a keen interest in life and an enthusiasm that many a younger man might envy. He is so associated with Dorsetshire that it is hard to picture him as living away from Max Gate, his home near Dorchester; but at the present time he is in London, where he hopes to stay until the middle of July. He may be observed, almost daily, an interesting and interested figure, passing through the London streets on his way to the Athenæum Club, 'doing' picture galleries with conscientious care, and attending service at St Paul's Cathedral or some of the City churches.

   The early years of his manhood were devoted to architecture, and his interest in that art to-day is as keen as ever. If asked what are his greatest pleasures he would probably say visiting cathedrals and hearing church music. His favourite exercise in the country is cycling, but in town he is an indefatigable walker. His so-called pessimism, he declares, is one rather of reason than of feeling. Certainly, in his ordinary life he is a person of average cheerfulness—one might almost say, of more than average cheerfulness.

   It is fairly well known that Mr Hardy's first literary ambitions were entirely in the direction of verse, and that only practical reasons led him to turn his attention to prose fiction. The earliest dated poems in his various volumes were written in 1866, when he was twenty-five, but as a matter of fact he attempted verse much earlier. The first serious verse he ever wrote was when he was about eighteen years of age, and this has never been printed, although it is in existence. It is entitled 'Domicilium', and is a description, in a very Wordsworthian manner, of the house in which was born and grew up, and its surroundings.[13] Yet his first work to be printed was a skit on an event that had stirred the burgesses of Dorchester. The manuscript was anonymously dropped into the box of a local newspaper. It was printed, much to the writer's surprise and even concern. The editor, wishing to ascertain the author, went to the post office and showed the manuscript to the clerk, who, comparing it with the superscriptions on letters, made the desired discovery. When Thomas Hardy, aged sixteen, next appeared to buy stamps, he was suddenly confronted with the proofs of his authorship,

---

[13] 'Domicilium' was first published, as a privately printed pamphlet, in 1916; cf. *LW*, p. 8.

and, with guilty blushes, received the first of this world's plaudits.[14] His early poems, written in London, were sent to various magazines, and were invariably 'declined with thanks'. He left London in 1867 and lived for some years at Weymouth. Here poetical attempts went on, but received no encouragement, and at length it became absolutely necessary to try something of greater commercial value.

It may not be generally known that portions of *Under the Greenwood Tree* were first written as episodes in a novel, *The Poor Man and the Lady*, that was destroyed. These, written before *Desperate Remedies*, are delightful pictures of rural life. It is somewhat surprising that the church musicians, who appear, with their humours, as if described from direct observation, were not personally known to Mr Hardy, who, indeed, never in his life saw or heard one of these village choirs. He lived, in childhood, in close contact with ancient worthies who had been members of such instrumental companies, and their narrated experiences keenly impressed him. The village choir was discontinued in his own parish before he was a twelvemonth old.

Mr Alexander Macmillan, one of the founders of the present firm of Macmillan, was the first to read Hardy's earliest novel. This was so long ago as 1868, and there came to the young author one of the most remarkable letters ever written by the eminent publisher and man of letters. He asked the very pertinent question, 'Are you young?' and, after dwelling upon the vigour with which some characters were delineated, ruthlessly criticised the point of view of the author. The novel submitted was a general indictment of fashionable and middle-class society, founded upon such observations as the young author could obtain from a Bohemian existence in London of five or six years. 'If the fashionable and educated classes', said Mr Macmillan, 'were really as artificial as you have painted them society would go to pieces in a week'.[15]

In the novel a working-man Socialist was made to lecture in Trafalgar-square on the inequalities of the human lot, and overheard by the lady of his affections as she drove past. The story of how Mr Hardy tried another novel, by the advice of George Meredith, is well known.

To come to the author's later work, the publication of *The Dynasts* has had one curious effect, inasmuch as it has brought letters to him from

---

[14] Cf. 1856.01 and *LW*, p. 37.

[15] See 1927.09, *LW*, pp. 59–60, and Charles Morgan, *The House of Macmillan (1843–1943)* (London: Macmillan, 1943), pp. 88–91.

descendants of many of the characters. For instance, in the scene (which occurs in the third part of the 'epic-drama') of the Battle of Salamanca, a captain's wife appears on the stage, searching for her husband's dead body. This lady had followed her husband to Spain with her two young children. In a footnote in the first edition Mr Hardy expressed wonder as to what had happened to the lady and her unfortunate infants.[16] The footnote brought a reply from a reader, who stated that they grew up, and that life had used them well. This is only one instance among many in which an account of the dead brought words from the living.

The Dynasts was written without any thought of its being acted, but several people approached Mr Hardy with schemes of production. The rather quaint comment of one well-known gentleman connected with the stage was that he only wished he were a millionaire, when the drama would immediately be produced. Although the length of *The Dynasts* is generally supposed to be portentous, it is only a little longer than the three parts of Shakespeare's *Henry VI.*, and has not so many lines of blank verse as Swinburne's *Bothwell*.[17]

The poem which attracted most attention in Mr Hardy's latest volume, *Time's Laughingstocks*, namely 'The Trampwoman's Tragedy', was refused by certain English magazines on the score of impropriety. If time and destiny permit, Mr Hardy will publish yet another volume of poems. Readers have almost given up hoping for another novel, although Mr Hardy has never distinctly stated that this will not appear. He feels that a condensed form of expression, as in poetry, attracts him more as the years go on. He does not think it probable that the 150,000 words or so of a novel will ever again come from his pen.

Mr Hardy has been called Quixotic in his insistence on the rights of animals, which, he says, have assumed a new aspect in his regard since the Darwinian theory showed the kinship of all animate creation. He would render illegal the caging of birds, the confinement of tame rabbits in hutches, and all performances of animals in public exhibitions. That even an ex-President of the United States[18] has any right to seek out and

[16] The footnote occurs in *The Dynasts*, Part Third (London: Macmillan, 1908), p. 22. TH incorporated these and other details when revising the footnote for the one-volume edition of *The Dynasts* published later in 1910, p. 338.

[17] These comparisons seem very characteristic of TH.

[18] Theodore Roosevelt (1858–1919), 26th president of the United States, made a much-publicized game-hunting expedition to central Africa in 1910.

kill lions in their native haunts he totally denies, and lady hunters of big game he declares to be his particular aversion.

Without any definite assurance, one may cherish the hope that a play by Mr Hardy, based upon one of his most popular novels, may appear before very long. Certainly there are good hopes that, on the Continent, appreciative audiences may make the acquaintance of Mr Thomas Hardy as playwright.[19]

[1910.06]

[Letter to the *Freethinker*]

> George William Foote (1850–1915), a leading secularist and editor of the *Freethinker*, discussed Hardy's work at some length in his 'Views and Opinions' editorial of 12 June 1910, pp. 369–70, praising him as 'unquestionably the first of living English writers', claiming him as a Freethinker on the evidence of *Tess* and *Jude*, and quoting with approval the central portion of his letter in the May 1910 *Humanitarian* (1910.03). Foote pointed out in the same editorial, however, that he and other members of the National Secular Society had long insisted that 'the moral rights of animals . . . are involved in the Darwinian demonstration of the kinship of life'. Hardy responded to Foote, 12 June 1910 (*CL* iv. 96–7), and that letter—minus its address and date—was published as below in the *Freethinker*, 19 June, p. 393, and reprinted in the *Humanitarian*, August 1910, p. 63.

Dear Sir,

I am much obliged to you for sending the copy of the *Freethinker*, in which I have read with much interest the article entitled 'Views and Opinions', and the generous appreciation it shows of my own defective writings. The letter to the Humanitarians[20] to which you refer was hurriedly written (so much is hurriedly written nowadays, I am sorry to

---

[19] TH was currently discussing with the actress Lillah McCarthy the possibility of a production of his own dramatization of *Tess*, and in a letter of 17 June 1910 (*CL* iv. 99–100) he offered to cancel in her favour a tentative agreement for the play to be produced in Brussels.

[20] For 'the Humanitarians' Hardy's MS reads 'the Humanitarian'.

say) or I should have expressed a deeper sense of what is being done in the cause of humanity by the more thoughtful of mankind. And though, of course, you are to be included among the 'few people'[21] who urge such questions, I fear that such ones do still remain few in proportion to the vast mass of people who never think of the subject.

Yours very truly,

Thomas Hardy.

[1910.07]

[Lloyd's Sixpenny Dickens]

> Hardy's indebtedness to the journalist James Milne for the placement of 'inspired' paragraphs was compounded in September 1910 by Milne's agreeing to publish in the *Daily Chronicle* 'Trafalgar! How Nelson's Death Inspired the Tailor', a weak Trafalgar Day piece by Hardy's young friend Florence Dugdale (*CL* iv. 117). Thanking Milne on 22 September 1910 (*CL* iv. 118), Hardy made the reciprocal gesture of accepting, and promising to write about, a set of the 'Sixpenny Dickens' currently being issued by the *Daily Chronicle* at sixpence for each of the thirty-four volumes: 'I shall be sure to say something about it—one can so safely say things about Dickens— which you can use as you please.' The result was an advertisement, headed 'A Letter from Mr. Thomas Hardy on the "Daily Chronicle" Sixpenny Dickens', that appeared alongside Milne's 'Books of the Day' column in the *Daily Chronicle*, 20 October 1910, p. 8; the text below is taken from that advertisement.

I am much obliged for the set of Lloyd's Sixpenny Dickens[22] just received, and one says on looking at it, 'Here is Dickens's message, at this small price.' Of course, no set of works by novelist or poet really presents life exactly as he saw it—only as near an approximation to his view as circumstances allowed him to present. But these thirty-four volumes contain everything that Dickens contrived to get printed about

---

[21] Quoted from TH's letter to the May 1910 *Humanitarian* (1910.03).

[22] Though the edition was being distributed by the *Daily Chronicle*, the publisher was Edward Lloyd, Ltd.; TH's set was sold as part of lot 184 at the H. Y. Duke & Son sale of the contents of Max Gate, 16 February 1938.

life, and all that his biographer printed about him,[23] remembering which, the size and the clearness of the type, and the compactness of the whole, are remarkable.

[1910.08]

[On Retiring as President of the Dorset Men in London]

Shortly before the 1909 annual meeting of the Society of Dorset Men in London Hardy indicated that he did not wish to serve a second term as the Society's president, and at the meeting itself, on 12 November, a vote of thanks to him as retiring president was moved and carried. William Watkins, secretary to the Society, then wrote to convey the members' appreciation of Hardy's services, and Hardy's letter of acknowledgement, 18 November 1909 (*CL* iv. 59), was subsequently reproduced in facsimile in *Society of Dorset Men in London* (Year-Book 1909–10), facing p. 82. The text below is based on that facsimile.

Max Gate, Dorchester. 18: 11: 1909

My dear Sir:

I am much gratified at hearing from you that the Society of Dorset Men in London has such a generous feeling towards me for my presidency of the Society during the last two years.

For myself I feel that I have filled the office very unworthily.[24] Authors do not, as a rule, make good official members of anything. They have 'the defects of their qualities'. If on the other hand there has been any slight advantage to the Society in my being pretty well known to the press of this country and others, it is a source of great satisfaction to me.

Believe me

Yours very truly
Thomas Hardy.

Wm Watkins Esq. Hon. Sec. Society of Dorset Men in London.

---

[23] Two volumes of the edition were devoted to John Forster's *Life of Dickens*, originally published in three volumes in 1872–4.

[24] TH had in fact attended no meetings of the Society during his two years as president.

[1910.09]

[Speech on Receiving the Freedom of the Borough]

In 1910, the year of his seventieth birthday, Hardy's reputation reached new heights. Long established as a novelist, more recently accepted as a poet, he was now also the author of *The Dynasts*, of which the first complete one-volume edition appeared that year. His investiture by the King as a Member of the Order of Merit was followed—more humbly yet scarcely less significantly—by his presentation, four months later, with the Freedom of the Borough of Dorchester. Hardy's appreciation of the latter occasion was signalled by his delivery of a prepared speech that—given his well-known aversion from public speaking—had scarcely been expected from him. The speech, delivered in the Corn Exchange, was reported, in the first person and evidently from copy supplied by Hardy himself, in *The Times*, 17 November, p. 12, the *Morning Post*, 17 November, p. 5, and the *Dorset County Chronicle*, 24 November, p. 6. None of these contemporary accounts appears to be complete, however, nor is the version in *Life and Work*, pp. 378–81, entirely comprehensive, even though derived from the cutting of the *Times* report inserted in Hardy's 'Personal' scrapbook (DCM), expanded by marginalia in his hand, and annotated 'Mr Hardy's complete speech'. The text below is therefore based on the most nearly complete of the early versions, that in the *Dorset County Chronicle*, but incorporates additional passages, duly footnoted, derived from the other authorial witnesses; such reportorial intrusions as '(Laughter.)' have been retained but are given in italics. Purdy, p. 272.

Mr Mayor and Gentlemen of the Corporation:—This is an occasion that speaks for itself; and so, happily, does not demand many remarks from me. In simply expressing my sincere thanks for the high compliment paid me by having my name enrolled with those of the Honorary Freemen of this historic town,[25] I may be allowed to confess that the freedom of the borough of Dorchester did seem to me at first something that I had possessed a long while—had helped myself to, to speak plainly. (*Laughter and hear, hear.*) For when I consider the liberties which I have taken with its ancient walls, streets, and precincts through the medium of the printing press, I feel that I have treated its external features with the hand of freedom indeed. True, it might be urged that my

---

[25] The passage 'for the high compliment . . . town' is absent from the *Chronicle*, but present in the *Morning Post* and *LW*, and added to the expanded *Times* account in TH's scrapbook.

'Casterbridge' (if I may mention seriously a name coined offhand in a moment, with no thought of it being localised) is not Dorchester, not even Dorchester as it existed 60 years ago, but a dream place that never was outside an irresponsible book. Nevertheless, when somebody said to me that 'Casterbridge' is a sort of essence of the town as it used to be, a place more Dorchester than Dorchester itself, I could not absolutely contradict him, though I could not quite perceive it. At any rate, it is not a photograph, that inartistic species of literary produce, particularly in respect of personages. But let me say no more about my own doings. If I may add another word or two, they shall be concerning the real town among whose Freemen I have the honour of being numbered (my distinguished precursors having been Sir Frederick Treves and the Bishop of Durham, all three of us born within two or three miles of this spot).[26] The chronicle of the town has vivid marks on it. Not to go back to events of national importance, lurid scenes have been enacted here within living memory, or not so many years beyond it—whippings in front of the town pump, hangings on the gaol roof. I myself saw a woman hanged not 100 yards from where we now stand,[27] and I saw, too, a man in the stocks in the back part of this very building. Then, if one were to recount the election excitements—Free Trade riots,[28] scenes of soldiers marching down the town to hear the proclamation of Sovereigns now crumbled to dust—it would be an interesting local story. Miss Burney, in her diary, speaks of its aspect when she drove through with the rest of King George's Court on her way to Weymouth. She says:—'The houses have the most ancient appearance of any that are inhabited that I have happened to see.'[29] This is not quite the case now, and though we may regret the disappearance of many of these[30] old buildings, I cannot be blind to the difficulty of keeping a town in what may be called working order while retaining all its ancient features. Yet it must not be forgotten that these are its chief attractions for visitors, particularly American visitors. Old houses, in short, have a far larger commercial

---

[26] The passage 'If I may . . . spot).' is present in the *Chronicle* but absent from all other witnesses, even *LW*, and Hardy may have departed from his prepared text at this point. Sir Frederick Treves, Bt (1853–1923), became surgeon to Kings Edward VII and George V; Handley Carr Glyn Moule (1841–1920), Bishop of Durham 1901–20, was the youngest son of the Revd Henry Moule of Fordington.   [27] Martha Brown, hanged in Dorchester prison in 1856.
[28] Widespread rioting, instigated by the Anti-Corn Law League, preceded the repeal of the protectionist Corn Laws in 1846: cf. TH's preface to *The Mayor of Casterbridge* (Wessex edn.), p. v.
[29] Accurately quoted from *Diary & Letters of Madame d'Arblay (1778–1840)*, ed. Charlotte Barrett and Austin Dobson, 6 vols. (London: Macmillan, 1904–5), iv. 294.
[30] For 'of many of these' *LW* reads 'of these'.

value than their owners always remember, and it is only when they have been destroyed, and tourists who have come to see them vow in their disappointment that they will never visit the spot again, that this is realised. An American gentleman came to me the other day in quite a bad temper, saying that he had diverged from his direct route from London to Liverpool to see ancient Dorchester, only to discover that he knew a hundred towns in the United States more ancient-looking than this. (*Laughter.*)[31] Well, we may be older than we look, like some ladies. (*Renewed laughter.*) But if, for instance, the original All Saints' and Trinity Churches, with their square towers, the Castle, and the fine mansion of the Trenchards at the corner of Shirehall-lane, the old Three Mariners Inn, the old Greyhound, the old Antelope, Lady Abingdon's house at the corner of Durngate-street, and other mediæval buildings were still in their places, more visitors of antiquarian tastes would probably haunt the town than even haunt it now. Old All Saints' was, I believe, demolished because its buttresses projected too far into the street. What a reason for destroying a record of 500 years in stone! I knew the architect who did it.[32] A milder-mannered man never scuttled a sacred edifice. Milton's well-known observation in his *Areopagitica*, 'As well kill a man as kill a good book',[33] applies not a little to a good old building, which is not only a book, but a unique manuscript that has no fellow. (*Hear, hear.*) But Corporations, as such, cannot help these removals. They can only be prevented by the education of their owners or temporary trustees, or, in the case of Churches, by Government guardianship,[34] and when all has been said on the desirability of preserving as much as can be preserved, our power to preserve is largely an illusion. Where is the Dorchester of my early recollection? I mean the human Dorchester—the kernel of which the houses were but the shell. Of the shops as I first recall them not a single owner remains. Only in two or three instances does even the name remain. As a German author has said, 'Nothing is permanent but change.'[35] Here in Dorchester, as

---

[31] *The Times*, unlike the *Chronicle*, did not record 'laughter' at this point, but TH pencilled a caret into the scrapbook cutting and added '(laughter)' in the margin.

[32] Benjamin Ferrey (1810–80), architect of the present All Saints' church, begun in 1843; for his connection with TH's father and with TH himself, see *LW*, pp. 40–1.

[33] Correctly, 'as good almost kill a Man as kill a good Book' (John Milton, *Areopagitica* (1644)).

[34] *LW*, following *The Times*, breaks off the sentence at this point and opens a new sentence and paragraph at 'And'.

[35] Ludwig Börne (1786–1837), German political writer and satirist; the passage beginning 'Nichts ist dauernd, als der Wechsel' from his *Denkrede auf Jean Paul* was used as the epigraph for Heine's *Die Harzreise*.

elsewhere, I see the streets and the turnings not far different from those of my schoolboy time, but the faces that used to be seen at the doors, the inhabitants, where are they?

Gentlemen, I turn up to the Weymouth road, cross the railway bridge, enter an iron gate to 'a slope of green access',[36] and there they are! There is the Dorchester that I knew best. There the names on the white stones, one after the other, recall the voices cheerful and sad, anxious and indifferent, that are missing from the dwellings and pavements. Those who are old enough to have had that experience may feel that, after all, the permanence or otherwise of inanimate Dorchester is[37] but the permanence of what is minor and accessory. As to the future of the town, my impression is that its tendency is to become more and more a residential town, and that the nature of its business will be mainly that of administering to the wants of private residents, as they are called. There are several reasons for supposing this. The dryness of its atmosphere and subsoil is unexcelled. It has the great advantage of standing near the coast without being on it, thus escaping the objections some people make to a winter residence close to the sea; while the marine tincture in its breezes tempers the keenness which is felt in those of high and dry chalk slopes further inland.[38] Dorchester's future will not be like its past—we may be sure of that. Like all other provincial towns, it will lose its individuality—has lost much of it already. We have become a London suburb, owing to quick locomotion, and though some of us may regret this, it has to be. I will detain you no longer from Mr Evans's comedy that is about to be played downstairs.[39] Ruskin somewhere says that Comedy is Tragedy, if you only look deep enough.[40] Well, that is a thought to remember, but to-night, at any rate, we will all be young and not look too deeply.

[36] Shelley's phrase for the Protestant cemetery in Rome (*Adonais*, stanza 49, line 7); although TH applied it here to the Dorchester cemetery he later reserved it for Stinsford churchyard.

[37] For 'is' *LW* reads 'concerns'.

[38] *Chronicle* ends the sentence at 'sea'; the passage 'while . . . inland' has been introduced here from *LW* and the expanded *Times* report in TH's scrapbook.

[39] The Freedom of the Borough ceremony, on the upper floor of the Corn Exchange, was followed on the ground floor by the first performance of *The Mellstock Quire*, a dramatization by Alfred Herbert Evans (see 1909.09) of Hardy's *Under the Greenwood Tree*.

[40] The reference—as Orel suggests (p. 274 n. 40) of its repetition in 1927.09—is apparently, if not very specifically, to Letter 82 of Ruskin's *Fors Clavigera: Volume VII*; see *The Works of John Ruskin*, ed. E. T. Cook and A. D. O. Wedderburn, 39 vols. (London: George Allen, 1902–12), xxix. 233–5. On an earlier occasion, however (*CL* i. 190), TH seems to have used the aphorism with little sense of its having a specific source; cf. Horace Walpole's '[T]his world is a comedy to those that think, a tragedy to those that feel'. See also the final stanza of TH's poem 'He Did Not Know Me' (*CPW* iii. 205).

[1910.10]

Some Old-Fashioned Psalm-Tunes Associated with the County of Dorset

Late in 1907, following his election as next President of the Society of Dorset Men in London, Hardy undertook to supply the Society with a collection of what he described to the historian A. M. Broadley as 'old Dorset psalm-tunes —either composed by Dorset men, much sung in Dorset, or bearing names of Dorset places' (*CL* iii. 285; see also iii. 286). He had, however, completed his term of office by the time a facsimile of his manuscript transcription of ten tunes with their titles and composers (when known), appeared under his own heading, as above, in the *Society of Dorset Men in London* (Year-Book, 1910–11), pp. [103–6]. Hardy's original manuscript is not known to survive, and only the names of the tunes are given in *Life and Work*, p. 363; reproduced below, therefore, are the headings and notes (though not the tunes) from the published facsimile. Purdy, pp. 313–14.

Wareham. (By William Knapp:[41] born at Wareham. Parish Clerk at Poole 39 years.) L. M.[42]

Blandford. L. M.

New Poole. C. M.[43]

Bridehead. (8.8.6.8.8.6) By A. H. Dyke Troyte[44]

Bridport. C. M.

Lulworth. C. M.

Charmouth. C. M. By Dr Wainwright.[45]

C. M. Frome.[46] (Psalm XVI. v 5, 6, 9, 10, 11) Bond:[47]

Rockborne. (Ps. V.) C. M. By Samuel Wakely.[48] (A Wessex Man)

Mercy. (Ps. I. or XIX.) C. M. By Samuel Wakely.

[41] For Knapp (1698–1768), see *CL* iii. 286 and n. Bernard Jones has pointed out that five of the tunes transcribed by TH—'Wareham', 'Blandford', 'New Poole', 'Bridport', and 'Frome'— appeared in volumes of psalm tunes published by Knapp between 1738 and 1753.

[42] i.e. Long Metre, a hymn stanza of four lines, each of eight syllables.

[43] i.e. Common Metre, a hymn stanza of four lines, alternately of eight and six syllables.

[44] Arthur Henry Dyke Troyte, formerly Acland (1811–57), amateur musician, several of whose hymn tunes are included in *Hymns Ancient and Modern*; he lived at Bridehead, near Dorchester, in his later years.

[45] Presumably Robert Wainwright (1748–82), Liverpool organist and composer; Charmouth is a Dorset village, but Wainwright's connection with the county, if any, remains unclear.

[46] The only one of TH's transcriptions to include any of the words.

[47] Unidentified, but just possibly the Revd Nathaniel Bond (1804–89) of Creech Grange, Dorset.

[48] Apparently of Bridport, Dorset; TH's grandfather subscribed to two volumes of Wakely's church music. Rockbourne is a village near Fordingbridge, just beyond the Dorset border.

1911

[1911.01]

'The *English Review* and the *Spectator*'

Austin Harrison (1873–1928), editor of the *English Review*, was the son of Hardy's old friend Frederic Harrison, the positivist, and appealed to Hardy for assistance when an anonymous article, 'The Great Adult Review', in the *Spectator*, 10 June 1911, attacked the *Review* for its announced commitment to freer, anti-Grundyist forms of expression. Hardy (*CL* iv. 158–9) judged the attack to be relatively mild, deserving of 'a little chaffing rather than an indignant protest', and offered some specific suggestions for a humorous response—one of which, based on a Du Maurier cartoon, Harrison incorporated into the first paragraph of his '*The Spectator*: A Reply', *English Review*, 8 (July 1911), pp. 666–70. Hardy's name headed the long list of contributors to the *English Review* with which Harrison's 'Reply' began, and it again appeared first among the fifty signatories of a letter in defence of the *Review* that the *Spectator* itself published—under the heading 'The *English Review* and *The Spectator*'—in its issue of 15 July 1911, p. 106. In a letter printed on the same page Harrison himself quoted—with added emphases—a passage from Hardy's letter to him of 25 June 1911 (*CL* iv. 161): '[H]aving read the programme of the *English Review*, as quoted in the *Spectator* article, I can see nothing to object to in it in the interests of *truth*, *morals*, and *honest literature*.'

[1911.02]

[Unattributed Report on Puddletown Church]

Hardy took seriously his membership of the Society for the Protection of Ancient Buildings (see 1906.07) and sought to keep the Society informed about the status of local buildings currently under threat. The 'letter by a member of the Society' quoted as part of the entry for 'Puddletown Church, Dorset' in *The Society for the Protection of Ancient Buildings. . . . Thirty-fourth Annual Report of the Committee . . . June, 1911* (London, 1911), p. 52, is identifiable as the correspondence card that Hardy sent on 8 October 1910 to the SPAB's Secretary, Thackeray Turner—who had earlier drawn upon one of Hardy's letters (*CL* iv. 73–4) when writing about Puddletown in *The Times*, 24 February 1910, p. 6. The text below is that of the SPAB report; for the original document, see *Collected Letters*, iv. 122. Beatty's *Conservation Architect* (see 1901.10) has a full account of the Puddletown situation (pp. 42–9).

In passing Puddletown Church about ten days ago I saw that the chancel [*i.e.*, the east wall][1] had been pulled down, also the east wall of the north aisle; the adjoining arch, being endangered by these demolitions, was propped up. Gravestones had been removed from the Churchyard, an extensive clearing made and foundations dug; and window-tracery and other Gothic details lay scattered about the Churchyard.

[1911.03]

'Mr. Thomas Hardy as Witness'

At the Dorchester Borough Petty Sessions of 1 September 1911 charges were successfully brought against Henry Mayo, a drover, for ill-treating a cow by driving it while it was in an unfit state, and against his employer, Charles Barrett, for causing the animal to be so driven and ill-treated. Hardy, himself a JP, had in effect instigated the case; his evidence was crucial, and at the end of the proceedings he was formally thanked by the Bench, the police, and the Royal Society for the Prevention of Cruelty to Animals for bringing the matter forward. The following summary of Hardy's evidence is extracted from the report, headed 'Driving a Tuberculous Cow.—Mr. Thomas Hardy as Witness', in the *Dorset County Chronicle*, 7 September 1911, p. 4. See *Collected Letters*, iv. 174–5.

The chief witness was Mr Thomas Hardy, O.M., who said that while he was walking into Dorchester from Max Gate on Saturday afternoon, August 26th, about four o'clock, and had reached that part of Prince of Wales'-road where it crosses Barnes-way, he saw a cow lying in the road

---

[1] Words within brackets inserted by Thackeray Turner.

and looking very exhausted.[2] The drover was prodding her with his stick, not cruelly, but just to stir her up.[3] There were some youths and boys around the animal, which did not seem able to get up. He suggested that a veterinary surgeon should be sent for. The drover said he would go and hunt for his master, and he went to do so. Witness followed, and went on to Cornhill, where he gave information to a policeman, who said that he would send for the inspector.

[1911.04]

[Anonymous Correction of Misstatements]

Sydney Carlyle Cockerell (1867–1962), director of the Fitzwilliam Museum at Cambridge, visited Max Gate for the first time in late September 1911 and suggested that Hardy should present his surviving manuscripts to selected institutional libraries. Hardy readily agreed, but left the choice of recipients and the practical business of distribution largely in Cockerell's hands (*CL* iv. 180–1, 184). On 23 October, however, the *Daily News*, in a sensational front-page article, headed 'Mr. Hardy's MSS.', claimed that only Cockerell's timely intervention had prevented the sale of all of Hardy's manuscripts to John Pierpont Morgan, the American banker, and their consequent departure for the United States. Hardy was described in the same item as cherishing theatrical ambitions and as writing a play for the actress Lillah McCarthy and another in collaboration with J. M. Barrie. Irritated by the article's mixture of truth and fiction, Hardy instigated (see *CL* iv. 185) anonymous publication of the following corrective paragraph in the 'Literary Gossip' column of the *Athenaeum*, 28 October 1911, pp. 523–4. The holograph draft or copy, dated 24 October and inserted into Hardy's 'Personal' scrapbook (DCM), shows that one trivial change (footnoted below) was made—perhaps by Hardy himself—before the item was printed. Purdy, p. 314.

A curious enlargement and embellishment of fact has appeared in some newspapers[4] this week concerning Mr Thomas Hardy's literary and

---

[2] The police inspector called to the scene testified in court that the cow was tuberculous—the worst case he had ever seen—and in very poor condition.

[3] TH evidently blamed the owner rather than the drover. The justices took the same position, fining Barrett 20 shillings plus 16 shillings costs and Mayo only 1 shilling inclusive.

[4] TH mentioned the *Daily News* item to Edward Clodd, 26 October 1911 (*CL* iv. 185–6), and inserted in his 'Personal' scrapbook (DCM) a cutting of a closely similar report from the *Globe* of 23 October 1911.

dramatic affairs. The detailed announcement relating to writing and collaborating for the theatre is wholly fictitious; and in respect of Mr[5] Hardy's manuscripts (of which nearly half have been lost), all that has occurred, so far as his responsibility goes, is that he has from time to time given single ones to friends who have asked for them for their private possession, and the remainder, or most, to another friend recently, at that friend's own suggestion, to distribute as he might choose; which he has done, or is doing.

[1911.05]

[Assistance to Saxelby's Hardy Dictionary]

Hardy in late 1910 did not at all welcome the news that F. Outwin Saxelby, of Birmingham, was preparing *A Thomas Hardy Dictionary*, and while he felt that he could not object to its publication he declined to authorize it in any way (*LW*, p. 384; *CL* iv. 133–4, [135]). When, however, Saxelby sent him a bound set of the page proofs in September 1911, Hardy took the trouble—and precaution—of reading those proofs (University of California, Berkeley) and pencilling in a series of corrections and expansions that were incorporated by Saxelby into the volume as published in London by George Routledge and Sons later that same year. At Hardy's insistence (*CL* iv. 172–3), Saxelby also toned down the wording of the original dedication.

[1911.06]

[Note on 'The Distracted Preacher']

Hardy's story 'The Distracted Preacher' was dramatized by Alfred Herbert Evans and produced in Dorchester by the Dorchester Debating and Dramatic Society in a double bill with *The Three Wayfarers*, Hardy's own dramatization of his story 'The Three Strangers', on 15 and 16 November 1911. There were subsequent single performances in London and Weymouth. As Keith Wilson shows in *Thomas Hardy on Stage*, p. 76, Hardy took an active interest in the production throughout, and on 29 October he supplied (*CL* iv. 187) 'Mr. Hardy's Note on the Story' for inclusion, as

---

[5] For 'respect of Mr' draft reads 'respect of that relating to Mr'.

below, in the theatre programme for *'The Three Wayfarers' and 'The Distracted Preacher,' Adapted from Thomas Hardy's 'Wessex Tales'* (Dorchester: Dorchester Debating and Dramatic Society, 1911), p. [6]. A similarly worded addition was made in 1912 to the preface to the Wessex edition of *Wessex Tales*, pp. vii–viii. Purdy, pp. 314–15.

The story entitled 'The Distracted Preacher',[6] which Mr Evans has chosen this year for the basis of his comedy, with some alterations of his own, is founded on certain smuggling adventures that occurred between 1825 and 1830, and were brought to a close in the latter year by the trial of the chief actors at the Dorchester Summer Assizes before Baron Bolland for a desperate armed resistance to the Custom-house Officers during the landing of a cargo of spirits.[7] The details of the tale were related to the writer in his boyhood by one or two of those who were engaged in the business, being then old men. Some incidents that came out at the trial are also embodied.

In the culminating affray, a little later than the episodes used in the story, the character called Owlett[8] was badly wounded; and several of the Preventive-men would have lost their lives through being overpowered by the far more numerous body of smugglers, but for the forbearance and manly conduct of the latter. This served them in good stead at their trial, in which Erskine[9] prosecuted, and the defending counsel was Earle.[10] Baron Bolland's summing up was strongly in their favour: they were merely ordered to enter into their own recognizances for good behaviour, and discharged.

---

[6] *Index*, HrT 1608, notes that TH's copy of the printed programme (DCM) carries at this point an insertion in his hand, 'published in 1879'.

[7] TH's 'Facts' notebook (DCM) contains, in Emma Hardy's hand, a four-page account—based on the report in the *Dorset County Chronicle*, 5 August 1830, p. [3]—of the trial of Emanuel Charles, William Wiltshire, and James Hewlett at the 1830 Dorset Summer Assizes. The presiding judge, Sir William Bolland (1772–1840), a baron of Exchequer 1829–39, had pronounced several sentences of death before extending leniency towards the smugglers.

[8] TH's name for James Hewlett, apparently the brother-in-law of one of TH's informants, James Selby, a mason who worked for TH's father.

[9] Thomas Erskine (1788–1864), barrister, later judge.

[10] Presumably William Erle (1793–1880), Dorset-born barrister, later chief justice of the Court of Common Pleas, knighted in 1845.

1912

[1912.01]

'Charles Dickens'

In February 1912 the London literary magazine the *Bookman* celebrated
the centenary of Charles Dickens's birth on 7 February 1812 by asking 'a
selection of representative authors, artists, and men and women eminent in
English public life' a number of questions about their personal recollections
of Dickens, his influence on their life or work, and their estimation of his
novels. Hardy's unilluminating reply—very much in line with his few other
recorded comments on Dickens—was given first place in the resulting article,
'Charles Dickens. Some Personal Recollections and Opinions', and thus
appeared, as below, in the *Bookman*, 41 (February 1912), p. 247. Purdy, p. 315.

In reply to your inquiries I regret to say that I have no information to
give that can be of much service to you. I did not know Dickens, though
when a young man in London I heard him read from his books in the
Hanover Square Rooms.[1]

But as I was thinking more of verse than of prose at that time, I do not
know that my literary efforts owed much to his influence. No doubt they
owed something unconsciously, since everybody's did in those days.

Your other questions I cannot answer.

[1912.02]

[On Greenhill Pond]

Alfred Pope (1842–1934), solicitor, brewer, and one of Dorchester's leading
citizens, was an old friend of Hardy's and shared his lively interest in the

---

[1] As briefly mentioned in *LW*, p. 54.

activities of the Dorset Natural History and Antiquarian Field Club. In October 1911, when Pope was drafting a paper on 'Some Dewponds in Dorset' for delivery at a Field Club meeting, he approached Hardy for information about Greenhill Pond, situated in a hollow on Puddletown Heath, about a mile from Hardy's birthplace. Hardy referred in his reply, 24 October 1911 (*CL* iv. 183–4), to 'an adventure' that had occurred to his grandfather beside the pond at least a hundred years before, and subsequently wrote out the anecdote in a manuscript (Thomas Hardy Society) that Pope quoted almost word for word in his lecture, both as originally delivered, in Hardy's presence, on 13 February 1912 and reported in the *Dorset County Chronicle*, 15 February 1912, p. 5, and as subsequently printed in—and off-printed from—*Proceedings of the Dorset Natural History and Antiquarian Field Club*, 33 (1912), pp. 22–33. The *Dorset County Chronicle* text is reproduced below, with departures from Hardy's MS indicated in footnotes.

By the courtesy of Mr Thomas Hardy I am permitted to give you in his own words an account of the following interesting adventure which happened to an ancestor of his (the author's grandfather[2]) beside this very pond, as nearly as possible a century ago.[3] He was crossing the heath, one midnight in June, by the path which then, as now, skirts the pond, when he became aware that he was followed by two men whom he had noticed watching him when he left Puddletown. He had now little doubt that they were bent on attacking and robbing him, for times were more lawless than[4] they are at present. It had so happened that while crossing a green field called 'Coomb' a little earlier in his journey, he had been struck by the great number of glow-worms that were shining in the grass, and being a young man, he had beguiled his walk by gathering several and placing them on the brim of his hat. As he was unarmed,[5] and the men were upon[6] him, the only way of escape that occurred to him was by playing upon their superstitious feelings. He accordingly rolled a furze faggot into the path, and, sitting down upon it took off his hat, placed it on his knees, stuck two fern-fronds on his head to represent horns, pulled from[7] his pocket a letter he chanced to have with him, and

[2] In the cutting of the *Chronicle* report in TH's 'Personal' scrapbook (DCM), the word 'grandfather' is underlined and 'great-uncle?' written in the margin alongside. TH certainly says 'grandfather' in his 24 October 1911 letter, however, and the scrapbook annotation seems not to be in his hand.

[3] The words 'beside . . . ago' inserted by TH into Pope's working manuscript (Thomas Hardy Society). TH's own MS begins at 'He was'. [4] For 'lawless than' MS reads 'lawless then than'.

[5] For 'was unarmed' MS reads 'was quite unarmed'.

[6] For 'were upon' MS reads 'were gaining upon'.

[7] For 'horns, pulled from' MS reads 'horns, and pulling from'.

began[8] reading it by the light of the glow-worms. The men approached, stopped suddenly, and then bolted at the top of their speed down the hill and disappeared. In a few days there was a rumour in the neighbourhood that the Devil had been seen at midnight by Greenhill Pond, reading a list of his victims by glow-worm light. He tried afterwards to discover who the men were, but they never revealed their identity.

[1912.03]

[Against the Use of Armed Airships]

Hardy was named in *The Times*, 6 February 1912, p. 6, as one of the many signatories of *A Memorial Against the Use of Armed Airships*, a four-page document (copy, BL) issued by the International Arbitration League following the vigorous campaign against aerial warfare conducted by John Galsworthy, the novelist and playwright. Returning his signed copy of the appeal to Galsworthy on 12 July 1911 (*CL* iv. 164), Hardy expressed the hope that it would 'prosper', but the doubts he had earlier voiced as to the practicability of the initiative (*CL* iv. 161–2) were shared—as H. V. Marrot shows in *The Life and Letters of John Galsworthy* (London: William Heinemann, 1935), pp. 698–701—by G. K. Chesterton, Arnold Bennett, George Bernard Shaw, and many others, and its failure to gain support outside the United Kingdom ensured that its 'ultimate effect was, as might have been expected, *nil*' (Marrot, *Life and Letters*, p. 320).

[1912.04]

'How Shall We Solve the Divorce Problem?'

The 1910–12 hearings of the Royal Commission on Divorce and Matrimonial Causes aroused a good deal of public interest, and on 6 January 1912 (DCM) Perriton Maxwell, editorial director of *Nash's Magazine*, invited Hardy to contribute to a symposium on the topic 'How Shall We Solve the Divorce Problem?' Hardy's original letter has not been located. The draft, however, dated 8 January 1912, that he pencilled on the back of Maxwell's

---

[8] For 'him, and began' MS reads 'him, began'.

letter (DCM), shows only minor divergences from the text published, as below, in *Nash's Magazine*, 5 (March 1912), p. 683, under the editorial subheading 'Laws the Cause of Misery'. A slight and obviously editorial alteration was made to the text for its inclusion in the somewhat different American version of the symposium published in *Hearst's Magazine*, 21 (June 1912), p. 2399, and reprinted in *Life and Art*, p. 120. Purdy, p. 315.

Max Gate, Dorchester.

I have[9] already said many times, during the last twenty or thirty years, that I regard marriage as a union whose terms should be regulated entirely for the happiness of the community, including, primarily, that of the parties themselves.

As the present marriage[10] laws are, to the eyes of anybody who looks around, the gratuitous cause of at least half the misery of the community, that they are allowed to remain in force for a day is, to quote the famous last word of the ceremony itself, an 'amazement',[11] and can only be accounted for by the assumption that we live in a barbaric age, and are the slaves of gross superstition.

As to what should be done, in the unlikely event of any amendment of the law being tolerated by bigots, it is rather a question for experts than for me. I can only suppose, in a general way, that a marriage should be dissolvable at the wish of either party, if that party prove it to be a cruelty to him or her, provided (probably) that the maintenance of the children, if any, should be borne by the bread-winner.

Thomas Hardy[12]

[1912.05]

[William Dean Howells at Seventy-Five]

Hardy first met the American novelist William Dean Howells (1837–1920) in London, at the Savile Club, in June 1883 (*LW*, p. 166) and remained

[9] For 'I have' TH's draft reads 'Dear Sir: In replying to your inquiry I may remind you that I have'.

[10] For 'the present marriage' *Hearst's* reads 'the English marriage'.

[11] In the Book of Common Prayer 'The Form of Solemnization of Matrimony' includes a homiletic passage on the duties of husbands and wives that concludes: 'even as Sarah obeyed Abraham, calling him lord; whose daughters ye are as long as ye do well, and are not afraid with any amazement'.

[12] Draft concludes 'Your obedient servant T. H.'; *Hearst's* also omits TH's address and signature.

sympathetically aware of him as a significant fellow-novelist, an influential magazine editor, and a leading American man of letters. When Howells's seventy-fifth birthday was marked by a special 'souvenir' supplement to the 9 March 1912 issue of *Harper's Weekly*, Hardy's letter of congratulation (p. 33) appeared as below among many such tributes; the one significant departure from the holograph original (Houghton), an obvious editorial alteration, is footnoted below. Purdy, p. 315.

Max Gate, Dorchester, February 16, 1912.

Dear Mr Howells,

It is with a movement of surprise that I recognize your being on the point of celebrating your seventy-fifth birthday. If you are at all the same man as he who kindly came to see me at my London flat about a year and half ago,[13] and revived a friendship of I should think thirty years' standing, you have no cause to complain of the clawing of time's 'crouch'.[14]

The experience and outlook of some of us may lead us to shuffle past such anniversaries with as little recognition of them as possible; but you have no need to fall into such shabby habits. I do not remember that a single word except of praise—always well deserved—has ever been uttered on your many labors in the field of American literature. You have, too, always beheld the truth that poetry is the heart of literature, and done much to counteract the suicidal opinion held, I am told, by young contemporary journalists, that the times have so advanced as to render poetry nowadays a negligible tract of letters.[15]

I hope you will long continue to fill the 'Easy Chair' of the MAGAZINE[16] to the edification of its readers, and am

Yours ever sincerely,
Thomas Hardy.

---

[13] For this visit of July 1910 see *CL* iv. 102.

[14] Apparently a reference to *Henry V*, Prologue, lines 6–8: 'at his heels | (Leashed in, like hounds) should famine, sword and fire | Crouch for employment.'

[15] TH's MS has an exclamation mark at this point.

[16] For '"Easy . . . MAGAZINE"' MS reads 'Easy Chair of your magazine'. Howells, in his capacity as associate editor, wrote many literary essays for the 'Easy Chair' section of *Harper's Monthly*.

[1912.06]

'The Blood Accusation in Russia'

Hardy, identified as the President of the Society of Authors, was listed in *The Times*, 6 May 1912, p. 7, among the very many British clergy, politicians, scientists, academics, writers, and journalists who had signed a protest against what the headline called 'The Blood Accusation in Russia'—the charges of ritual murder currently being brought against a number of Jews in Kiev. His name also appeared in the much more selective listing of signatories that accompanied the reprinting of the protest in *A Book of Jewish Thoughts*, edited by J. H. Hertz (London: Humphrey Milford Oxford University Press, 1918).

[1912.07]

'A Plea for Pure English'

The Academic Committee of the Royal Society of Literature decided early in 1912 to present Hardy with the Society's Gold Medal—previously bestowed upon Sir Walter Scott, George Meredith, and only a very few others—on the occasion of his seventy-second birthday. William Butler Yeats and Henry Newbolt made the presentation at Max Gate on 2 June, the actual birthday, in an awkward ceremony at which formal speeches were made despite the fact that no other persons were present, Hardy having insisted that even his wife be banished from the room. When Yeats and Newbolt offered to read Hardy's prepared speech for themselves, he replied that since the text had already been copied to the London newspapers his not delivering it orally would turn those papers into liars: see *Life and Work*, p. 385, and *The Later Life and Letters of Sir Henry Newbolt*, edited by Margaret Newbolt (London: Faber and Faber, 1942), pp. 166–8. The speech—of which no manuscript appears to be extant—is reproduced below from the report of the proceedings, headed 'Mr. Hardy on Literature. A Plea for Pure English', published in *The Times*, 4 June 1912, p. 7. Hardy's own title, however, may well have been '"The Encouragement of Pure English"', as assigned specifically to the speech, within quotation marks, in the *Dorset County Chronicle*, 6 June 1912, p. 5. Not surprisingly, Hardy was among the early members of the Society for Pure English when it was founded in 1913: see *CL* iv. 305.

In thanking the Royal Society of Literature and its Academic Committee very warmly for this interesting and valuable gift I need hardly say that the offer of it came quite as a surprise to myself, of which the Committee will be aware. I am, to be sure, rather an old boy to receive a medal, and am particularly unfortunate in having no younger boy to whom I can hand it on; so that, without undervaluing the receipt of it—rather, indeed, because I value it so highly—I have been thinking whether prizes of some kind could not be offered by the Society to makers of literature earlier in life to urge them to further efforts.

There is no doubt that any sort of incentive to the cultivation and production of pure literature is of immense value in these latter days, and awards by the Royal Society of Literature should be among the strongest. An appreciation of what is real literature, and efforts to keep real literature alive, have, in truth, become imperative, if the taste for it is not to be entirely lost, and, with the loss of that taste, its longer life in the English language. While millions have lately been learning to read, few of them have been learning to discriminate; and the result is an appalling increase every day in slipshod writing that would not have been tolerated for one moment a hundred years ago.

I don't quite like to say so, but I fear that the vast increase of hurried descriptive reporting in the newspapers is largely responsible for this in England; writing done by men, and still more by women, who are utterly incapable of, and unconscious of, that 'grin of delight' which, William Morris assured us,[17] comes over the real artist either in letters or in other forms of art at a close approximation to, if not an exact achievement of, his ideal. Then the increasing influx of American journals, fearfully and wonderfully worded, helps on the indifference to literary form. Their influence has been strongly apparent of late years in our English newspapers, where one often now meets with headlines in staring capitals that are phrases of no language whatever, and often incomprehensible at a casual glance. Every kind of reward, prize, or grant, therefore, which urges omnivorous readers and incipient writers towards appreciating the splendours of English undefiled,[18] and the desire of producing such for themselves, is of immense value.

---

[17] Probably, as Orel suggests, p. 273, a half-memory of the 'grin of pleasure' attributed to medieval artisans by William Morris in his paper 'The Art of the People', collected in *Hopes and Fears for Art: Five Lectures* (London: Ellis & White, 1882), p. 56.

[18] An allusion to Spenser's description of Chaucer as a 'well of English undefiled' in *The Faerie Queene*, bk. IV, canto ii, stanza 32, line 8.

For my own part I think—though all writers may not agree with me—that the shortest way to good prose is by the route of good verse. The apparent paradox—I cannot remember who first expressed it—that the best poetry is the best prose[19] ceases on examination to be a paradox and becomes a truism. Anybody may test it for himself by taking any fine lines in verse and, casting off the fetters of metre and rhyme that seem to bind the poet, trying to express the same ideas more freely and accurately in prose. He will find that it cannot be done; the words of the verse—fettered as he thought them—are the only words that will convey the ideas that were intended to be conveyed.

I know that it is said in Fleet-street that poetry is dead. But this only means that it is dead in Fleet-street. Poetry itself cannot die, as George Sand once eloquently wrote in her novel called *André*. I cannot do better than wind up these rambling remarks with some of her words on this question:—'Poesy cannot die. Should she find for refuge but the brain of a single man she would yet have centuries of life, for she would leap out of it like the lava from Vesuvius and mark out a way for herself among the most prosaic realities. Despite her overturned temples and the false gods adored among their ruins, she is immortal as the perfume of the flowers and the splendour of the skies.'[20]

[1912.08]

'Authors and Their Victims'

In the *Daily News and Leader*, 5 November 1912, p. 6, the journalist James Douglas (1867–1940) attacked Morley Roberts's recently published novel

---

[19] Cf. Wordsworth's statement, in his Preface to the Second Edition of the *Lyrical Ballads*, that 'some of the most interesting parts of the best poems will be found to be strictly the language of prose when prose is well written'. Byron, in 'English Bards and Scotch Reviewers', lines 241–2, refers to Wordsworth, 'Who, both by precept and example, shows | That prose is verse, and verse is merely prose'.

[20] The extended disquisition on poetry in the fifth chapter of *André* begins, 'On dit que la poésie se meurt: la poésie ne peut pas mourir' (Paris: Calmann-Lévy, [1882], p. 60). TH seems not to have owned a copy of *André* in either French or English, and the quotation here was perhaps adapted (as Bernard Jones has suggested) from the similarly worded extract from the novel translated on pp. 51–2 of *George Sand: Thoughts and Aphorisms from her Works* (London and Edinburgh: T. N. Foulis, 1911), compiled by Florence Dugdale's recently deceased friend Alfred H. Hyatt (see *Biography*, pp. 445, 500).

The Private Life of Henry Maitland on the grounds that it was an unacknowledged exploitation of the life of George Gissing, whom Roberts (1857–
1942) had known well, and thus exemplified 'a growing habit of converting
fiction into a public laundry for the washing of dirty literary linen'. On
6 November (DCM) Douglas sought Hardy's support for the position he
had taken; on 10 November Hardy responded with a personal letter of
endorsement (*CL* iv. 234–5); on 15 November that same letter, shorn of its
first two paragraphs, appeared under the heading 'Authors and Their Victims.
Mr. Thomas Hardy on the Modern Novel' in the 'Literature' section of
the *Daily News*, 15 November 1912, p. 6, with a prefatory acknowledgement of Hardy's having given permission for the publication of a private
communication. The text below is that of the *Daily News*; it occasionally
differs from the text in *Collected Letters*, but since the latter was based on a
draft (DCM) it remains unclear how far, if at all, the letter actually sent to
Douglas was revised as well as shortened prior to publication. The single
paragraph included in *Life and Work*, p. 386, is certainly drawn from the draft.

The point at issue seems to be: does such a book as *The Life of Henry
Maitland* injure the dead man's memory? In this case I feel that it may
possibly do so. But to set against that there is the fact (as I understand)
that Gissing authorised, or half-authorised, the book. Who is to tell?

What should certainly be protested against, in cases where there is no
authorisation, is the mixing of fact and fiction in unknown proportions.
Infinite mischief would lie in that. If any statements in the dress of
fiction are covertly hinted to be fact, all must be fact, and nothing else
but fact—for obvious reasons. The power of telling lies about[21] people
through that channel after they are dead, by stirring in a few truths, and
announcing by subterranean means that the book is true, is[22] a horror
to contemplate.

Such a development has been almost inevitable nowadays, when the
novelist has ceased to be an artist, but has become a mere reporter, and
is told that he must be nothing else. I have been gravely assured by a
critic in full practice that to write down everything that happens in any
household is the highest form of novel construction, being the presentation of a real 'slice of life' (a phrase which I believe I had the misfortune
to originate many years ago, though I am not sure).[23]

---

[21] For 'power . . . about' *LW* reads 'power of getting lies believed about'.

[22] For 'truths, . . . true, is' draft and *LW* read 'truths, is'; *LW* prints only this paragraph.

[23] For 'ago, . . . sure).' draft reads 'ago).' TH does not in fact seem to have originated the term
'slice of life'; he may have been half-remembering 'a picture of life in action' from 'The Profitable
Reading of Fiction' (1888.02).

I think you deserve great praise for having boldly opened up an inquiry into a matter so greatly affecting society and morals, and its ventilation may do much good. There can be no harm in your having stated one, your own, side of the case, strongly.[24]

Of course I am leaving untouched the question whether, even if every word be truth, truth should be presented (unauthorised) by so stealthy a means.[25]

[1912.09]

[Supplement to Obituary of Emma Lavinia Hardy]

Hardy's wife, Emma Lavinia Hardy (*née* Gifford), died suddenly at Max Gate early in the morning of 27 November 1912, three days after her seventy-second birthday. The short obituaries of her that appeared in *The Times*, p. 9, *Daily Chronicle*, p. 4, and other London newspapers the following day were almost certainly not written by Hardy himself, even though some of them were later inserted into his 'Personal' scrapbook (DCM). He clearly was responsible, however, for the supplementary obituary notice published, as from an unidentified 'correspondent', in *The Times*, 30 November 1912, p. 9, and reproduced below. Slight variations occurred in the same communication when printed, as from *The Times*, in the *Dorset County Chronicle*, 5 December 1912, p. 6, and since these could represent corrections supplied by Hardy himself it is the *Chronicle* text that is reproduced below. A final short paragraph about the funeral arrangements, present in *The Times* and possibly supplied by Hardy, was omitted from the *Chronicle*, the funeral having by that time already taken place.

She had lived with Mr Hardy at Max Gate since 1885, when they first took up their residence there in what was then a new house. She was a staunch Churchwoman, having been brought up by her mother in strong Evangelical principles which she never forsook, and to the last she lent her support to societies maintaining those principles. In her earlier married life she often assisted her husband by writing to his

---

[24] Draft inserts 'Yours very truly T. H.' at this point and sets out the next paragraph as a postscript.   [25] For 'means.' draft reads 'means. It has a sneaking look.'

dictation, particularly in the case of the novel entitled *A Laodicean*, which was almost entirely dictated to her from a sick-bed. She also used to accompany him to places which it was necessary for him to visit in the course of his work. It has been stated in the Press that Mr Hardy wished the performance of Mr Evans's dramatization of *The Trumpet Major* not to be postponed on account of his loss, but a more accurate statement would be that, appreciating the serious difficulties of a postponement on the very day of the performance, when many of the audience were arriving in the town from beyond London, he consented to there being no interference with the play.[26]

[1912.10]

[Death Notices for Emma Lavinia Hardy]

Hardy himself must have placed the following notice in the 'Deaths' column of *The Times*, 30 November 1912, p. 1, and an almost identically worded notice in the 'Deaths' column of the *Dorset County Chronicle*, 5 December 1912, p. 16.

HARDY.—On the 27th Nov., at Max Gate, Dorchester, after a very short illness,[27] EMMA LAVINIA, wife of THOMAS HARDY, and younger daughter of the late John Attersoll Gifford, of Plymouth.

---

[26] First produced in 1908, A. H. Evans's dramatization of *The Trumpet-Major* was scheduled to be revived by the Dorchester Debating and Dramatic Society on 27 and 28 November 1912. TH received much criticism locally for allowing the performances to go ahead as planned.

[27] For 'very short illness' *Chronicle* reads 'very brief illness'.

1913

[1913.01]

[On Funk and Wagnall's Dictionary]

Included in *Collected Letters*, iv. 258, 313, are two letters that Hardy wrote in 1913 to the European office of the American firm of Funk & Wagnall in praise of a new edition of its *New Standard Dictionary of the English Language*. The first, dated 3 February, responded to the receipt of specimen pages, the second, dated 26 October, to the arrival of the actual copy of the dictionary that he kept on his shelves for the rest of his life. Testimonials to the dictionary's quality were evidently being sought from literary and other figures, and although no publication has been traced for either of Hardy's letters, it is clear that both were written with just such a purpose in view.

[1913.02]

'The Conditions of Lasting Peace'

The Balkan Wars of 1912–13 caused much anxiety in western Europe, and in March 1913, at the request of Arthur G. Symonds of the Balkan War Relief Fund, Hardy signed a printed statement (Eton) of his willingness to be identified as a signatory of a memorial 'in favour of a lasting peace in the Near East'. This was presumably the memorial 'expressing the desire that the peace of the Near East may be concluded on a durable basis' that was reported and partly quoted in *The Times*, 27 March 1913, p. 5; if so, Hardy's name did not appear among the listed signatories, conceivably because his response arrived too late. The first Balkan War, in which Greece, Serbia, Bulgaria, and Montenegro were allied against Turkey, was in fact coming to an end at this moment, although a brief second war, in which Bulgaria attacked Serbia and Greece, began shortly afterwards.

[1913.03]

[Apology for Not Meeting Canadian Teachers]

Writing on 9 August 1913 to Henry A. Huxtable, the town clerk of Weymouth, Hardy apologized in advance for his absence from the civic welcome being planned for a visiting party of Canadian teachers on 15 August. A postscript to Hardy's original letter (*CL* iv. 294) makes it evident that he did not intend the document for general dissemination, but it presumably did not surprise him that its first four sentences were read out to the disappointed Canadians and published, as below, in the *Dorset County Chronicle*, 21 August 1913, p. 6. Clearly unanticipated, however, was the appearance of the second and third of those sentences in *The Times*, 16 August, p. 3, under the heading 'Mr. Hardy's Health', and Florence Dugdale, then staying at Max Gate, was obliged to assure an anxious Edward Clodd that Hardy was in fact in excellent health: 'The letter was meant to be a private one. Really he did not want to go to be stared at by three hundred American teachers' (*Letters EFH*, pp. 83–4; cf. *CL* iv. 298).

Max Gate, Dorchester, 9th August, 1913.

Dear Mr Huxtable,

I should much like to accept the Mayor and Mayoress's kind invitation to meet the 300 Canadian teachers at the Pavilion, some of whom doubtless are my readers. But I am sorry to say that the strain and stress of one thing and another of late have rendered me unable to attend functions, however attractive. In[1] fact, I have not gone out anywhere this year, and making a speech to the teachers, which would probably be imperative, would be utterly beyond me. Please, therefore, make my excuses to the Mayor and his company, and believe me, yours truly,

Thomas Hardy.

[1913.04]

[Assistance to Hermann Lea's *Hardy's Wessex*]

Hardy had assisted his friend Hermann Lea with his first guidebook in 1905 (see 1905.10) and clearly hoped that Lea's more ambitious *Thomas Hardy's*

---

[1] For 'me . . . In' *The Times*—departing from both *Chronicle* and draft—reads 'me quite unable to attend such functions, however attractive they may be. In'.

Wessex (London: Macmillan, 1913), published in a format uniform with that of his own Wessex Edition, would firmly establish itself as the standard source of information about the relationship between the Wessex locations invoked in his novels, stories, and poems and the actual topography of south-western England. His numerous letters to Lea (*CL* iv. 164, 173, 175, etc.) show that he was intensively engaged in all aspects and stages of the book's composition and illustration and that in August 1913 (*CL* iv. 280, 293–5) he read and corrected a complete set of proofs. Reproduced in *Complete Poetical Works*, ii. 525–8, are the preparatory notes for a never-published expanded edition of *Thomas Hardy's Wessex* that Hardy later inserted into his own copy (Beinecke).

[1913.05]

[On Sudermann's *The Song of Songs*]

In December 1910 Hardy was one of several writers consulted by John Lane, the publisher, as to whether he should, at the risk of a prosecution for obscenity, proceed with the publication of *The Song of Songs*, an English translation of the novel *Das hohe Lied* (1908) by the German novelist and dramatist Hermann Sudermann (1857–1928). Most thought the novel 'unpleasant' but not actually obscene; Hardy, however, writing on 15 December 1910 (*CL* iv. 131), suggested that the inadequacies of the translation undercut the novel's defensibility on grounds of literary distinction, and Lane in fact withdrew the 1910 edition and reissued the novel in a new translation in 1913. In an introduction to that volume Lane reviewed the earlier controversy and printed some of the relevant correspondence, Hardy consenting to publication of his December 1910 letter but returning the proof (Eton) with 'a sentence or two enlarged to make my meaning perfectly clear' (*CL* iv. 228). Those changes—more considerable than Hardy's comment suggests—duly appeared, as below, in *The Song of Songs*, translated by Beatrice Marshall (London: John Lane, 1913), pp. ix–x. Hardy acknowledged receipt of a copy on 24 July 1913 (*CL* iv. 288–9), but it was not published until October of that year. Purdy, p. 316.

Max Gate, Dorchester. December 15th, 1910.

Dear Mr Lane,

I am sorry to hear that you have been laid up with bronchitis, and hope that you are on the way to health again.

I finished reading last night the translation of Sudermann's novel, *Das hohe Lied*, that you sent me a few days back. I am not in a position to advise positively whether or not you should withdraw it, but I think that, viewing it as a practical question, merely, which I imagine to be your wish, I should[2] myself withdraw it in the circumstances.

A translation of good literary taste might possibly have made such an unflinching study of a woman's character acceptable in this country, even though the character is one of a somewhat ignoble type, but[3] unfortunately, rendered into the rawest American,[4] the claims that the original (which I have not seen) no doubt had to be considered as literature,[5] are largely reduced, so that I question if there is value enough left in this particular translation to make[6] a stand for.[7]

Believe me,

Yours very truly,

Thomas Hardy.

John Lane, Esq., The Bodley Head.

[1913.06]

'The Painless Slaughtering of Animals'

Hardy's letter, published under the above heading in the *Dorset County Chronicle*, 20 November 1913, p. 8, was prompted by the failure of the Wareham (Dorset) Council to act upon a proposal for the use of 'humane' instruments in the slaughterhouses within its jurisdiction. He wrote a similar letter, apparently not published, when the same issue arose in Blandford early in 1914, adding that the transportation and treatment of animals prior to slaughter was 'of little less importance than the actual killing' (*CL* v. 20).

[2] For 'question . . . should' TH originally wrote 'question I should'.

[3] For 'such . . . but' TH originally wrote 'such a story acceptable in this country, but'.

[4] Thomas Seltzer, American translator and, later, publisher, had put his name to the translation, but it had apparently been done by his wife, Adele: see Alexandra Lee Levin and Lawrence L. Levin, 'The Seltzers and D. H. Lawrence', in D. H. Lawrence, *Letters to Thomas and Adele Seltzer*, ed. Gerald M. Lacy (Santa Barbara: Black Sparrow Press, 1976), p. 173.

[5] For 'considered as literature' TH originally wrote 'considered literature'.

[6] For 'left . . . make' TH originally wrote 'left to make'.

[7] To the novelist George Moore (1852–1933)—who had seen, and deplored, the letter in its original form—TH wrote on 26 December 1910: 'If a protest against interference has to be made, it would be a wiser policy to do it in connection with some safer book' (*CL* iv. 133).

The *Chronicle* text of the Wareham letter, reproduced below, omits the salutation and valediction of the surviving typewritten original (G. Stevens-Cox)
but otherwise departs from it only in one (footnoted) detail.

Max Gate, Dorchester. 18th November 1913.

I regret to see from the report of the Wareham Town Council meeting that the excellent movement for the painless slaughtering of animals
for food should be obstructed in any way by a doubt as to particular
details on the practice of such humanity—which movement is belated
enough already in not being reached until after twenty centuries of what
is supposed to be a humane religion. Mrs[8] Filliter—who is a stranger to
me—deserves high commendation for her courage in bringing forward
the question. I also include those gentlemen who associated themselves
with her views. I may add that the Council of Justice to Animals[9]
(12, Old Burlington-street, London, W.) would give full information as
to the working of the instruments hitherto employed for such an end.

Thomas Hardy.

[1913.07]

[Tribute to Anatole France]

As President of the Society of Authors Hardy was almost automatically
named to the committee responsible for arranging a dinner at the Savoy Hotel,
10 December 1913, in honour of the French novelist and essayist Anatole-
François Thibault (1844–1924), better known under his pseudonym of
Anatole France. Hardy was familiar with France's work (*CL* iii. 53, 330) and
owned several of his books, and presumably stayed away from the dinner for
fear of having to get to his feet and speak. Writing to John Lane, France's
English publisher, on 7 December 1913 (*CL* iv. 326–7), he enclosed a

---

[8] A correction, presumably editorial, of the MS reading 'Miss'. Mrs Ellen G. Filliter, wife of the
town clerk of Wareham and secretary of the local branch of the Royal Society for the Prevention
of Cruelty to Animals, had been especially active in support of the proposal, and TH would have
seen the letter in the *Dorset County Chronicle*, 9 October 1913, p. 11, in which she urged the use of
the RSPCA's 'humane slaughterer' for the killing of pigs, the usual method being 'a disgrace to
humanity'.

[9] TH, encouraged by Florence Henniker, had recently become a member of the Council's
Central Executive Committee: see *CL* iv. 143.

separate 'letter of regret' that was subsequently read out at the dinner by the chairman, Sir Thomas Barclay. That letter was included, as below, in the report of the occasion published, under the main heading 'Anatole France', in *The Times*, 11 December 1913, p. 9, and reprinted verbatim in the privately printed pamphlet *Dinner Given in Honour of M. Anatole France at the Savoy Hotel, December 10, 1913* (December 1913), p. 4. The quotation from the letter in *Life and Work*, pp. 391–2, begins with the second sentence of *The Times* version; omitted from all published texts were the address, date, salutation, valediction, signature, and heading ('To the Chairman—') present in Hardy's original typescript (Texas). Reprinted (as from *The Times*) in *Life and Art*, p. 121. Purdy, p. 272.

I particularly regret that, though one of the committee, I am unable to be present to meet M. Anatole France at the reception on Wednesday. In these days when the literature of narrative and verse seems to be losing its qualities as an art, and to be assuming a structureless conglomerate[10] character, it is a privilege that we should have come into our midst a writer who is faithful to the principles that make for permanence, who never forgets the value of organic form and symmetry, the force of reserve, and the emphasis of understatement, even in his lighter works.

[1913.08]

'Performing Animals'

This letter—published as below under the editorial heading 'Performing Animals. Mr. Hardy's Protest' in *The Times*, 19 December 1913, p. 9—was written in response to an unsigned article, 'Performing Animals. The Psychology of Pain in Man and Beast' (*The Times*, 17 December 1913, p. 6), which insisted that animals did not possess 'a brain capable of great suffering' and could therefore legitimately be trained for human amusement. The letter was reprinted, as from *The Times*, in *Animals' Friend*, 20 (February 1914), p. 80. Purdy, pp. 316–17.

---

[10] For 'structureless conglomerate' *LW* reads 'structureless and conglomerate'.

Max Gate, Dorchester, Dec. 18.

Sir,

As I read your Correspondent's letter on the above subject, he confuses theory with practice in his arguments. Quite possibly some animals may be, and are, trained for performances without discomfort to themselves, but there is ample evidence to show that many trainers prefer short cuts to attain their ends, and that these short cuts are by the way of cruelty.[11] I have been present at dog performances at country fairs, where the wretched animals so trembled with terror when they failed to execute the feat required of them that they could scarcely stand, and remained with eyes of misery fixed upon their master, paralysed at the knowledge of what was in store for them behind the scenes, whence their shrieks could afterwards be heard through the canvas.

And there are cruelties of a more insidious kind produced by drugs. As to the caging of birds, the assertion that a caged skylark experiences none of the misery of a caged man makes demands upon our credulity. Anyhow, a caged skylark usually dies soon, while an imprisoned man will live out his natural years. There is, or was when I was young, a practice among boys of putting a nearly-fledged brood of young birds, with the nest, into a cage, and hanging the cage in the tree or bush where the nest was made. The parents come regularly to feed their young ones through the bars, and there seems no reason why they should not be successfully bred; but usually the young birds die. It used to be the tradition of schoolboys that the old birds poisoned their young at finding them imprisoned. However that may be, die they did.

It seems marvellous that the 20th century, with all its rhetoric on morality, should tolerate such useless inflictions as making animals do what is unnatural to them or drag out an unnatural life in a wired cell.[12] I would also include the keeping of tame rabbits in hutches among the prohibited cruelties in this kind.

Your obedient servant,

Thomas Hardy.

---

[11] TH told Florence Henniker on 21 December 1913: '[W]hat I object to most are perform-ances *with* animals—in which they are passive—e.g. bringing live canaries, rabbits, pigeons, &c. out of the sleeve or handkerchief. Every spectator can see that the wretched creature is in the greatest misery, & I believe that a great many are "used" in these tricks—that is, tortured to death' (*CL* iv. 330–1).

[12] Cf. TH's poem 'The Blinded Bird' (*CPW* ii. 181).

1914

[1914.01]

[Marriage Notices]

On 10 February 1914, rather more than fourteen months after his first wife's death, Hardy married Florence Emily Dugdale (1879–1937), with whom he had had a close relationship for eight or nine years. That it was Hardy himself who placed the following notice in the 'Marriages' column of *The Times*, 12 February 1914, p. 1, and *Enfield Gazette*, 13 February, p. 4, and an almost identical notice in the *Dorset County Chronicle*, 19 February, p. 16, is sufficiently confirmed by its overstatement of his new wife's Dorset connection: though her father came of Dorset-born parents, he was born in Portsmouth and always lived outside Dorset.

HARDY: DUGDALE. On the 10th Feb., at the Old Parish Church, Enfield, Middlesex, by the Revd. R. Howel Brown, Vicar, THOMAS HARDY, of Max Gate, Dorchester, to FLORENCE EMILY, second daughter of EDWARD DUGDALE, of Enfield, and formerly of Wareham, Dorset.[1]

[1914.02]

[On Nietzsche]

It is not clear what purpose or destination Hardy had in mind for the series of observations on Nietzsche's philosophy that he pencilled, some time in the early summer of 1914, in the white space of an undated but clearly pre-war circular (DCM)—written in German but with accompanying English

---

[1] For 'Wareham, Dorset.' *Dorset County Chronicle* reads 'Wareham.'

translation—that solicited support for celebrations of the seventieth anniversary of Nietzsche's birth (15 October 1914), including the funding of the
Nietzsche archives in Weimar and the erection of a monument nearby.
Hardy's hostility to Nietzsche was already well established by this date (see
1902.04 and note below), and these notes may well pre-date the August 1914
outbreak of the First World War and simply show Hardy jotting down
his grounds for declining to make a contribution. He did, however, include
the notes in *Life and Work*, p. 393, and the presence of his initials at the end
of the MS raises the possibility of its having been intended, and perhaps used,
during the latter part of 1914 as the basis of a public statement of some kind
(cf. 1914.05). The text below is that of the MS.

It is a question whether Nietzsche's philosophy[2] is sufficiently coherent
to be of great ultimate value, and whether the views of his which seem
so novel and striking are so only[3] because they have been rejected for so
many centuries as inadmissible under humane rule.

A continuity of *consciousness*[4] through the human race would be the
only justification of his proposed measures.

He assumes throughout the great *worth*,[5] intrinsically, of human
masterfulness.[6] The universe is to him a perfect machine which only
requires thorough handling to work wonders. He forgets that the universe is an imperfect machine, and that to do good with an ill-working
instrument requires endless adjustments and compromises.

[1914.03]

'Which is the Best Short Poem in English?'

The responses of several poets to the above question were published—under
the same heading—in the *New York Times*, 5 July 1914, section 5, p. 1.
Hardy's reply, reproduced below, was undated and shorn of its opening and
closing elements, but survival of the original typed MS (T. Trafton) shows

---

[2] Friedrich Wilhelm Nietzsche (1844–1900), German philosopher; for TH's response to
Nietzsche, see *LN* ii. 75, 444–51, and esp. 511–12, and Eugene Williamson, 'Thomas Hardy and
Friedrich Nietzsche: The Reasons', *Comparative Literature Studies*, 15 (December 1978), 403–13.

[3] For 'are so only' *LW* reads 'appear thus only'.

[4] Not emphasized in *LW*.   [5] Not emphasized in *LW*.

[6] MS originally read 'human development.'; the revision was evidently made at a later date,
perhaps just prior to the incorporation of the notes into *Life and Work*.

that it was in fact written on 30 March 1914 and signed 'Thomas Hardy per F.E.'—the initials being those used by the newly married Florence Emily Hardy when performing secretarial tasks on her husband's behalf. The second and third sentences of Hardy's letter were reprinted in the American magazine *Current Opinion*, 57 (August 1914), p. 131. Purdy, p. 317.

Max Gate, Dorchester.

In answer to your question on which is the best short poem I have read in the English language I can only say that I fail to see how there can be a 'best' poem, long or short; that is, one best in all circumstances. This attempt to appraise by comparison is, if you will allow me to say so, one of the literary vices of the time, only a little above the inquiry who is the biggest poet, novelist, or prizefighter, though not quite so low down as that deepest deep of literary valuation, 'who is the biggest seller'.[7]

Thomas Hardy.

[1914.04]

'Britain's Destiny and Duty'

The First World War began on 4 August 1914 and Hardy, despite his long-standing opposition to war as an instrument of national policy, was not immune to the patriotic fervour of the moment. Though reluctant at first to take any kind of position (*CL* v. 43), in early September he went to London for meetings designed by the government to produce 'public statements of the strength of the British case and principles in the war by well-known men of letters' (*LW*, p. 395). His presence at a Wellington House conference is recorded in *The Journals of Arnold Bennett*, edited by Newman Flower, 3 vols. (London: Cassell, 1932–3), ii. 103, and he is reported in the printed *Minutes* of that meeting (DCM) as suggesting 'that a list of German mis-statements should be drawn up and that these should be published together with answers to them in succinct language'. Later that month he was one of the fifty-two writers who put their names to the conventional statement of British war aims that appeared, under the above heading, in *The Times*, 18 September 1914, p. 3, and in the *New York Times* of the same date, p. 3. When returning his signed copy of the manifesto on 10 September (*CL* v. 47) Hardy said that he agreed with 'every word' of it. The extent of Hardy's further involvement

[7] Cf. 1919.07.

in such activities is unclear. His 28 September 1914 letter to the New York publisher Francis A. Duneka (*CL* v. 52) certainly included a paragraph directed towards encouraging American support for the British position, and Florence Hardy reported to Lady Hoare on 3 October 1914 (Wiltshire Record Office) that her husband was busily responding to a Government request that he 'write certain articles for the American papers—etc.'. But the fact that no such articles signed by Hardy have yet been discovered tends to suggest that few if any were written and published. Samuel Hynes, however, has pointed out in *A War Imagined: The First World War and English Culture* (New York: Atheneum, 1991), p. 27, that Hardy did promptly produce the patriotic poem 'Men who March Away', first published in *The Times*, 9 September 1914 (Purdy, pp. 157–8), and Hardy himself seems increasingly to have felt—as he told the Ministry of National Service on 7 March 1917 (*CL* v. 206)—that he could speak more effectively through 'a brief and condensed appeal in verse' than through 'an article in prose'. See also 1915.07, 1916.01, and D. G. Wright, 'The Great War, Government Propaganda, and English "Men of Letters" 1914–16', *Literature and History*, no. 7 (Spring 1978), pp. 70–100, esp. 72, 91–2.

[1914.05]

'Rheims Cathedral'

In September 1914 German shelling caused extensive damage to the great Gothic cathedral of Rheims, and Hardy—drawing upon his architectural knowledge and sensitivity and sharing in the general British outrage—issued a public statement that seems to have originated as a personal letter to Sydney Cockerell, even though the surviving typescript copy addressed to Cockerell (Princeton) clearly post-dates the public version. A heavily corrected pencil draft is also extant (Princeton), but there appear to be no near-final manuscripts or typescripts of the version that was widely printed on 7 October 1914, either in full (e.g. *Manchester Guardian*, p. 7, *Daily News and Leader*, p. 5, *Westminster Gazette*, p. 4) or in part (e.g. *The Times*, p. 10, *New York Times*, p. 2). When Clement Shorter proposed to publish 'Rheims Cathedral' and 'A Reply to Critics' (1914.08) in pamphlet form, Hardy declined to authorize the reprinting of what had been hurriedly written 'for the moment only on matters on which one's opinion is liable to be modified by new information' (*CL* v. 58). He nevertheless cooperated with the project, inscribing his corrections and expansions of 'Rheims Cathedral' on a cutting of the *Daily News* printing (DCM), and it is that latest and fullest version, as included in *Letters on the War* (privately printed, 9 November 1914), pp. [3–6], that is reproduced below. Reprinted (*Manchester Guardian* version) in *Life and Art*, pp. 136–8. Purdy, p. 159.

. . . .

Everybody[8] is able to feel in a general way the loss to the world that has resulted from this mutilation of a noble building which was almost the finest specimen of mediæval architecture in France. The late M. Viollet-le-Duc[9]—who probably knew more about French architecture than any man of his time—considered it to unite in itself in a unique degree the charms of beauty and dignity. But the majority of people have found comfort in a second thought—that the demolished parts can be renewed, even if not without vast expense. Only those who, for professional or other reasons, have studied in close detail the architecture of the thirteenth and fourteenth centuries are aware that to do this in its entirety is impossible. Gothic architecture has been a dead art for the last 300 years, in spite of the imitations thrown broadcast over the land, and much of what is gone from this fine structure is gone for ever.

The magnificent stained glass of the cathedral will probably be found to have suffered the most. How is that to be renewed? Some of it dated from the thirteenth century, and is inimitable by any handiworkers in the craft nowadays. Its wreck is all the more to be regretted in that, if I remember rightly, many of the windows had already in the past lost their original glass. Then the sculpture and the mouldings, and other details. Moreover, their antique history was a part of them, and how can that history be imparted to a renewal?

When I was young French architecture of the best period was much investigated, and selections from such traceries and mouldings as those at Rheims were delineated with the greatest accuracy; and copied by architects' pupils—myself among the rest. Sir Arthur Blomfield,[10] with whom I was working, first set me on the track of early French Gothic, of which he was a great admirer, and I won as an architectural prize the

[8] The initial line of spaced periods replaces in *Letters on the War* the line of spaced dashes that, in TH's holograph draft, intervenes between the opening 'My dear Cockerell' and the first word, 'Everybody', of the public text. The post-publication typescript (Princeton) begins, 'My dear Cockerell: I wonder how much you have learnt about the ghastly event that has happened? Everybody'.

[9] Eugène Emmanuel Viollet-le-Duc (1814–79), French architect, restorer of the cathedrals of Notre Dame, Amiens, Laon, etc.

[10] Sir Arthur William Blomfield (1829–99), architect; TH worked in his London office in 1862–7. The entire sentence 'Sir Arthur . . . subject' is absent from all newspaper texts and appears first in *Letters on the War*; it is present in the Cockerell typescript, and was added to TH's draft.

books of Nesfield and Norman Shaw[11] on the same subject. It seems strange indeed now that the curves we used to draw with such care should have been broken as ruthlessly as if they were a cast-iron railing replaceable from a mould.

If I had been told three months ago that any inhabitants of Europe would wilfully damage such a masterpiece as Rheims in any circumstances whatever, I should have thought it an incredible statement. Is there any remote chance of the devastation being accidental, or partly accidental, or contrary to the orders of a superior officer? This ought to be irrefutably established and settled, since upon it depends the question whether German civilisation shall become a byword for ever or no.

Should it turn out to be a pre-determined destruction—as an object lesson of the German ruling caste's Will to Power—it will strongly suggest what a disastrous blight upon the glory and nobility of that great nation has been wrought by the writings of Nietzsche, with his exemplifiers[12] Treitschke, Bernhardi,[13] &c.

I should think there is no instance since history began of a country being so demoralised by a single writer, the irony being that he was a megalomaniac, and not truly a philosopher at all.

What puzzles one is to understand how the profounder thinkers in Germany and to some extent elsewhere, can have been so dazzled by this writer's bombastic poetry—for it is a sort of prose-poetry—as to be blinded to the fallacy of his arguments—if they can be called arguments which[14] are incoherent assumptions. His postulates as to what life is on this earth have no resemblance to reality. Yet he and his school seem to have eclipsed for the time in Germany the close reasoned philosophies of such[15] men as Kant and Schopenhauer.[16]

---

[11] *Specimens of Mediaeval Architecture* (1862) by William Eden Nesfield (1835–88) and *Architectural Sketches from the Continent* (1858) by Richard Norman Shaw (1831–1912). The prize was that offered by the Architectural Association in 1863 for a design for a country mansion (*Biography*, pp. 80–1).

[12] For 'exemplifiers' newspaper texts (*Manchester Guardian*, *Daily News*, etc.) read 'followers'; the alteration of 'followers' to 'exemplifiers' in TH's draft was apparently a retrospective revision (cf. n. 10 above).

[13] Heinrich von Treitschke (1834–96), German historian; Friedrich von Bernhardi (1849–1930), German soldier and writer, whose *Deutschland und der nächste Krieg* (1912) caused a sensation in English translation.

[14] The *Letters on the War* reading 'arguments—which' has here been emended to conform to the clearly correct reading of TH's draft; newspaper texts follow the draft or insert a comma.

[15] For 'close reasoned . . . such' (also the reading of TH's draft) the *Manchester Guardian* reads 'close-reasoned philosophers, such'.

[16] The German philosophers Immanuel Kant (1724–1804) and Artur Schopenhauer (1788–1860).

It is rather rough on the latter that their views of life should be swept into one net with those of Nietzsche, Treitschke, and the rest, as 'German philosophy' (as has been done by some English writers to the papers) when they really differ further in ethics than the humane philosophers mentioned differ in that respect from Christianity.[17]

[1914.06]

'H.R.H. the Prince of Wales' National Relief Fund'

Early in the First World War the Prince of Wales gave his name, ostensibly in the role of Treasurer, to a National Relief Fund to 'meet the myriad cases of hardship and distress' occasioned by the war: see *The Times*, 7 August 1914, p. 6. Hardy was one of several writers named as supporting the appeals on behalf of the Fund placed in various journals—e.g. the *English Review*, 18 (October 1914), p. xiv—by a tributary organization called the Magazine-Readers' Half-Crown Fund, of which his friend Anthony Hope Hawkins ('Anthony Hope' the novelist) was the honorary secretary.

[1914.07]

[?Notes on the Lesser-Known Characters in *The Dynasts*?]

Prepared for the 1914 stage production of *The Dynasts* by Harley Granville Barker (1877–1946), and presumably slipped inside the theatre programmes, was a twelve-page leaflet headed 'Notes on some of the lesser-known Characters in the abridgment from "The Dynasts" presented at the Kingsway Theatre November 25th, 1914' (copy DCM). The historical information in the notes is often quite detailed, and it is tempting to think that they were Hardy's work. Their style, however, does not point at all strongly in that direction, nor can they readily be identified with the 'one or two other notes' mentioned in Hardy's letter to Barker of 28 October 1914 (*CL* v. 56). When the American writer Vincent Starrett (1886–1974) enquired about them at a later date, 14 November 1927 (DCM), Hardy replied (undated

---

[17] Cf. TH's letter to Cockerell, 26 September 1914 (*CL* v. 50–1).

draft, DCM) that he had never written any such leaflet and did not remember seeing it.

[1914.08]

'Mr. Hardy on Nietzsche. A Reply to Critics'

The *Manchester Guardian*'s publication of Hardy's letter about Rheims Cathedral on 7 October 1914 (1914.05) provoked responses from readers— Thomas Beecham, the conductor, among them—who deplored his endorsement of the hostility towards Nietzsche so prevalent in Britain at that time. On 11 October the newspaper published an editorial supportive of Hardy's views, and that same day Hardy wrote again to the editor in his own defence. There are no significant discrepancies between the text below, as printed under the heading 'Mr. Hardy on Nietzsche. A Reply to Critics' in the *Manchester Guardian*, 13 October 1914, p. 6, and either the pencil draft Hardy inserted in his 'Personal' scrapbook (DCM) or the version printed in Clement Shorter's pamphlet *Letters on the War* (see 1914.05), pp. [6–7]. Reprinted (as from the *Manchester Guardian*) in *Life and Art*, pp. 138–9. Purdy, pp. 159–60.

October 11.

Sir,

I would gladly, if at this stage of my life I could reopen what is an old subject with me,[18] reply to your correspondents who think I have misrepresented Nietzsche[19] (at the fag-end of a letter on an architectural subject, by the way). I will only remark that I have never said he was a German, or that he loved Germany, or that he lived before Treitschke; or that he did not express such sentiments as your correspondents and others—apparently young men chiefly—quote to the avoidance of other sentiments that I could quote, *e.g.*:

Ye shall love peace as a means to new wars, and the short peace better than the long. . . . I do not counsel you to conclude peace but to conquer. . . . Beware of pity.[20]

[18] See 1914.02.
[19] For the specific controversy, see Dennis Taylor, *Hardy's Poetry, 1860–1928* (London: Macmillan, 1981), pp. 185–6, and Nicholas Martin, 'Nietzsche under Fire', *The Times Literary Supplement*, 5 August 1994, p. 11.
[20] See Nietzsche, *Thus Spake Zarathustra: A Book for All and None*, trans. Alexander Tille (New York and London: Macmillan, 1896), p. 60.

He used to seem to me (I have not looked into his works for years) to be an incoherent rhapsodist who jumps from Machiavelli to Isaiah as the mood seizes him, and whom it is impossible to take seriously as a mentor. I may have been wrong, but he impressed me in the long run, owing to the preternatural absence of any overt sign of levity in him, with a curious suspicion (no doubt groundless) of his being a first-class Swiftian humourist[21] in disguise. I need hardly add that with many of his sayings I have always heartily agreed; but I feel that few men who have lived long enough to see the real colour of life, and who have suffered, can believe in Nietzsche as a thinker.

Yours, &c.,

Thomas Hardy.

[1914.09]

[List of Publications for the Authors Club of New York]

Hardy was elected to an honorary membership of the Authors Club of New York in 1908, and three sets of corrected proofs for 'Thomas Hardy' entries in the *Manual of the Authors Club* are in the Manuscripts Division of the New York Public Library. Although these proofs—evidently of different dates between 1914 and 1919—contain only standard bibliographical information, and are therefore not reproduced here, Hardy has corrected and expanded them with his usual attentiveness to the detail of public acts of self-presentation.

---

[21] For 'humourist' *Letters* and TH's draft read 'humorist'.

1915

[1915.01]

'Address and Presentation to Mr. Robert Ross'

Approached by his friend Edmund Gosse in January 1915 (*CL* v. 77), Hardy readily agreed to add his name to 'the memorial' to Robert Ross (1869–1918), friend and executor of Oscar Wilde (1854–1900). Subscribers later received a pamphlet, *An Address and Presentation to Mr. Robert Ross* (privately printed at the Chiswick Press, 2 June 1915), in which Ross was praised for his services to art and literature and as 'one who has proved a brave, loyal and devoted friend'. Hardy's is one of the more than 300 names listed in the pamphlet, and he is picked out as one of the more notable subscribers in the news item devoted to the *Address* in *The Times*, 29 March 1915, p. 5.

[1915.02]

[Praise for William Watson Sonnet]

William Watson's patriotic sonnet, 'To America, Concerning England', first printed in the London *Evening News* of 8 December 1914, was reprinted in *The Times* of 12 March 1915, p. 9, at the conclusion of a letter in which Watson (1858–1935) defended his poem against the criticisms of 'neutralist' voices in the United States. Hardy, reading the poem in that context, wrote Watson an extravagant letter of praise (*CL* v. 83) that Watson—impelled by pride, he told Hardy on 17 March (DCM)—sent on to the *Evening News*, where it was duly printed, 17 March 1915, p. 4, with an acknowledgement of Hardy's permission for the publication of a message originally 'of quite a private character'. The *Newspaper World*, 20 March, p. 17, reprinted the letter from the *Evening News* but commented adversely on its 'grammatical constructions'.

Max Gate, Dorchester, 12–3–1915.

Dear Mr Watson,

I have just read the sonnet, 'To America,' reprinted in *The Times*, (which I had never seen[1] before), and I think it one of the finest things— if not the very finest—you have ever written, and possibly any poet, both in craftsmanship and feeling. I hope you are well, and am, sincerely yours,

Thomas Hardy.

[1915.03]

'The War and Literature'

The London magazine *Book Monthly* for April 1915 published, under the heading 'The War and Literature', the responses of several writers to the question, 'What effects, so far as they can be estimated ahead, is the Great War likely to exercise on English literature?' Hardy's response, reproduced below, appeared on p. 434. Reprinted in *Life and Art*, p. 122. Purdy, p. 318.

Ultimately for good; by 'removing (from literature) those things that are shaken, as things that are made, that those things that cannot be shaken may remain.'—Heb. xii. 27.[2]

[1915.04]

[Two Translations for *The Book of France*]

Hardy was nominally a member of a committee supportive of the French Parliamentary Committee's Fund for the Relief of the Invaded Departments and presumably had little option but to associate himself—along with such

---

[1] For 'seen' TH's original (Texas) reads 'read'.
[2] Quotation from St Paul's Epistle to the Hebrews, slightly adjusted by TH.

colleagues as Henry James, H. G. Wells, and Edmund Gosse—with *The Book of France*, a 'charity-book' project involving the publication of essays by French writers both in the original French and in English translation. The editor of the volume, Winifred Stephens (d. 1944), a writer on French literature and history, was personally known to him as one of Edward Clodd's circle. Although Hardy could certainly read French, it is unclear to what extent he was directly responsible for the two translations attributed to him and reproduced below from *The Book of France* (London: Macmillan; Paris: Édouard Champion, 1915), pp. 12–15 ('Great Britain') and 61–2 ('Invasion'). The inflated style is curiously suggestive of that found in 1918.04 (q.v.), of which Florence Hardy appears to have been the principal author. Purdy, p. 318, gives the publication date as July 1915.

GREAT BRITAIN
(*A Frenchman's Reflections on British Character and Policy*)

For centuries England has been the most fortunate nation in Europe. Her very mistakes—and some of them have been grave—seem to have turned to her advantage. Her errors have done her no harm. In war-time she has shown herself capable of repairing the faults of an organisation often defective and sometimes deplorable. For example, she was totally unprepared for her struggle with Napoleon. Nevertheless she was by far the most formidable adversary of imperial France. At the opening of the Crimean War her army was quite out of date. In the Boer War she had foreseen neither the difficulties nor the new methods of warfare which were to prevail in that struggle, although she ought to have learnt them from the events of 1881.[3] England's success, therefore, has not always been the result of her foresight or of her prudence. It even involved a certain risk for which a less gifted nation might have had to pay dearly. It is *character* which, with the English throughout all ages, has repaired the errors and faults that have arisen from an overweening confidence in the resources of the three kingdoms. Into this national character enters, in addition to a relish for adventure and risk, a certain reasonableness which imposes limits, and, among the best, a certain dogged tenacity and indomitable will served by admirably clear vision. Hitherto no one in the world has known so well as the Englishman how to blend those qualities which inspire grand enterprises with the prudence which sees how to avoid haste, excess, and infatuation. And this it is which, combined with her insular position, has enabled Great Britain to organise

---

[3] A reference to the defeats inflicted on British forces in that year by the Boers of the Transvaal.

a dominion more vast than that of ancient Rome. Yet another cause—at least in modern times—has contributed to her success. I refer to England's tolerant attitude towards other European nations, great and small. It is long now—indeed ever since the opening of the industrial era—since England first learnt to respect the rights of other peoples. Take her own dominions, for example: she has put French Canadians into such an advantageous position that quite naturally they include themselves among the Empire's most loyal subjects. After the Boer War, the Boer general-in-chief became the political leader in South Africa.[4] In India the natives have been generously governed, and Great Britain has done her best to improve the lot of the poor and to put an end to the scourge of famine.

Towards foreigners England has behaved with equal justice. Holland has not been disturbed in her possession of vast colonies; Portugal peaceably holds her African possessions; and France, since 1871, has been able to build up a great colonial empire.

Besides favouring the liberation of Greece and Italy, England has always been kind to little neutral countries. All Europe never for an instant doubts that England grows more and more inclined to act justly towards all civilised nations; that, from the Balkans to the Atlantic, she aims at no territorial conquest, and that she is not moved by any tyrannical motives.

How can she avoid exercising a magnificent moral influence, at a time especially when another nation, formidable alike through its military and industrial power, is threatening all liberty, despising all rights, tearing up all treaties which have become inconvenient, recognising no rule save her own will, no laws save those dictated by her appetites, her pride, her scorn, or her ferocity?

To-day England's fate is intimately linked with that of Europe, far more intimately than in the beginning of the nineteenth century, for the French spirit did not then menace the very essence of the movement towards civilisation, which began at the Renaissance. With Germany victorious, *lasciate ogni speranza*! (give up all hope).[5] It would mean the end of a glorious epoch. . . . But the Allies will not be conquered. Heroic France has returned. England, the undaunted, out of her soil has miraculously caused armies to spring. Russia stands ready for gigantic battle.

---

[4] Louis Botha (1862–1919), commander-in-chief of the Boer forces during the war of 1899–1902, became in 1910 the first premier of the Union of South Africa.

[5] Dante Alighieri, *Divina Commedia*, 'Inferno', opening of Canto 3.

Once again England shall be happy England. From this terrific ordeal she will come forth greater, fairer, more beloved.

J. H. Rosny aîné,[6]
Translated by Thomas Hardy.

INVASION

At the beginning of this war I used to say to myself—and I have found many others who thought the same—that it might be less grievous if the fighting could be localised on the frontier, towards Belgium. That has certainly not yet happened. Nevertheless for those who, after the earliest events, expected the worst, the situation has vastly improved. But supposing my first wish had been realised, and the enemy had been driven back to the frontier departments, would our heart's wound have been less deep? Even with danger staved off Paris, the enemy would still have been encamped on a soil which is ours; and however limited the extent of his occupation, we should still have suffered the anguish of defilement. But at the present time we suffer something more than this, although the sense of defilement is the prevailing impression: there comes over us a feeling of outrage, of devastation, which corresponds only too well with facts. How have our fair towns been treated, those country scenes over which our minds loved to wander, and that beautiful demesne which has ceased to appear to us a demesne and over which we are lords no longer! As for the people, what are they but wanderers, hunted creatures lurking in forests or hiding amidst ruins! O the sorrow of it! Think, if you have no more personal recollections, of the homes you loved, of the little provincial towns, where beneath the park elms or the limes on the public square you imagined you had left an emotion which time would never dull, that would always await you there. To that spot you would wend in slow pilgrimage, returning melancholy perhaps, but yet happy. Now you must cease to think of it. Such thought has become impossible. *They* are there, and every memory they have put to flight. Where could memory linger? Everything is ruined. And though over this weeping desolation Spring may cast some semblance of

---

[6] Pseudonym of the French novelist Joseph-Henri Boëx (1856–1940), called 'aîné' (senior) because he once shared the 'Rosny' pseudonym with his younger brother Séraphin Justin François Boëx.

joy, though these frightful folk may perchance have left standing the house you remember, they will have polluted it in some way, rendering it more piteous perhaps than if it had been destroyed. How sorrowful the lot of those whose birthplaces and firesides have been thus infected. Poor hearts! For them I write these lines.

Remy de Gourmont,[7]

Translated by Thomas Hardy.

[1915.05]

[Obituary for Frank George]

Hardy took a strong interest in Frank William George (1880–1915)—the eldest son of Angelina George (*née* Hardy), his first cousin once removed and the widow of a Bere Regis publican—and thought him the most attractive and promising of his younger relatives. Immediately following the news of George's death in action at Suvla Bay in the Dardanelles in late August of 1915 (*LW*, pp. 400, 401; *CL* v. 120–5), Hardy wrote the poem 'Before Marching and After' (Purdy, p. 174) and sent to *The Times*—which routinely asked the relatives of dead officers to supply 'any biographical details in their possession'—the following unsigned obituary, duly published under the heading 'Fallen Officers' on 3 September 1915, p. 6. Florence Hardy, writing to Rebekah Owen on 1 September 1915 (Colby), spoke of typing the obituary that morning. The obituary was reprinted verbatim, with the subheading 'Thomas Hardy's Cousin Killed', in the Bere Regis section of the *Dorset County Chronicle*, 9 September 1915, p. 13.

SECOND LIEUTENANT FRANK WILLIAM GEORGE, 5th Dorset Regiment, barrister, who was killed in Gallipoli on August 22, was the eldest son of the late Mr William George, of Southbrook, Bere Regis, Dorset, and through his mother, *née* Hardy, was a cousin of Mr Thomas Hardy, O.M., of Max Gate, Dorchester. Mr George entered the service of the old Dorsetshire Bank (afterwards the Wilts. and Dorset, and now Lloyds), where he became assistant manager at the Bristol branch. He

---

[7] Rémy de Gourmont (1858–1915), French poet, novelist, and critic, was a leading Symbolist figure.

was called to the Bar by Gray's Inn two or three years ago. On the outbreak of the present war he enlisted in the 6th Gloucestershire Infantry. In the winter he volunteered for and was for a while attached to a division of the Midland Cyclist Company, till he applied for a transfer to the Inns of Court O.T.C., but being offered a commission in the Gloucesters, and also in the Dorset Regiment, he accepted the latter and was posted to the 5th Battalion, which he accompanied to the Dardanelles at the beginning of July last. He was unmarried.

[1915.06]

[Death Notice for Frank George]

Hardy evidently did not originate the formal notice of Frank George's death that appeared in the 'Deaths' column of the *Dorset County Chronicle*, 2 September 1915, p. 16. He was undoubtedly responsible, however, for the notice published, as below, in the 'Killed in Action' section of the 'Deaths' column of *The Times*, 3 September 1915, p. 1. He also persuaded Clement Shorter (*CL* v. 122) to publish a photograph of George in the *Sphere*, 25 September 1915.

GEORGE.—Killed in action, in Gallipoli, on Sunday, the 22nd Aug., SECOND-LIEUT. FRANK WILLIAM GEORGE, 5th Battn. Dorset Regt., son of the late W. George, of Southbrook, Bere-Regis, and cousin and friend of T. Hardy, Max Gate Dorchester.

[1915.07]

[?Support for Allied War Aims Statement?]

A card from Sir Frederick Pollock, Bt., 30 September 1915 (DCM), thanks Hardy for supporting some statement involving the reassertion of Allied war aims. Hardy had evidently questioned some detail of the wording but is assured by Pollock that '[a]greement to every word obviously is not implied'. The statement itself remains unidentified. See 1914.04.

[1915.08]

[Message for *The Times* Recruiting Supplement]

In the autumn of 1915 Britain's armies were still made up of volunteers, and Hardy supplied upon request a message published, under the subheading 'Mr. Thomas Hardy', in *The Times Recruiting Supplement*, 3 November 1915, p. 5. The message as printed consisted simply of the text of Hardy's adaptation (affecting only the last two lines) of a passage from Virgil's *Æneid* (book 11, lines 648–55) in the Dryden translation he had known from childhood (*LW*, p. 21); not included was the explanation of the adaptation present in his pencil draft (DCM) and presumably also in the message as dispatched. The text below is therefore that of Hardy's draft; the verses themselves were accurately reproduced in *The Times*, except that the draft's underlining of the words Hardy had altered was not indicated in any way.

A passage in the speech of Turnus, in the eleventh Book of the Aeneid,[8] as rendered by Dryden, becomes singularly apposite to the recruiting movement by the change of a very few words:—

> But if we still have fresh recruits in store,
> If our confederates can afford us more,
> If the contended field we have bravely fought,
> And not a bloodless inroad has been bought,
> (Their losses equall'd ours, and, for their slain,
> With equal fires they fill'd the shining plain)
> Why, thus unforc'd, should we not *up and go*,
> *And, ere compulsion comes, engage the foe?*[9]

[1915.09]

[Synopsis for *Far from the Madding Crowd* Film]

Visitors to the 16 November 1915 trade and press preview of the Turner Films production of *Far from the Madding Crowd*, adapted and produced by Larry Trimble and with Florence Turner as Bathsheba, were presented with

---

[8] Emended from MS reading 'Aenid'; Dryden's translation was first published in 1697.

[9] *The Times* adds, below the last line, 'Æneid XI. (Dryden's Translation)'. The words underlined by TH replace Dryden's 'so tamely yield; | And, e're the Trumpet sounds, resign the Field?'

a 'souvenir' booklet that contained a synopsis of the story written by Hardy himself and was illustrated on each of its ten unnumbered pages by a captioned still photograph from the film. The synopsis was reprinted, almost verbatim, in the *Kinematograph and Lantern Weekly*, 25 November 1915, p. 21. Both texts conclude with a florid paragraph-long characterization of Bathsheba that seems at odds with the subdued tenor of the preceding paragraphs of renarration: the 'souvenir', indeed, prints it on an eleventh unnumbered page typographically distinct from the synopsis proper, and its absence from Hardy's draft, headed 'Synopsis of the Story' (DCM), tends to confirm that it was not his work. That final paragraph has been relegated to a footnote in the following reproduction of the 'souvenir' text. Purdy, p. 318.

Gabriel Oak, who begins life as a Wessex shepherd, raises himself to the position of a small farmer, and as such woos, though unsuccessfully, the beautiful Bathsheba Everdene, a farmer's niece. Having the misfortune to lose his sheep by an accident he lapses again to shepherding, and in search of a place finds himself at the farm of the late Mr Everdene, which, to his surprise, is now managed by Bathsheba herself, whose inexperience threatens to bring her to grief. She engages him as her shepherd.

He has thus fallen into the tantalising position of being servitor to a woman with whom he is still desperately in love, and whose knowledge of his feelings causes her to throw mischievous little tyrannies into her commands to him.

She, meanwhile, by a coquettish freak, draws upon herself the attentions of a reserved bachelor, the rich Farmer Boldwood, who gets to love her with a moody and taciturn passion that rather alarms her.

A servant of Bathsheba's, Fanny Robin, mysteriously vanishes from the house, and, shortly after, the gay and careless Sergeant[10] Troy, who has wasted his education and opportunities, comes home to the village on furlough. His casual encounter with Bathsheba starts him on a courtship of her by all the flatteries his glib tongue can command. The shepherd warns her gently against Troy, and is promptly dismissed. Farmer Boldwood furiously chides her for deserting him, and threatens the Sergeant's life. She, fearing for her lover's safety, rushes off to tell him of his danger, Troy being temporarily absent at Bath.

When they reappear in the village they are married, Troy, for whom it is a good match, having persuaded her to this hasty step during her absence with him.

---

[10] Spelled 'Sarjeant' in draft, here and later.

He now buys his discharge and takes command of the farm, which soon begins going to ruin. Bathsheba's lost servant Fanny is brought home dead from the workhouse for burial. Bathsheba suspects some connection between her husband and the servant's disappearance, and in a scene by the open coffin of the latter discovers that it also contains a dead child of which Troy is the father. He, entering, confesses to it, and next morning deserts his wife and the farm, being heartily sick of bucolic life.

The rest is soon told. Bathsheba expects her husband to return, knowing that he has no money. Not so Farmer Boldwood, who by constant pressure wrings from her a vague promise that if Troy does not return in seven years she will marry him. Troy almost immediately enters. Boldwood, in rage and despair, snatches a gun from the rack and shoots Troy dead.

In after years, when a chastened woman, Bathsheba accepts Gabriel Oak, who has proposed again, and has succeeded to Boldwood's farm.[11]

[1915.10]

[?Commentaries on Illustrations to 'Autograph Edition'?]

In 1915 Hardy's American publishers, Harper & Brothers, published a limited signed 'Autograph Edition' of his works in twenty volumes (Purdy, p. 286). Hardy took an active interest in the edition, read the proofs of some of the volumes, and may have participated in choosing the four Hermann Lea photographs reproduced in each volume (see *CL* iv. 324). And while it was presumably Hermann Lea who wrote the contextualising commentaries on those photographs, Hardy is likely to have overseen and occasionally corrected Lea's work, much as he had done earlier with Lea's *Thomas Hardy's*

---

[11] The additional paragraph reads: '*Far from the Madding Crowd* is the life story of an impulsive, capricious, but fascinating woman upon whom tragedy and suffering is brought by her own actions. Her innate inability to refrain from misleading and torturing those whom she captivated by her alluring ways was the cause of the heartbreaking of Gabriel, of the death of Troy, and of the final doom of the morbid Boldwood. But, at the end of it all, the happiness of rest and peace must have been intensified by the turmoil that had gone before.' The first and third sentences were used in the programme (Beinecke) for the film's showing at the Cinema House, Oxford Street, London, in February–March 1916.

Wessex (see 1913.04), from which the photographs are taken. The same photographs and descriptions appear in the 'Anniversary Edition' published by Harper in twenty-one volumes (1920–1). Peter Lennon, who with Mark Simons provided the information for this entry, has pointed out that the descriptive commentaries, available only in these American editions, appear in several instances to supersede those in *Thomas Hardy's Wessex* and are therefore of some interest and importance.

[1915.11]

'Death of Miss Mary Hardy'

Hardy must have written the second paragraph—and some part at least of the opening paragraph—of the unsigned obituary of his sister Mary that appeared under the heading 'Death of Miss Mary Hardy. Sister of Mr. Thomas Hardy, O.M.' in the *Dorset County Chronicle*, 2 December 1915, pp. 8–9. A cutting of the obituary in Hardy's 'Personal' scrapbook (DCM) carries an alteration in his hand; another cutting (Beinecke), similarly altered, went to Sydney Cockerell with a letter in which Hardy's authorship was implicitly acknowledged (*CL* v. 135). Phrases from the obituary are echoed in the account of Mary Hardy's death in *Life and Work*, pp. 401–2, and it was plainly Hardy himself who supplied Clement Shorter with the revised version of the final three sentences of the obituary, attributed to 'a correspondent', that accompanied a photograph of a Mary Hardy self-portrait in the 'Literary Letter' section of the *Sphere*, 25 December 1915, p. 344. The text below is that of the *Dorset County Chronicle* printing, as emended in Hardy's scrapbook. Purdy, p. 318.

We regret to report that Miss Mary Hardy passed away on Wednesday, November 24th, in her 74th year, at 'Talbothays', West Stafford, where she lived with her brother, Mr Henry Hardy, and her sister, Miss Kate Hardy. The deceased lady, a sister of Mr Thomas Hardy, O.M., of Max Gate, the eminent man of letters, was born in the family home at Upper Bockhampton on December 23rd, 1841. She was educated at Miss Harvey's School, South-street, Dorchester, entered Salisbury Training College[12] in April, 1860, as a paying student (not having served as a pupil-teacher), and obtained her certificate in 1863. Her life was

---

[12] i.e. the Salisbury Church of England Diocesan Training College for teachers, located in the cathedral close.

devoted to educational work, and she was for many years Headmistress of the Dorchester Elementary Girls' School, her younger sister being one of her assistants. Miss Mary Hardy was endowed with a large share of the family taste and talent for art and music. While living in Wollaston-road she studied assiduously, and used her pencil and brush with skill at the Dorchester School of Art.[13] In her earlier career she had for years acted[14] as church organist. Under an often undemonstrative exterior she hid a warm and most affectionate nature.

In addition to Miss Hardy's long practical connection with school-teaching, there was a side to her activities of which less is known, except among her immediate acquaintances. This was her almost life-long devotion to sketching and painting, which, had it been developed and tended carefully, might have made a noteworthy artist of her. It took the direction of portraiture. Her facility in catching a likeness was remarkable, and hence, in respect of a family record on canvas—that which, whatever its shortcomings, is valued in proportion to its repro-duction for us of the faces of those we wish to remember—she painted to good purpose. Her picture in oils of her mother is a visible instance of this to those who recall the latter. It may be said indeed that her whole interest in the brush lay in this direction. In early life she was[15] often called upon to play the part of village organist, musicians not being so plentiful then in the country as they are now; and well the writer remembers her girlish consternation when, at the age of two-and-twenty, she was suddenly called upon to take the musical service in a strange church in a strange parish[16] on the following Sunday, upon an organ with pedals and two manuals, her previous experience having been entirely with piano and harmonium. How she got through her duty cannot now be estimated; but she speedily settled down to the instrument and performed regularly upon it as long as she resided in the parish, becoming an efficient choir-mistress amid the somewhat discon-certing vagaries of a rural choir. She was not, however, a born musician,

[13] Conducted in Handel House, now part of the Dorset County Museum. For a report of one of its annual exhibitions, including work by Mary Hardy, see the *Dorset County Chronicle*, 24 March 1904, p. 5.

[14] For 'Art. In . . . acted' *Chronicle* text reads 'Art, and acted'. This was the reading corrected by TH in the cutting sent to Cockerell.

[15] For 'In early life she was' the *Sphere*, beginning at this point, reads 'In early life Miss Mary Hardy was'.

[16] For 'service . . . parish' the *Sphere* reads 'service in a strange parish'; the allusion is to Denchworth, the Berkshire village where Mary Hardy first taught (see *CL* i. 4).

and her familiarity[17] with music decreased during the latter part of her life.

[1915.12]

[Death Notices for Mary Hardy]

Hardy must have been responsible for the following notice of his sister Mary's death, published in the 'Deaths' column of *The Times*, 27 November 1915, p. 1, and for the almost identical notice that appeared in the *Dorset County Chronicle*, 2 December 1915, p. 16.

HARDY. On the 24th inst., at[18] Talbothays, near Dorchester, Mary, elder daughter of the late Thomas and Jemima Hardy, and sister of Thomas Hardy, O.M., formerly headmistress of Church of England schools for many years, and sometime church organist, aged 73.

[1915.13]

[On Reading Good Books]

The brief unsigned message below, inscribed on a correspondence card in Hardy's hand (David Holmes), seems clearly to have been intended for early inclusion in some magazine or newspaper 'symposium'. Extensive search, however, has failed to locate the item in printed form and the text below is therefore drawn from the original document.

From Tho. Hardy, Max Gate, Dorchester. 18 Nov. 1915

In answer to your question I may say that I think the reading of good books—and particularly of good poetry—strengthens character. Such a poem as Wordsworth's 'Resolution and Independence',[19] for instance, is distinctly fortifying.

17 For 'musician . . . familiarity' the *Sphere* reads 'musician, as she was a painter, and familiarity'.
18 For 'On the 24th inst., at' *Chronicle* reads 'Nov. 24, at'.
19 Written in 1802, first published in 1807, and often referred to as 'The Leech-Gatherer'.

[1916.01]

[Manifesto of Friendship to Spain]

On 5 January 1916 (DCM) Sir Claud Schuster (1869–1956), permanent secretary in the Lord Chancellor's Office 1915–44, sent Hardy a copy of a manifesto expressive of British friendship towards Spain—where pro-German sentiment was strong—and asked him to co-sign the draft of a 'covering letter' designed to encourage 'people of standing' in Britain to sign the manifesto itself. Schuster's second letter (7 January 1916, DCM)—an assurance that most of the other signatories would be 'writers, learned men and artists' —was annotated by Hardy to the effect that he had signed the draft of the covering letter and returned it, together with the draft of the manifesto, on 8 January 1916. The manifesto itself, presumably issued only in Spain and in Spanish, has not been located. See 1914.04.

[1916.02]

'Which Is the Finest View in Dorset?'

When in 1914 the Dorset-born publisher Newman Flower (1879–1964) began editing the Year-Books of the Society of Dorset Men in London, he sought for his second issue the responses of leading Dorset figures to the question with which he headed the resulting article, 'Which is the Finest View in Dorset?' Hardy's typed letter of reply (21 July 1915, Texas), was pruned of its address, date, salutation, opening sentence, complimentary close, and signature for quotation, as below, in *Society of Dorset Men in London* (Year-Book 1915–16), pp. 31–2. Purdy, p. 318.

There[1] are views entirely inland, and views partly marine; also there are wide views with no near foreground, and bounded views in which the foreground plays a great part. I can only name a few embracing each kind that have struck me at different times as being good:—

1. From High Stoy, near Minterne.
2. From Bulbarrow, near Ansty.
3. From Castle Hill, Shaftesbury.
4. From the Purbeck Ridge above Creech Grange.
5. From Toller Down to Wynyard's Gap, between Maiden Newton and Crewkerne.
6. From the Highway between Dorchester and Bridport, at a point near Litton Cheney.
7. From Pilsdon.
8. From Golden Cap, near Chideock.

I am sorry to be unable to appraise them in order of merit.[2]

[1916.03]

Explanation of the Rural Scenes from *The Dynasts*

Hardy himself was very largely responsible for *Wessex Scenes from The Dynasts*, an adaptation of *The Dynasts* performed by the amateurs of the Dorchester Debating and Dramatic Society in Weymouth, 22 June 1916, and in Dorchester, 6 and 7 December 1916. He selected and adapted the episodes to be performed, participated in many aspects of the production, prepared the programme (*CL* v. 162), and wrote the following 'Explanation of the Rural Scenes from *The Dynasts*' for the guidance of the actors. Although the 'Explanation' is known to survive only as a pencil draft in the Dorset County Museum (*Index*, HrT 1631), Hardy's repeated direction that a 'white line' be left between paragraphs clearly indicates that he expected typed or printed copies to be made. If such copies indeed materialized, they have disappeared, and the text below is therefore that of the draft;

[1] For 'There' TH's original letter read 'I fear that it is beyond me to reply with conviction to your inquiry which in my opinion is the best view in Dorset. There'.
[2] TH's MS reads 'appraise these in the order of their merits, and I am, Yours truly, Thomas Hardy'.

ampersands are expanded and quotation marks standardized, in accordance with the edition's policies respecting MS materials, and Hardy's working revisions left unrecorded. See *Complete Poetical Works*, v. 404–5.

The scenes selected from the hundred and thirty that the complete Epic-drama contains are those and those only which are laid in this part of the country; for all the depicted events happen in spots that are not more than a mile from where the performance itself goes on[3] (though to help the historic consciousness Weymouth is periphrastically defined not by its own name but as 'The King's Watering-Place'.) This gives a curious sense of closeness to the action of each scene in point of place, although separated from it in time by more than 100 years.

A reference to the complete drama reveals that, of the five scenes put on the stage, the first is formed of three scenes from the first Act of the First Part in the book, the second of a scene from the second act of the same part, the third of a scene from the fifth act of the same part, the fourth of a scene from the fourth act of the Third Part, and the last of a scene from the sixth act.[4]

To lend some adequacy and coherence to this limitation—the only method which could possibly be adopted on a small stage with a small cast—and all of these representing characters of a quaint rural and country-town type—the plan adopted is that of interesting and impressing the spectator by exhibiting the reflex action on these characters of the great events which the spectator does not himself witness—tidings of them being brought in either by those who have taken part in them or have learnt of them. Thus at the moment of the convivial conversation at 'The Old Rooms Inn' on the Peace of 1814 and the Congress of Vienna, the attention of the Company is attracted to the adjoining barracks and camp by the unwonted movements and sudden marching off of the soldiery, which they watch in astonishment from the window, to be amazed in a few minutes by the entry of the recruiting sergeant (Mr Martin)[5] announcing that the reason of the stir is that Bonaparte has escaped from Elba.

---

[3] i.e. the Pavilion Theatre, Weymouth, where the first performance took place on 22 June 1916 (*LW*, p. 403).

[4] In performance the production seems also to have included material imported from *The Trumpet-Major* and the story 'A Tradition of Eighteen Hundred and Four'; see *Hardy on Stage*, pp. 98–104, and esp. p. 179 n. 51.

[5] Henry Austin Martin (d. 1949), Dorchester auctioneer and amateur actor.

To link together scenes, widely separated in the book, a few speeches are added here and there, and in one case there is a considerable development of a character—which is justified by her being a very charming one. This is the young girl[6] who sings 'My love's gone a-fighting', as she does in the book, but while there she does not appear till late in the Third Part, in the performance she enters near the beginning and has sundry emotional experiences with a young soldier. To make this gentle affair end happily before the fall of the curtain it is necessary that the soldier should get home on an early day after Waterloo, which is ingeniously contrived by making him the very sergeant who accompanied Major Henry Percy[7] in bringing news of the victory to England, on the famous occasion when he delivered the dispatches to the Prince Regent at Mrs Boehm's[8] ball in St James's Square.

The incidental airs are those which were popular in London from 1805 to 1815 and were danced to at the balls of the nobility at that date in country dances 20 couples long.

The performance is to be repeated to help the same cause[9] at Dorchester, Poole or Parkstone, and probably before the Society of Dorset Men in London.[10]

[1916.04]

[?'Hardy Play for Red Cross'?]

It seems highly probable—especially in light of 1916.03 and his friendship with Harold Child (see 1920.05)—that Hardy was either directly or indirectly responsible for at least the second and third paragraphs of the

---

[6] Played by Gertrude Adelia Bugler (1897–1992), a local actress to whom TH was already much attracted; she married Ernest Bugler, her cousin, in 1921.

[7] Henry Percy (1785–1825), Wellington's aide-de-camp, who brought to England Wellington's despatches reporting his victory at Waterloo.

[8] Apostrophe supplied. Mrs Boehm, the wife of a prominent merchant-banker, is said to have been much annoyed that the Battle of Waterloo spoiled her party.

[9] The Weymouth performance was in aid of 'British Red Cross Hospitals in Weymouth, and Russian Wounded'; the later Dorchester performances benefited the Dorset Red Cross and the Dorset Guild of Workers.

[10] The closeness of this final paragraph to the final paragraph of the review of the Weymouth performance in *The Times*, 23 June 1916, p. 11, combines with other similarities to suggest that the reviewer (presumably Harold Child) was familiar with TH's 'Explanation'.

following item, published under the above heading in *The Times*, 17 May 1916, p. 9.

Mention has been made in *The Times* of a performance to be given by the Dorchester Dramatic Society at Weymouth on June 22 of scenes from *The Dynasts* by Mr Thomas Hardy, in aid of Red Cross work.[11]

The scheme of the representation is quite different from that of Mr Granville Barker's selection of scenes from the same epic-drama last year.[12] The Weymouth production will consist entirely of the country scenes that occur in the ten-years' action of the book, the local backgrounds they require being in course of preparation by Mr T. H. Tilley, the stage manager.[13]

These scenes, taken from the poem, have been so linked together by Mr Hardy as to make an intelligible sequence, the great events on the Continent (which, of course, could not be presented on a country stage, or any other for that matter) being brought home to the spectators by messengers and other means, somewhat as in Greek plays.

[1916.05]

[Speech for Florence Hardy at Weymouth Performance of *Wessex Scenes*]

Among the papers in the Sanders Collection in the Dorset County Museum is a letter of 7 November 1916 in which J. H. Skillington, of Leicester, describes how Hardy, attending the 22 June 1916 Weymouth performance of *Wessex Scenes from The Dynasts* (1916.03) and learning that a speech would be expected from him, had slipped 'furtively' out of the audience 'after pencilling a short speech for his wife, which she was too nervous to deliver'. Accompanying the letter is a transcription of the original MS, said by Skillington to be in the possession of his 'friend at Weymouth'. The report of the occasion in the *Dorset County Chronicle*, 29 June 1916, p. 6, confirms

[11] Brief report, '*The Dynasts* for the Red Cross', *The Times*, 11 May 1916, p. 11.
[12] See Purdy, p. 135, *Hardy on Stage*, pp. 83–95, and 1914.07.
[13] Thomas Henry Tilley (1884–1944), alderman and sometime mayor of Dorchester, succeeded A. H. Evans as adaptor and producer of the Hardy plays for the Dorchester Debating and Dramatic Society. He adapted *The Return of the Native* (1920), *A Desperate Remedy* (1922), and two shorter pieces.

Hardy's departure from the stalls before the end of the performance but indicates that the speech was in fact delivered, on Florence Hardy's behalf, by Dr E. W. Kerr, then president of the Dorchester Debating and Dramatic Society. The text reproduced below from the *Dorset County Chronicle* differs only in details of punctuation from the Skillington transcription.

As my husband was obliged to leave before the end of the performance I hope you will allow me to thank you heartily in his name for your kind attendance to-day in such a worthy cause as the work of the Red Cross Society, and for your reception of the play. He desires me to say that owing to the pressure of other matters he was unable to give so much time to its preparation as he would have wished, and fears that it shows marks of hurried work in some places. This, fortunately for him, has been rendered less noticeable by the labours of Mr Tilley, the stage manager, whose efforts in the preparation of the play are worthy of all praise.

[1916.06]

[Support for the *Cambridge Magazine*]

The *Cambridge Magazine* was founded and edited by Charles Kay Ogden (1889–1957), linguist and (with I. A. Richards) the originator of Basic English. It provoked 'patriotic' hostility during the First World War by its policy of publishing, in each weekly issue, translated extracts from German and other foreign newspapers (see also 1917.02). Appealed to by Ogden (21 October 1916, DCM) for an expression of support, Hardy responded the next day with a typed letter (Magdalene College, Cambridge) that was promptly included, with messages from other leading British figures, in an advertisement for the *Magazine* in *The Times*, 1 November 1916, p. 4. The letter also appeared, as below, similarly stripped of its address, date, and signature, in the *Cambridge Magazine*, 11 November 1916, p. [97] under the heading 'Let us now be Praised by Famous Men'.

I read the *Magazine* every week, and turn first to the extracts from Foreign Newspapers, which transport one to the Continent and enable one to see England bare and unadorned—her chances in the struggle freed from distortion by the glamour of patriotism. I also admit a liking for the lighter paragraphs.

[1916.07]

'Remarkable Appeal to the Cabinet'

In the dark days of the First World War the heavy consumption of alcohol was increasingly perceived as having a deleterious effect not only on military personnel and munitions workers but on the well-being of the nation's children. A national debate ensued, the opening hours of public houses were sharply curtailed, the King banned alcohol in the royal household, the prohibition movement gained in strength, and an elaborately presented temperance 'Memorial'—occupying an entire page of *The Times*, 27 October 1916, p. 6—appealed to the Government to remove entirely 'the wasting-power of alcohol' and so 'put the Nation on its full strength'. Hardy's name appears at the head of the 'Literature, Music, Art' section of the supportive listing of '1000 Representatives of the Brain-Power of the Nation'.

[1916.08]

[Committee for an Intellectual *Entente*]

Hardy, who had long been a Fellow of the Royal Society of Literature, agreed in September 1916 (*CL* v. 179) to be named as a member of the Society's projected committee for promoting an 'intellectual entente' among allied and friendly countries, and he was so listed when the committee's formation was announced in *The Times*, 11 November 1916, p. 5. He seems not to have attended any meetings of the committee, but he did contribute, on 8 February 1917 (*CL* v. 202), an earnest letter—not, of course, made public at the time but reproduced almost verbatim in *Life and Work*, p. 405—about the need to expand 'the sentiment of *Patriotism*' to embrace the entire world and limit 'the sentiment of *Foreignness*' to beings from other planets.

[1916.09]

[Speech on *Wessex Scenes* Written for Mrs Hanbury]

For the first two Dorchester performances of *Wessex Scenes from The Dynasts* Hardy wrote introductory speeches, to be delivered prior to the rise of the

curtain by well-known local figures associated with the charities expected
to benefit from the production (*CL* v. 184–9). The first speech, delivered at
the evening performance on 6 December 1916 by Mrs Dorothy Hanbury
of Kingston-Maurward House, was reported by the *Dorset County Chronicle*,
14 December 1916, p. 6, in the third person and only in part, and it is
therefore transcribed below from Hardy's pencil draft, headed 'Speech
written for Mrs Hanbury', in the Dorset County Museum (*Index*, HrT 1632);
ampersands are expanded and Hardy's working revisions incorporated.
Purdy, p. 319.

Ladies and Gentlemen:

I have been asked to say a very few words by way of historical
introduction to the performance we are about to witness—thanks to
the generosity of the Dorchester Dramatic Society. The play, or rather
series of Scenes, that they are going to present on this stage is, as you
may know, a considerable abridgement of the complete drama as
written, which it would be impossible to act here, and almost impossible
on any stage.

The first point to which I wish to draw attention is that the scenes
chosen are confined to Wessex—and even to this part of Wessex—all
the action going on within a few miles of where we are now gathered.
They are so arranged and adapted as to show how the alarming events of
the war with Napoleon Bonaparte struck people at home at that date,
and, of course, are highly suggestive of our experiences at the present
day. Though it is a somewhat remarkable fact that when they were
written and published there was no thought in people's minds that
their production would so soon be followed by the terrible war we are
engaged in.

The scenes will take us through a period of nearly ten years, including the time between the alarms of invasion in 1805 and the Battle of
Waterloo in 1815. We shall see how people were living and feeling at
Weymouth in the first mentioned year, when the King and Court were
present in the town—living in that old red brick house now called the
Gloucester Hotel[14]—and how the town and country received the news
of the Victory of Trafalgar.

After which we skip forward through time to the still more exciting
year 1815, when the Battle of Waterloo put an end to Napoleon's power
for ever.

[14] Cf. *CL* v. 183–[5].

No further explanation is needed from me, and I leave the accomplished players themselves to exhibit to us the events and humours of the time.[15]

[1916.10]

[Speech on *Wessex Scenes* Written for Lady Ilchester]

> Because the Countess of Ilchester was unable to attend the second (matinée) performance of *Wessex Scenes from The Dynasts* in Dorchester on 7 December 1916, the speech Hardy had written for her was delivered by her 13-year-old daughter, Lady Mary Fox-Strangways (*CL* v. 193). The *Dorset County Chronicle*, 14 December 1916, p. 6, reported the speech in the first person, having presumably been supplied with a typescript made from Hardy's draft (DCM; *Index*, HrT 1633); that report, reproduced below, omits Hardy's heading, 'Town Hall Performances of "The Dynasts". Speech written for Lady Ilchester', and his opening directions to the speaker, but otherwise departs from the draft only in minor respects (see notes). Three slightly altered sentences from the speech had appeared earlier, under the heading 'Mr. Hardy on a War Contrast', in *The Times*, 9 December 1916, p. 11. Purdy, p. 319.

And now[16] as to the play itself. When the scenes are presently enacted, by the skill of members of the Dorchester Dramatic Society who have so kindly consented to their performance, we shall be struck most of all probably by the remarkable differences between the features of the great war with Napoleon that this play is meant to bring before us, and those of the greater war in which we are at present engaged. The contrast in point of humanity, honour, and chivalry between our enemies in the present struggle, and those of the struggle of 100 years ago, does not show altogether to the advantage of our modern methods of warfare

---

[15] The *Chronicle* report indicates that Mrs Hanbury went on to speak at some length about the Dorset Red Cross and Hospital Supply Depot, one of the charities that would benefit from the performances.

[16] TH's draft begins with a passage within square brackets: '[It is suggested that the speech should begin by remarks on any details of the Fund for the benefit of which the performances are given; continuing as follows]'.

and modern magnanimity. It is, indeed, no less than extraordinary that an additional century of civilisation and moral effort should have resulted in greater barbarities by far than any of those the much-abused Bonaparte ever put in force towards us.[17] They read like mildness itself by comparison with the mines, submarines, Zeppelin air-ships, gas-discharges, and other contrivances for taking human life that to-day are a common-place.[18] The difference between what may be called the legitimate weapons of war, of that time and now, is not less[19] remarkable. The guns were all muzzle-loaded, the cannon were all on wooden carriages, all small arms were fired by means of clumsy flint-locks, that missed fire as often as they went off, and every cartridge was bitten off at the end by the soldier's front teeth before it was used. Would that the present war laboured under such limitations! And Heaven grant that all its scientific slaughter may soon cease, and that a sense of its folly will ensure its disappearance for ever.

---

[17] 'The contrast . . . towards us.': *The Times* quoted these two sentences, with slight variations, then added the final sentence of the speech, again slightly adapted, without an intervening ellipsis.

[18] For 'life . . . common-place.' draft reads 'life.'

[19] For 'is not less' draft reads 'is no less'; for the thought here, cf. TH's poem 'Then and Now' (*CPW* ii. 299).

[1917.01]

[Reported Remarks on Poundbury Burials]

> Hardy was present at the annual meeting of the Dorset County Museum, 10 February 1917, and responded briefly to the Curator's announcement that recent digging on Poundbury Hill, just outside Dorchester, had unearthed two coffins made of Ham Hill stone that apparently dated from the Roman period. The account of the meeting in the *Dorset County Chronicle*, 15 February 1917, p. 5, included the following third-person summary of Hardy's remarks, in two separated passages, under the subheading 'The Find of Ancient Stone Coffins at Poundbury.—Mr. Thomas Hardy and the Accuracy of Tradition'. A brief report of the discovery and of Hardy's initial comment appeared in *The Times*, 15 February 1917, p. 4.

Mr THOMAS HARDY observed that the finding of these coffins tended in a very interesting manner to bear out the old tradition that Poundbury was a Saxon burying place. That was the idea prevalent when he was a boy. But then antiquaries said 'Oh, no; Poundbury was a Roman camp—because of its squareness.'

[*Curator*[1] *interjected that the coffins could well be Saxon.*]

Mr THOMAS HARDY added that it was interesting to observe how the establishment of one tradition tended to overthrow another. There was a belief when he was studying Gothic architecture that Ham Hill stone[2] was introduced into Dorset when St Peter's tower[3] was built, and that the builders only had it in time to finish off the tower. That was why, it

---

[1] Captain John Edward Acland (1848–1932), Curator of the Dorset County Museum 1904–32.
[2] Quarried in Somerset, just south of Yeovil.
[3] i.e. St Peter's church, in the centre of Dorchester.

was said, one saw Ham-hill stone only on the top of the tower; whereas in Fordington St George,[4] which was built a little later, they were able to make all the coigns and window dressings of Ham-hill stone. But now, if it was correct that these stone coffins were made of Ham-hill stone, it was obvious that this belief that Ham-hill stone was not introduced into Dorset until the 15th century was not accurate, for it must have been in use an indefinite time, many centuries earlier.

[1917.02]

[Renewed Support of the *Cambridge Magazine*]

The nine signatories of a letter headed 'Insidious Pacifist Propaganda' in the *Morning Post*, 24 February 1917, p. 6, launched a strong attack on the *Cambridge Magazine* for its reporting of what was being said about the war in foreign newspapers, including those hostile to the Allied cause, and accused it of being 'not a business undertaking but an organ of Pacifist propaganda'. Hardy had already supported the journal in 1916 (1916.06), and on 14 March 1917 (*CL* v. 207–8) he again agreed to sign a declaration in its defence, although he asked for some revision of the wording. Those revisions— visible in both his signed copy of the declaration (Lawrence of Crewkerne catalogue, 2 October 1980, lot 234) and his retained holograph copy of the declaration itself (DCM)—were almost all incorporated into the final statement published in the *Morning Post*, 17 March 1917, p. 9, under the same 'Insidious Pacifist Propaganda' heading, and then reprinted, under the heading 'Fighting with the Right People' and with a longer list of signatories, in the *Cambridge Magazine* itself, 24 March 1917, p. [445].

[1917.03]

'Shakespeare Monument in Rome'

Hardy agreed to join the Shakespeare Memorial Committee in 1905 (*CL* iii. 155–6), but played little part in its deliberations and eventually resigned in 1909 (*CL* iv. 27) over its commitment to the establishment of a Shakespeare

---

[4] See 1901.10.

Memorial theatre—a project he had already declined to support in 1908: 'Shakespeare in his literary aspect is really all I care about' (*CL* iii. 310, 313, and cf. vii. 149). In 1914 he accepted nomination to the British Academy's committee for commemorating Shakespeare's Tercentenary in 1917, but again emphasized his interest in 'Shakespeare the man of letters, & not Shakespeare the actor' (*CL* v. 33–4, and cf. 128–9) and went no further than to contribute his poem 'To Shakespeare after Three Hundred Years' to *A Book of Homage to Shakespeare*, published in 1916. He had always been willing to contemplate memorials to Shakespeare, however, and when *The Times*, 13 July 1917, p. 9, reported a proposal to erect a monument to Shakespeare in Rome following the end of the war, he was named as a member of the 'central committee to organize the movement'. In writing to Richard Bagot, the honorary secretary of the committee, on 7 June 1917 (*CL* v. 217–18), he had made his participation conditional on the removal of the word 'Christian' from the proposal itself.

[1917.04]

[Support for University Education in South-West England]

Arthur Eustace Morgan (1886–1972), university teacher and administrator, was at this date a lecturer in English at University College, Exeter, and in letters of 11 April and 6 May 1917 (DCM) he sought to enlist Hardy's support for a campaign to improve facilities for university education in south-west England once the war was over. In his reply of 8 May 1917 (draft, DCM) Hardy agreed to become a member of 'the Provisional Committee to further University Education in the South-West', and he was so listed in a report headed 'University Education in the South-West' in the *The Times Educational Supplement*, 18 October 1917, p. 400.

[1917.05]

'The Harper Centennial'

Hardy had a long association with the American house of Harper & Brothers as publishers both of books and of magazines, and when the firm celebrated its one-hundredth birthday in 1917 he contributed the following polite if somewhat tepid letter to *The Harper Centennial 1817–1917: A Few of the Greetings and Congratulations* (New York and London: Harper & Brothers, December 1917), p. 12. Purdy, p. 319.

Max Gate Dorchester May 29th, 1917

Mr Thomas Hardy has received with pleasure the Messrs. Harpers' card reminding him of the completion of their centenary as publishers. Although aware that they had handed on the torch for a good many decades it had not struck him that the period could be so long as it proves to be. He quite reciprocates their good wishes, and hopes that another such century of productivity will fall to their lot, and that they will be essentially unaffected by the shade of war now thrown over both continents.[5]

---

[5] The USA had entered the war against Germany on 6 April 1917.

1918

[1918.01]

'The Best Age'

Although the following letter to the novelist Hall Caine (1853–1931) was originally a private communication (*CL* v. 246–7), Hardy seems to have yielded quite readily to Caine's request, 31 January 1918 (DCM), that he permit its publication. It appeared as below, headed 'The Best Age', in the *Observer*, 3 February 1918, p. 3, and referred back, in a preliminary paragraph, to 'the correspondence published last week between Mr. Hall Caine and Sir Edward Clarke as to the time of life at which the human faculties reach their highest point'. Hardy never republished the letter, but a very similar passage occurs in *Life and Work*, p. 414, as part of a note dated 30 January 1918.

Max Gate, Dorchester, Jan. 29, 1918.

Dear Mr Hall Caine,

My thanks for the newspaper cutting.[1] If the mean age for the best *literary* work is thirty-seven[2] it must be owing to the conditions of modern life; for we are told that Homer sang when old and blind, while Æschylus wrote his best tragedies when over sixty, Sophocles some of his best when nearly ninety, and Euripides did not begin to write till forty, and went on to seventy; and in these you have the pick of the greatest poets who ever lived. The philosophers, too, were nearly always old.[3]

Yours very truly,

Th. Hardy.

---

[1] Of the Caine–Clark correspondence in the *Observer*, 27 January 1918, p. 3.

[2] As Clarke (1841–1931), a prominent lawyer and politician, had argued.

[3] Cf. stanza 9 of TH's poem 'An Ancient to Ancients', first published in 1922, and the first paragraph of his 'Introductory Note' to *Winter Words* (1928).

[1918.02]

[Speech Following Performance of *The Mellstock Quire*]

> Hardy and his wife entertained the 'Hardy Players' to tea following the afternoon performance of *The Mellstock Quire* on 1 February 1918. They were thanked for their hospitality by H. A. Martin (see 1916.03), the honorary secretary of the Dorchester Debating and Dramatic Society, and Hardy, obliged to respond, made the brief remarks reported as follows in the *Dorset County Chronicle*, 7 February 1918, p. 3. Hardy's letter to Florence Henniker of 7 February 1919 (*CL* v. 249–50) refers only to his wife's presence on this occasion, but it does appear that he did himself attend and say a few words.

Mr Hardy made a pleasant acknowledgment, and expressed his appreciation of the excellent manner in which the play had been performed.

[1918.03]

[?Inspired Paragraph on *Spoon River Anthology*?]

> When Florence Hardy told Sydney Cockerell (27 June 1918, Beinecke) that her husband found Clement Shorter 'useful', she cited Shorter's publishing in the *Sphere* (of which he was editor) a paragraph 'about the Spoon River Anthology' that Hardy 'particularly wanted mentioned'. Hardy was indeed irritated at the suggestion that he had been influenced by Masters (*CL* v. 314), and it seems very likely that he supplied Shorter with the material, if not the actual wording, for the second and third sentences of the paragraph reproduced below from Shorter's 'Literary Letter', *Sphere*, 15 June 1918, p. 202.

One of Miss Lowell's poets is, of course, Mr Edgar Lee Masters,[4] whose *Spoon River Anthology* struck me as peculiarly thrilling and interesting when it appeared, but I am rather surprised that Miss Lowell does not acknowledge the obvious indebtedness of Mr Masters in this, his one

---

[4] Masters (1869–1950), lawyer and poet, was among the writers discussed by the American poet Amy Lowell in her *Tendencies in Modern American Poetry* (New York: Macmillan, 1917), the topic of Shorter's preceding paragraphs.

successful book, to Mr Thomas Hardy. Mr Masters is careful to explain in the introduction to the *Spoon River Anthology*[5] that his verses appeared first in Reedy's *Mirror* for May, 1914, whereas Mr Hardy's *Satires of Circumstance* was published at the end of 1914; but Mr Masters must have been acquainted with the various poems in *Satires of Circumstance*, because these appeared first in *The Fortnightly Review* for 1911,[6] and also in American periodicals in that year, so that there cannot be the shadow of a doubt that Mr Masters was largely influenced by Mr Hardy's work. Yet by a curious irony of circumstance one critic actually suggested, in reviewing *Satires of Circumstance*, that the author was indebted to Mr Masters. I am the more surprised that Miss Lowell does not acknowledge this obvious indebtedness because I know that she is a great admirer of Mr Hardy, and actually paid him a visit in Dorchester in the summer of 1914 when she was motoring through England.[7]

[1918.04]

[?Appeal for Mrs Allhusen's Canteens?]

Dorothy Allhusen (1877–1965), the elder daughter of Lady St Helier, had known Hardy from her childhood, and in September 1918 she asked him to supply her with a letter she could use to solicit funds on behalf of the canteens for French soldiers she was operating in France. Having received through Florence Hardy (4 October 1918, Beinecke) Hardy's holograph manuscript of such an appeal, Allhusen supplemented it with a letterhead cut from an item of Max Gate correspondence, had some 300 facsimile reproductions made, and sent out an unknown number to friends and supporters. At a later date she presented Richard Purdy with Hardy's original MS and her sole remaining copy of the facsimile (both now Beinecke) and supplied him with the little additional information she could recall. Purdy, however, acknowledges (p. 209) the possibility that the appeal was 'in part the work of Mrs. Hardy', and reports (Notebooks, Beinecke) her as saying, shortly before her death, that Hardy had told her to write it herself by following his own practice of opening a volume of, say, Carlyle at random, reading a paragraph, and finding in it an initial idea. She did as he proposed, even to the choice of

---

[5] *Spoon River Anthology* (New York: Macmillan Company, 1915), p. vii.
[6] Eleven of the sardonic 'Satires of Circumstance' poems were first printed in the *Fortnightly Review*, NS 89 (April 1911), pp. [579]–83 (Purdy, pp. 164–5).   [7] See *LW*, pp. 420–1.

Carlyle, and wrote the appeal in its entirety, leaving him only the task of copying it out; any revisions he may have made would thus have been silently absorbed into the fair copy sent to Dorothy Allhusen. That copy—including the added Max Gate address—is transcribed below; ampersands have been expanded. Purdy, p. 209.

Max Gate Dorchester. October: 1918.

The sun as it shines on England falls indeed upon many a desolate home, upon shops and factories attenuated of their workers; but its rays still light up smiling valleys and fields. They strike upon no scene of desolation and destruction, no fair landscape laid utterly to waste. In France, how different!

At this moment, when the achievements of that wonderful country have filled our hearts with admiration, let us also consider how greatly she has suffered in comparison with our own land; and also how deep is our debt to France.

You are asked to give as a token of your grateful recognition of this debt—one which our people can never repay—a small sum to help the French 'poilus'[8] by affording them little comforts which they are unable to provide for themselves: such comforts as here we might be inclined to call necessities of life.

At Vertus, between Epernay and Chalons, in the Marne district, a canteen and rest-room for the French troops has been established by Mrs Henry Allhusen, who has already done much in France for the French wounded; and she is just starting another at Cire-les-Mello, near Senlis. At the canteen men are aided who are suffering from fatigue and other minor ailments sufficient to cause much discomfort, and even pain, but not bad enough for treatment at the hospitals. There is a great need for such canteens, and so far not a quarter of the number needed have been established. Coffee and bovril, biscuits and cigarettes, and other small luxuries, are provided for troops going to or returning from the front. Refugees, too, have been helped and given needful refreshment and clothing. No English man or woman whose heart is not of stone, and who has the power, can refuse help to these unfortunate people, driven from their houses and bereft of all they once had prized.

English soldiers have also been aided from time to time at this canteen; moreover the American combatant dying far from his home

---

[8] Literally, 'hairy ones'; during the First World War it was the popular term (cf. the British 'Tommy') for French soldiers serving in the ranks.

has found here in English helpers gentle and devoted hands to minister to his last wants, and kind-hearted English women to follow his coffin to its grave in French soil.

But the main object of this canteen, as also of the new one, is, as shown, to help and refresh the temporarily enfeebled French soldier. By thus doing surely the bond will be strengthened between the two countries, making for the brotherhood of nations, and universal peace.

Thomas Hardy.

[1918.05]

[Message to American Editors]

On 11 November 1918, Armistice Day, the editors among a group of American Trade Press Representatives then visiting London were being entertained at a dinner hosted by the newspaper proprietor Cecil Harmsworth (later Viscount Rothermere). Among the messages read out at the dinner was one from Hardy, reproduced below from the report in *The Times*, 13 November 1918, p. 5. Purdy, p. 320.

I much regret not being present. If I were I would speak to your guests in better words than my own by repeating what Edward said in *King Henry VI.*:—

> 'Now breathe we, Lords; good fortune bids us pause,
> And smooth the frowns of war.'[9]

[1918.06]

[Footnote to a Swinburne Letter]

Two letters from Swinburne that Hardy sent to Gosse 22 January 1915 (*CL* v. 77) were published, late in 1918, in *The Letters of Algernon Charles Swinburne*, edited by Edmund Gosse and Thomas James Wise, 2 vols.

---

[9] Shakespeare, *3 Henry VI*, II. vi. 31–2. The second line reads in full 'And smooth the frowns of war with peaceful looks'.

(London: William Heinemann, 1918), ii. 253–4, 265–6. Hardy may have been partly responsible for the footnotes on pp. 253 and 265, and is specifically acknowledged as the source of the footnote to p. 266, as below.

[Vol. 2, p. 266: Note on Swinburne's reference to The Dynasts, Part First, act 5, scene vii: 'I know the old story of "tapping the Admiral", but surely it was not Nelson, was it?']

I have always heard it related of Nelson.—T.H.[10]

[1918.07]

William Barnes

Hardy agreed in October 1916 (*CL* v. 181) to make and introduce a selection of William Barnes's poems for an added fifth volume of Thomas Humphry Ward's *The English Poets* (volumes 1–4 having been published in 1880), but warned that the introduction would inevitably 'not be much more than a paraphrase' of what he had said about Barnes on previous occasions. Six weeks later (*CL* v. 187) he sent Ward both the introduction and the texts of ten poems—the latter apparently in the form of tearsheets from his own selection of 1908 (1908.09)—but wartime publishing difficulties delayed correction of final proofs until October 1917 (*CL* v. 230) and actual publication until almost the end of 1918. The surviving five-page typescript of Hardy's introduction (David Holmes) carries corrections in his hand but also insertions in another hand (presumably Ward's) of additional biographical details that were incorporated into the text as printed in *The English Poets: Selections with Critical Introductions. . . . Volume V. Browning to Rupert Brooke*, edited by Thomas Humphry Ward (London: Macmillan, 1918), pp. 174–6. That text follows the typescript as edited by Ward, except in distinguishing typographically between the biographical and the critical portions of the introduction; the following reproduction of the published text eliminates that distinction, however, and omits (but footnotes) Ward's biographical insertions. Purdy, pp. 319–20.

[Born in 1801 at Rushay, near Pentridge, Dorset; educated at an endowed school at Sturminster-Newton; entered the office of Mr Dashwood, a solicitor of that townlet, in 1814 or 1815; left in 1818 for

---

[10] Cf. *CL* iii. 114.

the office of Mr T. Coombs, Dorchester. His first printed expression in verse was in *The Weekly Entertainer* in 1820. He took a school at Mere, Wiltshire, in 1823; married in 1827; opened a school at Dorchester in 1835; and in 1837 entered his name as a ten-years man at St John's College, Cambridge.[11] He gave up his school and was inducted rector of Winterborne Came in 1862, where he died October 7, 1886.[12]

Besides articles in the *Gentleman's Magazine*, 1831–1843, papers in the *Retrospective Review*, 1853–1854, and minor prose works, he published *Poems in the Dorset Dialect*, 1844; *Poems partly of Rural Life*, 1846; *Hwomely Rhymes* (a second collection of Dorset Poems), 1850;[13] *A Philological Grammar*, 1854; *A Grammar and Glossary of the Dorset Dialect*, 1863; *A Third Collection of Dorset Poems*, 1863; and *Poems of Rural Life in Common English*, 1868. An edition of the three series in one volume was brought out in 1879, and a selection by the present writer in 1908.]

The veil of a dialect, through which except in a few cases readers have to discern whatever of real poetry there may be in William Barnes, is disconcerting to many, and to some distasteful, chiefly, one thinks, for a superficial reason which has more to do with spelling than with the dialect itself. As long as the spelling of standard English is other than phonetic it is not obvious why that of the old Wessex language should be phonetic, except in a pronouncing dictionary. We have however to deal with Barnes's verse as he chose to write it, merely premising that his aim in the exact literation of Dorset words is not necessarily to exhibit humour and grotesqueness.

It often seemed strange to lovers of Barnes that he, a man of insight and reading, should have persisted year after year to sing in a tongue which, though a regular growth and not a provincial corruption, is indubitably fast perishing. He said that he could not help it. But he may have seen the unwisdom of such self-limitation—at those times, let us suppose, when he appeared to be under an uncontrollable impulse to express his own feelings, and to convey an ampler interpretation of life than his rustic vehicle would carry unenlarged, which resulted in his putting into the mouths of husbandmen compound epithets that certainly no user of the dialect ever concocted out of his own brain, and

---

[11] Following 'Cambridge.' Ward inserted: 'He was ordained in 1847.'

[12] Ward inserted at the end of the paragraph: 'His "Life" was published in the following year by his daughter, Mrs Baxter, writing under the name of "Leader Scott".' See 1887.02.

[13] Correctly, 1859.

subtle sentiments that would have astonished those husbandmen and their neighbours.

But though true dramatic artistry lies that way, the way of all who differentiate imaginative revelation from the blind transcripts of a reporter's note-book, it was probably from some misgivings on the score of permanence that now and then he would turn a lyric in 'common English', and once or twice brought out a little volume so written as an experiment. As usual, the prepossessions of his cocksure critics would not allow them to tolerate what they had not been accustomed to, a new idea, and the specimens were coldly received; which seems to have discouraged him. Yet in the opinion of the present writer the ordinary language which, as a schoolmaster, Barnes taught for nearly forty years, could soon have been moulded to verse as deftly as dialect by a man whose instinct it was to catch so readily the beat of hearts around him. I take as an example the lines (which I translate) on the husband who comes home from abroad to find his wife long dead:—

> The rose was dust that bound her brow,
>   Moth-eaten was her Sunday cape,
> Her frock was out of fashion now,
>   Her shoes were dried up out of shape—
> Those shoes that once had glittered black
> Along the upland's beaten track;[14]

and his frequent phrases like that of the autumn sun 'wandering wan', the 'wide-horned cows', the 'high-sunned' noons, the 'hoarse cascade', the 'hedgerow-bramble's swinging bow'.[15]

Barnes, in fact, surprising as it may seem to those who know him, and that but a little, as a user of dialect only, was an academic poet, akin to the school of Gray and Collins, rather than a spontaneous singer of rural songs in folk-language like Burns, or an extemporizer like the old balladists. His apparently simple unfoldings are as studied as the so-called simple Bible-narratives are studied; his rhymes and alliterations often cunningly schematic. The speech of his ploughmen and milkmaids in his *Eclogues*—his own adopted name for these pieces—is as sound in its syntax as that of the Tityrus and Meliboeus[16] of Virgil whom he had in

[14] Based on lines 5–10 of the last stanza of 'The Beäten Path'; lines 5–8 were quoted in TH's review of 1879 (1879.02).

[15] Quotations (mostly adapted into 'common English' by TH) from, respectively, 'The Maÿ-tree', 'Milkèn Time', 'Culver Dell and the Squire', 'Rural Nature', and 'Comèn Hwome'.

[16] Herdsmen in Virgil's *Eclogues*.

mind, and his characters have often been likened to the shepherds and goatherds in the idylls of Theocritus.

Recognition came with the publication of the first series of Dorset poems in 1844, though some reviewers were puzzled whether to criticize them on artistic or philological grounds; later volumes however were felt to be the poetry of profound art by Coventry Patmore, F. T. Palgrave, H. M. Moule,[17] and others. They saw that Barnes, behind his word-screen, had a quality of the great poets, a clear perception or instinct that human emotion is the primary stuff of poetry.

Repose and content mark nearly all of Barnes's verse; he shows little or none of the spirit of revolt which we find in Burns; nothing of the revolutionary politics of Béranger.[18] He held himself artistically aloof from the ugly side of things—or perhaps shunned it unconsciously; and we escape in his pictures the sordid miseries that are laid bare in Crabbe, often to the destruction of charm. But though he does not probe life so deeply as the other parson-poet I have named, he conserves the poetic essence more carefully, and his reach in his highest moments, as exampled by such a poignant lyric as 'The Wife a-lost', or by the emotional music of 'Woak Hill', or 'The Wind at the Door', has been matched by few singers below the best.

---

[17] Patmore wrote on Barnes on a number of occasions, beginning with the unsigned 'New Poems', *North British Review*, 31 (November 1859), pp. 339–52; the Palgrave reference is presumably to his review in the *National Review*, 8 (February 1887), pp. 818–39; TH's friend Horace Moule (see 1922.04) knew Barnes personally, invited him to speak at Marlborough College, and spoke in a letter of 22 January [1861?] (DCM) of reviewing a volume of Barnes's poems for the *Literary Gazette*.

[18] Burns and Béranger are both invoked in 1879.02 and again in 1886.02.

1919

[1919.01]

Foreword [to *A Book of Remembrance*]

Hardy's friend Alfred Pope (see 1912.02) was the patriarch of a large Dorset family whose active wartime record was memorialized in *A Book of Remembrance: Being a Short Summary of the Service and Sacrifice Rendered to the Empire during the Great War by One of the Many Patriotic Families of Wessex, the Popes of Wrackleford, Co. Dorset* (London: Privately Printed, 1919). Hardy agreed to write a Foreword and on 25 June 1918 (*CL* v. 270)—four and a half months before the war ended on 11 November 1918—he sent Pope the signed typescript that is still in the family's possession. Some revisions were evidently requested by Pope—even as Hardy made suggestions about the rest of the book (*CL* v. 287)—but since Hardy himself subsequently revised the Foreword and read it in proof, the following text, as published over his initials in *A Book of Remembrance*, pp. 5–6, in June 1919, can be accepted as effectively his; the more significant variations from the typescript are, however, recorded in footnotes. Purdy, p. 320.

The sturdy Dorset family of the Popes, a section of which has been grouped together for memorizing in the following volume, needs no apology for a modest appearance in a privately printed record based upon the varied achievements of one household, so to speak, in the present war—a household which has been for many years among my nearest neighbours.

Upon the family name it is not necessary to dilate. It has been known hereabouts—in Stalbridge, Marnhull, Corscombe, the Tollers and, later, Chilfrome—for[1] centuries; and it may be mentioned that when

---

[1] For 'Stalbridge . . . for' TH's typescript reads 'Stalbridge, Manston, Chilfrome, and elsewhere —for'.

John White went from Dorchester, England, to found Dorchester, Mass., U.S.A.,[2] he took with him some Dorchester Popes, whose descendants are now noteworthy people of Massachusetts.[3] That research might be able to trace consanguinity between the Dorset Popes and the poet Alexander has often been a conjecture of the present writer, based partly on the poet's interest in at least one corner of the county—Sherborne and its vicinity—of which, as is well known, he gives a long description in a letter to Miss Blount.[4]

The circumstances of the great conflict which, we may at least hope, is hastening to a close, differ so largely from those of the previous wars of this country, that it is impossible to infer how many, or even if any more than had already done so, of the eleven brethren[5] here marshalled would have deliberately chosen a military or naval career[6] in ordinary conditions. Yet[7] to read over their actions at this point of time conveys a fancy that they would all have fallen into line naturally:

> Though war nor no known quarrel were in question;
> . . . assembled and collected
> As were a war in expectation.[8]

However that may be, these chronicles, even when they become musty with age, may be interesting not only to descendants of the family but to others who are not of their blood or name. It often has happened that an account of what befell particular individuals in unusual circumstances has conveyed a more vivid picture of those circumstances than a comprehensive view of them has been able to raise.

September 1918.[9]

---

[2] John White (1575–1648), rector of Holy Trinity, Dorchester, known as the 'Patriarch of Dorchester'; a moderate puritan, he was largely responsible for the founding of the Dorchester colony in Massachusetts but never crossed the Atlantic himself.

[3] The passage 'and it may . . . Massachusetts' is not present in TH's typescript.

[4] *The Correspondence of Alexander Pope*, ed. George Sherburn, 5 vols. (Oxford: Clarendon Press, 1956), ii. 236–40. Pope is, however, a fairly common English surname and there seems to be no evidence to support TH's speculation.

[5] For 'if any . . . brethren' typescript reads 'if any, of the ten brethren'.

[6] For 'military or naval career' typescript reads 'military career'.

[7] For 'conditions. Yet' typescript reads 'conditions. Probably two or three at furthest might have done so. Yet'.

[8] Cf. Shakespeare, *Henry V*, ii. iv. 17, 19–20.   [9] TH's typescript is not dated.

'Message to the Aussies'

James Gibson's edition of *Thomas Hardy: Interviews and Recollections*, p. 118, includes an extract from an interview with Hardy that was first printed on the front page of the 14 March 1919 issue of *The Australian at Weymouth*, a paper for Australian troops stationed in the Weymouth area of south Dorset during and just after the First World War. The extract, however, stops short of the last two sentences of the interview's final paragraph, which is reproduced in its entirety below as constituting a specific message to the Australians as they prepared to depart. Though the interview is headed 'Thomas Hardy, the Wessex Novelist', it carries 'Message to the Aussies' as one of its subtitles. See also George Lanning, 'Through Australian Eyes: A Look at Life in Weymouth and Portland in 1918–19', *The Dorset Year Book for 1998*, pp. 47–52, esp. 52.

I have met a large number of Australians, and had the pleasure of spending two afternoons at the Australian Camp at Weymouth some time ago. Now that the Australians are going back home and will soon be leaving us, would you please tell them that I wish them a safe return and very good luck wherever they may go? I hope that very many of them will come back to the Old Country as visitors when things have smoothed down. We shall always be glad to see them, to welcome them and hold out the hand of not only friendship but kinship and fraternal greeting.

[1919.03]

[Association with *Clarté*]

In the summer of 1919 Hardy was invited (12 June, DCM) by the poet Georges Chennevière (1884–1929) to associate himself with 'Clarté'—a French left-wing pacifist movement (Ligue de Solidarité Intellectuelle pour le Triomphe de la Cause Internationale) named after a novel written by its leading figure, Henri Barbusse (1873–1935)—and with the journal, *Clarté*, it was about to launch. His reply, sent over his wife's name 15 June 1919 (draft, DCM), expressed approval of Clarté's ideas—he went so far as to write out an

English translation of the group's manifesto, sent by Barbusse himself on 19 July (DCM)—but regretted that increasing age prevented his taking 'any active part' in carrying them out. He seems not to have made any further response but was nevertheless identified in early issues of *Clarté* and elsewhere as a member of an international committee that also included H. G. Wells, Israel Zangwill, and Stefan Zweig. See Vladimir Brett, *Henri Barbusse: Sa marche vers la clarté, son mouvement Clarté* (Prague: Éditions de l'Académie Tchécoslovaque des Sciences, 1963), pp. 170, 176, 315.

[1919.04]

[Trade Unionism]

The *Shop Assistant* was the official organ of the National Amalgamated Union of Shop Assistants, Warehousemen and Clerks, and Hardy's message, published as below in its 'Special Textile Number' of 21 June 1919, p. 405, was one of a series of 'Messages to our Readers from Men of Distinction' that had been solicited in the hope of garnering expressions of support for the Union's campaign to organize workers in the textile industry. Purdy, p. 320.

I favour social re-adjustments rather than social subversions—remembering that the opposite of error is error still.

[1919.05]

[Unsigned Letter on the Plumage Trade]

H. J. Massingham (1888–1952), subsequently well known for his writings on the English countryside, was an active campaigner against the slaughter of exotic birds in order to obtain feathers for the decoration of women's hats. It was a cause with which Hardy also sympathized, but when, in July 1919, Massingham sought his support for a letter urging the Government to enact legislation against the 'plumage trade', he made his signature conditional on modifications to the wording of the document (see *CL* v. 317–18) that Massingham (21 July 1919, DCM) declared to be impossible of accommodation at so late a stage.

[1919.06]

'Mr. Gosse's 70th Birthday'

A report headed as above in *The Times*, 22 September 1919, p. 13, listed Hardy among the many signatories to the congratulatory address (written by the Marquess of Crewe) that was presented to Edmund Gosse, along with the promise of a bronze bust of himself, on the occasion of his seventieth birthday, 21 September 1919. Hardy had subscribed to the presentation on 15 May 1919 (*CL* v. 306) and referred to himself, in a personal letter to Gosse on 22 September (*CL* v. 324–5), as one of the 'conspirators against the repose of your 70th birthday'. He was not present when Gosse received the bust in November 1920, even though later included in Max Beerbohm's cartoon of the occasion: see Evan Charteris, *The Life and Letters of Sir Edmund Gosse* (London: William Heinemann, 1931), following p. 444.

[1919.07]

[On the *Canadian Bookman*]

It was a British journalist, Samuel Bensusan (1872–1958), who approached Hardy on behalf of the *Canadian Bookman* in May 1919 (DCM) and received in reply the letter now available—from Hardy's draft (DCM)—in *Collected Letters*, v. 305–6. And it was another British journalist, Sydney Walton (1882–1964), who made the text of that letter selectively public, as below, in the opening paragraphs of his article 'Two Great British Writers Speak to Canada', *Canadian Bookman* (October 1919), pp. 9–10—although in such a way as to create a false impression that the words being quoted had in fact been spoken by Hardy in the course of a face-to-face interview. The quotation in *Life and Work*, p. 422, evidently derives not from Walton's article but from Hardy's retained draft of the letter he actually sent.

[Mr Hardy] looked carefully through the second number of the *Canadian Bookman* and observed that the quarterly had made a promising beginning. He remarked that he was glad to see that the *Bookman* bestows a good proportion of articles upon poetry. 'This is as[10] it should be,' he remarked. 'Take care of the poetry and the prose will take care of

---

[10] Emended from the article's obviously erroneous 'at'.

itself. The articles are very suggestive. "Free Verse and the Parthenon,"[11] for instance, is particularly good, as is also that of Alfred Gordon on "What is Poetry?"[12] Such articles directly help real literature as distinct from commercial matters.'

From praise, Mr Hardy passed to criticism. 'Why', he asked, 'does the paper stultify its earlier articles by advertising "the best sellers"? Of all the marks of the unliterary journal this is the clearest.[13] If the *Canadian Bookman* were to take a new line, to advertise eulogistically the worst sellers, it might do something towards its object, as they are generally the best literature.' Mr Hardy added that he was compelled to say this, though he has occasionally been one among the guilty.

[1919.08]

[Speech at Opening of Children's Hospital]

> Hardy was one of a number of local dignitaries who attended, on 31 October 1919, the official opening of the Swanage War Memorial Children's Hospital, established by the Dorset branch of the Red Cross Society. Florence Hardy's sister Eva Dugdale had just taken up a nursing position at the hospital, but Hardy's participation in the ceremony had evidently been secured by Dorothy Hanbury of Kingston Maurward, county secretary of the Red Cross (see 1916.09). Writing to Sydney Cockerell, 2 November (Beinecke), Florence Hardy reported with some irritation that her husband had caught a cold as a result of his having 'to make a little speech of thanks to the Bishop, and also to stand with his hat off in a cold N.E. wind while the Bishop prayed'. Hardy also complained at the time (*CL* v. 338, 339) but later spoke of the weather as afflicting the 'overworked and worthy' Bishop of Salisbury (Frederick Edward Ridgeway) rather than himself (*LW*, p. 425). The report in the *Dorset County Chronicle*, 6 November 1919, p. 3, included the following third-person summary of Hardy's speech.

Mr Thomas Hardy said it afforded him great pleasure to second the vote. In going round the hospital one could not fail to be struck at the

---

[11] By Ramsay Traquair, *Canadian Bookman*, NS 1 (April 1919), pp. 23–6. Traquair was a professor of architecture at McGill University.

[12] 'What is Poetry?—A Synthesis of Modern Criticism', by Alfred Gordon, *Canadian Bookman*, NS 1 (April 1919), pp. 73–7. Gordon, trained in England as an engineer, published *Poems* (1916) and *Vimy Ridge and Other Poems* (1918).   [13] Cf. 1914.03.

enormous advance that had been made in hospitals since what he might call the first modern hospital was established in England. He referred to St Bartholomew's Hospital, familiarly called 'Bart's', which was established about 1540. In the matter of appliances he supposed that in those days they were considered good, and no doubt what they regarded as excellent modern appliances in the hospital that had been opened that day would be superseded some 25 years hence. The hospital was situated in the most healthy spot that could have been chosen, and as far as he could judge from his inspection of the interior it was most beautifully arranged.

[1919.09]

[Christmas Books]

The Christmas Number of the *Book Monthly*, December 1919, pp. 915–21, included a 'symposium', headed 'Old Yule Lamps and New', on the Christmas books the respondents had liked as children and the Christmas books they now liked as 'grown-ups'. Although Hardy had evidently declined to contribute, his name and the gist of his response were nevertheless incorporated, as below, into the article's headnote (p. 915).

Mr Thomas Hardy does not think there were any Christmas books when he was a child, eighty years ago.

[1919.10]

[Speech on Opening the Mellstock Club]

The speech that Hardy delivered on 2 December 1919, at the opening of the club room erected as a war memorial in Lower Bockhampton, seems not to have been published in his lifetime. The occasion was briefly mentioned in the *Dorset County Chronicle*, 11 December 1919, p. 6, but *Life and Work* notes in quoting the speech, pp. 427–9, that 'it was not reported in any newspaper'. What Hardy actually said in 1919 appears to be most accurately reflected in a lightly corrected two-page typescript in the Dorset County Museum:

headed 'Mr Thomas Hardys speech' in Hardy's own hand, it remains within an envelope addressed by him to his sister Katharine and postmarked 5 December 1919, just three days after the speech was delivered. That typescript is the source of the text below, significant *Life and Work* variants—generated on copy three, p. 562, of the preparatory typescript (DCM)—being recorded in footnotes.

I feel it an honour—and an honour of a very interesting kind—to have been asked by your President to open this Club as a memorial to the gallant men of the parish who fought in the last great war—a parish I know so well, and which is only about a mile from my own door.

It is, it seems, to be called 'The Mellstock Club'. I fancy I have heard that name of 'Mellstock' before. But we will let that pass.

Before I proceed to the formal function of starting the pendulum of the Club, so to speak, I may be allowed to say a word or two on the bygone times of this Parish and village, and the changes which led on to the present happy stage in the history of the place. There would be many things to interest us in the past of Bockhampton if we could only know them, but we know only a few.

It has had various owners. In the time of the Conqueror it belonged to a Norman Countess; later to a French Priory; and in the time of Queen Elizabeth to the Dean and Chapter of Exeter, who at the beginning of the last century sold it to Mr Morton Pitt.[14] What a lot[15] of scenes does this bare list of owners bring back!

At one time Bockhampton had a water-mill. Where was that mill, I wonder? It had a wood. Where was that wood?

However, to come to my own recollections. The village[16] contained several old Elizabethan houses, with mullioned windows and doors, of Ham-hill stone. They stood between General Balguy's[17] house and the withy bed. I remember seeing some of them pulled down,[18] but some were pulled down before I was born. To this attaches a story. Mr Pitt, by whose orders it was done, came to look on, and asked one of the men several questions as to why he was doing it in such and such a way.

---

[14] For 'Pitt. What' *LW* reads 'Pitt, a cousin of Pitt the Premier, who came, as we all know, of a Dorset family. What'. William Morton Pitt (1754–1836) inherited the Kingston Maurward estate in 1787 and purchased the hamlet of Bockhampton in 1803. TH's source here was evidently Hutchins's *Dorset* (see 1908.07), ii. 561.   [15] For 'lot' *LW* reads 'series'.

[16] For 'The village' *LW* reads 'From times immemorial the village'.

[17] Brig.-General John Henry Balguy (1859–1933), retired soldier, director of the Dorset Red Cross Society.   [18] For 'them pulled down' *LW* reads 'them in process of being pulled down'.

Mr Pitt was notorious for his shabby clothes, and the labourer, who did not know him, said at last, 'Look here old chap, don't you ask so many questions, and just go on! Anybody would think the house was yours!' Mr Pitt obeyed orders, and meekly went on, murmuring, 'Well, 'tis mine, after all!'

Then there were Poor-houses, I remember,—just at the corner turning down to the dairy. In[19] one of these lived an old man who was found one day rolling on the floor, with a lot of pence and half-pence scattered around him. They asked him what was the matter, and he said he had heard of people rolling in money, and he thought that for once in his life he would do it, to see what it was like.

Then there used to be dancing parties at Christmas and some weeks after. This kind of party was called a Jacob's Join, in which every guest contributed a certain sum to pay the expenses of the entertainment—it was mostly half-a-crown in this village. They were very lively parties I believe. The curious thing is that the man who used to give the house-room for the dances lived in a cottage which stood exactly where this Club house now stands—so that when you dance here you will be simply carrying on the traditions of the spot.

But though Bockhampton has had all these interesting features in the past it has never till now had a War Memorial—never had a Club room for social intercourse and reading. That had to wait till your kind-hearted friend and President, Mr Hanbury, and no less kind-hearted Mrs Hanbury,[20] came along, and in consultation with your valued friend Mr Cowley,[21] set it going; and here the thing is.

In conclusion I have now merely to say I declare the Mellstock Club and reading room to be open.

---

[19] For 'dairy. In' *LW* reads 'dairy. These were the homes of the parish paupers before workhouses were built. In'.

[20] Cecil Hanbury (1871–1937), the current owner of the Kingston Maurward estate; his wife, Effield Dorothy Hanbury (see 1916.09), was a connection by marriage of Hardy's first wife.

[21] The Revd Henry Guise Beatson Cowley, vicar of Stinsford 1911–33.

1920

[1920.01]

'To the Editor of *The Old Cambridge*'

> John North (1894–1973), a military historian, returned to Cambridge in 1919 after army service in the First World War. There he founded and edited *The Old Cambridge*, a short-lived weekly magazine in which the following letter appeared, as a separate item headed 'To the Editor of *The Old Cambridge*', on 28 February 1920, p. 5.

Max Gate, Dorchester. February 19th, 1920

Dear Sir,

In reply to your request I would, if I could, send you an arresting message or article, that would make all the people in Cambridge subscribe to your paper. But I have no more idea than a child unborn how to write any such message or article, having never learnt even the rudiments of journalism.

So that I can but baldly wish your adventure success.

Yours truly,
Th: Hardy

[1920.02]

[Palestine as a National Home for the Jewish People]

> Although *Life and Work*, p. 421, speaks of Hardy's signing, in February 1919, a declaration in support of '"the reconstitution of Palestine as a National Home for the Jewish People"', no such public statement has yet been

identified. Some fifteen months later, however, and in direct response to a request from the Central Office of the Zionist Organization (15 April 1920, DCM), Hardy did co-sign a message that urged the British government to accept the League of Nations' mandate for Palestine in furtherance of the Balfour Declaration's commitment to Palestine's 'being reconstituted the National Home of the Jewish People'. Publication of the message seems to have been rendered unnecessary by British acceptance of the Palestinian mandate on 26 April 1920, but similarities of phrasing suggest that Florence Hardy's undated transcription of it (DCM) may well have occasioned the reference in *Life and Work*.

[1920.03]

[To the Cambridge Vice-Chancellor]

Hardy received an honorary doctorate from Cambridge University in 1913 and was elected to an honorary fellowship at Magdalene College later that same year. It is not clear, however, that he would have expected publication, as below, in the *Cambridge Review*, 9 June 1920, p. 395, of a letter (*CL* vi. 21) thanking the current vice-chancellor, Peter Giles, Master of Emmanuel College, for good wishes on his eightieth birthday.

Max Gate, Dorchester. 3rd June, 1920.

My Dear Sir,

My sincere thanks for the kind message from yourself and the University on the occasion of my birthday.

I had hoped to be frequently in Cambridge after receiving the honour of the degree. But the war came and hindered travelling; and now I am almost past taking journeys.

Very truly yours,

Thomas Hardy.

[1920.04]

Prefatory Note [to *A Dull Day in London*]

Hardy knew Dora Sigerson (1866–1918), the Irish poet, not only through her marriage in 1896 to Clement King Shorter and but also through her friendship with his own second wife, begun when the latter was still Florence Dugdale and on the fringe of the circle centred upon the Irish writer Katharine Tynan (1861–1931). He had little enthusiasm for Sigerson's verse, and none for her views as an Irish nationalist, but evidently felt obliged to supply the 'Prefatory Note' reproduced below from pages 7–8 of her posthumously published collection of poems, *A Dull Day in London and Other Sketches* (London: Eveleigh Nash, 1920). Purdy speculates that Shorter was responsible for, and Hardy probably unaware of, the note's separate publication as a single-leaf private printing—independently set but without textual variants—with a claimed restriction to 'Twelve copies only' (Beinecke, Houghton). Purdy, pp. 210–11.

Many years ago when I chanced to be sitting by the sea in the company of the writer of the following charming sketches, I was struck by the evidences of her sympathy with the lower animal creation (as we are accustomed to call the less favoured of our fellow-mortals who are often nobler than ourselves). On opening, this week, these last pages of hers, the first thing I remark is the same sympathy further extended, till it seems to embrace all animate and inanimate nature.

Though not unfinished in execution, their brevity leads a reader to muse on what the author's achievements in the same kind on a larger scale might have been had she ever attempted such, for which her life could be supposed to have afforded her plenty of time. Whether if she had lived longer a constitutional impatience of sustained effort would always have prevented her building up her ideas on a broader artistic framework is a question that must now for ever remain unanswered.

[1920.05]

[?Inspired Article on *The Return of the Native* as Play?]

Hardy's friendship with Harold Hannyngton Child (1869–1945), poet, librettist, literary critic, and theatre reviewer for *The Times*, had practical advantages for both: Child always wrote generously about the Dorchester dramatizations of Hardy's novels and stories, and Hardy in turn provided material for Child's columns, and helped with the writing (*CL* v. 94–5)—and later the revision (see 1925.08)—of his *Thomas Hardy*, first published in 1916. With his 11 November 1920 letter to Child (*CL* vi. 45–6) about the forthcoming Dorchester production of *The Return of the Native* Hardy sent what he described as his wife's 'views' on the play, said that he agreed with them, and suggested that Child might perhaps 'make a preliminary paragraph of them'. That enclosure no longer accompanies the letter, but it is evident that the 'views' were in fact Hardy's own and that they very probably provided the basis and some at least of the actual wording for Child's unsigned article, ' "Return of the Native." Wessex Players' Version of a Hardy Novel', in *The Times*, 16 November 1920, p. 10. The relevant portion of that article is reproduced below, although if Child did indeed make direct use of the material Hardy supplied he could equally have done so in his follow-up articles in *The Times*, 18 November, p. 10, and 19 November, p. 8.

There will be great doings in Wessex tomorrow evening, when the Dorchester Debating and Dramatic Society resumes its operations with the production of yet another play adapted from a Hardy novel.

The novel selected on this occasion is *The Return of the Native*, and the stage version has been prepared by the honorary stage manager of the society, Alderman T. H. Tilley. Whatever may be the qualities of the play proper, there is one feature in it that is possibly unique on the stage—the introduction, into the second of the four acts, of the mumming play, *The Masque of Saint George*. In the novel, it will be remembered, the mumming play is ingeniously made use of (Book II., Chapter 5) by Eustacia as a means of seeing Clym, 'The Native', and the man who has attracted her. Their households are at variance, so that she cannot get into his presence in any other way than by the one she adopts, that of bribing the youth who plays the Turkish Knight in the mumming play to let her take his part. As the mummers' faces are covered, she can do this without being recognized; the plan is successful, and she turns herself into a knight of very picturesque appearance.

Thus the mumming is not an adventitious performance pitched into the middle of the play and suspending its action. On the contrary, the plot of the drama is directly advanced. The mummers are to go through their ancient masque precisely as it was done in Dorset and elsewhere in England 70 or 80 years ago, and great trouble has been taken by Mr Tilley to reproduce accurately the costumes, swords, staves, visors, helmets, and other accessories. There are seven characters in the mumming play, including Father Christmas, St George, who in turn slays the Turkish Knight and the Saracen, a Valiant Soldier, who is also killed, and a Doctor, who raises all three from the dead by fulfilling his boast—

> 'Yea more, this little bottle of alicampane
> Will raise dead men to walk the earth again.'[1]

The performance will take place at the Dorchester Corn Exchange, and will be repeated on Thursday.

[1920.06]

[On International Disarmament]

An editorial headed 'The Crime of Competitive Armament' in the New York *World*, 19 December 1920, p. 2E, launched a sustained campaign in support of contemporary American initiatives in the direction of international disarmament. Approached for a public endorsement by James M. Tuohy, London correspondent of the *World*, Hardy responded from Dorchester on 23 December with a telegram (draft on verso of Tuohy's telegram, DCM) that was then relayed by cable to New York, published as below on the front page of the *World*, 29 December 1920, under the heading 'Thomas Hardy Cables His Indorsement', and copied (as from the *World*) in *The Times*, 29 December, p. 8. The precise readings of Hardy's draft were restored, from the draft itself, in *Life and Work*, p. 441. A similar request from Tuohy was declined by Hardy in October 1921 (*CL* vi. 102). Purdy, p. 272.

London, Dec. 25.[2]

Yes, I approve of international disarmament on lines indicated by The World.[3]

Thomas Hardy.

---

[1] This couplet, absent from *The Return of the Native* itself, appears on p. 7 of *The Play of Saint George* (Cambridge: privately printed, April 1921), Florence Hardy's pamphlet containing TH's recension of a traditional Dorsetshire mumming play (Purdy, pp. 212–13).

[2] Presumably the address and date of the international cable; TH's original telegram was sent from Dorchester to the *World*'s London office on 23 December.

[3] TH's draft and (punctuation added) *LW* read 'Yes I approve of international disarmament on the lines indicated by the New York World.'

[Re-instatement of the Slade Professorship]

The Slade Professorship of Fine Art at Oxford, a non-permanent position, was suspended during the years of the First World War, and Hardy was asked, in a letter of 20 December 1920 (DCM), to sign a petition in support of its reinstatement. The letter is annotated in his hand '[Signed & returned registered.]'. The petition—never, perhaps, a fully public document—seems to have been effective, in that the decree of suspension was rescinded at a Convocation on 22 February 1921 (*The Times*, 23 February, p. 12).

1921

[1921.01]

'British'

Although Hardy declined, 8 December 1920 (*CL* vi. 50), an invitation to become a vice-president of the super-patriotic Royal Society of St George, the following slightly adapted version of the letter's final paragraph was promptly published, under the heading 'British', in the Society's organ, *The English Race*, no. 32 (January 1921), p. 5. Hardy's draft (DCM), used for the printing in *Collected Letters*, appears to be the only surviving pre-publication witness of this letter; there does exist (e.g. Maggs Bros cat. 1231, no. 86) a manuscript transcription of the original—as distinct from the published— form of the final paragraph, but the writing is clearly not Hardy's.

Congratulate the members of your Society upon[1] their wise insistence on the word 'English' as the name of this country's people, and in not giving way to a few shortsighted clamourers for the vague, unhistoric, and pinchbeck title of 'British', by which they would fain see it supplanted.

[1921.02]

'Proposed University for Wessex'

The Revd Albert A. Cock (1883–1953), Professor of Education and Philo-sophy at University College, Southampton, was a strong proponent of the proposed transformation of the College from a satellite of the University

---

[1] For 'Congratulate . . . upon' TH's draft reads 'All the same I may be allowed to congratulate its members upon'.

of London to a self-governing University of Wessex. On 12 January 1921 (DCM) he sent Hardy details of the scheme—which also envisaged the creation of a Thomas Hardy Chair of English Literature—and asked for an expression of support that could be reported to a public meeting on the issue to be held in Winchester on 18 January. The following extracts from Hardy's reply of 14 January (*CL* vi. 62–3) were quoted at the meeting and in the report of the occasion, headed 'Proposed University for Wessex', in the *Hampshire Observer*, 22 January 1921, p. 9. On 31 October 1921 (draft to C. J. G. Montefiore, DCM) Hardy agreed to be a member of the Honorary Appeal Committee of the existing institution. Despite his advocacy, subsequently renewed (see 1925.06), it was as the University of Southampton that the College was eventually granted its charter in 1962.

Max Gate, Dorchester. 14th January, 1921.

My Dear Sir,

I have read with much interest the outline you send of the project which would be carried out in establishing a University for this part of England. . . . That the name of the University should be 'Wessex' strikes me as being almost a necessity, no other short and easy name existing, so far as I see, that would denote a sphere of influence roughly conterminous with that of the ancient kingdom of the same title. . . . From this letter you will be able to inform all whom it may concern that I commend the work, and hope that all good fortune and success may attend it.

Yours very truly,
Thomas Hardy.

[1921.03]

Introductory Note [to *Wessex Worthies*]

Joshua James Foster (1847–1923), art historian and antiquary, was the son of a Dorchester bookseller and remembered Hardy as an older boy who used to come into his father's shop at the top of South Street. The connection was not actively kept up—Florence Hardy later recalled that her husband 'was always a little bored' by Foster (*Letters EFH*, p. 346)—but in 1917 Hardy did write the following 'Introductory Note' for Foster's biographical compendium *Wessex Worthies (Dorset)* (London: Dickinsons, 1920), p. [ix]. Purdy, pp. 320–1, gives publication date as February 1921.

Wessex—or at any rate the Dorset division of it—has not been regarded as a part of England in any way remarkable for the energy and resourcefulness of its natives. They have been supposed to pay for their advantages in point of climatic mildness, length of winter days, and nearness to the ports of fair France, by a lack of the driving power which is believed to be inherent in the folk of the northern latitudes of this island.

It is a question on which I cannot pronounce an opinion, but I venture to say that in the arts and sciences which soften manners and tend to make life tolerable the people of south-western England have certainly not been behind those of other counties.

The author of this book, who is himself Wessex born of a far-dating Wessex family, has devoted many years to the subject matter of its pages, and has had unique opportunities for his study[2]—in especial for the discovery and exhumation of the portraits of personages which were difficult of access, and in many cases supposed not to exist at all. His painstaking in this respect has surprised me, and has brought to light many curious details. These shadows of people of importance in their day[3] remind me of a remark of Leslie Stephen's when planning the *Dictionary of Biography*; that he was making it his object to get hold of the personal appearance of his characters whenever he could do so, holding that a few words on the look of a man as he walked and talked, so far as it could be gathered from portraits and traditions, was worth a page of conjecture on his qualities. There is also a passage in Carlyle to the same effect in which he says 'In all my poor historical investigations it has been and always is, one of the most primary wants to procure a bodily likeness of the personage enquired after—a good portrait if such exists; failing that, even an indifferent if sincere one. In short, any representation made by a faithful creature of that face and figure which he saw with his eyes, and which I can never see with mine, is now valuable to me, and much better than none at all.'[4]

Th: Hardy[5]

---

[2] When returning proof, 23 September 1920, TH told Foster, 'If you object to the word "hobby" you can insert "study"' (*CL* vi. 40).

[3] Cf. the title of Robert Browning's 1887 volume, *Parleyings with Certain People of Importance in their Day*.

[4] From Carlyle's essay, 'Project of a National Exhibition of Scottish Portraits' (1854), collected in *Critical and Miscellaneous Essays*, 3 vols. (London: Chapman and Hall, 1894), iii. 517. The quotation was evidently located and inserted by Foster at TH's suggestion: see *CL* v. 229–30.

[5] Hardy's signature is reproduced in facsimile.

[1921.04]

'A League of Thinkers'

In an article in the *New World* magazine, May 1921, pp. [500]–2, Léon Tolstoy, Jr., son of the novelist, proposed the formation of an international League of Thinkers that could provide the post-war world with the intellectual and moral basis for 'a real Society of Nations'. When the journalist Hamilton Fyfe wrote, 6 June 1921 (DCM), to seek public support for Tolstoy's initiative, Hardy enclosed with his reply (*CL* vii. 162, where the enclosure is wrongly reported as absent) a separate typescript (Eton) of the message subsequently published as follows, under the editorial heading 'A League of Thinkers: Some Replies to M. Tolstoy's Invitation', in the *New World*, 5 (July 1921), p. [109]. Purdy, p. 321.

I am much struck with the idea of a 'League of Thinkers'—which gives a distinctive name to what almost everybody must have felt during the late and present troublous years. Though I have not as yet had time to consider closely the ways and means of promoting it, or how the Thinkers are to get themselves listened to by the Doers, think they never so wisely,[6] I believe there are ways, and that it is only in those ways salvation lies, if there can be any salvation at all for a world that has got itself into such a deplorable welter, which seems to threaten a new Dark Age, to last may be for centuries before 'the golden years return'.[7]

[1921.05]

[Speech Opening Dorchester Hospital Fête]

The Dorset County Hospital, situated in Dorchester, was one of the local causes in which Florence Hardy was actively interested, and it was doubtless because of her involvement that Hardy accepted the invitation to 'open' the fund-raising fête held in the Dorchester Borough Gardens on 20 July 1921.

---

[6] The words 'think they never so wisely' evidently added in proof; they are absent from TH's typescript and present in his holograph draft (DCM) only as a late insertion. Initial capitals on 'Thinkers' and 'Doers' also added in proof.

[7] Shelley, *Hellas*, line 1061. The reference to 'a new Dark Age' was repeated in TH's 'Apology' in *Late Lyrics and Earlier* (1922).

The *Dorset County Chronicle*, 21 July 1921, p. 5, reported his speech, as below, in the first person, noting that he spoke 'in a clear and resonant voice'.

After Lord Ellenborough's[8] interesting and conclusive speech you will not expect me to say more than a few general words, my function this afternoon being merely to start the sale. I don't know why I should have been asked to do this—unless it be for the fact—two facts—connected with the hospital. That I can, of the very few people left in Dorchester, almost remember the original building of it—and that I knew the architect personally, the late Mr Benjamin Ferrey.[9] However, to come to the bazaar itself. I can assure you, ladies and gentlemen, that the objects gathered here represent a great deal of work, and thought, and money. I should also add, generous good will; and I do hope that you will be so kind as to respond, and show the promoters that they have not laboured in vain. (*Hear, hear.*)

Much may be said about bazaars—for and against. Some people say 'Pay down your donation and have done with it.' I fear I have occasionally spoken against them myself; but it is never too late to mend. In their favour there is this consideration, that what is superfluous in one house may be a useful article in another. And sometimes a person makes a thing, knowing it to be of great utility, and yet is not able to use it him or herself. This is a word to the wise. But you will be anxious to get to business. It therefore only remains for me to declare that the bazaar in aid of the County Hospital is now open. (*Loud applause.*)

[1921.06]

[Support for 'Magna Charta Day']

In August 1921 Hardy drafted and presumably sent the following message (draft, DCM) to J. W. Hamilton, of St Paul, Minnesota, the national secretary of an American-based movement for the annual observance of a 'Magna Charta Day' that would serve both to commemorate the signing of the charter in June 1215 and strengthen the solidarity of the English-speaking

---

[8] Cecil Henry Law, 6th Baron Ellenborough, was a retired professional soldier who lived in Dorchester and extended his patronage to many local charities.

[9] Work on the hospital was begun in 1839. Its designer, Benjamin Ferrey (see 1910.09, n. 32), executed several architectural commissions in the Dorchester area.

peoples. The movement's high point seems to have been the well-attended service held in the Cathedral of St John the Divine, New York, on 18 June 1922: *New York Times*, 19 June, p. 30; *The Times*, 20 June, p. 9. No public invocation of Hardy's name in this context has as yet been discovered.

August 27. 1921

Dear Mr Hamilton:

The scheme for emphasizing the essential unity of the English speaking nations by holding annually a 'Magna Charta'[10] day has a hopeful look, and I believe it may mature to a vast enthusiasm of acceptance.

Yours very truly

T——H——[11]

[1921.07]

'Mr. Frederic Harrison's 90th Birthday'

Hardy had known Frederic Harrison (1831–1923), the leading British positivist, at least since 1885 (*CL* i. 133–4), and always respected his work and ideas. Hardy was not himself a positivist, however, and when asked to sign an address on the occasion of Harrison's ninetieth birthday, he responded 'with great pleasure' but on the understanding that the other signatories would not be 'limited to one political party or denomination' (*CL* vi. 102). The address—headed ' "A Life Nobly Lived." Mr. Frederic Harrison's 90th Birthday.'—was published in *The Times*, 18 October 1921, p. 13.

[1921.08]

[?Inspired Letter on the Grey Squirrel?]

Florence Hardy was well accustomed to writing letters on her husband's behalf, and although the following letter, headed 'The English Squirrel', was

---

[10] TH, replying to Hamilton's letter of 10 August 1921 (DCM), adopted his American version of what in the UK would be called 'Magna Carta'.

[11] TH would have expected this draft to be typed, then returned to him for signature.

published over her name in *The Times*, 16 December 1921, p. 8, some aspects of its phrasing (e.g. the penultimate sentence) strongly suggest that Hardy may have had some part in its composition. Hardy mentioned the letter when writing to Florence Henniker on 19 December (*CL* vi. 110).

Max Gate, Dorchester, Dec. 13.

Sir,

Your interesting article on the foreign grey squirrel and its gradual acclimatization,[12] added to what I have learnt from other quarters, and another person's experiences,[13] of the lessening numbers of the native red squirrel in England, seems to show that the future squirrel of this country must be a choice between the latter, which has great beauty, and lives on hazel nuts, acorns, beech-mast, seeds, &c., or the former, which kills the red squirrel and by robbing wild birds' nests of their eggs may exterminate not only its rival, but our singing and other birds.

It might be possible at this date to exterminate the grey squirrel, and let the other be free to thrive as formerly. In a few years, when the grey breed has increased in large numbers, it will be too late. Even now, in plantations where 20 years ago the English squirrel could be seen leaping about in threes and fours on one tree, there is not one. Perhaps some correspondent of *The Times*, well informed on the whole matter, which I am not, could enlighten us.[14]

Your obedient servant,

Florence Hardy.

[1921.09]

'Peace and Goodwill'

Invited by telegram on 23 December 1921 (DCM) to contribute to *The Times* a Christmas message on the prospects for world peace, Hardy responded,

[12] 'Grey Squirrels in the London Parks. American Visitors Growing Acclimatised', *The Times*, 13 December 1921, p. 7.   [13] TH is evidently meant.

[14] Several letters did subsequently appear and *The Times* devoted a leading article to the subject in its issue of 20 December, p. 11. The grey squirrel has continued to increase its numbers and expand its territory, and the red squirrel now (AD 2000) survives in only a few British locations, typically self-contained habitats such as Brownsea Island in Poole Harbour.

also by telegram (pencil draft, DCM), with the following sentence, which was duly published, together with other such messages and under the above heading, in *The Times*, 24 December 1921, p. 11. The wording of the printed text is identical with that of Hardy's draft. Purdy, p. 321.

Though my faith in the bettering of nations was shattered by the brutal unreason of the Continental instigators of the war, the omens now seem favourable.[15]

---

[15] TH's optimism evidently reflected the promising developments being reported from the international disarmament conference then in progress in Washington.

1922

[1922.01]

[Tolstoy's Works]

Aylmer Maude (1858–1938), friend, disciple, and translator of Tolstoy, wrote to Hardy 17 March 1922 (DCM) to seek his signature to an appeal, written by George Bernard Shaw, for public support of the projected Oxford University Press multi-volume edition of Tolstoy's works in English translation—Tolstoy's waiving of translation rights having apparently resulted in the market's becoming flooded with cheap but often inadequate translations of his more popular titles. Hardy was sympathetic but—as he told Maude on 19 March (draft, DCM)—knew too little of the situation to endorse Shaw's letter in its entirety. Instead he sent, through Maude, a brief supplement to Shaw's letter that appeared with it, under the heading 'Tolstoy's Works', in *The Times*, 29 April 1922, p. 17, in the same day's *Daily Telegraph*, p. 8, and *Manchester Guardian*, p. 6, and elsewhere. Letter and supplement reappeared together in the undated eight-page brochure *Concerning the Proposed Centenary Edition of Tolstoy's Works* described in Dan H. Laurence, *Bernard Shaw: A Bibliography*, 2 vols. (Oxford: Clarendon Press, 1983), i. 160–1. The wording of the surviving draft in Hardy's hand (DCM) is identical with that of *The Times* as reproduced below. Purdy, p. 321.

Although I have no first-hand knowledge of the details mentioned in Mr Bernard Shaw's letter on translations of Tolstoy, I agree with the opinion that a good rendering of his works into English—so far as that is possible—should be made practicable by the concentration of effort on one production; and I believe that Mr Aylmer Maude's competence for the task is special and trustworthy.

[1922.02]

[On Slaughterhouse Reform]

Appealed to (3 July 1922, DCM) by the Duchess of Hamilton and Brandon (1878–1951), an active proponent of slaughterhouse reform (see e.g. *The Times*, 17 July 1922, p. 8, and 16 August 1922, p. 11), Hardy sent her a letter of support that was 'received', hence presumably read out, at a Westminster public meeting on behalf of the cause that she organized and chaired on 7 July 1922 (*Daily Telegraph*, 8 July 1922, p. 7). The draft survives (DCM) from which the letter sent to the Duchess would have been typed, and in the absence of that letter and of any known printed form of the message the draft must serve (cf. *CL* vi. 144) as the basis for the text below. See also Hardy's letter to the Duchess of 26 April 1925 (*CL* vi. 323).

July 5. 1922

Dear Duchess of Hamilton:

I am unfortunately unable to be present at the meeting, but I can say that slaughterhouse reform has my hearty support. A quick exit, with the minimum of suffering (mental and physical) is a right to which every victim is entitled, and if skilfully ensured may be less painful than the animal's natural death from age or infirmity—which is the only justification for killing such fellow-creatures at all. I fear that what among other things stands in the way in respect of many animals, such as pigs, is the belief that they must 'die slow' to produce a 'well-blooded' carcase—which of course really impoverishes the meat. I should welcome legislation that enforced humane killing.

Believe me

Sincerely yours

Thomas Hardy.

[1922.03]

[Negative Response to *Chapbook* Questionnaire]

Asked by Harold Monro (1879–1932) of the Poetry Bookshop to join other writers in answering three questions about the role and importance of poetry in the contemporary world, Hardy declined the invitation in the polite but firm letter of 16 June 1922 that is included in *Collected Letters*, vi. 137–8. No mention of his name accordingly appeared in Monro's article, 'Three Questions regarding the Necessity, the Function, and the Form of Poetry', published in *The Chapbook*, no. 27 (July 1922), pp. 3–5, nor can the library of King's College, Cambridge, find any trace of the copy of Monro's questionnaire with answers 'mostly in Hardy's hand' listed in the *Index* (HrT 1376) as accompanying the original of Hardy's 16 June letter.

[1922.04]

[Horace Moule]

On 13 June 1922 (*CL* vi. 137) Hardy sent John Collings Squire (1884–1958), editor of the *London Mercury*, a transcription of Horace Moule's 'Ave Caesar'—originally published in *Once a Week*, 6 September 1862, p. 294—for inclusion in the magazine's 'Reprints' series, dedicated to the resurrection of forgotten poems. He also supplied the following brief commentary on the poem and on Moule himself to accompany the poem's publication, under the heading 'Reprints—V', in the *London Mercury*, 6 (October 1922), pp. 631–2, although, as Purdy notes, Squire did not print the words Hardy added at the end of his transcription: 'It is hoped that this may be printed in any new edition of the Oxford Book of English Verse. T. H.' See *CL* vi. 160 and 1883.05, n. 51. Purdy, p. 321.

This fine poem was originally published in *Once a Week* in the summer of 1862, having been written after a short visit to the International Exhibition[1] of that year, in which was hung a picture by Gérôme of the interior of the Coliseum during the Empire.[2] The poem has never been reprinted.

The author of the verses was born at Fordington Vicarage, Dorchester, in 1832, died unmarried at Queen's[3] College, Cambridge, 1873, and

---

[1] Hardy accompanied Moule on that visit. The Exhibition, a successor to the Great Exhibition of 1851, was held mainly on the site now occupied by the Natural History Museum.

[2] Jean Léon Gérôme (1824–1904), French painter, especially of historical subjects. Moule's own note to the poem's original *Once a Week* printing reads: 'See the painting by Gérôme, in the International Exhibition, Foreign Gallery, No. 122. It was the custom, during the times of the Empire, for each successive troop of gladiators, before beginning their conflict, to advance to the Imperial box when the Emperor was present, and to salute him with the words, "Ave, Caesar Imperator; morituri te salutant." '   [3] Correctly, 'Queens' '.

was buried at Fordington. He was Hulsean prizeman at the University,[4] an accomplished Greek scholar and musician, and had early showed every promise of becoming a distinguished English poet. But the fates said otherwise. As a prose writer he was for many years on the staff of the old *Literary Gazette*, and on that of the *Saturday Review* in the eighteen-sixties under Cook and Harwood as editors.[5] He was also an occasional reviewer in the Quarterlies of that date.

[1922.05]

[Notes on Professor Chew's Book]

Samuel Claggett Chew (1888–1960) was a professor of English at Bryn Mawr College, near Philadelphia, and his *Thomas Hardy: Poet and Novelist* originally appeared in 1921 in the modest format of the 'Bryn Mawr Notes and Monographs' series published in New York by Longmans, Green. The Max Gate copy (DCM) of that first edition—apparently received prior to the visit that Chew and his wife paid to Max Gate in the summer of 1922—bears numerous marginal annotations in Hardy's hand, and these evidently served as the basis for the more systematic notes, typed up by Florence Hardy (top copy, Adams; carbon, DCM), that were mailed to Chew on 17 September 1922 (*CL* vi. 153–7) and subsequently incorporated, almost verbatim, into the more handsomely produced second edition of his book published in New York by Alfred A. Knopf in 1928.

[1922.06]

[Alderman J. C. Webber's 80th Birthday]

John Clark Webber (1842–1924) spent most of his adult life in Bournemouth, and served as its mayor in 1889–90, but he was born in Dorchester and had been one of Hardy's fellow-pupils at the British School in

---

[4] Moule won the Hulsean Prize at Cambridge in 1858 with his dissertation, *Christian Oratory; an Inquiry into its History during the First Five Centuries* (Cambridge: Macmillan, 1859).

[5] John Douglas Cook (1808?–68), edited the *Saturday Review* 1855–68 and was succeeded (1868–83) by his subeditor, Philip Harwood (1809–87).

Greyhound Yard. In recognition of that old association Hardy sent the following letter to be read out at a dinner in honour of Webber's eightieth birthday given at the Junction Hotel, Dorchester, on 10 October 1922. The text below is that of the letter's inclusion in the report headed 'Alderman J. C. Webber's 80th Birthday' in the *Dorset County Chronicle*, 12 October 1922, p. 5; the version published under the heading 'Mr. Thomas Hardy and an Old Schoolfellow' in *The Times* of 12 October, p. 15, omits the address, date, valediction, and signature and spells out the numerals.

Max Gate, Dorchester, Oct. 10th, 1922.

Dear Mr Webber,

I am informed that your 80th birthday is to be celebrated by a few friends this evening. I have a clear recollection of you as a small boy at school some 70 years ago, and though I have only, I fear, seen you once or twice during the long interval since then, I write to congratulate you on this anniversary, and on your marked success in business and municipal functions, and to express my sincere wish that you may live many more years to enjoy the fruits of your steadfastness.

Very truly yours,
Thomas Hardy.

[1922.07]

[Testimonial to Arts League of Service]

The *Dorset County Chronicle*, 19 May 1921, p. 2, reported that Hardy and his wife had attended on 12 May a Dorchester performance by a touring company of actors (Hermione Baddeley among them) sent out by the Arts League of Service, an organization dedicated 'to bring[ing] the arts into everyday life'. Hardy clearly enjoyed the occasion (see *CL* vi. 114) and formally expressed his approval in the following letter, published under his name in the 'Appreciations' section of *The Arts League of Service Annual 1921–1922* (London: Arts League of Service, [1922]), p. 14. In April 1923 he attended another Dorchester performance given by the League and was reported as having 'quite spontaneously' left his seat to congratulate the organizers (*Dorset Daily Echo*, 26 April 1923, pp. [1], [3]).

Max Gate, Dorchester, Dorset. May 17, 1921.

I have seen a performance by the theatrical company who are travelling under the auspices of the Arts League of Service and was quite surprised by its freshness and general merit, the absence of the lumber of the ordinary theatre being anything but a drawback.[6] The scheme of bringing dramatic art to the doors of the people seems to me to be deserving of the warmest support.

[1922.08]

Robert Louis Stevenson

Rosaline Masson (d. 1949), daughter of the Scottish scholar David Masson and herself a prolific author, wrote to Hardy 12 April 1922 (DCM) to invite his participation in a planned volume of first-hand recollections of Robert Louis Stevenson. Though Hardy's brief contribution was initially sent to the wrong person (*CL* vii. 163), it duly appeared, beneath the authorial heading 'Robert Louis Stevenson', in *I Can Remember Robert Louis Stevenson*, edited by Rosaline Masson (Edinburgh: W. & R. Chambers, 1922), pp. 214–16. Hardy wrote to acknowledge receipt of his copy (DCM) on 10 November 1922 (*CL* vi. 165–6). The text as printed, and as reproduced below, shows no significant differences from either the pencil draft in the Dorset County Museum or the lightly revised typescript in the National Library of Scotland. Purdy, p. 321.

The memories I have of Louis Stevenson are very meagre, as I saw him but a few times. I met him once—possibly on the first occasion—at Mr (now Sir) Sidney Colvin's house at the British Museum.[7] There were no other guests, and I can recall no particulars of the meeting further than that he said he liked wandering about the precincts of the Museum. A more distinct image of him accompanies my recollections of the first and last visit he paid me at Dorchester, in August, 1885. He came out to my house unexpectedly from the King's Arms Hotel in the town, where

---

[6] For TH's earlier objections to excessive theatrical scenery, see 1889.05 and 1892.13.

[7] Sidney Colvin (1845–1927), art and book critic, had an apartment at the British Museum by virtue of his position as Keeper of Prints and Drawings; he was knighted in 1911. This meeting with Stevenson, in June 1886, was in fact subsequent to Stevenson's visit to TH in Dorchester: see *LW*, p. 187.

he was staying for a day or two with Mrs Stevenson, her son, and a lady who was Louis's cousin.[8] He said that they were on their way to Dartmoor, the air of which he had been told would benefit him. He appeared in a velveteen jacket, with one hand in a sling. I asked him why he wore the sling, as there seemed nothing the matter with his hand: his answer (I am almost certain) was that he had been advised to do it to lessen the effort of his heart in its beats. He particularly wanted to see the room I wrote in, but as I had come into the house quite recently I had not settled into any definite writing-place, and could only show him a temporary corner I used. My wife and I went the next day to call on them at the hotel just before they left, where we bade them good-bye, expecting next to hear of them from Dartmoor. To our great surprise and regret a letter from Mrs Stevenson arrived about three weeks later, dated from an hotel in Exeter, and informing us that Louis had been taken ill on reaching that city, and could get no further; and that they were coming back to Bournemouth immediately he was well enough to travel.[9]

From this point my mind is a blank, excepting as to one fact—that shortly after the publication of *The Mayor of Casterbridge* in the May of the following year, he wrote to ask if I would permit him to dramatise it, as he had read the story, and thought Henchard 'a great fellow', adding that he himself was keeping unusually well. I wrote back my ready permission; and there the matter ended.[10] I heard no more about the play; and I think I may say that to my vision he dropped into utter darkness from that date: I recall no further sight of or communication from him, though I used to hear of him in a roundabout way from friends of his and mine. I should add that some years later I read an interview with him that had been published in the newspapers, in which he stated that he disapproved of the morals of *Tess of the d'Urbervilles*, which had appeared in the interim, and probably had led to his silence.[11]

[8] Katharine de Mattos, the sister of Robert ('Bob') Alan Mowbray Stevenson.
[9] See *LW*, p. 181, and *Biography*, pp. 270–1.   [10] See *LW*, p. 186.
[11] See 1923.04 and *LW*, pp. 259–60.

[1922.09]

[Message for Fédération Interalliée des Anciens Combattants]

Hardy responded with his usual promptitude to a request of 23 November 1922 (DCM) from the Paris-based Fédération Interalliée des Anciens Combattants—an umbrella organization for the veterans' associations of the wartime Allied Powers—that he supply an 'autographed dedication' for inclusion in 'an Album that is about to be published in all Allied Countries in order to perpetuate the heroism of the Allied Soldiers'. It is not clear that the Album ever appeared—in Britain it seems to have been superseded by the *British Legion Album* of 1924, to which Hardy also contributed (see 1924.03)—but Hardy's intended message is here transcribed from his draft, dated 26 November 1922, in the Dorset County Museum.

As warriors who have done gloriously they silently bid us to remember the chief thing: That the true glory of battle is, in the words of an old writer, 'to break battle out of the earth'.[12]

---

[12] TH's draft adds, within square brackets, 'the quotation is from Hosea II. 18.' In the Authorized Version the passage in fact reads 'I will break the bow and the sword and the battle out of the earth, and will make them to lie down safely'.

[1923.01]

Dorchester Dramatic Society

Reproduced below is Hardy's draft (DCM) of the statement, headed 'Dorchester Dramatic Society. Conditions of any other performance', that he issued to the amateur actors of the Dorchester Debating and Dramatic Society, who had for some years been performing dramatizations of his novels and short stories. It is not known whether the statement was duplicated for distribution to the Hardy Players (as they were now calling themselves) or delivered to them orally by the producer, T. H. Tilley (see 1916.04). Nor is the draft dated, although it seems clearly later than the November 1922 staging of *A Desperate Remedy*—see Keith Wilson's fully contextualized printing of the document in *Thomas Hardy on Stage*, p. 119—and probably belongs to the early months of 1923.

—That the novel selected for dramatization shall be approved by Mr Hardy.
—That the words 'New Wessex Play'—or 'New Tilley Play'—or 'New Play from a Wessex Novel'—are used instead of 'New Hardy Play' in all announcements and programmes (the latter having been misunderstood)
—That every programme contains this paragraph; 'The audience are respectfully asked to understand that Mr Hardy is not responsible for the choice, writing, or production of this play, beyond assenting to the Society's wish to undertake it.'
—That in view of Mr Hardy's age, he will not be expected to attend rehearsals, or a performance if too trying.
—The company to refuse to give any personal information whatever about Mr Hardy to reporters, etc., either in Dorchester or in London, and on whether he has attended or been interested.

[1923.02]

[Message to the PEN Club]

Hardy accepted Honorary Membership of the newly established PEN (Poets, Playwrights, Editors, Essayists, Novelists) Club in 1921 on the understanding that he would be unable to participate in its activities (*CL* vi. 107). He absented himself, accordingly, from the Club's first annual dinner on 2 May 1923, but sent to John Galsworthy (see 1909.07), as president, a letter (*CL* vi. 192) that Galsworthy endeavoured to convert into a message for oral delivery by isolating, on the MS, the extracts reproduced as the first item below. Following the event, however, he reported to Hardy (6 May 1923, DCM) that he had in fact read out—to 'acclamation'—only the statement about the 'exchange of international thought'. The second item below, following the line of asterisks, is the part of the same letter that Hardy himself chose to include, unaltered, in *Life and Work*, pp. 452–3.

I should have liked to meet the delegates of various nationalities who may be coming to the dinner. The exchange of international thought is the only possible salvation for the world. . . . I hope you will have a pleasant time.

*   *   *   *   *

The exchange of international thought is the only possible salvation for the world: and though I was decidedly premature when I wrote at the beginning of the South African War that I hoped to see patriotism not confined to realms, but circling the earth,[1] I still maintain that such sentiments ought to prevail.

Whether they will do so before the year 10,000 is of course what sceptics may doubt.

---

[1] TH's reference is to the last two lines of his poem 'Departure', dated October 1899 (*CPW* i. 117).

[1923.03]

'Tanks at Lulworth Cove'

When Herbert Weld-Blundell, owner of Lulworth Castle, wrote to Hardy on 10 May 1923 (DCM) about the Army's intention to retain in perpetuity the wartime firing range for tanks it had established on the Dorset coast near Lulworth Cove and Arish Mell, Hardy seems simply to have recommended that the matter be taken up with the local Member of Parliament and the National Trust. But an active protest movement—described in Patrick Wright, *The Village that Died for England: The Strange Story of Tyneham* (London: Jonathan Cape, 1995)—rapidly developed, and on 2 August 1923 J. L. Garvin, editor of the *Observer*, sent Hardy a pre-paid telegram (DCM) that prompted the response published with others in the *Observer*, 5 August, p. 5, under the heading 'Tanks at Lulworth Cove. Protests Against the Proposed Gunnery School'. No draft of the message has been discovered— Hardy's note on Garvin's telegram reads only 'Answer sent—that I join in the protest against the proposal'—and the text below is that of the *Observer*.

I join in the protest against such a foolish proceeding as establishing a gunnery school that will ruin a beautiful holiday spot enjoyed by millions since the reign of George the III., that monarch included.

[1923.04]

'Mr. Thomas Hardy and R.L.S.'

When Hardy responded, on 28 September 1923 (*CL* vi. 214–15), to an invitation (27 September, DCM) to become an honorary life member of the London branch of the Robert Louis Stevenson Club and bestow a 'bene-diction' on its inaugural meeting, he doubtless anticipated that his letter of polite refusal would be read out to the assembled enthusiasts. He perhaps had not expected that his correspondent, the Revd George Currie Martin, would communicate the letter to *The Times*, where it appeared as follows, shorn of its epistolary trappings and under the above heading, on 9 October 1923, p. 15. Reprinted in *Life and Art*, p. 140.

I much appreciate the suggestion of the Committee of the London R. L. Stevenson Club that I should become an honorary member, even though, as a matter of fact, I am not what would be called a Stevensonian,[2] in the full sense in which that expression could be applied to so many, probably all, of the club's members. However, the question of my sufficiency does not really arise. I have now reached a great age: one at which I find it necessary to abstain from further association with societies, even if only of an honorary kind, flattering as the connexion may be, and, therefore, I must decline the distinction of being elected one of the London branch of the club.

[1923.05]

[Assistance to Reviewer of *Queen of Cornwall* Production]

Hardy kept up his friendship of mutual convenience with Harold Child (see 1920.05, 1925.08), and wrote to him at some length (*CL* vi. 221–2) in advance of his coming to Dorchester to review the Hardy Players' production of *The Famous History of the Queen of Cornwall*. Child's review, *The Times*, 29 November 1923, p. 15, shows that he did make occasional, though not extensive, use of Hardy's observations. That Hardy himself regarded those observations as worth preserving is suggested by his inserting a partial, and somewhat altered, copy of the letter into his 'Memoranda II' notebook (DCM; slightly inaccurate transcription in *PN*, pp. 75–6), whence it was transferred by Florence Hardy to the penultimate chapter of *Life and Work*, p. 456.

---

[2] It is clear from *Life and Work*, pp. 259–60, that TH never quite forgave either Stevenson or Henry James for their shared hostility to *Tess of the d'Urbervilles*. See 1922.08.

1924

[1924.01]

[Message to the *Transatlantic Review*]

Ford Madox Ford, born Ford Hermann Hueffer (1873–1939), novelist and critic, had won Hardy's goodwill by publishing his controversial poem 'A Sunday Morning Tragedy' in the first number of the *English Review* in December 1908 (*CL* iii. 331). In October 1923, when Ford sought (DCM) a contribution or message to help initiate his projected *Transatlantic Review*, Hardy did not respond directly but drafted (DCM), for his wife to type and sign, the letter of 30 October 1923 that is given in full, from Hardy's draft, in *Collected Letters*, vi. 220. The first two paragraphs of that letter were quoted as below, over Florence Hardy's signature, in the first number of the *Transatlantic Review*, January 1924, p. 94.

Max Gate Dorchester.

Dear Mr Madox Ford,

As Mr Hardy continues rather unwell—which he has been the last fortnight, though not seriously except on account of his age—I reply to your last letter that you may not be inconvenienced by further delay.

In the circumstances he fears he can do nothing now beyond[1] sending the general message that, believing International understandings should become thorough for the good of mankind, he wishes every success to the *Transatlantic Review*, since it may help such understandings.

Yours truly

F. E. Hardy

---

[1] For 'nothing now beyond' TH's draft reads 'nothing beyond'.

[1924.02]

[Sir Walter Raleigh Memorial Fund]

Following the death of Sir Walter Raleigh (1861–1922), the Merton Professor of English Literature at the University of Oxford, Hardy responded positively to the request of Raleigh's colleague, H. W. Garrod (22 January 1924, DCM) that he support an appeal for contributions to a Raleigh Memorial Fund. When the fund was announced in *The Times*, 1 March 1924, p. 7, Hardy was among those named as signatories of the appeal.

[1924.03]

[Facsimile Quotation for *British Legion Album*]

On 22 October 1923 (*CL* vi. 218) Hardy gave permission for his previously submitted holograph inscription (from the poem 'I Met a Man') to be reproduced in facsimile in *The British Legion Album in Aid of Field-Marshal Haig's Appeal for Ex-Service Men of All Ranks*, compiled by E. Lonsdale Deighton (London: Cassell, n.d.) and published early in 1924. It appeared, as below, on the same unnumbered page as messages from Barrie and Kipling. The original album—containing the actual autograph messages, musical quotations, and drawings of a great many authors, artists, composers, scientists, politicians, etc.—became first prize in a 'draw' organized by the British Legion; more recently it was auctioned at Sotheby's, 10–11 July 1986, lot 299.

'Their plenteous blooms of promise shed Ere fruiting-time' . . .

(Moments of Vision.)[2]

Thomas Hardy.

Aug 1922.

---

[2] 'I Met a Man' was first published in 1917 and first collected in TH's *Moments of Vision* that same year.

[1924.04]

[On Rabbit-Coursing and Stag-Hunting]

Henry B. Amos, of the League for the Prohibition of Cruel Sports, asked Hardy on 12 March 1924 (DCM) if he would send 'a line in condemnation' that might be included in two of the League's pamphlets on rabbit-coursing. On 16 March (DCM) he wrote again to seek a further comment on the hunting of captive stags. No copies have been found of the pamphlets in question, but Hardy's two draft responses (DCM) are reproduced below in the light of Amos's assurance to Hardy, 16 November 1925 (DCM), that his messages of opposition to these practices had been 'most helpful' in moving preventive legislation through the parliamentary process.

[Ans.] I quite disapprove of rabbit-coursing

      *   *   *   *   *

[Ans.] 'And captive stag-hunting' may be added.

[1924.05]

[On the Old Theatre in Dorchester]

Writing to Harley Granville Barker, the dramatist and producer, on 28 April 1924 (*CL* vi. 248), Hardy expressed thanks for the information about Edmund Kean that Barker had sent, then added: 'I have now inked in the title-page of the visitors' book for Mr Godwin, and no doubt he will get some shillings by exhibiting the place.' The reference was to John Thomas Godwin's china shop (see 1902.06, n. 19) and to the continued visibility (at that time) of its past history as one of the town's oldest theatres. Hardy's holograph headnote to the visitors' book (now DCM) is transcribed below—ampersands and double quotation marks retained—on the grounds that, while a unique document, it was clearly intended for public exhibition.

The Old Theatre,
High West Street, Dorchester—

Down to 1820, & presumably to 1828, when the New Theatre was opened in North Square or Bull Stake.[3]

On this stage appeared as touring players many well-known London & other actors. Edmund Kean came here, on foot, in 1813, when Arnold the emissary from Drury Lane[4] witnessed Kean's performance as Octavian in "The Mountaineers",[5] & decided that he was the man for the London boards.—Kean's child died during his visit, & is buried in the churchyard opposite.[6]

T. H.

[1924.06]

'The Byron Centenary: A Practical Suggestion'

Hardy is named, along with Gosse, Masefield, Gilbert Murray, and others, at the foot of a one-page, single-sided leaflet headed as above and found by the Chicago bookseller Peter Lennon inside a copy of the *Poetry Review* for May–June 1924. The leaflet, undated but printed by Francis Meynell's Pelican Press, urged its readers to commemorate Byron's death at Missolonghi one hundred years earlier (19 April 1824) by funding 'a special memorial feeding centre' in Greece capable of providing direct assistance to Greek refugees from the recent war with Turkey. An item headed 'The Byron Centenary' in *The Times*, 15 April 1924, p. 13, reported not only that £2,000 was being directed to the establishment of 'a special feeding station for 2,000 refugees at Eleusis in memory of Byron' but also that the 'largest refugee camp near Athens' had been 'named Byronia in honour of the poet'.

---

[3] For TH's earlier comments on Dorchester theatres and Edmund Kean, see 1902.05, 1902.06, and 1902.08.   [4] Samuel James Arnold, then manager of the Drury Lane theatre.
[5] By George Colman the Younger (1762–1836); Barker had corrected Hardy's earlier identification of the play as *Coriolanus*.   [6] That of Holy Trinity, Dorchester.

[1924.07]

'Mr. Thomas Hardy and Weymouth'

Hardy's letter of 24 June 1924 to the Mayor of Weymouth, thanking him and the people of Weymouth for good wishes on his recent birthday, was printed in *Collected Letters*, vi. 260–1, from the original typescript. It is now known to have been published as follows, headed 'Mr. Thomas Hardy and Weymouth', in the Weymouth section of the *Dorset County Chronicle*, 3 July 1924, p. 4.

To the Mayor of Weymouth.

The delay in my reply to your letter has been caused by my large correspondence of late. I send my best thanks to yourself and the towns-people of Weymouth for your good wishes on my birthday and your kind words of appreciation.

Yours very truly,

Thomas Hardy.

[1924.08]

'Byron and the Abbey'

In a letter published in *The Times*, 14 July 1924, p. 15, Hardy joined Kipling, three former prime ministers, and a number of others (see *PN*, pp. 81–2) in urging that Byron, a century after his death, should at last be accorded a memorial in Poets' Corner in Westminster Abbey. When approached by Sir James Rennell Rodd, diplomat and scholar, on 26 June 1924 (DCM), Hardy had gladly agreed to be a signatory of the letter but suggested two minor alterations to its wording, both apparently adopted (*CL* vi. 262). The Dean of Westminster's rejection of the proposal for a memorial prompted Hardy's poem 'A Refusal' (*CPW* iii. 123–4 and n.).

[1924.09]

[Conditions for Performance of *Tess* Play]

Hardy had adapted *Tess of the d'Urbervilles* for the stage shortly after the novel was first published in the early 1890s, but that adaptation had for various reasons (*Hardy on Stage*, pp. 37–45) never been performed. That he chose to sanction and indeed promote its staging in Dorchester in the autumn of 1924 may be largely attributed to the national attention accorded previous productions of the 'Hardy Players' and to the appealing availability of the beautiful local actress Gertrude Bugler (see 1916.03) for the role of Tess herself. Hardy again (cf. 1923.01) required the company to accept a series of preconditions, and these were drafted (DCM) entirely in his own hand, typed up and signed by his wife as a letter from herself, and then read out to the players by the producer, T. H. Tilley. The letter as typed and signed by Florence Hardy has not been located, and the text below (as at *CL* vi. 269) is therefore based on Hardy's draft, with ampersands expanded and working corrections unrecorded.

24 Aug. 1924

Dear Mr Tilley—

We have thought that in meeting the Company of players on Monday evening it might be advisable for you to let them know the conditions on which Mr Hardy agrees to[7] their performing the Tess play, so that if they demur to them on your reading them over the idea of their doing the play can be abandoned, and he will not send the copy.

1. That performance in Dorchester only, is conceded at present, any question of performance elsewhere being left to be agreed on in the future.
2. Every announcement of the play is to include the statement that it was dramatized from the novel in 1894–5, (without stating by whom.)
3. The cast decided on is to have Mr Hardy's sanction, who is to be entitled to reject any actor that in his opinion is unfitted for the part, though this is not likely.

---

[7] For 'on . . . to' TH first wrote 'on which I agree to'.

4. Nothing is to be mentioned publicly or allowed to get into the press of its intended production till discussion of *The Queen of Cornwall* opera[8] has died down—say the end of September.

5. No more dialect or local accent than is written in the play is to be introduced by the performers, each part being spoken exactly as set down.

Of course Mr Hardy does not suppose there will be any objection at all to the above,[9] as it is merely what any author expects, and he is reading through the play to see it is all right for your putting it in hand.

Yours very truly

F. E. Hardy[10]

[1924.10]

[Message to *The Bermondsey Book*]

On 31 May 1924 (DCM) Lewis Hind, a former editor of the *Academy* (see 1897.02), wrote to Hardy on behalf of the proprietors of a new literary quarterly called *The Bermondsey Book*. In his reply of 8 June (*CL* vi. 255–6), Hardy excused himself from becoming a contributor but referred in positive terms to the journal itself; some five weeks later he agreed that his letter might be published, and the greater part of it duly appeared, as below, in the 'Editorial Notes' section of *The Bermondsey Book*, no. 4 (September 1924), p. 3.

I am so sorry to have left your letter over until now and not to have thanked you for *The Bermondsey Book*, which one would never guess from its title to be of such high quality. But, alas, for me I am now of an age at which I cannot promise anything to any publication. Nevertheless, I sincerely hope that this particular one will make its way in the literary world.

Most truly yours,

Thomas Hardy.

---

[8] Rutland Boughton's musical setting of TH's verse-play *The Famous Tragedy of the Queen of Cornwall* was first produced at the Glastonbury Festival, 21 August 1924, but with piano accompaniment only; TH saw a full-scale operatic performance in Bournemouth in April 1925.

[9] The minutes of the Dramatic Sub-Committee of the Dorchester Debating and Dramatic Society (Dorset County Record Office) show that TH's conditions were indeed unanimously accepted: see *Hardy on Stage*, p. 132.   [10] Signature also in TH's hand in the draft.

[1924.11]

'Ronsard Centenary'

A report headed 'Ronsard Centenary' in *The Times*, 18 October 1924, p. 14, listed Hardy among the signatories of an address in celebration of the 400th anniversary of the birth of the French poet Pierre de Ronsard that had been handed to the French ambassador at a ceremony in London the previous day. When invited to sign by Winifred Whale (*née* Stephens), one of the organizers of the address (28 April 1924, DCM), Hardy had replied that it seemed 'rather pretentious' for him to do so when he knew only 'two or three small lyrics' of Ronsard's, but if it meant no more than testifying to Ronsard's importance as the 'inventor' of French lyrical poetry he was willing to add his name (undated draft, DCM).

[1924.12]

[Speech between Performances of *Tess of the d'Urbervilles*]

Hardy's natural interest in the production of his own dramatization of *Tess of the d'Urbervilles* (see 1924.09) was intensified by his fascination with Gertrude Bugler in the part of Tess, and he attended not only the last of the five Dorchester performances of the play in late November 1924 but also the afternoon and the evening performances given in the Pavilion Theatre, Weymouth, on 11 December. Between these performances the mayor of Weymouth entertained Hardy, his wife, and the Hardy Players at a dinner in the Gloucester Hotel, and Hardy, with Gertrude Bugler on his right and the mayor on his left (photograph in *The Times*, 13 December 1924, p. 16), was reluctantly prevailed upon to make a brief speech—apparently in response to the toast of 'The Hardy Players'. Although *The Times*, 12 December 1924, p. 11, gave only a brief summary of the speech, the *Morning Post* of the same date, p. 8, reported it in full, and in the first person, as follows.

As I do not see that my wife is going to reply for me, I suppose I had better do so as well as I can. It will be done very badly. I have written in my time speeches for a great many people—a very great many, but when it comes to making one for myself I am quite nonplussed.

I can only say very briefly indeed that I thank you very much in my own name and my wife's and Mrs Bugler's and the players', and I should like, with them, to couple the name of Mr Tilley, who has done so much for the performances.

1925

[1925.01]

[Corrections to J. H. Fowler Introductions]

Early in 1923 John Henry Fowler, formerly a master at Clifton College, was commissioned by Macmillan to supply introductions to low-priced Indian editions of four of Hardy's novels (*CL* vi. 177). On 12 December 1924 (DCM) Fowler sent Hardy offprints of those introductions, bound together into pamphlet form as *The Wessex Novels of Thomas Hardy: Four Introductions Written for Indian Readers* but still independently paginated; Hardy responded on 19 January 1925 with a polite letter and an accompanying sheet headed 'Errata'; and Fowler (21 January 1925, DCM) undertook to make the recommended changes should the editions be reprinted. Hardy's letter and enclosure are both reproduced in *Collected Letters*, vii. 163–4, where it is wrongly assumed that Fowler had sent copies of the separate editions.

[1925.02]

[Speech to Dorchester Debating and Dramatic Society]

On 30 March 1925 Hardy accompanied his wife to a meeting of the Dorchester Debating and Dramatic Society at which she had agreed to share in judging the literary merits of papers presented by members. At the very end of the meeting, after all the scheduled business and speech-making had been concluded, he created what the *Daily Echo* reporter called 'the tensest silence' by suddenly and quite unexpectedly getting to his feet to acknowledge the thanks he had received for assisting the judges in reaching their final decision. His few words—said to have been followed by 'Loud applause'

—were reported as below, under the heading 'Thirty Words Speech', in the *Dorset Daily Echo and Weymouth Dispatch*, 1 April 1925, p. 4. A similar report, including an identical quotation, appeared in the *Dorset County Chronicle*, 3 April, p. 8.

I thank you for the kind remarks you have made. I must mention the extreme interest of all the papers, which made it so very difficult for us to decide.[1]

[1925.03]

[Inspired Letter about Ernest Brennecke's Biography]

Although Hardy thought well of *Thomas Hardy's Universe: A Study of a Poet's Mind* (London: T. Fisher Unwin, 1924), by the American critic Ernest Brennecke, Jr. (1896–1969), and even invited its author to call at Max Gate (*CL* vi. 259–60), he became alarmed, early in 1925, at the prospect of an English edition of Brennecke's ostensibly 'authorized' biography, *The Life of Thomas Hardy* (New York: Greenberg, 1925). He explained his concerns in a long letter to Sir Frederick Macmillan (*CL* vi. 318–19) that Macmillan, in collaboration with Sydney Cockerell, used as the basis for the letter published as follows, under the heading 'A "Life" of Thomas Hardy', in *The Times*, 11 April 1925, p. 11.

St Martin's-street, W.C.2, April 9.

Sir,

A book has recently appeared in America under the title of 'The Life of Thomas Hardy, by Ernest Brennecke', which is described by its publishers as 'authentic', and being 'the result of ten years of research and personal contact'.[2] We should like to be allowed to say that the

---

[1] The paper adjudged to be of the 'greatest literary merit' was 'Socialism and Happiness' by Mr T. R. Owens, reported as arguing that life in a Socialist state must be 'a hopeless march across an arid desert'; it did not, however, figure among the first three papers chosen 'by the popular vote of the audience'.

[2] This latter statement appears on the book's dust wrapper; the word 'authentic' does not so appear, but it is said of Brennecke's work that it 'will probably always stand as the most authoritative and comprehensive book on the subject'.

book in question has been published without Mr Hardy's authority or approval, and that the 'personal contact' referred to was confined to a single interview. The volume contains a certain amount of copyright matter, and it should be understood that any person selling or offering it for sale in this country runs the risk of prosecution for breach of copyright.[3]

Macmillan and Co., Limited.

[1925.04]

'Animals' Welfare Week'

Hardy was a co-signatory, along with George Bernard Shaw, Sybil Thorndike, and others, of a letter, headed as above, that was published in *The Times*, 25 April 1925, p. 8, and sought to draw attention to the national Animals' Welfare Week being planned for early May 1925. Henry J. Stone, organizing secretary of the National Council for Animals' Welfare Week, had asked Hardy to sign the letter 'on behalf of the National Council' (letter of 4 March 1925, DCM).

[1925.05]

[Message to Ramsay MacDonald]

The Liberal MP James Myles Hogge wrote to Hardy on 16 May 1925 (DCM) to ask if he would send a message to a non-partisan dinner being given in honour of James Ramsay MacDonald (1866–1937), leader of the Labour Party and Prime Minister in 1924 and 1929–35. Hardy was on friendly terms with MacDonald (*Letters EFH*, p. 333) and responded with the brief note transcribed below from his draft at the foot of Hogge's letter. Though not published, the message was certainly read at the dinner, the *Daily Herald*, 23 May, p. 3, reporting: 'And from Thomas Hardy came a cordial little note.'

---

[3] No English edition was in fact published.

May 19, 1925

Please convey my best wishes to Mr Macdonald, whose book I have just been reading.[4]

T. H.

[1925.06]

[Renewed Support for University of Wessex]

Hardy in 1921 had supported a campaign for the elevation of the existing University College in Southampton to a self-governing University of Wessex, and when he was again approached by Professor Albert A. Cock in April 1925 (*CL* vi. 321–2) he agreed that his letter as published in the *Hampshire Observer*, 22 January 1921 (1921.02), should be read out at another public meeting in Winchester and printed in a projected *Wessex Supplement*—apparently a publicity sheet for insertion in copies of local newspapers. No copy of the *Supplement* has yet been found, but the letter as reprinted in the reports of the Winchester meeting appearing in the *Hampshire Observer*, 23 May 1925, p. 7, and *The Times*, 23 May, p. 13, is identical with that of 1921, apart from the removal of all epistolary features and indications of elision.

[1925.07]

'Future of British Films'

At the invitation of Sir Robert Duncan (DCM), a former editor of the *Daily Chronicle*, Hardy joined Robert Bridges, Sir Edward Elgar, Cecil Harmsworth, Gordon Selfridge, and several others in signing a letter— published under the above heading in *The Times*, 20 June 1925, p. 11—that voiced alarm at the small percentage of British-made films being shown in British cinemas and appealed to the Prime Minister to set up an inquiry into 'the measures which should be taken to establish a film industry in this country on a sound foundation'. The same letter with the same signatures

---

[4] MacDonald's *Wanderings and Excursions* (London: Jonathan Cape, 1925); TH seems not to have owned a copy, however.

appeared, under a different heading, in the *Daily Telegraph*, 20 June, p. 10, and doubtless elsewhere. For a comment on the letter, see Rachel Low, *The History of the British Film 1918–1929* (London: George Allen & Unwin, 1971), p. 92.

[1925.08]

[Revision of Harold Child's *Thomas Hardy*]

Harold Child (see 1920.05) had gained Hardy's good opinion both by his sympathetic reviews in *The Times* of the productions of the 'Hardy Players' and by his critical study, *Thomas Hardy* (London: Nisbet, 1916). A typed attachment to Hardy's letter of 9 December 1924 offered corrections and suggestions for Child's 1925 reissue of his *Thomas Hardy*, and nearly all of these were incorporated into the published text. Letter and attachment are both accessible in *Collected Letters*, vi. 292–4; Hardy's holograph notes are loosely inserted at the back of the Max Gate copy of the original 1916 edition (DCM).

[1925.09]

[Revision to Untermeyer's *Modern British Poetry*]

In February 1939 the London bookseller Elkin Mathews offered for sale (Cat. 77, item 83) the Max Gate copies of both the first edition of *Modern British Poetry* (New York: Harcourt, Brace, 1920), edited by the American poet and anthologist Louis Untermeyer (1885–1977), and the revised and enlarged edition of 1925, Hardy's verse being represented in both editions. The present location of these volumes, both presentation copies (*CL* vi. 158, 333), is unknown, but the Mathews catalogue entry records that Hardy pencilled into his copy of the 1920 edition 'a marginal note about his poetry, twenty-four words long', and that those same twenty-four words appeared as part of the printed text of the 1925 edition. Hardy later suggested to Untermeyer (*CL* vii. 75) the titles of poems of his that might be included in an expanded third edition of the anthology.

[1925.10]

[Golden Wedding Message to Edmund Gosse]

Hardy's old friend Edmund Gosse (see 1889.01), knighted earlier in 1925, was at this date the principal literary reviewer for the *Sunday Times*, and on 6 August 1925 the paper's editor, Leonard Rees, asked Hardy by reply-paid telegram (DCM) to send a brief message for publication on the Sunday nearest to the Gosses' golden wedding anniversary on 11 August. Hardy's message, differing slightly from the draft scrawled on Rees's telegram (see note), was published as below, under the heading 'Sir Edmund and Lady Gosse. Golden Wedding Day This Week. Mr. Thomas Hardy's Message', in the *Sunday Times*, 9 August 1925, p.11.

That happiness may long continue to both is the wish of one[5] who thinks he has known you the whole time.—Thomas Hardy.

[1925.11]

[The Cerne Giant]

Hardy's suggestions for the proper care of the Cerne Giant—an ancient phallic figure cut into the chalk of a Dorset hillside—were neatly written out in his own hand before being sent by his wife to their friend Lady Hoare, of Stourhead, on 21 September 1925 (*CL* vi. 355), and the possibility of their having been intended for publication has been implicitly endorsed by the listing of the MS (as HrT 1526) in the *Index of English Literary Manuscripts*. It appears, however, that Lady Hoare's husband, Sir Henry Hoare, Bt, having already endowed the maintenance of the Giant through the National Trust, was simply seeking Hardy's response to some information received from the Trust's secretary in a private letter of 17 September 1925 (Wiltshire Record Office). Hardy's views on the Giant, expressed 'in the course of conversation', had earlier been invoked in an editorial article, 'The Giant of Cerne Abbas', *Country Life*, 18 October 1924, p. 612; see also *Siegfried Sassoon Diaries 1923–1925*, edited by Rupert Hart-Davis (London: Faber and Faber, 1985), p. 182.

---

[5] For 'That . . . one' TH's draft reads 'Continued happiness for both from one'; it is not clear whether the alteration was editorial or incorporated into the telegram TH actually sent.

[1925.12]

[Intended Tribute to Romain Rolland]

Romain Rolland (1866–1944), the French novelist, playwright, essayist, and outspoken pacifist, was known to Hardy not only as a significant literary figure but as the brother of Madeleine Rolland, who had translated *Tess of the d'Urbervilles* into French, visited Max Gate, and corresponded both with Emma Hardy and with Hardy himself. In anticipation of Rolland's sixtieth birthday Hardy was invited by the Swiss publisher Emil Roniger (20 October 1925; DCM) to contribute to the *Liber amicorum Romain Rolland*, a volume of tributes edited by Maxim Gorky, Georges Duhamel, and Stefan Zweig (Paris: Albin Michel; Zurich: Rotapfel-verlag, 1926), but his response—perhaps because of its brevity—was not included in the work as published. The text below is taken from the pencilled draft (DCM); the possibility that no letter was actually sent to Roniger seems rather remote.

22 October: 1925

Dear Sir:

   I join in the wish to offer homage to the distinguished man of letters and poet of goodwill, Romain Rolland, on the celebration of his sixtieth birthday.

   I much regret that circumstances compel me to limit my expression of the same to this brief note.

   I am, Dear Sir,

Yours very truly

M. Emil Roniger Rheinfelden Switzerland

[1925.13]

[*Tess of the d'Urbervilles* Re-Serialized]

In early October 1925 George Newnes, publishers of *John o' London's Weekly*, a popular literary magazine, contracted with Hardy's publishers, Macmillan, for a week-by-week re-serialization of *Tess of the d'Urbervilles* (*CL* vi. 356), Hardy himself to receive two-thirds of the £1,000 fee. The issue of 24 October 1925, in which the first instalment appeared, carried on its front page (p. [125]) 'A Message to Our Readers from Mr. Thomas Hardy' in a facsimile reproduction of Hardy's hand that is also the source of the text that follows. Purdy, p. 322.

October: 1925.

Gentle Reader:

The history of Tess of the d'Urbervilles is to the best of my belief, now published serially for the first time complete in all its details as primarily written, a fragment of one chapter here embodied having been discovered but a short while ago.[6]

It has been remarked that these experiences of the heroine could not have led to such an issue nowadays. Well: I for one am sceptical on this point, and think it just as likely to have happened last week as fifty years back, in which view I am supported by many men with large knowledge of the world, and perhaps by yourself.[7]

Thomas Hardy.

[1925.14]

[The Saturday Review]

The *Saturday Review*, founded in November 1856, had always been an important journal for Hardy: as early as November 1862 he was asking his sister Mary to be sure to keep for him the copies he was sending her from London (*CL* i. 2). When, therefore, the current editor, Gerald Barry, wrote on 19 October 1925 (DCM) to solicit a contribution to the *Review* on the occasion of its seventieth birthday—actually the beginning of its seventieth year of publication—Hardy drafted a prompt reply (DCM) that was shorn of its date and other epistolary features for publication, as follows, in the 'Letters and Messages of Congratulation' section in the *Saturday Review*, 7 November 1925, Supplement p. xiv. See, however, note 9 below for discussion of a biographical crux in the text as published. Purdy, p. 322.

I am sorry to be unable to send a special contribution to the number of the *Review* marking its arrival at the Psalmodic age[8] of three-score and

---

[6] TH's reference is to the pages describing the dance at the hay-trusser's, first reincorporated into the 'Wessex Edition' text of 1912 (Purdy, pp. 70, 77).

[7] The final period, absent from facsimile, is here supplied.   [8] Ps. 90: 10.

ten, but I may say that I am probably among its earliest readers still living, as I began to buy it when it was less than two years old.[9]

[1925.15]

[Tribute to William Watkins]

Hardy wrote the following public tribute to William Watkins (see 1904.16), founder and energetic Secretary of the Society of Dorset Men in London, on the occasion of his resigning the secretaryship in the spring of 1925. Watkins had died (*LW*, p. 461), however, by the time Hardy's letter was published, in holograph facsimile, in *The Dorset Year Book for 1925*, p. 4, and an obituary of him appeared in the same issue, pp. 12–13. The text below is based on the facsimile.

Max Gate, Dorchester. March: 1925

Dear Mr Watkins:

It is difficult to realize the Society of Dorset Men in London without yourself as the warm-hearted and enthusiastic Honorary Secretary. All these years—twenty-one I believe—you have been its mainstay, never sparing yourself for the good of every Dorset man who has needed your help. But we are glad to know that your friendly eye will still be up on the Society, and are sure that you will not be forgotten by Dorset Men in London, and Dorset Men in Dorset, and indeed, Dorset Men all over the world.

Yours most sincerely
Thomas Hardy.

---

[9] For 'buy it when' TH's draft reads 'buy it in 1862, when', and although it is possible that he began buying the *Review* in 1858, while he was still an apprentice architect in Dorchester, it seems more likely that in 1925 he miscalculated the journal's founding date, that editorial 'correction' compounded the error, and that his earliest purchases were indeed made in 1862, the year in which he first went to London.

[1926.01]

[London Message on Cruel Sports]

Henry B. Amos, secretary of the recently established League for the Prohibition of Cruel Sports, wrote on 16 November 1925 (DCM) to ask if Hardy could send 'a brief message of sympathy and goodwill' for the League's forthcoming Inaugural Public Meeting. And it was in the stripped-down form of a message that Hardy's responsive letter of 19 November 1925 (Princeton) was read out at the meeting and reported, as below, in the *Animals' Friend*, 32 (January 1926), p. 43. The message was later quoted in *Cruel Sports: The Official Journal of the League for the Prohibition of Cruel Sports*, 1 (March 1927), p. 27, and again, following Hardy's death, in *Cruel Sports*, 2 (February 1928), p. 15.

I do not[1] see that much can be done to hinder cruel sports while an appetite for cruelty is cultivated in the young; as, for instance, by teaching the children of the rich how to take life shortly after they are taught their letters.

[1926.02]

[Assistance to *Word-Lore*]

Douglas Macmillan (pseudonym 'D. M. Cary'), an authority on Somerset history and folklore, was in search of a name for a new magazine dealing with

---

[1] TH's letter began 'Dear Sir: In reply to your letter I can only say that I do not'.

dialect and folklore, and on 29 October 1925 (DCM) he wrote to ask Hardy for suggestions. Although Hardy's sympathetic reply of 1 November (*CL* vi. 365) did not directly supply such a title, his poem 'The Pity of It' was reprinted, with permission, on the title-page of the first issue (January–February 1926) of *Word-Lore: The 'Folk' Magazine*, and his interest in the new venture gratefully acknowledged. On page 2 of the same issue an editorial column, 'On Naming the Baby', made reference to the assistance of 'a number of literary people, some of them of considerable eminence', and silently incorporated a few words taken directly from Hardy's 1 November letter.

[1926.03]

'A Blake Memorial in St. Paul's'

Hardy gave immediate support (*CL* vii. 10, and see Jarndyce catalogue 124, item 13) to a proposal for a memorial to William Blake (1757–1827), poet and artist, to be placed in St Paul's Cathedral one hundred years after his death, and was listed as co-signing—along with Stanley Baldwin, Ramsay MacDonald, Sir Edward Elgar, and several others—the appeal for funds published under the above heading in *The Times*, 20 March 1926, p. 13.

[1926.04]

'New Shakespeare Theatre'

Despite earlier reservations about Shakespeare's plays in performance (see 1917.03), Hardy seems to have had no hesitation in co-signing an appeal—headed as above and published in *The Times*, 25 March 1926, p. 13 —for donations to help build a new Shakespeare Memorial Theatre at Stratford-upon-Avon to replace the one destroyed by fire on 6 March 1926. The appeal also appeared in the *Daily Telegraph* of 25 March, p. 11, and perhaps elsewhere. Strikingly reflective of Hardy's 'national' status was the fact that the only other signatories were the three leading statesmen of the day: Stanley Baldwin, the Conservative Prime Minister; Ramsay MacDonald, the Labour leader; and Lord Oxford and Asquith, the former Liberal Prime Minister.

[1926.05]

'An Appeal from Dorset'

The condition of the ancient bells of Stinsford Church became a source of active concern during the winter of 1925–6. Hardy saw and commented on a report by experts called in to estimate the cost of repairs (*CL* vii. 7–8) and provided information about the 'Mellstock' of his novels and poems that might form all or part of an appeal for funds (*CL* vii. 9). On 12 March 1926 a Stinsford Vestry meeting voted to send an appeal, 'with Mr Hardy's good-will', to the American press (Dorset County Record Office), but the vicar, the Revd H. G. B. Cowley, made little use of Hardy's suggestions in drafting the document, and Hardy pencilled only a somewhat tepid endorsement on Cowley's letter to him of 9 April 1926 (DCM). That same endorsement was nevertheless attached, as below, to the printing of Cowley's appeal, headed 'Letters from the "Herald's" Mailbag. An Appeal from Dorset', in the Paris edition of the *New York Herald Tribune*, 25 April 1926, p. 4. Although the appeal was mentioned in the *Daily Chronicle*, 10 September 1926, p. 9 (see note), in the London *Star*, 11 September 1926, p. 5, and probably in other British papers, it apparently attracted only one donation—from Margaret Kennedy, author of *The Constant Nymph* (Florence Hardy to Cowley, 4 October [1926], Dorset County Record Office). Purdy, p. 322.

I have lately visited Stinsford Church, and am quite in sympathy with the above appeal of the Vicar and Churchwardens.[2]

Thomas Hardy.

[1926.06]

[Hopkins's 'Thomas Hardy and His Folk']

On 2 June 1926, Hardy's eighty-sixth birthday, the *Dorset Daily Echo*, p. 6, published some extracts from an article by the journalist Robert Thurston Hopkins (1883–1958) that was being published in full in that day's issue of

---

[2] The *Daily Chronicle* article reported—accurately or otherwise—another version of this message as appearing in TH's hand below the copy of Cowley's *Herald Tribune* letter displayed in Stinsford church itself: 'I have lately revisited Stinsford Church and this appeal has my full and cordial support.—Thomas Hardy.'

the *Westminster Gazette*, p. 6, under the heading 'Thomas Hardy and His Folk'. Hardy took particular objection to Hopkins's baseless statements about his family—the subheading in the *Echo* read 'Mr. Hardy and His Folk. A Half-Brother Poet'—and demanded their withdrawal in a message (draft, DCM) that his wife delivered over the telephone to the *Echo*'s editor. The *Echo* published an apology in its issue of 3 June, p. 5; the *Westminster Gazette* added an apology to its publication of Hardy's undated letter, as below, under the heading 'Mr. Thomas Hardy', on 4 June, p. 6; while Hopkins himself, addressed by Hardy's solicitor (*CL* vii. 26–7, 28), apologized twice in the *Westminster*, on 8 June, p. 6, and (with reference to an earlier article in an American magazine) on 11 June, p. 6. Purdy, p. 322.

Max Gate, Dorchester, Dorset.

Sir,

An article in a local paper, copied from one in the Westminster, on 'Thomas Hardy and his Folk', by a Mr R. Thurston Hopkins, has been sent me, in which he writes of 'one of Mr Hardy's half-brothers . . . who is a gardener by trade', and gives various luminous particulars of this half-brother, and also of myself.

Mr Hopkins, whoever he may be, is a total stranger to me,[3] and his statements are absolutely false, there being no half-brother of mine in existence; nor have I either brother or half-brother who is a gardener or anything else by trade; or who is a poet,[4] as your contributor additionally states.

I suppose Mr Hopkins thinks it humorous to hoax an editor, and perhaps it is; but I must ask you to withdraw these misleading statements nevertheless.

Yours, etc.,

Thomas Hardy.

[3] TH may, however, have known Hopkins by name as the author of *Thomas Hardy's Dorset* (London: Cecil Palmer, 1922).

[4] TH's first cousin John Antell did have a local reputation as a poet; Hopkins's source for 'half-brother' was, as he acknowledged, a remark attributed to 'a native' in an article by Kathleen Woodward in the *New York Times Magazine*, 22 November 1925, p. 14 (see *CL* vii. 28).

[1926.07]

'Fate of Waterloo Bridge'

Waterloo Bridge, designed by John Rennie and built 1810–17, was acknowledged to be the handsomest of London's bridges, and in 1926 a government decision to pull it down rather than undertake expensive repairs generated much debate and many protests. Hardy, approached (DCM) by D. S. MacColl, the keeper of the Wallace Collection, sent a telegram on 31 May (Glasgow University Library) to register his support for a memorial urging the Prime Minister to take no decision on the fate of Waterloo Bridge until there had been an inquiry into 'the whole problem of London traffic and bridges'. He was listed among the memorial's many signatories in *The Times*, 5 June 1926, p. 11, and included also in the more selective listing on the front page of the same day's *Westminster Gazette*.

[1926.08]

'The Dram of Eale'

The following letter, published as below in *The Times*, 17 June 1926, p. 15, under the editorial heading 'The Dram of Eale', was prompted by a leading article in the newspaper's 15 June issue, p. 17, on the famous textual crux in *Hamlet*, I. iv. 36–8: 'the dram of eale | Doth all the noble substance of a doubt | To his own scandal'. Purdy, pp. 322–3.

Max Gate, Dorchester, June 15.

Sir,

Your leading article on the famous passage with which Shakespeare's printers have tantalized the poet's readers for the last 300 years reminds me that in the eighteen-sixties I worked at elucidating it, and marked in the margin of a copy I used my own conjectural reading.[5] I give it here,

---

[5] TH's suggested emendation is indeed inscribed, undated, in vol. ix, p. 171, of his ten-volume set of *The Dramatic Works of William Shakespeare*, ed. Samuel Weller Singer (London: Bell and Daldy, 1856), purchased in 1863 and now in the Dorset County Museum: see *Thomas Hardy's 'Studies, Specimens &c.' Notebook*, ed. Pamela Dalziel and Michael Millgate (Oxford: Clarendon Press, 1994), p. [91].

since it may pass in the crowd of conjectures on what Shakespeare really did write as being not much worse than the rest.

> The dram of ill
> Doth all the noble substance leaven down
> To his own scandal.

I am, Sir, your obedient servant,

Thomas Hardy.

[1926.09]

'Undergraduates from Overseas'

On 5 July 1926 Florence Hardy represented her husband at a lunch given in Dorchester Corn Exchange for a visiting party of 220 undergraduates from Canadian universities, delivering on his behalf the message he had written for the occasion. That message was reported in the third person in *The Times*, 6 July 1926, p. 13, under the heading 'Purity of the English Language', but the text below is taken from the somewhat fuller first-person account, headed 'Undergraduates from Overseas', in the *Dorset County Chronicle*, 8 July 1926, p. 2.

I bring this message from Mr Thomas Hardy. He much regrets his inability to be here in person to meet the undergraduates of the Universities of the Dominion of Canada, especially as he has relatives in Canada,[6] as have so many present. He realises that there are the strongest ties between the Dominion of Canada and Great Britain, and he feels more mentally related to Canadians through their admirable poet, Mr Bliss Carman,[7] who, he is glad to know, is still actively writing. He hopes that the Universities of Canada will continue to do their utmost to preserve the English language in its purity, so that the noble

---

[6] TH's mother's sister Martha, her husband John Brereton Sharpe, and their children emigrated to rural Ontario in 1851 (*PN*, pp. 12, 17).

[7] William Bliss Carman (1861–1929); TH inserted a 1906 review of Carman's poems into one of his literary notebooks (*LN* ii. 308–9).

inheritance of the works of Shakespeare and Milton, which belongs alike to Canada and Great Britain, may always be fully intelligible.[8] He hopes that our guests have enjoyed their visit to Dorchester.[9]

[1926.10]

To the Citizens of Weymouth, Massachusetts

Early in 1926 the citizens of Weymouth, Massachusetts, invited representatives of Weymouth, Dorset—port of embarkation for many of the earliest European settlers of Massachusetts—to visit their city for the Sesquicentennial Independence Day celebrations that July. Hardy, asked to compose a goodwill message for the Dorset delegates to carry with them (*CL* vii. 11–12), submitted two versions to Percy Smallman, the town clerk of Weymouth; a draft typescript of the version chosen, headed as above, still accompanies Smallman's reply of 4 June 1926 (DCM). The message was first reported, following its delivery, in *The Times*, 6 July 1926, p. 13; closer to Hardy's draft, however, and perhaps taken directly from the formal document (itself untraced), is the version printed under the heading 'The Delegation to Weymouth, Mass.' in the *Dorset County Chronicle*, 8 July 1926, p. 8, and reproduced below. Purdy, p. 323.

The Corporation of Weymouth, England, having accepted your friendly invitation to pay you a visit, it has been suggested that I, as their neighbour, write a message to be borne to you by the representatives of the ancestral Wessex town. This I readily do, and in the simplest shape, namely: Though we of Weymouth, England, call the Weymouth across the sea the newer Weymouth, we remember its venerable record as being the town second in antiquity in the State of Massachusetts, and its striking history of romantic and tragic vicissitude. And though[10] we may have vague ideas on whether it be similar or different in its enterprises, show less or more wise and learned men, less or more gifted and charming women, than the elder so designated, our greetings are sent to all

---

[8] Cf. 1912.07.   [9] The *Chronicle* report adds: '(Loud applause)'.
[10] The *Chronicle* reading 'vicissitude) and, though' is clearly erroneous, and the reading of TH's draft has here been editorially adopted.

within its walls, and good hope that for its name's sake it may be a continuing city[11] with a success not entirely of a material kind.

Thomas Hardy.

(For the aforesaid inhabitants of Weymouth, England.)[12]

[1926.11]

[Intended Protest against Banning of Broadcast by Shaw]

A minor controversy arose in the summer of 1926 following the British Government's decision to forbid the broadcasting of a speech by George Bernard Shaw at a dinner given by the Parliamentary Labour Party in celebration of his seventieth birthday. Ramsay MacDonald, presiding at the dinner, made a particular point of mentioning the decision (*Daily Herald*, 27 July 1926, p. 5), and Hardy asked his wife to include the following message in her letter to Sydney Cockerell of 1 August 1926 (Beinecke)—evidently in the expectation that Cockerell, a long-time friend of Shaw's, would make it public in some manner. Cockerell took no action, however, noting on the letter itself that existing rules against the broadcasting of political speeches had left the Government with no choice in the matter.

The crass stupidity of the Government in forbidding the broadcasting of G.B.S.'s speech has seldom been equalled.

[1926.12]

[Country Dances and 'The College Hornpipe']

E.F.D.S. News, the newsletter of the English Folk Dance Society, published in September 1926 an article entitled 'Dances Mentioned by Thomas

---

[11] Cf. Heb. 13: 14.

[12] Though placed in the *Chronicle* outside the quotation marks surrounding the body of the message, TH's parenthetical gloss on his signature was clearly intended as a part of that message and had in fact been a holograph addition to his draft typescript.

Hardy in *Under the Greenwood Tree'*, signed with the initials of William
E. F. Macmillan, a grandson of Alexander Macmillan, the co-founder of the
Macmillan publishing house. The article included the quotation, 'nearly *in
extenso'*, of the following letter—undated in its shortened form but acknowledged by Macmillan on 27 January 1926 (DCM). Hardy consented to
publication of the letter (3 March 1926; draft, DCM), but added an entirely
new third paragraph when returning proof of the Macmillan article (*CL* vii.
41; corrected proof at Cecil Sharp House). The text below is that of *E.F.D.S.
News*, no. 12 (September 1926), pp. 384–5; it includes what Macmillan introduced as 'the notation of the *College Hornpipe*, referred to in Mr. Hardy's
letter'. Purdy, p. 323.

I am interested to hear that you have been attracted by the old English
dances, which gave me much pleasure when I was a boy. The dance I was
thinking of in *Under the Greenwood Tree* must have been *The College
Hornpipe*, as that is the only one I remember beginning with six-hands-
round. I am sending you the figure as nearly as I can recall it sixty years
after I last danced in it.[13] This and other such figures have been revived
on the stage here by 'The Hardy Players' (as they call themselves) since
they began making plays out of my stories. Only very old country
people remember the dances now. I have many such figures in old music
books.[14]

These 'Country dances' were not the same as 'folk-dances', though
usually considered to be. They superseded and extinguished the latter
from a hundred to a hundred and fifty years ago, as being more 'genteel',
though sometimes the folk-dances were done within my memory,
the motions being more boisterous than in the Country dance, a distinguishing mark of them being the crossing of one leg over the knee of the
other, and putting the hands on the hips.

The history of the Country dance is puzzling. If it was the dance of
the country people, how comes it that new figures and tunes are first
heard of in London ball-rooms (*see* London magazines and musical publications throughout the eighteenth century), whence they gradually
spread into the rural districts? I for one cannot explain, and incline to
the belief that the now discredited opinion on the origin of the name

---

[13] This was also the dance TH specified for performance in *The Three Wayfarers* and, as Purdy
notes (p. 323), a similar—though by no means identical—figure was included in the edition of that
play published in New York by the Fountain Press in 1930, p. [vii].

[14] Some of the music books used by TH's grandfather and other members of the Hardy family
are now in the Dorset County Museum.

('contre-danse') may be after all the truth of the matter; and this would accord with the fact that these dances[15] displaced the simpler folk-dance.[16]

Many thanks for the *Country Dance Book*;[17] also for the two numbers of *E.F.D.S. News* . . .[18] The figure called *Bonnets so Blue*[19] was called *Hands across* here, and was probably the one I had in mind when Shiner would not cast off.[20] But it was mostly danced to a tune called 'Enrico'.[21]

I found a copy, or rather a leaf or two, of the original edition of *The Triumph* (to which you allude) among my grandfather's old music. The page is entitled 'New Dances for the year 1793', so that seems to be when it came out.[22]

* * * * *

THE COLLEGE HORNPIPE.
As formerly danced in Wessex.

(*First strain*). Top three couples six hands half-round and back again to places.

(*First strain repeated*). The same three couples, one hand joined of each, promenade full round to places.

(*Second strain*). Two top couples down the middle and up again, to places.

(*Second strain repeated*). The three couples whole poussette (both hands joined) leaving second couple at the top. (Tune ends).

(*Tune begins again*). The original top couple, being now in the second place, dance six hands round with the original third and fourth couples and so on through the figure as above, leaving original third couple above them. (Tune ends).

---

[15] The reading 'dances' in TH's holograph addition to the proof has been substituted for the clearly incorrect 'dancers' of the text as published.

[16] 'The history . . . folk-dance.' inserted in margins of proof in TH's hand.

[17] Cecil Sharp's *The Country Dance Book*, published in six parts (London: Novello, 1909–22); George Butterworth was co-author of parts 3 and 4, Maud Karpeles of part 5. Macmillan had sent TH the first part only.   [18] Macmillan's elision, not restored by TH on the proof.

[19] Described, like *The Triumph*, in *The Country Dance Book*, part 1, pp. 58, 57, and mentioned by Macmillan both in the introductory portion of the article and in his first letter to TH (19 January 1926; DCM).   [20] See *Under the Greenwood Tree* (Wessex edn.), p. 50.

[21] Briefly mentioned in *LW*, p. 19.

[22] TH's reference is apparently to the tattered and fragmentary copy of *Twenty four Country Dances for the Year 1793* now in the DCM: 'The Triumph' appears on p. [86].

(*Tune begins again*). The original top couple being now in the third place, do the same with the original fourth and fifth couple. (Tune ends, the original top couple being in the original fourth couple's place).

(*Tune begins again*). At the same time that the original top couple starts the figure again with the original fifth and sixth couples, the original second couple, which has been idle at the top, starts the same figure with the original third and fourth couples standing below them, so that the figure is now going on in two places, and later, if the line is a long one, in as many places as there is room for.

The original top couple at last finds itself breathless at the bottom of the dance; but gradually works up to the top as succeeding couples dance down and take places below.

[1926.13]

[Truro Message on Cruel Sports]

Hardy replied briefly to an appeal (4 October 1926, DCM) from Wilfred P. H. Warner, of the South Devon Branch of the League for the Prohibition of Cruel Sports, for a message that might be read out at a League meeting to be held in Truro, Cornwall, on 22 October 1926. The hostile tone of the report of that event in the *West Briton and Cornwall Advertiser*, 28 October 1926, p. 11, perhaps explains the absence of any reference to Hardy's message; on the other hand, Warner might himself have withheld it as constituting something less than a rallying cry. The text below is that of the correspondence card in Hardy's hand now in the Pierpont Morgan Library.

From Th. Hardy, Max Gate, Dorchester. 15 Oct. 1926

You have all my sympathy in protesting against cruel sports; but I fear that the human race has emerged so little as yet from a state of savagery that not much can be done.

T. H.

W. P. H. Warner Esq.

[1926.14]

[Message to Bournemouth Branch, National Union of Journalists]

Hardy responded positively in December 1926 to a request from the Bournemouth Branch of the National Union of Journalists for a message to be included in *Press Pie*, an occasional miscellany being published by the branch in connection with a Carnival Press Ball in aid of the Union's Widow and Orphan Fund. No copy of *Press Pie* has as yet been located, but Hardy was thanked for his help (20 December 1926, DCM) and the wording of the actual message—evidently reproduced in facsimile—was reported, as below, by the Dorset collector E. N. Sanders in a letter to Richard Purdy of 20 November 1953.

SUCCESS TO THE PRESS BALL.

T. H.

[1926.15]

'Commemoration Dinner of King's College'

Hardy corresponded in June 1926 with Dr Ernest Barker (1874–1960), political philosopher and principal of King's College, London, about the evening classes in French he had taken at the college in 1865–6 (*CL* vii. 30–1). Invited to the annual dinner of the college in December 1926, Hardy wrote a brief reply (*CL* vii. 50) that was read out by Barker at the dinner and imperfectly reported, as below, in *The Times*, 17 December 1926, p. 7, beneath the heading 'Commemoration Dinner of King's College'.

The PRINCIPAL, replying to the toast, read a letter from Mr Thomas Hardy, an old student of the college,[23] thanking him for an invitation to the dinner.

'It keeps alive', Mr Hardy wrote, 'a sense of my old relations[24] with you. I wish I could come. But I am getting more and more every year like an old vegetable which will[25] not bear transplanting.'

[23] TH, however, had been very much a part-time student, taking evening classes only and perhaps not completing them: see *Biography*, p. 90.

[24] For 'relations' TH's typed MS (King's College) reads 'relationship'.

[25] For 'like . . . will' TH's MS reads 'like a vegetable that will'.

[1927.01]

'Wessex University Scheme'

Informed by the Vice-Chancellor of University College, Southampton, of a forthcoming public meeting in Bournemouth to discuss the creation of a University of Wessex, Hardy responded on 25 February 1927 with a brief message of support (draft, DCM) that was read out at the meeting on 27 February and reported in still briefer summary, as follows, in *The Times*, 1 March 1927, p. 16. See 1921.02 and 1925.06.

Mr Thomas Hardy wrote wishing that the meeting would meet with great results.[1]

[1927.02]

[Taunton Message on Cruel Sports]

On 24 February 1927 (DCM) Henry B. Amos, Secretary of the League for the Prohibition of Cruel Sports, approached Hardy with a request for 'a brief message', to be read out at a meeting at Taunton on 4 March. Hardy promptly drafted a third-person reply, dated 25 February (DCM), to be sent by his wife on his behalf. The message itself, divested of the draft's opening comment that he believed he had 'already sent a message on his opinion of Cruel Sports' (see 1926.01, 1926.13), was published, as below, in *The Times*, 5 March 1927, p. 7, under the heading 'Protest Against Blood Sports.

---

[1] TH's draft reads: 'I am delighted to learn that the organizers of the movement for a University of Wessex have got so far as to hold a Public Meeting. I wish I could attend it, but in my inability to do so I send sincere wishes that it may lead to great results.'

Mr. Thomas Hardy's Message'; it also appeared in the *Morning Post*, 5 March 1917, p. 11, the *Animals' Friend*, 33 (April 1927), p. 79, and *Cruel Sports*, 1 (April 1927), p. 42. Purdy, p. 324.

The[2] human race being still practically barbarian, it does not seem likely that men's delight in cruel sports can be lessened except by slow degrees. To attempt even this is, however, a worthy object which I commend.[3]

[1927.03]

'The Preservation of Ancient Cottages'

In the autumn of 1926 the Royal Society of Arts enlisted Hardy's support for its campaign to halt the destruction of old cottages in the English countryside. He evaded, however, the request (27 November 1926, DCM) of the Society's secretary, George Kenneth Menzies, that he make a direct appeal for funds, and would later decline on grounds of age to broadcast on the campaign's behalf (RSA Minutes, 13 July 1927), but he did write and send what Florence Hardy, in a letter drafted by Hardy himself (undated, DCM), described as 'all that Mr Hardy feels able to say on behalf of the Ancient Cottages'. The document thus received by the Society in early December 1926 (RSA Minutes, 9 December 1926) was not, presumably, the extant fair-copy holograph manuscript headed '[Written for the Society of Arts]' (DCM) but rather a typescript made from it. But no typescript or other pre-publication form of the text, has been traced in the Society's archives, and in the absence of such evidence it is impossible to determine the extent of Hardy's responsibility for the several discrepancies between the fair-copy MS and the 'Note by Thomas Hardy, O.M.'—supplementary to the main appeal by the Prime Minister, Stanley Baldwin—that was published as below in *The Preservation of Ancient Cottages* ([London]: Royal Society of Arts), pp. 13–[16], in early March of 1927. Hardy's note was extensively quoted in *The Times*, 11 March 1927, p. 19, and reprinted in its entirety in the *Dorset*

---

[2] TH's draft begins 'Dear Sir: In reply to your letter Mr Hardy asks me to say that he thinks he has already sent a message on his opinion of Cruel Sports. In case however, he has not done so he repeats it—to the effect that the human . . .'.

[3] For 'which I commend'—the reading of all the printed texts listed above—TH's draft reads 'which he commends'; that the third-person wording of the draft was nevertheless preserved in the message actually sent is indicated by the return to 'which he commends' in *Cruel Sports*, 2 (February 1928), p. 15.

County Chronicle, 17 March 1927, p. 2; the text below, however, is that of the pamphlet, with the more substantial variations from the MS recorded in footnotes. Purdy, p. 323.

I can with pleasure support the appeal of the Royal Society of Arts for assistance in its plan towards preserving the ancient cottages of England, having been, first and last, familiar with many of these vener-able buildings in the West of England, and having also seen many of them vanish under the hands of their owners, through mistaken views not only on their appearance, but on their substantiality and comfort.

They are often as old as the parish church itself, but in consequence of a lack of distinctive architectural features in most, it is difficult to pro-nounce upon their exact date. In this district they continued[4] to be built in the old style down to about the middle of the last century, when they were ousted by the now ubiquitous brick-and-slate. By the merest chance I was able, when a child, to see the building of what was prob-ably one of the last of these old-fashioned cottages of 'mud-wall' and thatch. What was called mud-wall was really a composition of chalk, clay, and straw—essentially, unbaked brick. This was mixed up into a sort of dough-pudding, close to where the cottage was to be built. The mixing was performed by treading and shovelling—women sometimes being called in to tread—and the straw was added to bind the mass together, a process that had doubtless gone on since the days of Israel in Egypt and earlier.

It was then thrown up by pitch-forks on to the wall, where it was trodden down, to a thickness of about two feet, till a 'rise' of about three feet had been reached all round the building. This was left to settle for a day or two, and then another rise was effected, till the whole height to the wall-plate was reached, and then that of the gables, unless the cot-tage was hipped, or had a 'pinion' end,[5] as it was called. When the wall had dried a little the outer face was cut down to a fairly flat surface with a spade, and the wall then plastered outside and in. The thatch pro-jected sufficiently to prevent much rain running down the outer plaster, and even where it did run down the plaster was so hard as to be

---

[4] For 'date . . . continued' MS reads 'date. They continued'.

[5] A hipped roof has sloped instead of vertical ends. *OED* defines 'pinion-end' simply as 'gable', but the other Dorset spelling, 'pinning end', suggests it was used when a building had a hipped roof ending in a slope and thus did not require the end-walls to rise into gables; cf. *Two on a Tower* (Wessex edn.), p. 121.

unaffected, more lime being used than nowadays. The house I speak of is, I believe, still standing, unless replaced by a colder and damper one of brick-and-slate.

I can recall another cottage of the sort, which has been standing nearly 130 years,[6] where the original external plaster is uninjured by weather, though it has been patched here and there; but the thatch has been renewed half a dozen times in the period. Had the thatch been of straw which had passed through a threshing machine in the modern way it would have required renewal twice as many times during the existence of the walls. But formerly the thatching straw was drawn by hand from the ricks before threshing and, being unbruised, lasted[7] twice as long, especially if not trimmed; though the thatcher usually liked to trim his work to make it look neater.

I have never heard of any damp coming through these mud-walls, plastered and lime-whitened on the outside. Yet as everybody, at any rate every builder, knows, even when brick walls are built hollow it is difficult to keep damp out entirely in exposed situations.[8]

Landowners who have built some of these latter express their wonder that the villagers prefer their old dingy hovels (as they are regarded) with rooms only six feet high, and small dormer windows with little lead squares, to the new residences with nine-feet rooms and wide windows with large panes. The explanation is the simple one that in the stroke of country winds a high room is not required for fresh air, sufficient ventilation entering through the door and window, and that the draught through the hollow brick wall makes the new cottages cold in winter.

I would therefore urge owners to let as many as are left of their old cottages remain where they are, and to repair them instead of replacing them with bricks, since, apart from their warmth and dryness, they have almost always great[9] beauty and charm. Not only so, but I would suggest that their construction might be imitated when rebuilding is absolutely necessary.

---

[6] TH's reference is presumably to his own birthplace, built around 1800 in the Dorset hamlet of Higher Bockhampton.

[7] For 'threshing . . . lasted' MS reads 'threshing (the process being called "reed-drawing") and in its unbruised state lasted'; cf. *Tess of the d'Urbervilles* (Wessex edn.), pp. 370–3.

[8] For 'entirely in exposed situations.' MS reads 'entirely.'

[9] For 'have . . . great' MS reads 'have often—indeed almost always—great'.

[1927.04]

[Message to *The Countryman*]

John William Robertson Scott (1866–1962), journalist and author, founded the quarterly magazine of rural writing called *The Countryman* in 1927. On 23 April 1927 (DCM) Scott sent Florence Hardy a copy of the first number, regretted that Hardy had not felt able to contribute to it, and enclosed a postcard in the hope that he would nevertheless send 'a word or two' for reproduction in facsimile in the second (July) number. The wording of Hardy's draft response (DCM), dated April 1927 and pencilled onto Scott's letter, corresponds precisely to that of his actual holograph card as quoted in the Jenkins Co. of Austin, Texas, catalogue 48 (March 1972), item 234. Only Hardy's signature was in fact reproduced in facsimile in *The Countryman*, 1 (July 1927), p. 143, but the surrounding text referred to 'his postcard of greeting to us' and included the following third-person recension of the greeting itself.

Mr Hardy speaks of THE COUNTRYMAN'S 'promise', expresses his belief that the Review will be a success and says it 'makes one feel in the country'.[10]

[1927.05]

'Visit of South African Farmers'

During the summer of 1927 a group of eighty farmers from South Africa toured farms and agricultural institutions throughout England, Scotland, and Wales. Some twenty-five members of the group visited the Dorchester area on 13 and 14 July 1927 and were entertained to dinner on the 13th by the mayor, Wilfrid Hodges, and the Dorset Farmers' Union. Hodges, who knew Hardy well, asked him (DCM) for a message of welcome that could be printed on a souvenir menu for the dinner. No copy of that menu has been

---

[10] The front wrapper of the second issue, as of several later issues, bore the legend, '"The Countryman makes one feel in the country."—*Thomas Hardy*.' TH's draft read in its entirety: 'The first number of "The Countryman" is promising, & makes one feel in the country. The paper should be a success. Thomas Hardy.'

traced, but the message as printed under the heading 'Visit of South African Farmers' in the *Dorset County Chronicle*, 14 July 1927, p. 8—and as reproduced below—differs at only one point from the wording of Hardy's draft (DCM). Purdy, p. 324.

I send to your guests from South Africa—that beautiful country which has such an assured future before it—a few words which I am sorry to be unable to express orally; that I hope their visit to England and Europe will be a successful one,[11] and that the weather here, so uncertain by comparison with their own, will not unduly depress.[12]

[1927.06]

On Laying the Commemoration Stone of the New Dorchester Grammar School

Although Hardy never attended the Dorchester Grammar School as a boy, he served on the school's Board of Governors from 1909 to 1926, and accepted in February 1927 an invitation to lay the foundation stone of the school's new buildings on the outskirts of Dorchester (*CL* vii. 61). On the day itself, 21 July 1927, the weather was unseasonably windy and cold, and although Hardy reportedly performed his task 'with great vigour' and spoke 'in a clear resonant voice' (*LW*, p. 472), his doctor believed the exertion and exposure to have been directly contributory to Hardy's death less than six months later (*Letters EFH*, p. 265). The earliest version of the speech known to survive is the three-page fair-copy typescript prepared by Florence Hardy in several copies, one of which (Adams) was cut into half-sheets and used by Hardy when delivering the speech, while another (G. Stevens-Cox) supplied the basis for the full and accurate report of the speech in the *Dorset County Chronicle*, 28 July 1927, p. 2, and a third generated the report, also accurate, in *The Times*, 22 July, p. 11. Sydney Cockerell used *The Times* report as copy-text for the privately printed pamphlet that he took urgently in hand after receiving Florence Hardy's telegram of 23 July: 'PLEASE PRINT SPEECH OTHER APPLICATIONS RECEIVED' (Adams). Revisions made by Hardy on a proof and in a separately typed list of corrections (both Adams) were, however, incorporated into the pamphlet prior to its

[11] In TH's draft of a covering letter to Hodges—to be typed, signed, and sent by his wife—he suggested that if the message were over-long it could 'be abridged by leaving out all after "successful one"' (DCM).   [12] For 'depress.' TH's draft reads 'depress them.'

appearance, in twelve copies (Adams, Beinecke, DCM), as *Address Delivered by Thomas Hardy on Laying the Commemoration Stone of the New Dorchester Grammar School Twenty-First July 1927* (Cambridge: Printed for Florence Emily Hardy at the University Press, August 1927), and that text was later quoted, verbatim, in *Life and Work*, pp. 472–3. A London dealer named Joseph A. Allen, one of those specifically denied permission to reprint the speech (TH draft, 23 July 1927, DCM), nevertheless produced an unauthorized four-page leaflet (Adams, Beinecke, Houghton) entitled *The Two Hardys: An Address by Thomas Hardy, July 21, 1927* (London: printed for private circulation only, 1927). The text below is that of Florence Hardy's pamphlet; notes record significant variants found in earlier texts. Purdy, pp. 248–9.

I have been asked to execute the formal part of to-day's function, which has now been done,[13] and it is not really necessary that I should add anything to the few words that are accustomed to be used at the laying of foundation or dedication stones. But as the circumstances of the present case are somewhat peculiar, I will just enlarge upon them for a minute or two. What I have to say is mainly concerning the Elizabethan philanthropist, Thomas Hardy, who, with some encouragement from the burgesses, endowed and re-built this ancient school after its first humble shape[14]—him whose namesake I have the honour to be, and whose monument stands in the church of St Peter, visible from this spot. The well-known epitaph inscribed upon his tablet,[15] unlike many epitaphs, does not, I am inclined to think, exaggerate his virtues, since it was written, not by his relatives or dependents, but by the free burgesses of Dorchester in gratitude for his good action towards the town. This good deed was accomplished in the latter part of the sixteenth century, and the substantial stone building in which it merged eventually, still stands to dignify South-street, as we all know, and hope it may remain there.[16]

But what we know very little about is the personality of this first recorded Thomas Hardy of the Froome Valley here at our back, though his work abides. He was[17] without doubt of the family of the

---

[13] TH had already pronounced the words, 'I declare this stone well and truly laid' (*Dorset County Chronicle*, 28 July 1927, p. 2).

[14] For 'endowed . . . shape' all previous texts read 'endowed and probably built this ancient school in its first shape'.   [15] See *LW*, pp. 9–10.

[16] It has since been pulled down and replaced, in part by Hardye's Arcade.

[17] For 'He was' TH interlineated in the 'delivery' typescript 'He, like the rest of us Dorset Hardys, was'. The added words appear in no other form of the text and were presumably spoken on the day itself.

Hardys[18] who landed in this county from Jersey in the fifteenth century, acquired small estates along the river upwards towards its source, and whose descendants have mostly remained[19] hereabouts ever since, the Christian name of Thomas having been especially affected by them. He died in 1599, and it is curious to think that though he must have had a modern love of learning not common in a remote county in those days, Shakespeare's name could hardly have been known to him, or at the most but vaguely as that of a certain ingenious Mr Shakespeare who amused the London playgoers; and that he died before Milton was born.

In Carlylean[20] phraseology, what manner of man he was when he walked this earth, we can but guess, or what he looked like, what he said and did in his lighter moments, and at what age he died. But we may shrewdly conceive that he was a far-sighted man, and would not be much surprised, if he were to revisit the daylight, to find that his building had been outgrown, and no longer supplied the needs of the present inhabitants for the due education of their sons. His next feeling might be to rejoice in[21] the development of what was possibly an original design[22] of his own, and to wish the reconstruction every success.

We living ones all do that, and nobody more than I, my retirement from the Governing body having been necessitated by old age only. Certainly everything promises well. The site can hardly be surpassed in England for health, with its open surroundings, elevated and bracing situation, and dry subsoil, while it is near enough to the sea to get very distinct whiffs of marine air. Moreover, it is not so far from the centre of the borough as to be beyond the walking powers of the smallest boy. It has a capable headmaster,[23] holding every modern idea on education within the limits of good judgment, and assistant masters well equipped for their labours, which are not sinecures in these days.

I will conclude by thanking the Governors and other friends for their kind thought in asking me to undertake this formal initiation of the new building,[24] which marks such an interesting stage in the history of the Dorchester Grammar School.

[18] For 'doubt . . . Hardys' earlier texts read 'doubt one of the Hardys'.

[19] For 'and whose . . . remained' earlier texts read 'and have remained'.

[20] For 'Carlylean' earlier texts read 'Carlyle's'; the revision perhaps acknowledged that TH was not quoting Carlyle but momentarily adopting his style. Orel, p. 281, points to a possible specific source in bk. I, ch. 3, of *Sartor Resartus*.

[21] For 'might . . . rejoice in' earlier texts read 'might be that he rejoiced in'.

[22] For 'design' earlier texts read 'idea'.

[23] The headmaster, newly appointed, was Ralph William Hill, M.A., who remained in that position until 1955.

[24] The 'new building' has itself now been abandoned and the school moved to another site.

[1927.07]

'English Country-Dances'

Hardy's views on the history of the country dance (see 1926.12) had been challenged by members of the English Folk Dance Society as being at odds with those of Cecil Sharp (1859–1924), famous collector of English folk songs and dances and the Society's founder and first director. He therefore enlarged upon his views in a typed letter of 26 October 1926 (Cecil Sharp House) to N. O. M. Cameron, editor of *E.F.D.S. News*, and subsequently gave permission (*CL* vii. 62) for that letter to be published, as below, in the *Journal of the English Folk Dance Society*, 2nd series, 1 (1927), pp. 53–4, as part of an unsigned article headed 'English Country-Dances'. The printed text reproduces, lightly edited, the main body of the original letter but omits its epistolary features and opening acknowledgement of Cameron's letter of 9 October 1926 (DCM). Purdy, p. 323.

It is quite natural that my heretical query whether, after all, the country-dance might have been a successor to the true folk-dance, should meet with opposition. I hold no strong views, but I ask those who maintain otherwise to explain the following rather formidable facts:

1. Down to the middle of the last century, country villagers were divided into two distinct castes, one being the artisans, traders, 'liviers' (owners of freeholds),[25] and the manor-house upper servants; the other the 'work-folk', i.e. farm-labourers (these were never called by the latter name by themselves and other country people till about 70 years ago). The two castes rarely intermarried, and did not go to each other's house-gatherings save exceptionally.

2. The work-folk had their own dances, which were reels of all sorts, jigs, a long dance called the 'horse-race', another called 'thread-the-needle', &c. These were danced with hops, leg-crossings, and rather boisterous movements.

3. Country-dances were introduced into villages about 1800 onwards by the first group or caste, who had sometimes lived in towns. The work-folk knew nothing of the so-called folk-dances (country-dances), and had to be taught them at mixed gatherings. They would lapse

---

[25] *OED* defines 'livier' as 'One who holds a tenement on a lease for a life or lives', and TH so uses it, here and elsewhere; such villagers, however, were 'half-independent', as TH puts it in 'The Dorsetshire Labourer' (see final paragraph of 1883.04), rather than freeholders in the full sense.

back again to their own dances at their own unmixed merry-makings, where they never voluntarily danced country-dances.

4. That in the London magazines of the eighteenth[26] century, and by music publishers of that date, country-dances were printed, music and figures, as new dances.

Of course I speak only of the west and south-west of England; and don't wish to contest other explanations which may be possible. Also I speak of the Wessex village of seventy to eighty years ago, before railways, when I knew it intimately—and probably not many of your members did, not even the late Mr Sharp, who gave such good labour to the subject—and know little of its condition in the present century.

[1927.08]

[On Writing Poems]

Edward Wheeler Scripture (1864–1945), an American psychologist and phonetician teaching at the University of Vienna, collected material for his study of English verse forms by asking selected poets to answer a series of thirteen questions, beginning with '1. Describe your attitude toward the versification of the poem you are about to write' and ending with '12. How do you get your poems?' and '13. Why do you write them?' Hardy evidently ignored Scripture's indirect approach in July 1926 (*CL* vii. 36), but he did respond to a direct letter of 3 October 1927 (DCM) in which Scripture sought permission to quote from one of his poems before explaining that the accompanying questions were not intended to elicit answers but only a 'brief expression'. The first paragraph of Hardy's typed reply, 11 October 1927 (BL), granted the permission requested; the second provided the basis for the abbreviated and reworked quotation, reproduced below, that Scripture subsequently invoked in his *Grundzüge der englischen Verswissenschaft* (Marburg: N. G. Elwert, 1929), p. 1.

In respect of the questions I regret[27] to say that I am unable to answer them, and can only suggest in a general way that I write poems because I cannot help it.

Thomas Hardy.[28]

---

[26] Corrected in the *Journal* from the MS reading 'seventeenth'.

[27] For 'questions I regret' TH's letter reads 'questions you annex to your letter I regret'.

[28] TH's MS in fact closed with 'Yours truly, Th: Hardy', followed by Scripture's name and address. Scripture also omitted the letter's address, date, salutation, and first paragraph.

[1927.09]

G.M.: A Reminiscence

Writing to William Maxse Meredith 16 July 1927 (*CL* vii. 72), Hardy promised to 'try to say something' about Meredith's father, the novelist and poet George Meredith, on the occasion of the February 1928 centenary of his birth (see also *CL* vii. 78–9). The article—as completed in early October 1927 (fair-copy MS, DCM) and published after Hardy's death as 'G.M.: A Reminiscence', *The Nineteenth Century and After*, 103 (February 1928), pp. 146–8—proved to be more substantial than had been originally envisaged, and after the magazine proofs (Beinecke) had been corrected Florence Hardy passed on to Sydney Cockerell (3 November 1927, Beinecke) her husband's suggestion that unauthorized printings (cf. 1927.06) might be forestalled by advance publication of the article as a privately printed pamphlet. Cockerell acted with characteristic promptitude, the corrected magazine proof served as copy, Hardy made corrections at two subsequent proof stages (Beinecke), and the result was *G.M.: A Reminiscence*, privately printed in twelve copies (Beinecke, DCM, Houghton) for Florence Emily Hardy at the Cambridge University Press, 21 November 1929. Because Hardy's changes for the pamphlet were never transferred to the article, the text below is that of the former, with the more significant unrevised readings of the article recorded in footnotes. Purdy, pp. 250–1.

On the centenary of the birth of George Meredith it has been thought appropriate that I should say what few words I can say about so exceptional a man; and I have assented, not because I am well qualified to speak of one of such individual and brilliant achievement—indeed, far from it—but because I chanced to encounter him at a date that has now become very remote, and when he can probably have been known to few persons still alive who met him for purely literary reasons as I did, and not as members of his family or domestic friends.

Meredith is so modern that it may surprise his younger readers who have not given much thought to the matter to be reminded that he was living for four years as a juvenile contemporary of Sir Walter Scott, who at his birth had not published *The Fair Maid of Perth*, *Anne of Geierstein*, or *Count Robert*; that for six years he was a contemporary of Lamb and Coleridge, for fifteen years of Southey, and for twenty-two years of Wordsworth; and that *The Ordeal of Richard Feverel* was finished before Darwin settled the question of the Origin of Species.

It is hopeless to attempt to get back all the way from effects to causes in terrestrial affairs as in celestial, but at any rate a proximate cause of my knowledge of Meredith was the late Mr Alexander Macmillan.[29] He had been the first to read the manuscript of my first novel—if it could be called a novel (essayed after I had[30] dabbled in verse for years)—and, being apparently in some doubt about it, suggested that I should let it be seen by Messrs Chapman & Hall, to which firm of publishers he gave me an introduction. He may have had it in his mind that by sending me there the troublesome manuscript would be read by Meredith, but he did not tell me so. Anyway, thither I went, left the novel, and some weeks later received a letter from the firm, asking me if I could 'meet the gentleman who has read your MS., as he would like to speak to you about it'.

Hence it happened that on a winter afternoon hard upon sixty years ago—to be precise, in January 1869[31]—I was shown into a back room of Messrs Chapman & Hall's premises in Piccadilly, and found Meredith awaiting me there. I felt that he was an unusual sort of man to discover in a back office in London, though I knew nothing about his personality, Mr Frederick Chapman, who presented me to him, not having told me his name.

He was then a little over forty[32] years of age, and was quite in the prime of life. At that time he had by no means escaped the shots of reviewers who were out to suppress anything like originality. The criticisms bestowed upon his writings were, indeed, as various probably as those upon any author before or since whose treatment by the press can be remembered. Only six or seven years earlier the *Spectator's* pronouncement was, 'Mr Meredith may be a very clever man, but he is not a genius', or words to that effect,[33] which provoked Swinburne into writing an expostulatory letter to that paper,[34] the editor, I must add, honestly printing the letter intact, despite his own opinion. At about the same time—though[35] I cannot quite remember the exact sequence of events—the *Saturday Review* also treated Meredith's volume entitled *Modern Love, and Poems of the English Roadside*, in this fashion:

[29] Alexander Macmillan (1818–96), co-founder with his brother Daniel (1813–57) of the Macmillan publishing house; for his response to TH's MS of 'The Poor Man and the Lady', see 1910.05 and *LW*, pp. 59–60.   [30] For 'novel . . . had' article reads 'novel (though I had'.

[31] *LW*, p. 62, gives the date, correctly, as March 1869; cf. *Biography*, pp. 114–15.

[32] For 'He . . . forty' article reads 'He must have been then about forty'.

[33] The *Spectator* review of *Modern Love* (24 May 1862, p. 580) in fact stated: 'Mr. George Meredith is a clever man, without literary genius, taste, or judgment'.

[34] *Spectator*, 7 June 1862, pp. 632–3; reprinted in *The Swinburne Letters*, ed. Cecil Y. Lang, 6 vols. (New Haven: Yale University Press, 1959–62), i. 51–3.

[35] For 'opinion. At . . . though' article reads 'opinion. And about five years before—though'.

His strong thought and quaint expression remind us here and there—though at a considerable interval—of Robert Browning. . . . However, a perusal of Mr George Meredith's more ambitious productions, and especially of *Modern Love*, leads one reluctantly to the conclusion that he has entirely mistaken his powers, and has utterly marred what might have been a rare and successful volume. . . . It is, as we have said, bad enough that a writer of real ability and skill should allow himself to associate this kind of fustian with poems of worth and merit. But Mr George Meredith's descent from his 'roadside' style of thought and composition to his lyrical mood is, we regret to say, only trifling compared with the change which he undergoes when he indulges in an elaborate analysis of a loathsome series of phenomena which he is pleased to call 'Modern Love', . . . a choice of subject involving a mistake so grave as utterly to disqualify the chooser from achieving any great and worthy result in art.[36]

Thus we see that the two leading weekly reviews of that mid-Victorian decade during which I made his acquaintance were practically in accord about Meredith, and doubtless they were strong enough to put a damper on the circulation of *Modern Love* till years later.

However, as above stated, I was not aware that my adviser at the interview was the man who had undergone these bludgeonings, and was just then emerging from them triumphantly. Unfortunately I made no note of our conversation: in those days people did not usually write down everything as they do now for the concoction of reminiscences; and the only words of his that I remember were, 'Don't nail your colours to the mast just yet.' But I well recall his appearance—a handsome man with hair and beard not at all grey, and wearing a frock coat buttoned at the waist and loose above.

Many years were to elapse before I saw him again—this time as himself, and not 'as the gentleman who has read your MS.'—when he had been accepted and had become familiar to those who could enjoy his writings as 'chaos illuminated by flashes of lightning',[37] full of epigrams of thought and beauty. Our meetings were then continued at irregular intervals that covered a long span of time, till there came a last, of which I can only recall one trifling incident. A literary lady of rank had asked me if I would take her to see him, which she said she was dying to do. I did not wish to take her, but I put the question to him as I was leaving.

---

[36] *Saturday Review*, 24 October 1863, p. 562. TH quotes accurately, except that for 'subject . . . mistake' the *Review* reads 'subject which we cannot help regarding as involving a grave moral mistake—a mistake'.

[37] Oscar Wilde, 'The Decay of Lying: A Dialogue', *Nineteenth Century*, 25 (January 1889), p. 40: 'Ah! Meredith! Who can define him? His style is chaos illumined by flashes of lightning.'

To his warm invitation to me to come again soon, which I promised to do, he added drily: 'But don't bring the lady.'

As is so often the case with such intentions, before I had gone again I was confronted one afternoon by a newspaper placard—almost close to the spot in Piccadilly where I had first met him forty years before—announcing in large capitals: 'DEATH OF MR GEORGE MEREDITH.'[38]

I am not able to say what influence Meredith may be exercising over the writings of the present generation. Some of his later contemporaries and immediate successors certainly bear marks of his style and outlook, particularly in respect of the Comic Spirit,[39] most of them forgetting, as he did not forget (though he often conveniently veiled his perception of it), that, as I think Ruskin remarks, 'Comedy is Tragedy if you only look deep enough.'[40] The likelihood is that, after some years have passed, what was best in his achievement—at present partly submerged by its other characteristics—will rise still more distinctly to the surface than it has done already. Then he will not only be regarded as a writer who said finest and profoundest things often in a tantalising way, but as one whose work remains as an essential portion of the vast universal volume which enshrines as contributors all those that have adequately recorded their reading of life.

[1927.10]

[Preface for French Translation of *The Dynasts*]

Yvonne M. Salmon, a lecturer in French at University College, Reading, visited Hardy at Max Gate in February 1925 in her capacity as secretary of the British branch of Alliance Française (*CL* vi. 304–5). She subsequently embarked, with Hardy's approval, on a French translation of *The Dynasts*, and Hardy wrote—apparently in mid-November 1927 (*CL* vii. 83)—a special preface to the two segments of her translation scheduled for publication in a forthcoming Thomas Hardy issue of *La Revue hebdomadaire*. Following Hardy's death on 11 January 1928, however, the *Revue hebdomadaire* material

---

[38] Cf. 1909.06.

[39] For 'the Comic Spirit' article reads '*The Comic Spirit*'. Meredith's lecture, *On the Idea of Comedy and the Uses of the Comic Spirit*, was first published in 1877.   [40] See 1910.09, n. 40.

was incorporated into a special 'Hommage à Thomas Hardy' double issue of *La Revue nouvelle* (nos. 38–39, January–February 1928), and Hardy's Preface—in French translation, headed 'Préface de l'auteur pour la traduction française', and dated December 1927—appeared there, as follows, on pp. 40–1. The apparent non-survival of the original English version of the Preface has prompted speculation that the pedestrian and perhaps excessively literal translation was Hardy's own work. But Salmon was inexperienced, as her letters to Florence Hardy (DCM) clearly show, and had Hardy indeed translated the piece it seems inconceivable that its French editors and publishers would not have announced and celebrated the fact. In any case an editorial footnote in *La Revue nouvelle* not only refers to 'la traductrice' but quotes a sentence in her praise that Hardy had included in 'l'original' but she had modestly omitted. Translations of the Preface back into English have appeared in the *Colby Mercury*, 6 (June 1936), pp. [86]–87, and, more recently, in *Complete Poetical Works*, v. 398–9. The *Dynasts* project itself, announced as forthcoming by a correspondent in *The Times*, 24 February 1928, p. 10, was not realized in print until 1947, when *Les Dynastes*, translated into French prose by Yvonne Salmon and Philippe Neel, was published in Paris by Éditions Stock. Hardy's Preface reappeared, pp. [7]–8, in a new and livelier translation and with the sentence about his translator reinserted as a final paragraph. Purdy, p. 324.

Lorsqu'on me suggéra que *Les Dynastes* étaient un drame qui paraissait particulièrement susceptible d'intéresser les lecteurs français, je fus frappé par la vraisemblance de la suggestion; c'est pourquoi je me prêtai au projet de traduction du drame, formant tous le vœux pour que l'entreprise pût être conduite à terme, tout en redoutant que le labeur qu'elle impliquait ne fût quelque peu écrasant. En fait, il se révéla moins écrasant que je ne m'y attendais.

En y réfléchissant il m'apparut qu'il y avait une raison toute spéciale pour qu'une version de ce drame fût donnée en français. Combien de fois, au cours des siècles, les deux pays de France et d'Angleterre n'avaient-ils pas été entraînés dans des conflits en vertu de codes ou de gouvernements irresponsables, alors que les peuples eux-mêmes eussent, comme de juste, préféré vaquer à leurs propres affaires! Tel fut notamment le cas à l'époque où se situe ce drame,—de 1805 à 1815. Je me disais qu'avec le recul du temps la perception de ce fait induirait les lecteurs français à affronter les événements sans passion ni parti-pris. Le spectacle entier, en vérité, peut maintenant être envisagé tant en France qu'en Angleterre, comme un phénomène singulier dans lequel, comme dans toute guerre en général, la raison humaine eut peu de part.

Une autre considération encore faisait taire toute objection,—je veux dire le cadre ou *merveilleux* philosophique, Napoléon est un personnage particulièrement adapté à être traité par le dramaturge comme une marionnette du Destin: en fait lui-même s'est souvent regardé comme tel; et comme tel peut-être pouvons-nous lui pardonner certaines de ses erreurs et de ses ambitions, en attendant que dans l'avenir nous puissions en arriver à lui tout pardonner (ainsi qu'aux autres tempéraments combatifs!) si la théorie *moniste* des Causes et des Effets, adoptée dans ce drame, en vue de motifs principalement artistiques, comme la force de propulsion qui meut les personnages, se découvre être la vraie théorie de l'univers. Sur ce point toutefois, auquel d'ailleurs se trouve liée toute la question du libre arbitre, je n'ai point qualité pour prophétiser. En tout cas les compatriotes de Descartes[41] sauront apprécier cette théorie comme système dramatique, même s'ils ne l'acceptent pas en tant que philosophie.[42]

Décembre 1927.

[1927.11]

[Recommendation for *Tarka the Otter*]

The novelist Henry Williamson (1895–1977) recalled in his autobiographical *Goodbye West Country* (London: Putnam, 1937), p. 273, that, following an unheralded visit he had made to Max Gate in the autumn of 1927, Florence Hardy wrote to the publisher (Putnam) of the first commercial edition of his *Tarka the Otter* to say that her husband would like his opinion of the book to be quoted in an advertisement. Williamson's signature is indeed present in the Max Gate visitors' book for 31 October 1927 (BL), and the following words duly appeared, alongside brief recommendations by John Galsworthy and Arnold Bennett, in an advertisement for *Tarka the Otter* in the *Spectator*, 3 December 1927, p. 1005.

Mr Thomas Hardy writes: 'A remarkable book.'

[41] René Descartes (1596–1650), French philosopher and mathematician.
[42] The note on p. [40] of *La Revue nouvelle* quotes the sentence of Hardy's that 'la modestie de la traductrice a cru devoir supprimer': 'Je dois ajouter que j'ai grande confiance dans ma traductrice dont le courage, en s'attaquant à une tâche aussi difficile, mérite tous les éloges; je la félicite ici de son heureux achèvement.'

[1927.12]

[Final *Who's Who* Entry]

Among the numerous books from the Max Gate library listed in William P. Wreden's Catalogue 11 of 1938 is a copy—current location unknown—of *Who's Who* for 1926 (item 136) in which the Thomas Hardy entry is described as having been extensively revised in Hardy's own hand. Hardy supplied his first *Who's Who* entry in 1897 (1897.01), updated it on several occasions over the succeeding years—a revised copy of the 1907 edition appears as item 135 in the same Wreden catalogue—and sometimes made changes as well as additions: the 1918 edition, for example, listed his 'Recreations' as 'architecture, old church and dance music'. No attempt has been made to record such variants, but the text of the Hardy entry in *Who's Who 1928* (London: A. & C. Black, [1927]), p. 1309, is reproduced below as representing Hardy's final act of self-description in his own lifetime. Of particular interest are the references to Florence Hardy's writings and the explicit rejection of cruelty to animals.

HARDY, Thomas, author; O.M. 1910; Hon. LL.D. Aberdeen; Litt.D. Cambridge and D.Litt. Oxford; LL.D. St Andrews and Bristol; Hon. Fellow Magdalene College, Cambridge, and Queen's College, Oxford; J.P. Dorset; *b.* Dorsetshire, 2 June 1840; *s.* of late Thomas and Jemima Hardy; *m.* 1st, 1874, Emma Lavinia (*d.* 1912), *d.* of J. A. Gifford, and *niece* of Archdn. Gifford; 2nd, 1914, Florence Emily, J.P. for Dorchester, *d.* of Edward Dugdale, and author of numerous books for children, magazine articles, and reviews. *Educ.*: Dorchester; King's College, London. Pupil of John Hicks, ecclesiastical architect, 1856–61; read Latin and Greek with a fellow-pupil, 1857–60; sketched and measured many old country churches now pulled down or altered; removed to London and worked at Gothic architecture under Sir A. Blomfield, A.R.A., 1862–67; prizeman of Royal Institute of British Architects, 1863; the Architectural Assoc., 1863; wrote verses, 1865–1868; gave up verse for prose, 1868–70; but resumed it later. Holds Gold Medal of Royal Society of Literature; Member of the Council of Justice to Animals; is against blood-sport, dog-chaining, and the caging of birds. *Publications*: Prose—Desperate Remedies, 1871; Under the Greenwood Tree or The Mellstock Quire, 1872; A Pair of Blue Eyes, 1872–73; Far from the Madding Crowd, 1874; Hand of Ethelberta, 1876; Return of the Native (with map), 1878; The Trumpet-Major, 1879; A Laodicean,

1880–81; Two on a Tower, 1882; The Life and Death of the Mayor of Casterbridge, 1884–85; The Woodlanders, 1886–1887; Wessex Tales (collected), 1888; A Group of Noble Dames, 1891; Tess of the d'Urbervilles, 1891; Life's Little Ironies (collected), 1894; Jude the Obscure, 1895; The Pursuit of the Well-Beloved, serially 1892, revised and rewritten as The Well-Beloved, 1897; A Changed Man, etc. (collected), 1913. Verse—Wessex Poems (written 1865 onwards), 1898; Poems of the Past and the Present, 1901; The Dynasts (epic-drama), Part I., 1903; Part II., 1906; Part III., 1908; Select Poems of William Barnes, with Preface, 1908; Time's Laughing-stocks and other Verses, 1909; Satires of Circumstance (serially), 1911 (with Lyrics and Reveries), 1914; Selected Poems, 1916; Moments of Vision, 1917; Late Lyrics, 1922; Queen of Cornwall (Play), 1923; Human Shows, 1925; definitive Wessex edition of works in prose and verse with new prefaces and notes, 1912 onwards; complete Poetical Works, 2 vols., 1919; limited Mellstock Edition of works, 1920. *Address*: Max Gate, Dorchester, Dorset. *Club*: Athenæum.

APPENDIX:
HARDY AS MEMORIALIST

It seems appropriate to include in this edition a supplementary, if less formal, record of another category of public statements for which Hardy was directly responsible—namely, the many tombstones and memorials which he designed and sometimes directly commissioned. In 1881 he gave knowledgeable advice on the design of a headstone for his deceased uncle, John Antell senior (*CL* i. 92), and on numerous subsequent occasions he devoted much time and trouble to making sketches and detailed working drawings for tombs and memorials, most but by no means all of them for members of his own family. He also set up headstones for the animals interred in the pets' cemetery at Max Gate itself, sometimes—as his 1904 request to Hamo Thornycroft for a sculptor's chisel clearly shows (*CL* iii. 137, 138)—carving the names with his own hands.

In 1903, as in the leaflet he prepared for his father's funeral (1892.11), Hardy had recourse to the unchangeability of Latin, as a dead language (*LW*, p. 517),[1] for the wording of a brass tablet to be installed in Stinsford Church in commemoration of the extended participation of his grandfather, father, and uncle James in the old west gallery 'quire'. The transcription below is taken from the brass itself; the text in *Life and Work* (*LW*, p. 342), though accurate as to the wording, slightly misrepresents the punctuation and fails to indicate that the actual inscription is entirely in capitals:[2]

> MEMORIAE SACRUM THOMAE HARDY PATRIS, JACOBI
> ET THOMAE FILIORUM, QUI OLIM IN HAC ECCLESIA
> PER ANNOS QUADRAGINTA (MDCCCII-MDCCCXLI)
> FIDICINIS MUNERE SUNT PERFUNCTI. PONENDUM
> CURAVERUNT THOMAE IUNIORIS FILII ET FILIAE
> THOMAS HENRICUS MARIA CATHARINA. MDCCCCIII.

---

[1] Cf. Samuel Johnson's dictum that the epitaphs of learned men should properly be 'in an ancient and permanent language' (*Boswell's Life of Johnson*, ed. George Birkbeck Hill, rev. L. F. Powell, 6 vols. (Oxford: Clarendon Press, 1934–50), iii. 84, n. 2).

[2] Omitted here, as elsewhere, are the raised medial points conventionally used to separate one word from another in capitalized inscriptions.

Hardy's full-size drawings for the tablet are in the Dorset County Museum, as are the transcriptions with accompanying translations (both word for word and discursive) that he wrote out for his mother and siblings. In the following example the words within square brackets correspond to words that Hardy in his manuscript circled as being 'understood' in the Latin version, and not actually present:

[A] Sacred [monument] to the memory of Thomas Hardy the father, of James and of Thomas the sons, who formerly in this church for forty years (from 1802 to 1841) performed the office of violinist.—Thomas, Henry, Mary, Katharine, the sons and daughters of the junior Thomas, caused [this] to be placed [here] 1903.

In the Adams collection is Hardy's design for a headstone to be erected to mark the grave in Stinsford churchyard of his paternal grandfather:

Sacred
to the Memory of
THOMAS HARDY
of Puddletown & Bockhampton
Born October 26: 1778:
Died August 1: 1837.
He was the Son of
JOHN HARDY: Born 1755:
Died June 11: 1821: & of
JANE his Wife: Born 1757:
Died July 16: 1825.

Accompanying the drawing of his grandfather's stone is Hardy's transcription, with measurements, of the already existing Stinsford headstone of his paternal grandmother, born Mary Head, who died in 1857. It is not known when this latter stone was erected nor whether Hardy, aged 16 at the time of his grandmother's death, made any contribution to its design: from the pencilled reckoning on the verso of this second drawing by the Dorchester stonemason Walter Hounsell (from whose firm these items came), it would appear that Hardy had simply asked him to repair Mary Head's stone at the same time as the new stone for her husband was being cut and set in place. The Dorset County Museum has similar drawings, one of them on tracing paper.

Also in the Dorset County Museum are Hardy's simply worded designs, drawn to a scale of 1: 8 with a few letters given full size, for his parents' tomb in Stinsford churchyard:[3]

---

[3] On the tomb itself the month of TH's mother's birth is given in full.

THOMAS HARDY OF BOCKHAMPTON SON OF THOMAS
AND MARY HARDY: BORN NOV: 18: 1811: DIED JULY 20: 1892

JEMIMA WIFE OF THOMAS HARDY: BORN AT MELBURY OSMUND
SEPT: 21: 1813: DIED AT BOCKHAMPTON APRIL 3: 1904

The horizontal tomb was evidently first erected soon after the death of Hardy's father in 1892. Following Jemima Hardy's death in April 1904—so Walter Hounsell's surviving day-book indicates—the tomb was reopened and reset upon a new base, the new inscription added, and the existing lettering recut and repainted.[4]

Both in the Museum and in the Adams collection are examples of Hardy's detailed designs for the second horizontal tomb in Stinsford churchyard, closely modelled on the one beneath which his parents were buried, that he commissioned following the death of his first wife in late November 1912. Some of the drawings are to scale, others actual size, so that Florence Dugdale, staying temporarily at Max Gate, could tell Hounsell on 26 March 1913 (Adams) that until he had received Hardy's 'full size' specification of the lettering he 'need not take the trouble to mark it in'. Those final drawings of the inscription to Emma Hardy's memory, on the tomb's north face, were sent to Hounsell two days later, and the work was finished—accurately in all essentials and at a total cost of £29 10*s*. O*d*.—before the end of April:[5]

HERE IS BURIED EMMA LAVINIA WIFE OF THOMAS HARDY O M
AND DAUGHTER OF JOHN ATTERSOLL GIFFORD
HE WAS BORN AT PLYMOUTH NOV 24 1840 LIVED AT ST JULIOT CORNWALL 1868–1873
DIED AT MAX GATE DORCHESTER NOV 27 1912

Among other drawings in the Adams collection are those in which Hardy, in 1919 (*CL* v. 294, 316), instructed Hounsell to install an additional sloping slab at the base of the north face of Emma Hardy's tomb and incise upon it the following supplementary message:

THIS FOR REMEMBRANCE

Drawings of later date in the Dorset County Museum incorporate Hardy's drafting of the inscriptions in respect of himself and his second wife that would eventually be required for the same tomb. In the surviving drawings the inscription for Florence Hardy, destined for the south face, is sketched only in the barest outline; the one for Hardy himself, to be located on the narrower west-facing head of the tomb, is annotated 'open to modification' but complete as it stands apart from the space left in the last line for the date of death:

---

[4] I gladly acknowledge my indebtedness to Bill and Vera Jesty for details of the Hounsell day-books (currently in the possession of Mr Harry Hounsell).

[5] *CL* iv. 262, 270–1, and Hounsell day-book.

HERE RESTS ALSO

THOMAS HARDY O M

POET & NOVELIST

HE WAS THE SON OF THOMAS & JEMIMA HARDY:

WAS BORN JUNE 2 1840 & DIED

Because, in the event, Hardy's cremated body was interred in Westminster Abbey and only his heart buried at Stinsford, these words were deemed inappropriate and replaced by the following inscription, probably (though not certainly) composed by Sydney Cockerell:[6]

HERE LIES THE HEART OF

THOMAS HARDY O M

SON OF THOMAS AND JEMIMA HARDY

HE WAS BORN AT UPPER BOCKHAMPTON 2 JUNE 1840

AND DIED AT MAX GATE DORCHESTER 11 JANUARY 1928

HIS ASHES REST IN POETS CORNER WESTMINSTER ABBEY

When Mary Hardy died in 1915 Hardy commissioned a third horizontal tomb at Stinsford, and drawings of his in the Dorset County Museum and in the Adams collection detail the design for the tomb and the wording of the inscription along its north face:[7]

SACRED TO THE MEMORY OF MARY ELDER DAUGHTER OF THOMAS & JEMIMA HARD

BORN AT BOCKHAMPTON DEC 23 1841 DIED AT TALBOTHAYS NOV 24 1915.

Two letters to Hounsell of May and September 1916 (*CL* v. 161, 180) show Hardy's concern for the depth of the incised lettering ('so that when the rain splashes up from the ledger it will not wash out') and for the precise location of this new tomb in relation to the two family tombs that were already in place.[8] Hardy's other siblings, Henry (died 1928) and Katharine (died 1940), were subsequently commemorated, one above the other, on the south face of the same tomb, but Hardy seems not to have drafted any anticipatory inscriptions.

Following his first wife's death, Hardy became keenly interested in locating and preserving the graves of members of her family, and the Dorset County Museum possesses his designs for a new tombstone to be placed over the

[6] The lettering of 'THOMAS HARDY O M' is substantially larger than that of the remainder of the inscription: see photograph in Timothy O'Sullivan, *Thomas Hardy: An Illustrated Biography* (London: Macmillan, 1975), pp. [184–5].

[7] No attempt has been made to reproduce either the variations in the size of the lettering in this inscription or the placement of 'TO' over 'THE'.

[8] The resulting relationship can be seen, for example, in the photograph in Tom Howard, *Hardy Country* (London: Regency House Publishing, 1995), p. 32.

damaged grave of Emma Hardy's parents, John Attersoll Gifford and Emma Gifford, in the churchyard of Charles Church, Plymouth (*CL* iv. 311; and see *LW*, p. 387). As the somewhat sketchy drawings show, he took the opportunity to add a reference to Emma herself:[9]

> ALSO IN MEMORY OF THEIR
> DAUGHTER EMMA LAVINIA
> WIFE OF THOMAS HARDY O M
> SHE WAS BORN IN PLYMOUTH
> 1840 DIED AT DORCHESTER
> 1912 AND IS BURIED AT
> STINSFORD DORSET

The new tombstone, evidently in place by the early summer of 1914 (*CL* v. 32), was subsequently destroyed when Plymouth was bombed during the Second World War, and Charles Church itself now survives only as a roofless ruin dedicated as a war memorial.

Of particular biographical interest are two wall tablets that Hardy designed for Emma Lavinia Gifford and himself and that now hang, as intended, in the Church of St Juliot in Cornwall, the occasion and location of their romantic first meeting in March 1870 (*LW*, pp. 387–90). The original designs, including full-size working drawings, are in the Berg Collection of the New York Public Library. Hardy revisited St Juliot in March 1913, four months after Emma's death, and by 3 April of that year he had commissioned Joseph Geach, a Plymouth monumental mason, to supply and erect a tablet in 'Sicilian Marble on Carsew Granite' worded as follows:

> TO THE DEAR MEMORY OF
> ## EMMA LAVINIA HARDY born GIFFORD
> WIFE OF THOMAS HARDY AUTHOR: & SISTER
> IN LAW OF THE REV C HOLDER FORMERLY
> INCUMBENT OF THIS PARISH: BEFORE HER
> MARRIAGE SHE LIVED AT THE RECTORY
> 1868–1873 CONDUCTED THE CHURCH MUSIC
> & LAID THE FIRST STONE OF THE REBUILT
> AISLE & TOWER: SHE DIED AT DORCHESTER
> 1912 & IS BURIED AT STINSFORD DORSET:
> ERECTED BY HER HUSBAND 1913

[9] The drawing is tentative and incomplete and the actual inscription may not have followed precisely this wording or layout.

At some later date Hardy designed a companion (and closely similar) tablet recording his own association with St Juliot, and within a year of his death his widow had arranged for that design to be realized in the same stone and style as Emma's tablet and hung on the same wall inside the church. The tablet as completed reads:

THOMAS HARDY: O M: LITT D:

AUTHOR OF MANY WORKS IN VERSE
& PROSE & IN EARLY LIFE ARCHITECT
MADE DRAWINGS IN MARCH 1870 OF
THIS CHURCH IN ITS ANCIENT STATE &
LATER FOR THE ALTERATIONS & RE-
PAIRS EXECUTED 1871-2 WHICH HE AS-
SISTED TO SUPERVISE: HE DIED 1928
& IS BURIED IN WESTMINSTER ABBEY:
ERECTED 1928 AS A RECORD OF HIS ASSOCIA-
TION WITH THE CHURCH & NEIGHBOURHOOD.

In Hardy's full-size drawing of the tablet—on architect's tracing paper and annotated 'This Tracing is to be used for working from'—the years of death and of the tablet's erection are necessarily left blank; the place of burial, however, is lightly dotted in as 'STINSFORD DORSET', just one letter shorter than the 'WESTMINSTER ABBEY' that Hardy perhaps already guessed might be his actual destination.[10]

Hardy seems to have had little success in suggesting street names for Dorchester (*CL* iii. 19–20; also *intra* 1893.02, 1905.16) or in urging the placement of an historical plaque on the Gloucester Hotel in Weymouth, once the summer residence of King George III (*CL* iv. 294–5, v. 183–4, 244–5, and see the reproduction of Hardy's sketch at v. 185).[11] He may, however, have chosen the quotation (from 'Culver Dell and the Squire') for the plaque on the statue of William Barnes erected outside St Peter's Church in Dorchester, and he certainly supplied in 1923, nearly forty years later, both the quotation ('That swift sympathy . . . which quicks the world', from his own poem 'At an Inn') and the facsimile signature for the bronze plate formerly located at the entrance to the Dorset County Hospital, subsequently set into the wall of one of the buildings just off Princes Street.[12]

[10]　This drawing is reproduced in *A Descriptive Catalogue of the Grolier Club Centenary Exhibition 1940 of the Works of Thomas Hardy, O. M. 1840–1928* (Waterville, Me.: Colby College Library, 1940), facing p. 13. Photographs of both completed tablets are in Kenneth Phelps, *The Wormwood Cup: Thomas Hardy in Cornwall* (Padstow: Lodenek, 1975), facing p. 159 and following p. 172.

[11]　For the wording of the brass plaque later installed at the hotel entrance, see *CL* iv. 295.

[12]　I am particularly grateful to Lilian Swindall for her assistance in locating this initially elusive item. The plate has now (AD 2000) been removed from the Princes Street location and will presumably be transferred to the new hospital site in due course.

In 1920 Hardy seems to have been given sole charge of the design and wording of the memorial tablet to the eleven members of the staff of the Dorchester Post Office who had died in uniform during the war of 1914–18 (*CL* vi. 44). Florence Hardy reported to Sydney Cockerell on 5 September 1920 (Beinecke) that her husband was busy with the design and seemed 'to enjoy doing it'. The tablet itself, signed 'T HARDY DEL.' and incorporating the line 'None dubious of the cause, none murmuring' from his poem 'Embarcation', remains visible at the Dorchester Post Office—although not in its original location. Full-scale drawings of the design exist in the Dorset County Museum and the library of Colby College, Maine, but it is here reproduced from a photograph of the finished tablet:[13]

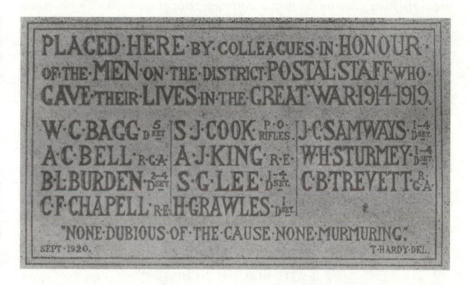

In 1924 Hardy provided the epitaph for the headstone in the Dorchester cemetery of Sir Frederick Treves, the famous Dorchester-born surgeon, adapting for the purpose—and at Lady Treves's request[14]—the closing lines of 'In the Evening', the eulogistic poem that he had published in *The Times* of 5 January 1924, just three days after Treves's funeral.[15] Hardy is also said to have designed, in the same year and for the same cemetery, the tombstone of William Watkins, the long-serving secretary of the Society of Dorset Men in London,[16] and he was

---

[13] Photographs appeared in the *Builder*, 3 December 1920, p. 625, and the *Sphere*, 25 December 1920, p. 302; cuttings of both are in TH's 'Personal' scrapbook (DCM).

[14] Letter to TH of 16 February 1924 (DCM). Treves's stone has weathered considerably and I am especially grateful to Bill and Vera Jesty for their recovery of he inscription.

[15] The original last stanza was both revised and expanded prior to the poem's republication in *The Dorset Year-Book for 1924*, p. 3 (see *CPW* iii. 144–5).

[16] *The Dorset Year Book for 1953–4*, p. 104.

undoubtedly responsible for its carrying a biblical quotation ('What man is there that is fearful and faint hearted?')[17] neatly reminiscent of the Society's motto, 'Who's a-feär'd?', that he had himself suggested many years earlier (1905. 04). In 1925, in response (*CL* vi. 357) to a request from the mayor of Dudley, in Worcestershire, he became partly responsible for the words carved into that town's war memorial.[18] In June 1926 he responded to a more personal request from his old friend Dorothy Allhusen for an inscription to be placed in the Junior Combination Room of Trinity College, Cambridge, which she was having restored in memory of her husband, Henry Allhusen, and their son, Henry Christian Stanley Allhusen. Unfortunately, the suggestions he sent no longer accompany his covering letter (*CL* vii. 27), and while the Latin of the actual memorial inscription on the marble chimney-piece of the restored room seems sufficiently straightforward to have been within Hardy's scope, there is no clear evidence that it was in fact of his composition.

Early in 1927, just a year ahead of his own death, Hardy performed the melancholy task of designing a headstone for Wessex, the troublesome but much-loved Max Gate dog, who had died in late December 1926 and been buried in the pets' cemetery in the garden.[19] Hardy's full-scale preparatory sketch of the design (DCM) is annotated 'Portland Stone. Edges & Back may be left rough—letters to be cut deep'. The actual working drawings, however, remain with Mr C. Grassby of the local firm of monumental masons which executed Hardy's design in every detail, as follows:[20]

THE

FAMOUS DOG

WESSEX

AUG. 1913–27 DEC. 1926.

FAITHFUL, UNFLINCHING.

One final act of memorialization, less poignant than the stone for Wessex but still deeply personal, was his design (later faithfully executed) for the plaque affixed to the house in South Street, Dorchester, in which William Barnes had lived and conducted his school.[21] Modestly, but in the circumstances somewhat absurdly, his letter accompanying the sketch of the design insisted that he was 'no authority on such things'.[22]

---

[17] Deut. 20: 8.

[18] See William W. Morgan, 'Verses Fitted for a Monument: Hardy's Contribution to the Dudley War Memorial', *Thomas Hardy Journal*, 1 (January 1985), pp. 25–32.

[19] See the photograph following p. 400 of *Biography*.

[20] A slightly inaccurate transcription of the inscription was incorporated by Florence Hardy into the typescripts of 'Life and Work': see *LW*, p. 469.

[21] The house adjoins the one (also bearing a plaque) in which TH served his apprenticeship to the architect John Hicks.   [22] TH to H. O. Lock, 29 August 1927 (H. E. F. Lock).

INDEX

Principal entries are indicated by *italics*.